THE MEMORIES OF A RUSSIAN YESTERYEAR
Volume 3

Compiled & Presented by

TONY ABBOTT

AUTHOR OF
'NICHOLAS II - TSAR TO SAINT'
'THE MEMORIES OF A RUSSIAN YESTERYEAR VOLUME 1'
'THE MEMORIES OF A RUSSIAN YESTERYEAR VOLUME 2'

19 ILLUSTRATIONS

New Angle Publishing

Copyright © Tony Abbott 2024
First Published April 2024
email@tonyabbott.co.uk

INDEPENDENT PUBLISHING NETWORK
ISBN 978-1-80517-623-7
Paperback Edition (cream paper)

CONTENTS

SECTION		PAGE
01	PUBLIC DOMAIN BOOKS	3
	COPYRIGHT	5
	PHOTOGRAPHS	5
	ACKNOWLEDGEMENTS	5
02	INTRODUCTION	6
	I Sergei Witte	11
	II Mikhail Rodzianko	22
03	BOOK ONE	29

THE MEMOIRS OF COUNT WITTE
By COUNT WITTE
(Translated by Abraham Yarmolinsky
Preface by Countess Witte)

04	BOOK TWO	381

THE REIGN OF RASPUTIN:
An Empire's Collapse
By M. V. Rodzianko
(President of the Russian State Duma)
Translated by Catherine Zvegintzoff
Preface by Sir Bernard Pares

05	VOLUME & SERIES INFORMATION	599

To my friend
Carlos Alexander Johnson
Who passed away one month before this book was published
Rest In Peace

PUBLIC DOMAIN BOOKS

A consideration when reprinting memoirs is how faithfully to keep to the original work in terms of styling. Any misspellings and typographical errors in the original version can give an indication of quality but even the best typesetters let a few through the net. This series of volumes is no different and might contain a new typo here or there. It's a nit-picking exercise that serves only to reveal the rush to get the manuscript to print.

Since Alfred the Great up until this last century, special characters were used widely in Europe to carry dialect in vowels (acute accent), having originated from the Germanic tongues of the fifth century and perhaps even earlier. In this volume, you'll come across á, ä, and ă, but their aid to pronunciation has faded and become obsolete in the UK, for example. Word usage too, can be confusing and the antiquated form mistaken for a misspelling, for example, the word 'employees' appearing twice in a paragraph for Book 1, (page 57 of the original work and page 76 in this volume) gives one instance with an accent and the other without one. The former, employés, is used throughout and so in this case the latter is the typo.

You'll also come across 'æ' and 'œ', sounds made from the ligatures of two vowels; the former a diphthong of Germanic origin to do with phonetics and the latter a grapheme of Greek origin to do with writing. Both perhaps deriving from Classical Latin and having spread in Europe during Roman expansionism. Still, they were in use up until the last century when these memoirs were written.

Of course, print errors are down to the typesetter and should be corrected on re-printing. But it would be wrong to adjust grammar, which is the expression of the author, rightly or wrongly laid down, and this is especially important to preserve when the work has been translated. In typesetting for re-printing, it can be taxing when story issues popup like random characters appearing out of nowhere and mentioned once or twice; like in Book 2, (page 501) where it says, "*Before doing so I wished to speak to Krivoshein, and telephoned to him at his villa on Elagin.*" But who is Krivoshein? If we were overly attentive, on page 479 it was said, "*Krivoshein, Sukhomlinoff and Goremykin approved of the idea of a conference . . .*", so Krivoshein has been declared as a Minister, but we need to wait for page 569, to learn that he was indeed the Minister for Agriculture; despite these issues, the work must be faithfully reproduced as is.

CORRECTIONS

For the most part of Witte's book it is error-free with a concentration of misspellings in the last third, leaving evidence of the fleeting moments a typesetter was visited by absent-minded thoughts. Rodzianko's book contains fewer errors. Both authors are guilty of mixing American English and International English, seemingly at random. For example, Witte uses both 'favorable' and 'favourable'. Is this an indication the work passed through the hands of several typesetters and editors, each with their language preference, and is it an inconsequential oversight. These are issues that modern word processing can eliminate.

The following list are the corrections made to this volume:

1) Witte (page 45), "*So great an emperor as Alexander III*". Should be 'Alexander II' as correctly stated on page 49.

2) Witte (page 65), 'APPELATION' corrected to 'APPELLATION'.

3) Witte (page 70), 'VYHSNEGRADSKI' corrected to 'VYSHNEGRADSKI'.

4) Witte (page 87), 'DIASASTROUS' corrected to 'DISASTROUS'.

5) Witte (page 148), 'CIRCUMSATNCES' corrected to 'CIRCUMSTANCES'.

6) Witte (page 149), 'OPINON' corrected to 'OPINION'.

7) Witte (page 150), 'NECCESSARY' corrected to 'NECESSARY'.

8) Witte (book 183), 'FYORODOROVNA' corrected to 'FYODOROVNA'.

9) Witte (page 216), 'DICATOR' corrected to 'DICTATOR'.

10) Witte (page 228), typo, "There were hundreds of casualties *in* killed and wounded." - Removed the word 'in'.

11) Witte (page 287), 'PRECIPATING' corrected to 'PRECIPITATING'.

CORRECTIONS

12) Witte (page 376), Index, 'RACHKOVSKY' corrected to 'RACHKOVSKI'. As the latter is used in the text on pages 187-8 and 288.

13) Witte (page 379), Index for Wilhelm II, typo "directly appealed to *to* speed up work of Algeciras Conference, 265;" – Removed second 'to'.

14) Rodzianko (page 415), typo, "This proved that such an honest man as Makaroff undoubtedly was *was* nevertheless not entirely free from servility when it came to shielding Rasputin." – Removed second 'was'.

15) Rodzianko (page 507), typo, "By way of an *an* answer . . ." Removed second 'an'.

Copyright:
This volume as a whole, incorporating two books of memoirs with additional images is in its completion the sole work of the author. The books themselves are in the public domain, and the material in this volume has been meticulously examined with numerous errors corrected. The typesetting differs from the original and the way footnotes and menus appear also differ from the originals. Prior permission should be obtained from the copyright holder and author, before reprinting the material contained in this volume.

Photographs:
All the images in this volume have been sourced from public domain image archives. They inevitably required some editing for reprinting, but they can be reproduced at will from this volume if desired, with no restrictions. Restoration and removing noise can be an arduous process and so, in this new age of AI (artificial intelligence), some images have undergone a pass to smooth or improve, but most have been touched up by hand in the reliable old-fashioned way.

Acknowledgements:
I would like to thank the Internet Archive for excellent digital copy and Yandex for public domain stock photographs.

INTRODUCTION

THE two books in this volume were written by prominent politicians in the reign of Nicholas II. The authors; Sergey Yulyevich Witte and Mikhail Vladimirovich Rodzianko, raised their heads above the parapet, not afraid to speak out and give their opinions, plainly and honestly to the Tsar. Their empirical evidence gives invaluable insight in to the Government and Imperial Duma, and sheds some light on the goings on of Prime Ministers and other notaries at the heart of managing the Russian Empire.

These authors slightly overlap their careers; in 1911 Witte was in the twilight years when Rodzianko became the 5th Duma President and began his parliamentary career. Witte is forever reminiscent of happier times when he was in the service of Alexander III, and his account is relevant from the accession of Nicholas II in 1894 to the First Revolution and the manifesto that he helped to write in 1905. Rodzianko, on the other hand, enters the sphere of the Tsar during the slightly less turbulent times of the 3rd Duma (Chairman 1911-1912) and up until he persuaded the Tsar to abdicate in 1917. Between the authors, they cover the full reign of Nicholas II.

Both men were similarly tall and physically large in stature; their presence was felt in any room. Rodzianko introduced himself to the Tsarevich Alexei, in his deep bass voice, as, 'the biggest and fattest man in Russia'. They shared a similar way of thinking up to a point, as all intelligent people do: Witte striving to reform the Monarchy and Rodzianko living to reform the Government's priorities; each believing in that absolute need for major changes to be implemented alongside economic growth. They were staunch monarchists fiercely loyal to their country and preached unity of the institutions and in all walks of life; they were men of the people. They witnessed first-hand the injustices and cruelty perpetrated against the Jews and other minorities, by the Tsarist regime. They served amid the corruption employed at every level, that also extended to the Tsar's beloved military and the untouchable manipulators in the nobility.

The uphill struggles they faced led ultimately to frustration over their failures, as career-long humanitarian efforts proved ineffective and opposed by a Tsar who worked only to increase his powers. The revelation came that the régime condoned racial cleansing which was the incontrovertible proof that they were victims of turbulent and unprecedented times, and they felt slighted by it.

INTRODUCTION

Both were noblemen from distinguished families; Witte on his maternal side from a long line of Dolgoruky princes and Rodzianko a wealthy landowner of note. They considered it their privilege to be afforded due respect but it was not always forthcoming and it filled them with indignation that the Tsar preferred his counsel from the nefarious elements, often leaving his ministers, and the like, in the dark. In their memoirs they take a fair share of potshots at the Imperial couple, fully aware that they were disliked and for what the Empress had misinterpreted as their continuing efforts to undermine the status of the Tsar and the autocracy – a state of affairs that could not have been further from the truth.

The autocratic structure was simple enough – Government and Parliament operated as appendages of the monarch; the former being an arm to manage the empire justly, and the latter for guiding the people spiritually and morally. These precepts had existed for centuries before becoming muddied by the Tsarina, whose unappreciativeness of how the Supreme Power worked, by her interference caused the rifts that estranged the Tsar from his means to rule effectively. This instability is examined as Witte and Rodzianko attempt to confront the Tsar but underestimate the influence of a Russian empress. It was neither the Tsar's, Witte's nor Rodzianko's vision for Russia that prevailed, only the residue remained of a revolution that came out of the political melee.

Their level of radicalism for reforms were similar but the level of pacifism very different. Witte was against all war, rather akin to a CND activist of the 1980s, whereas Rodzianko had encouraged the Tsar to take the Bosphorus Strait, saying, "*A war will be joyfully welcomed...*" They were equally philanthropic men, but of course their political allegiances were not aligned. Witte was no supporter of Pyotr Stolypin, the great reformer Prime Minister until his assassination in 1911, who had also dissolved the Second Duma in June 1907. Yet, Rodzianko attended the memorial service in Kieff and said, "*Gutchkoff, who laid a wreath at the foot of the memorial, merely bowed to the ground in silence. This silent homage expressed more eloquently than words the profound sorrow caused by Stolypin's death.*" Rodzianko therefore, held Stolypin in high regard. Perhaps Witte felt he had done enough whereas Rodzianko aimed to show that he could do more. Nevertheless, their cries for attention were fruitless in the eyes of the Imperial couple who regarded them equally in low esteem.

INTRODUCTION

Witte witnessed mysticism arriving at the Court and speaks with some authority when blaming the Tsarina for the free rein given to such notables as Master Philippe and Papus and of the religious obsession that similarly struck her. However, it is not dwelled upon and Witte mentions but once; Hermogenes, Iliodor and Rasputin. The heyday of mysticism at the Court, i.e. 1910 to 1916, was already well established when Rodzianko arrived at the Duma and as its Chairman he was uniquely placed to voice the nation's concerns about Rasputin to the Tsar during their personal audiences.

Witte served under two emperors and his book is therefore the longer, encompassing political activity right up until he died from a brain tumour in 1915. His first calling was to be a mathematician, but he became established in logistics within the transport sector under advisement from his father who considered it a more fitting career for a nobleman.

The railways project started by Alexander III and completed by Nicholas II linked Europe to the Far East for the first time and cost an inordinate sum. The financing was largely facilitated by Witte during his tenure as Minister of Finances. It was the greatest Russian construction achievement, albeit hampered by increasing costs and therefore lacked the foresight for longevity in its design. During the Russo-Japanese War, it was realised that a single track could not transport troops and supplies in both directions at the same time, and a second track had to be built alongside. During World War I it was realised that investment of the Siberian Railway had been to the detriment of railway infrastructure elsewhere, particularly to connect to strategic points. For example, coal that was discovered in Donbas in 1721 and the huge pig iron deposit there, was not exploitable until the railway arrived in 1869. By 1913 Donbas was producing 87% of coal and 74% of pig iron across the Russian Empire. However, during World War I the railway was unable to supply factories in sufficient quantities which meant that armaments to the front actually stopped.

Russian modernism came in the form of large infrastructures but lacked the underlying logistical support and corruption was the linch pin preventing the economic wheels from turning. Nonetheless, Witte succeeded, significantly improving the railways and extending his contribution to the opening of schools that everyone could access, particularly for Poles, Jews and other minorities. For this overextension of his remit he was redeployed as the Minister of Finances.

INTRODUCTION

It was essentially a promotion that provided a larger scope, not quite what had been intended for him. He diligently set about reforming the banking system, making the ruble convertible to gold and securing the largest loans ever made in Europe, from France, Great Britain, Germany and other investors. This time, for his bold but necessary overextensions, which had brought with it a temporary financial crisis, he was again steered by the Tsar, in August 1903, from his ministerial role to a political appointment as Chairman of the Committee of Ministers. It was a bewildering appointment to him because when he felt he was most needed to prepare the country for war with Japan, he had been taken away from effective government and placed in a nominal role – seemingly out of sight and out of mind.

Witte witnessed every faux pas made by the Tsar and enacted by the Government. His release from ministerial exile arrived with the position of Chief Plenipotentiary for the peace negotiations that concluded the costly defeat by Japan. He was subsequently rewarded with the Premiership (6 November 1905 – 5 May 1906) during which time he helped suppress the Soviet uprisings, workers' strikes, and troop mutinies that would nevertheless eventually brim in to the First Revolution 1905. At the inception of the First Duma, Witte was insistent that session details not be made publicly available due to the increasing criticism of the Tsar. Yet, despite his efforts to protect the monarchy he remained a thorn in their side, advising to accept a new constitutional monarchy and persuading the Tsar to sign the October Manifesto of 1905, that Witte had written himself.

In hindsight, Witte was the only statesman that could have implemented the railways, secured foreign loans, reformed the country's financial system, brokered a peace deal with Japan, and turned a revolution in to a smooth transition for the monarchy. But, he had attracted enemies over his open views on the rights for minorities and in opposing the hard-line monarchists who he blamed for corrupting the Supreme Power to gleefully sanction the pogroms and Russification.

Despite his achievements, spanning a career from 1892 to 1906, the Tsar forced Witte to resign from service altogether. While he convalesced abroad with his family, to alleviate health concerns, he received the Tsar's wishes in the form of a letter from the Court Chancellor, Baron Frederichs, advising him not to return to Russia. Witte disregarded that notion and at once returned to resolve the matter with the Tsar. Witte's book is discussed further on in detail, but as already mentioned, he does introduce random characters at times, such as on page 319 when he says, "*As for Shcheglovitov, he was little more than Stolypin's valet, Przeradski said so that it was quite useless to expect any independent action from him.*" This assumes the reader is familiar with the right-wing politician who served as the Minister of Justice and chairman of the State Council.

Rodzianko has a briefer range, from the first meeting of the Duma in May 1906 to the Tsar's abdication in 1917 and does not broaden his horizons as much as Witte. His account though, is no less impressive considering the significance of that period in Russian history. Unlike Witte, Rodzianko wrote several books, the one here being concerned with the effect Rasputin had on the Tsar's decision making, enabled by an impressionable Tsarina. Rodzianko delves in and out with references to Rasputin, trying to keep him connected as the underlying theme for the book, but it is not a book *per se* about Rasputin, despite its title. However, the book does provide invaluable insight of Rasputin's power at Court over the Tsarina and in the workings of the Government, which in other contemporary accounts has been contested.

Whereas Witte kept his distance on the subject, Rodzianko confronted the Tsar with the Duma's concern over Rasputin and his influence over the Tsarina. At one sitting, he asked why mention of Rasputin was banned in the media while there were no restrictions for members of the Imperial Family and ministers. Rodzianko was alluding to the interventions of the Tsarina to protect Rasputin from allegations made against him and for which intrusion he attributes the Tsarina's hatred towards him.

As the Tsar stayed away from the capital for longer periods he repeatedly disregarded Rodzianko, who in retrospect was in the Corps des Pages (1859), and a former lieutenant in the Imperial Guards Cavalry regiment (1878-1882) and served as a justice of the peace and then Head of the Judiciary in Ekaterinoslav. This was before he became a founding member of the Octobrist Party and was elected to the Duma. The Tsar had little appreciation for his experience or affiliations with the people through the military, the zemstvos and the duma. It was perhaps a reason why Rodzianko supported the Grand Duke Nicolai Nicolaevitch when the Tsar replaced him as Supreme Commander of the Russian Army fighting on the Western Front.

INTRODUCTION

This decision the Tsar made following a communiqué from General Alexei Brusilov: "*In recent battles a third of the men had no rifles. These poor devils had to wait patiently until their comrades fell before their eyes and they could pick up weapons. The army is drowning in its own blood.*" General Brusilov also wrote separately: "*In a year of the war the regular army had vanished. It was replaced by an army of ignoramuses.*"

Rodzianko's judgement is by no means definitive. The Grand Duke Nicolai Nicolaevitch, although highly respected, was not a great leader and had resigned himself to the logistical aspects of fighting in World War I. Brusilov's comments are evidence enough of the major problems for supply, which even at that, the Grand Duke had not capitalised on his rank and peerage to resolve. With ineptitude all around him, and having much less clout than the Tsar, Grand Duke and ministers, Rodzianko used his chairmanship to connect with the local authorities and resolve the restrictive issues facing manufacturers and suppliers. But it was too much for one man to accomplish and as Witte had once been instrumental in the Tsar's signing of the October Manifesto 1905, Rodzianko was instrumental in the Tsar's abdication following the February Revolution 1917, after which Rodzianko resigned from the Government.

Rodzianko, like the Tsar, had not conceived of the possibility for the largest army in the world to be defeated by Austria-Hungary and Germany. He joined the White forces for a brief spell; one of his sons was shot by the Bolsheviks in 1918, and with the collapse of the civil war in 1920, Rodzianko fled with his family to Serbia where he died in 1924, aged 64.

The term 'Zemstvo' is used liberally by both authors. In the first paragraph of Rodzianko's introduction it is stated that he was a former President of the Provincial Zemstvo Executive. The zemstvo was a product of the 1864 reforms of Alexander II. They were councils across the provinces of Russia and primarily collected taxes for construction projects like roads, schools and hospitals. They acted equally as money lenders to farmers and peasants and generally were supportive of district social and economic concerns.

* * *

INTRODUCTION

I - SERGEI WITTE (b.1849-1915)

Sergei Witte's second wife writes the preface to these memoirs, affording herself the opportunity to address the American people to thank them for their kindness during the Portsmouth 'declaration'. She tells of her husband writing his drafts in secret and how the Tsar's police went to Europe in search of locating them.

The work was completed three years before Witte's death in February 1915, and as such there is no mention of World War I, although he had been voicing his opposition to that escalation. The book ends with the rising issues of Turkey and the wider political wrangling for Russian power in Persia, which had reached the inevitable conclusion that Russia had lost all influence in the region, as they became entangled within the political astuteness of Great Britain, Germany and France.

Witte starts with recollections of the famed Theosophist Madame Blavatski, his first cousin. He describes her enormous azure coloured eyes, *"never in my life have I seen anything like that pair of eyes, and possessing the gift of hypnotizing both her hearer and herself into believing the wildest inventions of her fantasy."* In Book Two, Rodzianko will apply a similar description to Rasputin.

Although from a noble family, Witte by no means grew up in splendour and he started out working on railway platforms, making his way to senior levels within the transportation industry and much later moving to Imperial service and the Government. He leads the reader in great detail through his railway journey up to the assassination of Alexander II when he suggests ways for dealing with Revolutionists, which brought him to the immediate attention of Alexander III. He was soon recruited in to "The Holy Brotherhood," a secret society created by Alexander III, from Witte's suggestions on how to deal with the Revolutionists.

His favour with the Emperor propelled him to Paris on a quest for the brotherhood until it dawned, upon his arrival, that he had been sent there to supervise an assassination. Witte was no murderer and retreated to St, Petersburg. Murder was performed without abandon in those times, even racial cleansing and genocide were not crimes against humanity. Witte first mentions the pogroms on page 51 stating that Government did not incite the population against the Jews, indirectly pointing to the far right groups and the sanction given to them by a complicit and approving Tsar.

INTRODUCTION

Witte viewed the Government and the Emperor as two distinct entities, each with their own morals and interpretation of justice. Or at least that was true in the beginning and he certainly changed his opinion after Nicholas II ascended the throne. As the book progresses, the institutions drift apart while power is concentrated to the centre, the same situation being also given in Rodzianko's account.

Tiflis, where Witte lived (modern day Tbilisi), is 770 miles, as the crow flies, from Odessa on the opposite side of the Black Sea, in and around where Witte had started his railway career, and where the main activity of the pogroms took place - Odessa being an area containing a great population of Jews.

He rose to be the Director of the South-Western Railroads, albeit his offices were in St. Petersburg. Still in Chapter 1, he mentions the Borki rail disaster which Alexander III and his immediate family survived, but which left the emperor with an undiagnosed liver injury that eventually took his life in later years. Witte's thorough investigation in to that rail disaster saw him promoted to Director of the Department of Railway Affairs, for simply establishing that the train was travelling too fast. Having reached the pinnacle of that career in 1888, he set about regulating freight tariffs and took greater control of the private railroads, both being operated under blatant corruption. Chapter 1 ends with his promotion to the Minister of Finances.

In his appraisal of Alexander III, the man whom he gives his undying loyalty, Witte points out that his reign was uninterrupted of peace; the Turkish war was over and the Japanese war was yet to come. This may have given Witte the belief that an empire could be maintained without resorting to war and the use of aggression determined solely under *jus ad bellum*. It certainly had sculptured his pacifism and he always voiced his anti-war sentiments, opposing all discussions about the waging of war. Alexander III had told him personally, "*I am glad that I have taken part in natural warfare and seen with my own eyes the horrors inevitably cemented with military action.*" What exactly was the meaning of natural warfare?

Witte said of him, "*It was his steadying influence that kept Europe at peace.*" This trait Witte employed in his statesmanship. He describes a softer side to the great emperor, who was physically large and thunderous by nature, and who was viewed with caution and suspicion by the West, notably by Queen Victoria. Witte states, "*He was, indeed a man of few words, but his pronouncements carried weight."* Witte extols his Emperor's irreproachable honour and attributes great wisdom to him, *"He raised her* [Russia] *by his wisdom and firmness, to an enviable position of power and prestige among the nations, without shedding a drop of Russian blood."*

Up to the accession of Nicholas II in 1894, Witte was used to getting his way using his calm persuasiveness. His meticulous planning propelled him to head the entire railway network which he credits to Alexander III for backing his vision of the railways, *". . . the Throne had complete confidence in me and extended entire approval to my actions."* Witte was therefore ideally placed when Nicholas II started out, but it would take several years for the young Tsar's skulduggery to emerge and be a concern to Witte.

At first he believed that Nicholas II valued him as much as his father Alexander III had done. Their collaboration started when Witte petitioned for the Tsarevich Nicholas to direct the massive Siberian Railway project. In coronation year, 1896, Witte placed the country on the gold standard enabling the ruble to be exchangeable for the first time and opening up access to global bankers like Morgan and Rothschild. He started a tariff war on German industrial imports to counter their increased tariffs for Russian agricultural imports. Germany being an industrial superpower and Russia by comparison a nation of peasant farmers, Witte determined that in their mercantile relations, the Russians could hold out on industrial purchasing for longer than the Germans could hold out on the need to sell. Witte was proved correct and tariffs were dropped by both sides soon after the standoff.

The Tsar was easily swayed by his wife, his uncles and closest advisors, who pushed him to strengthen the autocracy and the anti-Jewish policy. As a result he became acquainted with the extremist element of the Black Hundred which placed him on opposite sides to Witte and Rodzianko who were working towards resolving the Jewish problem, as it was termed.

"Many of my antagonists were undoubtedly moved by a desire to frighten the Emperor into withdrawing his approval of my actions, thus abandoning me to certain failure and lasting discredit."

Witte was plagued by paranoia, always looking over his shoulder assuming duplicity from everyone. He attributes his harsh treatment by the Imperial couple entirely to the Tsarina's utter dislike of him.

INTRODUCTION

Witte's achievements are his lasting legacy. He claimed that since his appointment as Minister of Finances in 1892, the country's credit stood higher than ever in markets at home and abroad. The resolution of his tariff war led to the first commercial treaty between Russia and Germany in 1894 and became a template for Russian trade negotiations in the decades that followed. The move to a gold standard in 1896 was followed by a financial crisis, but he states, "*It was not my fault that our military adventures have so thoroughly injured our credit.*" – A reference to the war with Japan 1904-1905.

Strange as it was, war with Japan was not the most devastating event for Russia in that final decade of Witte's life; World War I was on the horizon. Witte expressed his opposition to involvement in the great war up until his death on 13 March 1915. "*She [Russia] is poor, for the reason that the history of the country is a continuous chain of wars, not to speak of other reasons.*" That statement explains why he believed Russia was not ready for war, despite his years developing the transportation infrastructure and industrial base which were as good if not stronger than any other country.

His policies as Minister of Finances were hugely successful in spite of the financial crisis and it was during his tenure that a statesman was forged from his visits abroad. He first mentions the flamboyant Chinese ambassador Li Hung Chang, on page 97; that relationship with China was key to keeping a finger on the Chinese pulse. The Kwantung Peninsula was seized by Russia and other parts of China had been occupied by Japan, and the European Powers since 1898. By 1900, a rebellion that started in the south and rapidly gained momentum in the north, left the encircled government secretly in support of the rebels.

It was known as the Boxer Rebellion, during which came the demise of Li Hung Chang due to public opinion after power had been restored to the Chinese Government. Russia had remained in Manchuria much to the consternation of the European Powers, which undid the once good relations between the two countries. It followed that in March 1902 an agreement was made for Russian troops to withdraw by the end of September 1903.

Witte states, "*Accordingly a copy of the agreement was handed to Li Hung Chang's assistants and I took the other one and began to scan it, suspecting no evil.*" But Russia was being duplicitous, the Tsar had already sent an envoy to investigate the exploitable opportunities for natural resources in Manchuria.

INTRODUCTION

Witte explains how General Kuropatkin was petitioning to remain in Manchuria and operate the Manchurian railroad, i.e. The Eastern-Chinese Railway. Both these activities were a violation of the agreement for Russia to leave China despite the Russian political body being largely in agreement not to annex Manchuria. The political opposition forced General Kuropatkin to give up ambitions of securing the south and he looked to possible territorial gains in the north.

On page 125 Witte quotes from a letter in which he prophetically announced that technologically advanced western countries would devour the vast but dormant weaker countries of the Far East. China was the largest territorial conquest and alongside the UK and France, the Western powers carved up China – Witte's view being that Russia deserved the 'Lion's share'. But Japan was an entirely different foe, the only oriental state that had been advancing militarily and with convictions to the West, namely in forging its relationship with the UK and developing an alliance with France that would become the Franco-Japanese Treaty of 1907. It was Japan's alliance with the UK and its French (financial) connection, that made it formidable.

About the half way mark, Chapter VI, when Witte takes the road along the last ten years of his life, he is a well respected foreign dignitary and one of the most influential men in the autocratic system, albeit without any official direct connection to the Tsar. He describes his frustration at having to make appointments through the Tsar's aides to be granted an audience. It was a bizarre situation to find oneself held in such esteem abroad but at an arm's length back at home.

He was by no means a socialist, neither liberal in his beliefs, and perhaps leaned more toward conservatism when one considers his efforts to protect the status quo and preserve the autocracy. Yet, if one believes his claims of conspiracies working against him and an undermining Tsar, then why his intriguing appointment to Chief plenipotentiary on the 29 July (OS) 1905, which invested him with the full powers of the monarchy and government to negotiate the country's finances as well as war and peace treaties.

On the outward journey to New York for the peace negotiations that followed the defeat by Japan, Witte and his family passed through France to public cries of *Faites la Paix* (make peace). He was taken aback by the negative views on the Tsar. The French sensed in the few years preceding World War I, the looming inevitability of war and this ebbing fear was perhaps what Witte detected from a people who regarded Russia as the instigator for having attacked Japan; a country that was considered to be, at least by the UK, an Asian outpost – Russia had jeopardised the relative peace that existed in Europe since the end of the Napoleonic wars.

On the ship to America, Witte was interviewed by French and American newspaper reporters, Dr. Dillon being the most notable as he telegraphed the interview. It was the first press communiqué to be transmitted by wireless telegraph, a full five years before that technology was used again to apprehend the American homeopath Dr. Hawley Harvey Crippen, for the murder of his wife Cora, Treasurer of the Music Hall Ladies' Guild and a singer who performed under the stage name Belle Elmore.

In Dr. Crippen's case, he was en route to Canada aboard the North Atlantic liner SS Montrose, when the ship's captain, Henry George Kendall, sent word of his suspicion to the Montreal Star newspaper. His first official message was transmitted on 22 July 1910 informing London that Dr. Crippen and his mistress (his typist since 1900 when she was just 17) were in disguise travelling under the names of Mr and Mrs Robinson. When the ship docked at Pointe-au-Père (Father Point), Quebec, it was the first time that a wireless telegraph had been used to arrange for an arrest. Dr. Crippen was hanged at Pentonville prison, Caledonian Road, London, and the mistress, Ethel Le Neve, was acquitted after her twenty-minute trial. She settled in Croydon (South London), and started a family who knew nothing of her past until after she died of heart failure in Dulwich Hospital in 1967, aged 84.

As for Witte's arrival in America for the peace negotiations, which in reality were a tacit deal on the terms for a surrender, he was well aware that America had been the chief financier to Japan and that Great Britain backed Japan as an ally since the Anglo-Japanese Treaty of Alliance 1902, which had been the first treaty of its kind against a European rival and which circumstance Japan used to advance as a world power. Therefore, when Witte arrived in America, he was not exactly on neutral soil.

It's a wonder that Russia and Japan accepted to meet in America, ostensibly for peace talks, but in actual fact they had been steered to Portsmouth by President Roosevelt who had contrived with Japan to further American interests in the Far East. History credits Japanese

Foreign Minister Baron Jutaro Komura, through his plenipotentiary Kogoro Takahira, for having formally asked Roosevelt to act as the intermediary, and despite his disguised political motive, Roosevelt won the Nobel Peace Prize for his effort.

A delicate diplomatic balance was called for, lest perchance there should arise a cultural impasse to threaten the negotiations. For example, Witte expressed his concern that the toast to the Japanese Emperor (the Mikado), might come before the toast to the Russian Emperor - The solution was to make the toasts simultaneously. Witte saw a gluttonous man in Komura, and warned him not to gorge himself on the cold food the Americans were serving. Komura did not heed the warning and contracted an intestinal variety of typhus. In Witte's opinion, the Americans had no culinary taste and described the food at his hotel in West Point as "*exceedingly bad*", this being the reason his intake was limited to bread and vegetables.

On page 162 he says, "*During my stay in the United States I ate only one decent luncheon and dinner, and that was on board Morgan's yacht, on the day of my visit to West Point.*" i.e. J.P. Morgan the banker. But having scowled Komura for his gluttony, Witte himself became ill in the last days of the Portsmouth Conference. On page 155 he states that unlike his opposite number who had been restricted to bed (Komura), "*. . . in spite of my illness I had to be constantly in the limelight and play the part of a conqueror.*"

Perhaps Roosevelt was the only one who could accommodate the friction that existed between the chief plenipotentiaries. Komura was a previous ambassador to St. Petersburg and knew of Witte, but did not reciprocate to him the same level of courtesy. This was a forced peace and Komura was there to officiate the surrender as Japan had been victorious and were the conquerors. Witte likewise harboured the same disillusion and instead of appeasing Japan he was negotiating territorial claims, driven by the Tsar's stipulation that he concede no territory that was held by Russia at that time.

The reality was that both nations had been almost bankrupted by the war and neither could continue for much longer. Japan could neither push in to Russia nor remain in Manchuria because they teetered along the borders of Korea and Manchuria, unable to commit to either whilst a state of war existed between Russia and Japan. Russia, equally depleted of resources, had been brutally defeated on land and sea and could neither engage nor defend. Yet, each believed they held the high ground in Portsmouth. Of course, it was Japan that had the best cards and they demanded 60 million rubles in reparations. But Witte was the better negotiator, not least because the Tsar had promised to make him a count if he pulled off the talks without further humiliation. The story goes that once the Tsar knew Witte had made a deal, he ordered him to break off the talks, to renege on his pledge. Witte continued to the end, crediting himself for bringing about a good deal for Russia out of an impossible situation. Nevertheless, for his disobedience Witte ascribes it as another reason why the Imperial couple regarded him with such contempt.

It certainly was the case that Witte had warned against the war from the very start. On page 154 he says, "*. . . I did all I could to oppose it . . . .*" But it had been his way back to the world stage and his effort was considered an overriding success for Russia as the Japanese could have been firmer and secured a much better deal for themselves. Although the signing of the second Anglo-Japanese Alliance was in August 1905, Japan at that time also had its own problems at home. Just twenty-four days before the Russo-Japanese Peace Treaty was signed on 5 September 1905, the Hibiya Riot started, in protest to the Portsmouth Treaty, and the following day martial law was enforced in Tokyo to suppress it. In mid-October 1905 the treaty was ratified by Japan and although Russia had not technically surrendered, they had lost their Manchurian and Chinese Assets to Japan.

However, Roosevelt told Japan that over-zealous expansionism was not advisable for a new world power and said, (page 153), "*Let her manifest her superiority in the question of ethics, no less than in military affairs. An appeal is made to her in the name of all that is lofty and noble and to this appeal, I hope, she will not remain deaf.*" Almost at once, The Japan-Korea Treaty of 1905 was agreed upon, making Korea a protectorate of Japan which would ultimately lead to annexation in 1910. Japan had no intention of being constrained by the Americans, and their interests would collide again during the Russian Civil War. Having lost no more territory than Russia had gained, Witte returned with his head held high and the Tsar awarded him the title of Count (slightly higher than a baron).

Still disgruntled by the attempt to keep him in Europe, Witte again tendered his resignation and a second time the Tsar declined it. The next thing for Witte to get involved with were the troubles that had developed at home, and the Tsar needed him now more than ever. One might see how in 1905, the end of the war with Japan was followed by the start of the First Revolution, but this is an over-simplification as war and revolution ran in tandem, the former to a large extent fuelling the latter. There were severe shortages and starvation from which rural pockets of rebellion rapidly grew in to urban revolution. It must have been a momentous occasion when Witte realised that the reforms he had always called for were now the necessary component to stave the revolution.

While Witte had been the statesman in Europe, the war with Japan and the riots at home had broken out in 1904. The first rioting occurred in the Spring, in Odessa, then Kiev in the summer and Baku in the winter. By December 1904 rioting reached St Petersburg's which continued in to January 1905. The attempt to appease the rioters with reforms was discussed at the Conference of December 12th, 1904. Witte says of it, "*It clearly demonstrated to the intelligent classes that the emperor and his government were either unable or unwilling to grant reforms.*" It would have been unthinkable to contemplate at the time, but it was the beginning of the end for the autocratic system.

The October Manifesto 1905 was a necessary correction which gave ordinary Russians some rights. Unfortunately, lessons were not learned, and at the same time that law was duly enacted in 1906 a rescript was issued which completely removed the powers that had been granted. In one account it has been attributed to the Tsarina's doing and in another to the Black Hundred. The resulting political discombobulation split the new constitutional parties and kept the Tsar in perpetual power by enabling the Okhrana (police) and the Black Hundred, as well as the army, to be used to supress the revolutionary elements. Witte said of it, "*Thus one and the same day witnessed the enactment of two diametrically opposed legislative measures.*" And he added, "*Under these circumstances it is no wonder that the country underwent the trials of a revolution.*"

Witte had convinced the Tsar that he needed to sign the Manifesto to survive the revolution, and had these reforms been taken seriously it might have marked a defining time for the good, but the whole affair was sordid and so the revolution continued.

Witte was Prime Minister (1905-1906), "*immediately upon the publication of the historical manifesto.*" Even his elevated position could not quell the national discontent and the unruly element in the Government. It must have been a huge frustration for a man that thrived in a controlled environment. For this he blames the Tsar and the nobility in general and is relentless with his criticisms. "*It is in the Emperor's nature to act like a pendulum, swinging between two extremes.*" And also, "*He* [the Tsar] *was always fond of taking his counsellors by surprise.*" And a subtle dig, "*. . . for like all weak people . . .* " in referring to the Tsar.

Discussing the Tsar's acceptance of and communication with Alexander Dubrovin, the president of the Russian People's Union (Black Hundred), Witte says, "*This telegram, coupled with the manifesto which dissolved the Second Duma, revealed all the poverty of this autocratic Emperor's political thought and the morbidity of his mind.*" Likewise, Witte says of the Tsarina on page 184, about her conversion to Russian Orthodoxy, "*she knew about Russian Orthodoxy no more than a new-born babe knows about the theory of the perturbations of heavenly bodies.*"

Admittedly a hereditary nobleman, Witte says of the nobility, "*the majority is politically a mass of degenerate humanity.*" He tells of how they evolved unchallenged since medieval times and their unwillingness to engage the 20th Century made a rod for their back and enabled the uprisings of 1905, "*Rulers and politicians who do not grasp this simple truth prepare a revolution with their own hands.*" The Government did not escape Witte's criticisms either, "*All revolutions occur because governments fail to satisfy in time the crying needs of the people and remain deaf to them.*"

Prince Svyatopolk-Mirski, the Minister of the Interior, is credited for introducing Liberalism in the Government and the reforms which Witte called for. The problem was that measures to help the plight of the peasantry were blocked by ministers Plehve and Sipyagin (both would be assassinated), and the eminent Konstantin Petrovich Pobiedonostsev, a statesman perhaps equal in political stature to Witte. These three men according to Witte, steered the Emperor away from social reforms to benefit minorities. At one meeting for agrarian issues the committee would only allow discussion from the stance of the nobility, for which Witte says, "*As was usually the case with conferences conducted under His Majesty's presidency, the meeting came to no definite decision.*" He goes on to mention the Finns, Slavs, Polish Jews and Crimean Jews, and blames the criminal element in Siberia for the internal struggles and proudly recalls the arrest of an entire Soviet of 190 members.

INTRODUCTION

Witte said of the Soviet arrests, "*In general, I attributed no importance to this Soviet.*" Little could he know how they would come to dominate the next eight decades. Aside from this, he did make an assessment of what would happen following the granting of the constitutional manifesto of 17th October: If a popular assembly had appeared, it would have demanded the Tsar's abdication and broke out a Fratricidal Civil War, with the occupation of a portion of Russian territory by foreign troops. Russia would then become a constitutional régime which would come about by peaceful efforts or out of torrents of blood. His vision transpired after the Tsar's death; the abdication and civil war came and foreign troops occupied Crimea and Siberia.

Finally, he resigned as Prime Minister, at which time the First Duma was dissolved. It was while he sojourned at Aix-les-Bains in France that he received a message from Baron Frederichs advising him to stay out of Russia. The Tsar wished for him to act as a foreign ambassador, befitting a seasoned statesman. In another example of Witte's paranoia, he interpreted it negatively and was infuriated. He responded to Baron Frederichs by yet again threatening to withdraw completely from government service, stating, "*I propose to offer my services to private institutions.*" The Tsar then asked for their intimate correspondence to be returned, which Witte later regretted doing. The Tsar's trepidation was over a concern that his private conversations would find their way in to Witte's memoirs.

Could the Tsar simply have been trying to help Witte in keeping him away while at home he was blamed for Russia's problems and was a candidate for assassination. Indeed, he received a telegram in October 1906 with a warning to remain in political exile, or, "*come here if you wish to die.*" But, once more back in Russia, he talks about Stolypin's animosity towards him while in his speeches to the Imperial Council, Witte is most definitely the attacker, accusing Stolypin of institutional murder through the promulgation of field court-martials and wisely states, "*. . . problems involving the historical prejudices of the masses which are based on race peculiarities, can be solved only by degrees and slowly.*" He also advises the Tsar against Stolypin's bill to reduce the supreme power. It resulted in Stolypin tendering his resignation which the Tsar declined. Was Witte a victim of his own airs and graces?

INTRODUCTION

II - MIKHAIL RODZIANKO (b.1859-1924)

Sir Bernard Pares gives an adequate introduction to Mikhail Rodzianko's memoirs covering the period of 'Rasputin's Reign.' But you'd be mistaken for assuming it is a biographical work in any real sense and Rasputin's usurpation appears to be a marketing ploy. Of course, events do cover Rasputin's flowering years but the book's subtitle, 'An Empire's Collapse', is a better descriptor as Rodzianko blames Rasputin, the Empress, and to a considerable degree the Emperor as well, for the demise of the Monarchy. Like Sergei Witte, Rodzianko cannot disguise his disgruntlement for the country he loved which he felt had let him down. It was a time when all men were belittled before the Tsar and Rodzianko felt the effect of the Imperial couple's scorn much like Witte had.

Chapter 1 begins with the Imperial couple introducing occultism at the Court due to Tsarina Alexandra's obsession with it. It was a remarkable opening for such opportunists as Master Philippe and Papus and which challenged the influence of the ascetic archbishop and theologian Feofan, the confessor to the Imperial couple, who was deeply rooted in the Orthodox Church. Rasputin's background is outlined and he is described as a man 'greedy' for material gain. Strangely, this is the trait that biographers have not tended to agree with; Rasputin was not impervious to the acquisition of personal wealth - although it cannot be overlooked that much of his labours resulted in financial gain, albeit arguably for the benefit of others.

In the pursuit of his aims Rasputin was utterly unscrupulous, there is no disagreement about that. From the start, (page 396), Rodzianko assigns to Rasputin the role of Emperor's lampkeeper - which according to Baroness Sophie Buxhoeveden in her subsequent memoirs says, was a non-existent post. A few pages later (page 398) and this time instead of creating a myth he dispels one by confirming the Empress was never sexually compromised by Rasputin, which he knew from reading the Imperial couple's war correspondence, which to all that read it, would have proved that:

"The blameless nature of the family life of the Imperial couple was patent to all, while those who, like myself, became acquainted with their private evidence during the war it was proved by documentary evidence. Nevertheless, Gregory Rasputin became the Empress Alexandra Feodorovna's oracle, and for her his opinion was law."

INTRODUCTION

On the same page it's generally accepted that the Tsar was weak-willed and controlled by his wife and thereby Rasputin. He states:

"On the other hand she, herself strong-willed, almost despotic by nature, exercised over her august consort, who lacked all traces of will or character, an unlimited, almost overwhelming influence."

It is reiterated succinctly on page 407 as, "*The Emperor's feeble will.*" This perceived weakness meant that, "*Nicholas II was organically incapable of adopting any anti-Rasputin policy.*" Not only did Rasputin control the Empress and through her also the Emperor, but his followers of Rasputinites along with the parties of the Extreme Right, "*laid the foundations of the Russian Revolution.*"

In Chapter III Rodzianko has a first audience with the Tsar at Tsarskoe Selo in his capacity as Chairman of the Duma. Somewhat inappropriately, in hindsight, Rodzianko broached on concerns about Rasputin. The Tsar seemed remarkably well informed during Rodzianko's full report but the revelations about Rasputin took him aback, according to the Palace Commandant, General V. N. Dediulin, who later said the Tsar became considerably affected by it and had asked Dediulin to entrust Rodzianko to conduct a discreet investigation in to the allegations made against Rasputin. A chance encounter occurred when the Tsarevitch Alexei passed by, affording Rodzianko the opportunity to meet him for the first time. At the next Duma sitting, Rodzianko gave the representatives a verbatim account of his audience with the Tsar and Tsarevich, which was gladly received by all the parties and at that time all appeared to be going well. Rodzianko's job at first was to build good relations between the Duma and the Tsar, which he had done.

During his investigation in to Rasputin, Rodzianko secured the file on Rasputin from the Church officials at the palace, thereby inadvertently pitting himself against the Tsarina, Rasputin's greatest supporter. She instructed the church officials to retrieve the file. But Rodzianko remained unwavering in his sense of duty, refusing to hand it back and rebuking the officials for their cowardice. The Tsarina had the investigation supressed and blocked Rodzianko's attempts to report to the Tsar on his findings. He had been firm but was yet to learn who held the reins of influence at the palace.

The standoff with the Tsarina and Rasputin, Rodzianko cites as the main reason for the Tsarina's growing hatred towards him. In

INTRODUCTION

Chapter IV he describes the relationship between the Duma and the Emperor and in Chapter V the focus returns to Rasputin about his returning to St Petersburg from exile. So, at this point, Rodzianko has claimed that the Tsarina, the Tsar and Rasputin, each in their own measure, had it in for him, and even the High Procurator of the Holy Synod is accused of slandering him to the Tsar.

In Chapter VI these underlying tensions become the hostility of the Government against the Duma. He makes sarcastic remarks here and there, partly borne out of his resentment for being treated disrespectfully; for example, when he comments, "*Thus the most uncomfortable compartment was reserved for me on the official train.*" The chapter ends with a divided Duma and Rodzianko's intention to resign the chairmanship and establish a new party of moderates called the Zemstov-Octoborists. He does not seem to appreciate that his position demanded a high level of compromising mediation in order to represent the collective voice of the Duma and that his word was not in itself the law, as was the case with the Tsar. There's a taint of manic depression when things don't go entirely his way, opposed by others or blocked by the Tsar.

As the outbreak of World War I approaches, the Duma is re-called. Sergei Witte, was out of the political arena with a year left to live; Rodzianko was in to his final ten years, a more confident phase when he was convinced that he was better suited to steering Russia through the current turmoil, more so than the Tsar who in his remissness to lead had left the country in the political doldrums. The double Nobel Prize winner (1903 Physics, 1911 Chemistry,) Marie Curie, née Maria Sklodowska, was also in Poland shortly before Rodzianko (1913), soon to be appointed Director of the Curie Laboratory in the Radium Institute of the University of Paris (1914). She wrote to her brother dated 18 March 1894, the year that Nicholas II acceded the throne, "*One never notices what has been done; one can only see what remains to be done.*"

Rodzianko easily foresaw Austria's invasion in to Serbia and the ensuing declarations of war, yet, he headed out to Warsaw where he fell upon the fiasco of 18,000 Russian wounded soldiers being deposited on railway platforms, mostly laying in mud and medically untreated since their removal from the front. One can hardly imagine being left outside, day and night, without much hope of deliverance. There were around 100 Polish volunteers making the best of it, no military staff and no transportation passing through. On further investigation Rodzianko found a nearby hospital with a Red Cross presence of doctors and nurses that were doing nothing other than waiting around for hospital trains to be arranged. His priority turned to expediating the wounded by putting the Red Cross staff to work and bringing medical trains to the platforms.

General Nikolai Vladimirovich Russky was an infantry and cavalry officer in command of the Third Army in the Kiev Military District, that from September 1914 commanded the entire northwestern front. He would receive orders in 1917 to meet the detoured Imperial train at Pskov, a city in northwestern Russia located about 12 miles from the Estonian border, to facilitate the Tsar's abdication. Rodzianko first mentions him when they meet in Warsaw and he learns of the severe boots shortage and lack of munitions to the front; indeed, many soldiers were fighting without footwear, without rifles and with silent artillery behind them. Rodzianko reports to the supreme commander of the armies in the West, Grand Duke Nicolai Nicolaevitch, the grandson of Nicholas I and uncle to Nicholas II, that he was, "*oppressed by the incompetence of the commanding staff.*"

Some accounts attribute all blame to Grand Duke Nicolai for the poor logistics and his, "*leaving of things*" such that the manufacture of boots, rifles and munitions, being a matter for the War Office and Artillery Department, had not been overly chased and given ultimatums but instead the entire fiasco he blamed on Rasputin. It's hard to fathom how Rasputin could or would act to prevent supplies to the front, even though he was against the war, unless to imply that Rasputin was a German agent. The Grand Duke had respect but was neither a gifted leader nor tactician, leaving these qualities for his subordinates at the Stavka. As for the Government, it was hindered by the Tsarina's constant changes of ministers. The military's issue was that it could only make requests through the relevant Government departments, which were stifled in a sea of corruption that filled the space left by all the bureaucratic confusion.

Rodzianko saw the problem of supplying the front as a combination of failures from the Emperor down to the boot manufacturer and rifle maker. This tragedy in logistics is regarded as the main factor that caused the Great Retreat. He wanted to by-pass the red tape and make arrangements with the zemstvos who were eager to help supply the front, but were restricted by legislation preventing the free movement of goods; i.e., a product made in one district could not be transported through another district to its destination. In addition, many State factories were still run by German subjects and should the workers turn against them, the whole manufacturing base would be lost. Rodzianko was organising with the Zemstvos and other organisations outside of the control of the Government, which politicians like Minister Maklakoff had persuaded the Tsarina that they had anarchistic aims. Maklakoff in particular, was an avid opponent of the Duma and its chairman and sought to limit their powers to a 'consultative' institution only.

Much procurement by the Artillery Department was done through the Grand Duke Sergei Mikhailovitch, a grandson of Nicholas I and a brother to Alexander, the husband of the Tsar's sister Xenia. He fell in love with the ballerina Mathilde Kshesinskiai (aka Kschessinska), the woman the Tsar had been seeing before his marriage to the Tsarina. Kshesinskiai did not reciprocate Sergei's affections and used him for her own financial gain, acting as the go-between in arms deals. It was a highly lucrative enterprise because private firms were forbidden to supply the war effort. Yet, the Grand Duke's team could only source one fifth of what was possible and so the front fell short. This was the problem Rodzianko was trying to get around, "*The principal danger which the country was menaced lay not outside but within.*"

Another grandson of Nicholas I was Grand Duke Nicolai Nicolaevitch, the Commander-in-Chief at the front, who at the outbreak of World War I had pledged his loyalty to the Duma chairman. When the Tsar removed him to take command at the front himself, Rodzianko believed it to be a grave mistake and blamed the Tsarina for it. An audience with the Tsar imploring him to reconsider was fruitless and Rodzianko, "*had a heart attack in consequence.*" Princess Zinaida Yusupoff visited Rodzianko at his home and told his wife, Anna Golitsyna, that it would all lead to revolution, and indeed it did, a little over a year later. Princess Zinaida was mother to Felix Yusupoff, the man who would arrange the murder of Rasputin in December 1916, which was secretly backed by his mother and the Grand Duchess Elizabeth Feodorovna, sister to the Tsarina.

When the Tsar arrived at Stavka he issued an ukase to his Prime Minister Goremykin that sanctioned the dissolution of the Duma. According to Rodzianko, "*to lower the prestige of the President of the Duma in the eyes of the representatives of the people.*" In effect the parliament had been prorogued at a time when Russia was at war. He wrote to Goremykin to 'dissavow' any culpability of the war being badly managed by him or the Duma, saying with his customary measure of sarcasm, "*We, the members of the Duma, possess a merely consultative voice, and cannot, therefore, be held responsible for the inevitable and imminent collapse.*" In so doing, Goremykin was added to the list of Rodzianko's enemies.

Rodzianko received The Order of St. Anne, first class, not for his Duma chairmanship which he held from 1911 to 1915, but for 'special services' for the types of military accomplishments that he had previously been instructed by the Tsar to keep his nose out of. This marks the half way point in the book and it now moves in to a detailed view of the Duma during war time, keeping Rasputin's presence lingering in the background. Rodzianko is appalled by the corruption he has seen in the supply chain from the military and nobility alike and notes the utter incompetence of the Government. The final straw came from within the Duma when his vice-president, Alexander Protopopoff, was promoted to Minister of the Interior and became an avid supporter of the Tsarina and Rasputin and further allied himself with Prime Minister Sturmer to dissolve the Duma.

Protopopoff had fallen in with spiritualism and Rodzianko says of him, "*His behaviour was in general very peculiar, and at times he gave the impression of not being quite normal.*" In fact, "*. . . since he became Minister, Protopopoff had positively gone mad.*" Rodzianko warned him not to compromise himself but to no avail. Eventually, Protopopoff believed that he alone was entrusted to save Russia and thereafter, he was not received well by the Duma.

Rodzianko attributes the February Revolution 1917 to Rasputin whereas other accounts say that Rasputin had no influence at all. In this book that Rodzianko dedicates to Rasputin, he attests to the extensive influence the *Starets* had. However, one must guard against these strong opinions in memoirs, as for example, when Rodzianko states the troops were totally loyal to the Emperor and "*willingly sacrificing their lives for their country,*" that was simply not true. Most men were fighting without any care for the Tsar at all and knew not what they were fighting for other than to survive the horrors of war. As initial victories turned in to a long and costly retreat, patriotism was left in the mud and revolution ripped through the trenches.

BOOK ONE

These are the secret memories of Count Sergei Witte, a Russian statesman who served two Emperors. They were completed in 1912 and consequently there is no reference to World War I, for which he was quite outspoken, in favour of peace at all cost.

Original book published by Doubleday, Page & Company, 1921
Published in New York and Toronto
445 printed pages – manuscript held at Columbia University Library, Bakhmeteff Archive.
Digitised by Internet Archive in 2007. Public Domain.

The Memoirs of
COUNT WITTE

TRANSLATED FROM THE ORIGINAL RUSSIAN
MANUSCRIPT AND EDITED BY
ABRAHAM YARMOLINSKY

GARDEN CITY, N.Y., AND TORONTO
DOUBLEDAY, PAGE & COMPANY
1921

EDITOR'S NOTE

Unless otherwise indicated, the dates in the text are according to the Russian, or "old style" calendar. In some cases the corresponding Western, or "new style" date is given in parentheses. To convert a Russian (Julian) to a Western (Gregorian) date add twelve days to the former, for dates preceding the year 1900, and thirteen days for later dates.

In spelling the Russian names an attempt is made to follow a consistent system of transliteration, in keeping with the best modern practice, due allowance being made for forms consecrated by usage.

CONTENTS

CHAPTER		PAGE
I	My Youth and Early Career	35
II	Memories of Alexander III	60
III	My Work as Minister of Finances	69
IV	Dealing with Li Hung Chang	95
V	Origins and Course of the Russo-Japanese War	112
VI	The Peace of Portsmouth	134
VII	Nicholas II and Alexandra	170
VIII	The Czar's Attempts at Reform	192
IX	The Manifesto of October 17, 1905	216
X	Bloody Sunday and the First Soviet	226
XI	The Loan that Saved Russia	253
XII	My Premiership	277
XIII	Stolypin's Reactionary Régime	314
XIV	My Experiences with the Keiser	343
INDEX		369

PREFACE

Not without hesitancy have I resolved to write a few lines as a foreword to the memoirs of my late husband. I cannot be impartial in my estimate of this work, to which Count Witte attributed so much importance; and the biased judgment of his wife can hardly be of any interest to the reader. I confess, however, that I have not been able to resist the temptation to take advantage of this occasion to convey to the American public the gratitude which the late Count Witte felt toward the Government, press, and people of the United States for the sympathy they had shown him at the time of the Portsmouth Conference. America's recent declaration of its resolve to defend Russia's incontestable interests at the critical period of its temporary weakness has shown that this sympathetic attitude toward him at that time was not an accident.

I should like to explain to the reader the significance which my husband attributed to his work. I also wish to say a word about the motives which urged him to present his thoughts and reminiscences in the form of a book not destined to be published while he and his contemporaries were alive. Count Witte was neither a courtier flattering the monarch, nor a demagogue flattering the mob. Although a nobleman, he did not defend the privileges of the nobility; and while aiming in his political activities mainly at improving the condition of the peasantry in accordance with the dictates of justice, as a statesman he remained alien to that theoretical "populism" with which the majority of the Russian intellectuals was infatuated. He was not a Liberal, for he did not sympathize with the striving of the Liberals to reorganize the political system all at once, with a single stroke. Nor was he a Conservative, for he despised the coarseness and backwardness of the political thinking which was characteristic of Russia's ruling bureaucracy. My husband repeatedly said to those intimate with him: "I am neither a Liberal nor Conservative. I am simply a man of culture. I cannot exile a man to Siberia merely because he does not think as I do, and I cannot deprive him of civil rights because he does not pray in the same church as I do. . . ."

For this reason Witte had many enemies in all camps. At the Court, among Conservatives, among Liberals, in the democratic circles, everywhere Count Witte was considered "an alien." He sought to serve his country in a way all his own, and that is why he had but few constant companions. Justice compels one to acknowledge that my husband's gifts in the field of statesmanship were not contested. As a matter of fact, they were valued in all the circles of Great Russia. Nevertheless, for the reason just mentioned, no other statesman has ever been the object of so many varied and contradictory, yet persistent and passionate, attacks. At the Court he was accused of republicanism, while the Radicals attributed to him the desire to curtail the rights of the people to the Monarch's advantage. The landowners ascribed to him a desire to ruin them for the benefit of the peasants, while the radical parties upbraided him for a fancied desire to deceive the peasants for the benefit of the land-owners. The author of the Constitution of October 17th, which forms the opening of new Russian history, was too inviting a target for intrigues and slanders; on the other hand, the many-sided and complex personality of a great statesman could not easily be forced into a simplified formula and, therefore, it gave rise to misunderstandings, which were at times entertained in good faith.

To engage in controversies with his opponents, to refute slanders, to clear away misunderstandings through the press, my husband did not desire. He would not demean himself by taking a hand in an undignified wrangle. Besides, the censorship conditions of the old régime, which were more stringent for the Czar's Prime Minister than for an ordinary citizen, as well as a desire to spare the feelings of his contemporaries, prevented Count Witte from expressing his thoughts fully and openly. Hence his decision to let the next generation judge his activity; hence these Memoirs.

My husband wrote his Memoirs only abroad, during the months of his summer or winter rests at the foreign health resorts. He was not quite confident that his study on the Kamenny-Ostrov Prospect in Petrograd was sufficiently secure from the eye and arm of the Secret Service. At any moment, by searching the house, they could deprive him of his manuscripts. He knew that too many persons of power were interested in his work. All the time the manuscripts were kept in a foreign bank in my name. My husband feared that in the event of his death the Court and the Government would seek to take possession of his archives, and he begged me to insure the safety of the Memoirs in time. I did so by transferring the manuscripts from Paris to Bayonne and depositing them there in another person's name. The precautions were not in vain. Immediately upon the death of my husband, in February, 1915, his study was sealed and all his papers examined and taken away by the authorities.

PREFACE

Shortly afterwards the Chief of the General Staff, a General-Adjutant, came to me in the Emperor's name and said that His Majesty, having perused the table of contents of my husband's Memoirs, had become interested in them and wished to read them. I replied that to my regret I was unable to present them to His Majesty, because they were kept abroad. The Emperor's messenger did not insist, but some time afterwards an attaché of the Russian Embassy in Paris appeared in our villa at Biarritz, and in the absence of the owners made a very careful search. He was looking for the Memoirs, which at that time, as I said before, were quietly lying in a safe of a bank at Bayonne.

The Memoirs do not touch upon the events of the great war, for they were completed in 1912. For this reason I shall say a few words about the popular legend which attributes to Count Witte a particular Germanophilism. The legend is entirely without foundation. Generally speaking, my husband had no sentimental biases in politics. He was guided by reason alone. He had no particular love or hatred for any country or nation. He was only a Russophil, in the sense that he placed above all else the interests of his country and people. It is true that he was a most resolute opponent of wars in general and of this war in particular. He said that it would end with a catastrophe for Russia, and that it would ruin Europe for a century. Long before the war he stood for a rapprochement between Germany and France with the energetic assistance of Russia. When the war began, he was deeply worried by it, and he expressed himself in favour of the immediate convocation of a peace conference. "Let the armies fight, since they have already started that madness, but let the diplomats immediately begin their work of making peace," he would say to his friends. This circumstance must have given rise to the legend of my husband's Germanophil tendencies. Whether or not he was right in his views of the great war, I do not know, but I do know that all his thoughts and feelings were instinct with love for Russia, and that he wished well-being and order to the whole world.

COUNTESS WITTE.

Bruxelles, October 1st, 1920

THE MEMOIRS OF COUNT WITTE

CHAPTER I

MY YOUTH AND EARLY CAREER

I WAS born in the year 1849 in the city of Tiflis. My father, Yuli (Julius) Fiodorovich Witte, was of Baltic origin, although officially he belonged to the gentry of the province of Pskov. His ancestors were Dutchmen who emigrated to the Baltic provinces at the time when that region was under Swedish rule. My mother, on the contrary, came of pure Russian stock. She was the daughter of Princess Yelena Pavlovna Dolgoruki, the last representative of the older branch of that ancient and high-born race. Her father was Andrey Mikhailovich Fadeyev, who began his career as Governor of the province of Saratov and ended as a member of the Main Board of the Viceroy of the Caucasus. At the marriage ceremony they were blessed with an ancient cross, which, according to the family tradition, belonged to Mikhail of Chernigov, a mediaeval Russian prince, martyred by a Tatar Khan and canonized by the Orthodox Church.

At the time when my grandfather held the post of Provincial Governor, the young Witte, who had studied agriculture and mining in Prussia, arrived in Saratov in the capacity of expert agronomist. There he fell in love with my mother and married her. My father was born a Lutheran, and as my mother's family was arch-Orthodox, he was forced to embrace her faith as an indispensable condition of the union. He became completely submerged in his wife's family and retained but little contact with the Wittes. When his father-in-law went to the Caucasus at the invitation of Viceroy Prince Vorontzov, he followed him and served there in the capacity of Director of the Department of State Property. The two families settled in Tiflis and lived in close intimacy. My grandparents played an important part in my early life. My grandmother was my first teacher. She was an exceptionally cultured woman and a botanist of no mean achievement.

She gathered a vast collection of specimens of the Caucasian flora and supplied a scientific description of each plant. She taught me reading and also the first principles and dogmas of the Orthodox Church. She was very old and palsied, so that she had to be wheeled into the children's room seated in an armchair for the lesson. As she could not move, I would kneel by her with a primer in my hands. In this manner she also taught my two brothers, Alexander and Boris. I was grandfather's pet, and his death he departed this life at the age of seventy was a heavy loss for me.

Brother Alexander chose a military career and was fatally wounded in the last Turkish War. Major Witte was a brave, modest, and lovable man. The memory of him is still green in his regiment, and the favourite regimental songs are those which sing of his exploits. I loved him dearly and took care of him during his fatal sickness. He used to tell me, I recall, his war experiences and also how he once fought a duel and killed his adversary. Brother Boris did not distinguish himself. Of my two sisters one died two years ago (1909).

Several members of my mother's family were prominent in one way or another. One of my aunts, who married a Colonel Hahn, achieved some fame as a writer. Her older daughter was the celebrated theosophist known under the name of Madame Blavatski. The personality and career of my cousin Yelena Petrovna Blavatski deserves to be treated at some length.

As I was many years her junior, I could not have any recollecttions of Yelena in her youth. From the stories current in our family I gather that when Mrs. Hahn, her mother, died, she and her sister came to live with my grandfather at Tiflis. At an early age, such is the family tradition, Yelena married a certain Blavatski, Vice-Governor of the province of Erivan, and settled in the city of the same name, but soon abandoned her husband and came back to her grandfather. When she appeared in his spacious mansion he immediately decided to send away the troublesome young person at the earliest possible moment to her father, who was an artillery colonel stationed in the vicinity of St. Petersburg. As there were at that time no railways within the territory of the Caucasus, the problem was not without its difficulties. It was solved in this wise. Two women and as many men, including grandfather's trusty steward, were selected from the large staff of domestic serfs, and under this convoy the future theosophic celebrity proceeded in the direction of Poti, enthroned in a capacious four-in-hand. From Poti it was planned to ship the fugitive by sea to some port connected by rail with the interior of Russia. When the company arrived in Poti, several steamers, including an English craft, lay in the harbour. Young Mme. Blavatski, so the story runs, immediately struck up an acquaintance with the captain of the English vessel. To make a long story short, one fine morning the convoy discovered to their horror that their mistress and charge had vanished into the air. Stowed away in an English ship, she was on her way to Constantinople.

The subsequent developments of her amazing career appear as follows: At Constantinople she entered a circus as an equestrienne and it was there that Mitrovich, one of the most celebrated opera bassos of the time, fell in love with her. She gave up the circus and accompanied the singer to one of the European capitals where he was engaged to sing. Shortly afterwards, grandfather was the recipient of letters from the singer Mitrovich, who asserted that he had been married to Yelena and styled himself "grandson." The famous basso apparently was not disconcerted by the fact that she had not been properly divorced from her legal husband, the Vice-Governor of Erivan. Several years later a new "grandson" accrued to my grandparents. A certain Englishman from London informed them in a letter bearing an American stamp that he had been married to Mme. Blavatski, who had gone with him on a business trip to the United States. Next she reappears in Europe and becomes the right hand of the celebrated medium of the sixties, Hume. Then her family caught two more glimpses of her dazzling career. They learned from the papers that she gave pianoforte concerts in London and Paris and afterwards became the manager of the royal choir, maintained by King Milan of Serbia.

In the meantime some ten years had passed. Grown tired, perhaps, of her adventures, the strayed sheep decided to return to the fold. She succeeded, at the end of that period, in getting grandfather's permission to return to Tiflis. She promised to mend her ways and even go back to her legitimate husband. It was during that visit of hers that I saw her first. At that time she was but a ruin of her former self. Her face, apparently once of great beauty, bore all the traces of a tempestuous and passionate life, and her form was marred by an early obesity. Besides, she paid but scant attention to her appearance and preferred loose morning dresses to more elaborate apparel. But her eyes were extraordinary. She had enormous, azure coloured eyes, and when she spoke with animation, they sparkled in a fashion which is altogether indescribable. Never in my life have I seen anything like that pair of eyes.

It was this apparently unattractive woman that turned the heads of a great many society people at Tiflis. She did it by means of spiritualistic séances, which she conducted in our house. Every evening, I remember, the Tiflis society folks would foregather in our house around Yelena Petrovna. Among the guests were Count Vorontzov-Dashkov, the two Counts Orlov-Davydov and other representatives of the jeunesse doree, which at that time was flocking to the Caucasus from the two capitals in quest of pleasure and adventure. The séance would last the whole evening and oftentimes the whole night. My cousin did not confine the demonstrations of her powers to table rapping, evocation of spirits and similar mediumistic hocus-pocus. On one occasion she caused a closed piano in an adjacent room to emit sounds as if invisible hands were playing upon it. This was done in my presence, at the instance of one of the guests. Although a young boy, my attitude toward these performances was decidedly critical and I looked on them as mere sleight-of-hand tricks. I should like to add that these séances were kept secret from my grandparents and that my father, too, entertained a negative attitude towards the whole business. It was Hume, I believe, to whom Madame Blavatski owed her occult knowledge.

Mme. Blavatski made her peace with her husband and went as far as establishing a home at Tiflis, but it was not given to her to walk the path of righteousness for any length of time. One fine morning she was accosted in the street by Mitrovich. The famous basso was now declining, artistically and otherwise. After a brilliant career in Europe, he was forced to accept an engagement at the Italian Opera of Tiflis. The singer apparently had no doubts as to his rights to my cousin, and did not hesitate to assert his claims. As a result of the scandal, Mme. Blavatski vanished from Tiflis and the basso with her. The couple went to Kiev, where under the guidance of his "wife" Mitrovich, who by this time was approaching sixty, learned how to sing in Russian and appeared with success in such Russian operas as "Life for the Czar," "Rusalka," etc. The office of Governor-General of Kiev was held at that time by Prince Dundukov-Korsakov. The Prince, who at one time served in the Caucasus, had known Yelena Petrovna in her maiden days. I am not in a position to say what was the nature of their relationship, but one fine morning the Kievans discovered a leaflet pasted on the doors and telegraph posts which contained a number of poems very disagreeable for the Governor-General. The author of this poetic outburst was no other person than Mme. Blavatski herself, and as the fact was patent, the couple had to clear out.

She was heard of next from Odessa, where she emerged in the company of her faithful basso. At the time our entire family was settled in that city (my grandparents and father had died at Tiflis), and my brother and I attended the university there. The extraordinary couple must have found themselves in great straits. It was then that my versatile cousin opened in succession an ink factory and retail shop and a store of artificial flowers. In those days she often came to see my mother and I visited her store several times, so that I had the opportunity of getting better acquainted with her. I was especially impressed by the extraordinary facility with which she acquired skill and knowledge of the most varied description. Her abilities in this respect verged on the uncanny. A self-taught musician, she was able to give pianoforte concerts in London and Paris, and although entirely ignorant of the theory of music, she conducted a large orchestra. Consider also that although she never seriously studied any foreign languages, she spoke several of them with perfect ease. I was also struck by her mastery of the technique of verse. She could write pages of smoothly flowing verse without the slightest effort, and she could compose essays in prose on every conceivable subject. Besides she possessed the gift of hypnotizing both her hearer and herself into believing the wildest inventions of her fantasy. She had, no doubt, a literary talent. The Moscow editor, Katkov, famous in the annals of Russian journalism, spoke to me in the highest terms of praise about her literary gifts, as evidenced in the tales entitled "From the Jungles of Hindustan,! which she contributed to his magazine, The Russian Messenger (Russki Vyestnik).

Mme. Blavatski's ventures in the field of commerce and industry proved, of course, dismal failures. It was then that Mitrovich accepted an engagement to sing at the Italian Opera at Cairo and the couple set out for Egypt. By that time they presented a rather sorry sight, he a toothless lion, perennially at the feet of his mistress, an aged lady, stout and slovenly. Off the African coast their ship was wrecked and all the passengers found themselves in the waves. Mitrovich saved his mistress, but was drowned himself. Mme. Blavatski entered Cairo in a wet skirt and without a penny to her name. How she extricated herself from that situation, I do not know, but she was next discovered in England, where she founded a Theosophic Society. To strengthen the foundations of the new cult, she travelled to India, where she studied the occult science of the Hindus. Upon her return from India she became the centre of a large group of devotees of the theosophic doctrine and settled in Paris as the acknowledged head of the theosophists. Shortly afterwards she fell ill and died. The teachings of theosophy, however, are still thriving.

Let him who still doubts the non-material origin and the independent existence of the soul in man consider the personality of Mme. Blavatski. During her earthly existence, she housed a spirit which was, no doubt, independent of physical or physiological being. As to the particular realm of the invisible world from which that spirit emerged, there may be some doubt whether it was Inferno, Purgatory or Paradise. I cannot help feeling that there was something demoniac in that extraordinary woman.

As I wander back in memory to the formative period of my life, I perceive that I was brought up in an atmosphere of absolute loyalism. One of my earliest reminiscences is of a room where I am with my nurse and which is suddenly filled with the members of the family weeping aloud. The cause of that sorrow was the news of the death of Emperor Nicholas I. Alone the loss of a very dear friend could make people weep with such genuine grief. My devotion to the monarchs whom I served and to the monarchistic principle generally must be indeed an inherited characteristic....

Speaking of my early upbringing, I must say that while my parents hired for us boys, gouverneurs and tutors without stinting money, they failed to give us enough of their personal attention. As a result, we were not sufficiently safeguarded against harmful and depraving influences. As a child I witnessed ugly scenes between my foster-mother (my mother did not suckle me herself) and my nursery-maid and their respective husbands who happened to be drunkards. When brother Boris, who was one year my senior, and myself somewhat grew up, we were entrusted to the care of a tutor, a retired Caucasian veteran, who was a heavy drinker. Subsequently we were left in the charge of a French gouverneur, a former officer of the French Navy. After a short while the Frenchman was deported by the authorities as a result of a scandalous love affair of his. He was succeeded by a Swiss, who became enamoured of our governess, and was in his turn supplanted by a German imported by my father from Dorpat. Herr Paulsohn taught us, among other subjects, history, geography, and German. For some reason or other, I have not profited by his instruction in German, and in fact I have never learned to speak that language. French, on the contrary, I learned to speak early in life. In fact, I spoke it with more ease than Russian.

Simultaneously several instructors of the local classical Gymnasium (secondary school preparing for the university) were busy coaching us for the entrance examinations to that school. We were finally admitted as non-matriculated students to the fourth class (the course of instruction comprised seven classes or years), and we passed from one class to another without examination. I was an extremely poor student and, in fact, I played hookey most of the time. The teachers indulged me partly out of consideration for my family and partly because they were not responsible either for my instruction or behaviour. I was consumed at that time by a passion for music and devoted most of my time to practice and lessons in the local Conservatory. Besides, both brother Boris and myself were enthusiastic sportsmen. We rode a great deal on horseback and at the in(*si*)stance of Uncle Rostislav we studied fencing. At the final examinations I could hardly give a satisfactory answer in any subject. Nevertheless, I received the Certificate of Maturity, which entitles one to admission to the University. The certificate contained, however, a very low mark for deportment. At that time I was coming seventeen.

The moment had now come when I was to bid farewell to the place where I spent my childhood and adolescence and journey to some distant university town. I was entering upon a new period of existence. The impression which those years left upon my mind is one of great opulence and freedom. To characterize our mode of living, it is enough to point out that the family kept as many as eighty-four domestic serfs. Needless to say that our house was the meeting place of "society," including men like Metropolitan Isidor, Exarch of Georgia, who used to dine with us.

At first father intended to send Boris and myself to the University of Kiev, but finally his choice fell on Odessa, where a university had just been opened. In the Fall, accompanied by both father and mother, we set out for Odessa. There I discovered that I was too young to be admitted to the University and that, besides, the mark in deportment would also be in my way. It was then decided that I would for one semester attend the local Gymnasium of Richelieu. Father and mother returned to Tiflis, and we remained alone.

Just then it suddenly dawned upon me that neither brother nor I was doing any serious work and that should this idling continue we were bound sooner or later to go to the dogs. It was then that for the first time I gave evidence of that independence of judgment and sturdiness of will which have afterwards never deserted me. I formed a definite plan of action. The two of us were to leave Odessa, which because of its many distractions and temptations was no place for serious study, and go to Kishinev, where we would be entire strangers. There we would engage several reliable Gymnasium instructors as coaches, work hard as long as necessary and take the maturity examinations once more. I won over my brother to this plan, we went to Kishinev, and at the end of six months of strenuous, honest work we obtained Certificates of Maturity from the local Gymnasium. Thereupon we returned to Odessa and entered the university, in the year 1867, if I remember rightly. I matriculated under the Faculty of Physico-Mathematical Sciences.

At the end of our first University year, we set out for Tiflis with a view to spending the summer vacation at home. At Poti we were met by a relative who imparted to us the sad news that father had suddenly died. Father's death resulted in the complete financial ruin of the family. This is how it happened. Viceroy Baryatynski made various attempts to develop the natural resources of the Caucasus. The production of cast-iron he entrusted to a certain Lippe, the consul of Baden at Odessa. This German set up a number of mills, but soon died and left them in a lamentable state. At the Viceroy's suggestion, father, who had studied mining in Prussia, took over the management of the mills, and in trying to develop the business he was forced to invest in it his own funds. As he had no fortune of his own, he drew upon mother's capital, with her permission, of course. Thus he spent all mother possessed and in addition incurred enormous debts. The informal understanding was that the Government was sooner or later to take over the mills and reimburse father for all his expenses. But when father suddenly died, the understanding proved of no value. The liabilities on father's estate were so great that we found it advisable to waive the inheritance. Thus we were left without any resources, barring a small pension granted by the Viceroy to mother, and a modest sum which grandfather willed to Uncle Rostislav and which the latter generously turned over to mother Under these circumstances it was decided that it would be best for the entire family to settle at Odessa. This we did the next Fall. Only

Alexander, who at that time had already his commission, remained in the Caucasus. This sudden transition from opulence to what was practically poverty was very painful for mother. Our situation was, indeed, very difficult. It was only owing to a monthly stipend of fifty rubles that brother and I were enabled to complete our studies.

At the University I worked day and night and achieved great proficiency in all my studies. I was so thoroughly familiar with the subjects that I passed all my examinations with flying colours without making any special preparations for them. My final academic thesis was entitled "On Infinitesimal Quantities." The work was rather original in conception and distinguished by a philosophic breadth of view. Two years ago I noticed a French translation of it in a show window of a Parisian book shop. I was getting ready to write another thesis, on an astronomical subject, but I fell in love with an actress and lost all desire to compose dissertations.

During my University years I had but little time for politics. Generally speaking, I remained faithful to the principles of monarchism and the dogmas of Christianity, which my upbringing had impressed upon me. In this respect I stood apart from the general student body, which in those years was swayed by extreme political ideas and the philosophy of atheistic materialism. Nevertheless, my seriousness and learning commanded the respect of my comrades. In spite of my extreme monarchistic sympathies, I was, in fact, elected to the board which was in charge of the Students' Fund. This innocent savings-fund was subsequently closed down as a dangerous institution and the members of the board including myself were brought to trial. An indictment was drawn up by Attorney-General Orlov, which threatened us with exile to Siberia. We were saved by the aristocratic so-called English Club!

This is what happened: Orlov applied for membership in that club, but was voted down. The Minister inquired why that happened. He was told that the members of the club objected to the preposterous indictment Orlov had drawn up against the students. As a result, instead of being exiled to some distant corner in Siberia, we were each fined twenty-five rubles by a Justice of the Peace.

The faculty of the University of Odessa included men like Mechnikov and Sechenov in biology who later achieved world-wide fame, but the teaching staff of the mathematical department did not shine. We had only one professor who possessed the rare gift of mathematical thought in its purest and highest form, but he was a heavy drinker. Nevertheless, in spite of his handicap, he exerted a great influence on his students. I was his favourite pupil and, to a certain extent, assistant.

Looking back at my student years, I cannot help feeling that I am greatly indebted to my *alma mater*. I have a high regard for university scholarship and university life. By its very definition, a university is dedicated to the study of the whole sum of human knowledge as it exists at a given moment. This enables the student, while specializing along a definite line, to live, to a certain extent, in intellectual contact with the main currents of science. But academic scholarship must be assured complete freedom. In saying this I do not wish to advocate that false "freedom" of the universities, which would turn them into a forum for political discussion envenomed by passion, falsehood, and vulgar cynicism. A true university is the best medium for the growth of that broad-mindedness which is the pre-requisite for fruitful scientific work and all other forms of constructive activity.

I left the university with a firm intention to prepare myself for an academic career, notably for the chair of pure mathematics. My decision was very distasteful both to my mother and to Uncle Rostislav. They argued that a professorial career did not befit a nobleman. Finally, uncle persuaded me to accept a nominal position in the chancery of Count Kotzebue, Governor-General of Odessa, while continuing my academic studies. This circumstance gave me access to the Count's parlour, where among others I met Count Vladimir Bobrinski, then Minister of Ways of Communication. Apparently at Gen. Fadeyev's suggestion, Bobrinski repeatedly spoke to me of the great advantages of the career of a railroad man. Tempted by his words, I told him that I was going to give up my academic career and take an examination for the degree of traction engineer. To my surprise, the Count strenuously opposed my latter intention. To his mind, the caste of engineers was a great evil. The Government railroad service needed, he said, not narrow specialists, but men with a good liberal education, preferably with a training in mathematics. Instead of going through the theoretical work necessary to obtain the degree, he advised me to learn the technicalities of railroading in practice. I yielded to his arguments and entered the service of the Odessa Government Railroad.

I donned the military uniform worn in those days by the railroad employés who had a definite rank and began to study railroading by actually doing the routine work essential to the various forms of railroad service, beginning with the humblest. I sold passenger tickets, studied freight traffic, worked as assistant station-master and full-fledged station-master and acted as train inspector. At the end of six months I was promoted to the position of Director of a Traffic Bureau.

In those years the principle of private exploitation of railways became popular in the high Government circles, and the Odessa road was turned over to a private corporation, "The Russian Steamship and Commerce Society," headed by Admiral Chikhachev. The new administration discharged the traffic director, a rather competent man, for no other reason than his Jewish birth, and appointed me in his stead; Baron Ungern-Sternberg, traction engineer, was appointed Director of the road. Shortly after the corporation took possession of the road we had a most serious accident, known in the history of Russian railway accidents as the "Telegul Catastrophe."

On the border between the provinces of Podolya and Kherson there lies a ravine known as Telegul. A railroad runs along this ravine, branching off into three different directions. On a December day in 1875, a fatal accident, in which many lives were lost, took place at that point, which is 186 versts from Odessa. A section of the rail had been removed for repair. The spot, however, was not marked by danger signs, nor were the neighbouring stations warned of this condition of the track. A blinding blizzard was raging over the steppe, and the workmen had gone into a shanty by the road to warm themselves and take some hot tea. Just then a train loaded with recruits, and bound for Odessa, was heading full speed for this spot. On reaching it the whole train was precipitated into the ravine. As it was sliding down it caught fire, and the gale fanning the flames, a part of the train was burned to ashes. We were immediately informed of the catastrophe. Accompanied by Baron Ungern-Sternberg, I took a special train and rushed to the scene. We found that most of the recruits had been burned to death, and that the injured had been removed to hospitals. I do not remember how many lives were lost, but the number of victims certainly exceeded one hundred.

This disaster attracted wide attention. Public opinion in those days was envenomed by that spirit of liberalism which is essentially hatred against those who stand out, either because of position or wealth, the spirit which animates the revolutionary mob, and which several years later was responsible for the revolting assassination of so great an emperor as Alexander II. Therefore, to pacify the popular indignation, it was necessary to find a scapegoat among the higher officials indirectly responsible for the accident. The choice fell upon Admiral Chikhachev, Director of the Odessa Railroad, and myself, for I was considered the leading spirit of the railroad management. As a matter of fact, the repair of the roads was entirely outside of the sphere of my supervision. Of course the real culprit, the man in charge of the repair, was also arraigned, but he lost his mind and ran away. The prosecution was conducted in a manner which was clearly unfair, and designed to create the impression that the judicial authorities were thoroughly imbued with the spirit of liberalism. The Attorney-General of the Odessa District Court refused to sanction the indictment for the reason that, properly speaking, we had committed no crime, nor could we be proved accomplices of the real culprit. The case was then transferred to the Kamenetz Criminal Court, which was of the old type. There we were each sentenced to four months in prison.

Then war with Turkey broke out. Grand Duke Nikolai Nikolaievich, who had come to Kishinev, with a brilliant staff, promised me that should I succeed in transporting the army successfully, he would intercede for me before the Emperor to the end of voiding my sentence. To dispose of this incident completely, I wish to add the following: At the end of the war I received a telegram from the War Minister, that in consideration of our distinguished services, both Chikhachev and myself were freed from serving our prison terms. Thereupon I went to Petrograd and settled down with my wife, whom I had recently married. One night I was awakened by my valet and told that an officer of the gendarmes, accompanied by a detachment of policemen, had invaded the house and were asking for me. I was taken to the police station and thence to the Winter Palace. There I discovered the cause of my sudden arrest. The Minister of Justice, it appeared, had reported to the Emperor that the abrogation of our sentences was unlawful. The Emperor can amnesty but not invalidate a court sentence. The Minister pointed out that public opinion was greatly aroused on account of the fact that nobody had been punished in connection with the Telegul catastrophe. The Emperor compromised by ordering my arrest for two weeks in the guardhouse. I was at that time engaged in drafting Regulations concerning the field management of railroads. Besides I was serving on Count Baranov's Commission. Count Baranov reporting to the Emperor that I was indispensable to him, I was allowed my freedom during the day, but was obliged to spend the nights in the guard house.

When the Russo-Turkish war broke out, in 1877, I was practically the head of the Odessa Railroad. Being of a great strategic importance, it was subjected directly to the authority of Grank Duke Nikolai (Nicholas) Nikolaievich, Commander-in-Chief of the active forces. My particular task was the transport of the troops to the front. In the preceding year I successfully handled the numerous volunteers who were flocking southward to join General Chernyayev's forces. In those days I was an enthusiastic adherent of the "Slav idea," and I dreamed of the capture of Constantinople. I was, in fact, vice-president of the Slavonic Society at Odessa. We maintained a special office which handled the transportation of volunteers. Curiously enough, one of the clerks who worked in that office at 20 rubles a month was the man to whom King Ferdinand of Bulgaria owes his throne and who in the end became the president of the Bulgarian Cabinet. It was Stephan Stambulov.

The task of transporting the army divisions to the front was by no means an easy one. The railroad was extremely inefficient. There existed definite, carefully elaborated plans for the transportation of the army, but the plans could not be carried out because of insufficient rolling stock. Nevertheless, as I said, I acquitted myself with success of my difficult task. I owed my success to energetic and well-thought-out action. Faced by a serious shortage of locomotives, I invented and applied the traffic system which had long been in practice in the United States and which is now known as the "American" system. It consists in working the locomotives day and night, using shifts of machinists. Under the pressure of necessity I also introduced other technical improvements.

The railroads in the Southwest yielded no profit. When the war was over, three of them, including the Odessa Railway, combined forming the Corporation of Southwestern Railroads. This resulted in my appointment as Director of the Exploitation Department of the newly formed railroad system. As my office was located in St. Petersburg, I settled in the capital and married Madame Spiridonov, née Ivanenko, a very beautiful woman and the daughter of the Marshal of the nobility of the Chernigov province. I met my future wife at Odessa, where she resided after having left her husband, who was a profligate and a worthless fellow generally. With my assistance she obtained her divorce and followed me to St. Petersburg. Out of consideration for my wife, I adopted the girl who was her only child, with the understanding, however, that should our marriage prove childless she would not succeed me as heiress.

Those years were the golden age of private railroad construction and operation in Russia. They witnessed the growth of huge fortunes in the hands of several railroad kings. I have known some of them, for instance, Guboñin, a plain peasant with a great deal of horse sense, old Polyakov, a Jewish patriarch, the head of a dynasty of financial and railroad leaders, von Meek, a stiff German, Derviz. The latter's fabulous wealth turned his head. In the palazzo which he built for himself in Italy he maintained a complete operatic company and had operas produced for himself as the only audience.

Blioch, the head of our railroad corporation, made a rather remarkable career. An apparently insignificant and totally untutored Jew, he started as a small railroad contractor. When he prospered he had the intelligence to withdraw from the country for the purpose of getting an education. He went as far as attending a German university. Thereupon he returned to Russia, and married a beautiful society girl at the price of conversion to Catholicism. He settled in Warsaw and began to build railroads. At the time when I entered the service of the Corporation of South-Western Railroads, Ivan Alexeyevich Vyshnegradski, later Minister of Finances, was his chief agent in St. Petersburg. In the end Blioch lost all interest in railroading and began to dabble in scholarship and politics. He published several learned works, including a "History of the Russian Railroads," i.e., they were issued under his name but were written by specialists whom he hired for the purpose. He also became a propagandist of pacifism. I am told that he made an effort to convert to his pacifistic faith Empress Alexandra soon after her marriage to His Majesty, but that it was labour lost.

Vyshnegradski was nominally head of the Management of the South-Western Railroads. I was shocked to see how he cringed before his superior, Blioch. As Vyshnegradski was busy with a number of other things, the administration of the affairs of the South-Western Railroads was practically in the hands of a young engineer by the name of Kerbedz and myself. In addition to my serving in the Management, I was also a member of Count Baranov's Railroad Commission. In fact, I was the leading spirit of the Commission. Its only tangible achievement was the drafting of a set of Railroad Statutes, the text of which is almost entirely my work. In spite of considerable resistance on the part of the Minister of Ways of Communication, these statutes became a law and are still in force.

In the meantime, the roads continued to yield a deficit. It was consequently decided to send me to Kiev, in the hope that my presence there might help improve matters. I went to Kiev and reorganized the entire management of the roads with a view to centralizing it. The corporation announced its intention to appoint me Director of the roads, but the Government refused to confirm the appointment on the pretext that I did not have the degree of Traction Engineer. Soon after my arrival in Kiev, Vyshnegradski was appointed Minister of Finances, and a certain Andreyevski succeeded him as Director of the South-Western Railroads. As he proved unsatisfactory, the Government was again asked to approve my appointment as director. This time the Government yielded. I was the first director of a large railroad system without a technical education in engineering.

The assassination of Alexander II (March I, 1881) found me at Kiev. Under the influence of the disastrous event, I wrote to General Fadeyev a letter in which emotion prevailed over reason. In that message I argued that the Government was powerless against the revolutionists because it hurled too huge a missile at too small an enemy. The revolutionists, I wrote, must be combated with their own weapon, namely, by means of a secret organization which would make it its business to answer each terroristic letter with a counter blow of a similar nature. To attempt, I said, to overcome the enemy by using the whole weight of the State machinery would be like trying to crush a grain of dust with a huge steam hammer.

Several days later my uncle informed me that my letter was on the Emperor's desk and that I would probably be summoned before His Majesty. In effect, shortly afterwards the Court Minister requested me to come to St. Petersburg for a conference with him. In the course of it he inquired of me whether I still held the opinion which I expressed in my letter to General Fadeyev. Upon receiving an affirmative reply, he introduced me to his aide-de-camp, Count Shuvalov. The count took me to his mansion, and as soon as I entered his study he produced a Bible and asked me to swear allegiance to the secret society which had been formed in accordance with my suggestion, under the name of "The Holy Brotherhood." Surprised and nonplussed, I went through the ceremony of taking the oath with a feeling of doing a rash and thoughtless act. Thereupon Shuvalov announced to me that I had been appointed chief organizer for the Kiev district, and initiated me into some of the secrets of the organization. Each member was to form a group of five and the groups were not supposed to know of the existence of each other. "The Holy Brotherhood" was a strictly secret body, not unlike the societies which existed in the Middle Ages in Venice. Shuvalov supplied me with a code and explained to me the secret to be used by the members of the society. Thereupon, I immediately returned to Kiev.

Soon afterwards I was ordered by the Brotherhood to go to Paris where I was to get further instructions. I obeyed the order. In Paris I was informed by letter that a member of the society, by the name of Polyanski, was living in the hotel where I had stopped (Grand Hotel, opposite the Grand Opéra) and that he had the mission of assassinnating the revolutionist Hartman, who two years previously made an attempt on the life of Emperor Alexander II. I knew this man. He was a dashing officer of the Uhlans. I had previously met him at Odessa in the company of actresses.

Upon ascertaining each other's membership by means of secret signs, Polyanski accosted me and astonished me by the following declaration:

You have come to Paris to kill me if I fail to do away with Hartman, haven't you? I assure you, if I have not killed him yet it is because I have received instructions from St. Petersburg to postpone the execution. This may have something to do with your arrival here. But let us get up tomorrow at 5 o'clock in the morning and I shall prove it to you that it is within my power to kill Hartman any moment. The matter depends solely upon me.

Early next morning we made our way to the Quartier Latin and stationed ourselves in the street before a house which my companion bade me watch. After waiting a considerable while we noticed Hartman himself as he emerged from the gates. Two *apaches* (gunmen) who had been lingering nearby followed him. After a while the *apaches* returned, accosted Polyanski and declared indignantly that they were sick of the whole business and were going to quit it. It appears that they had been hired by my fellow conspirator to start a quarrel with Hartman and dispatch him *ad patres* in the squabble. But as Polyanski kept on postponing the final order, the men were growing more and more impatient. Polyanski somehow pacified the worthy cut-throats, and explained to me that the order not to kill the man came from

Zograf, the son of the former Ambassador to Greece. "Let's go to the restaurant 'Le Voisin,'" he suggested. "Zograf will be there. He told me he was expecting some news from St. Petersburg."

We found Zograf in the restaurant. He declared to us that Adjutant-General Wittgenstein was coming to Paris to settle the affair. That was the last drop in the bucket. I told my comrades then and there that I was not going to wait for Wittgenstein and I took the next train for Kiev. The preposterous incident thoroughly disgusted me. Besides, I learned that all manner of riff-raff and ambitious climbers was flocking into the secret "brotherhood," in the hope of acquiring valuable connections. "The Holy Brotherhood" was in fact becoming the tale of the town. I felt that something had to be done to put an end to this ridiculous, if not disgraceful, situation.

Accordingly I wrote to Count Vorontzov-Dashkov, saying that the society for the existence of which I was partly responsible had rapidly degenerated and that the situation had become intolerable. Nevertheless, since I had sworn allegiance to the society, I wrote, I did not consider it proper for me to withdraw from it. To remedy the situation I suggested that the statutes of the society as well as a list of its members should be published in *The Governmental Messenger* and other papers, thus exposing the members to the vengeance of the revolutionists. Naturally, I stated, those members who were not sincerely devoted to the aims of the society would withdraw, and the organization would thus be thoroughly purged. I concluded the letter by declaring that I would wait a month for a reply, after which period I should no longer consider myself a member of the "brotherhood." A month passed, but no answer came. I returned the secret code and other material in my possession, and that put an end to the "Holy Brotherhood" incident.

I wish to record here another reminiscence of the early eighties, namely, the anti-Jewish riots which I witnessed at Kiev and Odessa. In those days, it must be admitted, the Government had the right attitude toward the pogroms. It is certain that the authorities did not incite the population against the Jews. The movement was spontaneous. The Government did not hesitate to suppress the lawlessness of the mob with a firm hand. General Kotzebue, Governor-General of Odessa, took against the rioters the most ruthless measures, including bayonet attacks upon the mob. As a result, I remember, the disorder did not spread.

To return to my activities as Director of the South-Western

Railroads, I must say that I was fortunate in securing the services of a number of prominent railroad men as my assistants. Quite a few of them were Jews and Poles, for the simple reason that the Southwest of Russia is the homeland of a great Jewish and Polish population. With the rise of the senseless nationalistic policy in recent years, a great many of these highly competent men were ousted from the service. My efforts were crowned with success. The financial situation of the railroads soon improved, so that instead of suffering losses the corporation was before long in a position to pay substantial dividends.

My activities at Kiev included also sporadic literary work. I contributed occasional articles to such papers as Katkov's *Moksovskiya Vedomosti* (Moscow Bulletins) and Aksakov's *Rus* (Russia), and I took part in founding a Kiev daily, where I conducted a polemic on railroad and financial subjects. I advocated private ownership and exploitation of railroads as opposed to Government exploitation and Government interference in railroad matters generally. As a result of these discussions, I decided to elaborate a theory of railroad tariffs. This I did in a book entitled "Principles of Railroad Tariffs," which I wrote at Marienbad, while taking a cure there. I kept on revising the successive editions of this work, and I understand that it is still used as a manual by railroad tariff experts.

I remember Emperor Alexander's visit to Kiev soon after his accession to the throne. He was accompanied by his immediate family and his two brothers, Grand Dukes Vladimir and Alexey. In my official capacity I was on board the Emperor's train on his way back. Before the train left, the Imperial passengers gathered in the waiting room. The heir apparent and Czarevich George, then mere boys, were very troublesome. They scampered between the legs of the numerous men arrayed in gorgeous uniforms, who had come to see the Imperial guests off. Seeing this, Grand Duke Vladimir seized one of the boys by the ear and boxing it said: "I say behave yourself." Thirteen years later this boy became the Autocrat of all the Russias. On the way, the two boys were a source of constant worry to their gouverneur. As soon as the train came to a stop they would alight and run to look at the engine. I was constantly in fear that they might be left behind at some station.

In my capacity of Director of the South-Western Railroads I accompanied the Emperor in his travels in the South on two more occasions, notably when he reviewed manoeuvring troops near a station situated between Brest and Bielostok, and in the Summer of 1888, when he travelled to Yalta. As a rule, the schedule for the Imperial trains was worked out by the Minister of Ways of Communication, without consulting the directors of the local railways. According to the schedule, which I received in due time, the Imperial train was to make the distance between the stations Rovno and Fastovo with a speed which was safe only for a light passenger train. As a matter of fact, several hours before the arrival of the train I was informed by wire that it consisted of a great many large, heavy cars. To run such a train at the speed demanded by the schedule, it was necessary to use two freight engines. I was perfectly aware that a train of this weight running at such a speed was in danger of being smashed up at any spot where the road was not in perfect condition. Nevertheless, nothing was left to me but to follow the schedule. I boarded the train at Rovno and took it to Fastovo. I spent the night in the car of the Minister of Ways of Communication, which was in the rear and had no communication with the rest of the train. While everyone was soundly asleep, I lay feverish with constant expectation of a disaster.

To my great relief, we reached Fastovo safely. Upon my return to Kiev, I sent a report to the Minister of Ways of Communication, stating that not wishing to create a scandal I had followed the schedule of the Imperial train, but that I considered the speed impossible and highly unsafe. In support of my statement I cited technical data. In conclusion, I declared that I refused all responsibility for the safety of the Imperial train on its way north if the speed was not reduced in accordance with the proper standards of safety. The Minister's reply was to the effect that the schedule would be changed in compliance with my desire.

When I boarded the Imperial train on its backward journey, I noticed that everyone looked at me askance. Count Vorontzov-Dashkov, who had been on good terms with my family and had known me since my boyhood, pretended not to have recognized me. I understood what it all meant when Adjutant-General Cherevin, Minister of Ways of Communication, approached me and said: "His Majesty has ordered me to inform you of his displeasure with the service on the South-Western Railroads."

I started to explain what had happened, when the Emperor came up to us and said, addressing me: "What are you trying to say? I have travelled on other roads with the same speed, and nothing ever happened. One cannot get any speed on your road, simply because it is a Jewish railway" (the Emperor was alluding to the fact that the head of the corporation which owned the road was a Jew). His Majesty walked off, and we continued our unpleasant conversation. The Minister's main argument was that the Emperor had ridden on other roads with the same speed, and no one had ever objected to it. At last, unable to restrain myself any longer, I snapped brusquely:

"Your Excellency, let others do as they please, but I do not wish to endanger His Majesty's life. In the end you will break his neck."

The Emperor, no doubt, heard my words and must have been displeased by my impertinence, but he said nothing. Anticipating upon the course of events, I may say that Alexander III was the only man in whose presence I spoke my mind with complete unrestraint and with that bluntness which is rooted in my temperament. It is noteworthy that while my natural sharpness and looseness of speech has always stood between me and Emperor Nicholas II, those traits of my character never aroused the displeasure of Alexander III throughout the years of my service as his Minister. In this respect, as in many others, the now reigning Czar is the direct contrary of his most august father.

Two months passed. On the night of October 16, I received a dispatch informing me that the Imperial train was on its way to Fastovo, whence the Emperor would proceed to Kiev. I immediately ordered a special train and made ready to set out for Fastovo. But before I left Kiev, I received a second telegram to the effect that the route of the Imperial train had been changed. I soon learned what was the cause of this sudden change. Before several hours were over I received a third telegram instructing me to go immediately to Kharkov, there to act as expert in the investigation of the causes of an accident which had just happened with the Imperial train. I went straightway to Kharkov and thence to the scene of the catastrophe, near the village of Borki, province of Kharkov.

The investigation which I conducted convinced me that the Borki accident was exactly what I feared at the time when I accompanied the Imperial train on its way from Rovno to Fastovo. Here is what, I believe, had occurred. The train was running with two freight engines and at a speed to which I had previously objected. Freight train engines are not built for high speeds. When such an engine runs at an excessive speed, it sways and is thus apt to thrust a loose rail off the track-bed and wreck the train. That is exactly what happened. The train jumped the track and rolled down the embankment. Twenty-one lives were lost and thirty-seven people wounded. At the moment of the catastrophe the Emperor with his family was in the dining-car. This car being completely smashed, its entire roof fell on him, yet owing to his great strength he supported it with his back, thus saving everyone in the dining-car from injury. In this grave danger he did not lose his habitual presence of mind and kind-heartedness.

In reporting my findings, I did not hesitate to put the blame on the Minister of Ways of Communication, who was responsible for the schedule of the Imperial trains, and also on the inspector of those trains, Baron Sherval. As a result, both the Minister and the Inspector were soon afterwards compelled to tender their resignations. It is worth mentioning that the Emperor parted with them without any ill-feeling. They were forced to resign because public opinion was incensed by the Borki catastrophe. The Emperor also dismissed the Chief of the Railroad Management, whom he considered chiefly responsible for the accident and against whom he bore a personal grudge.

Shortly after these changes had taken place, Finance Minister Vyshnegradski offered me the newly-created post of Director of the Department of Railroad Affairs. The offer came to me as a complete surprise. That department was established as a division of the Ministry of Finances in pursuance of the Statutes which I had elaborated as a member of the Baranov Commission. Within its province came the finances and, generally, the economic side of the entire railroad system of the country, including the tariffs, a matter of high importance indeed.

I informed the Minister that I did not intend to change my independent and lucrative position with a private corporation for the Government post of a department director. To this Vyshnegradski replied that it was the Emperor's personal desire to have me take that post, and that His Majesty designed me for higher Government positions. It appears that Alexander had not forgotten the incident which resulted in my being rebuked by General Cherevin. In his letter, Vyshnegradski quoted the terms in which the Emperor referred to me in insisting on my appointment to the post in question. "It is that blunt fellow," His Majesty said, "who nearly to my face told the Minister of Ways of Communication that he would in the end break my neck. But everything happened just as he said. I mean to make good use of that man."

I hastened to inform the Minister that I did not wish, of course, to go counter to His Majesty's desire. I asked him, however, to report to the Emperor that I had no income whatsoever besides my salary, which now amounted to more than 50,000 rubles a year, and that I could not live comfortably on the 8,000 which a department director gets. The Emperor agreed to pay me, in addition to the latter sum, another 8,000 rubles from his own pocket, and I accepted the appointment. The year 1888 thus marks the beginning of my career as a high Government official.

My service necessitated my presence in St. Petersburg. Accordingly, we settled again in the capital. The change was not at all after my wife's heart, because we could not live on as rich a footing as we did at Kiev, and also because the Northern climate did not agree with either of us. Upon my arrival in St. Petersburg, I was received by the Emperor, together with several other men. The reception took place at His Majesty's residence at Gatchina. The Emperor told me that he was pleased to see me and that he was glad that I had accepted the post of Director of the newly-created department. His Majesty had a long private conversation with one of our party, a lean man in a colonel's uniform. Its subject, as I learned afterwards, was the comparative advantages of various reducing diets. It appears that the Emperor was greatly worried by his growing embonpoint. As he had known the colonel when the latter was stout, he detained him and plied him with questions as to how he succeeded in reducing his fat.

The Department of Railroad Affairs contained a financial section and a section of tariffs. In addition, there also existed in connection with the Department a Tariff Committee, which examined all the proposed tariffs, and a Council on Tariff Affairs, under the presidency of the Minister of Finances, which dealt with tariff questions requiring legislative sanction. My main achievement, as Director of the Department, was the imposition of order upon the chaos which prevailed in the field of tariff regulations. The statutes defined the maximum tariffs. Except for this restriction—and most of the Russian railways were in those days owned privately—the companies did what they pleased. For purposes of competition the corporations resorted to drastic reductions of the freight tariffs, and since the Treasury guaranteed the profit on a part of the capital invested in the railroads, the result was a loss to the State, that is, to the Russian taxpayer. As the corporations were not compelled to publish their tariffs, they established secret tariffs and indulged in other practices which added to the confusion.

I put an end to this deplorable situation by introducing Governmental control over railroad tariffs. At first, my efforts in this direction aroused the animosity of the private corporations. They considered my attempt to regulate the tariffs as an encroachment upon their rights. As the corporations soon perceived, however, that the order which I had introduced actually benefited them, their ill-feeling toward me disappeared. The tariff regulations which I put into effect eventually succeeded in eliminating the railroad deficit amounting to 48,000,000 rubles. These regulations are still in force.

Early in 1892 I was appointed Minister of Ways of Communication to the astonishment of the official circles of the capital. A word must be said about my predecessors in that post. Posyet, Minister during the Borki catastrophe, had been appointed for the reason that he was the naval instructor of Grand Duke Alexey. He was very honest but remarkably unintelligent. His ignorance of rail-road matters was prodigious. He had a peculiar weakness. His inspection of the roads was confined to an examination of the toilet rooms. If he found them in an insanitary condition he was furious, but if they were clean he felt satisfied and looked at nothing else. My immediate predecessors were Pauker and Gübbenet. The latter was a bureaucrat with no knowledge of railroading. In his administration the railroad traffic was greatly demoralized. A certain Colonel Wendrich was appointed to combat the freight jams, but upon the whole his activity only made the confusion worst confounded.

As a rule, I do not like to make many changes in the staff, when I am appointed to a new position. Here, however, I insisted on the removal of Colonel Wendrich. During the revolution of 1905, he came again to the surface with the aid of Grand Duke Nikolai Nikolaievich. For a whole year he raged on the railroads, discharging men and evolving various ill-starred schemes for the suppression of the unrest among the railway workers. I secured the services of two experienced railroad directors and of several local railroad men. My acquaintance with the country's highways and waterways was rather superficial, yet I was aware that laxity and corruption thrived in the department which controlled that section of the Ministry's work. I started a campaign against these corrupt practices, but as my administration of the Ministry was very brief, my efforts bore no fruit. The memory of the Borki catastrophe still being fresh in my mind, I drafted a set of new rules regulating the movement of the Imperial trains, to the end of insuring their safety. Although these regulations, to a certain extent, limited the comforts of the Emperor's attendants, they were readily approved by His Majesty and are still in force.

Although in those years I was tied down to my bureaucratic office in the capital, I did not lead an entirely sedentary life. In the fall of 1890, I accompanied Minister Vyshnegradski in his trip to Turkestan. We inspected the Transcaspian Railway and visited Samarkand. That part of Asia profoundly impressed me with the vastness of its natural resources, which in those days were entirely undeveloped. Since that time the cotton industry has grown up in this region, but the mineral resources are still lying dormant in the soil of Turkestan.

We also visited the Imperial Domains at Murgab, Transcaspia. The Government was just then attempting to convert these vast estates into a sort of agricultural experimental station for the cultivation of cotton and other valuable industrial plants. To make the soil fertile it was necessary to irrigate it with water drawn from the Amu-Darya River. This worked great hardships on the population of this region where water is exceedingly scarce and is considered the most precious of gifts. For this reason the local population was extremely hostile to the undertaking. The people were embittered by what they thought was an effort on the part of the Russian Czar to take away a part of their water after he had appropriated to himself vast stretches of their land. Of course, neither Alexander II who originated the idea of the Murgab experimental station, nor Alexander III were aware of this aspect of the matter. We telegraphed to the Court Minister, reporting that when irrigated the Murgab steppe would perhaps be fit for the cultivation of cotton, but that the local population and also the Governor of the region had assumed a hostile attitude toward the project for the reason that the irrigation of the Murgab Domains would considerably reduce the water resources of the region and thus endanger the agricultural industry by which the population subsisted. I doubt whether the telegram was shown to the Emperor.

On our way to Turkestan we visited the Caucasus, and I spent two days with my wife at Kislovodsk, the celebrated health resort, where she was taking a cure. When I left her she was in high spirits and very hopeful as to her health. We agreed to return to St. Petersburg at about the same time. But instead of going directly north after she had completed her course of treatment, my wife visited her brother in the latter's country estate in the province of Chernigov and wrote me that she had a very pleasant time there. In the meantime I returned to St. Petersburg. Shortly after my arrival there I received a telegram informing me that my wife had died at Kiev from a heart attack. I hastened to that city and assisted at her burial.

About a year after my wife's death I saw for the first time Madame Lisanevich, the woman who shortly afterwards divorced her husband and became my wife. As I was aware that the Emperor considered it improper for a member of the Government to marry a divorced woman, I attempted to resign from my ministerial post shortly before my marriage. His Majesty, however, who had been initiated into all the circumstances of the case, assured me that in his judgment I acted properly and that my step would only add to the respect he had for me. Nevertheless, for many years Court circles could not be reconciled to my marriage, and it is only since 1905 that my wife has been received at the Court and in high society generally.

As Minister of Ways of Communication I made an extensive trip along the Volga, in the spring of 1892, when an epidemic of cholera broke out in that region. I undertook the trip at the Emperor's suggestion for the purpose of seeing what measures were being taken to combat the plague in the stricken provinces. I travelled from town to town, from hamlet to hamlet, inspecting hospitals and dispensaries, coming in close contact with the patients. What struck me most was the scarcity of doctors. Nearly the entire burden of medical work lay on senior medical students, and it must be said to the glory of the Russian student body that they gave without stint both their energies and their lives in the heroic task. I sent the Emperor frequent reports from the field. When I returned to St. Petersburg, His Majesty told me that he was happy to hear of the self-sacrificing service of the students and that they had thus proved themselves to be the most noble-minded element of the intellectual class. As a matter of fact, this incident completely broke down the Emperor's hostility toward the student body, which he had regarded early in his reign as the hotbed of sedition and revolution.

My administration of the Ministry of Ways of Communication lasted some six months. In August I was appointed Minister of Finances. At this point of my narrative I wish to present a brief sketch of the personal traits of Emperor Alexander III and a view of the general character of that great monarch's reign.

CHAPTER II

MEMORIES OF ALEXANDER III

THE unfortunate brevity of Alexander Ill's reign, thirteen years in all, did not prevent the full growth and display of his noble, outstanding personality, to which the whole world paid homage on the day of his death. His Russian contemporaries and the succeeding generation did not highly esteem him, however, and many looked upon his reign with a scorn altogether unjustifiable, especially in view of the unhappy conditions of his youth and the deplorable circumstances under which he ascended the throne.

To begin with, his education and training were largely neglected, since the older brother, Nicholas, was the heir apparent during that period of Alexander's life. In addition, the family environment was unfavourable. The future emperor's sensitive moral feelings were grievously hurt by his father's late re-marriage at the age of sixty, when he already had numerous grown-up children and even grandchildren. Then his uncompromising honesty was outraged by the prevalence in higher Government circles of a traffic, in privileges and concessions to mercantile associations and particularly by the implication of Alexander II's morganatic wife, Princess Yuryevski, in this barter.

Consider, too, the unpropitious national situation. Having turned his back upon reform during the latter part of his reign, the .Great Liberator (Alexander II) drove the liberals into the ranks of the revolutionists, so that when the heir apparent began to take an interest in politics, he was confronted with the existence of an extremely radical party and strongly impressed, therefore, with the necessity of stern measures to suppress subversive movements. The Heir was encouraged in this attitude by his preceptor, Pobiedonostzev.

Furthermore, the war with Turkey had weakened the country and hindered its development in spite of apparent military successes. After conquering more by weight of numbers than by superior strategy and tactics, we concluded a very advantageous treaty, only to be robbed of the fruits of our victory by the Congress of Berlin. Threatened with a ruinous war by Austria, Russia was constrained to accede to the nullification of the favourable San-Stefano agreement with Turkey, a humiliation which left a painful and lasting impression upon the future Alexander III, who had taken part in the war as a detachment commander.

This war retarded our financial development twenty years, as it frustrated the labours of the Minister of Finances, Reitern, who had endeavoured to establish the gold standard in Russia in order to raise to par the value of the silver ruble, which had remained at a low level ever since the Sebastopol war. It was not until I occupied the post of Minister of Finance, a score of years later, that the Imperial system of currency was placed on a firm basis.

Finally, let it not be forgotten that the last years of Alexander II's reign were marred by a long chain of terroristic acts, culminating in the murder of the Emperor himself by a bomb on March 1, 1881. Emperor Alexander III had to take his place on a throne, stained, so to speak, with paternal blood, and the horrible event left an indelible scar upon his memory.

Alexander III was undeniably a man of limited education. I cannot agree, however, with those who would class him as unintelligent. Though lacking perhaps in mental keenness, he was undoubtedly gifted with the broad sympathetic understanding which in a ruler is often far more important than rational brilliancy.

Neither in the Imperial family nor among the nobility was there anyone who better appreciated the value of a ruble or a kopeck than Emperor Alexander III. He made an ideal treasurer for the Russian people, and his economical temperament was of incalculable assistance in the solution of Russia's financial problems. Had not the Emperor doggedly warded off the incessant raids upon the Russian treasury and checked the ever-present impulse to squander the public funds accumulated by the sweat and blood of the people, Vyshnegradski and myself could never have succeeded in putting the nation back upon its feet financially.

Alexander III's prudence in government expenditures was matched by his personal thrift. Abhorring luxury and lavish spending, he led an extremely simple life. When he grew tired of his own table, he would ask for a common soldier's or a hunter's meal. This economy was sometimes carried too far. The Imperial table was always relatively poor, and the food served at the Court Marshal's board was sometimes such as to endanger the health. Alexander III was extremely economical with his wearing apparel. I had a curious proof of this when I accompanied the Emperor on one of his railway trips. Since I found it impossible, on account of my responsibility, to sleep of nights, I would often catch glimpses of His Majesty's valet mending the Emperor's trousers. On one occasion I asked him why he didn't give his master a new pair instead of mending the old so often. "Well, I would rather have it that way," he answered, "but His Majesty won't let me. He insists on wearing his garments until they are threadbare. It is the same with his boots. Not only does he wear them as long as possible, but he refuses to put on expensive ones. If I should bring him patent leather boots, he would angrily throw them out of the window." The Emperor's dislike of the expensive included gorgeous rooms. For this reason he never stayed at the Winter Palace, but always occupied the unpretentious quarters of Anichkov or Gatchina. There he took small rooms and lived frugally. He tolerated the Court's luxury as an unavoidable formality, but he always longed for a different mode of existence and created it for himself in his private life.

The entire Imperial family respected and feared Alexander III, who wielded the influence of a veritable patriarch. He believed that the royal family must set a moral example for the whole nation both in their private and social life. In his time dissolute conduct by Russian Grand Dukes in foreign countries, so common now, was very rare. Transgressing members of the Imperial family were sure to incur the Emperor's heavy displeasure. Remarriage was severely frowned upon in the case of anybody connected with the Government.

Alexander III himself led an unimpeachable life and his family was a splendid example of the old-fashioned, god-fearing Russian type. He was a stern father and while the children did not fear him, they were uneasy and constrained in his presence with the single exception of Mikhail, the favourite son, who was not only unrestrained, but even inclined to take liberties, as the following amusing anecdote, related to me by his valet, will indicate. Becoming impatient at the boy's impertinence and inattention during a stroll in the gardens early one Summer morning, Alexander III snatched up a watering hose and gave Mikhail a good dousing. Without further ado they went in to breakfast, the youth changing his drenched clothing. After that the Emperor retired to work in his study and as usual indulged in his habit of occasionally leaning out of the window, but was met with an altogether unusual deluge from the upper window, where Misha had stationed himself with a pailful of water in anticipation of the Imperial appearance fenestral.* There is very little doubt that none but Mikhail would have dared to think of such a stratagem, and there is no doubt whatsoever that nobody else could have executed it with impunity.

As a ruler, Alexander III made important contributions to the welfare and prosperity of his subjects and the international prestige of the empire. In the first place, he practically reconstructed the army, which had been thrown into a state of serious disorganization by the war with Turkey in the seventies. During the time that I was Director of Railways and later Minister of that department under Alexander III, railroad building, which had practically ceased some years before, was resumed with excellent results and plans were laid for future development. Alexander III also made possible the financial rehabilitation of Russia, in which I had the honor of participating as Minister of Finances. His salutary influence in this matter extended beyond his reign. In fact, it was only due to this that I was able to retain my position eight years after his death and thus complete the work, for Nicholas II was incapable of appreciating my endeavours and simply relied upon his deceased father's confidence in me.

I now come to a subject which furnishes a striking refutation of those who would have us believe that Alexander III was incompetent and dull-witted. I refer to the inauguration of the system of protective tariff in order to encourage and promote Russia's manufacturing industries. Thanks to his Imperial insight, Alexander III had an absolutely clear understanding of a fundamental situation which was obscure to many who possessed the technical and formal education that the Emperor lacked. He comprehended that Russia must produce industrial as well as agricultural commodities before she could enjoy prosperity. Perceiving that protection was essential to the initiation and growth of manufacturing plants, he persisted until an adequate tariff was established. This called for no mean determination and confidence, for the plan met with tremendous opposition on the part of the ruling and educated classes of the coun-

---

* *Ed.* 'Fenestral' is an architectural term used as a noun which describes a window sash closed with cloth or paper instead of glass. Not as transparent as glass but less opaque than a heavy curtain. In comparison it could also be used to describe a thinning transparent spot such as the wings of butterflies and moths.

try. Only a monarch of Alexander III's rare wisdom and firmness could have succeeded in such a task. The Emperor's achievement was a great gift to the empire as its rapidly expanding industries, attest, and the day is not far off when Russia will be among the leaders of the world in manufacturing.

Of the measures passed during Alexander III's reign there are two which are almost invariably looked upon with disfavour. One of these is the University Code of 1884, which displaced that of the sixties. It was put through at the instance of Count Tolstoy and a group of ultra-conservatives. I myself considered its passage a bad blunder, and it is significant that K. P. Pobiedonostzev, a former professor and, on the whole, more conservative than Count Tolstoy, expressed himself vigorously against the code, both in the Imperial Council and in a private conference under his chairmanship. The measure provoked no outbreaks, however, and university life was in general very quiet under Alexander III with a single exception toward the beginning of his reign, when several prominent professors, among them the renowned Mechnikov, lost their chairs because the Minister of Public Education, Count Delyanov, thought them too liberal.

The second provision for which Alexander III is often condemned relates to the institution of the *Zemski Nachalnik*, that is, Rural Chief of Police, which entailed a policy of paternalistic guardianship over the peasants on the theory that they are eternally under age, so to speak. This belief seems to me profoundly erroneous. It has already made trouble and is fraught with disastrous consequences for the future. The measure was undoubtedly a serious mistake, but I can vouch that the Emperor had the best of intentions. His attitude toward the peasantry was one of profound sympathy. He shared their joys and sorrows and protected the helpless and weak, thus realizing the ideal of the Christian monarch.

Realizing at last that the deep unrest prevalent during the least years of the preceding reign had been due principally to his father's unstable character, Alexander III's outlook began to change. As he became convinced that Russia was in reality far from a revolution, he grew more liberal in his ideas and actions. It is my firm belief that had Alexander III been granted a longer life, he would have inaugurated an era of liberalism, but God called him away before this could be.

The chief merit of Alexander III's reign lies in the fact that during its entire thirteen years the empire enjoyed unbroken peace. The Emperor's attitude toward war is defined in the following remarks, which he made to me in connection with a report on the frontier guards:

"I am glad," he said, "that I have taken part in actual warfare and seen with my own eyes the horrors inevitably connected with military action. After such an experience, not only will a ruler never desire war, but he will employ every honourable means of sparing his subjects the trials and terrors of armed conflict. Of course, if the strife is forced upon him, he will accept the challenge, confident that the curse and guilt of the sanguinary struggle will fall upon the heads of the instigators."

These were no empty words. Emperor Alexander III detested phrase making and ostentatious pledges of international friendship. His deep-rooted honesty forbade such shams. For this reason there were very few royal visitors to Russia during his reign. Europe was puzzled at the gentleness of this mighty giant and continually wondered whether he might not at any moment break out in words of thunder. He was, indeed, a man of few words, but his pronouncements carried weight. The whole world trusted and respected him. It was soon recognized that he was not in search of conquests. He was too modest and loved his subjects too well to desire to illumine the pages of his reign with brilliant victories purchased with the lives and happiness of his people. Alexander III was great enough to pursue successfully a policy of profitable peace with irreproachable honour. He never sacrificed a single jot or tittle of the empire's rights and interests. On the contrary, finding Russia in a very unfavourable situation, he raised her, by his wisdom and firmness, to an enviable position of power and prestige among the nations, without shedding a drop of Russian blood.

Alexander III is known in history as "the Peacemaker." This epithet did not come from the mouth of the people. It occurs for the first time in a decree issued by his son soon after his death. Emperor Nicholas rather disliked this appellation. "The word does not fit my father," he told me on one occasion. "Count Vorontzov-Dashkov submitted to me the act where it occurs, and I signed it thoughtlessly." As a matter of fact, the greatness of Alexander III is not that he was a peacemaker, but that he was firm as a rock and honest in the highest sense of the word.

Alexander III's internal national programme was just as noble and enlightened as his external policy. His attitude toward the non-Russian races of the empire was one of broad-minded sympathy. While he did not, of course, abandon the historical Russian viewpoint and tradition, his native good sense made him realize that these people must be granted the privilege of living a normal life, since their union to the empire made them his subjects to be treated as such. Naturally, he loved the Russians best, but he was kindly disposed towards all his subjects. His treatment of Poland is an example in point. When he visited that territory, he displayed admirable good will, but without giving any encouragement to separatist tendencies. Gurko and Drenteln, the Governor-Generals of Poland, during Alexander III's reign, showed the same spirit. They ruled firmly but justly, avoiding religiously all jingoistic measures of hatred and intolerance. The results fully justified this policy, for the Poles were loyal in those days and they still revere the memory of Alexander III and his governor-generals. Had this noble-hearted Emperor lived in these times, he would have surely risen in wrath against the mad persecution of all those Russian subjects who do not share the blind and blatant patriotism of the Black Hundreds.

Unfortunately for Russia, Emperor Alexander III's reign was comparatively short. His health began to fail him in the late '80's. He appeared pale and anaemic. On Easter Sunday of 1894 an incident occurred in the Winter Palace which superstitious people regarded as a foreboding of evil. It is customary for the Court to hold a grand levee during the morning of that holiday. All the electric lights in the palace went out suddenly on this occasion and it was necessary to go through the ceremony by candle light. By this time the Emperor looked seriously ill and he grew gradually worse, especially after the catastrophe at Borki, to which I have already alluded. I had my last interview with His Majesty during the Summer of 1894 when I reported to him regarding my trip to Murman. At this meeting his haggard appearance made a heartbreaking impression upon me, for I worshipped his personality and was attached to him with profound devotion.

The Emperor's disease was undoubtedly aggravated by his extreme antipathy to medical treatment, a very common characteristic among the members of the Imperial family. The famous Moscow professor, Zakharin, who was summoned to St. Petersburg, pronounced His Majesty was suffering from nephritis. Shortly afterwards the Emperor went to Yalta, where he was treated by the renowned

German specialist, Leiden. Both of these physicians later told me that though Alexander III displayed a very cheerful and even temperament, he was an extremely difficult patient to handle on account of his utter lack of faith in medicine.

Just before the Emperor left for Yalta I found it necessary to go abroad to Vichy, where I stayed a few weeks. On my return, I immediately communicated with His Majesty, as was customary, requesting his permission to resume my work as Minister of Finances. His formal consent came promptly by telegraph. Some time after the Emperor passed away, I inquired at the Court for the original of this telegram because I desired to have it as a remembrance if it had been written by His Majesty personally. Such was in fact the case and I now have the message in my archive. Although composed only about ten days before his death, it is written in a very firm hand. It was the last communication to me from the Emperor.

As his end drew near, Alexander III became very anxious to have the Crown Prince wed and he accordingly sent him to fetch the Princess of Darmstadt as his bride. The Emperor waited impatiently for the Prince's return and was, I have been told, supremely happy when the pair arrived, although he had refused his consent to the match on a previous occasion.

On October 19 (31), as the result of an alarming report from Yalta regarding His Majesty's critical condition, a special prayer was ordered at the Kazan Cathedral. Members of all classes of the population, including the students, thronged the church and prayed fervently for the Czar's life. The next day the people received the sad news that the Emperor had passed away. He died with beautiful equanimity, mindful only of the welfare of the dear ones left behind.

The Emperor's body was taken from Yalta to St. Petersburg. On the way it lay in state for a day at the Uspensky Cathedral in Moscow, whose inhabitants flocked to do final homage to their revered ruler. When the body reached the northern capital, there was a solemn procession from the station to the Cathedral of St. Peter and Paul. The ceremonies were highly impressive, yet marked at every point with the noble simplicity which had characterized Alexander III's reign. Several times, once throughout the night, I was among those who stood guard over the Emperor's body at the Cathedral and I saw the people come in masses to pay the last honours to their beloved monarch.

Under the burden of grief of those days the Empress bore up

wonderfully well. It was only toward the end of the Metropolitan's funeral sermon that she broke down for a little while and became somewhat hysterical, crying out "Enough! Enough! Enough!" When I visited her a short time afterwards, she received me very kindly, indeed, although she had treated me rather coldly after my marriage in 1892. I remember her saying to me on this occasion: "I believe you are deeply grieved by His Majesty's death, for he truly loved you."

During his short rule Alexander III won for himself the esteem and gratitude of the whole world. It was his steadying influence that kept Europe at peace. The anxious eyes of the continent were fixed on Yalta as the Emperor's life ebbed, and when he passed away, everybody felt that a mighty power for good had departed from the earth. At his death all parties and factions, even the extreme radicals, joined in his praise. In truth, Alexander III was a great emperor and he amply merited his high position, for he was undoubtedly the noblest personality in the empire.

Emperor Alexander III

CHAPTER III

MY WORK AS MINISTER OF FINANCES

WHEN I assumed the administration of the country's finances, we had not as yet recovered from the terrible famine of 1891, when the crops reached the lowest level known in the second half of the nineteenth century. The Treasury was practically empty. As the 20th of September (the 20th of the month is the pay-day in Russia) was approaching, the Director of the Treasury informed me that there was no money wherewith to pay the officials and troops. There was no other way out than to print several million rubles of paper money. When this was done, old Bunge, ex-Minister of Finances, paid me a visit and declared to me that I was entering upon a road which was bound to ruin Russia. I assured my visitor that this was a temporary and exceptional measure, necessitated by our desperate financial situation, but the venerable old statesman shook his head sceptically.

Before taking up in detail my activity as Minister of Finances, I wish to say a word about my predecessor, Vyshnegradski. In the early part of 1892, he had an apoplectic fit. Although he was very reluctant to give up his work, he agreed to take a sick leave in the hope that he might recover his health. The administration of the ministry automatically passed into the hands of his associate, Terner, a man of rather limited Germanic intelligence and very high moral principles. Vyshnegradski's health did not improve, and when he came back he tendered his resignation and was appointed member of the Imperial Council. Two or three years later he sustained another fit, which proved fatal. Soon after Vyshnegradski's resignation I was appointed his successor (on August 30 / September 11 1892).

Vyshnegradski knew his work thoroughly. He was cautious and prudent, but he lacked that breadth of imagination which is so necessary in transacting business on a large scale. The following incident is characteristic of the methods he sometimes employed.

Shortly before my appointment as Minister of Finances, Emperor Alexander III handed me a memorandum by Tzion charging Vyshnegradski with having taken graft to the amount of 500,000 francs from the Rothschild banking house at the conclusion of our loan in France. In spite of the document's presentation of authentic facsimiles from Rothschild's books indicating the payment of this sum to Vyshnegradski, I expressed to His Majesty my unwillingness to lend any credence to the accusation. I stated that I could not believe in the possibility of such an act on the part of a Russian Minister of Finances, since, living, so to speak, in a glass house, his every move is constantly under the scrutiny of his subordinates. As the Emperor shared my views in the matter, no official action was taken, the note remaining in my possession.

First I shall explain briefly the accuser's underlying motive. Tzion, of Jewish origin, by the way, had been a professor of physiology under the famous Sechenov before entering the service of the Ministry of Finances under Bunge in the early '80's. During those years our principal financial source was England, and, to a limited extent, Holland and Germany. As a consequence, however, of the policy of Franco-Russian rapprochement, inaugurated with Alexander III's ascension to the throne, the French financiers assumed an important role in this field. The first relatively large Russian loan to be floated in France was negotiated through Tzion by a financial group under the leadership of Hoskier, an old-established but second-rate banker. Discovering some time afterwards that Tzion had received from this French syndicate a commission amounting to some 200,000 francs, Vyshnegradski demanded and forced his resignation. As a result of this, Tzion harboured a bitter grudge against Vyshnegradski.

The second Russian loan subscribed in France was handled by Vyshnegradski, and it was in connection with this transaction that Tzion presented his memorandum to the Emperor. Not long after taking up the duties of Minister of Finances, I succeeded in unravelling the mystery of the 500,000 francs in question. The details were revealed to me by a banker, Rothstein, who, together with Laskin, a Director of the International Bank, had acted as Vyshnegradski's agent in negotiating the loan. It appears that Vyshnegradski had insisted that the Hoskier group be invited to participate in the second loan, since he had given Hoskier a verbal promise that they would be asked to take part in any further loans contracted in France. Rothschild, however, flatly refused to allow Hoskier to share in the operation on the ground that he had never done, and did not wish to do, business with this banker. Vyshnegradski was constrained to acquiesce, but at the conclusion of the negotiations he demanded a commission of 500,000 francs. Rothstein, to whom the request was made, felt deeply mortified to find a Minister stooping to graft. Nevertheless, he and Laskin telegraphed to Rothschild and obtained his consent to meet Vyshnegradski's wishes. The next day they told Vyshnegradski that Rothschild had placed 500,000 francs to his credit. Rubbing his hands with glee, Vyshnegradski replied ironically: "Now, gentlemen, please be so kind as to take these 500,000 francs and distribute the sum among the members of the Hoskier group in proportion to their share in the first loan. You see, I gave my word to those people that they would be granted an opportunity of participating. Since Rothschild and the others saw fit to dispose otherwise, I thought it only just that they should pay 500,000 francs to the Hoskier syndicate for the pleasure of excluding them."

Astonished by this story, I asked Rothstein whether he could furnish proof of the actual distribution of the money to the members of the Hoskier group. In answer he submitted the individual receipts. I showed them to the Emperor, who was gratified to have conclusive proof of his Minister's integrity. His Majesty remarked, however, that Vyshnegradski's method in this case was improper, to say the least.

In concluding my reminiscences of Vyshnegradski, I wish to say a word about his great fondness for arithmetical calculations of all sorts and his phenomenal memory for figures. On one occasion, in my presence, he read a page in a table of logarithms and then repeated it all from memory without making so much as a single mistake.

To return to my administration of the Ministry of Finances, I wish to say that I enjoyed the privilege of having under me a number of gifted assistants. The celebrated scientist Mendeleyev served in the capacity of Director of the Chamber of Measures and Weights. In recognition of his great scientific merits, I gave every possible assistance both to him and to the institution he headed. With his expert help I succeeded in considerably improving the Chamber. A very able and reliable assistant I had in the person of Malishevski, who at my instance was appointed Director of the Credit Chancery, in spite of his being a patriotic Pole. The post of secretary of the Department of Economy was held by Kokovtzev. Later I promoted him to the office of my associate.

Under my administration the Ministry grew greatly in scope. In addition to financial matters proper, it came to include commerce and industry and also railroading in all its aspects, except the purely technical. This state of affairs had its obvious drawbacks, and so in 1905, at my suggestion, a separate Ministry of Commerce and Industry was formed, which included a railroad department. It happened that the Minister of Commerce mishandled the railroad tariffs to such an extent that it was found necessary to transfer the railroad affairs back to the Ministry of Finances.

The construction of railroads fell entirely within the authority of my Ministry. In those years the Russian railroad system was in a process of continuous and rapid growth. Naturally, the numerous concession seekers kept flocking to my reception room. Among them there were a great many members of our highest aristocracy. It was then that I found out of what inferior stuff all these people with ancient names were made. Unlimited greed seemed to be their chief characteristic. These men who at Court functions wore princely airs were ready to crawl on all fours in my office, provided they could thus obtain some financial advantage. For many years some of these scoundrels and hypocrites have been holding the highest Court positions and, at least outwardly, they have been intimate with the Imperial family.

Speaking of railroad building it must be borne in mind that in those years the Government was pursuing a consistent policy of railroad construction and operation by the State. This policy involved a series of transactions designed to redeem the privately owned roads and turn them over to the State.

It will not be an exaggeration to say that the vast enterprise of constructing the great Siberian Railway was carried out owing to my efforts, supported, of course first by Emperor Alexander III, and then by Emperor Nicholas II. The idea of connecting European Russia with Vladivostok by rail was one of the most cherished dreams of Alexander III. He spoke to me about it in the course of one of my first conferences with him following my appointment as Minister of Ways of Communication. As is known, Czarevitch Nicholas, the present Emperor, during his trip through the Far East, inaugurated, on May 19, 1891, the construction of the Ussurian Railroad, connecting Vladivostok with Khabarovsk. The Emperor complained that in spite of his efforts, which extended over ten years, his dream had failed to materialize owing to the opposition of the Committee of Ministers and the Imperial Council. He took my promise that I would bend my energies to the accomplishment of his desire.

In my capacity of Minister of Ways of Communication and later as Minister of Finances, both during the reign of Alexander III and afterwards, I persistently advocated the idea of the necessity of constructing the great Siberian Railway. As much as the former Ministers thwarted the plan, so I, remembering my promise to the Emperor, sought to advance it. As Minister of Finances, I was in a peculiarly favorable position with regard to furthering the project, for what was most needed for the construction of the railway was money. Had I remained Minister of Ways of Communication, I would have had to face the opposition of the Minister of Finances.

I devoted myself body and soul to the task, yet Emperor Alexander III did not live to see the realization of his dream, and it was only under Nicholas II that the immense railroad was completed. I was aided by the circumstance that the young Emperor took a personal interest in the matter. At my instance, while his father was still alive, he was appointed head of the Siberian Railroad Committee, which I had formed to promote the construction of the railroad. This committee was empowered to eliminate all manner of unnecessary delay and had the authority over both the administrative and the legislative matters involved in the construction. For the young heir-apparent this task was something in the nature of a preparatory school of statesmanship. He worked under the guidance of the vice president of the committee, Bunge, who was also his tutor. This was a very happy arrangement. The future ruler took his appointment in earnest and worked with enthusiasm. When he became Emperor, he retained the title of President of the Siberian Committee and did not lose his interest in the matter. This enabled me to complete the work within a few years.

Soon after my appointment as Minister of Finances the Emperor told me on one occasion that in addition to the construction of the Trans-Siberian he wished to put in my charge another matter which had for a long time been on his mind, namely the reorganization of the vodka traffic. He also confided to me that the heavy drinking prevailing among the people was a matter of great concern to him and that it was necessary to take some drastic measures to curb it.

This matter attracted the attention of the government at the end of the reign of Alexander II, but only half measures were taken, for it was considered that the existing system of vodka traffic, the so-called excise system, was the best possible, and that it was not advisable to change it in substance. As is known, under the excise system, the production and sale of alcohol and vodka are more or less free. The State merely controls the business to the extent of levying the excise, that is, an indirect tax upon the product. During the latter part of the reign of Alexander II, several conventions met to draft measures which, while not doing away with the excise system, would nevertheless restrict the freedom of selling alcoholic drinks. Since, however, the excise system is largely incompatible with substantial restriction upon vodka traffic, these measures came to nothing.

Emperor Alexander III was anxious to help his people in this respect. After lengthy discussions he arrived at the conclusion that palliatives would not avail; consequently, he resolved to effect a measure, absolutely unprecedented and vast in its scope, namely, the so-called vodka monopoly. Its basic idea is that the State has the monopoly of selling alcoholic drinks and that the production of those beverages must be limited to the amount sufficient to meet the needs of the State as the sole buyer. I do not know who originated this plan. Some people attribute it to Katkov, the editor of a Moscow daily. I am inclined to the belief that the thought originated with the Emperor himself.

Alexander III told me that he had spoken about this plan to Minister of Finances Bunge, but that the latter, as a learned financial expert, had found the project neither desirable nor feasible. Thus under Bunge nothing was done to reorganize the existing system. Nevertheless, the idea of the necessity for such a reorganization struck root in his administration. Bunge's successor, Vyshnegradski, was also approached by the Emperor on this subject, but his reply, although not altogether negative, was nevertheless discouraging. Alexander III told me that he relied upon my youth, my character and my personal devotion to him, to take up this idea and carry it to a successful consummation. Thus the introduction of the vodka monopoly was another great task bestowed upon me by the late sovereign. This task I succeeded in achieving while he was still alive. I transferred the entire vodka traffic into the hands of the government. The refinement of liquor also became a State monopoly. Only the production of the unpurified alcohol remained in the hands of private manufacturers, but they could not produce more than the Government specified.

By 1903, when I left the Ministry of Finances, the vodka monopoly had been established nearly throughout the extent of Russia, except some of the distant border provinces. Nevertheless, the reform was not as yet entirely completed. The introduction of the monopoly was stubbornly opposed by the interests which suffered from the reform. Grand Duke Vladimir Alexandrovich, Commander-in-Chief of the Guard, was assured, I remember, that on the day when the monopoly would be introduced in St. Petersburg bloody disturbances would break out in the city. The Grand Duke took up the matter with His Majesty and the latter began to hesitate as to whether the reform should be effected in the capital, although all the preparations for it had been completed. I succeeded, however, without difficulty in allaying the Emperor's alarm, the monopoly was introduced, and of course the city remained perfectly quiet.

The vodka monopoly, as conceived by Alexander III, was essentially a measure intended to reduce the consumption of alcohol. In 1899, I travelled in the central provinces for the purpose of inspecting the work of introducing the vodka monopoly, which was going on there. In my talks with the officials I emphasized the fact that the reform was designed not to increase the State income, but to reduce the consumption of alcohol, and that the activity of the officials would be judged not by the amount of income derived by the State from the monopoly but by the beneficent effect of the measure upon the morals and health of the people. But when the Japanese war broke out and Kokovtzev became Minister of Finances, he completely distorted the meaning of the reform. Under the pressure of the huge war expenditures he began to treat the monopoly as a source of income for the State. To have the sale of vodka yield as large a profit as possible, was the sole purpose of his efforts in this direction. The amount of income derived from the monopoly became the measure of the worth of the excise officials. Not to restrict but to increase the consumption of vodka became the aim of the Government. Accordingly, no police measures were taken against drunkenness. The scale of prices was changed. The prices became high enough to ruin the habitual consumers, but not so high as to render the vodka inaccessible to the masses. The number of vodka shops was doubled. During the war there was some justification for this policy, but when the war was over it was the Minister's duty to remember the late Emperor's original purpose in carrying out his vodka reform.

Speaking of the vodka monopoly, I recall the opinion about it of an inspector of the French financial department, who accompanied me in my inspection tour through the central provinces. He believed that it was an admirable measure and that from the standpoint of the State it was likely to be highly beneficent. He was of the opinion that the reform could be applied in France with equal success. He was aware, however, he said, that only an absolute monarch of an unusually firm character could carry out such a measure in France. The Frenchman was perfectly right. No parliament will ever pass such a measure, for it is detrimental to the interests of too many moneyed people. During my recent prolonged stays in France I noticed that in the elections to the Chamber of Deputies a predominant part was played by people who in one form or another were financially interested in the liquor industry.

Vyshnegradski bequeathed to me a bill providing for the responsibility of factory and mill owners for the death or injury of their employees. When the matter came up for discussion in the Imperial Council, Pobiedonostzev made a long speech against it, pointing out that the bill was socialistic in tendency. He asserted that in Russia the relationship between employers and employés was purely patriarchal, that the factory workers were substantially peasants who had lost their connection with the soil, and that the measure in question would tend to create a nomadic homeless proletariat. The other member of the Council who spoke against the bill was Polovtzev. He had invested his funds in industrial enterprises and was afraid that the proposed legislative act would reduce his profits. As I had not personally taken part in the drafting of the bill, I declared that, although I did not share Pobiedonostzev's opinions, I was ready to withdraw the project and revise it. In the course of my next audience with the Emperor (Nicholas), he assured me that he was decidedly in favour of the factory law. On this occasion His Majesty warned me not to fall under Pobiedonostzev's spell. The latter, he said, was an excellent critic, but incapable of any constructive measure. For that reason, the Emperor said, he had long since ceased to heed Pobiedonostzev's counsels.

I must say that, as a rule, His Majesty refused to support me in my efforts to organize a system of factory inspection. The latter had always been regarded by the Government with suspicion as a liberal institution inclined to uphold the rights of the workers against those of the employers. This suspicion was fostered by those of the factory owners who, being of noble birth, had access to those in power. In general, all the efforts to improve the lot of the factory workers in

Russia by legislative means were strenuously opposed by the reactionaries. This policy naturally increased the friction between the workmen and their employers and led to the spread of extreme views of a socialistic and revolutionary character among the city proletariat.

My financial activities proper included, first of all, the conversion of our loans, transactions consisting in passing from loans at a higher rate of interest to loans at a lower rate. In addition to these very extensive financial operations, I negotiated several direct loans, exclusively to cover the expenses of railroad construction and to increase our gold resources in connection with the introduction of the gold standard of currency. In all these enterprises I enjoyed the unqualified support of His Majesty.

Among my purely financial reforms the first place belongs, no doubt, to the introduction of the gold standard of currency. This measure definitely established Russia's credit and put her financially on an equal footing with the European Powers. It was owing to this reform that we weathered the wretched Japanese War and the subsequent domestic upheaval. Without it, an economic and financial collapse would have occurred at the very beginning of the war, and all the economic achievements of the recent decades would have been annihilated.

In a slight measure my immediate predecessors, Bunge and Vyshnegradski, prepared our finances for the introduction of the gold standard, but it was left to me to elaborate a detailed and final plan for the currency reform. I worked against great odds, and if I succeeded in carrying the plan into effect it is because His Majesty, Emperor Nicholas, had full confidence in me and because he offered me his support without stint.

In the beginning, nearly the whole of thinking Russia was opposed to the reform. Very few of our financial and economic experts had any theoretical or practical knowledge of the matter in its entirety. The subject was not taught in our institutions of higher learning, and there were no good books in Russian on currency problems. As we had lived under the régime of paper currency since the Crimean War, the very notion of metallic currency had become obscured in the press and in the minds of educated people generally. We had grown accustomed to paper currency as one gets used to chronic disease, in spite of the fact that gradually it ruins the organism.

I was strenuously opposed by those elements of the population which were interested in the export of commodities, especially the farmers. They imagined that paper currency was advantageous for them, because with the depreciation of our money they obtained more for their products exported abroad, i.e., in terms of our depreciated money. Of course, this opinion was erroneous, for the exporter had to pay higher prices for whatever he purchased. Not being an economist, he failed to grasp the correlation of phenomena.

I received but scant help from my own subordinates. The chief reason why I selected Professor Antonovich as my associate was the fact that he had written a doctoral dissertation on Currency, in which he firmly advocated the metal standard. But I had overestimated the man's character. He turned out to be more interested in his own career than in the fate of the currency reform. Noticing the strong opposition to the reform, he began to tergiversate * and ended by expressing himself against it.

Of course, there were people who realized the advantages of the metal standard of currency. Nevertheless, they opposed, fearing my energetic and resolute manner of action. Besides, among the advocates of the metallic standard there was no uniformity of opinion as to whether gold, silver, or both should be made the basis of currency. To the bi-metallists abroad belonged Alphonse Rothschild, head of the Rothschild firm in Paris, and his friend, Leon Say, Minister of Finances under Thiers. It is noteworthy that the French Government did not hesitate to carry on an intrigue against my plan to make gold the standard of Russian currency. Through the French Ambassador in St. Petersburg, Meline, President of the French Cabinet of Ministers, transmitted to His Majesty two memoranda, one of his own composition, the other drafted by the well known economist Theyri. The two authors warned the Emperor that the introduction of the gold standard would ruin Russia. They advocated a bi-metallic standard, similar to the one which existed in France. Such an interference with our domestic affairs on the part of Meline I considered highly improper. Neither the Russian Emperor nor the Government stood in need of his advice. His Majesty turned these memoranda over to me, without reading them.

In interfering with my reform the French were prompted by purely purely selfish reasons. France had an enormous amount of silver

---

* abandon a principle

money and she was much interested in raising the price of silver. If Russia had based its currency on both gold and the depreciated silver, the price of the latter metal would have risen and the wealth of France increased by hundreds of millions of francs. Fortunately, however, Russia did not enter the road pointed out by Meline, in spite of all the obstacles, the great reform, the glory of the present reign, was successfully carried out.

I laid the bill for the introduction of the gold standard of currency before the Imperial Council in April, 1896. The bill met a strong opposition, and it soon became clear to me that the Council would not pass the measure. I withdrew it and changed my tactics. When I felt that the time was ripe for the inauguration of the reform, I asked His Majesty to call a special session of the Financial Committee, which was then examining the details of the proposed reform, under his own presidency and with the participation of some of the members of the Imperial Council, including Grand Duke Mikhail Nikolaievich, its president. At this extraordinary session, which took place on January 2 (14), 1897, the Committee passed the bill, owing chiefly to His Majesty's confidence in me. The decree enacting the reform was promulgated the following day. It may truly be said that Russia owes the gold standard solely to Nicholas II.

Speaking of my currency reform, it is often asked why I based it on the depreciated ruble and why I did not adopt a smaller unit than the ruble. Nominally the ruble was worth four francs, but on January 3 (15), 1897, when the reform was enacted, the rate of exchange was 2.66 2-3 per ruble. To avoid a perturbation in the economic life of the country, I adopted the latter rate. As a result, the transition to the new standard of currency passed practically unnoticed by the population. As for the desirability of adopting a smaller monetary unit, at one time I thought, indeed, of introducing a unit much lower in value than the ruble. That unit I christened "*rus*" and I went as far as having a sample "*rus*" coined. In the end, however, I gave up the idea of substituting the "*rus*" for the ruble, fearing the effect of the reform upon the ignorant peasant masses. The adoption of a smaller monetary unit would have, no doubt, lowered the cost of living, especially for the city population, but the country as a whole would hardly have profited by the substitution.

The very first year of my administration of the Ministry was marked by an event which will no doubt be reckoned among my most notable achievements in statesmanship. I have in mind the conclusion of a commercial treaty with Germany.

For a long time Germany's industrial products enjoyed free entry into Russia, enormous quantities being imported regularly without duty. The foundation of a protective tariff system for the Russian Empire was not laid until the concluding years of Alexander II's reign, when customs dues were fixed on iron, steel and their manufactures. Naturally, this measure displeased the Germans, and protests came from many quarters, among others, from the great Bismarck, who was still Chancellor. Meeting Giers at a watering place shortly after the establishment of the new imposts, he touched upon the subject and warned him that such taxes on our part would provoke Germany to retaliate with tariffs on agricultural products and raw materials. The Iron Chancellor's remark is somewhat inaccurate and misleading. As a matter of fact, while it may be true that our moves hastened the raising of her tariff wall, Germany's import duties on farm products had been put into effect long before we took any action. The author and leader of the protectionist movement in the German Empire was Frederick List, the famous economist, about whom, by the way, I wrote a brochure while I was Manager of the South-Western Railways.

The principal reason for the long-continued absence of formal commercial treaties between the two empires is to be found in the intimate dynastic relations existing between them. It is well known that rivers of Russian blood were shed in the struggles connected with the aggrandizement of the Prussian Kingdom, which culminated in the welding together of the German Empire. When Alexander III ascended the Russian throne, however, he turned the ship of state toward France and our relations with Germany underwent a decided change. Alterations in the conditions of commercial intercourse between the two countries followed swiftly upon the political transition. It was at about this time, in 1891, to be exact, that we devised a scale of import duties, partly intended to counter the tariffs which Germany had already imposed upon agricultural products, especially upon wheat, but mainly designed to foster our domestic industries and eventually liberate us , from our extreme dependence upon Germany's manufactures.

The immediate effect of these preliminary steps was a feeling of extreme irritation and dissatisfaction on both sides. We were particularly displeased because of Germany's evident discrimination against us in comparison with her treatment of other nations. Having instituted a double set of import duties, that is, a minimum and a maximum scale, Germany declared that all countries that had concluded, or were negotiating, commercial treaties with her would be charged the minimum rates, while all others would have to pay the maximum. Although this provision was couched in general terms, it was doubtlessly aimed directly and exclusively at us, for Russia was practically the only state of any consequence that had neither made, nor was engaged in drawing up, a mercantile agreement with the German Empire. Such unfair tactics worked a severe hardship upon us, as can be easily understood. If a country, say, Germany, collects a tax of 30 kopeks indiscriminately on every pood of imported grain, no matter from which foreign land it originates, then, while every exporter of this class of merchandise will be hampered to some extent, the burden will be proportionately distributed among all, so that none will be seriously harmed. When a certain country, for instance, Russia, is singled out, however, and compelled to pay more than the others, for example 45 kopeks per pood, then a ruinous and unjust burden falls upon the disfavoured nation. Under such circumstances it would be far better for Russian grain exporters to bear a levy of 60 or 80 kopeks, or even a whole ruble on every pood they sent to Germany, provided that the same duty was charged to all other countries.

It is self-evident that the unfavourable conditions under which we laboured in this respect made it urgently desirable for us to conclude a commercial pact with the German Empire, all the more so because the informal agreements governing our trade relations had another serious disadvantage for us. These irregular arrangements consisted of verbal promises and understandings interchanged between the rulers and their ministers. Now, the Germans insisted on the one hand upon interpreting our promises and concessions to them in the widest and most favourable sense possible, while, on the other hand, they invariably managed to foist upon our authorities the most limited meaning of their own statements. Add to this the fact that our Government frequently forgot or neglected to utilize privileges granted to us.

Although pourparlers looking toward a commercial treaty had been begun during Vyshnegradski's administration, nothing of any importance had resulted, largely, it seems, on account of the lack of interest and energy displayed by the embassy officials through whom the negotiations were conducted. When I was appointed Minister of

Finances, these listless consultations were still dragging on. At the time the German Ambassador to the Court of St. Petersburg was General Werder. In spite of the fact that the Emperor was very favourably disposed toward him, General Werder played a very insignificant role by reason of his want of political ability, and he took no part at all in the formulation of our trade compact. Count Pavel Shuvalov, our Minister in Berlin, was a man of much higher calibre. As an adjutant-general he had distinguished himself in our war with Turkey during the 70's. He had enjoyed an excellent education, and besides possessing tact and social charm, his otherwise Russian nature was gifted with characteristic Polish shrewdness, doubtlessly inherited from his mother, who was of Polish origin. Count Shuvalov made an extremely successful ambassador and was highly esteemed by the German Emperor. When it came to negotiating a commercial treaty, however, he could make no headway, his enthusiasm and diligence notwithstanding. This failure can be attributed to two causes. In the first place, he was much too eager to avoid all the disagreeable international friction and personal clashes inevitably incident to transactions of this sort. In the second place, economic problems were altogether alien to his personality and consequently out of his sphere of useful activity. In order to provide competent assistance for Shuvalov, we sent Vasili Ivanovich Timiryazev, who later became Minister of Commerce and Industry and is now a member of the Imperial Council. Timiryazev, Vice-Director of the Department of Commerce and Industry at the time, certainly knew his business. Unfortunately, while he possessed the ability to negotiate, he lacked the proper point of view to attain success. Furthermore, he made his keen anxiety to effect a compact so apparent to the Germans that they took advantage of it, assuming a very bold stand and offering us practically no concessions though demanding every conceivable privilege for themselves.

Germany made audacious use of her double-scale tariff in the preliminary conferences with us. In effect she said to us: "If you will grant us all the privileges we are asking, your goods will be admitted subject to the minimum rates; otherwise you must continue submitting to the maximum." Nothing more than this was offered to us in return for the many concessions demanded, and it must be borne in mind with regard to this that the minimum duties were by no means light. Finding myself faced with this manoeuvre upon undertaking direction of the negotiations as Minister of Finances, I quickly decided that only by employing Germany's own tactics against her could we secure an equitable agreement. Accordingly I requested His Majesty, Emperor Alexander III, to permit me to put a double scale tariff through the Imperial Council, retaining the existing rates as the minimum and adding approximately 20 percent to form the new maximum level. Since the blow was aimed at Germany, the increases were levied almost solely on industrial articles which she was exporting to Russia.

When introduced into the Imperial Council, this measure caused a great stir. In general the members feared that a sharp move of this sort was bound to lead to diplomatic, and, possibly, military complications. In addition there was a spirited protest from Giers, our Minister of Foreign Affairs, on the ground that a step thus seriously affecting our external relations should not have been taken without his previous consultation and assent. Then, too, my vigorous action produced great excitement in Berlin, and Count Shuvalov transmitted a pointed report to St. Petersburg, criticizing me severely and warning of impending diplomatic difficulties. Despite threats from abroad and misgivings at home, I resolutely insisted upon the passage of the measure. In my stand in this matter I enjoyed the Emperor's unqualified support. His Majesty paid no heed to the pretensions of Foreign Minister Giers and ordered Shuvalov to be informed that the Throne had complete confidence in me and extended entire approval to my actions. Before the Imperial Council I argued that the act was merely an emergency one, intended more for persuasive effect than for retaliatory execution. I pointed out that Germany, seeing two could play at her game, would immediately realize the futility of her unfair tactics and assume a reasonable attitude. Thanks to the logical soundness of my position and to the Emperor's powerful support, the measure went through the Imperial Council without delay.

We were now able to say to Germany: "Unless you agree at once to charge us the minimum rates, we will subject to the new maximum tariffs all German goods imported into Russia. If you consent to place us thus on the same level with other nations, we shall then be glad to negotiate a commercial treaty with you on a just basis of take and give." Such was, in fact, the proposition we laid before them. Our Teutonic neighbours, thinking, it seems, that I would not dare to carry out my program, brazenly pursued their original methods. Without the least hesitation I cut short the commercial pourparlers and ordered the immediate imposition of the maximum duties on German goods. Our adversaries swiftly retorted by raising the maximum rates already in effect against Russian products. We straightway went them one better. And so we found ourselves engaged in an extremely bitter tariff war. I had no doubt whatever that we would emerge the victors in this bloodless strife, since in such a struggle a country like Russia, little advanced in manufacturing, could endure much more than a highly developed industrial nation like Germany, whose very existence is dependent upon a quick commercial turnover.

The tense situation at this time, when mercantile relations between Germany and Russia had practically ceased, did not fail to cause some alarm. I can perhaps give no better illustration of the prevailing feeling than the general attitude evinced toward me at a celebration of Empress Maria Feodorovna's name's-day in Peterhof on July 22, 1894. A national holiday had been declared, and the nobility, government officials and court attendants thronged the great palace, where the grand mass, thanksgiving prayer and procession were to be held. When I entered the great hall, almost everybody moved away from me and shunned me as though I were some gruesome plague carrier. Dark rumours flew about that I, through my temerity and lightheadedness, had dragged Russia to the brink of war with Germany, that the latter's inflexibility would inevitably result in a conflict which was bound to precipitate all of Europe into a sanguinary struggle.

I cannot forget that, besides His Majesty, the only prominent government official to stand by me at this crisis was Piotr Semyonovich Vannovski, our Minister of War. He understood the necessity of showing decisiveness and firmness if we were ever to rid ourselves of Germany's overweening behaviour. In connection with this lack of official support I must say that the opposition was not all due to fear of embroilment with Germany. Many of my antagonists were undoubtedly moved by a desire to frighten the Emperor into withdrawing his approval of my actions, thus abandoning me to certain failure and lasting discredit. Their best endeavours were all in vain, however, for Alexander III was not the man to be taken in by such a stratagem and he upheld me to the end without faltering.

Our steadfastness was crowned with success before long, for Germany, notwithstanding her loud protestations at the outset, requested a renewal of negotiations. Pourparlers were accordingly resumed in Berlin, not, however, before Germany had placed us upon the same basis as other favoured nations in return for our withdrawal of the new maximum duties.

Germany acted through Caprivi, Bismarck's successor as Chancellor of Germany, and Marschall von Bieberstein, the Secretary of Foreign Affairs, who was later appointed Minister to Constantinople after Caprivi's retirement. On our side the transactions were conducted by Timiryazev and other attachés of my ministry. It is important to note that our representatives in Berlin acted merely as agents, no decisions being made except under my orders and instructions or with my permission and consent. Count Shuvalov, our Ambassador in Berlin, played no role on this occasion. When Germany acceded to our demands, he frankly admitted that he had been wrong in his estimate of the situation. We were always good friends after that, both during the remainder of his ambassadorship and during the time he was Governor-General of Poland. When he suffered an apoplectic stroke during his tenure of this post, he was retired and appointed a member of the Imperial Council.

The commercial treaty finally drawn up by the conferees was without doubt advantageous and just to both parties. The Germans, however, were bitterly disappointed with it on account of their original expectations of having everything their own way. Our vigour, our determination and our success in securing an equal share of the concessions and privileges was a rude shock to those who had set their hearts on the lion's share. There was much talk of serious opposition in the Reichstag, but it did not materialize and the compact was ratified with no modifications worth mentioning. It was our first commercial treaty with Germany and we had good reason to be well satisfied with it. The agreement included certain political features intimately related to the execution of the trade arrangements.

Throughout the transactions Emperor Wilhelm II of Germany acted with tact and good will. As soon as he realized that I was in earnest and enjoyed the Russian Emperor's confidence and support, he adopted a very conciliatory attitude and exercised his influence over the ministers and the Reichstag for a peaceful solution. To one unacquainted with the real cause, it may, therefore, seem strange that the German Emperor should have dismissed Caprivi apparently on account of dissatisfaction with this very treaty. In point of fact, Wilhelm II merely seized upon the treaty as an opportune pretext. He availed himself of a good chance to kill two birds with one stone.

By discharging Caprivi he pleased the Junkers, who were enraged at the outcome of the negotiations, and at the same time he gracefully disposed of a chancellor who was, in the Imperial estimation, disgracefully peaceable and dangerously liberal. Caprivi was made a Count and Hohenlohe was appointed in his place.

Emperor Alexander III was highly content with my conduct of the negotiations and their successful termination. I could easily have obtained a title as a reward, and in reality the Emperor himself broached the subject to me. Now, the German Ambassador had, shortly before that, paid me a visit, in the course of which he had hinted broadly that His Majesty, Emperor Wilhelm II, would be delighted to be presented with the Russian admiral's uniform. Evidently I was expected to convey Wilhelm's wish to Alexander III. Therefore, when His Majesty mentioned honours to me on this occasion, I said: "If Your Highness will permit me to express an opinion in this matter, I wish to state that I think it would be an excellent idea to bestow the Russian admiral's uniform upon Emperor Wilhelm II in appreciation of his liberality during the transactions." Smiling good-naturedly, His Majesty answered: "Your desire shall be fulfilled at the first convenient opportunity. Wilhelm has, indeed, behaved very tactfully in this instance. For the first time I have found him sincerely anxious to avoid a break with us." Emperor Alexander III evidently did not take this request very seriously, as decorative conceit was altogether foreign to his character. In Wilhelm II, on the contrary, this trait is very prominent and he esteems nothing more highly than uniforms, orders, medals and titles. As a result of Alexander III's death shortly after his promise, the German Emperor was constrained to wait several years for the coveted uniform. When Nicholas II ascended the throne, I told him about this conversation and the deceased Emperor's promise. Nicholas listened with a smile but deigned no reply. A few years later he presented the admiral's uniform to Wilhelm II. Whether the matter had slipped his mind during all that time, whether the Kaiser's request was renewed or whether Nicholas II had some special reason of his own for making the gift at last, I do not know. All this, by the way, happened before the Russo-Japanese War, while the Russian naval uniform still enjoyed great prestige.

The negotiation of this commercial treaty was my debut on the stage of world politics. Everybody in Europe was surprised at the performance. A short while afterwards Harden, the German writer and publicist, came to St. Petersburg to make my acquaintance. He was on intimate terms with Bismarck, paid him frequent visits and sometimes set forth his views in newspaper and magazine articles. In his conversation with me Harden stated that he had come to see me at the suggestion of Bismarck, who had said to him: "It will be well worth your while to go and get acquainted with that man. He is the first one I have ever heard of during the last decade who knows what he wants and has the character and will power to get it. You will see him achieve a great career as a statesman." Bismarck recognized that I had won a cleancut victory over German diplomacy. On parting with Harden I said to him: "When you see Bismarck again, tell him that I was highly flattered to hear his good opinion of me, especially his prophecy regarding my future." I never had an opportunity of meeting Bismarck, but I have been told by Count Shuvalov and Count M. N. Muraviov, at that time Counsellor to our Embassy in Berlin and later Minister of Foreign Affairs in Russia, that the old Chancellor was always very much interested in me and never failed to talk about me with the Russians he met.

This first commercial treaty between Russia and Germany, concluded in 1894, formed the basis of succeeding treaties with other countries, both for ourselves and for Germany. The duration of the agreement was fixed at ten years. The expiration of this period found us engaged in the disastrous war with Japan and at a stage when the unfavourable outcome for Russia was already clear. Unscrupulously taking advantage of our unfortunate situation, Germany refused to renew the compact under the same conditions and extorted from us highly important concessions, which we certainly should never have yielded to her under normal conditions.

The economic wealth and consequently the political strength of a country depend upon three factors: natural resources, capital, and labour, physical and intellectual. With regard to natural resources, Russia is extremely rich, although she is unfavourably situated because of the rigorous climate in many of her sections. In capital, that is, accumulated values, she is poor, for the reason that the history of the country is a continuous chain of wars, not to speak of other reasons. Considering her population, she is rich in physical labour and also in intellectual resources, for the Russians are a gifted, sensible, and God-fearing people. All these factors of production are intimately correlated in the sense that only their concerted and co-ordinated action can produce wealth. At present, owing to the development of communication, natural resources are easily transported, and owing to the growth of international credit, capital is even more easily shifted. In view of this, labour has acquired an exceptional importance in the creation of wealth. It follows that I had to give especial attention to the development of both capital and labour. In the first place, it was necessary to stabilize the national credit. I hope that financial history will acknowledge the fact that never did Russian credit stand higher in both domestic and international money markets than at the time when I was Minister of Finances. It was not my fault that our military adventures have so thoroughly injured our credit. The other day I read in some Russian papers arguments to the effect that it does not matter to the foreign bankers and holders of our securities what régime prevails in our country, provided an end is put to anarchy. This is rather a naïve idea. It is of the utmost importance to both the foreign and the domestic investor that we should have a governmental régime under which adventures like the Japanese War would be impossible, and that the nation should cease to become the object of experiments in the hands of a self-seeking and irresponsible court camarilla. Our creditors can have no faith in a régime under which they lost twenty per cent, of their investments.

During my administration of the country's finances, I increased the state debt approximately nineteen hundred million rubles, and I spent even more on railroads and amortization of the debts of the Imperial Bank for the purpose of restoring the gold standard of our currency. Thus the money borrowed was expended for productive purposes exclusively. That money has increased the country's capital.

Owing to the confidence of foreign capital in Russia's credit, which I built up, our country obtained several billion rubles of foreign capital. There are people, and their number is not small, who hold this against me. Oh, folly and ignorance! No country has ever developed without foreign capital. Throughout my administration I have defended the idea of the usefulness of foreign capital. In this respect, I had to contend with such statesmen as I. N. Durnovo, Plehve, and other members of the Committee of Ministers. Nicholas, as usual, favoured now one, now the other viewpoint. He went as far as calling a special session to discuss the advisability of importing foreign capital. At this session I declared that I was not afraid of foreign capital, that on the contrary I considered it beneficial for Russia. What I feared, I said, was that our régime is so peculiar that but few foreigners would care to have anything to do with us. Of course, foreign capital would have entered the country more abundantly if so many obstacles had not been created against it during my administration.

A great many people, including the Emperor, opposed the importation of foreign capital to Russia for purely nationalistic considerations. They argued that Russian natural resources should be exploited by "true" Russians and with the aid of Russian money. They overlooked the fact that the amount of available capital in Russia was very small. As a result, industrial concessions were usually granted to "true" Russians, who subsequently sold them to foreigners and pocketed a round sum of totally unearned money. Thus, for instance, I recall that a certain retired Colonel, by the name of Vonlyarlyarski, obtained a concession for mining gold on the Kamchatka Peninsula. Several months later he sold it to a foreign corporation.

The development of our national labour was another great problem. The productivity of Russian labour is exceedingly low, this being due to the climate, among other reasons. For the latter reason, tens of millions are idle several months during the year. The scarcity of ways of communication is another factor lowering the productivity of labour. After the Turkish War of the '70's railroad construction was suspended, and it fell to my lot to resume the building of railways. In this respect, I have succeeded in achieving a good deal, for during my administration I doubled the railroad mileage. It is noteworthy that the Ministry of War was constantly thwarting my efforts. This Ministry supported me only when I proposed to build railroads of a strategic importance. Often strategic railroads were built counter to my recommendation. Besides, the direction of non-strategic railroads was often distorted to suit the purposes of the War Ministry. In this respect, General Kuropatkin, and especially the former Chief of Staff Obruchev, did a great deal of harm. The latter was a gifted and well-educated man, but strategic railroads were his monomania. It often happened that the railroads which, at the moment of their construction, were recognized as of strategic importance, two or three years later were declared to have no such importance.

Thus I strained every effort to develop a railroad net. Military considerations, with which his Majesty often naturally sided, prevented me from building the lines most productive economically. As a result, the system yielded a deficit.

After dealing with the railroads for forty years, I can say that in most cases the strategic considerations of our War Ministry regarding the direction of the road are pure fantasy. The country will be best off if, in building railroads, it is guided by purely economic considerations. On the whole, such railroads would also meet the strategic needs. It is my opinion that this should become a basic principle of railroad construction. For thirty years we were building railroads with a view to a war in the West, and we have wasted no end of energy in that section. In the end the war broke out in the Far East.

To create new sources for the application of labour, it was more than desirable to develop our industry. Alexander the Third, with his characteristic firmness and wisdom, was the first to recognize and carry out this policy. In this respect I was his faithful assistant. It was imperative to develop our industries not only in the interest of the people, but also of the State. A modern body politic cannot be great without a well-developed national industry. As Minister of Finances, I was also in charge of our commerce and industry. As such, I increased our industry threefold. This again is held against me. Fools! It is said that I took artificial measures to develop our industry. What a silly phrase! How else can one develop an industry? Whatever men do is to a certain extent artificial. The measures taken by me were much less artificial and drastic than those practised by many foreign countries. The only thing I did was to support the protectionist tariff introduced by Vyshnegradski under Alexander III. This I did in the face of a strenuous opposition on the part of the large landowners. All my efforts to facilitate the formation of joint-stock companies were systematically thwarted by the Ministry of the Interior and Plehve particularly. I have also been blamed for having issued industrial loans from the Imperial Bank. In reality, these loans amounted only to some 50,000,000 rubles. Besides, a considerable portion of this sum was lent, without my approval, to members of the court camarilla or their friends. I must say that but few people in Russia grasped the full significance of my work of building up the nation's industries. Among those few, be it mentioned in passing, was Mendeleyev, our great scientist and my lifelong friend.

Railroad construction and industrial expansion diverted some four or five million men from agriculture, thus increasing, so to speak, the country's land resources by 20,000,000 to 25,000,000 desiatins. Much more will have to be done in the future to fertilize Russian labour. The very conditions under which the people live and work will have to be changed. At present a Russian works as he drinks. While he drinks less than a member of any other nationality, he gets drunk more frequently. While he works less, he overworks himself more frequently than anyone else.

Until 1905 matters pertaining to industry and commerce were within the province of the Ministry of Finances. In my capacity of director of that Ministry, I did a great deal to promote commercial and industrial education. Owing to my efforts the system of secondary commercial schools was considerably extended. I also conceived and carried out the plan of founding a number of polytechnical institutes, that is, institutions of higher learning teaching all the branches of commercial and technical knowledge. In 1899 I raised the question of opening such a school in St. Petersburg. With the aid of my assistants I drew up the statutes of the Polytechnic, and had them approved by the Imperial Council not without difficulty. It was argued that we had our hands full with the schools of higher learning already in existence, and that the new Polytechnic would be an additional hotbed of unrest. I succeeded in opening two more such schools, one in Kiev, the other in Warsaw.

During my administration of the country's finances, their condition left nothing to be desired. Not only did we have no deficit, but each year there was a considerable excess of State income over State expenditures. This circumstance enabled me to keep in the Treasury large sums of free cash amounting at times to several hundred million rubles. This policy of mine was oftentimes criticized. It was pointed out that neither France, England or Germany kept unemployed cash in their state treasuries and it was argued that it would be much more advisable to invest these funds profitably. My critics merely demonstrated their ignorance of Russia's national economics. Given the Russian Empire's huge foreign debts, by far exceeding the indebtedness of any of the above-cited Western countries, it was necessary to keep a reserve fund in order to check, in a case of emergency, a panicky fall of Russian securities abroad. It must also be taken into consideration that Russia is essentially an agricultural country. The year's crops, its chief wealth, depend on the capricious elements and are an uncertain factor. This again necessitates the keeping of a reserve fund in anticipation of the lean years. I must also say that I was prompted to keep large sums of free cash in the Treasury by the feeling, which never left me after the ascension of Emperor Nicholas to the throne, that sooner or later a bloody drama would be staged in this or that part of the country.

When I left the post of Minister of Finances, the free cash funds in the Treasury amounted to 380,000,000 rubles. This sum enabled the Empire to exist without a loan when the Russo-Japanese War broke out soon afterwards. It also enabled us, later, to conclude a loan on terms more favourable than we would have been forced to accept, had we not been in a position, thanks to this cash surplus, to make the world feel that our need was not urgent and immediate.

His Majesty expressed his appreciation of my work in an Imperial rescript, dated January 1, 1903, on the occasion of the tenth anniversary of my service as Minister of Finances:

Sergey Yulyevich!

Ten years ago my Father, now resting in God, summoned you to the post of Minister of Finance. Despite the burdensome consequences of the bad harvest of 1891, you undertook with firm faith in the economic power of the Russian State and with persistent energy the task of rehabilitating the Russian finances, begun by your predecessor; and you had the consolation of justifying the confidence and meriting the gratitude of Emperor Alexander III.

Now with the lapse of a decade of your activity as Minister of Finances, I take pleasure in expressing my appreciation to you of all that you have done within the past eight years to justify my confidence as well. With equal faith in the energies of the Russian people, and with equal devotion to the throne, not alone did you lighten my efforts to realize my chief cares relating to the strengthening of the country's power and defence and the prosperity of the State entrusted to me by God, but also you aroused to spontaneous activity the best forces of Russia. You solidified the independence and stability of the currency, increased the resources of the Treasury, thereby enabling us from year to year to meet the demands of the growing budget, and aside from your varied official duties, you have executed to my complete satisfaction the task which I imposed upon you of instructing my Heir and beloved Brother, Grand Duke Mikhail Alexandrovich in state economy.

Hoping for the further continuation of your service, so useful to the State and to me, at the head of the Ministry entrusted to you, I remain

Unalterably well-disposed* to you,
(Signed)   NICHOLAS.

* On the original His Majesty wrote in his hand "and thankful".

In the meantime the clique headed by Bezobrazov and Plehve was vigorously pushing its militaristic plots in the Far East and the Emperor was gradually falling under the influence of those unscrupulous men. In 1903 it became clear to me that war with Japan was inevitable. Whenever the Far-Eastern adventure came up for discussion, I severely condemned it. I admit, in fact, that the language I used in His Majesty's presence was often too sharp. The Emperor went even as far as endeavouring to win me over to his side, but his efforts were in vain.

I felt that if, under these circumstances, I continued to hold my ministerial post, the entire blame for the impending war would have been placed upon me. Russia knew my temperament and the firmness of my character, and the public would refuse to believe that I had remained a member of the Government although opposed to its military policy. On the other hand, it was obvious to me that, since I completely disagreed with the course of action espoused by the Emperor, he could not very well let me hold one of the most important posts in the Government.

On August 16 (29), 1903, I received a note from the Emperor asking me to report to him the following morning at Peterhof and take along Pleske, Director of the Imperial Bank. The request came to me as a complete surprise. I suspected that His Majesty intended to appoint Pleske to some post, but I could not understand why the Emperor's choice should have fallen on this man, with whom he was not personally acquainted. Pleske called on me in the morning and we went together to Peterhof. I left him in the reception room and entered the Emperor's study. His Majesty received me graciously. The audience lasted about an hour. I reported to him several plans and asked his permission to make a trip in some of the provinces where the vodka monopoly was just then being introduced. His Majesty approved of my desire to see personally that the important reform was carried out. Finally, when I rose to take leave, the Emperor asked me whether I had brought Pleske. I replied in the affirmative. "What do you think of him?" the Czar continued. I said that I had the highest opinion of the man. In fact, I thought very highly of Pleske both as a man and a financial expert. All through my administration he was one of my nearest assistants.

"Sergey Yulyevich," the Emperor said after a pause, "I should like to ask you to accept the post of President of the Committee of Ministers; as your successor I wish to appoint Pleske." I could not conceal my surprise at this sudden decision. "Are you dissatisfied with this new appointment?" His Majesty then said, seeing my astonishment: "Don't forget, the post of President of the Committee of Ministers is the highest office in the Empire." I assured the Emperor that if this appointment was not a sign of disfavour I was glad of it, but that I thought I had a greater opportunity to be useful in my former capacity than at my new post. I took leave of the Emperor and left his study.

General Aleksey Nikolayevich Kuropatkin
Minister of War (January 1898 to February 1904)

CHAPTER IV

DEALING WITH LI HUNG CHANG

TOWARD the end of the reign of Alexander III, relations between Japan and China became extremely strained, and finally war broke out between the two countries. At that time we had but few troops in the Far East. Our detachments stationed at Vladivostok were moved to Kirin for fear that military operations might spread northward and affect Russian possessions or interests. That was the only step we took. The war ended in Japan's complete victory. By the peace of Shimonoseki (1895), as is known, the Japanese acquired the peninsula of Liao-Tung, including the harbours of Ing-Kow and Port Arthur, and secured various other advantages.

With the exception of two serious misunderstandings, good neighbourly relations have existed between China and Russia for the past two and a half centuries. This traditional friendship found expression in connection with Japan's exactions at Shimonoseki. In those years very few statesmen in Russia had a clear notion about Korea, Japan, and, especially, China and their mutual relations. Prince Lobanov-Rostovski, Foreign Minister, knew no more about the Far East than the average schoolboy. Inasmuch as I was in charge of the construction of the Trans-Siberian Railway, I gave a good deal of attention to Far-Eastern affairs. In fact, I was the only Russian statesman familiar with the economic and political situation in that region.

The peace of Shimonoseki we justly regarded with alarm. It gave Japan a footing on the continent, in the neighbourhood of our own sphere of interest. Emperor Nicholas, who had in the meantime ascended the throne, was anxious to spread Russian influence in the Far East. Not that he had a definite program of conquest. He was merely possessed by an unreasoned desire to seize Far-Eastern lands. As for myself, I clearly saw that it was to Russia's best interests to have as its neighbour a strong but passive China, and that therein lay the assurance of Russia's safety in the East. Therefore, it appeared obvious to me that it was imperative not to allow Japan to penetrate into the very heart of China and secure a footing in the Liao-tung peninsula, which to a certain extent occupies a dominating position. Accordingly, I insisted on the necessity of thwarting the execution of the peace treaty between Japan and China. To discuss the matter a conference was called by His Majesty under the presidency of Admiral-General Grand Duke Alexey Alexandrovich. At this conference I advocated the principle of the integrity of the Chinese Empire. Russia's best interests demanded, I pointed out, that China remain unchanged and that no power be allowed to increase its territorial possessions at China's expense. I was supported by Minister Vannovski. Obruchev's attitude was rather indifferent, for he was exclusively interested in military possibilities in the West. The other members of the conference expressed no definite opinion.

When we came to discuss the practical ways and means whereby the policy I had recommended could be carried out, I proposed to present to Japan an ultimatum to the effect that we could not suffer her to violate the principle of the unity and territorial integrity of the Chinese Empire and that we could not, therefore, agree to the treaty concluded between Japan and China. I suggested that we ought to permit Japan, as the victorious nation, to recover her war expenditures by imposing a more or less considerable indemnity upon China. Should Japan fail to comply with our demands, there was no other course left to us, I said, than to open active operations. I did not explain the exact nature of the measures which I proposed to take, but it was my opinion that we might go as far as bombarding some of the Japanese ports. Although I clearly formulated my policy and made definite recommendations as to the practical means for its execution, the conference ended in nothing. All the while Prince Lobanov-Rostovski held his peace.

Thereupon the Emperor called a conference under his own presidency, to which he invited only General Vannovski, Prince Lobanov-Rostovski, Grand Duke Alexey Alexandrovich and myself. In the presence of His Majesty I reiterated my opinion and, as it met practically no opposition, the Emperor accepted my suggestions. This special committee on Sino-Japanese affairs reached the following conclusions on March 30, 1895:

(1) —To seek to preserve the status quo ante bellum in northern China and in pursuance of this to advise Japan, at first amicably, to desist from the occupation of southern Manchuria, for such an occupation would injure our interests and would be a constant menace to

the peace of the Far East; in case of Japan's refusal to follow our advice, to declare to the Japanese Government that we reserve to ourselves freedom of action and that we shall act in accordance with our interests.

(2) —To issue an official statement to the European Powers and to China to the effect that, while on our part we do not seek any seizures, we deem it necessary, for the protection of our interests, to insist on Japan's desisting from the occupation of southern Manchuria.

His Majesty instructed our Foreign Minister to carry out this program. Prince Lobanov-Rostovski must be given credit for the skill with which he acquitted himself of his task. He immediately secured the agreement of Germany and France to Russia's demand, whereupon he hastened to send our ultimatum to Japan. The latter was forced to accept it, and instead of the Liao-Tung peninsula she demanded and obtained an indemnity.

Simultaneously, I entered into negotiations with China and offered her our services for the conclusion of the large loan which she needed in order to pay the Japanese indemnity. As China's credit was not sufficient to enable her to contract the loan, I agreed to pledge Russia's resources as security for the Chinese loan. Furthermore, I took practically complete charge of negotiating and arranging for the transaction on the French money market. The banking firms which took part in floating the loan included Banque de Paris, Banque des Pays Bas, Crédit Lyonnais, and the Hotenger house. The representatives of these banks secured my promise to help them in their financial activities in China in return for the service they had done me in connection with the loan to China.

As a result I founded the Russo-Chinese Bank, in which the French financiers were the chief shareholders. At first, the Chinese government and also our Treasury invested heavily in the institution, but lately our interest in it had been practically negligible. After the wretched Russo-Japanese War we lost our prestige in China and the bank began to decline. Recently it was merged with the Northern Bank, the combination being known as the Russo-Asiatic Bank.

Li Hung Chang was sent to Russia as China's Ambassador Extraordinary. He had been Governor-General of the province of Chi Li and at the time of his appointment occupied the post of First Chancellor, the most exalted office in the Empire. It seemed fantastic that the first dignitary of China should be sent as an emissary to a foreign sovereign and the unprecedented event caused a sensation. The distinguished envoy arrived in St. Petersburg on April 18 (30), 1896, three weeks before the coronation solemnities. By sending such a high dignitary to witness this ceremony the Chinese wished to express their gratitude to our youthful Emperor for all his benefactions to the Chinese Empire.

In the meantime the great Trans-Siberian Railway, which was under construction, had reached Transbaikalia and the question arose as to the further direction which the railroad should follow. I conceived the idea of building the road straight across Chinese territory, principally Mongolia and northern Manchuria, on toward Vladivostok. This direction, I calculated, would considerably shorten the line and facilitate its construction. Considering the enormous mileage of the Trans-Siberian, it was natural to seek to shorten the route. Technically the Amur section presented great difficulties. Besides, the road would run along the Amur River and would thus compete with the Amur steamship companies. The Manchurian route would save 514 versts. In comparison to the Amur region this section also possessed the advantage of a more productive soil and a more favourable climate. The problem was how to get China's permission for this plan, by peaceful means based on mutual commercial interests. The idea appealed to me strongly and I found occasion to draw His Majesty's attention to it. The court physician, Badmayev, a Buriat by birth, who wielded a considerable influence over the Emperor, on the contrary, stood for the Kyakhta-Peking direction. I could not sympathize with his project, first, because I considered Vladivostok as the most desirable terminus for the Trans-Siberian, and, second, because I believed that a railroad to Peking would arouse the whole of Europe against us. It must be borne in mind that the great originator of the Trans-Siberian had no political or military designs in connection with the road. It was an enterprise of a purely economic nature. Alexander III wished to establish communication by the shortest possible route between the distant Maritime Province and Central Russia. Strategically, both Alexander III and his successor attributed a strictly defensive importance to the road. Under no circumstance was the Trans-Siberian to serve as a means for territorial expansion.

When Li Hung Chang on his journey to Russia reached the Suez Canal, he was met by Prince Ukhtomski, at that time one of the Emperor's intimates. This was done at my instance. It had come to my knowledge that England, Germany and Austria were eager to decoy Li Hung Chang and that they wanted him to go to St. Petersburg through western Europe. I, on the contrary, desired to prevent him from visiting any other European country before his arrival in Russia, for it was clear to me that while in Europe Li Hung Chang was bound to become the object of various intrigues on the part of the European statesmen.

Prince Ukhtomski met the Chinese dignitary and apparently succeeded in establishing cordial relations with him. In spite of the fact that Li Hung Chang was showered with invitations to various European ports, he boarded the *Rossiya*, a steamer of the Russian Steamship and Commerce Corporation, specially prepared for us for the purpose, and proceeded straight to Odessa, accompanied by his retinue and Prince Ukhtomski. In that city he was given an honorary guard consisting of a detachment of our troops. At my instance, he was allowed to go directly to St. Petersburg, although Prince Lobanov-Rostovski was of the opinion that Li Hung Chang should be kept waiting for the coronation at Odessa. Inasmuch as our Minister of Foreign Affairs was entirely ignorant of our Far-Eastern policy, I was empowered by His Majesty to conduct the negotiations with our Chinese guest.

I was told that in conducting negotiations with Chinese officials it was necessary, above all, not to show any haste, for they consider that very bad taste, and business must be transacted slowly and ceremonially. Li Hung Chang was the first to pay me a visit in my capacity of Minister of Finances. When he entered my reception room, I came out to meet him in my official uniform. We greeted each other and bowed. Then I led the way to a second reception room and ordered tea served. Tea was served with great and elaborate pomp. My guest and myself sat, while all the members of his retinue as well as my attendants remained standing. When we had taken our tea, I inquired of Li Hung Chang whether he did not want to smoke. He emitted a sound not unlike the neighing of a horse. Immediately two Chinamen came running from the adjacent room, one carrying a narghile and the other tobacco. Then began the ceremony of smoking. Li Hung Chang sat quietly inhaling and exhaling the smoke, while his attendants with great awe lighted the narghile, held the pipe, took it out from his mouth and put it back. It was apparent that Li Hung Chang wanted to impress me with all these solemn ceremonies. On my part, I made believe that I did not pay the slightest attention to all these proceedings.

Of course, during the first visit no attempt was made to talk business. Li Hung Chang kept on inquiring about the health of His Imperial Majesty, Her Imperial Majesty, and each of their children, while I evinced a profound interest in the state of health of the Chinese Emperor, his mother and all their nearest relatives. Our next meeting was of a different nature. Seeing that the elaborated ceremonies made no impression upon me, he gave them up and became less formal in his intercourse with me. Afterwards, during the coronation days in Moscow, we met without the slightest display of pomp, and he was quite outspoken and business-like. I hold a very high opinion of him. During the active period of my life I had occasion to come in contact with a great many statesmen whose names will forever remain in history. His intelligence and common sense give Li Hung Chang a prominent place among those men. In recent Chinese history his importance is very great. For many years he was practically the ruler of that vast empire.

In my conferences with Li Hung Chang I dwelt on the services which we had recently done to his country. I assured him that, having proclaimed the principle of China's territorial integrity, we intended to adhere to it in the future; but, to be able to uphold this principle, I argued, we must be in a position, in case of emergency, to render China armed assistance. Such aid we would not be able to render her until both European Russia and Vladivostok were connected with China by rail, our armed forces being concentrated in European Russia. I called to his attention the fact that although during China's war with Japan we did dispatch some detachments from Vladivostok, they moved so slowly, because of the absence of railroad communication, that when they reached Kirin the war was over. Thus I argued that to uphold the territorial integrity of the Chinese Empire, it was necessary for us to have a railroad running along the shortest possible route to Vladivostok, across the northern part of Mongolia and Manchuria. I also pointed out to Li Hung Chang that the projected railway would raise the productivity of our possessions and the Chinese territories it would cross. Finally, I declared, Japan was likely to assume a favourable attitude toward the road, for it would link her with Western Europe, whose civilization she had lately adopted.

Naturally enough, Li Hung Chang raised objections. Nevertheless, I gathered from my talks with him that he would agree to my proposal if he were certain that our Emperor wished it. Therefore, I asked His Majesty to receive Li Hung Chang, which the Emperor did. It was practically a private audience and it passed unnoticed by the press. As a result of my negotiations with the Chinese statesman, we agreed on the following three provisions of a secret pact to be concluded between Russia and China:

(1) The Chinese Empire grants us permission to build a railroad within its territory along a straight line between Chita and Vladivostok, but the road must be in the hands of a private corporation. Li Hung Chang absolutely refused to accept my proposal that the road should be either constructed or owned by the Treasury. For that reason we were forced to form a private corporation, the so-called Eastern Chinese Railroad Corporation. This body is, of course, completely in the hands of the Government, but since nominally it is a private corporation, it is within the jurisdiction of the Ministry of Finances.

(2) China agrees to cede us a strip of land sufficient for the construction and operation of the railway. Within that territory the corporation is permitted to have it own police and to exercise full and untrammelled authority. China takes upon herself no responsibilities with regard to the construction or operation of the road.

(3) The two countries obligate themselves to defend each other in case Japan attacks the territory of China or our Far-Eastern maritime possessions.

I reported the results of my negotiations to His Majesty and he instructed me to take up the matter with the Foreign Minister. I explained to Prince Lobanov-Rostovski that I had come to an oral agreement with Li Hung Chang regarding the provisions of a secret Russo-Chinese pact, and that the only thing left now was to embody the agreement in a formal written instrument. After listening to my statement of the terms of the agreement, the prince took a pen and wrote the text of the treaty. The document was drafted so skilfully that I approved it without the slightest reservation. The prince told me that the following day he would submit the document to His Majesty and return it to me if it was approved by the Emperor.

When the text of the treaty came back to me, I discovered, to my great surprise, a substantial alteration in the paragraph dealing with the Russo-Chinese union against Japan. The words *par le Japon* (by Japan) were missing from the text. In its altered version the pact provided for the mutual defence of the two countries in the event of an attack upon either of them not by Japan alone, but by any other

Power. I was actually frightened. The alteration was of momentous importance. A defensive alliance against all the other Powers was quite different from such an alliance against Japan. Several European Powers, including France, our ally, and England, have interests in China, and to obligate ourselves to defend China from all those countries meant to arouse them all against us and to invite no end of trouble.

I immediately went to see the Emperor and laid the matter before him. He instructed me to ask Prince Lobanov-Rostovski to make the necessary correction in the text of the agreement. The situation was very delicate. I was much younger than the Foreign Minister and much below him in official rank. For me to correct what he had done was to affront him and arouse him against me. I made known my apprehensions to His Majesty and asked him personally to take up the matter with the prince. He agreed. Soon afterwards we all went to Moscow to attend the solemnities of the coronation.

In Moscow I devoted much time and attention to Li Hung Chang, for I considered it a matter of primary importance to the State to bring our negotiations to a successful consummation. The Russo-Chinese alliance meant two things: first, a great railroad extending as far as Vladivostok on a straight line without curving northward along the Amur River; and, second, firmly established peaceful relations with our neighbour, the Chinese Colossus.

The Emperor assured me that he had spoken to the Foreign Minister and that the latter had promised to restore the original version of the treaty. His Majesty spoke so definitely that no doubts were left in my mind on the subject. After this I met Prince Lobanov-Rostovski several times, but neither of us referred to the matter.

In the meantime I continued my negotiations with Li Hung Chang to the end of inducing the Chinese Government to grant the concession for the construction of the Eastern Chinese section of the Trans-Siberian to the Russo-Chinese Bank, which was already functioning. At the same time I prepared an agreement with this Bank, whereby it ceded the concession to the Eastern Chinese Railroad Corporation soon to be formed by the Russian Government.

Finally, we set the day for the signing of the secret agreement, the signatories on the Russian side being Prince Lobanov-Rostovski and myself, and on the Chinese side Li Hung Chang, who had received instructions directly from Peking. It was agreed that we would meet in the office of the Foreign Ministry and there sign the document with all the formalities prescribed by law and etiquette. On the appointed day the Russian plenipotentiaries with the officials attached to them and Li Hung Chang with his retinue gathered in the office of the Ministry and were seated around a table. Prince Lobanov-Rostovski opened the session and declared that both sides were familiar with the text of the agreement, that the instrument had now been carefully copied by the secretaries and that it could be signed without reading. Nevertheless, he said, he was perfectly willing to let the Chinese re-read the document, if they so wished. Accordingly a copy of the agreement—the document was to be signed in duplicate—was handed to Li Hung Chang's assistants. I took the other one and began to scan it, suspecting no evil. Suddenly, to my horror, I noticed that the paragraph relating to our defensive alliance with China had not been changed, notwithstanding His Majesty's assurance, and that, unlike my version, it provided for an obligation on our part to defend China from an attack by any Power.

I approached Prince Lobanov-Rostovski, called him aside and whispered in his ear that the provision regarding the defensive alliance had not been changed in accordance with His Majesty's will. "My God!" he exclaimed, striking his forehead, "I clear forgot to tell my secretary to insert that paragraph in its original wording." Nevertheless, he was not in the least taken aback. He looked at his watch. It was a quarter past twelve. He clapped several times to call the servants and said, turning to the gathering: "It is past noon. Let's take luncheon. We will sign the agreement afterwards."

We all went to have luncheon, except the two secretaries, who, while we were lunching, copied the document and made the necessary corrections. These new copies were quietly substituted for the ones which had been circulated before luncheon and were duly signed by Li Hung Chang, on one side, and by Prince Lobanov-Rostovski and myself, on the other.

The agreement was an act of the highest importance. Had we faithfully observed it, we would have been spared the disgrace of the Japanese war and we would have secured a firm foothold in the Far East. Anticipating upon the course of events, I may say here that we ourselves broke the agreement and brought about the situation which we are now facing in the Far East. It was an act in which treachery and giddy-headedness were curiously mingled.

The agreement was ratified without further delay by both the Chinese and our Emperor. This agreement was to serve as a basis for our relations with China and for our status in the Far East generally.

For some time after the signing of the agreement Li Hung Chang remained in Moscow. Once, I remember, while I was visiting him, the Emir of Bokhara was announced. The Chinaman immediately assumed his most important air, and seated himself majestically in an armchair. When the Emir entered the reception room where Li Hung Chang sat, the latter rose from his seat, took several steps toward him and greeted him. As I knew both men very well, I did not withdraw. The Emir was visibly shocked by Li Hung Chang's important air and he gave him, first of all, to understand that he, the Emir, was a royal personage and that he paid Li Hung Chang a visit merely out of respect for the latter's sovereign, the Chinese Emperor. He kept on inquiring about the health of the Emperor and of the Emperor's mother and evinced no interest in the person of his host, which according to Chinese notions is very insulting.

On his part, Li Hung Chang kept questioning the Emir as to what was his faith. He explained that the Chinese adhered to the religious teachings of Confucius, and he wondered, he said repeatedly, what was the religion of the Emir and his subjects. The Emir declared that he was a Moslem and went so far as to present the principles of the religion founded by Mohammed. When the visit was over, Li Hung Chang accompanied his guest to the very carriage in which the Emir had come. When the carriage was already in motion, Li Hung Chang shouted to the interpreter who was with the Emir: "Please tell the Emir that I forgot to say to him that the Mohammed he spoke about had been in China. There he was found out to be a convict and they chased him out of the country. Then he must have gone to the Emir's people and founded his religion among them." This sally was so unexpected that the Emir was taken aback and retorted nothing. Having thus retaliated for the offence the Emir had done him, Li Hung Chang returned to his reception room in high spirits.

Not the slightest information penetrated into the press regarding our secret agreement with China. The only thing Europe learned was the bare fact that China had agreed to grant the Russo-Chinese Bank a concession for the construction of the Eastern Chinese Railway, a continuation of the Trans-Siberian. The concession was drawn up under my instructions by the Assistant Minister of Finances, Piotr Mikhailovich Romanov, in consultation with the Chinese Minister in St. Petersburg, who was also China's envoy to Berlin.

Winter and spring he usually spent in St. Petersburg, while the rest of the year he stayed in Berlin. Since it was then summer-time, Romanov went to Berlin and it was there that the terms of the concessions were drafted. The project was subsequently ratified by the two contracting Governments. At the time it was rumoured in Europe, I remember, that Li Hung Chang had been bribed by the Russian Government. I must say that there is not a particle of truth in this rumour.

The terms of the railroad concession granted by China were very favourable for Russia. The agreement provided for China's right to redeem the road at the expiration of, 36 years, but the terms of the redemption were so burdensome that it was highly improbable that the Chinese Government would ever attempt to effect the redemption. It-was calculated that should the Chinese Government wish to redeem the road at the beginning of the 37th year, it would have to pay the corporation, according to the terms of the concession, a sum not less than 700 million rubles.

In his informal talks with me Li Hung Chang reiterated that, as Russia's friend, he advised us not to go south of the line along which the Trans-Siberian Railroad was to run. Any movement southward on our part, he assured me, might result in vast and unexpected perturbations which would be disastrous both for Russia and China. In the interior of the country, he said, the ignorant masses regard every white as an enemy. Li Hung Chang's efforts to persuade me that it was necessary for Russia to refrain from any designs of conquest were indeed unnecessary. As the devoted servant of the Emperor to whom his son had justly (albeit inadvertently) applied the epithet "Peace-Maker," I have always been a most sincere advocate of the idea of peace. I believe that the teachings of Christianity will not become effective until mankind learns to execute Christ's chief commandment, namely, that no human being has the moral right to kill other human beings. I mention this to show what an eminently sane statesman was Li Hung Chang, this representative of what to the Europeans appeared to be a semi-civilized people.

In those days the young Emperor carried in himself the seeds of the best that the human mind and heart possess, and I did not judge it necessary to report to him Li Hung Chang's advice. I was certain that, in concluding the secret agreement with China, the Emperor pursued exclusively peaceful designs.

In passing, I may note the origin of Nicholas's appeal to the

Powers for partial disarmament. In the middle of 1898 Kuropatkin informed Foreign Minister Muraviov that, according to his information, Austria was about to increase and re-arm her artillery. This necessitated a re-arming of our own artillery, which would have been exceedingly burdensome, for we were at that time in the process of rearming our entire infantry. For this reason the War Minister suggested that we should open negotiations for the purpose of inducing Austria to give up her plan, with the understanding that we, too, would obligate ourselves to refrain from either increasing or perfecting our artillery. Muraviov asked me to give him my opinion on the matter. The step, I declared, could bring us nothing but harm. It would achieve no practical results and it would merely reveal our financial weakness to the whole world. In speaking to the Minister I expatiated on the incalculable harm which the growing militarism was doing to the peoples of the world and on the boon which would be conferred on humanity by limiting the armaments. These rather trite ideas were new to the unsophisticated Minister and apparently produced on him a profound impression.

Several days later the Foreign Minister called a conference to consider the question of appealing to the Powers for partial disarmament and a limitation of military expenditures. Muraviov informed us that His Majesty favoured the plan, and read a draft of the appeal. Naturally enough, Kuropatkin opposed the project. On the contrary, I approved the plan, as I would any scheme tending to settle international conflicts by peaceful means. At any rate, I pointed out, it was much less im-practicable and odd than the plan for an agreement with Austria, previously suggested by the War Minister.

The appeal was issued August 12 (24), 1898, and the following year a peace conference took place at the Hague. I had an occasion to discuss the matter with His Majesty. I congratulated him upon having taken the initiative in the great and noble task of bringing about universal peace, but I pointed out that the conference was not likely to have any practical results. The sacred truths of the Christian faith were enounced by the Son of God some two thousand years ago, and yet most of the people are still indifferent to these precepts. Likewise many centuries will pass before the idea of peaceful settlement of international conflict will be carried into practice. Five years later we ourselves showed that our talk about disarmament and peace was but empty verbiage.

During the coronation solemnities in Moscow we signed another agreement bearing on our Far-Eastern policy. I have in mind the treaty with Japan regarding Korea, which sanctioned Russia's dominating position in Korea and determined Japan's sphere of influence in that country. This treaty granted us the right to keep military instructors and several hundred of our soldiers in Korea. The agreement also gave us a preponderating influence upon Korea's state finances. We had the right to appoint the financial counsellor to the Korean Emperor, i.e., practically the Korean Minister of Finances. As for Japan, the treaty guaranteed her certain commercial and industrial rights and privileges in Korea. Thus the treaty demarcated the spheres of influence of the two states in independent Korea (the Sino-Japanese treaty provided for the independence of that country).

After the Sino-Japanese war and the subsequent increase of our Pacific fleet, the Naval Department began to look for a harbour to be used by our warships, for, in view of strained relations with Japan, it was no longer safe to rely upon the Japanese ports. In 1895, the Chinese Government agreed to open to us the port of Kiao-Chow, but as a matter of fact we did not take advantage of this privilege, for we found the harbour inconvenient.

The question of a harbour for our warships remained open till late in 1897, when Germany landed an armed force at Kiao-Chow, on the southeastern coast of the Kwantung peninsula. The news came to me as a complete surprise. The Foreign Minister, however, was not altogether surprised by Germany's step. Several days afterward the German diplomats issued a statement to the effect that Germany's vessels had entered the port in order to punish the Chinese for the assassination of a German missionary, which had taken place some time previously. It appeared odd, however, that this punishment should have necessitated the occupation of the entire port by a considerable armed force landed by a strong naval squadron.

On receiving the news of the landing, the Chinese Government asked for a detachment of Russian warships to be sent to Kiao-Chow for the purpose of watching the actions of the Germans. At first our Chargé d'affaires at Peking was notified from St. Petersburg that the warships had been dispatched to the Chinese port in question, but the following day that order was cancelled. In informing Li Hung Chang about these developments, our Chargé d'affaires stated that negotiations were, no doubt, going on between St. Petersburg and Berlin, which would result in the speedy settlement of the misunderstanding at Kiao-Chow.

The Foreign Minister, Count Muraviov, conceived the idea of taking advantage of this situation for the purpose of securing a base for our navy. It would be easy, he believed, to justify our occupation of some point on Chinese territory by our need of a strong base for our navy, should events develop in a direction unfavourable to China.

Early in November, several Ministers, including myself, received a memorandum drawn up by Count Muraviov. It pointed out that the occupation of Kiao-Chow by the Germans offered a favourable occasion for us to seize one of the Chinese ports, notably Port Arthur or the adjacent Ta-lieng-wan. After a while we received an invitation to a conference called for the specific purpose of taking up Count Muraviov's suggestion. The conference was presided over by His Majesty himself and was attended, besides the author of the memorandum and myself, by the War Minister, Vannovski, and the Director of the Naval Ministry, Tyrtov.

Count Muraviov declared that Russia needed a Pacific port in the Far East and that the moment was opportune for the occupation, or, more correctly, the seizure of Port Arthur or Ta-lieng-wan. He pointed out that these ports had an enormous strategical importance. I indignantly protested against this measure. I reminded my hearers that we had declared the principle of China's territorial integrity and that on the strength of that principle we forced Japan to withdraw from the Liao-Tung peninsula, which comprises Port Arthur and Ta-lieng-wan. I further pointed to the fact that we had concluded a secret defensive alliance with China, thus obligating ourselves to defend her from Japan's encroachments upon her territory. Under these circumstances, I declared, the seizure of a Chinese port would be the height of treachery and faithlessness. Aside from these considerations of an ethical order, I said, the proposed measure would be extremely dangerous even from the standpoint of our self-interest. I called the attention of the conference to the fact that we were engaged in building a railroad on Chinese territory and that our step would arouse the country against us, thus endangering the railroad construction. Besides, the occupied ports, I said, would have to be connected by rail with the trunk line, which circumstance would drag us into complications likely to have disastrous results.

Minister of War Vannovski staunchly supported Count Muraviov. The Navy Minister declared that a port on the Korean coast, nearer to the open ocean, would be preferable to either Port Arthur or Ta-lieng-wan. My arguments did not have any effect upon either Vannovski or Muraviov, but the Emperor was visibly impressed by my heated denunciation of the project and he refused to sanction the plan of occupation.

Several days afterwards I had an audience with His Majesty. "You know, Sergey Yulievich," said the Emperor to me, evidently somewhat put out, "I have decided to occupy Port Arthur and Ta-lieng-wan. Our ships with troops are already on their way there. Here is why I have taken this step. After the conference the Foreign Minister reported to me that, according to his information, British warships were cruising off the ports in question and that if we did not occupy them, the English would do so." Muraviov's information was, of course, false, as I later found out from the British Ambassador.

The news greatly upset me. On leaving the Emperor's study, I met Grand Duke Alexander Mikhailovich. He was *au courant* of the developments in the Far East. "Your Highness," I said, "remember this day: this fatal step will have disastrous results."

Directly from His Majesty I went to see Tschirsky, counsellor of the German Embassy in St. Petersburg, and asked him to telegraph to the German Emperor that in the interests of both my country and Germany I counselled and urged him to withdraw from Kiao-Chow, after having punished those guilty of the assassination of the missionaries. The Kaiser's answer was substantially as follows: "I see from Witte's words that some very important details relating to the matter are unknown to him. Therefore, we cannot follow his advice." Later I found out what were the "important details" the German Emperor had referred to. During his visit to Peterhof in the summer of 1897, he had practically forced from Emperor Nicholas a tacit agreement to Germany's occupation of Kiao-Chow.

In the early part of December, 1897, a squadron of our warships occupied Port Arthur and Ta-lieng-wan. This, as I have said, took place in consequence of the Foreign Minister's report to the effect that if we failed to occupy these seaports, they would be occupied by the English.

Foreseeing all the disastrous consequences of the decision which His Majesty had taken, I did not give in and continued to advocate withdrawal from Port Arthur. In this connection I had several sharp explanations with the Minister of Foreign Affairs. As a result, my relations with Count Muraviov became strained and remained so until his very death. All my efforts were in vain. It was natural for the young Emperor to follow the advice of his Foreign Minister and Minister of War, which was in agreement with his own thirst for military glory and conquests.

Count Muraviov instructed our Chargé d'affaires in Peking to inform the Chinese Government that we had no intention of seizing Chinese territory, that we had occupied Port Arthur in order to protect China from the Germans and that we would leave as soon as the Germans had left. At first the Chinese were reassured and offered their services to supply coal for our warships.

In the meantime parties of engineers began to arrive in Manchuria. By March, 1898, the preliminary investigation was so far advanced that it was possible to draft construction plans. The Eastern Chinese Railroad was designed exclusively for cultural and peaceful purposes, but jingoist adventurers turned it into a means of political aggression involving the violation of treaties, the breaking of freely given promises and the disregard of the elementary interests of other nationalities.

On the 1st of January, 1898, General Alexey Nikolaievich Kuropatkin was appointed Director of the Ministry of War, supplanting Vannovski. I hoped that the new War Minister would adopt my policy and that we would withdraw from Port Arthur. My hope was vain. At a conference under the presidency of Grand Duke Alexey Alexandrovich, called in order to determine the demand made upon China, the General showed himself entirely opposed to my views. The demands upon China, he said, were to include not alone the cession of Port Arthur and Ta-lieng-wan, but also that part of the Liao-tung peninsula which is known as the Kwantung Province. This he considered to be a strategic necessity. The conference drafted a set of demands in this aggressive spirit. It provided for the lease of the Kwantung Peninsula to Russia for 36 years, without any compensation to China, and also the construction of a branch linking them with the Trans-Siberian.

Shortly afterwards I asked His Majesty to set me free from my ministerial office, in view of my disagreement with the Far-Eastern policy of the Government. His Majesty refused to comply with my request. He pointed out to me that he had implicit confidence in my abilities as Minister of Finances and that personally he valued my services very highly. As for the occupation of the Chinese ports, he said, the matter had already been settled beyond recall and that the future would show whether it was a right or wrong step. In the meantime the Emperor asked my assistance in carrying out his newly inaugurated policy in the Far East.

The Chinese Government was reluctant to comply with our demands. The Empress Regent, together with the young Chinese Emperor, had gone to her summer residence, in the vicinity of Peking. Under the influence of English and Japanese diplomats, she obstinately refused to make any concessions. Seeing that under the circumstances, should we fail to reach an agreement with China, bloodshed was likely to take place, I wired to the agent of my ministry in Peking to see Li Hung Chang and Chang Ing Huan, another high official, and to advise them in my name to come to terms with us. I instructed the agent to offer these two statesmen valuable presents amounting to 500,000 and 250,000 rubles respectively. This was the first time that I resorted to bribing in my negotiations with Chinamen.

Largely under the influence of the fact that a number of our warships, cleared for action, lay off Port Arthur, the two statesmen went to the Empress intent on persuading her to yield. Finally, the Empress consented to sign the agreement. This came as a pleasant surprise to His Majesty. The agreement was signed on March 15, 1898, by Li Hung Chang and Chang Ing. Huan, on the one hand, and our Chargé d'affaires, on the other. The act was a violation of our traditional relations with the Chinese Empire. In speaking to the German Ambassador, Prince Radolin, about our occupation of Port Arthur, I remember, I characterized our policy as "child's play which will end disastrously." It was a fatal step, which eventually brought about the unhappy Japanese War and the subsequent revolution. On the other hand, the Chinese Empire is tottering and, out of the civil war now raging, a republic is bound to arise. The fall of the Chinese Empire will produce an upheaval in the Far East and will be felt for many years to come.

CHAPTER V

ORIGINS AND COURSE OF THE RUSSO-JAPANESE WAR

IT is certain that by the seizure of Kiao-Chow Emperor William furnished the initial impetus to our policy. Perhaps he was not clearly aware to what consequences our step would lead, but the German diplomats and the German Kaiser were clearly making every effort in those days to drag us into Far-Eastern adventures. They sought to divert our forces to the Far East, so as to insure the safety of their Eastern frontier. During the war the Kaiser was, in a sense, the defender of our frontier in the West. We paid for this service by a commercial treaty highly unfavourable to us.

Speaking of our Far-Eastern policies, I recall that in 1898 we built a large ice-breaker, with a view to carrying on navigation in the Baltic during the Winter, but chiefly for the purpose of discovering an Arctic sea route to the Far East. The ice-breaker was built with the close participation of Admiral Makarov, who during the Japanese War met his death heroically at Port Arthur. The admiral undertook an Arctic expedition on the ice-breaker, but did not go farther than Nova Zembla.

The problem of an Arctic sea route to the Far East greatly interested our celebrated scientist Mendeleyev. I recall a conference on the subject, which I had with Admiral Makarov and Mendeleyev in my study. The great chemist advocated a daring plan. He spurned the idea of reaching Sakhalin by sailing parallel to the Arctic coast. The safest and shortest route, he asserted, lay across the North Pole. Admiral Makarov, on the contrary, considered this to be a very risky project and thought it more prudent to skirt our Northern coast. Mendeleyev was so certain of the feasibility of his plan that he expressed his willingness to accompany the expedition on board the ice-breaker, should his route be adopted. He refused, however, to join the expedition if it were to follow the admiral's route. The clash between the two men actually assumed a personal character, and they never met again. In the end neither plan was carried out.

Admiral Makarov was soon appointed commander of the port of Kronstadt and when the Russo-Japanese war broke out he was made Commander-in-Chief of the Far-Eastern Navy.

Our occupation of the Kwantung Peninsula alarmed the Powers which had vested interests in China. England immediately seized Wei-Hai-Wei, and Japan renewed its encroachments upon Korea. France seized some territory in the South of China, and on February 17, 1899, the Italian Ambassador, Martino, made a demand upon China for the cession of the harbour of Sang-Ming to Italy and for the recognition of the province of Che-tzian as the sphere of Italian influence. In this case the Chinese Government showed an unusual firmness, and Italy was obliged to give up its claim. In a word, Germany's act was a signal for the pillaging of Chinese territory by all the Powers. To pacify them we obligated ourselves to build a free commercial port in the vicinity of Port Arthur. This failed to satisfy the Japanese. Fearing a clash with that country, we were forced to yield ground to it in Korea. We withdrew our soldiers and military instructors from that country and we recalled our counsellor to the Korean Emperor, who in a short time had acquired complete influence over the finances of the country. Our agreement with Japan, dated April 13, 1898, sanctioned the dominating position of that country in Korea. If we had faithfully adhered to the spirit of this agreement, there is no doubt but that more or less permanent peaceful relations would have been established between Japan and Russia. We would have quietly kept the Kwantung Peninsula while Japan would have completely dominated Korea, and this situation could have lasted indefinitely, without giving occasion to a clash.

The cession of the Kwantung Peninsula to Russia and the subsequent seizure of China's territory by European Powers profoundly aroused Chinese public opinion. Li Hung Chang, who signed the agreement of March 15, 1898, had to give up his high post and accept a Governor-Generalship in Southern China. As for Chang Ing Huan, he was exiled during the Boxer Rebellion into the interior of the country, where he was throttled or strangled. It is also known that the Chinese Ambassador to St. Petersburg and Berlin, a respectable and conscientious official, was publicly executed on his return to Peking.

The most violent form, however, assumed by popular discontent in Russia Boxer Rebellion, so-called. The year 1898 witnessed the beginning of disturbances. The following year the movement grew considerably stronger, and in 1900 it called forth repressive measures on the part of the European Governments. It originated in the South and spread North. Chinese bands attacked the Europeans, looted their property and, in some cases, endangered their very lives. The Chinese Government secretly assisted the rebels. At any rate, it is certain that the authorities had neither the desire nor the means to combat the rebellion.

On the day when the news of the rebellion reached the capital, Minister of War Kuropatkin came to see me at my office in the Ministry of Finances. He was beaming with joy. I called his attention to the fact that the insurrection was the result of our seizure of the Kwantung Peninsula. "On my part," he replied, "I am very glad. This will give us an excuse for seizing Manchuria." I was curious to know what my visitor intended to do with Manchuria, once it was occupied. "We will turn Manchuria," he informed me, "into a second Bokhara."*

In taking repressive measures against the Boxers, we went hand in hand with the other European Powers. We took upon ourselves the initiative of the march on Peking, after the failure of Admiral Seymour's attempt to free the Embassies in Peking, which were practically besieged. Here again I disagreed with Kuropatkin. I pleaded with His Majesty to refrain from active intervention in China and to let the other Powers quell the riots in Peking. Kuropatkin, on the contrary, insisted that we should play the leading part in the punitive expedition against Peking. I argued that it was essential for us not to irritate the Chinese, so as to protect our position in Manchuria, in which we were vitally interested.

My counsel went unheeded. With the assistance of the Japanese troops we took Peking, after the Empress Dowager and the young Emperor had fled from the capital. A number of private residences and, especially, the Imperial palace were pillaged. It was rumoured that Russian army officers took part in the looting, and I must say, to our shame, that our agent in Peking unofficially confirmed these rumours to me. One lieutenant general, who had received the Cross of St. George for the capture of Peking, returned to his post in the

---

* Ed. The Russian conquest in Central Asia was largely centred around the khanates of present day Uzbekistan and was a series of conquests of which the invasions of Bukhara in 1868 and Khiva in 1873, were the significant annexations so that by 1876 the region was the protectorate of the Russian Empire and by 1885 was fully incorporated.

Amur region with ten trunksful of valuables coming from the looted Peking palaces. Unfortunately, the General's example was followed by other army men.

The pillaging of the Imperial palaces was accompanied by the seizure of Chinese State documents of the highest importance. Among the papers taken there was, curiously enough, the original copy of the agreement signed in 1896 by Prince Lobanov-Rostovski and myself, on one side, and Li Hung Chang, on the other. It appears that the Empress Dowager attributed such a high importance to this document that she kept it in her bedroom in a special safe. When Peking was besieged, the Empress was forced to flee from the palace in such a great haste that she left the precious document behind. At my recommendation, this agreement, which we had so treacherously violated, was returned to the Chinese Government.

After the capture of Peking we came to our senses and withdrew our troops from the capital, at the instance of the Foreign Minister and of myself.

Unfortunately, the Boxer movement spread to Manchuria. The attitude of the authorities and the population of that province toward our activities there was at first, on the whole, satisfactory. But after we had occupied Port Arthur, the situation underwent a change. Especially in Southern Manchuria the population showed a great deal of hostility toward us. Both the population and the officials sought to interfere with the building of the railroad, and at times we had to deal with armed attacks. There were various reasons, some of them purely economical, for this hostility, but it is significant that since our occupation of Kwantung the local authorities had made no efforts to allay this hostility or to keep it in check.

The Chinese administration was markedly passive when it came to punishing offenders against Russian life or property. Only upon receiving direct and repeated instructions from Peking would the local administration take the necessary punitive measures, and that reluctantly. The connivance of the local authorities went so far that on one occasion there were regular Chinese soldiers with field guns and military insignia among the rebels who attacked a group of our railway employes*. In some cases the officials themselves instigated attacks on us and acted as ring-leaders. Early in 1899, the Governor of Mukden issued a proclamation to the people of that province, which accused the Russians of oppressing the population in various

* employe is a dated U.S. and European form of the word employee.

ways and of illegally occupying land for the construction of the city and of the port of Ta-lieng-wan. The proclamation caused considerable unrest in that region. In seeking to hinder us, the Chinese resorted to their favourite method of setting us against the British, our rivals in the Far East. The central Chinese Government clearly favoured the English and was hostile toward us.

At the first sign of trouble in Manchuria Kuropatkin made ready to dispatch our troops stationed in the Amur region to the scene of the disturbances. I made every effort to stay Kuropatkin's hand, but soon the riots in Manchuria assumed a threatening character, and I was forced to urge the General to shift our troops to Manchuria. In this case, too, Kuropatkin acted with his customary flightiness and characteristic lack of foresight. He brought into play an all too large contingent of troops, although it was obvious that the most insignificant military force was sufficient to restore order. He went as far as dispatching troops from European Russia. By the time a part of them reached Port Arthur the riots were quelled, so that they were immediately turned back. Both Northern and Southern Manchuria were occupied by our troops.

The administration of our Manchurian railway was decidedly in a peaceful frame of mind. It advocated a policy of fair play toward China, and they were eager to make up for past transgressions against that country. Kuropatkin was entirely out of sympathy with that policy. Our army behaved in Manchuria as in a conquered country, thus preparing the ground for a catastrophe. The forces of the Boxers in Manchuria were practically insignificant. General Subotich defeated the strongest Boxer band without any difficulty, for which exploit he was decorated with the Cross of St. George. This practically put an end to the disturbances. Yet the War Ministry persisted, under one pretext or another, in keeping our troops in Manchuria. For a year and a half this was the cause of differences between the Ministry of Finances, the administration of the Eastern-Chinese Railroad, and the agents of the Foreign Ministry, on one side, and the War Ministry, on the other. His Majesty vacillated and rendered inconsistent decisions. On one hand, he did not definitely condemn the view held by the Ministers of Finances and Foreign Affairs. On the other hand, he seemed to countenance General Kuropatkin and his group.

After the suppression of the Boxer rebellion, the military elements obtained a dominating influence upon our relations with China. They sought to utilize the trouble for the purpose of promoting their professional interests and they kept on hatching various plans of conquest. Excerpts from a memoir written in 1902 by one Hirshman, an engineer who built the Southern section of the Kharbin-Port Arthur line, will best illustrate the activities of our militarists in Manchuria.

Speaking of the campaign of 1900, Hirshman notes the incredibly exaggerated character of the official accounts of military engagements and the extraordinary lavishness with which all manner of rewards were showered upon the Manchurian "heroes." "Furthermore," he writes, "it is an open secret that from the very beginning of the campaign it was the desire of the military party not only to punish the Boxers but also permanently to annex Manchuria." Describing the conduct of the military operations in Manchuria, he very aptly observes that we were pillaging a region in whose economic prosperity we were vitally interested. Punitive expeditions were undertaken with no other end in view than to furnish an excuse for new promotions and new looting. He cites, as a striking example, the expedition against a rebel band led by a Khing Tzang. It became known to General Tzerpitzky that this band had established its headquarters in the vicinity of the town of Kulo in Mongolia, and he decided to exterminate it. In view of the excellent relations which existed between the Russians, on one hand, and the Mongolian population and authorities, on the other, the expeditionary forces were provided with reliable Chinese officials and safe-conducts. The goal of the expedition was the town of Kulo with its ancient monastery revered throughout Mongolia and renowned for its riches. Everything ran smoothly. The attitude of the population toward the troops was friendly and hospitable, and the expedition would have been a very peaceful affair indeed, if the General in command had not been possessed by a thirst for military laurels and also loot.

"The story was related to me by General Tzerpitzky himself," writes Hirshman, "in the presence of several witnesses. When the expedition approached Kulo, the General simulated sickness and declared that he could not enter the town the same day. When night came and the Chinese officials attached to the expedition went to sleep, after having taken the necessary precautionary measures, the General suddenly recovered and entered the town in the dead of the night. Under the pretext of a rifle shot fired at the troops, it was most probably one of those shots which the town night guards are in a habit of firing as a sign of their watchfulness, the monastery was taken by force, a considerable number of monks and laymen were slaughtered and the sanctuary pillaged. The valiant General's share of the booty included some two hundred ancient sacred statues of gilt bronze."

The author of the memoir reaches the following conclusion: "It is possible, without the slightest apprehension, to let the Chinese administration itself, which is more experienced in these matters, disperse the robber bands and restore order. It is also certain that the withdrawal of our troops presents no danger."

Interesting sidelights on the Far-Eastern policy of our central Government during the period of the suppression of the Boxer movement are contained in a series of letters, which I wrote to Minister of the Interior Sipyagin in 1900, while he sojourned abroad for the sake of his health. This is from a letter, dated St. Petersburg, August 10, 1900:

> The march on Peking came as a surprise to Count Lamsdorff. Kuropatkin kept on assuring us that Peking could not be taken now, that operations could not be begun before September and that only by that time a sufficient number of troops would be available. It transpired, however, that while Kuropatkin thus kept on reassuring Lamsdorff, he removed Admiral Alexeyev, to whom the Foreign Minister all the while gave instructions, appointed Linevich in his stead and, without Count Lamsdorff's knowledge, ordered him to march on Peking . . . But that is not all. In spite of official and public assurances that our only intention is the restoration of order, Grodekov suddenly declares the right shore of the Amur River to be ours. The Emperor extends his thanks, and this is published to the world! Then they seize the highly important harbour of New-Chang, hoist the Russian flag and establish a Russian administration there. The same thing is done in Kharbin. The result is distrust on the part of the Chinese, jealousy and malevolence in Europe and alarm in Japan. In addition, every day Kuropatkin summons foreign military agents and tells them that we are waging war, that we want to occupy the entire North, that we shall not tolerate Japan in Korea and so forth. Under these circumstances I took the liberty of writing again to His Majesty to the effect that Kuropatkin was leading him to a disaster; that he, the Emperor, must not declare publicly through the Foreign Minister one thing and do another; that our only business in China is to restore order on the Eastern-Chinese Railroad, after which we must withdraw; that by waging war against China we are making eternal enemies out of the Chinese; . . . that should we penetrate further into Manchuria, some unpleasant surprise would surely be sprung on us either on the Western or the Asiatic frontier; that the Far-Eastern

campaign arouses no enthusiasm among the people; that all this is very dangerous, for *internal psychological epidemics may develop in the country*. . . . In conclusion, I implored His Majesty to instruct the War Ministry to carry out, faithfully and without ambitious plans, his original program and not to drag us into further international complications.

As it was a very sharp letter, I showed it to Pobiedonostzev. He said that it was my duty to send it to the Emperor, which I did. Probably under the influence of my letter, the Emperor summoned Count Lamsdorff. The latter corroborated the views expressed in my letter and complained against Kuropatkin's methods. He was especially bitter in denouncing the occupation of Peking and the way in which it was done. . . . His Majesty was gracious to the Minister, but often interrupted him saying that, after all, the Asiatics deserved the lesson which they had been taught. . . . As you see, the situation is discouraging. There is no definite policy, no firmness, no adherence to one's word, and Kuropatkin is in a state of chronic rage. . . . I have done all I could to prevent a disaster. . . . The course of events does not depend upon me. . . .

And here is an extract from a letter dated August 31, 1900:

Jesting apart, Count Lamsdorff and myself are more afraid of Kuropatkin than of the Chinese. . . . Aside from the unnecessarily large army contingents he is using, the huge expenditures, and the useless measures relating to telegraphs and railroads, which he is taking, my indignation is roused by his communiques, reporting fantastic battles with no casualties or very insignificant ones on our side, and with hundreds of Chinese killed or wounded. . . . And to think that Kuropatkin set the whole of Russia agoing and mobilized upward of 200,000 men to deal with this opponent! I wish all this were nothing but folly and giddiness, but I fear that the General has something up his sleeve. Recently I have had several discussions with him, but to no purpose: he says one thing, and does another. Perhaps, the clue to his behavior is this. The other day he dined with us and, among other things, he said that the Commander-in-Chief alone was competent to determine the requisite number of troops. I was curious to know who was the Commander-in-Chief he had referred to. He replied to the effect that although many people insisted on the necessity of appointing a Commander, His Majesty and himself had decided at the very beginning of the campaign that the Emperor himself would act as Commander-in-Chief and he, Kuropatkin, as his Chief of Staff. . . . Judge for yourself what it all means.

General Kuropatkin was self-seeking and glib-tongued and he possessed, no doubt, a measure of personal bravery. He was clever enough to take advantage of the fact that he had been appointed

Minister by the young Emperor himself. He soon perceived that as war chief he was destined to become the right hand of the ruler of an essentially military Empire. In fact Kuropatkin at once became His Majesty's favourite. While the Ministers appointed under Emperor Alexander III were rarely invited to take luncheon with their Majesties, this high honour was frequently bestowed upon Kuropatkin and also Foreign Minister Muraviov. The latter amused the Empress by telling poor jokes, while the former pleased His Majesty. It soon occurred to the General, however, that it was important for him to please Her Majesty as well. On one occasion, I remember, shortly after he was appointed Minister I called upon him, knowing that the following day he was to report to the Emperor. I wanted to ask him to speak to the Emperor about a certain matter. I found him in his study at a desk littered with books. Having stated my business, I rose to depart, but he asked me to stay and have a chat. I said I was not in a hurry, but did not wish to keep him from his work, whereupon he assured me that his report was ready. "But after the report," he said, "I am invited to lunch with their Majesties. So, you see, I must prepare some interesting conversation for the Empress. All the books you see here are novels and stories by our best writers, especially Turgenev. The subject of my talk tomorrow will be woman, in general, and the fine types of Russian women, in particular."

The next year the Emperor spent a part of the Spring at Yalta, Crimea, and some of the Ministers, including General Kuropatkin and myself, had come to stay there. There was a spell of bad weather, I remember. One morning on his way from the Emperor's palace the General stopped at my summer-house. "This morning," he declared, "I have succeeded in cheering up His Majesty. While I was reporting to him, the sky was overcast, and the Emperor was gloomy. Suddenly Her Majesty, in a gorgeous dressing-gown, appeared on one of the balconies. 'Your Majesty,' I said, seeing that the Emperor did not notice her, 'look, there is the sun!' 'Where do you see the sun?' he exclaimed. 'Please turn around,' I said. He did, noticed the Empress, and smiled. His gloom was gone."

Both as commander and military organizer Kuropatkin lacked creative talent and originality. He always worked with other people's ideas and suggestions. But it must be conceded that he possessed a great deal of assiduity and diligence.

The beginning of the century witnessed the formation of an unofficial force, which gradually became a highly important factor in our Far-Eastern policy. A certain Bezobrazov, a retired captain of cavalry, appeared on the stage. He advocated the necessity of regaining our influence in Korea by means of securing various concessions in that country, ostensibly private, but in reality backed and directed by the Government. Bezobrazov succeeded in winning over to his side Count Vorontzov-Dashkov and Grand Duke Alexander Mikhailovich. These two men introduced the captain to His Majesty. They were in favour of annexing Korea in the spider-like fashion advocated by their protege. The Prince was not intelligent enough to see the consequences of such a policy, while the Grand Duke was actuated by a weakness for all those schemes which promised to bring him to the foreground and give food to his restlessness.

Early in 1900 Bezobrazov conceived an idea of forming a semi-official Eastern-Asiatic industrial corporation, with the financial participation of the Treasury, for the purpose of exploiting the Korean forests. Seeing that the enterprise had all the earmarks of a politico-industrial adventure, I strenuously opposed it. This time I scored a victory. Although the statutes of the corporation were confirmed (in June, 1901), the corporation was not formed.

The Korean problem was one of the storm-centres of our Far-Eastern policy. My views on this subject are best expressed in a letter written by me to the Foreign Minister and dated November 28, 1901:

> It is my profound conviction that unless we remove our misunderstandings with Japan in a peaceful fashion and by making mutual concessions, we shall not only be under the constant menace of an armed clash with that Power, but we shall also be unable to stabilize our relations with China, who is bound to seek Japan's support against us, just as she sought our support and co-operation during the war with Japan. An armed clash with Japan in the near future would be a great disaster for us. I do not doubt that Russia will emerge victorious from the struggle, but the victory will cost us too much and will badly injure the country economically. Furthermore, and that is most important, In the eyes of the Russian people a war with Japan for the possession of distant Korea will not be justified, and the latent dissatisfaction may render more acute the alarming phenomena of our domestic life, which make themselves felt even in peace time. . . . I consider it my duty to say that, according to my opinion, when the worst comes to the worst, it may be advisable to give up Korea altogether. . . . Between the two evils, an armed conflict with Japan and the complete cession of Korea, I would unhesitatingly choose the second.

The Manchurian situation was another source of trouble. We occupied Manchuria ostensibly for the purpose of upholding the authority of the Peking Government and quelling the Boxer revolt. The disturbances ended, the Government resumed its seat in the capital, but we still remained in Manchuria. It was natural for China to turn for support to Japan and to the other Powers which had interests in the Far East. All these countries joined in demanding our withdrawal from Manchuria. As a result, on March 26, 1902, we concluded an agreement with China, providing for the gradual evacuation of Manchuria by our troops within the year ending on September 26, 1903.

In the middle of 1902, I visited Manchuria to inspect the Eastern-Chinese Railway and to solve on the spot some of the problems relating to its construction and operation. Upon return, I submitted a report to His Majesty, in which I emphasized the advisability of evacuating Manchuria and of securing our influence in the Far East by peaceful means exclusively. The report failed to impress His Majesty. Had he followed my advice, we would have avoided the unhappy Japanese war with all its disastrous consequences.

According to our agreement with China, we evacuated a part of Manchuria, but in 1903 there arose a movement against clearing the rest of the province without securing a set of guarantees from China, which would insure our interests in Manchuria. At a conference of Ministers, which was called to consider the matter, Kuropatkin expressed himself to the effect that he "could not help looking at Manchuria as a territory which, in part, must become a Russian possession in the future." According to his opinion, "it was necessary not to hinder the manifestations of hostility on the part of China and the other Powers and not to protest against the direct violation of our expressly stipulated rights, in order thus to secure an excuse for not carrying out our obligations toward Manchuria."

A set of guarantees was drawn up, the evacuation of Manchuria being conditioned upon them. The Imperial Chinese Government refused to grant our demands.

In the meantime Bezobrazov's influence was rapidly growing, although he had been abandoned by his high protectors. He succeeded in enlisting the sympathies of the Emperor himself. In November, 1902, he was sent to the Far East to study the possibilities of exploitting the natural resources of the region. I was instructed by His Majesty to place a sum amounting to 2,000,000 rubles at Bezobrazov's disposal in the Russo-Chinese Bank, and to keep this transaction in strict secrecy. Bezobrazov spent two months in the Far East. He declared himself to be a personal representative of the Emperor. His presence in Port Arthur introduced an element of confusion into the administration of the region. Everywhere he advocated the policy of industrial aggression backed by military force.

In those days two currents became clearly distinguishable in our Far-Eastern policy: one, official, represented by the Ministers and moderate in character, the other, secret, inspired by Bezobrazov and led by the Emperor himself. The plans of the Bezobrazov group were the subject of several Ministerial conferences. In all the discussions I figured as the implacable enemy of the Korean adventures. I did not try to spare anyone's sensibilities, and I used the harshest and most scathing terms in denouncing Bezobrazov. At the conference of March 26, 1903, I pointed out that, having reached the shores of the Yellow Sea under the jealous eyes of several foreign Powers, we must halt our forward movement and entrench ourselves in our present positions. Upon the whole, the conference was hostile to Bezobrazov's plans and did not approve of them.

Seeing that Bezobrazov's influence on His Majesty was constantly growing and knowing that the opinion of a certain Prince Meshchersky, a notable journalist, had considerable weight with the Emperor, I overcame my aversion to the prince, went to see him, and asked him to write to His Majesty warning him of the dangers of the course of policy which he was pursuing in the Far East. Prince Meshchersky complied with my request. The Emperor's reply clearly showed that he was not impressed by Meshchersky's warnings. The note ended with an enigmatic phrase to the effect that on the 6th of May it will be seen what opinion I hold on the subject. As a matter of fact, on that day Bezobrazov was promoted to the rank of Secretary of State, while his collaborator, Vogak, was made General of His Majesty's retinue. These promotions were very exceptional and significant.

The following day a new conference was called to consider Bezobrazov's projects. The Emperor was exceedingly amiable with me. He offered me one of his cigars and lighted a match for me. He obviously hoped thus to disarm me, but I only reiterated my opinion on the subject with my customary bluntness. Count Lamsdorff insisted that the conduct of Far-Eastern negotiations must be left to our diplomats and that all the treaties and legitimate interests of the parties concerned must be respected. To this Plehve replied that, not diplomats, but bayonets had made Russia; and that the Far-Eastern problems must be solved by bayonets, not diplomatic pens. It must be said, however, that upon the whole the conference viewed rather favourably Bezobrazov's plans.

Bezobrazov succeeded in forming an industrial corporation for the purpose of exploiting the forest in Yalu River basin. The corporation hired a number of Chinese robber bands and used them as guards, but the Chinese Government regarded them as outlaws and there were frequent clashes between the guards and the regular Chinese troops. Relations between the representatives of the corporation and the Chinese authorities were very strained. Our activities in the Yalu region began to attract the attention of foreign diplomacy. Japan appealed to Great Britain and especially to the United States. In the middle of 1903 all the Powers concerned were carefully watching our activities there.

About that time Bezobrazov took another trip to the Far East. This time he travelled, not as a private person, but in a luxurious special train, accompanied by a numerous retinue. Minister of War Kuropatkin also happened to be in the Far East at the time, and a number of conferences dealing with the chief problems of our Far-Eastern policy took place at Port Arthur. The decisions did not materially differ from those reached at the spring conferences held in St. Petersburg. The idea of annexing Manchuria was rejected, but it was decided to demand guarantees from the Peking Government intended to safeguard Russia's interests in Manchuria. With the exception of Bezobrazov, the members of the conference were against an aggressive policy. General Kuropatkin, on his return to St. Petersburg, submitted a report to His Majesty. Speaking about our activities in Korea, he said:

> I do not dare conceal from your Imperial Majesty my apprehension that now that our enterprise in the Yalu region has become known to the whole world and that the high interest of the Autocrat of Russia in the undertaking has also become a matter of common knowledge, both at home and abroad, it is no longer possible to present this enterprise as a purely commercial venture, and in the future it will inevitably preserve a great and alarming political importance. Therefore, however great the commercial advantages of the enterprise may be, it appears advisable for us to sell it to foreigners if we do not wish to maintain a constant source of danger of a break with Japan.

Kuropatkin concludes his memoir by stating that we must, above all, take the necessary measures to insure good relations with Japan, and that with this in view we must give up the idea of securing a lodgment in Southern Manchuria, contenting ourselves with strengthening our influence in Northern Manchuria.

In July, 1903, I also submitted a report dealing with the Far-Eastern situation. On the essence of the Far-Eastern question and on the general character of our problem in the Far East I had this to say:

Rapid ways of communication have drawn the yellow races into the whirlpool of international intercourse. Beginning with the middle of the last century, industrial overproduction and the colonization urge directed the eager attention of Europe and America to the vast dormant countries of the Far East. Here, naturally enough, clashes arose, not only among themselves, but with the native states, which for thousands of years lived without any intercourse with the rest of the world and had developed their own culture. Given the technical and military superiority of the Westerners, it is not difficult to foretell the outcome of the conflict for those native states. Only those countries will survive which, like Japan, will have speedily acquired those achievements of European culture that are necessary for self-defence; the more inert countries will fall a prey to the powerful invaders and will be divided up between them.

Such is the essence of the Far-Eastern problem. Accordingly, the problem of each country concerned is to obtain as large a share as possible of the inheritance of the outlived oriental states, especially of the Chinese Colossus. Russia, both geographically and historically, has the undisputed right to the lion's share of the expected prey. The elemental movement of the Russian people eastward began under Ivan the Terrible. Continuing ever since, it has lately stopped with the occupation of the Kwantung peninsula. Obviously, neither this territory nor Manchuria can be Russia's final goal. Given our enormous frontier line with China and our exceptionally favourable situation, the absorption by Russia of a considerable portion of the Chinese Empire is only a question of time, unless China succeeds in protecting herself. But our -chief aim is to see that this absorption shall take place naturally, without precipitating events, without taking premature steps, without seizing territory, in order to avoid a premature division of China by the Powers concerned, which would deprive Russia of China's most valuable provinces.

From this viewpoint, I insisted, the Manchurian problem must be solved. I argued that after securing certain guarantees we must evacuate the province.

In July, 1903, it became a matter of urgent necessity to come to a definite decision regarding the Manchurian situation. At the same time Japan renewed the negotiations with us regarding the division of our respective spheres of influence in Korea and Manchuria. Nevertheless, no definite decision was taken. The situation remained indefinite till the very beginning of the war. That is why the war found us unprepared.

I found that the Japanese proposal was, upon the whole, acceptable. A conference called on August 1 to consider the Japanese terms reached essentially the same conclusion.

In the meantime a sudden break occurred in our Far-Eastern policy. Without the knowledge of the Ministers of War, Finances, and Foreign Affairs, who had previously been in charge of the Far-Eastern affairs, an Imperial decree, on July 30, instituted the post of His Imperial Majesty's Viceroy in the Far East. That official was given the administrative and military power in the entire territory east of Lake Baikal and was also entrusted with the conduct of diplomatic relations with China, Japan, and Korea. The appointee to the new post was Admiral Alexeyev, Governor of the Kwantung peninsula. At first, I believe, Alexeyev was opposed to Bezobrazov, but seeing that power was on the latter's side, he had apparently gone over to him. From that time on I considered my cause lost and a disastrous war inevitable.

It was obvious to me that I could no longer remain a member of the Government. I have already related the circumstances under which I left my Ministerial post. My dismissal did not affect the course of our policy. We were headed straight for a war and at the same time we did nothing to prepare ourselves for the eventuality. We acted as if we were certain that the Japanese would endure everything without daring to attack us. In those years the constant preoccupation of the War Ministry was the possibility of a war with the Teutonic Empires. Several months before the outbreak of hostilities in the Far East we were busy preparing for what appeared an inevitable war with Germany and Austria-Hungary. We went as far as appointing army commanders. Grand Duke Nikolai Nikolaievich was nominated Commander-in-Chief of the forces which were to face the German army, while General Kuropatkin was appointed to command the troops on the Austrian front.

I deem it my duty to say that as long as the responsible Cabinet Ministers were unanimous in their negative attitude toward an aggressive policy in Korea, the Bezobrazov coterie remained powerless, in spite of its influence upon His Majesty. The situation radically changed when Minister of the Interior Plehve openly joined Bezobrazov. It was only then that the Emperor went over to Bezobrazov. For some time a duel had been going on between the latter and myself, and His Majesty was hesitating as to whether he should sacrifice him or me.

With the creation of the post of viceroy, Alexeyev and Bezobrazov openly took into their hands the direction of our Far-Eastern policy. They elaborated grandiose fantastic schemes of exploiting our Far-Eastern possessions, among which they reckoned Manchuria and northern Korea. For that purpose they intended the Eastern-Chinese Railway Corporation and the Russo-Chinese Bank. It was contemplated also to attract foreign investors. While I was still Minister, Bezobrazov visited me several times and explained to me his fantastic projects. He found nothing but indifference, on my part, and an unwillingness to let him spend Treasury funds. The 2,000,000 rubles credit granted to him early in 1903 was soon exhausted, and the various enterprises started by him in Manchuria were left in pecuniary straits, for the colossal profits from the forest business existed only on paper and the other enterprises also proved a failure. They only aroused against us the Chinese and deepened the suspicions of the Japanese.

In September the Emperor went to Germany and stopped at Darmstadt. By that time the influence of the Foreign Minister on the Far-Eastern affairs had been almost completely eliminated. His Majesty conferred directly with Viceroy Alexeyev, without resorting to Count Lamsdorff's offices. At Darmstadt His Majesty ratified the statutes of the Far-Eastern Committee and appointed Bezobrazov and Abaza members of that Committee.

While the Emperor sojourned at Darmstadt, I went abroad. In Paris I found much optimism regarding the Far-Eastern situation. The French were certain that there would be no war with Japan, for Foreign Minister Delcassé declared on every occasion that, according to his information, the war was impossible. As a matter of fact, he obtained his information from our Ambassador in Paris. He had no diplomatic intelligence from either Peking or Tokio, which circumstance indicates what a poor diplomatic service the French had in the Far East. On the contrary, the German Foreign Office was very well informed regarding the Russo-Japanese situation. Berlin was aware that Japan was making strenuous military preparations and that war was considered inevitable there. It appears that my withdrawal from the Ministry of Finances finally convinced the Japanese that nothing could avert the conflict, for they knew that I was the chief opponent of our reckless militarists.

While His Majesty was visiting at Darmstadt, the German Emperor wrote to him to the effect that preparations were being made in the Far East for an armed conflict. His Majesty's reply was very characteristic. He told the Kaiser that there would be no war, because *he* did not wish it. What he meant, apparently, was that Russia would not declare war and that Japan would not dare do it.

The Emperor returned to Tsarskoye Selo on November 21 (December 4), and three days later Minister of Finances Pleske was taken ill. He was succeeded by his associate Romanov, a man of excellent principles, absolutely honest, and of broad financial erudition. Given these qualities, he could not naturally remain at his post for any length of time. He was soon succeeded by Kokovtzev.

The year 1904 was marked by several important appointments. Early in January there was an evening party at the Winter Palace. In the course of it Kurino, the Japanese Ambassador, approached me and asked me to impress the Foreign Minister with the necessity of replying to Japan's latest note without the least delay. He told me that the negotiations with his country were being conducted neglectfully, with the obvious intention of delaying the solution of the Korean and Manchurian problems. Japan was at the end of her patience, he declared, and if within a few days no reply was given, hostilities would break out. Indeed, on our part, the negotiations were conducted in a fashion which seemed to indicate our desire to compel the Japanese to resort to armed force. While our opponents repeatedly proved their willingness to yield on several points, we were intractable. In spite of the fact that we recognized the essential justice of the Japanese demands, we kept on systematically protracting the negotiations.

I had known Kurino for some time. A month before my dismissal from the post of Minister of Finances he submitted to us an outline of a Russo-Japanese agreement which would have obviated the war. In spite of my support, the project was forwarded to the viceroy for consideration, and endless negotiations ensued. I conveyed Kurino's words to Count Lamsdorff. "I can do nothing," he replied. "I take no part in the negotiations."

We failed to reply in due time, and on January 26 (Russian style), the Japanese warships attacked our naval squadron off Port Arthur and sank several of our vessels. The following day war was declared. There was a court reception and a solemn church service, prayers being offered for victory. There was no enthusiasm noticeable among those present. Gloom and silence reigned in the palace and it was as if a heavy burden weighed down upon the people.... At the Emperor's return to the palace a feeble hurrah was heard, but it soon died down. The following day a series of street demonstrations was organized by the administration, but they met with no sympathetic response on the part of the population. It was apparent that the war was highly unpopular. No one wanted it, and many cursed it. This was an ominous sign.

Viceroy Alexeyev was appointed Commander-in-Chief of the fighting forces. The appointment was the height of absurdity. He was not an army man. He could not even ride on horseback. Nor did he in any way distinguish himself in the naval service. He made his career in a rather peculiar way. As a young navy officer he accompanied Grand Duke Alexey Alexandrovich in his voyage around the world. It is said that at Marseilles the merry travellers had a drinking bout, in the course of which the youthful Grand Duke behaved so indecorously and violently that he was arraigned by the police. It appears that Alexeyev succeeded in persuading the authorities that it was he and not the Grand Duke who was guilty of the offence. He paid a fine, and won the friendship of the Grand Duke. Under Alexander III, Alexeyev became Admiral General, and owing to the Grand Duke's efforts was appointed Governor of the Kwantung province. I believe, however, that the Grand Duke never dreamed that his protégé could be made Commander-in-Chief of a fighting army several hundred thousand strong, which was soon to be increased to a million.

Under the pressure of public opinion, which assumed a highly distrustful attitude toward Alexeyev, on February 8 (21) General Kuropatkin was appointed commander of the armies in the Far East. The appointment resulted in a duality of authority which was bound to produce no end of confusion and trouble. Kuropatkin's departure was very pompous. He made public speeches and behaved generally like a victor. It would have been more tactful to depart quietly and come back with pomp and triumph, but fate decreed otherwise.

The evening before his departure General Kuropatkin spent with me, and we had an occasion to discuss the situation. Knowing my familiarity with Far-Eastern affairs, he asked my advice regarding the general conduct of the war. Before expressing any opinion on the subject, I wished to know what were the General's plans. He explained that we were totally unprepared for the war and it would take many months before we could muster enough troops to oppose the enemy. Until then it was his intention to retreat slowly and steadily in the direction of Kharbin and to leave Port Arthur to its fate. Having reached Kharbin and effected a juncture with the fresh auxiliary troops from European Russia, he would then open an offensive against the Japanese and annihilate their army. This plan of action appeared to me sound and I approved it.

Before taking leave the General turned to me and said: "Sergey Yulyevich, you are a man of extraordinary intelligence and many talents. What advice will you give me before I leave?"

"I have a good piece of advice for you," I replied. "Only you would not take it."

He insisted on hearing what I had to say.

"Who is going with you to the Far East?" I asked him. He explained that he was accompanied by several adjutants who would later form his staff.

"Are they altogether reliable?"

"Certainly," he replied.

"If such is the case," I said, "here is my advice to you. Admiral Alexeyev is at present at Mukden. Of course, you will go straight there. Now this is what I would do if I were you. On arriving at Mukden I would send my staff officers to Admiral Alexeyev with orders to arrest him. In view of your prestige in the army your order would no doubt be obeyed. Then I would immediately send him with a convoy to St. Petersburg on the first west-bound train. Simultaneously I would send to His Majesty a dispatch reading, in substance, as follows: 'Your Majesty, for the sake of the successful execution of the great task that you have imposed upon me, I found it necessary upon arriving at the front first of all to arrest the Commander-in-Chief and dispatch him to St. Petersburg. Otherwise the successful conduct of the war is unthinkable. I beg your Imperial Majesty either to order me shot for such a transgression or else to forgive me for the sake of the country.' "

The General burst out laughing, waved his hand and said: "You are always joking, Sergey Yulyevich." I assured him that I was quite in earnest and that I foresaw trouble as a result of the dual authority which his arrival at the front would create.

The commander of the Far Eastern army, Kuropatkin, considered Alexeyev, not without ground, a complete nonentity and, above all, a self-seeking office-hunter, while, on his part, the Commander-in-Chief hated Kuropatkin and at heart wished to see him fail. The two made contradictory reports to the central Government, but in practice Kuropatkin compromised so as to avoid a final break. In his inmost feelings, the Emperor sympathized with the tactics advocated by Alexeyev, but as usual he could not make up his mind and he kept on acting as if his main purpose was to deceive both of his Generals. Kuropatkin afterwards told me that he had in his possession a series of telegrams which would present in their true light the failures of the first part of the campaign, that is, up to Alexeyev's dismissal. In an attempt further to justify himself, Kuropatkin also told me that stupid Generals had been forced on him and that the central authorities had constantly interfered with him. To these complaints I replied that it was all his fault, for he had not followed the advice I had given him on the eve of his departure for the front. If he found, I said, that he could have no freedom of action, he should have resigned.

To what extent optimism prevailed among our military leaders at the beginning of the war and how we undervalued the fighting capacity of the Japanese, may be seen from the following circumstance. In discussing the size of the army which was to be put on the front, General Kuropatkin disagreed with former War Minister Vannovski. While General Kuropatkin believed that the proportion of our army to the Japanese should be two to three, the former Minister thought that one Russian soldier would hold his own against two Japanese.

Throughout the year 1904 the Emperor reviewed all the army contingents which were being sent to the front. To that end he visited Bielgorod, Poltava, Tula, Moscow, Kolomma, Penza, Syzran. In September he visited a number of western cities and inspected the warships at Reval. In October he went to Suvalki, Vitebsk and neighbouring points. In December he visited a number of points in the south. The Emperor usually delivered a short speech wishing the departing troops a good voyage. Then he, as well as Her Majesty, distributed among the soldiers various icons, including the icon of the recently canonized St. Seraphim of Sarov. Inasmuch as throughout the year we had nothing but defeats, this gave General Dragomirov an occasion to coin a very sarcastic *mot*, which went the rounds of the country. "We are attacking the Japanese with icons," he said, "while they use bullets against us."

The course of the war in 1904 presents itself as follows (the dates are according to the Russian calendar) : On March 31, our flagship Petropavlovsk was sunk, and Admiral Makarov and a part of the crew went down with the ship. That catastrophe condemned our entire Far-Eastern fleet to complete inaction. In the middle of April we lost the battle of Turenchen. At the end of May we were defeated in an engagement off Port Arthur. In August we lost an important battle near Liao-Yang and began our retreat toward Mukden. When we reached that city, Kuropatkin declared in his order of the day that we would not retreat another step. On December 20, Port Arthur fell. Then we were defeated near Mukden and were forced to retreat in the direction of Kharbin.

As I had foreseen, there was constant friction between Kuropatkin and Alexeyev. The former followed a definite plan of systematic retreat. The latter, on the contrary, advocated the tactics of aggression. Sitting in his luxurious study he spoke glibly of marching on Port Arthur and licking the Japanese. Neither plan was carried out with any degree of consistency. Both appealed to St. Petersburg for instructions and many of the military measures taken were ordered from the capital. The result of this absurd method of conducting war was a successive series of most shameful defeats. In the end the Commander-in-Chief was dismissed and ordered to go to St. Petersburg, while General Kuropatkin was appointed in his stead.

The loss of the battle of Mukden revealed the complete incompetence of General Kuropatkin as a Commander-in-Chief. He was succeeded by General Linevich, who had distinguished himself by the capture of Peking and the looting, of the Imperial palace there. General Linevich, personally a brave soldier, could do nothing to remedy the situation. The army was completely demoralized and revolutionized. No sane man could help seeing that on land we had lost all chances of victory. I believe that the cause of our continual defeats lay in our complete unpreparedness, and also in the duality of our military authority. General Rediger, who had become War Minister before Kuropatkin was dismissed, openly expressed the opinion that we had lost the war.

THE RUSSO-JAPANESE WAR

When I stayed in Germany and conducted the negotiation for the renewal of the commercial treaty I still believed that, while our navy would be defeated, our army would be victorious. I had confidence in Kuropatkin, although I had no illusions as to his abilities as a military leader. It appeared to me impossible that Japan should keep on inflicting one defeat after another upon us. But when I returned to St. Petersburg I clearly perceived that the war was lost. From that time on my efforts were directed toward the speediest conclusion of peace. But my efforts were in vain and it was only after we had been defeated on all sides that we decided to open peace negotiations.

After the defeat of Mukden, the people, who are guided not by reason but by all manner of mystic impulses, conceived the hope of changing the destinies of war in our favour by sending our Baltic fleet to the Far East. They believed that under the command of Admiral Rozhdestvensky our Baltic fleet would defeat the Japanese. Of course, it was a wild fantasy. It was a thoughtless plan, dictated by hope rather than by cold reason. It was clear to every sane observer that the fleet was doomed. After the fall of Port Arthur, the situation of Rozhdestvensky's fleet became more precarious, for it could expect no help from anywhere and it had no port in which to seek refuge in emergency. On May 14, 1905, there occurred the disastrous Tsushima battle and our entire fleet was buried in the Japanese waters. It was the death blow to our ambitions in the Far East. After this crushing defeat His Majesty became inclined toward the idea of peace.

The Tsushima defeat was a signal for the abolition of the Far Eastern Committee and the dismissal of Admiral Alexeyev from the post of Viceroy of the Far East. It was something in the nature of a funeral service for the dead body of Bezobrazov's adventure. The admiral was decorated with the Cross of St. George, although he had never smelled powder. During the war he had stayed in his palazzo at Mukden and was more preoccupied with his bodily comforts than with the state of the army. The ways whereby Russians receive high appointments and military decorations are past finding out.

CHAPTER VI

THE PEACE OF PORTSMOUTH

ON the morning of July 29 (Russian style), 1905, I was appointed chief plenipotentiary for the purpose of conducting peace negotiations with Japan. Muraviov, our Ambassador to Rome, was summoned to St. Petersburg and appointed plenipotentiary. I had a frank conversation with him in the course of an evening which he spent with me on his arrival in the capital. He was aware, he told me, that the task of conducting the peace parley was a thankless one, for, whatever the outcome, he would be the target of numerous attacks. Nevertheless, he said, he decided to sacrifice his personal career and accept the Emperor's offer. A stay abroad in a country living under a parliamentary régime, he declared, had convinced him that a constitution alone would save Russia. The Ambassador did not show any signs of ill health, and he said that he felt fit as a fiddle.

Several days later Count Lamsdorff approached me and informed me that the Emperor had asked him to find out privately whether I would accept the post of first plenipotentiary and conduct the negotiations with Japan. It appeared that on the previous day Muraviov came to His Majesty and, alleging ill health, implored the Emperor to free him of the task with which he had been entrusted. The count had a definite theory as to why Muraviov refused the post. In the first place, Count Lamsdorff declared, Muraviov was completely unprepared for the task, and he was intelligent enough to perceive that he was running great risks in undertaking it. In the second place, he was rather disappointed to find that His Majesty had fixed the plenipotentiary's emolument at 15,000 rubles. He had expected 100,000.

Count Lamsdorff appealed to my patriotism. He explained that he could not go himself, for he was needed at his place of duty. As for his associate, Prince Obolensky, the count thought him unfit for the task. In the end I declared to the count that I would not decline the mission if the Emperor in person either asked me or ordered me to accept. The following day I was summoned to the Emperor. He received me very amiably and asked me to take upon myself the conduct of the peace negotiations. I replied that I was always ready to serve my Emperor and country. His Majesty thanked me, and said it was his sincere desire that the *pourparlers* should result in peace. He added, however, that he would not pay a kopeck of indemnity or cede an inch of Russian territory.

Several days later I set out for the United States of America. At the time of my departure our financial situation was as follows. We had exhausted all our means and had lost our credit abroad. There was not the slightest hope of floating either a domestic or a foreign loan. We could continue the war only by resorting to new issues of paper money, that is, by preparing the way for a complete financial and consequently economic collapse. As a matter of fact, during the war the amount of paper currency had grown from 600,000,000 to 1,200,000,000 rubles. This lamentable situation was the result of Kokovtzev's lack of experience, on one hand, and of our optimism regarding the outcome of the war, on the other.

Personally I am convinced that Kuropatkin and Linevich prayed to God for the success of my mission. Indeed, peace was the only way out for them, for then they could say: "Yes, it is true that we were repeatedly beaten, but were it not for this peace we would have come out on top in the end."

The mission included the following members: Martens, Professor Emeritus of international law at the University of St. Petersburg, and honorary member of many foreign universities, a man of great knowledge but by no means broad-minded; Planson, of the Ministry of Foreign Affairs, a typical bureaucrat, above all anxious to please his superiors; Pokotilov, our Ambassador to China, a gifted statesman who had always opposed our aggressive policy in the Far East; Shipov, who was later to become Minister of Finances and who represented that Ministry; General Yermoloy, who represented the War Ministry and was the official guardian of the dignity of our valiant but brainless army; Colonel Samoylov, the second representative of the War Ministry, who believed that our cause was lost and that it was necessary to conclude peace at any price; Captain Rusin, delegated by the Naval Ministry, whose views were essentially in agreement with Samoylov's. With Baron Rosen, the second plenipotentiary, I became acquainted only upon my arrival in America. He had the mediocre intelligence of a Baltic German and the manners of a perfect gentleman. He was not abreast of the affairs in Russia and, until he heard Colonel Samoylov's and Captain Rusin's tales of the situation at the front he vacillated in his attitude toward peace. While he took no active part in the negotiations, he did all he could to be of service to me.

It was arranged that part of my retinue should meet me at Cherbourg, where I was to embark, and that the rest should join me in New York. I left St. Petersburg accompanied by my wife with our several-months-old grandson, Leo Naryshkin, and a body of servants. We stopped in Paris, where I spent several days. In the French capital my feelings as a Russian patriot were hurt at every step. The public treated me, the chief plenipotentiary of the autocrat of all the Russias, as a representative of some political nonentity. Some a slight minority sympathized with me, others did not conceal their joy at our misfortune; but the majority treated me with complete indifference. At the station in Paris cries of *Faites la paix* were heard. The attitude of the radical press toward the Emperor and our country were insulting.

I left Paris for Cherbourg accompanied by my wife, our daughter and her husband, Naryshkin, and also a host of journalists. I had intended to go aboard our steamer in the evening, but the ship was delayed by a storm and I did not embark until the next morning. We spent the night at an hotel, which was so crowded that we could barely secure two uncomfortable rooms. At Cherbourg the disdainful attitude of the French toward us was even more marked. It may well be, however, that, in my delicate role as representative of a country which had by chance become entangled in an unfortunate position, I was inclined to be morbidly sensitive and suffer from imaginary affronts and animosities.

The steamer on which we were to make our passage was, if I remember rightly, the *Wilhelm der Grosse* of the Hamburg Steamship Company, one of the largest and fastest ocean-going vessels. On board we were met by the captain and the crew with great pomp, the band playing the Russian national hymn when I reached the deck. Some of my associates, namely, Colonel Samoylov, Planson, Nabokov, Korostovetz and Martens, were already on board. A number of the journalists who accompanied us I knew personally. Such were Bryanchaninov, a young man not without ability, but essentially an amateur and a giddy chatterbox, and Suvorin, a charming youth both Russians. Of the foreign correspondents I knew Dr. Dillon, a prominent and able English publicist and a man of honour and sincerity, known to fame both in England and America. A graduate of a Russian university, he had at one time taught comparative philology at the University of Kharkov. He speaks and writes Russian very well and his familiarity with Russian conditions, especially recent, is very great indeed. He has connections in all our political parties and social groups. Among the journalists was also Mackenzie Wallace, special correspondent for King Edward. To judge by the fact that until just the moment of signing he asserted that the treaty would not be concluded, he must have been constantly misleading His Majesty, the King of England. At one time Wallace was political editor of the *Times*. He may be a good publicist, but he has always misinformed his compatriots about Russia. He speaks Russian well. He has a weakness for everything aristocratic. When in Russia he stays with aristocratic families and hobnobs with the smart set exclusively. All he hears there he takes for gospel truth and faithfully transmits it to his countrymen. No one takes him seriously in England though. Some time ago he wrote a book about the Russian peasantry, in which he sang paeans* to our *obshchina* (communal land system).

Six months before the outburst of our revolution (1905-1906), he issued a new edition of this work, where he asserted that, owing to the wise *obshchina* (communal) organization of our peasantry, a revolution in Russia was an impossibility. The winter of 1906-1907 he spent in St. Petersburg and, I was told, referred to me in his reports in terms far from flattering. He must have been influenced by the circle with which he rubbed elbows. The fact that I slighted him in America may also account for the ill-will he bears me. On one occasion I told him that his work on the Russian peasantry showed how even intelligent people may err when looking at things through other people's eyes.

We also had with us Hadémant, who wrote for the *Matin*. An able professional newspaper man, he was well disposed to us. There were also other correspondents, but as far as Europe was concerned

---

* A pæan is a loud and jolly song to solicit a victory or mark a triumph. The *ash* (i.e. æ), perhaps had its roots in ancient Greek but is more notable in the Anglo-Saxon that spread across Scandinavia. It denotes a variant sound of an e, with the a part being probably originally looking like a flick off the e to mark an accent for placing emphasise on the desired sound.

the information regarding the course of the negotiations was practically controlled by Hadémant and Dr. Dillon. The German press had no prominent representative at the Conference.

Our voyage lasted six days. The ocean was very calm, so that I felt none of the discomforts of sea travel. We took our meals apart from the general public, and several times I invited some of the newspaper men to dinner. A couple of times I dined in the general dining-room. I discovered that among the passengers there were quite a few seekers of strong sensations who were sailing to Portsmouth out of sheer curiosity to witness the political joust between myself and Komura.

From mid-ocean Dr. Dillon flashed over the wireless telegraph his interview with me relating to the coming negotiations. It was the first case in the history of the world press of an interview transmitted by wireless from a ship on the high seas. The interview appeared in all the European papers and contributed a great deal toward acquainting the world with my views on the nature of my task.

Hardly two weeks had passed since my unexpected appointment as plenipotentiary and during all those days I was constantly rushed and unable to collect my thoughts. But on board ship I had ample opportunity to remain alone and reflect. It was there that I prepared myself for the diplomatic duel and determined my plan of battle. I resolved to base my tactics on the following principles: (1) Not to show that we were in the least anxious to make peace, and to convey the impression that if His Majesty had consented to the negotiations, it was merely because of the universal desire on the part of all countries to see the war terminated; (2) to act as befitted the representative of the greatest empire on earth, undismayed by the fact that that mighty empire had become involved temporarily in a slight difficulty; (3) in view of the tremendous influence of the press in America, to show it every attention and to be accessible to all its representatives; (4) to behave with democratic simplicity and without a shadow of snobbishness, so as to win the sympathy of the Americans; (5) in view of the considerable influence of the Jews on the press and on other aspects of American life, especially in New York, not to exhibit any hostility toward them,—which conduct was entirely in keeping with my opinion on the Jewish problem. This program of action I followed strictly throughout my stay in the United States, where I lived, as it were, in a glass house, always in everybody's sight like an actor on the stage. I believe I owe 1 my diplomatic success partly to that program. On board our liner I began to put my plan into effect, and, as a result, there was soon established between me and the numerous passengers a relationship of cordiality, which, spreading from the steamer into the public and the press, created an atmosphere favourable to myself and Russia. Not only did I not shun the reporters, but, on the contrary, I was always at their disposal and I actually met them half-way in their desire to keep the world abreast of what was going on at the Conference. Naturally, I had to be constantly on the alert, carefully weighing every word I uttered, in order to secure the best results for the cause which I was championing.

It is an open secret that nearly all of Japan's war loans were floated on the American money market, so that America practically financed Japan in her clash with us. Furthermore, American public opinion, upon the whole, was on our enemy's side. Such was the situation which I found on my arrival in the United States. Anticipating upon the current of events, I may say that I succeeded in swerving American public opinion over to us. By my course of action I gradually won the press over to my side, and, consequently, also to the side of the cause which the will of my Monarch had entrusted to my charge, so that when I left the transatlantic republic practically the whole press was our champion. The press, in its turn, was instrumental in bringing about a complete change in the public opinion of the country in favour of my person and of the cause I upheld.

In this regard the Japanese plenipotentiary, Komura, committed a grave blunder, which is all the more surprising since he was brought up in the United States and knew the spirit of the country. He rather avoided the press, endeavouring to keep from it many circumstances of the matter. On my part, I took advantage of my adversary's tactlessness to stir up the press against him and his cause. At the very beginning of the negotiations I moved that the discussions should be wholly accessible to the representatives of the press, as if to say that I was ready to take the whole world into my confidence and that in my capacity of plenipotentiary of the Russian Czar I had no secrets or side purposes. I knew, of course, that the Japanese would oppose me. As a matter of fact, at the instance of my opponents, the newspaper men were not admitted to the sessions. This incident immediately became known to the journalists and greatly prejudiced the cause of Japan in their eyes. It was decided to issue brief statements for the press after each session. These were written by the secretaries and passed by the plenipotentiaries. Before long the reporters found out that it was the severity of the Japanese censorship which was responsible for the brevity and scarcity of the bulletins. The American people's friendship toward Russia was growing, while their sympathy for the Japanese cause was constantly on the wane.

My personal behaviour may also partly account for the transformation of American public opinion. I took care to treat all the Americans with whom I came into contact with the utmost simplicity of manner. When travelling, whether on special trains, government motor cars or steamers, I thanked everyone, talked with the engineers and shook hands with them,—in a word, I treated everybody, of whatever social position, as an equal. This behaviour was a heavy strain on me as all acting is to the unaccustomed, but it surely was worth the trouble. Not only did it not detract from my dignity as the chief plenipotentiary of the Russian Emperor, but, on the contrary, greatly enhanced my prestige. The Americans were accustomed to think of an emissary from the autocrat of all the Russias as a forbidding and inaccessible personage, not unlike the other foreign officials who visited the country. And here they discovered, not without keen pleasure, that one of the highest dignitaries of the Russian Empire, the President of the Council of Ministers and the Ambassador Extraordinary of the Emperor himself, was a simple, accessible and amiable man, treating the most humble citizen as his equal.

As we entered the New York waters, on the sixth day of our journey, we were met by a whole flotilla of small vessels and motor boats. They were filled with newspaper men and curious people who were anxious to see the Russian plenipotentiary. The reporters boarded our steamer and greeted me in the name of the American press. I, on my part, gave expression to the feeling of joy which animated me, I said, on the threshold of the country which had always been on friendly terms with Russia. I also said a few flattering words about the press, which plays such a prominent part in America. From that moment until my departure from the United States I was under the surveillance, so to speak, of the newspaper men, who literally watched my every step. During my stay I was the object of innumerable snapshots taken with kodaks. All sorts of people, especially ladies, would approach me and ask me to remain quiet for a moment in order to be snapped. Every day I would receive numberless written requests, coming from every part of the country, for my autograph. These autograph hunters, especially ladies, would also call on me in person. I cheerfully satisfied everyone and, generally, I tried to show every possible attention to my visitors, above all to representatives of the press.

On disembarking we were met by Ambassador Rosen, second plenipotentiary, with his assistants. He took me in his car to the best hotel in New York, situated on the city's principal street. A suite of rooms, consisting of two studies, a large parlour, a dining-room, a bedroom, a dressing room and a room for my valet, was kept in readiness for me at this hotel. The charge for the apartment was 380 rubles a day. Over the balcony adjacent to my room fluttered a huge Russian flag, which attracted everybody's attention. The weather was extremely sultry, and a great many New Yorkers were out in the country.

At President Roosevelt's order several secret service agents were detailed to guard me. They looked, spoke and behaved like gentlemen, these American sleuths. There was nothing to mark off these plain-clothes men from other men on the street,—at least to a foreigner's eyes. In Europe it is very easy to recognize a secret agent. In St. Petersburg he dresses like an ordinary mortal, but you can spot him from afar: he wears a stiff hat and carries a large black umbrella. The appearance of this guard was an unpleasant surprise to me. There were rumours, Baron Rosen explained to me in response to my inquiry, that an attempt upon my life might be made by the agents of a certain group of extreme Japanese militarists who were seeking to thwart the conclusion of peace. It was also rumoured, he said, that an attempt on my life might come from another quarter, namely, from the Jews swarming in New York. They had emigrated after the pogroms which followed in the wake of the Kishinev pogrom organized by Plehve. After the treaty was signed, the secret guard was reinforced, for the reason that the Japanese residing in the United States were believed to be preparing an attempt upon my life.

On the day following my arrival in New York I took an automobile and, accompanied by an Embassy official, I visited the Jewish ghetto, populated mostly by Russian emigrants. By that time the Jewish population of New York had reached half a million. The Jews soon recognized me. At first they looked askance at me, but when I greeted several of them and exchanged a few words in Russian with others, the ice was broken, and most of them began to treat me kindly. Upon my return to the hotel I found the agent who was assigned to accompany me during my visits. When he learned that I had visited the ghetto and remained unharmed, he was somewhat taken aback, for, according to the information in possession of the police, there was a great deal of animosity toward me among the Jews.

The same day I paid a visit to President Roosevelt, at Oyster Bay, within one hour's ride from the city. Baron Rosen accompanied me. Roosevelt occupied a small house of his own, in which he still lives, having retired into private life. It looked like an ordinary summer house of a burgher* of small means. All the servants at the house were black. Roosevelt has been a life-long advocate of full equality of the negroes and the whites and he has always championed the cause of the coloured population of the United States. Naturally, the negroes' attitude toward him is one of respect and love, while, on the other hand, he is attacked by a portion of the whites, which is small, however. I had a, long business talk with the President. He was displeased by my attitude. He declared that my views on the subject precluded the possibility of an agreement with Japan. It seemed to him that after the initial formulation of diametrically opposed and irreconcilable viewpoints by the two sides, the Conference would be dissolved. Then we had luncheon, at which, besides the host and the two guests, there were the President's wife, his daughter by his first wife, and her husband. The luncheon was more than simple and, for a European, almost indigestible. There was no tablecloth, and ice water instead of wine. A little wine was served to Baron Rosen as an exception. I noticed that, generally speaking, people ate very poorly in America. What surprised me most was that the host, and not the hostess, was the first to seat himself at table and the first to rise, and that the courses were served first not to his wife but to himself. I also noticed that the hostess walked behind the President. All this is quite contrary to European manners and customs. The principle of "ladies first" applies to the wife of the French President, just as to any other woman. Priority is given to the French President only at a strictly formal function, but then his wife usually does not

---

* A privileged individual of the middle class from which the municipal leaders were selected or the upper social class collectively known as the bourgeoisie.

participate in them.

After luncheon, we resumed our conversation, but, as the President's wife took part in it, it was not in the nature of a business talk. It was agreed that the next day I would meet the Japanese plenipotentiary with his retinue on board the President's yacht in his presence. After a meeting on the yacht and a formal exchange of greetings Baron Rosen and I were to sail in one warship, and Komura with his retinue in another, direct to Portsmouth, where the Conference was to take place.

At the appointed hour I left the hotel and made my way to the docks, where crowds of people greeted me in silence. We boarded a small steamer and set out for the President's yacht. Our way was marked by continuous roaring and shrieking of sirens and factory whistles, which is a peculiar American way of saluting. It is curious to note that the progress of the Japanese was not marked by any such manifestation. When we reached our destination, we were saluted by the Presidential yacht in the conventional way. Japan's representatives were greeted in the same manner.

As soon as we reached the deck, the President went through the ceremony of introducing us to our opponents and forthwith invited us to luncheon. We took it standing, so as to avoid all delicate questions of priority in seating the guests. I expressed to Baron Rosen my apprehension that the Japanese would be given some advantage over us. I pointed out to the Baron, for instance, that I would not suffer a toast to our Emperor offered after one to the Mikado. I feared that the President, as a typical American inexperienced in and careless of formalities, would make a mess of the whole business. Baron Rosen took up the matter with the assistant Secretary for Foreign Affairs who had served for a long time in St. Petersburg at the American Embassy. He was appointed to take care of the Conference and arrange the ceremonial so as to avoid all friction. As for the toast, it was offered in connection with the President's speech simultaneously in honour of the two monarchs. My first meeting with the Japanese was morally very painful to me, for, after all, I represented a country which, although the greatest empire on earth, had been defeated in war. The interview was formal and very stiff. As we were leaving the stateroom, our group, including the President, myself, Baron Rosen, Komura and the second Japanese plenipotentiary, the Japanese Consul in New York, Takahira, was photographed, in accordance with President Roosevelt's wish. The photograph was then given to every member of the Conference and reproduced in all the American newspapers. After taking leave of the President and the Japanese, we went on board a warship sailing directly to Portsmouth.

Inasmuch as I am not a lover of sea travel and as, furthermore, I was anxious to see Boston, I landed at Newport in the company of one of my secretaries with a view to making the remainder of my way to Portsmouth by land. The rest of the party continued their journey on board the warship.

After having luncheon with the commander of the port, I went out riding to see the sights of Newport. The town proper is rather small and by no means remarkable, but it is surrounded by country houses which are the most luxurious and palatial in the land. It is the summer residence of all the New York millionaires and the meeting-place of America's rich and, to a certain extent, of wealthy Europeans.

Although the hour was early, I noticed a great many equestrians. Their attire somewhat surprised me. The men wore light, coloured shirts, light trousers and leather gaiters, and were bareheaded in spite of the hot sun. The women were also hatless and wore light and rather short riding habits.

The port commander,—he returned my visit two years later at Homburg, near Frankfort, Germany, told me that originally the American Government planned to have the peace conference meet at Newport, which with respect to comforts, luxuries and amusements is, of course, much superior to Portsmouth. Finally, however, he said, Portsmouth was chosen, for the following reason. It was feared, and not without ground, that the "smart set" at Newport would cultivate the Russian representatives and féte and pamper them, while the Japanese would be neglected. This was inevitable, for, whatever the political sympathies of the Americans might be, as members of the white race they could not help feeling socially attracted to us Russians and repelled from the Japanese.

From Newport I proceeded to Boston in a special train. I arrived there in the evening and was immediately recognized. The next day I drove through the streets of the city and visited Harvard University, one of the best and oldest institutions of higher learning in the country. President Roosevelt is a Harvard alumnus. On one occasion he told me that he did not wish to run for the office of president the next term. His ambition was, he added, to be elected

THE PEACE OF PORTSMOUTH

president of Harvard University. I was met by the president of the university and some of the professors and I had lunch with them. On my way back I visited some sections of the city, returned to the hotel and then drove to the railway station, intending to take a train for Portsmouth. The secret service men, who accompanied me in another automobile, asked me to use a side passage in making my way to the train. They saw fit to escort me to the train under a special guard. The station was crowded with people of the Jewish type, and apparently the American authorities feared a demonstration or an attack upon me on the part of the Jews. My guardian angels also begged me not to leave the car, but since a great many people were visibly anxious to speak to me, I stepped on the platform. The men near me took off their hats. I followed their example, approached one group and struck up a conversation. They were Jews who had emigrated from Russia. We spoke Russian, and I still vividly recall the substance of the talk I had with them. Some of them were American-born or had come there during childhood, they told me, but most of them had been in America only a few years. They had not been able, they said, to withstand the oppression any longer. I was anxious to know how they were getting on economically. They explained to me that in America they enjoyed full liberty and equal rights, and for that reason had no great difficulty in securing a more or less comfortable living. I then inquired whether they were satisfied with their lot. The men nearest to me began to talk fast. No, they were very homesick and they longed for Russia. Russia's soil, they said, held the bones of their ancestors, and so she would forever remain their fatherland. They had become American citizens, they remarked, but they could never forget Russia and when they were alone and thought of life and death, their hearts naturally turned to their ancestors and thus to Russia. "We do not love the Russian régime," they told me, "but we love Russia above all else. Therefore, please, do not believe those people who will tell you that we side with Japan. We wish you success at the Conference, as the representative of the Russian people, and we shall pray to God for you." The land of Russia is to them the dearest land on earth. As I took leave of these people, a loud "Hurrah!" resounded in the air. A similar attitude toward Russia I found also among the Jews of Portsmouth.

In the evening of the same day I reached Portsmouth, which is a combination of a naval base and a small town, the latter being the summer residence of middle class people. At the hotel I found some of the members of my retinue, who had preferred to come to Portsmouth by rail instead of by sea. The warships which carried the diplomatic missions were due at Portsmouth the next morning. Our vessel was the first to arrive. Earlier in the morning I had stolen *incognito* into the naval port and, as soon as our warship entered the harbour, I made my way to her in a motor boat, boarded and later disembarked accompanied by Baron Rosen and the rest of our group. A naval crew, headed by the port authorities and a military band, were ashore to salute us.

From the port we proceeded straight to the Naval Building. One of the two wings was assigned to us for our offices, the other to the Japanese. The two wings are connected by a large hall, in which the sessions of the Conference took place. Opposite that hall there were vast rooms where the members of the Conference had tea and lunch. After our arrival in Portsmouth we were considered the guests of the American people, and so we were housed and fed at the expense of the United States Government. We also had government motor cars at our disposal. All the members of the Conference were accommodated in the largest available hotel, but the hotel and the town in general were so overcrowded that I, the chief plenipotentiary of the Emperor of Russia, was assigned but two tiny rooms for myself and another small one for my two valets. My study was almost a glass room, so that all I did there was plainly visible not only from the many hotel rooms and adjacent balconies, but even from the road to passers-by. Naturally, that road was constantly thronged by curious people who were anxious to catch a glimpse of the Russian plenipotentiary at work. Needless to say, the press correspondents hung around the place all day. Not satisfied with keeping in constant touch with my secretaries, they solicited me ceaselessly for personal interviews, the reporters of each paper endeavouring to secure a separate interview so as to obtain an exclusive story.

After the first morning session of the Conference was over, we had luncheon with some of the port officials and their wives, to whom we had previously been introduced. Afterward it became customary for the first and second plenipotentiaries on each side to have luncheon at one table. We also had with us two interpreters, ready to assist us should the Japanese resort to their own language. Literally dozens of courses were served, but the dishes were mostly cold. It appears that the government had ordered hundreds of various luxuriously prepared dishes and stored them in refrigerators to feed us on them. I soon noticed that one must be very careful with his food. Two or three days later I decided to refrain completely from eating it, and for a time I touched nothing but bread and some vegetables. Komura, on the contrary, ate everything with great appetite. On one occasion I called his attention to the danger lurking in our food, but he wanted to display his Japanese intrepidity and said that he was not afraid, that he could eat everything, and kept on eating. As a result, while I left Portsmouth hale and hearty, Komura was taken ill at the end of the Conference and developed an intestinal variety of typhus, so that when I visited him before my departure from the United States, I found him sick in bed.

After the first session we set out for the City Hall, riding in open landaus, which formed a solemn procession. The road was lined with spectators and troops who saluted us. I recall one incident of that parade which is rather out of keeping with our notion of a disciplined army. As I was riding past one of the detachments I suddenly heard the traditional Russian military greeting: "I wish you good health, your Excellency." I looked back and noticed a soldier presenting arms to me. It must have been an American soldier of Russian-Jewish extraction. What surprised me was that the officers did not react to this breach of discipline. At the City Hall we were met by the local mayor and other municipal officials, and exchanged greetings with them.

At first we Russians dined at a separate table in the general dining-rooms of the hotel. Later we found it more comfortable to have our dinner served in a separate room adjacent to my apartment. The food was prepared by special order in accordance with our instructions, for it is highly dangerous to eat the ordinary food which is served in America. I have arrived at the conclusion that Americans have no culinary taste and that they can eat almost anything that comes in their way, even if it is not fresh, provided the food is properly seasoned and properly served.

The next day the business sessions of the Conference began. It may be appropriate to say a few words here about my chief opponent, Komura. I had previously met him in St. Petersburg while he was Japanese ambassador. I was also acquainted with some of the members of his staff. Komura is, no doubt, a man of prominence, but his appearance and manners are rather unattractive. In the latter respect he is inferior to the other Japanese statesmen I have had occasion to meet, for instance: Ito, Yamahata, Kurino, Montono.

Those were strenuous and painful days. An enormous responsibility rested upon me. I understood perfectly well that should I return home with empty hands, the military operations would be resumed, a new debacle would follow, and the whole of Russia would curse me for not having obtained peace. On the other hand, patriotism made my heart revolt against a peace imposed upon us by a victorious foe.

It seems to me—and the whole civilized world will uphold my opinion—that I did all it was possible to do under the circumstances by means of diplomacy; in fact, I achieved more than was expected of me. Nevertheless, it must not be forgotten that, after all, I represented the defeated side and that my situation had its inexorable logic, against which I could do nothing.

The manner of the Japanese at the sessions was correct but cold. They often interrupted the proceedings to hold private consultations. In addition to three secretaries on each side, the Conference was attended by the plenipotentiaries alone, that is, myself, Baron Rosen, Komura and the Japanese Ambassador at Washington. Most of the talking was done by myself and Komura, the second plenipotentiaries but rarely taking part in the debates. My tone and manner were such that on one occasion Komura exclaimed: "*You talk as if you represented the victor.*" To which I retorted: "There are no victors here, and, therefore, no defeated."

It was my desire to have the assistant plenipotentiaries, too, attend the conferences, but Komura, for a reason unknown to me, resolutely opposed me. Some of the assistants attended no more than one session. The Japanese plenipotentiaries kept their assistants in the rooms adjacent to the conference hall, and Komura constantly kept in touch with one of them, an American, a former lawyer in Japan, who was attached to the Ministry of Foreign Affairs. Socially we Russians met the Japanese only in the course of the short luncheon.

I carried out the instructions given to me by my Monarch fully and strictly. The cession of Southern Sakhalin was the only infringement upon the principle of no territorial cessions,—but for that step His Majesty alone is responsible. It was a correct step, for otherwise we would have failed to obtain peace, but I would probably not have taken it on my own initiative.

As for President Roosevelt, at first he tried to scare me into making considerable concessions by pointing out to me that otherwise the treaty would not be concluded. But he met with a firm determination on my part not to make any such concessions. At that time, there were two clashing parties within the body of the Tokio Government. One, headed by Ito, advocated the acceptance of my conditions; the other insisted on an indemnity and was ready to continue the war, should we fail to accede to that demand. Then Roosevelt, seeing that American public opinion was becoming favourable toward Russia and fearing that the unsuccessful end of the parley might turn the sympathies of the people away from him and from the Japanese, telegraphed to the Mikado, describing the trend of public opinion in America and advising him to accept my conditions. Komura was instructed to yield, but as he personally was opposed to this, he requested a personal instruction from the Mikado. Hence the confusion and delay which marked the end of the Conference.

The course of the Conference may be indicated by quoting the following interchanges of cablegrams and letters. On August 13th, I cabled the Foreign Minister at St. Petersburg as follows:

We have begun the discussion of the Japanese terms point by point. I think the Japanese are temporizing, either expecting some events to happen or for the purpose of making arrangements with Tokio, or perhaps London. We adhere to the opinion that they will not desist from their principal demands. It is my profound conviction that we must so conduct the negotiations as to win over to our side not only the Russian people but also the public opinion of Europe and America. Only in that case shall we be able to overcome the enemy with God's help, if we are destined to become engaged in a prolonged war. If Europe and America cease rendering Japan material assistance and side morally with us, we shall come out victorious. Consequently, in conducting the negotiations three things are absolutely indispensable: 1. We must so act as to be able, with clear conscience, to publish all the documents and submit the whole matter to the judgment of humanity, in case peace is not concluded; 2. We must let Japan have all those gains which she has obtained owing to her good luck in this war and which do not injure either the dignity of Russia as a great Power or the feelings of the Russian heart; 3. We must be fair in our estimate of the situation, inasmuch as fairness is practicable in such cases. I am convinced that, no matter what the outcome of the negotiations is, in conducting them thus I shall serve my Monarch and my country as much as is within my powers, provided of course I have the necessary support.

Four days later I cabled the Foreign Minister as follows:

At present the situation is as follows: We have reached no agreement regarding the payment of indemnities, Sakhalin, the reduction of the navy, and ships in neutral waters. On Monday or Tuesday there will be the decisive session, after which, if neither side yields, we shall have to break off the negotiations. What the Japanese think is not known to anyone, I believe. They are an impenetrable wall even to their white friends.... In view of the infinite importance of the matter, it is necessary, it seems to me, to gauge the situation again and to take an immediate decision. I have not the slightest doubt but that a continuation of the war will be the greatest disaster for Russia. We can defend ourselves with more or less success, but we can hardly defeat Japan.

The Emperor's autographed remark on the margin of this telegram: "It was said—not an inch of land, not a ruble of indemnities. On this I shall insist to the end."

On August 21st, I cabled the Foreign Minister:

... I believe that after the Conference, when the world learns what happened there, the peace-loving public opinion will recognize that Russia was right in refusing to pay a war indemnity, but it will not side with us on the subject of Sakhalin, for facts are stronger than arguments. As a matter of fact, Sakhalin is in the hands of the Japanese, and we have no means to recover it. Consequently, if we wish the failure of the Conference to be laid to Japan, we must not refuse to cede Sakhalin, after having also refused to indemnify Japan for her war expenditures. If it is our desire that in the future America and Europe side with us, we must take Roosevelt's opinion into consideration, in giving a final answer.

The following day I received his reply, as follows:

Unfortunately, it appears from your last telegrams that in spite of the readiness which you manifested in the conferences to come to an amicable agreement on each point, the Japanese plenipotentiaries continue to insist on peace terms, which, being incompatible with Russia's dignity, are altogether inacceptable.

In view of this His Majesty has ordered you to cease further conferences with the Japanese delegates, if the latter are not empowered to desist from the excessive demands which they are now making.

. . . Thus the negotiations are being broken off because of the intractability of the Japanese as regards the question of indemnities; we must stop then and there. Under these conditions, the further discussion of the altogether inadmissible cession of Sakhalin becomes unnecessary.

True, Sakhalin is at present occupied by the Japanese and we shall not soon be able to dislodge them from the island; nevertheless, there is a great difference between a forceful occupation of this territory and a formal documental cession of this island which has a brilliant future.

President Roosevelt used his influence with the Japanese delegates to restrain them from pressing their demand for an indemnity, as is witnessed by the two letters following, which came into my possession.
[These letters as here reproduced are re-translated into English from the translation into Russian as they appear in Count Witte's papers.—The Editor] :

Oyster Bay, August 22, 1905.

Dear Baron Kaneko:

I deem it my duty to inform you that on every hand I hear doubts, expressed by Japan's friends, as to the possibility of her continuing the war for a large indemnity. One of the prominent members of the Senate Committee on Foreign Relations, who absolutely sides with Japan, writes me:

"It seems to me that Japan is hardly in a position to continue the war only for a large indemnity. I would not blame her, if she should break the negotiations for the purpose of occupying Saghalien. But if she will resume the military operations exclusively for the purpose of obtaining money, she will not obtain the money and besides she will soon lose the sympathies of this and other countries. I deem it my duty to say that I do not consider her demand for an indemnity just. She has occupied no Russian territory except Saghalien, and the latter she still has to retain."

Your Excellency should understand, I believe, that in America, among people who hitherto were well-disposed toward Japan, a very considerable majority would share the opinion expressed in the above cited lines. The consent to restore the North half of Saghalien gives Japan some hope of getting a certain amount of money in addition to the sums for the Russian war prisoners which are justly due to her, but I do not think she can demand or obtain anything like the sum which she set as indispensable, namely six hundred millions. You know how urgently I advised the Russians to conclude peace. With equal firmness I advise Japan not to continue the war for the sake of war indemnity. Should she do so, I believe that there will occur a considerable reversal of public opinion against her. I do not believe that this public opinion could have a tangible effect. Nevertheless, it must not be altogether neglected. Moreover, I do not think that the Japanese people could attain its aims if it continued the war solely because of the question of an indemnity. I think that Russia will refuse to pay and that the common opinion of the civilized world will support her in her refusal to pay the enormous sum which is being demanded or anything like that sum. Of course, if Russia pays that sum, there is nothing else for me to say. But should she refuse to pay, you will see that, having waged war for another year, even if you succeeded in occupying Eastern Siberia, you would spend four or five hundred more millions in addition to those expended, you would shed an enormous quantity of blood, and even if you obtained Eastern Siberia, you would get something which you do not need, and Russia would be completely unable to pay you anything. At any rate, she would not be in a position to pay you enough to cover the surplus expended by you. Of course, my judgment may be erroneous in this case, but it is my conviction expressed in good faith, from the standpoint of Japan's interests as I understand them. Besides, I consider that all the interests of civilization and humanity forbid the continuation of the war for the sake of a large indemnity.

This letter is, of course, strictly confidential, but I will be glad if you wire it to your Government and I hope that you can do it. If the message is transmitted at all, it should be done immediately.

Sincerely yours,
(Signed) THEODORE ROOSEVELT.

Oyster Bay, Aug. 23, 1905.

Dear Baron Kaneko:

In addition to what I wrote you yesterday, I wish to bring the following to the attention of the Ambassadors of His Majesty the Japanese Emperor:

It seems to me that it is to the interests of the great Nipponese Empire to conclude peace for two reasons: 1st, its own interest; 2nd, the interest of the whole world, toward which Japan has certain duties. You remember, I am not speaking of the continuation of the war for the purpose of keeping Saghalien, which would be right, but of the continuation of the war for the purpose of getting from Russia a large sum of money, which in my opinion would not be right. Of course, it is possible that you may get it, but I am convinced that you would have to pay too dear a price for that success. If you fail to obtain the money, no further humiliations and losses inflicted upon Russia would redeem your expenditures in blood and treasure.

1. It is in Japan's interests now to end the war. She has acquired domination in Korea and Manchuria; she has doubled her own fleet by destroying the Russian fleet; she has obtained Port Arthur, Talienwan, the Manchurian Railway; she has obtained Saghalien. There is no advantage for her in continuing the war for money, for the continuation of the war would absorb more money than Japan could in the end get from Russia. She will be wise if she will now put an end to the war with triumph and take her place as a leading member in the council of nations.

2. From the ethical standpoint, it seems to me Japan has a certain obligation toward the world in the present crisis. The civilized world expects from her the conclusion of peace; peoples believe in her; let her manifest her superiority in the question of ethics, no less than in military affairs. An appeal is made to her in the name of all that is lofty and noble, and to this appeal, I hope, she will not remain deaf.

With profound respect,
Sincerely yours,
(Signed) THEODORE ROOSEVELT.

On August 27th, I cabled the Foreign Minister:

... In view of the fourteen-hour difference in time, he asked me to call the next session not to-morrow, but the day after to-morrow (Tuesday). I replied that I did not think I had the right to refuse his request, but I declared to him in a most categorical fashion that we would not in any case or under any circumstance renounce the decisions taken in accordance with His Majesty's latest instructions, that this was the last concession granted by His Majesty, and that any new proposal I would reject on the spot without submitting it to my Government. Consequently, I said, if they hoped that we would yield, they were wasting their breath and time and keeping the world in uncertainty.

The Emperor wrote the following remark on the margin of this dispatch:

Send Witte my order to end the parley to-morrow in any event. I prefer to continue the war, rather than to wait for gracious concessions on the part of Japan.

Dated Peterhof, August 28, 1905.

The following day I could say, in a message to the Foreign Minister:

> Before the beginning of to-day's session, at half past nine, Baron Komura wished to have a private conversation with me. In the course of it I said that, according to instruction I had received, to-day's session must be the last one and that the only thing left to them is either to accept or reject the final and irrevocable decision of our Emperor. I am almost certain that they will yield to His Majesty's will.

And later in the day, I conveyed joyful news in the following despatch:

> I have the honour to report to your Imperial Majesty that Japan has accepted our demands regarding peace conditions. Thus peace will be restored owing to your wise and firm decisions and in exact conformity with your Majesty's plans. Russia in the Far East will remain a Great Power, which she has been hitherto and which she will forever remain. In executing your orders we have exerted all the powers of our intelligence and Russian heart. Graciously forgive us for not having been able to achieve more.

The peace treaty was signed September 5, 1905, at 3 p. m.

On the eve of the last day of the Conference I had been still in the dark as to whether the treaty would be signed by the Japanese. My sleep was obsessed with nightmares and interrupted by intervals of praying and weeping. My mind was a house divided against itself. I was aware that the conclusion of peace was imperative. Otherwise, I felt, we were threatened by a complete débâcle, involving the overthrow of the dynasty, to which I was and am devoted with all my heart and soul. I knew I did not bear the slightest particle of guilt for this terrible war. On the contrary, I did all I could to oppose it. Yet it fell to my lot to be instrumental in concluding this treaty, which, when all is said, was a heavy blow to our national *amour-propre* *. I knew that all the responsibility for the treaty would be placed on me, for none of the members of the ruling clique, let alone Emperor Nicholas, would confess the crimes they had committed against their country and against God. Naturally, I could not help being greatly depressed. I do not wish my worst foe to go through the experiences which were mine during the last days of the Portsmouth Conference. To crown my miseries I was taken ill, but in spite of my illness

---

* a sense of one's own worth, confidence, values and self-esteem.

I had to be constantly in the limelight and play the part of a conqueror. Only a few of my collaborators understood my state of mind.

The signing of the treaty was announced by cannon-shots. Immediately the town bedecked itself with flags. Straight from the Conference I drove to one of the local churches, where I used to go in default of an Orthodox temple. All along our way throngs greeted us enthusiastically. Near the church and in the adjacent streets, the crowd was so dense that we had great difficulty in making our way through it. Many tried to shake hands with us,—the usual expression of attention with Americans.

Having worked our way into the church, we found it so crowded that we had to place ourselves behind the grate of the raised platform on which the service is performed. We beheld a wonderful spectacle: ministers of various creeds and faiths, including our Orthodox priest from New York and several rabbis, had formed a solemn procession and were moving across the church toward the altar, headed by a choir which was chanting a peace hymn. The procession reached the raised platform and then the Russian priest and the Protestant minister offered short thanksgiving prayers. During the service the Bishop of New York came to join the other clergymen, straight from the railway station. He and the Russian priest delivered short sermons. Then the clergy with the several choirs present sang a church hymn, while many of the people wept. Never did I pray with more fire than at that moment. The celebration effected that unity of all the Christian churches and of all Christians, which is the dream of all the truly enlightened followers of Christ. We were all welded by the heat of our enthusiasm for the great principle: " Thou shalt not kill! " Seeing American men and women thank God with tears in their eyes for the peace He had granted to Russia, I asked myself how it concerned them. The answer was: "Are we not all Christians?" When the service was over, the choirs started singing, "God, save the Czar." To the sounds of that hymn we left the church. As I moved slowly through the crowd, many tried, apparently in accordance with a local custom, to force various presents into my pockets. When I reached the hotel, I found in my pockets some very valuable gifts, in addition to a great many trinkets of no worth.

I acquitted myself of my task with complete success and I was extolled and praised up to the skies, so that in the end Emperor

Nicholas was morally compelled to reward me in an altogether exceptional manner by bestowing upon me the rank of Count. This he did in spite of his and, especially, Her Majesty's personal dislike for me, and also in spite of all the base intrigues conducted against me by a host of bureaucrats and courtiers, whose vileness was only equalled by their stupidity.

Several circumstances combined to enable me to achieve a peace which the whole world proclaimed to be the first Russian victory after more than a year of uninterrupted disgraceful defeats. In the first place, while I was in the United States my behaviour awakened in the Americans the consciousness of the fact that we Russians, by race, culture, and religion, were akin to them, and that we had come to their country to go to law with a race alien to them in every essential respect. Furthermore, the American people discovered that, although the personal representative of the autocrat of all the Russias and a high dignitary, I was much like their own public leaders and statesmen. The favourable impression was enhanced by the fact that all the other members of our group caught that general democratic attitude from me. I have already had the occasion to explain how I treated the American press and how it stood me in good stead. I also had the support of the American Jews, for they knew both from my past career and from their conferences with me in the course of my stay in the United States—these conferences are described below—that I was one of the rare Russian statesmen who in recent years have advocated a humane treatment of Russian Jewry. I have already mentioned the fact that President Roosevelt's sympathies were with the Japanese. To enhance his own popularity and to gratify his self-love as the initiator of the Conference, he wanted peace, but a peace advantageous for the Japanese. It did not occur either to the President or to the American people generally that the excessive growth of Japan's strength was not exactly to the best interests of America. I should like to observe in this connection that, upon getting acquainted with President Roosevelt and other American statesmen, I was struck by their ignorance of international politics, generally, and European political matters, in particular. I heard the most naive, to use a mild term, judgments regarding European politics from some of the most prominent American statesmen and public leaders. Here is one gem: "There is no room in Europe for Turkey, because it is a Moslem country, and it does not matter who gets its European possessions." And another: "Why not restore a strong, independent Poland? This would be both just and natural."

Upon the whole, the international situation favoured the successful outcome of the Portsmouth Conference. With a view to her own immediate interests, France was very anxious that we, her ally, should make peace with Japan. It is true that Great Britain wished a peace more or less favourable to Japan. This, the English hoped, would teach Russia a lesson and be of service to them when it came to regulating certain moot points of the Anglo-Russian relations. On the other hand, however, the English perceived that the excessive growth of Japan was fraught with dangers in the future and therefore undesirable. At that very time, it happened, the term of the Anglo-Japanese treaty elapsed. Negotiations for the renewal of the treaty were begun in London, and it was decided that the final formulation of the pact would depend upon the outcome of the Portsmouth Conference. I called the attention of Count Lamsdorff, our Minister of Foreign Affairs, to that circumstance, but we were unable to find out why the London parley had been linked with our Conference. The financial circles also favoured the termination of hostilities, for the reason that the Russo-Japanese war greatly upset Europe's finances. The Christian churches were on our side, for they regarded the Japanese as heathens, although it should be stated in all fairness that these heathens were sustained by an all-powerful faith in God and an unshakable belief in immortal life. Finally, the successful termination of the Portsmouth parley was also to the best interests of Emperor William of Germany.

At Portsmouth I received, among other deputations, a group of representatives from American Jews. The deputation included Jacob Schiff and Seligman, two great bankers, and Oscar Straus, who has in recent years served as American Ambassador to Constantinople. Two years ago this diplomat conceived a desire to visit Russia. In spite of his high station and the universal respect he enjoys in America he was forced to enter into protracted negotiations with the Russian police and it was only under special surveillance and for a strictly limited period of time that he was allowed to come to Russia. I recorded in detail my conversation with the Jewish delegates in a number of official dispatches which I sent to the Minister of Foreign Affairs, and I shall state here merely the substance of the talk. I received them very cordially and listened with attention to what they had to say. The spokesman of the deputation called my attention to the exceedingly painful situation of the Jews in Russia and to the necessity of putting a stop to the present deplorable state of affairs by granting them full rights. I pointed out that the horrors of the Jewish situation in Russia had been presented to the world in a somewhat exaggerated light, but I did not deny that the Jews in Russia were in a very difficult position. Nevertheless, I argued, an immediate and complete removal of their legal disabilities would, in my opinion, do them more harm than good. To this remark Jacob Schiff made a sharp retort, which was, however, toned down by the more balanced judgments of the other members of the deputation, especially Dr. Straus, who made an excellent impression on me.

Among the many visitors I received at Portsmouth was Jeremiah Curtin, an American Russophile, whom I had known since my boyhood. He was a friend of my uncle, General Fadeyev, and frequented our family whenever he came to Tiflis (Caucasus). Later I met him in St. Petersburg, where he served in the American Embassy as a secretary, and where he frequently came for long stays, after he had given up his diplomatic career. An intimate friend of the famous Procurator of the Holy Synod, Pobiedonostzev, he was deeply interested in our Orthodox faith. He mastered the Russian language and wrote a good deal about our country which he sincerely loved. At Portsmouth he made every effort to promote our cause. I saw him twice during my stay in America: the old man looked still hale and hearty, but several months after my departure from his country I received the news of his death.

Upon the signing of the treaty, our mission left Portsmouth. Some members of the group took trains for the interior of the country, anxious to catch a glimpse of America, and, particularly, to visit Niagara Falls. Baron Rosen and I returned straight to New York. The baron had previously insisted that at the end of the Conference I should undertake a tour of the chief cities of the United States in order to strengthen the sympathy between the United States and Russia, for which I had laid a foundation. The American Government, too, regarded this plan with favour. I communicated about this matter with Count Lamsdorff, pointing out to him the political significance of the tour. I received a rather evasive reply. On the one hand, His Majesty granted me his permission to undertake the tour and even seemed to be anxious to see the plan carried into effect; on the other hand, certain conditions were imposed which made me believe that the project was looked at askance in St. Petersburg. As I am not accustomed to such replies, and as, besides, by temperament I am literally unable to bear such treatment, I made no bones about wiring back to Count Lamsdorff that I did not wish to undertake the tour. Knowing, as I did, the atmosphere which surrounded His Majesty, I immediately grasped the situation. The reception which I was given in America was, of course, well known in St. Petersburg and disturbed many a courtier's sleep. Naturally, intriguing began. It was, no doubt, insinuated within His Majesty's hearing that I was aiming at becoming the president of the Russian Republic. "Look how easily he wins the sympathy of the masses," some of my well wishers probably told His Majesty. "He must not be allowed to increase his popularity." The Emperor himself on one occasion had been heard to say: "Witte is a hypnotist. No sooner does he open his mouth in the Imperial Council or any other meeting than he gains the support of his very enemies." The plotters also tried to spoil my relations with Count Lamsdorff by insinuating that I was seeking to eclipse and finally supplant him, but they could not prevail against our true friendship and the count's noble-heartedness.

Upon my arrival in New York, Baron Rosen and I went to pay a farewell visit to President Roosevelt at Oyster Bay. We dined with the President in his family circle, as during our first visit, and I conversed a great deal with our host both before and after the dinner. I had a pleasant surprise in store for him. Previous to the outbreak of the Russo-Japanese war the United States imposed a differential duty on imports of our sugar. We protested against this measure, which was not in agreement, we thought, with the position of Russia as a most favoured country, but in vain. At that time I held the office of Minister of Finances. We retaliated by establishing differential duties on several American imports,—which step naturally displeased the United States. Before I left for America I obtained His Majesty's permission to inform the United States Government that these differential duties were abolished. Before and during the Conference I did not deem it advisable to make use of this permission, for I did not want to create the impression that we curried* favour with America. The signing of the treaty set my hands free, and I took advantage of my last visit to Oyster Bay to break the news to the President. He was visibly pleased. The next

* An act of insincerity in paying homage or placating an authority in order to gain some political advantage.

day the story of the abolition of the duties was published in all the papers and made an excellent impression.

I have already had occasion to refer to the fact that throughout the Conference my relations with President Roosevelt were not particularly harmonious or cordial. Finding me intractable, he finally refused to deal with me and began to communicate directly with Emperor Nicholas. For this reason some of the points of the controversy were settled by His Majesty in person. I feel it to be my duty to state here that none of my Monarch's decisions were essentially at variance with my own policy, although I would not perhaps have been resolute enough to make the concessions which His Majesty made. However, this is only natural, for I am but one of our sovereign's servants, while he is the autocratic monarch of the Russian Empire, responsible for his deeds to God alone.

Throughout our conversation, especially before the dinner, President Roosevelt was visibly at pains to smoothe away the impression of unpleasantness which had marked our official relations. He assured me that he used his influence on the Japanese in our favour. To corroborate his statement, he showed me his telegram to the Mikado, which I mentioned above. Generally speaking, the conversation was conducted in a very amiable tone. Toward the end of the visit, 1 asked the President to give me his autographed photograph, which he agreed to do with evident pleasure. We took leave of our host and his family, and in the evening returned to New York. The photograph was forwarded to me at my hotel in New York the following day, accompanied by a letter, which read [Re-translation from Russian version] :

Oyster Bay, Sept. 10, 1905.

Dear Mr. Witte: ——

I beg you to accept the enclosed photograph, together with my hearty greetings.

I thank you sincerely for His Majesty's message, which was transmitted to me, informing me of his noble-hearted intention henceforth to interpret the article about the most favoured nation in such a manner as to put America on an equal footing with the other Powers.

Please convey to His Majesty my sincere gratitude for this act.

In the course of our conversation, which took place last evening, I urged you to give your attention to the questions of issuing passports to respectable American citizens of the Jewish faith. It seems to me that if that could be done, there would be eliminated the last cause of irritation between the two peoples, for the perpetuation of whose historical mutual friendship I should like to do everything in my power. You can always refuse to issue a passport to some American citizen, Jew or Gentile, if you are not quite certain that the issuance of the passport will not harm Russia. But if your Government found a way to permit respectable American citizens of the Jewish faith, whose intentions you do not distrust, to enter Russia, just as you permit it to respectable Americans of Christian faith, this would be, it seems to me, in every respect fortunate.

Assuring you again of my profound respect and renewing my felicitations to you and your country on the conclusion of peace, I beg you to believe me,

     Sincerely yours,
(Signed)   THEODORE ROOSEVELT.

Mr. Sergius Witte,
Hotel St. Regis, New York.

The remaining few days of my stay in the United States I spent very pleasantly. Immediately upon the termination of the Conference I divested myself of the title of plenipotentiary and ambassador extraordinary and became a plain citizen. As such I took a more modest suite of rooms at the hotel, paying only 82 rubles a day for it, instead of 380 rubles as formerly. Life is very expensive in America. For instance, you cannot give the elevator-boy a tip less than a dollar (two rubles in terms of our money), so. that at the large hotels small coin does not exist, as it were. Naturally, I had to lay out quite a few thousand rubles from my own pocket, in addition to the twenty thousand rubles which was my allowance for the trip to the United States.

Wherever I went in New York I was met with much enthusiasm and much pomp. For instance, when I appeared in the Stock Exchange, to honour me all business was stopped for ten minutes. Among other institutions, I visited the military academy (West Point) which supplies the American army with officers. The school is situated on the Hudson River, at the distance of some three hours from New York City, and is luxuriously equipped. I was received there with great pomp, and the cadets, all full-grown men in smart uniforms, were reviewed for my benefit. I was not the only one visiting the academy that day. It happened, as a matter of chance, that the Japanese army officers attached to Komura had also come there to see the school. I noticed that they were very unhappy, for the reason that no one paid any attention to them. Having taken notice of their awkward predicament, I approached them, greeted them and asked them to join me. They thanked me and kept close to me all the while, forming a part of my retinue, as it were. The parade was very beautiful, and at one time the cadets marched to the strains of "God Save the Czar." When the sounds of that wonderful hymn burst forth, I bared my head and so did all those present.

I came to West Point on board J. P. Morgan's yacht. I met that famous banker and industrial king several times during my stay in the United States. A man of fabulous wealth, he is the most influential financier in America. Morgan has a palace in New York City, but he practically lives on board his yacht. In that craft he crosses the ocean, cruises in the Mediterranean, etc. He believes, not without reason, that life on the sea is the healthiest mode of living and accordingly he tries to spend most of his time at sea. During my stay in the United States I ate only one decent luncheon and dinner, and that was on board Morgan's yacht, on the day of my visit to West Point. At the hotel we paid fabulous sums for our dinner (30 to 40 rubles per plate), and yet the food was exceedingly bad.

The purpose of my visits to Morgan was to induce him to take part in the foreign loan which we were preparing to conclude for the purpose of liquidating the war. He showed himself open to inducement and, in fact, offered me his services himself, insisting that I should not enter into any negotiations with the Jewish group of bankers headed by Jacob Schiff. I relied upon his promise of assistance and did not attempt to interest the Jewish bankers in the loan. I have described elsewhere under what circumstance the loan was concluded, how the German bankers were prohibited by Emperor William from participating in it, and how the group of banking firms headed by Morgan also backed out, probably under the pressure of the German Government.

Morgan is afflicted with a nose disease which greatly disfigures him. He has on his nose a large growth resembling a beet. Before leaving his yacht, I took advantage of a moment when we were left alone and said to him:

"Let me thank you for your hospitality and volunteer a little service. The celebrated Professor Lassar of Berlin is a good friend of mine. I was under his treatment for a skin disease of which I suffered and I saw at his clinic a number of patients with morbid nose formations such as yours. He removed these growths surgically and restored the noses of his patients to their normal state."

My host thanked me and said that he had heard about that operation and even knew the professor I mentioned, but that he was not in a position to be operated upon. I thought that the banker was afraid, but I was mistaken.

"No," he said, "I am not a bit afraid. I know how skilful that surgeon is, and I do not doubt the result. But, my dear sir, how shall I show myself in America after the operation? Do you know that I would never be able to return to these states?"

I was puzzled.

"Don't you see?" he went on. "If I come to New York with my nose cured, every street boy will point at me and split his sides laughing. Everybody knows my nose and it would be impossible for me to appear on the streets of New York without it."

All this was said in a serious tone. The banker, it was apparent, sincerely regretted that he was not in a position to get rid of his beet.

Upon my return to New York from Portsmouth, Columbia University in the city of New York bestowed upon me the honorary degree of Doctor of Laws. I spent a whole morning at that institution of higher learning, examining the buildings and talking to the professors. They received me very cordially, and I was greatly flattered by their attention. Externally, Columbia University is richer than Harvard. I also caught a glimpse of the student body, for the university was already open. I was greatly impressed by the importance attributed in America to physical education. Columbia University includes a large building entirely devoted to gymnastics and games.

While examining the economics division of the Columbia library, I remember, I asked the professor of political economy whether he expounded to his students Henry George's single tax doctrine. He assured me that Henry George was studied in his classes very carefully. "In the first place," he said, "Henry George is one of our most gifted writers. Besides, I consider it useful to acquaint my students with his views on the land problem, for the purpose of exposing its fallaciousness." Many of our home-spun economists and also our great writer but naive thinker, Leo Tolstoy, would do well to go to school to that American teacher.

I was also curious to know whether student riots and disturbances, such as are customary in Russia, were possible in the American universities. The idea apparently never occurred to the professors. Should any student attempt, they said, to devote himself at the university to other activities than study, he would be immediately cast out of the school by his own comrades.

I took a trip to the city of Washington, which is the official capital of the United States. There I visited the President's White House, the Senate, the Congress and the Congressional Library. In the vicinity of that city there is the house where the great Washington, the maker, so to speak, of the present United States of America, lived and died. It is situated on the banks of a river. The ships sailing by salute it and the passers-by take off their hats to it. It may be said that the Americans revere this building like a sacred relic. They surely know how to honour their great men. Visitors to George Washington's house and little farm are usually shown the spot where he and his wife are buried. One can also see the room where the great man died and the apartment occupied by the French General Lafayette, who helped build up the new-born republic. Near the house there is a special enclosure for trees, each planted by a prominent visitor. I, too, was asked to plant a tree there. I do not know what has become of it.

It happened that I arrived in the capital on Sunday, when Washington's house is not open to visitors. As I was anxious to return to New York on the same day, I asked President Roosevelt to allow me to visit the house as a special favour. I was told that all the historical monuments and buildings in the United States were in the custody of a special Women's Society. This organization has large means and bears all the expenses incident to the maintenance of the monuments. The society is so independent, I was told, that even though President Roosevelt should appeal to its president in person, she might refuse to grant his request. I was, therefore, advised to appeal to her directly for permission to visit the house. I wired to the lady and received a very courteous reply, giving me the freedom of Washington's house. I went there on board a government steamer, and representatives of the Society acted as my guides.

While sightseeing in New York I was struck by the appearance of the sky-scrapers. I even ventured to go up in an elevator to the top of one such monster, thirty-seven stories high. There was a light breeze blowing and I could feel the top room swaying.

Some of the peculiar features of American life greatly amazed me. Thus, for instance, I could not for a long time get accustomed to the idea that most of the waiters in the hotels and restaurants which I visited were university students. Attracted by the high wages, —they often amount to as much as a hundred dollars a month, — the students cheerfully enter the service of hotels and restaurants and earn enough during the summer months to keep them afloat during the winter. These students did not seem to be ashamed of the menial duties of their occupation. They wore the waiters' outfit, served the guests and removed the dishes from the tables, all without the slightest embarrassment; but, once the meal was over, they would change their clothes, sometimes put on their fraternity insignia, court the girls who stayed at the hotel, walk with them in the park, play tennis, etc. Then when meal time came, they would again put on their regulation outfit and be metamorphosed into waiters. This is altogether impossible in Russia. Our students would live on ten or twenty rubles a month or even starve, rather than demean themselves by doing the work of a servant. This probably holds true of other European countries.

I was also shocked to see girls of good families, who stayed at our hotel, promenading in the dark in the company of young men. A girl and a youth, téte-á-téte, would walk away into the forest, the park, and stroll there for hours alone or else they would take out a boat and row on the lake, and no one would find that reprehensible. During our stay at Portsmouth, some of the members of the mission, including myself, were often with two charming young girls who lived with their mothers in the neighbourhood of our hotel. We would have tea with them, and the young folk stayed in the house far into the night. I noticed that no one considered their behaviour either unusual or improper. At Portsmouth, for purposes of recreation, I often spent an hour or so on the open beach, watching the surf. At Biarritz in Europe the ocean is impressive enough, but it lacks the grandiose quality and the magnificence with which it is invested at the American shores.

I was surprised to see the attitude of the American public to the secret service. One day I was riding in an automobile in New York, accompanied by one of the secret service agents who were attached to my person. We reached a congested thoroughfare where ordinary mortals usually wait quite some time before they can proceed on their way. The agent showed his badge to the traffic policeman, the latter waved his hand, the stream of traffic stopped as if by magic, and we drove on. I imagine the storm of indignation which such an action of the police would raise in Russia, in monarchist Russia.

Before I left the United States, President Roosevelt handed me a letter with a request to transmit it to Emperor Nicholas. The missive began by referring to the gratitude His Majesty had previously expressed to the President for his assistance in bringing about the peace. Now, the author of the letter went on, he was asking a favour of His Majesty. The commercial treaty of 1832 between the United States and Russia, the President said, was interpreted by the Americans as providing for the free entrance of all United States citizens into Russian territory, it being understood that limitations of that right were to originate exclusively from the necessity on Russia's part to protect herself from harm, material and otherwise. As a matter of fact, however, the Russians seemed to interpret the treaty in a different spirit. In recent years, the President pointed out, it had become the practice of the Russian Government to discriminate against the American citizens on the basis of religion and refuse admittance to Jews of American allegiance. To this discrimination, President Roosevelt emphatically asserted, Americans would never consent. Therefore, the letter concluded, to continue the friendly relations which had been inaugurated by my visit to the United States, it was necessary for the Russian Government to give up the reprehensible practice of excluding the American citizens of Jewish faith from Russia. This letter I transmitted to His Majesty and in due course it reached the Minister of the Interior. In my premiership a special commission was appointed to study the matter. The commission after long deliberations recommended to give up the interpretation of the treaty clause which offended the Americans, but this recommendation led to no practical consequences. In the end the United States Government abrogated* the treaty, and we lost the friendship of the American people.

I made my return trip to Europe on board a German steamer which was even faster and more luxuriously equipped than the one

* to do away with a law or formal agreement.

which took me to the United States. The people of New York gave me a hearty farewell, and on the steamer the passengers treated me with much kindness and deference. In the first military port which we entered a military salute was fired in our honour.

The following is the text of the letter in which Czar Nicholas informed me of his decision to honour me with the title of Count and expressed his appreciation of my services in successfully concluding an honourable treaty of peace:

October 8, 1905.

Count Sergey Yulyevich:

In my constant solicitude for Russia's peaceful prosperity, I agreed to accept the amicable proposal of the President of the North-American United States for a meeting of Russian and Japanese plenipotentiaries for the purpose of determining the possibility of putting an end to the miseries and horrors of a protracted war, which has already involved so many sacrifices on both sides. My confidence has imposed upon you the mission of going to the United States as my first plenipotentiary and of entering into negotiations should Japan's terms prove admissible, for the purpose of concluding peace on the basis of principles which I had elaborated with precision.

Both in the detailed discussion of the preliminary terms and in the final drafting of the peace treaty you acquitted yourself brilliantly of the task confided to your charge. You acted firmly and with the dignity which befits a representative of Russia, and thus you have obtained just concessions, having demonstrated the inadmissibility of terms which could offend the patriotic consciousness of the Russian people or injure the vital interests of our country. Having duly acknowledged the consequences of the successes achieved by our opponent, you have, nevertheless, declined, according to my instructions, to pay, in one form or another, the expenses for the conduct of the war, which was not begun by Russia, and you have only agreed to return to Japan the Southern part of Sakhalin, which belonged to her prior to 1875. Thus, the task of restoring peace in the Far East has been successfully accomplished for the common good.

Highly valuing the skill and statesmanlike experience manifested by you, I herewith bestow upon you the rank of count of the Russian Empire, as a recompense for your high and great service to the country. I remain unalterably well-disposed to you and sincerely thankful,

(Signed) NICHOLAS.

At one point in my negotiations with the Japanese for peace I became aware that we could obtain better terms if the peace treaty were complemented with a treaty of alliance with Japan. Very cautiously I alluded to the matter and received an evasive answer from Komura. It was clear, however, that the Japanese were not averse to a partial alliance with us. I telegraphed to Count Lamsdorff that, in my opinion, the negotiations should be conducted with a view to a Russo-Japanese alliance. As the Minister's reply was evasive and rather hostile to my suggestion, I dropped the matter. And so, when the parley was over, we parted from the Japanese not as friends determined to support each other, but as enemies who had agreed to suspend the struggle for an indefinite period of time.

On returning to Russia I perceived why my suggestion had not been welcomed by the Government. As a matter of fact, in those days the idea of *revanche* * prevailed among a considerable number of influential people, mostly speculators enriched by the war. It was preached by such powerful organs of the press as *Novoye Fremya* and favoured by the highest court circles, including the Emperor. One of the chief agencies of the *revanche* movement was the Committee on State Defence, presided over by Grand Duke Nikolai Nikolaievich. It actually took under consideration a number of measures aiming at the realization of the *revanche* dream.

Premier Stolypin was, of course, with the militarists. He conceived the plan of building the Amur Railroad, so that we might have a railway which, running within Russian territory, would be secure from seizure by the Japanese. The project was laid before the Duma and was welcomed by the notorious Defence Committee headed by Guchkov. In order to impress the Duma with the necessity of the road, it was told that war with Japan was imminent and that it would indeed break out not later than 1911 or 1912, at the latest. And so the Duma authorized the construction of this line, which will constitute a heavy financial burden on the Russian people and which will in the end bring nothing but harm. Under the influence of the same argument the Imperial Council, too, gave its consent. I vigorously opposed the project, pointing out that in the event of war the new road would not be any safer from seizure by the Japanese than the Eastern-Chinese Railway. Besides, I argued, the railway would increase the influence of the Chinese in the Amur

* a policy for reclaiming lost territory (as Japan viewed Sakhalin since it was ceded to Russia in the 1875 Treaty of St. Petersburg. Although largely ignored by Japan, the opportunity arose during the Russo-Japanese War to retake the elongated island of Sakhalin which was officially reclaimed at the Portsmouth Peace Conference 1905, that ended the Russo-Japanese conflict in the Far East.)

province to a dangerous extent. Above all, I insisted, the new line meant the expenditure of huge sums which could be spent, with better results, on defending our Far-Eastern possessions and the existing Eastern-Chinese Railroad. But my arguments were in vain.

The international situation was considerably affected by the Russo-Japanese War. For several decades previous to the war the relations between France and Great Britain were rather strained, this being due to rivalry in African and Asian colonial regions adjacent to the Mediterranean. After the Franco-Prussian war England almost wholly supplanted France in Egypt and snatched, as it were, the Suez Canal from her hands. Then Great Britain became France's rival in those regions of Northern Africa which were either within the French sphere of influence or gravitated toward French colonial possessions. Several years before the war a certain Colonel Marchand hoisted the French flag in a territory in Northern Africa, which he had explored. Great Britain in a rather unceremonious form forced France to give up the claim to that territory. The incident produced a great stir in France, and the Government appealed to Russia for support. We advised France not to bring the matter to a break, and she yielded. Thereupon Foreign Minister Delcassé came to St. Petersburg to devise a means whereby England might be held in check. He urged us to hasten the construction of the Orenburg-Tashkent Railway, which would enable us to threaten India in case of emergency. To this we agreed, and France in return obligated itself to assist us in floating a loan. With the progress of the Russo-Japanese War Delcassé perceived that France could not rely on Russia and that, under the circumstances, it was no longer safe to have strained relations with both Germany and England. As a result, Delcassé inaugurated a rapprochement with Great Britain. With Russia's knowledge he concluded a treaty with Great Britain, which regulated the relations of the two countries in those regions where their interests clashed. Ever since then France has been cultivating England's friendship.

CHAPTER VII

NICHOLAS II AND ALEXANDRA

WHEN, in 1894, I learned of the death of Emperor Alexander III, I went to share my grief with I. N. Durnovo. In those days he was Minister of the Interior, while I held the office of Minister of Finances. Both of us had been greatly attached to the deceased monarch, and, naturally, we were in a very dejected mood. In the course of our talk Durnovo asked me what I thought of our new ruler, Nicholas II.

My reply was to the effect that I had but rarely discussed business matters with him, that I knew him to be inexperienced in the extreme, but rather intelligent, and that he had always impressed me as a kindly and well-bred youth. As a matter of fact, I had rarely come across a better-mannered young man than Nicholas II. His good-breeding conceals all his shortcomings. I hoped, I added, that our young monarch would learn his business, and in that event, the Ship of State would float on safely.

Durnovo looked at me slyly and said: "Well, Sergey, I am afraid you are mistaken about our young Emperor. I know him better, and let me tell you that his reign has many misfortunes in store for us. Mark my words: Nicholas II will prove a modernized version of Paul I."

I suspect that Durnovo owed his fine knowledge of the Emperor's character not so much to his perspicacity, but to the fact that perlustration of letters is one of the tasks with which the Minister of the Interior is entrusted. It appears that Durnovo perlustrated with great diligence. He told me himself, with candour, that he had surrendered the portfolio of Minister of the Interior, for the reason that the Dowager Empress protested to her son against Durnovo reading her private correspondence. Such being the attitude of the Empress, he explained, he could not remain in office.

About the same time I also had a talk with the celebrated Procurator of the Holy Synod, Pobiedonostzev. He was deeply grieved by Alexander's death. As for Nicholas, he spoke of him in vague terms, although he was one of his preceptors. What he feared most was that, owing to his youth and lack of experience, the Emperor might fall a prey to evil influences.

At my first audience, Emperor Nicholas treated me very cordially. I had enjoyed his favour ever since my participation in the Siberian Railway Committee, over which young Prince Nicholas had presided. The subject we discussed during that first official conference was the construction of a naval base for our Northern Fleet. That was one of the tasks bequeathed to the young Emperor by his deceased father. Largely owing to my influence, Alexander III had chosen the Yekaterina Harbour on the Murman Coast for that purpose, in preference to Libau. His Majesty declared to me that he was going to carry out his late father's will and would immediately decree the construction of the Murman base.

Two or three months passed, and suddenly I found in the Governmental Messenger an Imperial decree ordering the construction of the naval base at Libau, to be called Port of Emperor Alexander III, in consideration of the fact that this was the late Emperor's wish. I was taken completely by surprise, for several months before his death Alexander III expressly stated his preference for the Murman base.

Shortly afterwards I learned that immediately upon the publication of the decree His Majesty went to Grand Duke Konstantin and, with tears in his eyes, complained that Admiral General Grand Duke Alexey had forced him to sign a decree which was contrary to his own views and to the view of his late father.

The man who was chief advocate of the idea of constructing the naval base at Libau was not, however, Grand Duke Alexey, but N. M. Chikhachev, the Minister of the Navy. It is he who was chiefly responsible for the Grand Duke's insistence on Libau, and the Emperor knew it. So that while he yielded to the external pressure he, nevertheless, harboured a secret grudge for the person who was the source of that influence. Hardly a year passed before Chikhachev was dismissed. It was clearly an act of revenge.

Unhappily, the behaviour of Nicholas II in this instance is only too characteristic of His Majesty, and, as Prince Mirski has remarked, his character is the source of all our misfortunes. A ruler who cannot be trusted, who approves to-day what he will reject to-morrow, is incapable of steering the Ship of State into a quiet harbour. His outstanding failing is his lamentable lack of will power. Though benevolent and not unintelligent, this shortcoming disqualifies him totally as the unlimited autocratic ruler of the Russian people. Poor, unhappy Emperor! He was not born for the momentous historical role which fate has thrust upon him.

The coronation of Emperor Nicholas II, which took place on May 14 (Russian style), 1896, was marked by a sad and ominous occurrence; nearly two thousand people perished on the Khodynka Field, in Moscow, where refreshments and amusements had been prepared for the populace. A few hours after the Khodynka disaster their Majesties attended a concert conducted by the celebrated Safonov. I vividly recollect a brief conversation which I had at that concert with the Chinese plenipotentiary Li Hung Chang, who was at that time in St. Petersburg on official business. He was curious to know the details of the catastrophe and I told him that nearly two thousand people must have perished.

"But His Majesty," he said, "does not know it, does he?"

"Of course, he knows," I replied. "All the facts of the matter must have already been reported to him."

"Well," remarked the Chinaman, "I don't see the wisdom of that. I remember when I was Governor-General, ten million people died from the bubonic plague in the provinces confined to my charge, yet our Emperor knew nothing about it. Why disturb him uselessly?"

I thought to myself that, after all, we were ahead of the Chinese.

A gorgeous evening party was scheduled for the same day, to be given by the French Ambassador, Marquis de Montebello. We expected that the party would be called off, because of the Khodynka disaster. Nevertheless, it took place, as if nothing had happened, and the ball was opened by their Majesties dancing a quadrille.

The Emperor's character may be said to be essentially feminine. Someone has observed that Nature granted him masculine attributes by mistake. At first any official coming in personal contact with him would stand high in his eyes. His Majesty would even go beyond the limits of moderation in showering favours upon his servant, especially if the latter had been appointed by him personally and not by his father. Before long, however, His Majesty would become indifferent to his favourite and, in the end, develop an animus against him. The ill-feeling apparently came from the consciousness that the person in question had been an unworthy object of his, Nicholas's, favours. I may observe here that His Majesty does not tolerate about his person anybody he considers more intelligent than himself or anybody with opinions differing from those of the court camarilla*.

There is an optimistic strain in His Majesty's character, and he is afflicted with a strange near-sightedness, as far as time and space are concerned. He experiences fear only when the storm is actually upon him, but ss soon as the immediate danger is over his fear vanishes. Thus, even after the granting of the Constitution, Nicholas considered himself an autocratic sovereign in a sense which might be formulated as follows: "I do what I wish, and what I wish is good; if people do not see it, it is because they are plain mortals, while I am God's anointed."

He is incapable of playing fair and he always seeks underhand means and underground ways. He has a veritable passion for secret notes and methods. Even at the most critical moments, such as the period which immediately preceded the granting of the Constitution, His Majesty did not relinquish his "Byzantine" habits. But inasmuch as he does not possess the talents of either Metternich or Talleyrand,† he usually lands in a mud puddle or in a pool of blood.

The following incident well illustrates the Emperor's unscrupulous tendencies. When Sipyagin, one time Minister of the Interior, was assassinated by a revolutionist, in 1902, P. N. Durnovo, his colleague, and Adjutant-General Hesse were entrusted with the task of setting his papers to rights. These were sorted out, and the documents of a private nature were handed to the late Minister's widow. She knew that her husband had kept a diary, consisting of two books, one covering the period of his Ministry, the other—the time when he headed the Commission of Petitions. As the diaries were not returned to her, she inquired of Durnovo what had become of

* Courtiers favoured by the monarch who have his ear and have great influence behind the scenes, usually without themselves holding office or other official responsibilities.

† Metternich and Talleyrand were prominent statesmen respected for their political acumen and diplomatic skills. Klemens von Metternich was the Chancellor of Austria from 1809 to 1848 and significantly helped to maintain peace in Europe after the Napoleonic wars. Charles Maurice de Talleyrand similarly used his influence to maintain order in France and bring about the Treaty of Paris which ended the Napoleonic Wars. The European peace accords lasted until World War I.

them and was told that they were in General Hesse's hands. (The subsequent developments of the incident I have from Mme. Sipyagin herself and her brother-in-law, Count Sheremetyev). Several days later the widow went to the Court to thank their Majesties for their attentions. In the course of the audience the Emperor told his guest that he had received the diaries of her late husband, and found them so interesting that he would like, with her permission, to retain the books and read them. Mme. Sipyagin naturally gave her consent.

Several months passed, and the diaries were still in the Emperor's hands. Mme. Sipyagin then turned to her brother-in-law, Count Sheremetyev, who was the Emperor's aide-de-camp and former chum, asking him to remind His Majesty of her late husband's notes. Shortly afterwards Mme. Sipyagin had an audience with the Empress, and when she was on the point of leaving, Her Majesty asked her to wait awhile, because the Emperor wished to see her. Several minutes later the Emperor entered the room and handed her a package, saying that he was returning her late husband's interesting memoirs and thanking her for the opportunity of reading them. At home, Mme. Sipyagin discovered, however, that only one set of diaries had been returned to her, namely, the one covering the time when her husband presided over the Commission of Petitions. Mme. Sipyagin again resorted to Count Sheremetyev's good offices to have the matter straightened out. The Count turned to General Hesse, but received a rather sharp reply to the effect that too much fuss was being made about these diaries.

Several days later His Majesty went to Moscow, where he prepared for the sacrament, and spent the first days of the Easter week. At one of the official dinners Count Sheremetyev happened to sit next to General Hesse. The latter assured the Count that he had handed both sets of Sipyagin's diaries to His Majesty. On returning to St. Petersburg, the Emperor summoned Count Sheremetyev and had a talk with him, which was afterwards related to me by the Count himself. He had learned, His Majesty had told the Count, that one set of Sipyagin's diaries was lost and he wondered whether Count Sheremetyev could account for it. The Count pointed out to His Majesty that neither Durnovo nor Hesse denied that they had received two books of diaries. He was, however, unable to explain the loss. Then the Emperor observed that Hesse had been on bad terms with Sipyagin. The General must have found in the diaries,

His Majesty said, some unpleasant passages relating to himself and decided to destroy the book so as to prevent his monarch from reading it. "As a matter of fact," the Count said, concluding his tale, "I know for a fact that it was His Majesty himself who destroyed the book of Sipyagin's diaries." After the act of October 17, 1905, I may add in passing, Count Sheremetyev ordered all the Emperor's portraits in his palace turned face to the wall—which circumstance led to a break between us.

Here is another incident of a similar nature which concerns me personally:

In view of the persistent rumour that I had forced the Manifesto of October 17th upon the Emperor, I composed a memoir giving the exact facts of the matter, and presented it to His Majesty through the Minister of the Court. The Emperor kept it about a fortnight and returned it, saying to Baron Frederichs: "The facts in Witte's memorandum are described correctly. However, do not make this statement to him in writing, but orally." The Baron reported these amazing words to Prince Obolensky and the latter to me. And to think that these words were spoken by the son of Alexander III, the noblest and most truthful of monarchs! . . . Of course, I never received a written reply to my memorandum.

The Emperor's part in shaping our foreign policy, especially with regard to the Russo-Japanese War, I have dealt with elsewhere. Suffice it to say here that, when all is said, he alone is to be blamed for that most unhappy war, if indeed it is possible to condemn a man who is responsible for his deeds to none but God.

At heart, His Majesty was for an aggressive policy, but as usual his mind was a house divided against itself. He kept on changing his policy from day to day. He tried to deceive both the Viceroy of the Far East and the Commander-in-Chief of the army, but, of course, most of the time he deceived nobody but himself.

He became involved in the Far Eastern adventure because of his youth, his natural animosity against Japan, where an attempt had been made on his life (he never speaks of that occurrence), and, finally, because of a hidden craving for a victorious war. I am even inclined to believe that, had there been no clash with Japan, war would have flared up on the Indian frontier, or, most probably, in Turkey, with the Bosphorus as the apple of discord. From there it would have spread to other regions. After His Majesty's coronation and his trip to France, Nelidov, then our ambassador at Constantinople, all but dragged us into a war with Turkey.

In the latter part of the year 1896, there was a massacre of Armenians in Constantinople, preceded by a similar massacre in Asia Minor. In October His Majesty returned from abroad, and Nelidov, our Ambassador to Turkey, came to St. Petersburg. His arrival gave rise to rumours about various measures which were going to be taken against Turkey. These rumours forced me to submit to His Majesty a memorandum in which I stated my views on Turkey and advised against the use of force. On November 21 (December 3) I received a secret memoir drafted by Nelidov. The Ambassador spoke in vague terms about the alarming situation in Turkey and suggested that we should create incidents which would afford us the legal right and the physical possibility to seize the Upper Bosphorus.

Nelidov's suggestion was discussed by a special conference called two days later and presided over by His Majesty. The Ambassador insisted that a far-reaching upheaval was bound to occur in the near future in the Ottoman Empire and that, to safeguard our interests, we must occupy the Upper Bosphorus. He was naturally supported by the War Minister and the Chief of Staff, General Obruchev, for whom the occupation of Bosphorus and if possible of Constantinople was a veritable *idée fixe*. The other Ministers refrained from expressing their opinion on the subject, so that it fell to my lot to oppose this disastrous project, which I did with vigour and determination. I pointed out that the plan under consideration would eventually precipitate a general European war and shatter the brilliant political and financial position in which Emperor Alexander III left Russia.

The Emperor at first confined himself to questioning the members of the conference. When the discussion was closed he declared that he shared the Ambassador's view. Thus the matter was settled, at least in principle. Namely, it was decided to bring about such events in Constantinople as would furnish us a specious pretext for landing troops and occupying Upper Bosphorus. The military authorities at Odessa and Sebastopol were instructed immediately to start the necessary preparations for the landing of troops in Turkey. It was also agreed that at the moment which Nelidov would consider opportune for the landing he would give the signal by sending a telegram to our financial agent in London requesting him to purchase a stated amount of grain. The dispatch was to be immediately transmitted to the Director of the Imperial Bank and forwarded by the latter to the War Minister and also to the Minister of the Navy.

The minutes of the session were drawn up by the Director of the Foreign Ministry Shishkin. They presented the decisions of the conference as accepted unanimously. I notified Shishkin that I could not sign the minutes, for the reason that, in my opinion, the decisions of the Conference threatened Russia with disastrous consequences. I requested him to obtain His Majesty's permission either to insert a summary of my view of the matter in the minutes or else to state briefly that I completely disagreed with the conclusions arrived at by the conference. I did not wish, I said, to bear the responsibility for this adventure before history. Shishkin wrote to His Majesty and was instructed to insert the following statement at the beginning of the minutes: "In the opinion of Secretary of State Witte the occupation of Upper Bosphorus without a preliminary agreement with the Great Powers is, at the present moment and under the present circumstances, very risky and likely to lead to disastrous consequences." His Majesty signed the minutes on November 27 (December 9) and penned on the margin a few words to the effect that he was in complete agreement with the opinion of the majority.

Nelidov left for Constantinople eager to carry out his long cherished plan. It was expected that the signal might come at any moment, so that one of the secretaries of the Director of the Imperial Bank kept vigil all night long, ready to receive the fatal telegram and instructed to transmit it immediately to the Director. Fearing the consequences of the act I could not refrain from sharing my apprehensions with several persons very intimate with the Emperor, notably Grand Duke Vladimir Alexandrovich and Pobiedonostzev.

The latter read the minutes of the session and returned them to me with the following note: "I hasten to return the enclosed minutes. Thank you for having sent them to me. *Alea jacta est.* May God help us!"

I do not know whether it was the influence of these men or the influence of that Power which rules the whole world and which we call God, only His Majesty changed his mind and instructed Nelidov soon after the latter's departure for Constantinople to give up his design. It is significant that for some time after this incident the Emperor bore a grudge against me.

It is noteworthy that at the time of the Russo-Japanese War the attitude of the court clique and of the Emperor himself toward England was one of strong hostility. This was due to England's agreement with Japan and also to the fact that she furnished refuge to the Russian revolutionists. To the Japanese His Majesty was in the habit of referring as macacoes (monkeys), using this term even in official documents. The English he called Jews. "An Englishman," he liked to repeat, "is a zhid (Jew)."

To illustrate further His Majesty's views and sympathies, I shall cite also this striking incident. During my premiership (1906) I received a dispatch from Governor-General Sologub, describing the measures taken to suppress the uprising in the Reval district and requesting me to exert a moderating influence upon Captain Richter of the punitive expedition, who was executing people indiscriminately without the least semblance of legality. I submitted the dispatch to His Majesty, who returned it to me with the following words jotted down opposite the lines describing the captain's bloody deeds: "Fine! A capital fellow!" Afterwards he asked me to send back this telegram to him. He never returned it to me. Some time after I left the post of Prime Minister, His Majesty received me very amiably and asked me to return all letters and telegrams with his autographed commentaries which were in my possession. I did so, and I now regret it. These documents would shed a remarkable light on the character of this truly unhappy sovereign, with all his intellectual and moral weaknesses.

When, in the course of my official conferences with His Majesty, I referred to public opinion, His Majesty oftentimes snapped angrily: "What have I got to do with public opinion?" He considered, and justly, that public opinion was the opinion of the "intellectuals." As for the Emperor's view of the intellectuals, I recall a story related to me by Prince Mirski. When Nicholas was visiting the Western provinces, the Prince, in his capacity of local Governor-General, accompanied His Majesty and dined with him. Once at table someone referred to the *intelligentsia* (intellectuals). The Emperor caught the word and exclaimed: "How I detest that word! I wish I could order the Academy to strike it off the Russian dictionary."

The Emperor was made to believe that the people as a whole,

exclusive of the intellectuals, stood firmly with him. That was also Her Majesty's conviction. On one occasion, discussing the political situation with the Empress, Prince Mirski remarked that in Russia everybody was against the existing régime. To this the Empress sharply replied that only the intellectuals were against the Czar and his government, but that the people always had been and always would be for the Czar. "Yes," retorted the Prince, "that is true enough, but it is the intellectual class that makes history everywhere while the masses are merely an elemental power; to-day they massacre the revolutionary intellectuals, tomorrow they may loot the Czar's palaces."

The Emperor was surrounded by avowed Jew-haters, such as Trepov, Plehve, Ignatyev, and the leaders of the Black Hundreds. As for his personal attitude toward the Jews I recall that whenever I drew his attention to the fact that the anti-Jewish riots could not be tolerated, he either was silent or remarked: "But it is they themselves, i.e., the Jews (His Majesty always used the opprobrious *zhidy*, instead of *yevrei*) that are to blame." The anti-Jewish current flowed not from below upward, but in the opposite direction.

In December, 1905, an atrocious anti-Jewish pogrom broke out at Homel. I requested Durnovo, the Minister of the Interior, to institute an investigation. It revealed that the bloody riot was organized, in a most efficient manner, by secret service agents under the direction of the local officer of gendarmes, Count Podgorichani, who did not deny his rôle in the affair. I asked Durnovo to report the findings of the investigation to the Council of Ministers. The Council sharply condemned the activity of the governmental secret service and recommended that Count Podgorichani should be dismissed and tried. The opinion of the Council was recorded in the minutes of the session, but in a very mild form. The minutes were in due course submitted to His Majesty. With visible displeasure he wrote the following words on the margin: "How does all this business concern me? The case of Count Podgorichani is within the province of the Minister of the Interior." Several months later I learned that Count Podgorichani was chief of police in one of the Black Sea cities.

In his attitude toward the Jews, as in all other respects, the Emperor's ideals are at bottom those of the Black Hundreds. The strength of that party lies precisely in the fact that their Majesties have conceived the notion that those anarchists of the Right are their salvation.

The party of "True Russians," as the Black Hundreds style themselves, is fundamentally patriotic, which circumstance, given our universal cosmopolitanism, should command our sympathy. But the patriotism of "the Black Hundreds" is purely elemental; it is based not on reason, but on passion. Most of their leaders are unscrupulous political adventurers, with not a single practical and honest political idea, and all their efforts are directed toward goading and exploiting the low instincts of the mob. Being under the protection of the two-winged eagle, this party may be able to cause appalling riots and upheavals, but its work will necessarily be purely destructive and negative. It is the embodiment of savage, nihilistic patriotism, feeding on lies, slander, and deceit, the party of savage and cowardly despair, devoid of the manly and clear-eyed spirit of creativeness. The bulk of the party is dark-minded and ignorant, the leaders are unhanged villains, among whom there are some titled noblemen and a number of secret sympathizers recruited from the courtiers. Their welfare is made secure by the reign of lawlessness, and their motto is: "Not we for the people, but the people for the good of our bellies." It should be pointed out, however, that the "Black Hundred" leaders, be they secret or patent, constitute a negligible minority of Russian nobility. They are its outcasts feeding on the crumbs, rich crumbs indeed, which fall from the Czar's table. And the poor misguided Emperor dreams of restoring Russia's grandeur with the aid of this party! Poor Emperor!

In this connection I recall the Emperor's shameful telegram to that notorious sharper, Dubrovin, the president of the Russian People's Union (a "Black Hundred" organization), dated June 3, 1907. In this most gracious dispatch, His Majesty expressed his approval of Dubrovin's actions in his capacity of president of the Russian People's Union and assured him that in the future, too, he would lean upon that band of cut-throats. This telegram, coupled with the manifesto which dissolved the Second Duma, revealed all the poverty of this autocratic Emperor's political thought and the morbidity of his mind.

Alexander III was a very thrifty ruler. Throughout his reign the budget of the Ministry of the Court remained stationary. With the ascension of Nicholas II to the throne that budget began rapidly to increase. According to the law, the budget was to be fixed by the Imperial Council in the regular way. But in practice the estimate was the result of an understanding between the Minister of the Court and the Minister of Finances, and the figure thus arrived at was, as a rule, ratified by the Imperial Council. With Nicholas's ascension to the throne, Count Vorontzov-Dashkov, then Minister of the Court, began greatly to increase the expenditures of the Ministry. As he ignored my remonstrances, I submitted a report to the Emperor. His Majesty told me that it was his desire to be as economical as his father had been. He must have subsequently told something unpleasant to Count Vorontzov-Dashkov, because the latter came to me and practically confessed himself in the wrong. Several months later the Count left his post and was succeeded by Baron Frederichs. Shortly afterwards I received an Imperial decree abolishing the then existing regulations concerning the fixation of the budget of the Ministry of the Court and establishing the following order of estimating the expenditures of that Ministry: the estimate is drawn up and submitted for Imperial confirmation by the Ministry of the Court alone; the final figure is communicated to the Minister of Finances, who inserts it in the general budget, without allowing it to be discussed in the Imperial Council. The decree concluded with a provision that the new law should not be published, to avoid needless discussion, but in the next edition of the statutes the articles pertaining thereto should be modified accordingly. Such an illegal procedure had been unknown in Russia since the days of Paul I, and he, too, would have perhaps hesitated to do what practically amounted to forging the laws of the land.

Speaking of their Majesties' attitude toward my own person, I should like to say that I am aware of having been the object of Alexandra's particular enmity. I believe it goes back to an incident which occurred in 1900, if I remember rightly. That year, in the course of a stay at Yalta, Crimea, the Emperor was taken ill and developed intestinal typhus. Nicholas II had a distaste for medical treatment. This is, I believe, a family trait with the Romanovs. It is my conviction that his father died prematurely for the reason that he started a serious course of treatment when it was too late. The court physician of Emperor Nicholas was a certain Hirsch, a much esteemed gentleman, who had inherited rather than earned his position. He had practically no professional standing either as physician or surgeon.

As chance would have it, Sipyagin, Minister of the Interior, and myself happened to be at Yalta at the time when the Emperor fell ill. We immediately sounded the alarm and summoned a medical celebrity from St. Petersburg. When the disease reached its critical stage, I was asked by Sipyagin to come to see him in the hotel where he stayed. Besides the host, I found in the study Grand Duke Mikhail Nikolaievich, Count Lamsdorff, Minister of Foreign Affairs, and Baron Frederichs, Minister of the Court. They were in the course of discussing the situation which would be created by His Majesty's death while there was no heir. At that time Czarevich Alexey was not yet born. It was suggested that, since the Empress might be with child, she should be declared regent until the time of her delivery. I opposed that plan, insisting that the letter of the law should be followed, that is, that the Emperor's next of kin, his brother Grand Duke Mikhail Alexandrovich, should ascend the throne. I succeeded in winning over to my side all the members of this improvised conference. It was decided that, in the event of the Emperor's death, we would immediately take an oath of allegiance to Mikhail Alexandrovich. This incident, which ended in nothing because Emperor Nicholas recovered from his illness, was interpreted by Her Majesty as an underhand intrigue on my part against her, whence her animosity against me. When I surrendered my post of Prime Minister, Her Majesty expressed her satisfaction, I was told, by an interjection of relief.

Despite my many and invaluable services to himself and his Empire, the Emperor's attitude to my person, except during the early part of his reign, was essentially in keeping with Her Majesty's profound distaste for me. Since my resignation as President of the Council of Ministers I have had but two audiences with His Majesty. The first occurred in 1906, after my return from abroad, where I was practically in exile, and lasted about twenty minutes. We spoke about the monument to Alexander III, which was at that time in the course of construction. An interval of six years separates this interview from the second audience. Since 1912 I have not been received by the Emperor.

During the early part of his reign Nicholas was under the ascendancy of the Grand Dukes and partly also of his mother, Empress Dowager Maria Fyodorovna. The influence of Grand Duke Nicholas Nikolai Nikolaievich, Junior, probably lasted longest. The circumstance may be due to the fact that he was possessed of that mysticism complex with which Empress Alexandra had infected her husband.

An incident in my relations with Grand Duke Nicholas will

illustrate this phase of his character. I had made his acquaintance at Kiev, in the house of his mother, Grand Duchess Alexandra Petrovna, which I frequented. At that time I was director of the South Western Railroads, while he was a colonel attached to the General Staff. Sometimes we played cards. His mother was an excellent woman, but also affected by the craze of occultism. Later I saw him repeatedly, but never had an occasion to converse with him. When I became Minister, he sent me his visiting card on holidays, or left it at the house. Some time after my appointment as President of the Committee of Ministers I went to see him. The conversation turned upon the Emperor.

"Tell me frankly, Sergey Yulyevich," he said suddenly, "is the Emperor, in your judgment, merely a human being or is he more?"

"Well," I retorted, "the Emperor is my master and I am his faithful servant, but though he is an autocratic Ruler, given to us by God or Nature, he is nevertheless a human being with all the peculiarities of one."

"To my mind," remarked the Grand Duke, "the Emperor is not a mere human being, but rather a being intermediate between man and God." We parted.

The influence of the Empress Dowager (Maria Fyodorovna) upon her son was, I believe, a power for good. But after his marriage, his mother's influence rapidly waned and Nicholas fell permanently under the spell of his wife, a woman hysterical and unbalanced, yet possessed of a sufficiently strong character to master him completely and infect him with her own morbidity.

Several years before the death of Alexander III an ineffectual attempt was made to find a wife for the future Emperor Nicholas II. In that connection Princess Alix of Darmstadt was brought to St. Petersburg for inspection. She was not liked, and at the time the project of marrying the heir apparent came to nothing. That was a grave mistake. Young Nicholas, naturally enough, sought illicit pleasures and took up with the ballet dancer Kszesinska. His liaison with that woman remained unknown to his august father, but it could not escape the attention of those nearest to the Emperor. They urged him to hasten the marriage of the heir. In the meantime His Majesty was taken ill and, as a result, became anxious to see his son married without any further delay. It was then the rejected bride, Princess Alix, was remembered, and the heir was dispatched to Darmstadt to ask her hand.

I got a premonition of the fateful character of this decision from Count Osten-Sacken, our present envoy to Germany, who told me the following story in the course of an intimate talk which took place in Berlin. "Under Alexander II," the esteemed count said, "I was attached to the court of Darmstadt in the capacity of Chargé d'affaires, and was well acquainted with the Grand Duke's family. Under Alexander III the post of Chargé d'affaires was abolished, and I was transferred to Munich. When the Heir Apparent went to Darmstadt I was ordered to join him there. The first day after my arrival in Darmstadt I had a talk with the old Ober-Hoffmarschall with whom I was on friendly terms at the time when I was attached to the court. The conversation turned upon the Princess. 'When I left Darmstadt,' I said, 'Princess Alix was a little girl. Tell me frankly, what do you think of her, now that she is grown up?' The old courtier rose, examined all the doors to make sure that no one was eavesdropping and said: 'What a piece of good luck it is for Hesse-Darmstadt that you are taking her away!' "

She accepted Nicholas—of course, she did—and expressed her regret, no doubt sincerely, that she would have to change her religion. She knew about Russian Orthodoxy no more than a newborn babe knows about the theory of the perturbations of heavenly bodies, and, given her narrowmindedness and stubbornness, it was, I do not doubt, hard for her to forsake the religion into which she was born. One must keep in mind that her conversion was due not to any lofty motives but to purely mundane considerations. However, having embraced Orthodoxy, she seems to have succeeded in convincing herself that it was the only true religion known to mankind. Of course, the religious essence of Orthodoxy still is and will perhaps always be a sealed book to her, but she is spellbound by the external forms of our ritual, such as captivate her eye at the solemn church services in the various court chapels. She worships the forms, not the spirit of our religion. It is easy to see how the religion of such a woman, who lives in the morbid atmosphere of Oriental luxury and is surrounded by a legion of perennially cringing retainers, was bound to degenerate into crude mysticism, and into fanaticism unrelieved by loving kindness. Hence, the far-famed "Dr." Philippe, the cult of St. Seraphim of Sarov, imported mediums, and home-bred "idiots" passing as saints—all of which I shall discuss presently.

Emperor Nicholas was married to Princess Alix on November

13, 1894, soon after his ascension to the throne. Alexandra does not lack physical charms. She has a strong character and she is a good mother. She might have been a good enough consort for a petty German prince, and she might have been harmless even as the Empress of Russia, were it not for the lamentable fact that His Majesty has no will power at all. The extent of Alexandra's influence upon her husband can hardly be exaggerated. In many cases she actually directs his actions as the head of the Empire. On one occasion, I recall, Nicholas referred to Her Majesty as "a person in whom I have absolute faith." The fate of many millions of human beings is actually in the hands of that woman. Surely the poor Emperor, and all of us who are his devoted servants, and, above all, Russia, would have been much happier had Princess Alix married a German Duke or Count.

Now to return to that strange and crude mysticism, which, as I have said above, took hold of Empress Alexandra and with which she infected her august spouse. In the course of my stay in Paris in 1903 I had long talks with Baron Alphonse, the septuagenarian head of the Rothschild house. Our conversation mostly revolved around the preoccupation with the occult and the mystic which had taken root at the Russian Court, this being, in the Baron's opinion, a bad symptom. He repeatedly returned to this subject. History shows, he pointed out, that great events, especially of an internal nature, were always and everywhere preceded by the prevalence of a bizarre mysticism at the court of the ruler. He even sent me a book on the subject, in which the author presented an array of historical evidence in support of this view. The Baron told me that the influence of a certain Dr. Philippe, of Lyons, upon their Majesties and some Grand Dukes and Duchesses was being much talked of in France. He repeated some of the rumours which were abroad, adding that much was probably exaggerated, but that, no doubt, the charlatan Philippe often saw their Majesties, was worshipped by them as a saint and exerted a substantial influence upon their inner life.

All these stories, bruited abroad in France, made a painful impression on us Russians. Of course, I heard a good deal about Philippe in Petrograd, too. I shall set down here all the authentic information on the subject which I have in my possession. Philippe originally resided at Lyons, France. He had completed no course of study. When his daughter married a physician, Philippe began to practise as a quack doctor and, as is often the case, was sometimes successful. Besides quackery, he also practised fortune telling. Those who knew him reported that he was clever and possessed a peculiar occult power over men and women who were of a flabby will or were afflicted with diseased nerves. As a result of his charlatan activities, he had several lawsuits. He was forbidden to practise by the government and several times prosecuted. Nevertheless, he succeeded in securing a group of admirers, mostly among the nationalists. It included our military agent in Paris, Count Muraviov-Amursky. There is no doubt but that the count was practically out of his mind. He tried to involve us in a quarrel with the republican Government which he hated whole-heartedly.

It was this Count and other admirers of Philippe who declared this impostor a saint. At any rate, they asserted that he was not born in the usual commonplace way, but that he had descended direct from heaven and would make his exit from life in the same extraordinary fashion. In France, Philippe was introduced to a Russian Duchess. It was either by the wife of Grand Duke Peter, Militza, the Montenegrin Princess No. 1, or the wife of Prince Leuchtenberg, Anastasia, the Montenegrin Princess No. 2; I do not know which one it was.

(The other day, the Montenegrin Princess No. 2, at the instigation of the spirits and with their Majesties' permission, divorced the Prince of Leuchtenberg and married his cousin, Grand Duke Nicholas.)

This friendship of the two Montenegrin princesses for Dr. Philippe was of vast importance to Russia, for they were the most intimate confidantes of the Empress. It is worth while to trace their entrée to the Russian Court, upon which they exerted such a baleful influence. While very young they were placed by their father, Prince Nicholas of Montenegro, in the Smolny Institute, where they attracted but little attention. They were graduated from the Institute at the time when Alexander III broke the traditional bonds which attached Russia to Germany, and when the union with France was yet in the incipient stage. It was at that time that Alexander II, at a dinner given in honour of Prince Nicholas of Montenegro, proposed the famous toast: "To my only friend, Prince Nicholas of Montenegro." This toast was proposed not so much out of love for Prince Nicholas, as with the intention of informing the world that the Emperor neither had nor needed any friends.

On his part, Prince Nicholas of Montenegro did everything in his power to ingratiate himself in the favour of the Emperor. It was natural that the latter should bestow his good graces upon this representative of a knightly race, which of all the Slavic peoples manifested the greatest attachment to us Russians. Under these circumstances, it was quite proper for Emperor Alexander to show some attention to the Montenegrin princesses. This was sufficient for some of the members of the Imperial family to come forward as suitors. By that time, it will be remembered, we were already in possession of a whole drove of Grand Dukes. Grand Duke Peter, the sickly youngest son of Grand Duke Nicholas (Nikolai Nikolaievich, Senior), who commanded our armies in the last Turkish War, married the Montenegrin Princess No. 1, while the Princess No. 2 was married to Prince Yuri of Leuchtenberg.

Thus, owing to Alexander III, the Montenegrin Princesses were married off to second-rate dukes. The story would have ended then and there, had not Nicholas II ascended the throne and married Alix. Her Majesty was met by the Dowager Empress and by the Grand Duchesses very cordially, indeed, but yet not as an Empress. The Montenegrin Princesses were the only ones to bow before her as before an Empress and to flaunt a most abject admiration and infinite love for her. It happened that the Empress contracted a stomach disease, and they took advantage of this occasion to display their devotion. They clung to her day and night, sent away the chambermaids and took upon themselves the latter's rather disagreeable tasks. In this fashion, they ingratiated themselves into the favour of Her Majesty and became her closest friends. Their influence upon their Majesties grew in proportion as the influence of the Dowager Empress decreased.

It was these Montenegrin Princesses who became zealous devotees of Dr. Philippe. While in Paris, one of them summoned the head of our secret police at Paris, Rachkovski, and expressed a desire that Philippe should be allowed to practise his art and given a medical diploma. Naturally, Rachkovski explained to the swarthy Duchess all the naivete of her demand. As he spoke of the charlatan in terms not sufficiently courteous, he gained for himself a dangerous enemy at the Court.

And it was through the good offices of these Montenegrins that Philippe gained access to the Grand Dukes, and later to their Majesties. Empress Alexandra was on intimate terms with none of the female members of the Imperial family except those Montenegrin women, who were to her a cross between bosom-friends and chambermaids. For months Philippe secretly lived in St. Petersburg and in the Summer residences of his high patrons. Consultations and mystic séances were continuously going on there with the participation of their Majesties, the Grand Dukes, and their Montenegrin wives.

While in Russia, Philippe was in the care of the Court Commandant, Adjutant-General Hesse, who, just like the present commandant, had his own secret service. Hesse found it necessary to inquire from Rachkovski about Philippe's personality. Rachkovski drew up a report which presented Philippe as the charlatan that he was. This report he brought with him to St. Petersburg, when he came there on business. Before submitting it to Hesse, he read it to Sipyagin. The latter told him that officially he knew nothing of the report, inasmuch as it was not addressed to him. Privately, he advised Rachkovski to throw it into the fire which was burning on the hearth. Nevertheless, Rachkovski did submit the report. With Plehve's appointment to the ministerial post, Rachkovski was dismissed and forbidden to reside in Paris and, if I remember rightly, in France generally. Plehve explained to me that he had been forced to do this. Hesse made every effort to protect Rachkovski, but in vain. Under Trepov's régime, however, which was a sort of dictatorship, Rachkovski was again summoned to occupy an important post in the Police Department.

Since Philippe did not succeed in getting a diploma in France, the St. Petersburg Military Medical Academy was forced to bestow upon him the degree of doctor of medicine, in flagrant violation of the law. This happened at the time when Kuropatkin was Minister of War. Furthermore, "Dr." Philippe was actually granted the rank of Councillor of State. All this was done in secrecy. The saint paid a visit to a tailor and ordered an army physician's uniform.

The night séances with Philippe, though kept secret, greatly annoyed the Dowager Empress Maria Fyodorovna. The Prince of Leuchtenberg and Grand Duke Nicholas, the first and the second husbands of the Montenegrin Princess No. 2, when asked by inquisitive friends about Philippe, replied that in any event he was a saint. Little by little, a small group of illuminists formed around "Dr." Philippe.

Empress Alexandra fell completely under the influence of the impostor. Among other things she actually believed that "Dr."

Philippe had an enchanted life and could not be harmed by physical means. Nothing will better illustrate the extent and nature of his ascendancy over the Empress than the following incredible, yet well authenticated, incident. At the time when she was under the sway of the charlatan she was very anxious to have a son, because the four children who had previously been born to their Majesties were all girls. Dr. Philippe made Her Majesty believe that she was going to give birth to a boy, and she convinced herself that she was pregnant. The last months of the imaginary pregnancy came. Everybody noticed that she had grown considerably stouter. She began to wear loose garments, and ceased to appear at court functions. Everyone was sure that Her Majesty was pregnant, the Emperor was overjoyed, and the population of St. Petersburg expected, from day to day, to hear the cannon shots from the Petropavlovsky Fortress, which, in accordance with an ancient custom, announce the birth of Imperial off-spring. Finally, the Empress ceased to walk, and the court accoucheur, Professor Ott, with his assistants, came to stay in the palace at Peterhof. But time passed without the confinement taking place. Finally, Professor Ott asked Her Majesty's permission to examine her. She agreed, and the physician, after a thorough examination, declared that the Empress was not pregnant.

It is easy to see what havoc such an hysterical woman could work, when invested with the tremendous power which an autocratic régime places in the hands of the ruler.

At the Summer residence of Grand Duke Peter, Philippe met a number of ecclesiastics, among them the notorious Father John of Kronstadt. It was apparently there that the project was hatched of canonizing the *staretz* (saintly man) Seraphim of Sarov.

This incident was related to me by K. P. Pobiedonostzev himself. One fine morning he was invited, he told me, to take luncheon with their Majesties. The invitation came unexpectedly, because at that time relations between their Majesties and Pobiedonostzev were rather strained, although he had been instructor both to the Emperor and his most august father. After breakfast, at which Pobiedonostzev was alone with his Imperial hosts, the Emperor, in the presence of the Empress, asked his guests to submit to him a decree canonizing Father Seraphim, on the day when the memory of that saintly man is celebrated, which was a few weeks off. Pobiedonostzev replied to the effect that canonization lay within the province of the Holy Synod and must be preceded by a thorough investigation of the candidate's life and of the people's views on the subject, as expressed in oral traditions. To this the Empress replied by remarking that "everything is within the Emperor's province." This opinion I, have heard from Her Majesty on various occasions. Nevertheless, the Emperor gave heed to his guest's arguments, and Pobiedonostzev, on the evening of the same day, received from the Emperor an amiable note, expressing agreement with the opinion about the impossibility of immediately canonizing Seraphim, and ordering Pobiedonostzev to carry out the canonization the following year.

Pobiedonostzev obeyed. Their Majesties were present at the ceremony of consecrating the relics. In the course of that celebration there were several cases of miraculous recovery. At night the Empress bathed in a healing fountain. The conviction prevailed, it was said, that the Sarov saint would give Russia an Heir Apparent, after four grand duchesses. This momentous event did take place and established the absolute faith of their Majesties in the efficacy and holiness of Saint Seraphim. A portrait-icon of that saint appeared in the Emperor's study. During the revolutionary days which followed the act of October 17th, Prince A. D. Obolensky, then Procurator of the Holy Synod, repeatedly complained to me about the interference of the Montenegrin Princesses in the affairs of the Holy Synod. On one occasion, he said, he spoke of Saint Seraphim to the Emperor in connection with that matter, and His Majesty said: "As for Saint Seraphim's holiness and the authenticity of his miracle, I am so fully convinced of them that no one will ever shake my belief."

A number of men made their careers through the Saint Seraphim incident. Among them was Prince Shirinski-Shakhmatov, who staged the ceremony of consecrating the relics. Following close upon that solemnity he was appointed Governor of Tver. In that capacity he distinguished himself by requesting the priests to vouch for "the political reliability" of the population. As a result, Prince Mirski, the then Minister of the Interior, dismissed him, thus bringing upon himself the displeasure of His Majesty. As soon as Prince Shirinski-Shakhmatov arrived in St. Petersburg, the Emperor received him, listened to his insinuations against Prince Mirski and, contrary to all regulations, appointed him senator. When I was forced, after the First Duma met, to surrender the office of President of the Council of Ministers, Prince Shirinski was appointed Procurator of the Holy Synod in Goremykin's Cabinet. The collapse of this cabinet and the appointment of Stolypin as President of the Council led to Prince Shirinski's dismissal. His Majesty immediately appointed him member of the Imperial Council. At present he sits in the Imperial Council as the head of the Black Hundreds. Prince Shirinski has all the defects and vices of Pobiedonostzev, without having, in the slightest degree, his good points, such as education, refinement, experience, knowledge, and political decency.

Philippe died before the end of the Russo-Japanese War. His devotees asserted that, having fulfilled his mission on earth, he ascended, alive, to Heaven.

Tsar Nicholas II and Tsarina Alexandra Feodorovna
Emperor and Empress of the Russian Empire

CHAPTER VIII

THE CZAR'S ATTEMPTS AT REFORM

I SHALL now deal with the devious course of the movement, within the governmental circles, for legislative and administrative reforms during the reign of Nicholas II, which culminated in the Constitutional Manifesto of October 17, 1905, after passing through many stages of pathetic failure and ineffectiveness.

While his most august father was still reigning, Nicholas gave proof of sincere sympathy for the lot of the peasant. Thus, in 1893, in his capacity of chairman of the Committee on the Siberian Railroad, he sided with me in my efforts to encourage migration of landless peasants to Siberia, which measure was opposed by the landowners as tending to deplete the supply of cheap agricultural labour. When Nicholas ascended the throne, I thought that he would inaugurate an era marked by a policy of fairness and intelligent care for the peasant, in keeping with the admirable traditions of his grandfather, the Emperor-Liberator. But my hopes were to be shattered. It soon became apparent that the young Emperor had fallen under the sway of powers inimical to the interests of the peasantry. The effect of the addresses delivered by some of the deputations from the nobility and the zemstvos which came to congratulate the young sovereign may have been responsible in part for His Majesty's change of heart. The feelings and desires voiced in these addresses were akin to those which swept Russia in the revolutionary days of 1905-1906. The spokesmen of these delegations, I believe, should have been more restrained in the expression of their wishes. Minister of the Interior I. N. Durnovo and the famous Procurator of the Most Holy Synod Pobiedonostzev took advantage of this tactlessness, and as a result the Emperor rebuked the liberals by referring to their wishes, which were couched in the most respectful and loyal terms, as "vain dreams." Ten years later these vain dreams were to come true.

In the early days of the present reign I made several attempts to draw His Majesty's attention to the peasant problem, pointing out the necessity of forming a special commission for the study of that problem. But my efforts were constantly thwarted by Plehve, and, to my complete surprise, instead of a peasant commission, a conference was created in 1895 for the study of the needs of the landed gentry. I. N. Durnovo, President of the Committee of Ministers, was put at the head of the conference, but Plehve soon became its leading spirit. The membership of that body was such that it was clearly intended to raise the economic status of the private landowners alone, and especially of our debt-ridden and artificially supported nobility. In my capacity of Minister of Finances, I, too, was a member of the conference. At the very first session of the conference I declared that, as the peasant was our chief landowner and agricultural toiler, especial attention should be given to his needs. Peasant prosperity, I argued, would mean prosperity for the class of landed proprietors generally. The chairman interrupted me and did not let me terminate my speech. He had consulted the Emperor, he announced at the opening of the subsequent session, and His Majesty had expressed himself to the effect that he had appointed the conference for the purpose of examining the needs of the nobility exclusively. Consequently, His Majesty ordered the conference, Durnovo declared, to confine itself to that specific task.

This decision was equivalent to a death sentence for the conference. It lasted some three years, the problems upon which it deliberated being mostly various privileges for the nobility and financial assistance to them to be derived from the public treasury. I opposed most of these schemes, and made every effort to expose the greed of the nobility. I aroused thereby the ire of that part of the nobility which looks at the Russian Empire as a cow to be milked by them. All the while Plehve played the part of the champion of ultra-feudal tendencies. In his speeches he constantly made incursions into Russia's past to show that the Russian Empire owed its existence chiefly to the nobility. Plehve found in me an implacable opponent. I confess I did not spare his amour-propre, so that on several occasions he appealed to the chairman for protection. Needless to say, the conference achieved practically nothing. Durnovo received a generous prize and several small financial concessions were given as a sop to the nobility, but a certain element among the nobility could never forget my opposition to the plans of the conference. It goes without saying that I have never entertained any hostile feelings against the nobility as a class. I am myself an hereditary nobleman and was brought up on genteel traditions. I am aware that there are among our landed aristocracy many truly noble and unselfish men and women, imbued with the spirit which should animate every true nobleman, namely, that of protecting the weak and serving the people generally. All the great reforms of the 'Sixties were carried out by a handful of noblemen, and in our own days there are aristocrats who do not separate their welfare from the welfare of the people and who sometimes serve the cause of the nation at the peril of their very lives. Yet such noblemen are in the minority. The majority is politically a mass of degenerate humanity, which recognizes nothing but the gratification of its selfish interests and lusts, and which seeks to obtain all manner of privileges and gratuities at the expense of the taxpayers generally, that is, chiefly the peasantry.

It is noteworthy that the minutes of the sessions of the conference have hitherto remained unpublished. Should these documents become known, even the unscrupulous third Duma would blush with shame. Although they are not by any means a faithful report of the debates, their publication, as well as the publication of the memoranda which were addressed to the conference, would throw a great deal of light upon many aspects of the disaster which befell us after the Japanese War. At the beginning of the 20th century it is impossible to pursue with impunity a mediæval course of policy. When the nation becomes, at least partly, conscious of its dignity and needs, it is impossible to follow the policy of a patently unjust encouragement of the privileged minority at the expense of the majority. Rulers and politicians who do not grasp this simple truth prepare a revolution with their own hands. At the first weakening of the Government's power and prestige, it bursts out with the violence of an uncontrollable explosion. Our revolution took place because our Government was blind to the fundamental fact that society moves onward. It is the duty of the rulers to regulate this movement and hold it in check. When they fail to do so and, instead, dam the current, the result is a revolutionary flood. This flood is made more dangerous in Russia by the fact that 35 per cent. of the population consists of non-Russian, conquered nationalities. Anyone who has intelligently read recent history knows how difficult the development of nationalism in the past century has rendered the task of welding together heterogeneous national elements into a uniform body politic.

THE CZAR'S ATTEMPTS AT REFORM

Upon the dissolution of the Noblemen's Conference I again called His Majesty's attention to the peasant problem in my yearly report relating to the State budget for the year 1898. Taking advantage of the fact that the State Comptroller* several months later also touched upon that matter in his yearly report to the Emperor, I laid before the Committee of Ministers a proposal for the formation of a special conference for the study of the peasant problem, to be made up of high State officials under the presidency of a statesman appointed by the Emperor, or, better still, of His Majesty himself. Goremykin raised no objections, but Plehve and, consequently, Durnovo, strenuously opposed this measure. Nevertheless, the Committee of Ministers expressed itself in favour of the plan, and it was decided to form a special conference "to study the problems relating to the extension and development of the legislation about the peasant class." The Emperor neither sanctioned the minutes of the session, nor definitely declined to sign them, and the matter remained in abeyance. In the meantime, Summer came. The Emperor left for Crimea. I addressed to him the following letter, emphasizing the importance of the conference, and imploring him not to give up the plan :

The Crimean War opened the eyes of those who could see. They perceived that Russia could not be strong under a régime based on slavery. Your grandfather cut the Gordian knot with his autocratic sword. He redeemed the soul and body of his people from their owners. That unprecedented act created the colossus who is now in Your autocratic hands. Russia was transformed, she increased her power and her knowledge tenfold. And this in spite of the fact that after the emancipation a liberal movement arose which threatened to shatter the autocratic power, which is the very basis of the existence of the Russian Empire. . . . The crisis of the 'eighties was not caused by the emancipation of the serfs. It was brought about by the corrupting influence of the Press, the disorganization of the school, the liberal self-governing institutions and, finally, the fact that the authority of the organs of the Autocratic power had been undermined as a result of constant attacks upon the bureaucracy on the part of all manner of people. . . . Emperor Alexander II freed the serfs, but he did not organize the life on the firm basis of law. Emperor Alexander III, absorbed by the task of restoring Russia's international prestige, strengthening our military power, improving our finances, suppressing the unrest, did not have the time to complete the work begun

* an official who supervises expenditures.

by his most august father. This task has been bequeathed to your Imperial Majesty. It can be carried out and it must be carried out. Otherwise the growth of Russia's grandeur will be impeded. . . .

Your Majesty has 130 million subjects. Our budget before the Emancipation amounted to 350 million rubles. The Emancipation enabled us to increase it to 1400 million. In proportion to our population, we could have a budget of 4200 million, if we were as wealthy as France, or a budget of 3300 million, if our economic prosperity were on a level with that of Austria-Hungary. Why is our taxpaying capacity so low? Chiefly because of the lamentable state of our peasantry. . . .

The peasant was freed from his landowner. . . . But he is still a slave oh his community as represented by the *mir* meetings and also of the entire hierachy of petty officials who make up the rural administration. The peasant's rights and obligations are not clearly defined by law. His welfare and his very person are at the mercy of the arbitrary rulings of the local administration. The peasant is still flogged, and that at the decision of such institutions as the *volost* (rural district) courts. . . . The peasant was given land. But his right to it is not clearly defined by law. Wherever the communal form of landownership prevails, he cannot even know which lot is his. The inheritance rights are regulated by vague customs. So that at present the peasant holds his land not by law, but by custom, and often by arbitrary discretion. The family rights of the peasants have remained almost completely outside of the scope of law. . . .

The peasant was but slightly affected by the legal reform of Emperor Alexander II. Justice is meted out to him not by the common courts of the land, but by special rural courts on the basis of customary law, or plainly speaking, by arbitrary discretion. The raising of taxes is no better organized. It is governed by the arbitrary will of the local administration. . . . The principle of mutual responsibility for taxes makes the individual peasant responsible for the whole community and at times results in his complete irresponsibility. The zemstvos tax the peasants according to their own discretion, and the Government has no means of checking them if they choose to tax the peasant beyond his powers. Arbitrariness and confusion prevail also in the raising of the *mir* dues, which have lately shown a tendency to excessive growth. These taxes are entirely outside of the Government's control.

And what of popular education? It is an open secret that it is in the embryonic stage and that in this respect we are behind not only many European countries, but also many Asian and Transatlantic lands. However this is not an unmitigated evil. There is education and education. What education could the people have received during the period of liberal aberrations, which extended from the 'sixties to the death of

Alexander II (1881)? That education would have probably meant corruption. It is imperative, nevertheless, to push the cause of education, and this must be done energetically. From the fact that the child may fall and injure itself it would be erroneous to infer that it must not be taught how to walk. Only the education must be completely in the hands of the Government.

Thus, the peasantry, while personally free, is still a slave to arbitrariness, lawlessness, and ignorance. Under these circumstances the peasant loses the impulse to seek to improve his condition by lawful means. The vital nerve of progress is paralyzed in him. He becomes passive and spiritless, thus offering a fertile soil for the growth of vices. Single, even though substantial, measures will not remedy the situation. Above all, the peasant's spiritual energies must be aroused. He must be granted the plenitude of civil rights which I the other loyal sons of your Majesty enjoy. Given the present condition of the peasantry, the State cannot advance and achieve the world-importance to which the nature of things and destiny itself entitle it.

This condition of the peasantry is the fundamental cause of those morbid social phenomena which are always present in the life of our country.... A great deal of attention is given to the alleged "land crisis." It is a strange crisis, indeed, seeing that prices of land are everywhere on the increase. Widespread discussion also centres around the comparative merits of the individual classes which go to make the nation. An effort is made to ascertain which of them supports the throne. As if the Russian Autocratic Throne could possibly rest on one class and not on the entire Russian people! ... On that unshakable foundation it will rest forever. .. The root of the evil is not the land crisis, or unorganized migrations, or the growth of the budget, but rather the confusion and disorder which prevail in the daily life of the peasant masses... In a word, Sire, it is my profound conviction that the peasant problem is at present the most vital problem of our existence. It must be dealt with immediately.

I do not know what impression my letter made on His Majesty. He did not answer it, and upon his return to St. Petersburg never referred to it. Thereupon, in response to Durnovo's report, His Majesty decreed that the aforementioned measure passed by the Committee of Ministers, and approved by himself, should only be carried into effect at his express order. That order was never given. Thus the Plehve-Durnovo clique again thwarted my effort to improve the peasant's lot by way of legislative reforms.

I succeeded, however, in carrying out, in 1894, two reforms which to a certain extent improved the legal status of the peasant class, namely, the abolition of mutual responsibility in taxation, and the mitigation of the passport regulations.

When the peasants were emancipated, the mutual responsibility for direct taxes was introduced for purely fiscal purposes. The underlying principle was that it is easier to govern communities than individuals. Mutual responsibility meant in substance the responsibility of the thrifty for the shiftless, the hard workers for the idlers, the sober for the drunk. A crying injustice, it demoralized the population and undermined its conception of right and of civic responsibility. Since the Ministry of the Interior in its defence of mutual responsibility usually alleged the needs of the Ministry of Finances, I declared in the Imperial Council, in my capacity of Minister of Finances, that my Ministry was opposed to this principle. Then I submitted a project for the levying of taxes on the peasants, providing for the abolition of mutual responsibility and the transfer of the task of levying from the police to the agents of the Ministry of Finances, notably the tax inspectors. Goremykin, Minister of the Interior, insisted that this task should be intrusted not to the tax inspectors, but to the rural police chiefs. The majority of the Imperial Council, however, supported my proposal. The next thing Goremykin did was to complain to His Majesty that I sought to lower the prestige of the rural police chief in the eyes of the peasants. Thereupon I wrote to the Emperor that should the project approved by the majority of the Imperial Council be rejected I would be forced to tender my resignation. In the end mutual responsibility was abolished and the task of collecting the taxes from the peasants was imposed upon the tax inspectors. Nevertheless, the new law was not entirely free from provisions which betrayed the conviction of the legislator that peasants could not be treated like all the other elements of the population.

The passport regulations, which tied the peasant hand and foot, were also defended on the ground of the financial benefit derived from the passport tax. I declared to the Imperial Council that the Ministry of Finances was willing to do without this benefit, and I laid before the Council a new passport law which to a considerable extent did away with the restrictions upon the freedom of the peasant's movements. The new law was passed, but at the instance of the Minister of the Interior it was modified so as to make it more conservative. When I was appointed president of the Council the Minister of the Interior elaborated a more liberal passport status, but for some reason it never became a law.

When, in 1900, Sipyagin succeeded Goremykin as Minister of the Interior I impressed upon him the importance of the peasant problem. So long, I argued, as the peasant question remained unsolved in the liberal sense, on the basis of the principles of individual prosperity and personal freedom, all the other reforms would be as a house built on sand. Sipyagin took up the matter with His Majesty, and as a result I was commissioned to form what was officially known as "The Special Conference on the Needs of the Agricultural Industry," i.e., a committee for the purpose of ascertaining the needs of the agriculturists and especially the peasants. The conference consisted of statesmen whose reputation for conservatism was beyond suspicion. There were among others: Count Vorontzov-Dashkov, Viceroy of the Caucasus; Adjutant General Chikhachev; Gerard, who was later appointed Governor-General of Finland; Prince Dolgorukov, Lord High Marshal, and Count Sheremetyev, His Majesty's master of the hunt. The conference lasted from January 22, 1902, to March 30, 1905, that is, upward of three years. In the course of an audience which I had with His Majesty, at the time when the conference had just been formed, he told me that he wished me to study and solve the peasant problem in the spirit of the principles which were carried out under Alexander II. The first year we spent in classifying and summing up the reports of the provincial and district committees. We hoped thus to gather a mass of information on which to base our solution of the peasant problem. The two types of local committees functioned under the presidency of Governors and Marshals of Nobility respectively, which circumstance naturally tended to restrict their freedom of discussion. Nevertheless, for the first time in many years, they presented to the local population the opportunity to voice their opinions with comparative freedom. Both the Emperor and the Minister of the Interior expected that the committees would attack the financial and economic policy of the Government and that these bodies would thus prove to be a trap for their own originator. To their surprise, however, the unanimous complaints of the committees were aimed at the internal policy of the Government, in general, and the legal disabilities which weighed down upon the peasantry, in particular.

Three Ministers of the Interior succeeded each other during the existence of the conference. No sooner did the Agricultural Conference, supplied with the necessary factual material, open its deliberations preparatory to taking practical steps, than Sipyagin was assassinated and Vyacheslav Konstantinovich von-Plehve appointed in his stead. He immediately visited his wrath on some of the leaders of the local committees who were too outspoken in the expression of their opinions. Thus, Prince Dolgorukov, chairman of the District Board of the Government of Kursk, was discharged, while Shcherbina, a well-known statistician, was exiled from the government of Voronezh. The small fry was treated even more unceremoniously. In endeavouring to intercede for a peasant who was arrested and exiled from the Tula province because of the opinions he expressed before one of the local committees, Count Leo Tolstoy accused me, not without some ground, of provocation. (His letter is filed in my records.) Then Plehve obtained His Majesty's permission to elaborate a system of laws and regulations relating to the peasants in a special conference attached to the Ministry of the Interior, and immediately proceeded to form another set of provincial committees under the presidency of provincial governors. The personnel of these new committees was made up with great care, so as to include only men accustomed to say nothing but what pleased the authorities. As there was no direct decree forbidding the Agricultural Conference to deal with the needs of the peasant class, and as I was certain that the Plehve conference would come to nothing, I assumed an attitude of watchful expectation. In the meantime, my conference was studying general problems relating to grain commerce, railroads, small credit, etc.

By a curious coincidence, Plehve met his fate in the same way as did his predecessor. As soon as he was assassinated and succeeded by Prince Svyatopolk-Mirski, a man of honour, but too weak for his responsible post, the Agricultural Conference took up the various aspects of the peasant problem. A motion was made to recommend the abolition of the redemption payments, but my successor, Minister of Finances Kokovtzev, objected, and His Majesty decided to postpone the matter until the termination of the war. The redemption payments, be it mentioned in passing, were abolished in 1906 in my premiership, under the direct pressure of the revolutionary upheaval. The conference then attacked some other problems relating to the peasantry, the general tendency of the discussion being in favour of removing the burden of legal disabilities from the peasant. It is also noteworthy that the conference preferred the individual form of land ownership to the communal (*obshchina*). I had the support of men whom no one would suspect of liberalism, while the opposition consisted of members of the court camarilla who later put themselves at the head of the Black Hundreds either openly or secretly.

One of the members of the conference was Goremykin. Ostensibly, he sided with me, but behind my back he conducted an underhand plot against me with the aid of that office-hunter, Krivoshein, now member of the Imperial Council, and General Trepov. These plotters succeeded in persuading His Majesty that the conference was "unreliable." As a result, one fine morning, March 30, 1905, to be exact, I was informed over the telephone by the director of one of the Departments of the Ministry of Finances that the Agricultural Conference had been closed by a special decree and that a new conference was formed under the presidency of Goremykin, and with the participation of men of his type. Although I was president of the conference and a very active president too, this act came to me as a complete surprise. We were treated as if we were a revolutionary club. As late as two days before the publication of the decree dissolving the conference His Majesty approved the minutes of its session. Of course, he never told me he was dissatisfied with the work of the conference, nor did he warn me of its dissolution. Afterwards he never referred to the conference. Such is His Majesty's character. Yet, if the authorities had allowed the conference to complete its work, much of what happened later would have been avoided. The peasantry would not have been as deeply stirred up by the revolution as it actually was. The agrarian disturbances would have been greatly reduced in scope and violence, and many innocent lives saved.

Naturally, Goremykin's conference failed to interest anyone, and resulted in nothing. As for our conference, it left behind a vast contribution to Russian economic literature in the form of memoranda written by competent members of local committees and well-digested systematic material relating to the various sides of Russia's economic life. The general impression an investigator derives from all this material is that in the years 1903-1904, one definite idea fermented the minds of the people, namely that to avoid the miseries of a revolution, it was necessary to carry out a number of liberal reforms in keeping with the spirit of the times. It was this feature of the activity of the conference that accounts for its dissolution.

When the revolution broke out, the Government, in its agrarian policy, was forced to go much beyond what was projected by the Agricultural Conference. But it was too late. The peasant problem could no longer be solved by way of liberal reforms. It assumed an acute, a revolutionary form. All revolutions occur because governments fail to satisfy in time the crying needs of the people and remain deaf to them. No Government can neglect these needs with impunity. For many years our Government kept blazoning forth with great pomp that it had the people's needs at heart, that it was constantly striving to render the peasantry happy, etc., etc. All that was mere lip service. Since the death of Alexander II, the Government's treatment of the peasants has been determined by the representatives of the landed nobility at the court, and, as a result, the peasantry is now assaulting the nobility, without distinguishing the right from the wrong. Such is the nature of man.

The appointment of Prince Svyatopolk-Mirski as Minister of the Interior opened an era of liberalism. Not that the prince was a liberal by conviction, or career, or birth. He was merely an intelligent, sober-minded man and a loyal servant of his monarch. Mirski opened his campaign for liberal reforms by submitting a report to His Majesty and appending to it a rough draft of a ukase decreeing a number of liberal reforms. In December (1904) His Majesty called a conference at Tsarskoye Selo to discuss the prince's report. In addition to the Minister of the Interior, a limited number of high officials were present. His Majesty, I was told, did not wish to invite me, but Svyatopolk-Mirski persuaded him to do so.

His Majesty opened the conference by declaring that the revolutionary movement was on the increase and that it was necessary to decide whether the Government should meet the moderate element of society half-way or whether it should pursue the policy which brought about the assassination of two Ministers, Sipyagin and Plehve. I happened to be the first speaker. I expressed myself vigorously to the effect that persistence in the reactionary policy would lead us straight to ruin. The majority sided with me. Pobiedonostzev, naturally enough, assumed a critical attitude toward my views, but, as usual, he concluded his speech by declaring that it would be best to do nothing. Among other subjects, the conference discussed the restoration of the authority of law in the Empire, and also the abolition of the stringent regulations directed against the Old Believers and of the other laws which are not in keeping with the principle of toleration and religious freedom. It was also pointed out that it was necessary to increase the authority and scope of the zemstvos and of the organs of municipal self-government. But the storm-centre of the debates was the question whether representatives elected by the people should be allowed to take part in the work of legislation. The majority spoke in favour of this measure. I expressed myself to the effect that our governmental order was out of keeping with the needs of the country and the consciousness of nearly all the intelligent classes of the population. Therefore, I said, I could welcome the proposed reforms. I did not wish, however, to conceal from His Majesty, I concluded, that the constant and regular participation of the representatives in legislative work was bound, in my opinion, to lead to what is known as a constitutional régime. As was usually the case with conferences conducted under His Majesty's presidency, the meeting came to no definite decision. The Emperor ordered Secretary of State Baron Nolde to draft, under my supervision, a decree in agreement with the prevalent views expressed at the conference. It was also decided that the projected reforms were to be discussed and elaborated by the Committee of Ministers.

The decree was drafted the following day and its definitive wording was discussed at a second conference, called on December 6th or 7th. The final version included a rather vaguely worded provision for the regular admission of elected representatives to participation in the legislative activity of the government. This version was laid before His Majesty and, after some deliberation, he changed the article dealing with the representatives in the sense that they were to be elected not by the people but by the Government. Thereupon I was summoned before the Emperor and asked what I thought of the modified article. I pointed out that, in its altered form, the article meant practically nothing, for the existing regulations provided for the participation of experts, summoned for the purpose, in the deliberations of the Imperial Council. I advised His Majesty to strike out the article from the decree altogether. If His Majesty entertained doubts, I observed, as to the advisability of summoning elected representatives and thus inaugurating what amounted to a constitutional régime it was best to drop the matter completely. His Majesty followed my advice, and the expurgated version of the ukase was signed and published on December 12, 1904.

The decree of December 12, 1904, imposed upon the Committee of Ministers the duty of elaborating the necessary measures tending to establish legality, extend freedom of speech, religious toleration and the scope of local self-government, to reduce the disabilities of the non-Russian national groups and to do away with all manner of extraordinary laws. The decree also emphasized the necessity of bringing to a satisfactory completion the work of the Agricultural Conference. The Committee of Ministers was to establish the general principle, while the detailed elaboration of each question was to be the task of special commissions appointed by the Emperor and responsible directly to him. In my capacity of President of the Committee of Ministers, I did everything in my power to see the reforms outlined in the decree carried into effect with the greatest possible expediency and thoroughness. In every question I took the initiative and my staff supplied ample material pertaining to the particular subject under consideration. By speedily carrying out the decree of December 12, I hoped to check the spread of discontent and unrest in the country. The obstacles I had to cope with were at first apathy, then intriguing on the part of the courtiers, and, all the time, His Majesty's profound distrust of the reforms outlined in the decree. To make a long story short, the results of the decree were practically a negligible quantity. The only legal measures enacted related to religious toleration, the schools in the western provinces, and the legal status of the sectarians.

The principles of legality established by the Committee of Ministers have never been carried into effect. I succeeded in forming a conference for the revision of the censorship regulations, with a membership which included men of high competence and moderately liberal views. Several days after the appointment of this body, His Majesty, without the knowledge of either myself or the chairman of the conference, named two new members : Prince Golitzyn-Muravlin, now member of the Union of the Russian People (Black Hundreds), and Yuzefovich, a notorious pervert and a man without honour. The conference achieved nothing. The conference on religious toleration met a similar fate, after having removed from the Old Believers some of the legal disabilities that had oppressed them for centuries. At heart, the Emperor always sided with these sectarians, but they had a powerful and stubborn enemy in the person of Pobiedonostzev, who for twenty-five years was an insurmountable obstacle to the liberal solution of the sectarian problem.

While the conference on religious toleration was discussing the legal status of the sectarians, the Holy Synod raised the question of calling a church assembly and restoring the patriarchate, abolished by Peter the Great. Under the influence of K. P. Pobiedonostzev, the convocation of a church assembly was indefinitely postponed by His Majesty. At the same time the reactionary newspapers began to shout that Metropolitan Antonius, member of the Committee of Ministers, and I were intent on undermining the authority of the Czar, that by advocating the restoration of the patriarchate we sought to create two Czars, a civil and an ecclesiastical one. After I had assumed the office of President of the Imperial Council, the question of convoking a church assembly was raised anew. A preliminary conference attached to the Synod was appointed for the purpose of elaborating the program of the convention. But with my resignation and Prince Obolensky's dismissal from the post of Procurator of the Holy Synod, the matter was again dropped. In my opinion, the greatest danger confronting Russia is the degeneration of the official Orthodox church and the extinction of the living religious spirit of the people. If Slavophilism has performed any real service to the country, it is by emphasizing this truth as far back as fifty years ago. The present revolution has demonstrated it with exceptional clarity. No body politic can exist without higher spiritual ideals. These can only sway the masses if they are simple, lofty, and accessible to everyone, in a word, if they bear the imprint of the divine. Without a living church, religion becomes philosophy and loses its power to enter into the life of men and regulate it. Without religion the masses turn into herds of intelligent beasts. Our church has unfortunately long since become a dead, bureaucratic institution, and our priests serve not the high God of lofty Orthodoxy, but the earthly gods of paganism. Gradually we are becoming less Christian than the members of any other Christian church. We have less faith than any other nation. Japan has defeated us because she believes in her God incomparably more than we do in ours. This is just as true as the assertion that Germany owed her victory over France in 1870 to her school system.

In pursuance of the decree of December 12, the Committee of Ministers also discussed the labour problem, but did not go further than recommending the introduction of obligatory workers' insurance. With a view to carrying out the provisions of the decree, the Committee decided to call a convention of representatives from the provincial and district zemstvos and municipal dumas, and empower them to elaborate a new set of regulations relating to the zemstvos and the organs of municipal self-government. The minutes of the session where the decision of the Committee was recorded in detail were signed by His Majesty, but the decision was never carried out. The Committee also stated that the arbitrary rule of the administration, in general, and "the extraordinary and reinforced rule," so-called, in particular could not be tolerated. That rule was proclaimed early in the '80's as a set of temporary regulations and has persisted until this very day, expanding geographically and growing in scope. Nothing, however, was accomplished in this direction. Finally, the Committee declared that the Jewish problem must at least receive a definite solution and that there was no solution except a gradual abolition of the Jewish disabilities. The Committee also advocated the idea that the Jewish question, in view of its acuteness, could not be solved without the participation of representatives from the population which lives now in contact with the Jews or which, with the abolition of the anti-Jewish restrictions, will be brought in close contact with them.

Seeing that no serious measures would be taken as a result of the decree of December 12th, I hastened, to His Majesty's visible satisfaction, to put an end to the activities of the Committee of Ministers in pursuance of the decree. Thus, a measure which could have become a blessing for the country proved useless, if not harmful. It clearly demonstrated to the intelligent classes that the Emperor and his Government were either unable or unwilling to grant reforms.

In the meantime, Prince Svyatopolk-Mirski lost his prestige in the Emperor's eyes and was succeeded by Bulygin, an apathetic, upright man and mediocre statesman, who owed his appointment to the fact that he had previously served as assistant to Grand Duke Sergey Alexandrovich, the Moscow General Governor. Shortly before, at the suggestion of Baron Frederichs, Minister of the Court, General Trepov was appointed Governor-General of St. Petersburg, He was given this newly created important post because he had an imposing martial appearance and because, like Baron Frederichs, he had served in the Cavalry Guards, but above all because he had severely criticized Mirski's policy in His Majesty's presence. It is in the Emperor's nature to act like a pendulum, swinging between two extremes. Thereupon, General Trepov, without resigning his

Governor-Generalship, became, against Bulygin's will, associate Minister of the Interior with special privileges. Thus we had two Ministers of the Interior, or, more precisely, a dummy minister and a veritable dictator. No other term could describe the General's position and role. Trepov completely dominated His Majesty and enjoyed the favour of the Empress, which favour he owed to the good offices of Her Majesty's sister, Grand Duchess Elizabeth Fyodorovna. It was during his dictatorship that the revolution of 1905-1906 gathered sufficient impetus to come to the surface.

While Trepov wrote to His Majesty daily reports about matters relating to both our home affairs and foreign policy, Bulygin sat quietly in his office learning from the papers about the course of our internal policy, which he was nominally directing. It must be said that he bore his cross not without equanimity. When asked under what circumstance this or that measure was taken, he would answer with composure: "I do not know, have not been told yet," or: "I have just read about it in the papers myself."

The only serious, though dead-born, reform with which Bulygin's name is associated is an attempt to create a parliamentary body with consultative powers. All the work in connection with this reform was done by the Council of Ministers, better known as the Solski Conference. Until October 17, 1905, there were two administrative bodies which sometimes acted in a legislative capacity, i.e., elaborated legal measures previous to laying them before the Emperor, namely the Committee of Ministers and the Council of Ministers. The Council met very rarely, as a rule under the presidency of the Emperor. In January, 1905, His Majesty convened the Council and at the end of the session remarked in a casual manner, speaking to Count Solski: "I beg you, Count, to call the Council for the discussion of all the questions either raised by the ministers or pointed out by me." After that all the subjects relating to the projected reforms came under the jurisdiction of the Council, which became known as the Solski Conference. This body survived the reforms which followed the constitutional manifesto of October 17, 1905, and functioned alongside of the Imperial Council. It was this conference that raised again the question of admitting elected representatives to the legislative institutions. The measure received the support of Kokovtzev, among others. He declared that without this measure it would be difficult to contract the loan necessitated by the war. Bulygin, on his part, opined that the internal situation of the country made this reform an imperative necessity. As a result of this discussion, His Majesty asked Bulygin to draft a rescript empowering him, i.e., Bulygin, as the Minister of the Interior, to work out a plan of summoning representatives elected by the population to take part in the work of legislation.

The next session, which was to take up Bulygin's draft of the rescript, was set for the following day, if I remember correctly. In the morning some of the members of the conference, including myself, met at a station on their way to Tsarskoye Selo, where the meetings took place. We were all greatly upset and indignant. The morning papers contained the text of a manifesto which had come to us as a complete surprise. Minister of Justice Manukhin explained that last night the manifesto was sent to him for publication. He had intended to observe all the prescribed formalities and promulgate the document through the Senate, but the chief of His Majesty's Chancery requested him in the Emperor's name to publish the manifesto in the morning issue of the *Governmental Messenger*. Like all manifestoes, it overflowed with grandiloquent phrases, but in substance it was a variation on the old theme: "Everything will be as before; forget your vain dreams." No one knew who was the author of the manifesto. At Tsarskoye Selo we learned that the document had been submitted on the previous day to Pobiedonostzev and enthusiastically commended by him. Later it became known that the manifesto had been transmitted to His Majesty by the Empress who, in her turn, had received it from Prince Putyatin. Who actually composed the document, I have been unable to ascertain. It was probably written by some Black Hundred leader.

His Majesty appeared at the meeting with an air of perfect serenity, as if nothing had happened. I suspect that internally he was greatly amused by our upset appearance. He was always fond of taking his counsellors by surprise. As he made no reference to the manifesto, Bulygin read his draft of the rescript, which provided for a more or less extensive participation of the people's representatives in legislation, thus inaugurating principles diametrically opposed to the ones publicly and officially proclaimed several hours before. After a brief period of discussion, which bore mostly on the wording of the rescript, the luncheon recess was announced. As was usually the case, His Majesty took his luncheon with the Empress, apart from all the other members of the conference, who lunched together. In the course of the luncheon I remarked that those present would start an endless debate about the wording of the rescript and in the end it would fall through. But everyone was so indignant at the manifesto trick, that it was agreed to accept Bulygin's version without discussion. We kept our agreement, to His Majesty's great surprise. There was nothing left to him but to sign the rescript, which he did. Prince Hilkov was moved to tears, and Count Solski delivered a brief speech overflowing with emotion and gratitude. Thus, one and the same day witnessed the enactment of two diametrically opposed legislative measures. Under these circumstances, it is no wonder that the country underwent the trials of a revolution. Russia was and still is being played with like a toy. In the eyes of our rulers was not the Japanese campaign itself a war with toy soldiers?

After that incident I no longer took any active part in the work on the Bulygin project. The Solski Conference approved its main outlines. After I left for the United States, the matter came up for final discussion before a conference, called at Peterhof under His Majesty's presidency. The gathering was attended, besides Count Solski, by several Grand Dukes and by such staunch supporters of conservatism as Pobiedonostzev, Ignatyev, Naryshkin, member of the Imperial Council representing the nobility, Count Bobrinski, formerly Marshal of the St. Petersburg nobility, and others. On the 26th of August, 1905, a manifesto was published, together with a decree providing for the establishment of an Imperial Duma. The decree defined this institution, in substance, as follows:

1. The Duma is a permanently functioning institution, similar to western parliaments.
2. All the laws and regulations, both permanent and provisional, as well as the budget, must be brought before the Duma for discussion.
3. The Duma is an exclusively consultative institution, and it enjoys complete freedom in expressing its opinions on the subjects under discussion.
4. The electoral law is based chiefly on the peasantry, as the element of the population predominant numerically and most reliable and conservative from the monarchistic standpoint; the electoral law cannot be modified without the consent of the Duma.

5. The franchise does not depend on nationality and religion.

Such was this typical invention of our bureaucratic eunuchs. It had all the prerogatives of a parliament except the chief one. It was a parliament and yet, as a purely consultative institution, it was not a parliament. The law of August 6th satisfied no one. Nor did it in the least stem the tide of the revolution, which continued steadily to rise.

During my absence in the United States the universities were granted autonomy. It was one of those sudden, ill-calculated acts which characterized the fitful course of the Government's policy. As a result, all the institutions of higher learning in St. Petersburg became the meeting-place of the revolutionists of various classes. Most extreme ideas of anarchism and militant socialism were preached at those meetings. The speeches of the orators were punctuated with outcries, "Down with the autocracy!" and similar revolting expressions directed against the head of the empire and the dynasty. The only thing the Government did was to throw around the university buildings a cordon of troops to prevent the revolutionary fire from spreading to the streets. The academic authorities, on their part, declared that the only way to put an end to the meetings was for the Government to permit the population to hold meetings elsewhere. According to these authorities, the students said that they considered it their duty to share their privilege (freedom of assemblage) with the rest of the citizens. Thus, the university autonomy was the first breach in the Government's fortifications, through which the revolution burst forth into the open. Soon afterwards the Government did issue a set of regulations relating to the right of assemblage, but the measure remained ineffective.

The coördination of the work of the various ministries, by means of an institution not unlike a Cabinet of Ministers, was another problem which arose during my stay in America. It was also discussed in Count Solski's Conference. I returned from the United States at the very beginning of the discussion and found the participants almost unanimous in recognizing the necessity of bringing unity into the actions of the ministers. Most strenuously opposed to this measure was the Minister of Finances, Kokovtzev, who, realizing that the plan entailed the appointment of a chairman or president of ministers and foreseeing that he could not possibly obtain this post for himself, did everything in his power to thwart the execution of the project, an attitude so very characteristic of this small-minded man. The rest of those who objected to the measure did so neither on account of disapproval of the general idea nor, like Kokovtzev, for personal reasons, but because they feared that the existence of a body with such a powerful functionary at its head would tend to impair the prestige of the Emperor in the eyes of the people. Finally the conference decided to set up a Council of Ministers to take the place of the existing council, established in accordance with a decree promulgated in the reign of Alexander II, which had provided that the Emperor himself should be its president. As previously mentioned, Nicholas II had, however, given this office to Count Solski in contravention of the law.

The new decree, having been elaborated, was put into force by the Emperor shortly before October 17th and actually did unite the ministers to a certain extent, although everything that had resulted from Count Solski's Conferences was vague and fragmentary, largely because of the compromises to which the count liked to resort in order not to trouble the Emperor with controversies. To avoid the suggestion of a liberal western constitution, Solski called the new body Council of Ministers instead of Cabinet. I was appointed its first Presiding Minister. Now, as an organization called a council had previously been in existence, everything enacted by it, such as Bulygin's Duma law, was attributed to me. Even to this day the great majority of the public makes no distinction between the present council and the former council, which sometimes was out of session for years at a stretch.

Although the need of coordination was the ostensible cause of the formation of the new council and the abolition of the old, I have reason to believe that the change was due largely to the fact that Count Solski, perceiving that the turbulence of the masses was increasing rapidly and that the storm was about to break, desired to retire into obscurity and thus be relieved of the burdensome responsibilities attached to the role of presiding over the former council in the Emperor's stead. This desire is not only comprehensible, but also pardonable, since the count had been an invalid for many years—he was even unable to walk. Indeed, under the circumstances, it is astounding that he should have been able to hold all the important and highly responsible offices with which he was entrusted and which included those of President of the Imperial Council, chairman of the Financial Committee and President of the

Council of Ministers. Because of his weak will and poor health, he had lately been much under the influence of his numerous assistants and secretaries.

By the end of September, the militant revolution was so far advanced that the question "What should be done?" assumed extraordinary urgency. During the first half of the following month the political events developed with astonishing rapidity, culminating in the publication of the constitutional manifesto of October 17. Here is the text of that historical document:

Unrest and disturbances in the capitals and in many regions of our Empire fill our heart with a great and heavy grief. The welfare of the Russian Sovereign is inseparable from the welfare of the people, and their sorrow is his sorrow. The unrest now arisen may cause a profound disorder in the masses and become a menace to the integrity and unity of the Russian State. The great vow of Imperial service enjoins us to strive with all the might of our reason and authority to put an end within the shortest possible time to this unrest so perilous to the State. Having ordered the proper authorities to take measures for the suppression of the direct manifestations of disorder, rioting, and violence, and for the protection of peaceful people who seek to fulfil in peace the duties incumbent upon them, We, in order to carry out more effectively the measures outlined by us for the pacification of the country, have found it necessary to unify the activity of the higher Government agencies.

We impose upon the Government the obligation to execute our inflexible will:

1. To grant the population the unshakable foundations of civic freedom on the basis of real personal inviolability, freedom of conscience, of speech, of assemblage, and of association.

2. Without stopping the appointed elections to the Imperial Duma, to admit to participation in the Duma those classes of the population which have hitherto been deprived of the franchise, in so far as this is feasible in the brief period remaining before the convening of the Duma, leaving the further development of the principle of general suffrage to the new legislative order (i. e., the Duma and Imperial Council established by the law of August 6, 1905).

3. To establish it as an unshakable rule that no law can become effective without the sanction of the Imperial Duma and that the people's elected representatives should be guaranteed a real participation in the control over the lawfulness of the authorities appointed by us.

We call upon all the faithful sons of Russia to remember their duty to their country, to lend assistance in putting an end to the unprecedented disturbances and together with us make every effort to restore quiet and peace in our native land.

Simultaneously there was published my report addressed to His Majesty in reply to his order requesting me, in my capacity of president of the Committee of Ministers, to unify the activity of the ministers. The text of the report follows:

The unrest which has seized the various classes of the Russian people cannot be looked upon as the consequence of the partial imperfections of the political and social order or as the result of the activities of organized extreme parties. The roots of that unrest lie deeper. They are in the disturbed equilibrium between the aspirations of the thinking elements and the external forms of their life. Russia has outgrown the existing régime and is striving for an order based on civic liberty. Consequently, the forms of Russia's political life must be raised to the level of the ideas which animate the moderate majority of the people.

The first task of the Government is immediately to establish the basic elements of the new order, notably personal inviolability and the freedom of the press, of conscience, of assemblage, and of association, without waiting for the legislative sanction of these measures by the Imperial Duma. The further strengthening of these foundations of the political life of the country must be effected in the regular legislative procedure, just as the work of equalizing all the Russian citizens, without distinction of religion and nationality, before the law. It goes without saying that the civic liberties granted to the people must be lawfully restricted, so as to safeguard the rights of the third persons and peace and the safety of the State.

The next task of the Government is to establish institutions and legislative principles which would harmonize with the political ideals of the majority of the Russian people and which would guarantee the inalienability of the previously granted blessings of civic liberty. The economic policy of the Government must aim at the good of the broad masses, at the same time safeguarding those property and civil rights which are recognized in all the civilized countries.

The above-outlined foundations of the Government's activity will necessitate a great deal of legislative and administrative work. A period of time is bound to elapse between the enunciation of a principle and its embodiment in legislative norms or, furthermore, the introduction of these norms into the life of the people and the practice of the Governmental agents. No Government is able at once to force a new political régime upon a vast country with a heterogeneous population of 135 million, and an intricate administration brought up on other principles and traditions. It is not sufficient for the Government to adopt the motto of civic liberty to inaugurate the new order. Alone the untiring and concerted efforts of a homogeneous Government, animated by one aim and purpose, will bring it about.

The situation demands that the Government should only use methods testifying to the sincerity and frankness of its intentions. Consequently, the Government must scrupulously refrain from interfering with the elections to the Imperial Duma, and also sincerely strive to carry out the reforms outlined in the decree of December 12, 1904. The Government must uphold the prestige of the future Duma and have confidence in its work. So long as the Duma's decisions are not out of keeping with Russias's grandeur, the result of the age-long process of her history, the Government must not oppose them. In accordance with the letter and spirit of his Majesty's manifesto, the regulations relating to the Imperial Duma are subject to further development, in proportion as the imperfections of that institution come to light and as new demands arise. Guided by the ideas prevalent among the people, the Government must formulate these demands, constantly striving to satisfy the desires of the masses. It is very important to reconstruct the Imperial Council on the basis of the principle of elected membership, for that alone will enable the Government to establish normal relations between that institution and the Imperial Duma.

Without enumerating the other measures to be taken by the Government, I wish to state the following principles which, I believe, must guide the authorities at all the stages of their activity:

1. Frankness and sincerity in the establishment of all the newly granted rights and privileges.
2. A firm tendency toward the elimination of extraordinary regulations.
3. Coordination of the activities of all the Governmental agents.
4. Avoidance of measures of repression directed against acts which do not threaten either Society or the State, and
5. Firm suppression of all actions menacing Society or the State, in strict accordance with the law and in spiritual union with the moderate majority of the people.

It goes without saying that the accomplishment of the outlined tasks will only be possible with the broad and active coöperation of the public and on the condition of peace, which alone will enable the Government to apply all its forces to fruitful work. We have faith in the political tact of the Russian people. It is unthinkable that the people should desire anarchy, which, in addition to all the horrors of civil war, holds the menace of the disintegration of the very State.

While these two documents, which saw the light of day simultaneously, are identical in spirit and general tendency, they are badly coordinated and vary greatly in scope. The question arises, why did His Majesty find it advisable to issue two statements instead of expressing his will in one pronouncement? This and a number of other questions bearing upon the origin of the manifesto are answered by the subjoined memorandum on the manifesto of October 17, 1905 [see Chapter IX], written early in January, 1907. I composed it in order to nail to the barndoor the legend current among the court circles to the effect that I had forced the manifesto upon the unwilling monarch. It is a concise and scrupulously accurate history of the eleven days which preceded the publication of the manifesto. In another place I have told how I submitted it to His Majesty and how meanly he acted in this matter.

Vyacheslav Konstantinovich von Plehve
Minister of Interior (1902-1904)

Plehve was responsible for applying the Tsar's Russification plan in the provinces and also supported the pogroms. Having destroyed numerous uprisings he was eventually assassinated in 1904.

CHAPTER IX

THE MANIFESTO OF OCTOBER 17, 1905

IN view of the outbreak of deep unrest in all parts of Russia, especially in St. Petersburg and some other large cities, during September and the early part of October, 1905, following upon several years of continual ferment and political assassinations, Count Witte, the President of the Committee of Ministers, on the 6th of October, 1905, asked His Majesty to receive him and hear an analysis of the extremely alarming situation then existing. This request was made at the urgent instance of Count Solski, the President of the Imperial Council. On the 8th of October His Majesty wrote to Count Witte, stating that it had been his intention to summon him to discuss the actual state of affairs and directing him to come on the next day, the 9th of October, at about six o'clock in the evening.

On the 9th of October the President of the Committee of Ministers appeared before His Majesty and presented a hastily prepared memorandum, in which he expressed his views regarding conditions. At the same time he pointed out that in his opinion there were two courses of action: either to adopt the method outlined in his communication, orally submitted on that occasion, or to invest with complete power a responsible person (a dictator), who, with unremitting energy, might by dint of physical force suppress the turbulence in all its manifestations. For this task, he remarked, it would be necessary to select a man of resolute character and military training. He added that though the first measure seemed to him the more appropriate, his judgment might very well be erroneous, and, therefore, it would be desirable to consider this problem in conference with other government officials and with the members of the Imperial family, whom this matter might touch very closely. His Majesty, having listened to Count Witte, refrained from revealing his opinion.

On returning from Peterhof, Count Witte, together with N. I.

Vuich, at that time temporary chairman of the Committee of Ministers, reëxamined* the rapidly drafted report which had been presented to His Majesty, and made a few corrections, adding at the end that there was another way out: to breast the current, but that it would have to be done resolutely and systematically. Stating that he doubted the success of such a course, but that he was perhaps mistaken, he went on to say that in any case the fulfillment of this or the other line of action should be undertaken only by one who had complete faith in it.

The next day, October 10th, at three o'clock in the afternoon, Count Witte again had the honour of appearing before the Emperor, and, in the presence of Her Majesty, Empress Alexandra Feodorovna, related all his conclusions in detail, explaining the addition to his note and at the same time reviewing the alternate plan, which he had already laid before the Emperor. Their Majesties did not express their opinions, but His Imperial Majesty remarked *that perhaps it would be best to publish the substance of the report in the form of a manifesto.*

During the 12th and 13th of October Count Witte had no news from Peterhof. At about this time during one of the conferences at Count Solski's the discussion turned, among other things, to the very dangerous situation due to the turmoil, which was fast becoming a revolt, whereupon Adjutant-General Likhachov and Count Palen asserted their firm conviction that above all it was necessary to crush by force of arms every sign of turbulence. Count Witte did not hesitate to inform His Majesty of this fact in a special note, recommending at the same time that officials with such beliefs should be given a hearing. Some time afterwards Adjutant-General Likhachov inquired of Count Witte whether it was not at his suggestion that the Emperor had been good enough to summon him, to which Count Witte answered that he could not say, but that he had, indeed, considered it his duty to notify His Majesty that some of the functionaries had formed a clear conception of the course of action required by existing conditions, and that in his estimation it would doubtless be very helpful for His Majesty to give them an audience. On the 11th and 12th of October, Count Witte was told, his program was brought up for discussion; and on the 13th he received the following telegram from the Emperor:

* The mark over a vowel with a double-dot is called a diaeresis and indicates a separate syllable, e.g. as in Brontë.

"Until the confirmation of the Cabinet Law, I direct you to coordinate the activities of the ministers, whom I instruct to restore order everywhere. Only in the tranquil current of the Empire's life will it be possible for the Government to cooperate in constructive work with the future freely chosen representatives of my people."

By reason of this message Count Witte again went to Peterhof on the morning of the 14th and insisted that it would be impossible to allay the unrest merely through uniting the ministers holding different views, and that circumstances demanded the adoption of resolute measures in either of the directions already indicated. On this occasion, due to His Majesty's previous remark as to the desirability of publishing the substance of the note in a manifesto, Count Witte laid before His Majesty a summary of his report with a foreword explaining that the abstract had been drawn up at the order and direction of His Majesty, to whom it would be presented for official sanction in case it met with approval. As for the publication of a manifesto, which is proclaimed in all the churches, Count Witte pointed out that it was unadvisable to go into the necessary details in such a document, whereas it would be quite prudent to do so in an imperially sanctioned report, which would imply nothing more than the simple approbation by the Emperor of the program outlined therein, no responsibility devolving upon His Majesty in this way, since the burden of recommending the measures would fall upon Count Witte.

At this time in St. Petersburg, just as in many other municipalities, the strike of factory workers, as well as the employés of the railways and other public service utilities, was in full swing, so that the city was left without light, business facilities, street car and telephone service and railway communication. This state of affairs and the abovementioned telegram from the Emperor led Count Witte to call at his house a conference of some of the ministers, including General Rediger, General Trepov, Assistant Minister of the Interior and Governor-General of St. Petersburg, and Prince Hilkov, Minister of Railways, in order to discuss the steps to be taken for reëstablishing St. Petersburg's rail connections, even though only with neighbouring points. At this meeting the Minister of War and General Trepov, who was in command of the St. Petersburg garrison, affirmed that although there were sufficient forces in the city to suppress an armed uprising, should such occur there and in the nearby residence of the Emperor, not enough troops were available to restore railway traffic even between St. Petersburg and Peterhof. In a general way the Minister of War stated that, in addition to the regular military units, there had been ordered into the active army a large number of soldiers and officers who had been retained in European Russia. The forces were at the time filled up with men from the reserve, among whom general dissatisfaction had arisen because they had been kept in the army after the conclusion of peace. This circumstance, together with the lengthy period of service, had in large measure demoralized the troops of the Empire.

During the evening of the 14th, Prince Orlov informed Count Witte by telephone from Peterhof that he was asked to attend a conference called by His Majesty for the 15th at eleven o'clock in the morning, and that he should take along a draft of the manifesto, since it was essential that "everything should come from the Emperor personally and that the reforms sketched in the report should be transferred from the sphere of promises into the field of actualities granted by the Emperor." Although he judged it safer not to go beyond an Imperial sanction of his report and hoped that there would be no need of a manifesto, Count Witte, feeling ill that evening, requested Prince A. D. Obolensky, a member of the Imperial Council, who happened to be his guest at the time, to draw up a plan of the manifesto for the next morning.

Inviting Prince Obolensky and the chairman of the Committee of Ministers to accompany him, Count Witte again set out for Peterhof on the morning of October 16th. Baron Frederichs, the Court Minister, was travelling on the same steamer. In the presence of these people Prince Obolensky read his draft of the manifesto. Count Witte made a few observations, but, as they were nearing Peterhof at the moment, he asked Prince Obolensky and Vuich to try to formulate a more or less final version of the manifesto on the basis of their conversation, while he himself went to the court with Baron Frederichs. There he met Grand Duke Nikolai Nikolaievich and General Rediger. At eleven o'clock His Majesty received these four persons and directed Count Witte to read the report previously mentioned. Then Count Witte stated that to the best of his knowledge and belief there were but two ways out of existing difficulties, either to institute a dictatorship or to grant a constitution, on the road to which His Majesty had already started with the manifesto of August 6th and the subsequent decrees. His report recommended the second method, which, if sanctioned, must lead to the legislative enactment of measures that would broaden the law of August 6th and inaugurate a constitutional régime. During the reading Grand Duke Nikolai Nikolaievich, with His Majesty's permission, asked a great many questions, in answer to which Count Witte gave detailed explanations, adding, in conclusion, that he did not expect quiet to return quickly after such a bitter war and such wild turmoil, but that the second course promised to accomplish this result sooner.

At the termination of the report the Emperor asked Count Witte whether he had prepared a manifesto. Count Witte replied that during the trip to Peterhof he had examined a draft of the manifesto, which was then being revised; but that in his opinion it would be more expedient for the Government to limit themselves to a sanction of the report he had just read. At one o'clock His Majesty dismissed all those present, instructing them to return at three and directing Count Witte to bring the proposed manifesto.

The conference was resumed at three o'clock and, after a continuation of the exchange of ideas regarding the report, Count Witte read the draft of the manifesto. None of those present raised any objections.

On the evening of October 16th Baron Frederichs gave Count Witte to understand that he would visit him to discuss the manifesto. The Baron, together with the Director of his Chancery, General Mosolov, arrived after midnight and said that His Majesty, aside from conferring with those present at the meeting the previous day, had advised with others and that Goremykin and Budberg, members of the Imperial Council, had formulated two plans for the manifesto, with which the Emperor had commissioned them to acquaint Count Witte. In the first place Count Witte inquired whether all this was known to General Trepov, who controlled the police of the entire Empire and shouldered the responsibility for the outward order of the country, so that any comprehensive measure, if not confided to him beforehand, might result in very unpleasant events. Baron Frederichs replied that he was so late precisely because he had been at General Trepov's to inform him of everything. Then he presented the two drafts* to Count Witte, who observed that the sketch drawn to his attention as the more suitable was unacceptable to him for two reasons: first, on account of its direct

*These drafts were taken away by Baron Frederichs and I was unable to get possession of them again.

direct announcement that His Majesty granted all the privileges from the day of its publication, whereas in his project the Emperor merely asked the Government to carry out his determined desire to confer these liberties, thus presupposing preliminary work by the Government; secondly, because of its omission of many important provisions outlined in his report and because of its incompatibility with the simultaneous publication of the report, the soundness and power of whose principles would at once be subject to doubt. For these reasons he requested Baron Frederichs to declare to the Emperor that in his opinion as he had already pointed out, it was unnecessary to publish a manifesto, but that it was sufficient and more prudent to proclaim His Majesty's approbation of the report. To this the Baron retorted that the question as to whether or not the reforms suggested in the report should be announced to the people in the shape of a manifesto had been decided once and for all. Upon hearing this reply, Count Witte asked Baron Frederichs to tell His Majesty that, since the office of President of the Cabinet must be conferred upon a person with an acceptable program and he felt that His Majesty entertained certain doubts as to the accuracy of his judgment in this matter, it would, under the circumstances, be advisable to abandon any idea of appointing him prime minister; furthermore, in the event of the final rejection of the plan of selecting a dictator to suppress the unrest by force, to choose a man with a more satisfactory policy for the task of coordinating the activities of the ministers. He added that if the manifestoes he had just read were recognized as adequate, one of the authors should in his estimation be appointed President of the Cabinet. In conclusion Count Witte requested Baron Frederichs to report to His Majesty that in case of need, as he had already stated to the Emperor, he was ready to serve the common cause in a secondary capacity, even though it be as governor of a province.

The next day, the 17th of October, Count Witte was again summoned to Peterhof, and, on arriving, he immediately went to Baron Frederichs. The Baron informed him that it had been decided to accept his draft for the manifesto and to sanction the report presented by him, adding that this decision had the unqualified support of Grand Duke Nikolai Nikolaievich, who had affirmed that on account of the lack of troops it was impossible to institute a military dictatorship.

At about six o'clock Count Witte and Baron Frederichs went to the palace, the Baron taking with him the manifesto, which had been copied in his office. Grand Duke Nikolai Nikolaievich was in the palace. His Majesty signed the manifesto and sanctioned Count Witte's report in their presence. Both of these documents were announced to the people on the same day with the knowledge of General Trepov.

I have in my possession two other memoirs relating to the period covered in my memorandum and written respectively by N. I. Vuich, formerly secretary of the Council of Ministers and now senator, and Prince N. D. Obolensky, His Majesty's secretary and practically associate Minister of the Court. These two men had an exceptional opportunity to observe the inner court circles and they were abreast of all that was happening around the Emperor in those critical days. It is, therefore, gratifying for me to find that their story tallies in every respect with my own account of the events which led up to the act of October 17.

I shall now relate some of the episodes and state some of the thoughts, for which there was no room in my Memorandum in view of its conciseness and purely factual character.

I was struck by the indifference to the fate of the country and the dynasty, which the Grand Dukes displayed during those decisive days. Nikolai Nikolaievich was out hunting in his estate and did not arrive in St. Petersburg until the 15th, while Peter Nikolaievich was staying in the Crimea. I am certain, however, that had any member of the Imperial family shown an active interest in the political situation and made an attempt to direct the course of events, he would have been politely told to mind his own business.

When His Majesty for the first time referred to the manifesto, I assumed an attitude toward it which was at first one of skepticism and later became one of decisive hostility. I feared that it might defeat its purpose and throw the country into a confusion worse confounded instead of pacifying it. Nor did I have faith in the efficacy of a dictatorship. If I did hope for it internally, it was, I confess, for purely selfish reasons. A dictatorship would, of course, deliver me from the necessity of assuming the reins of power. I had no illusions as to the thanklessness of the task. I knew that should I succeed I would be destroyed because the Court would be afraid of my success, and that, should I fail, friend and foe would be equally glad to fall upon me and undo me. Afterwards I found out the reason

MANIFESTO OF OCTOBER 17, 1905

why His Majesty insisted on issuing a manifesto. As a matter of fact, he had been persuaded by his satellites that I was aiming at becoming neither more nor less than the first President of the All-Russian Republic. This assertion of mine may appear fantastic, but it is nevertheless true. I was seeking, His Majesty was told, to associate my own name, and not his, with the measures which were to pacify the Empire. To thwart my evil plans, it was necessary to publish the manifesto. "Let us make use of Witte's ideas; later on we can get rid of him." That is how, I imagine, the Emperor's intimate counsellors argued.

While negotiating with me, His Majesty was secretly conferring with other statesmen. In fact, he simultaneously conducted two independent sets of conferences with two political groups holding strongly opposed views and headed respectively by myself and Goremykin, the man who was destined to succeed me as Prime Minister. This double-dealing exasperated me. It was clear to me that even in these critical circumstances His Majesty was incapable of playing fair. Had Emperor Nicholas in those decisive days acted with uprightness and good faith, as behooves a Russian Czar, much misunderstanding and misery would have been avoided. Had Goremykin and I been given a chance for an open and frank exchange of opinions, the common feeling of responsibility would have surely compelled us to take a more or less balanced decision, in spite of the wide divergence of our political views and sympathies. But as we were engaged in a hide-and-seek game, events were naturally developing by fits and starts, and documents of historic importance were drawn up hurriedly and without the care and caution which the significance of the subject demanded.

On October 16 I had a telephonic conversation with Baron Frederichs. It had come to my knowledge, I told him, that conferences were taking place in Peterhof with Goremykin and Baron Budberg, and that a number of alterations in my version of the manifesto were being contemplated. I had nothing against these changes, I assured him, but should they be effected His Majesty would have to abandon the idea of putting me at the head of the Government. I reiterated that, in my judgment, it was entirely unnecessary at this time to publish anything in the nature of a public manifesto. The baron gave me his assurance that the contemplated changes related exclusively to the wording of the document and were altogether insignificant. He promised to show me the altered version in the evening. When the baron came to me,—it was past midnight,—I found that the suggested changes were so substantial that in reality there were two different versions of the manifesto. I decided to put an end to this unworthy game. With my customary bluntness, I asked the baron to inform His Majesty that I flatly refused to accept any version of the manifesto which did not agree with my program, and that if he did not have sufficient confidence in me he had better put at the head of the Government one of the men with whom he was having secret conferences. I was in a rather excited state when the baron left me. Remaining alone, I prayed to the Most High that He should deliver me from this tangle of cowardice, blindness, craftiness, and stupidity.

Here is what Baron Frederichs told me the next morning, when I came to see him at Peterhof: "This morning I repeated to His Majesty the conversation I had with you last night. He made no reply. He was apparently waiting for Grand Duke Nikolai Nikolaievich. I left him. As soon as I returned to my quarters, the Grand Duke came to see me. I told him what had happened, concluding my story with these words: 'It is necessary to set up a dictatorship and you must be appointed dictator.' In reply he produced a revolver from his pocket and said: 'Do you see this firearm? I will now go to the Emperor and beg him to sign the manifesto and Witte's program. He will either do it, or I will blow my brains out with this very weapon!' With these words he left me. After a while the Grand Duke returned and transmitted to me His Majesty's order to prepare clean copies of the manifesto and your report and, when you come here, to take these documents to the Emperor who will sign them."

I understood then that there was no way out for me. The same morning General Mosolov, Director of the Chancery of the Court Ministry, had a conversation with Baron Frederichs just after the end of the latter's interview with the Grand Duke. General Mosolov afterwards reported to me the substance of the baron's words. "All the while," the baron said, "I was hoping that the situation would end in a dictatorship, with Grand Duke Nikolai Nikolaievich as the natural dictator, for it seemed to me that he was brave and absolutely devoted to the Emperor. Now I find that I was mistaken. He is a mean-spirited and unbalanced man. Everyone shirks the responsibilities of a dictatorship; we have all lost our heads, and so we must give in to Witte, whether we like it or not."

For a long time I did not know why the Grand Duke was so resolutely in favour of the act of October 17. I was sure, of course, that he had not been prompted either by liberalism or by an understanding of the country's internal state. His sympathies had always been with autocracy of the most unlimited and arbitrary character. As for his rational powers, they had long since been befogged by an inordinate passion for occultism. At any rate, I was convinced that, whatever may have been the precise reason, cowardice and mental confusion played an important part in determining the course of the Grand Duke's actions. P. N. Durnovo, who was unusually well informed about a variety of confidential matters for the reason that he was in charge of the perlustration division of the Ministry of the Interior, told me, in 1907, that the Grand Duke's attitude toward the constitutional manifesto was to be accounted for by the influence exerted upon him in those days by a certain Ushakov, a labour leader. I knew this man as one of the few workmen who did not lose their heads during the revolutionary days and who refused to join the Soviet in 1905. I had a talk with him and at my request he composed a memorandum for me, describing his relations with Nikolai Nikolaievich and, in general, the role he played in the October days. According to this document, which is in my possession, Ushakov had gained access to the Grand Duke through Prince Andronnikov and a certain Naryshkin, and on the eve of October 17, 1905, Ushakov had an interview with him, in the course of which he insisted on the granting of a constitution as the only way out of the critical situation. I have told elsewhere how short-lived was the Grand Duke's affection for the new-born Russian constitution. A few weeks after the publication of the manifesto I learned that he was conspiring with the head of the Black Hundred Party, the ill-famed Dubrovin.

CHAPTER X

BLOODY SUNDAY AND THE FIRST SOVIET

IN the early days of the Russo-Japanese war, General Kuropatkin on one occasion reproached Plehve, I recollect, with having been the only Minister to desire the Russo- Japanese war and make common cause with the clique of political adventurers who had dragged the country into it. "Alexey Nikolayevich (i.e., Kuropatkin)," retorted Plehve, "you are not familiar with Russia's internal situation. *We need a little victorious war to stem the tide of revolution.*"

History made a mockery of the calculations of Plehve and his like. Instead of enhancing the prestige and increasing the physical resources of the régime, the war, with its endless misery and disgrace, completely sapped the system's vitality and laid bare its utter rottenness before the eyes of Russia and of the world generally, so that the population, whose needs had been neglected for many years by a corrupt and inefficient government, finally lost its patience and fell into a state of indescribable confusion.

I shall begin my narrative of the revolutionary upheaval of 1905-1906 with my reminiscences relating to the events of January 9, 1905, a day which in the annals of the Russian revolution is known as Bloody Sunday.

A certain Sergey Zubatov, a notorious agent-provocateur, is responsible for the idea of combatting the revolution by applying the principle of "knock out one wedge with another." He inaugurated a system which aimed at fighting the revolution with its own weapons and tactics, and which might be described as police socialism. The revolutionists are winning over the workmen to their side by preaching the doctrine of the socialistic millennium to them, he argued;—let us, therefore, imitate the methods and the language of the socialistic agitators, and we shall have the masses with us. And Zubatov proceeded to organize a veritable "labour movement," with trade-unions, workers' meetings, lecture clubs, etc., all under the auspices of the Secret Service. The city of Moscow, with its large industrial population, was Zubatov's headquarters, and his activities had the coöperation and unqualified approval of both Grand Duke Sergey Alexandrovich, Governor-General, and General Trepov, Governor of Moscow. Both the department of factory inspection and myself, in my official capacity, were strenuously opposed to Zubatov's scheme, but we could do nothing against the all-powerful Grand Duke. Sipyagin, Minister of the Interior, merely succeeded in restricting Zubatov's efforts to Moscow.

When Sipyagin was assassinated (in 1902), his successor Plehve extended the experiment with police socialism to St. Petersburg. He began to organize there workmen's societies of a counter-revolutionary nature, on the model of the Moscow organizations, in order to keep the labouring masses under the influence of the department of police. The task of organization was entrusted to Father Gapon, who soon succeeded in gaining the entire confidence of the Governor of St. Petersburg. Then, of course, the inevitable happened. The preaching of the socialists and anarchists gradually demoralized the workmen, and they began instinctively to strive to carry into effect the extreme program of socialism. Not only was Gapon unable to stem this movement, but gradually he, too, became infected with the revolutionary spirit. A storm was brewing, while neither Prince Mirski nor I, in my capacity of President of the Committee of Ministers, nor the Government knew anything about the matter.

On January 8th, I was told by the Minister of Justice that in the evening there would be a conference at Prince Mirski's for the purpose of deciding what to do with the workmen who intended the next day to march to the Palace Square and present a petition to His Majesty. The Minister assured me that I would be invited to the conference because of my familiarity with the labour problem, but, as a matter of fact, owing to the opposition of the Minister of Finances, I was not invited to the conference. In the evening a deputation of public-spirited citizens came to see me. I received the committee and recognized among the delegates the academician Shakhmatov, the author Arsenyev, and also Maxim Gorki. The spokesman of the delegation begged me to see to it that the Emperor should appear before the workmen and receive their petition. Otherwise, they said, a great disaster was inevitable. I refused to do anything, for the reason that I had no knowledge whatever of the matter and that it was not within my province. The men left, indignant at the fact that at such a critical time I stood on formalities. As soon as they were gone I informed Prince Mirski over the telephone about the delegation. The next morning, from my balcony, I could see a large crowd moving along the Kamennoostrovski Prospect. There were among it many intellectuals, women, and children. Before ten minutes were over shots resounded in the direction of the Troitzky Bridge. One bullet whizzed past me, another one killed the porter of the Alexander Lyceum. The next thing I saw was a number of wounded being carried away from the scene in cabs, and then a crowd running in disorder with crying women here and there. I learned afterwards that it was decided at the abovementioned conference not to allow the marchers to reach the Square, but apparently instructions were not issued in time to the military authorities. There was no one present to speak to the workmen and make an attempt to bring them to reason. I do not know whether the same thing happened everywhere, but on the Troitzky Bridge the troops fired rashly and without rhyme or reason. There were hundreds of casualties killed and wounded, among them many innocent people. Gapon fled and the revolutionists triumphed: the workmen were completely alienated from the Czar and his Government.

Afterwards, when Trepov was appointed Governor-General, he conceived the happy project of removing the horrible impression of Bloody Sunday on the workmen. Having secured from the employers the names of those workmen who were reliable to the extent of being willing to do a spy's work, he took a dozen of them to Tsarskoye Selo and introduced them to His Majesty as representatives of the St. Petersburg workmen. The "delegates" expressed their loyal feelings to the Emperor, and His Majesty delivered before them a speech, written out beforehand, assuring them that he had their needs at heart and would do for them everything within his power. Thereupon, the "delegates" were dined and taken back to St. Petersburg. On the working masses of the capital the whole farce produced no effect whatever, and some of the "delegates" got such a hot reception from their comrades that they were forced to leave the factories where they were employed.

When I became President of the Council of Ministers, an effort was made to have me meet Father Gapon, who, I was told, regretted his part in the disaster of January 9, 1905, and, now that a constitution had been granted, was anxious to help pacify the country. I refused to see him and informed Manuilov-Manusevich, who approached me on his behalf, that if Father Gapon did not leave St. Petersburg within twenty-four hours he would be arrested and tried. The following day I was informed that Gapon was ready to go abroad, but that he lacked the necessary funds. I gave Manuilov 500 rubles with the understanding that he would see Gapon out of Russia. Some time later I was again asked to allow Gapon to return to Russia. It was asserted that, in view of his influence on the workmen, he could be exceedingly useful in the struggle against the anarchists and revolutionists. My reply was to the effect that I would never have anything to do with that man. In March, 1906, I heard from Minister Durnovo that Gapon was in Finland and that Rachkovsky, the chief of the Secret Service, was negotiating with him about his, Gapon's, proposal to betray the entire fighting organization of the central revolutionary committee into the hands of the Government. Gapon asked 100,000 rubles for that service; Rachkovsky offered 25,000. I observed that the price was a matter of, no importance but that generally I had no confidence in the man. I next heard that he had been assassinated in Finland.

After the January disaster events followed with ominous rapidity, and by September, 1905, when I returned from my peace mission in America, the revolution was in full swing. A great deal of harm was done by the press. Having started to get out of hand at the beginning of the war, the press grew bolder and bolder as defeat followed upon defeat in the East, and in the month preceding October 17th it kicked over the traces altogether, not only the liberal, but also the conservative organs. Although not with the same ultimate ends in view, all preached revolution in one way or another and adopted the same slogans: "Down with this base, inefficient government." "Down with the bureaucracy!" "Down with the present régime!" The St. Petersburg papers, which had set the pace for the whole Russian press and still do, though not to such a great extent, emancipated themselves completely from the censorship and went so far as to form an alliance based upon a tacit agreement to disregard the censor's orders. Almost all the newspapers joined this league, even the conservative, including *Novoye Fremya*. In this connection it is interesting to note that later on, when the revolution was crushed, *Novoye Fremya*, forgetting its past behaviour, was the first to accuse the Government of weakness and the press of demoralization.

On October 19, 1905, if I remember rightly, I had a conference with the representatives of the press. The chief spokesman of the delegation was the editor of *Birzheviya Viedomosti,* a Jew by the name of Propper. He spoke very boldly and with that arrogance which is characteristic of a certain type of educated Russian Jew. The tenor of his speech was to the effect that the press had no confidence in the Government. He demanded that the troops be removed from the capital and that the preservation of order in the city be entrusted to the municipal militia. He also demanded complete freedom of the press, universal amnesty, and the dismissal of General Trepov. That this man, who used to spend long hours in the ante-chambers of influential persons, in an effort to obtain a government advertisement or some other privilege for his sheet, that this man should speak to me, the head of the Government, in such a tone was sufficient proof that Russia was possessed by a peculiar sort of dementia. No, I could not lean upon the press in my effort to placate the country.

The newspapers informed the public of the many unions which had been organized throughout the country and coordinated by a central union of unions. About the proceedings of some of these organizations, for instance about the Academic Union, the papers gave extensive reports, but regarding the rest they limited themselves to stating that such and such a union had held a meeting somewhere and had taken important measures. Besides these bodies, there was, of course, the Union of Zemstvo and Town Delegates, with its permanent bureau, which played an important rôle. With this society were connected the leaders of the so-called public workers, some of whom became reactionary after experiencing the "amenities" of the revolution. Guchkov, Lvov, Prince Galitzin, Krasovsky, Shipov, Stakhovich, Count Heyden, and others of the same class belonged to this union, as well as secret republicans and idealistic politicians, some of them persons of great literary and oratorical ability, such as Hessen, Miliukov, Gredeskul, Nabokov, Shakhmatov, member of the academy, etc. All these unions, despite wide differences in composition and aims, joined in the preliminary task of overthrowing the existing régime. In endeavouring to accomplish this they acted in accordance with the maxim that the end justifies the means. Consequently they were not squeamish about their tactics, especially about blazoning forth palpable lies in the press. In fact, at the time the newspapers were nothing but a mass of falsehoods, the conservative as well as the radical. But it must be admitted that when the revolution broke out and anarchy was rampant, the conservative sheets outdid the radical in spreading lies, slander and wild rumours.

The Government took no measures, or only ineffectual ones, to counteract and stop the subversive activities of the unions and of the press. Probably it did not have the necessary information regarding the aims and doings of many of the unions. Very likely, too, it was misled by incompetent advisers. For instance, I was told afterwards that the Union of Railway Workers, which later brought on the railroad strike, was vigorously, defended by Prince Hilkov on the ground that this organization was purely economic and fraternal in character without any anti-Government tendencies. As far as the enforcement of the censorship is concerned, the difficulty of the task was tremendously increased by the existence of a widespread secret press, which turned out and distributed millions of copies of all sorts of revolutionary pamphlets, programs and proclamations.

What prevented the Government from coping promptly and successfully with the revolutionary outbreaks was the lethargy, incompetence and timidity prevalent among executive and administrative officers. To begin with, the Minister of the Interior, Bulygin, was altogether apathetic because he was aware that in reality not he, but General Trepov, ruled. In his turn, Trepov was almost out of his mind. He worked in starts and fits and writhed with apprehension as he saw the storm come sweeping on. Broken in health and spirit, he longed to escape from the whole incomprehensible nightmare. He told me that he could stay no longer at his post of Associate Minister of the Interior, actually a position of dictatorship, which he had created for himself. Indeed, the desire to retire from the places of responsibility was very common at this time. The sagacious and skeptical K. P. Pobiedonostzev, for instance, abandoned the whole business except that he corresponded with the Emperor. The rest of the ministers, a colourless insignificant lot, Kokovtzev, Schwanebach, General Glazov, and General Rediger, kept silent and did nothing.

The revolution made its appearance first in the border territories, the Baltic provinces being the earliest to show signs of deep unrest. In that region it took the form of agrarian disturbances. The chief reason for this was the policy of Russification which the Government pursued in that territory. The lower classes of the population of the Baltic provinces consist, as is known, of Letts, while the upper class is made up of Germans. In trying to Russify the region, our Government has succeeded, during the last several decades, in destroying the elements of culture which the German masters had forced upon the Letts. This was done through the instrumentality of the Russian school, with its liberal spirit, so thoroughly opposed to the mediæval traditions in which the German nobility educated the Lettish peasant. As a result, the effect of the Russification policy was to pit the Lettish plebeian against the German aristocrat. Small wonder that, when the revolutionary wave reached the narrow-minded, staunch Letts, they responded to it by a veritable orgy of burning and looting the German landowners' property. In consequence, the leaders of the Baltic nobility, for instance, Budberg and Richter, the President of the Court of Appeals, urged the Government to establish military rule in that territory. As a matter of fact, at Mitau and in the southern districts adjacent to that city there was already something in the nature of martial law. I did not wish, however, to grant the desire of the Baltic barons.

To remedy the situation I created a provisional General-Governorship for the territory comprising the Kurland, Estland and Livland districts, with Lieutenant General Sologub as Governor-General. In that capacity, General Sologub, who was appointed at my instance, won my unqualified approval. He acted courageously and openly and endeavoured to restrain the unbridled cruelty of some of his subordinates. Thus, he saved Riga from the punitive detachment headed by Her Majesty's favourite, General Orlov. It was perhaps for this reason that General Sologub was forced to give up his post. He was succeeded by General Meller-Zakomelski, who had more faith in the efficacy of a policy of ruthlessness.

As early as the beginning of 1905, Finland was in a state of latent conflagration. Upon ascending the throne, Nicholas II by a special manifesto solemnly proclaimed his intention to respect the privyleges granted to Finland by his predecessors. Such was indeed his sincere desire. During the first year of his reign he expressed his willingness to permit the Finns to establish a direct connection between the Finnish and Swedish railroads, although I pointed out to him that his most august father was opposed to that measure for strategic reasons. He did not doubt, he said, the loyalty of his Finnish subjects, and he had complete confidence in them.

When General Kuropatkin became Minister of War, he raised the question of Russifying Finland. He wished to distinguish himself.

As long as Count Heyden, the Finnish Governor-General, was alive he held Kuropatkin's zeal in check. But soon the count died, and General Bobrikov was appointed to succeed him. When I congratulated him upon his nomination, he remarked that his mission in Finland was analogous to that of Count Muraviov in Poland. The comparison was rather unexpected, and I could not refrain from observing that while Count Muraviov had been appointed to suppress a rebellion, he was apparently commissioned to create one. . . . That was our last friendly conversation. . . .

Soon afterwards Kuropatkin hatched a project of a military reform in Finland. Simultaneously an Imperial manifesto was issued decreeing that all the legislative matters affecting the interests of the Empire should be passed upon by the Imperial Council. This was a violation of the Finnish constitution granted by His Majesty's predecessors and confirmed by himself. Kuropatkin laid his project before the Council, in the hope that this body would pass it, in spite of the opposition of the Finnish Diet. I vigorously opposed the reform as the Minister of War conceived it, and I drafted what I considered to be an acceptable version of the project. I had behind me the majority of the Imperial Council and also the public opinion of Finland. Nevertheless, the Emperor sanctioned Kuropatkin's project, which was naturally supported by Bobrikov and Plehve.

In the meantime, the Russification of Finland was being carried into effect. The Russian authorities took a number of measures, which from the Finnish standpoint were clearly and aggressively illegal. The Russian language was forced upon the Finnish schools, the country was flooded with Russian secret agents, Finnish senators were dismissed and replaced by men who had nothing in common with the people, and those who protested were deported from the country. As a result Bobrikov was assassinated, the terroristic act being committed not by anarchists but by Finnish nationalists, and the country became a hotbed of unrest.

In consequence, the outbreak of the revolution in Central Russia was a signal for the beginning of the revolution in Finland. Prince Obolensky, the Governor-General, immediately gave up the struggle and after a while resigned. I was aware that a Finnish insurrection would greatly complicate the revolutionary chaos in Russia. On the other hand, I was always opposed to the policy of persecution inaugurated in Finland by Nicholas II. Therefore, when the Finnish representatives came to me and assured me that the Finns would forget all their grievances and quiet down, if the Russian Government would conscientiously observe the privileges granted to the duchy by the Emperor Alexander I and Alexander II,—I, on my part, expressed my conviction to His Majesty that it was imperative to revert to. the Finnish policy of his predecessors. I pointed out to him that the Finns had always been loyal as long as they were treated decently, and that it was highly dangerous to create a second Poland close by the gates of St. Petersburg. I urged His Majesty to respect the liberties granted to the Finns by Emperors Alexander I and Alexander II. At my recommendation, the Emperor appointed Gerard as Governor-General of Finland, to succeed Prince Obolensky, who had tendered his resignation. Upon Gerard's appointment Finland ceased to be the stage for the rehearsal of revolutionary tragedies intended for Russia. At present, it seems, Russian militant chauvinism is again turning against Finland, in the hope of making trouble. It is noteworthy that the Empress Dowager Maria Fiodorovna was completely out of sympathy with Bobrikov's policy. She repeatedly intervened before the Emperor in behalf of the persecuted Finns.

At this juncture Poland was also permeated with a spirit of revolt, but the malcontents were forced to keep under cover and disturbances occurred only sporadically because of the comparatively large army stationed there. It was commanded by Governor-General Skalon, who, while not a marvel, was at least a brave, straightforward man. He had been chosen shortly before when his predecessor, General Maximovich, a petty character, appointed on the recommendation of the Court Minister, Baron Frederichs, was removed because he deserted to his country villa near Warsaw, whence he did not emerge till after the storm had blown over. He had been recommended merely in return for a favour rendered to Baron Frederichs at the time of the latter's marriage, which was a misalliance.

When I became President of the Cabinet of Ministers, in October, 1905, I found Poland in a state of complete anarchy, assassinations and other terroristic acts happening daily. The disturbances were partly agrarian, partly industrial, in character. The situation was complicated by the nationalistic movement which united all classes of the population by a common aspiration for national independence, some dreaming of a separate Polish kingdom united to the Empire only in the person of the monarch, but most hoping for local autonomy. In view of all this, I conferred with the Governor-General and declared the country in a state of war, which measure aroused more indignation among the radical Russians than among the Polish masses. It was condemned by the Russian liberals, and it served as a pretext for the socialists to call a second general strike, which was, however, unsuccessful. It was clear to me that in our enthusiasm for political emancipation, we Russians had lost all respect for our glorious history and its product, the great Russian Empire. The radicals confused emancipation from the misrule of bureaucrats and courtiers with emancipation from all the traditions of our historical existence.

A Polish delegation came to see me and made an attempt to persuade me to lift the state of war in Poland. Their chief spokesman, a well-known Polish lawyer, impressed me as very intelligent. He was aware, he said, that Poland's separation from Russia was a fantastic dream and that the Russian Government had no choice but to take stringent measures against the outbreaks of anarchy in Poland, but, he asserted, the Russian régime and culture were alone to blame for the intolerable state of affairs in the Polish provinces. For that reason the Poles, he said, were anxious to keep away from the Russians. "The labor problem," he went on, "is of long standing in Poland, but, as in the west, it had developed in an orderly, evolutionary fashion. The revolutionary germ we owe to you Russians. After the pogrom organized by Plehve at Kishinev and the subsequent anti-Jewish riots, a great many Jewish artisans and workmen emigrated to Poland, where the Jews are treated more humanely. It was these Russian emigrants who imbued our workmen with their militant, embittered anarchism and their terroristic methods of political struggle. Your Jews have debauched ours, just as wild animals would infect domesticated ones with their savagery. And, of course, your Jews cannot help being wild, since you deny them the sum of human feelings and aspirations. Our schools are infested with socialistic propaganda, the product of Russian nihilism. Where did those obnoxious ideas come from? From your schools and colleges. Our children respect their parents and their elders. They revere their religion, their culture, their language, their literature, they have faith in their nationality and they believe that 'Poland has not yet perished.' The only result of your attempt to Russify us was to de bauch our children and to deprive them of those sacred traditions which alone form a strong nation. You have taken our dearest possessions and, in exchange, you have given us nothing but your nihilism, in its various aspects." He finished his philippic by a plea for reconciliation and for the lifting of the state of war. I found it, however, impossible to grant his desire, for I was assured from an authoritative Russian source that those Poles who had anything to lose would at heart regret the removal of martial law.

Odessa, too, was seething with rebellion. There were two special causes for the extreme disorder in this city. In the first place, the Jews, who formed a large proportion of its inhabitants, supposed that, by taking advantage of the general confusion and the undermining of the Government's prestige, they would be able to obtain equal rights through revolution. At this time only a comparatively small number of the Jews were active, but the overwhelming majority, having lost patience long before by reason of the many injustices practised against them, sympathized with the so-called emancipatory movement, which was now adopting revolutionary tactics. In the second place, the uprising was largely provoked by the brutality of the Municipal Governor, Neidhart, who was bitterly hated by most of the inhabitants. Fitted neither by education nor by experience for such an important position, he had been appointed simply because he was Stolypin's brother-in-law, the same reason for which he was later made senator. The appointment may also have been due partly to the fact that the Czar had taken a liking to Neidhart as the buffoon officer of the Preobrazhensky regiment, in which His Majesty served during his youth. Neidhart, though not stupid, was very superficial and ignorant, but he had a high opinion of himself and excited such hostility by his arrogance and harshness toward his subordinates and the people that I had to remove him soon after the 17th of October, an action for which he and his sister, Premier Stolypin's wife, have been my enemies ever since.

In the southeastern territory, Governor-General Kleigels had become inactive and when the October days came, he abandoned his post altogether. Previously he had been Governor of St. Petersburg. He was a dull-witted individual, but the Emperor liked him very much, wholly, I imagine, because of his knightly appearance and his imperturbable demeanour. As police chief, Kleigels was perhaps in the right place, but he was totally unfit to occupy such an important place as the governor-generalship of Kiev; and when the Emperor appointed him, all who had not given up the attempt to follow the course of events were greatly astonished.

In the Caucasus both the country districts and the towns were in full blaze, and all sorts of excesses were committed daily. The lieutenant, Count Vorontzov-Dashkov, tried to pursue a policy of conciliation, but all he actually put into practice was a perpetual interchange of liberal and reactionary measures. On the whole, the count, though not very intelligent, meant well and was endowed with common sense, but he failed principally on account of his inability to choose capable subordinates.

The whole of Siberia was in a terrible turmoil. This was due to the fact that this territory had been for a long time, as it still is, a reservoir for criminals, exiles and restless people generally. Furthermore, being nearer to the theatre of war, Siberia felt its shame more keenly, and having witnessed the traffic to and from the battlefields, was more deeply horrified at its disasters. Besides, here, too, the situation was aggravated by the presence of an inefficient governor-general. Kutaisov, who held the office and had his headquarters at Irkutsk, did not lack intelligence, but he was not a man of action and wasted his time in talking continually and to no purpose. It was said that he had been appointed merely to satisfy the wish of the Empress, Alexandra Fyodorovna, who, as a girl, while visiting her grandmother, Queen Victoria, had become acquainted with Kutaisov during the time that he was our military attaché in London. The administration's power in Siberia was also impaired by the frequent disputes between Kutaisov and Sukhotin, the Governor-General at Omsk, who was dependable, straightforward and clever, but somewhat irascible.

The border provinces were clearly taking advantage of the weakening of Central Russia to show their teeth. They began to retaliate for the age-long injustices which had been inflicted upon them and also for the measures which, although correct, outraged the national feeling of the peoples which we had conquered but not assimilated. They were ardently waiting for what appeared to them as their deliverance from the Russo-Mongolian yoke. For this situation we alone were to blame. We failed to perceive that since the days of Peter the Great and, especially, since the reign of Catherine II, we had been living not in Russia, but in the Russian Empire. The dominating element of the Empire, the Russians, fall into three distinct ethnic branches: the Great, the Little, and the White Russians, and 35 per cent, of the population is non-Russian.

It is impossible to rule such a country and ignore the national aspirations of its varied non-Russian national groups, which largely make up the population of the Great Empire. The policy of converting all Russian subjects into "true Russians" is not the ideal which will weld all the heterogeneous elements of the Empire into one body politic. It might be better for us Russians, I concede, if Russia were a nationally uniform country and not a heterogeneous Empire. To achieve that goal there is but one way, namely to give up our border provinces, for these will never put up with the policy of ruthless Russification. But that measure our ruler will, of course, never consider. On the contrary, not content with all these Poles, Finns, Germans, Letts, Georgians, Armenians, Tartars, etc., etc., within our borders we conceived a desire to annex a territory populated by Mongolians, Chinese and Koreans.

I assumed the duty of ruling the Russian Empire in the capacity of President of the Committee of Ministers in October, 1905. At that time the country was in a state of complete and universal confusion. The Government was in a quandary, and when the revolution boiled up furiously from the depths, the authorities were completely paralyzed. They either did nothing or pulled in opposite directions, so that the existing régime and its noble standard bearer were almost completely swept out of existence. The rioting grew more fierce, not daily but hourly. The revolution came out openly on the streets and assumed a more and more threatening character. Its urge carried away all classes of the people.

A general feeling of profound discontent with the existing order was the most apparent symptom of the corruption with which the social and political life of Russia was infested. It was this feeling that united all the classes of the population. They all joined in a demand for radical political reforms, but the manner in which the different social groups visioned the longed-for changes varied with each class of people.

The upper classes, the nobility, were dissatisfied and impatient with the Government. They were not averse to the idea of limiting the Emperor's autocratic powers, but with a view to benefiting their own class. Their dream was an aristocratic constitutional monarchy. The merchants and captains of industry, the rich, looked forward to a constitutional monarchy of the burgeois type and dreamed of the leadership of capital and of a mighty race of Russian Rothschilds. The "intelligentzia," i.e., members of various liberal professions, hoped for a constitutional monarchy, which was eventually to result in a bourgeois republic modelled upon the pattern of the French State. The students, not only in the universities, but in the advanced high school grades, recognized no law, except the word of those who preached the most extreme revolutionary and anarchistic theories. Many of the officials in the various governmental bureaus were against the régime they served, for they were disgusted with the shameful system of corruption which had grown to such gigantic proportions during the reign of Nicholas II. The zemstvo and municipal workers had long before declared that safety lay in the adoption of a constitution. As for the workmen, they were concerned about filling their stomachs with more food than had been their wont. For this reason they revelled in all manner of socialistic schemes of state organization. They fell completely under the sway of the revolutionists and rendered assistance without stint wherever there was need of physical force.

Finally, the majority of the Russian people, the peasantry, were anxious to increase their land holdings and to do away with the unrestrained arbitrary actions on the part of the higher landed class and of the police throughout the extent of its hierarchy, from the lowest gendarme to the provincial governor. The peasant's dream was an autocratic Czar, but a people's Czar, pledged to carry out the principle proclaimed in the reign of Emperor Alexander II, to wit, the emancipation of the peasants with land in violation of the sacredness of property rights. The peasants were inclined to relish the idea of a constitutional monarchy and the socialistic principles as they were formulated by the labourite party, which party emphasized labour and the notion that labour alone, especially physical labour, is the foundation of all right. The peasants, too, were ready to resort to violence in order to obtain more land and, in general, to better their intolerable condition.

It is noteworthy that the nobility was willing to share the public pie with the middle class, but neither of these classes had a sufficiently keen eye to notice the appearance on the historical stage of a powerful rival, who was numerically superior to both and possessed the advantage of having nothing to lose. No sooner did this hitherto unnoticed class, the proletariat, approach the pie than it began to roar like a beast which stops at nothing to devour its prey.

Anticipating upon the course of events, I may say that when the nobility and the bourgeoisie beheld the beast, they began to fall back, or rather face to the right. Suvorin, the head of *Novoye Fremya*, who three years before had prophesied the coming of the "spring" and rejoiced in relishing its fragrances in advance, turned into a charlatan shouting every day at the top of his voice: "I want a constitution, but for the good of Russia all should be done in accordance with the will of His Majesty and of us, who have incomes of a hundred thousand rubles." In a word, for a hundred years the nobility had dreamed of a constitution, but for itself alone. When they discovered that the constitution could by no means be a noblemen's constitution, they embraced the political faith of scoundrels like Dubrovin, Purishkevich, and other Black Hundred leaders.

I have already told how the aliens,—and in the empire 35 per cent, of the population consists of non-Russians,—seeing this great upheaval, lifted their heads and decided that the time was ripe for the realization of their dreams and desires. The Poles wanted autonomy, the Jews equal rights, etc.; and all of them longed for the annihilation of the system of deliberate oppression which embittered their existence. To cap the climax, the army was in an ugly mood. Discipline had been undermined and morale shaken by the terrible defeats of the war, which the soldiers blamed on the Government, and justly so. Besides, there was a great deal of trouble about demobilization. Due to the enormous demands of the war in the east, the military forces in European Russia had been reduced to a minimum, so that when peace was concluded, the Government considered it inadvisable to fulfil its promise of demobilizing all those who had been called to the colours during the war. Enraged at the breaking of this pledge, the soldiers mutinied in many places, and frequently small detachments fought the Government under the orders of revolutionary leaders. Many of the officials, concluding from these disorders that the whole army was unreliable, had deep misgivings about the return of the forces stationed in the east. It was this apprehension that led to a project of retaining at least a part of the eastern army in Siberia, bribing the men into acquiescence by granting them free land in that territory, ostensibly as a reward for their services to the country.

Anarchistic attacks directed against the lives of government officials; riots in all the institutions of higher learning and even in the secondary schools, which were accompanied by various excesses; trouble in the army; disturbances among peasants and workmen, involving destruction of property, personal injury and loss of life;

and finally strikes, such were the main conditions with which the authorities had to cope. On October 8, 1905, traffic on the railroads adjoining Moscow ceased completely. It took the railway strike but two days to spread to the Kharkov railroad junction, and on October 12th, the St. Petersburg junction was tied up. In the subsequent days traffic ceased on the remaining railroads. By October 17th, nearly the entire railway net and the telegraph were in a state of complete paralysis. About the same time almost all the factories and mills in the large industrial centres of Russia came to a standstill. In St. Petersburg the strike in the factories and mills began on the 12th day of October, and on the 15th the business life of the capital was completely tied up.

Thus all these ills came to afflict the land at one and the same time and such terrible confusion resulted that one can truthfully say that Russia's soul cried out in agony for relief from the torment of chaos. The universal exclamation was: "We can live like this no longer. The present insane régime must be done away with." To accomplish this purpose, leaders and fighters, both of thought and deed, arose from every class of the people, and not a handful, but thousands and thousands. While it is true that they were after all only a small minority, nevertheless their might was irresistible, for almost everybody sympathized with them and longed for their success.

The city of St. Petersburg, the intellectual capital of the country, with its large industrial population was, naturally enough, one of the chief storm centres of the revolution: It was there that the council (Soviet) of Workmen's Deputies came into being. The idea of setting up this institution was born in the early days of October, and the press began to agitate for it among the working population of the capital. On October 13th, the first session of the Soviet took place in the Technological Institute. At this session an appeal was issued to the workmen of the capital, urging them to strike and to formulate extreme political demands. The second session took place in the same building the following day. At this session a certain Nosar, a Jew and an assistant attorney-at-law, was elected president of the Soviet. Nosar, for purposes of propaganda, worked as a weaver at Chesher's factory and was known there under the name of Khrustalev. The working population of St. Petersburg, almost in its entirety, carried out the decision of the Soviet with complete submission. On October 15th, the Soviet met again in the same building, this session being attended by several professors and a few members of other liberal professions, who took an active part in the discussions. The next day, in consequence of the publication of new rulings concerning public meetings, the school and university buildings were closed down. For this reason the Soviet could not meet that day. On October 17th, the Soviet held a session in the hall of the Free Economic Society. By that time it counted upward of two hundred members.

The historical manifesto which granted the country a constitution was issued on the 17th of October, 1905, and on the same day "The Bulletins (*Izviestiya*) of the Soviet of Workmen's Deputies," a purely revolutionary organ, began to be printed in turn in several printing houses. Needless to say, this was done in spite of the owners of the presses, who were far from being revolutionaries.

At the time when I entered upon my office (the 18th of October), this Workmen's Soviet appeared at the first glance to be a considerable power, for the reason that it was obeyed by the working masses, the printers included. The last circumstance was of particular importance, for it meant that the newspapers were to a certain extent controlled by the Soviet, since the publication of the papers depended, in the last account, upon the willingness of the printers to work. The printers' devotion to the Soviet affected most intimately A. S. Suvorin, the editor and publisher of *Novoye Vremya*. This great newspaper was first of all a profitable business establishment and had for a long time been treated as such by its owner. He was a talented publicist and a patriot, but with the growth of his profits and vast fortune, he was willing to sacrifice more and more of his ideals and talents to the interests of his pocket. He started his journalistic career without a penny to his name and died the owner of a fortune estimated at five million rubles. Yet several months before he died he expressed his dissatisfaction with Russia. Had he lived and worked in America, he complained, he would have accumulated tens of millions, while in Russia he had made but a miserable fortune of some two or three million rubles.

The Workmen's Soviet met on October 18th and decided to declare a general strike, as an expression of the workmen's dissatisfaction with the manifesto. Nevertheless, the strike movement in Moscow and elsewhere began to wane and railroad traffic was soon restored to normal conditions. Under these circumstances the Soviet, at its session of October 19th, decided to call off the strike two days later. During the days following closely upon the publication of the manifesto, frequent clashes took place in the streets of the capital between the revolutionaries, on one side, and the troops, the police, and counter-revolutionaries, on the other. During these clashes, several people were killed and wounded. Among them was Professor Tarle, of the St. Petersburg University, who was wounded in the head, near the Technological Institute. The Soviet attempted to organize demonstrations in connection with the funeral of the fallen workmen, but the Government did not permit it. After October 17th, I gave orders to allow all peaceful processions arranged in connection with the manifesto, but to suppress the demonstrations at the first sign of disorder and violation of the public peace. The demonstration which was to accompany the funeral was clearly intended to cause disorder and consequently was not permitted.

Generally speaking, several days after October 17th St. Petersburg quieted down, and throughout the six months of my premiership I did not enact a single extraordinary measure relating to the administration of St. Petersburg and its, district. Nor was there a single case of capital punishment. All the extraordinary measures were taken later, when Stolypin inaugurated the policy of undoing the reform of October 17th.

One of the faults with which I have been charged is that during my premiership I did not shoot enough people and kept others from indulging in that sport. Whoever hesitates to shed blood, it was argued, should not hold so responsible a post as I did. But, on my part, I consider it a special merit that during the six months when I was in power only a few dozen people were killed in St. Petersburg and no one executed. In the whole of Russia fewer people were executed during those months than in several days under Stolypin, when officially law and order prevailed in the country. History will condemn the reign of Nicholas II for the indiscriminate courtmartialing of men and women, adults and adolescents, for political crimes committed two, three, four, and even five years previous to the execution.

Elsewhere in Russia, however, the demonstrations connected with the manifesto were accompanied by disorders. Thus, for instance, on October 26th, riots broke out at Kronstadt. They were not quelled until October 28th. Kronstadt, a city administered by the Ministry of the Navy, was revolutionary to an extraordinary degree. The spirit of revolt was rooted deeper among the sailors than in the army. Even before October 17th, this spirit manifested itself in military pronunciamentos among the sailors at Sebastopol and partly at Nikolayev and Kronstadt. This revolutionary spirit became rampant among the sailors because of the naval authorities' misrule and also because the sailors were recruited from the more intelligent elements of the population, which fall an easier prey to revolutionary propaganda. It must be borne in mind that in those days the revolutionizing process was going on among vast masses of people.

The publication of the manifesto gave rise to numerous joyful demonstrations all over the country. They were met by counter-demonstrations conducted by bands known as Black Hundreds. These bands, which were so nicknamed because of their small numbers, were made up of hooligans. But as they were supported in some places by the local authorities, they soon began to grow in number and weight, and then it all ended in a pogrom directed mostly, if not exclusively, against the Jews. Furthermore, as the extreme Left elements were also dissatisfied with the manifesto because of its insufficient radicalism and also indulged in rioting without meeting sufficient moral opposition on the part of the liberals, the hooligans of the Right, that is, the Black Hundreds, soon found support in the central administration and then also higher up.

In connection with the Department of Police a printing press was set up for turning out pogrom proclamations intended to incite the dark masses mostly against the Jews. This activity, to which I put an end, was revealed to me by the former Director of the Police Department, Lopukhin, who is now in exile in Siberia. But in the provinces this activity was going on as before. Thus, in my premiership a pogrom was perpetrated against the Jews at Homel. The riot was provoked by the gendarmerie. When I discovered this shameful incident, and reported it to the Council of Ministers, His Majesty wrote on the memorandum about this affair that such matters should not be brought to his attention (as too trivial a subject).... The Emperor must have been influenced in this case by the Minister of the Interior, Durnovo.

After the strike was over, beginning October 27th, the workmen in several mills started to introduce by direct action the eight-hour workday. The Workmen's Soviet took advantage of the situation and decreed the forceful introduction of the eight-hour day. The Soviet felt that it was losing its prestige among the workmen. On November 1st it called a second general strike, emphasizing the necessity of this measure as a protest against the introduction of martial law in Poland and also against the manner in which the Government suppressed the riots at Kronstadt. I learned about this step that same night and I wired at once to the workers of several mills, warning them to cease obeying persons who, clearly, were leading them to ruin and starvation. In my dispatch I told the workers that I was advising them in a spirit of comradeship. The phrase was rather unusual in mouth of the head of the Government addressing the workmen. Some of the newspapers, *Novoye Vremya* included, took up the phrase and began to make sport of it. On the other hand, the labour leaders, touched to the quick by the influence my dispatch exerted upon the workers, grew furious. Nevertheless, the strike proved a failure, the workmen ceased to obey the Soviet and their leaders, and, therefore, on the 5th of November the Soviet decided to call off the strike. Generally speaking, the strikes were over by November 7th, and the Emperor wrote to me on that same day: "I am glad that this senseless railroad strike is over. This is a great moral triumph for the Government."

On November 13th, the Soviet again considered the proposition of declaring a general strike. The plan was rejected, and the Soviet was also constrained "temporarily" to discontinue the forceful introduction of the eight-hour workday. From that time on the authority of the Soviet began rapidly to decline and its organization to decay. It was then that I found it opportune to have Nosar arrested. The arrest was made on November 26th. Thereupon the Soviet elected a presidium of three to replace Nosar. This presidium held secret sessions, while the body of the Soviet did not meet at all. I had intended to have Nosar arrested at an earlier date, but Litvinoff-Falinski, now in charge of one of the departments of the Chief Management of Commerce and Industry, persuaded me to refrain from so doing. He argued that it was necessary to postpone the arrest till the workmen would welcome it, that is, until Nosar and the Soviet would have lost all prestige. In this fashion we would avoid an unnecessary clash with the workmen, a clash which might prove bloody. This was judicious advice. After Nosar was taken, I ordered the arrest of the whole Soviet, which order Durnovo carried out on December 3rd. Durnovo feared that the members would disperse and escape if he started arresting them separately. He therefore waited for the Soviet to meet, which the latter hesitated to do. Their fears were well founded, for as soon as the body gathered on December 3rd in the Hall of the Free Economic Society, the members, 190 in all, were rounded up and arrested. After Nosar's arrest the Soviet had attempted to put through a plan for a general strike as a protest against the arrest, but their efforts were in vain.

Thus ended the affair of the Workmen's Soviet and its leader, Nosar. The matter was greatly overdrawn by the press, for the simple reason that these strikes, involving, as they did, the printers, touched the pockets of the newspaper people. Of course, there were among the journalists men who sympathized with the "Workers' Revolution," but those were impecunious* journalists, mostly dreamers. Revolution always and everywhere brings forth such fanatical idealists.

Since 1905 there have been no serious strikes in Russia. The strike movement during the revolution taught the workers to assume a very skeptical attitude toward leaders like Nosar. It also taught the employers a lesson. To a certain extent they have bettered the conditions of the workers. The Government, too, learned a lesson. This year the Government has enacted a workmen's insurance law, despite the masked opposition of some of the representatives of industry sitting in the Imperial Council and Duma. This law was practically approved about twenty years ago, when I was Minister of Finances, but met with constant obstruction. Nevertheless, the revolution appears not to have taught any lesson to the gendarmerie and secret police. This very year an officer of the gendarmes, Tereschenko by name, if I remember rightly, caused upwards of 200 Lena miners to be shot, although the men tried to better their intolerable condition by peaceful means and only after their patience had been tried for many years. The local administration was apparently in the pay of the rich gold mining corporation and did nothing to thwart its predatory greed. The Minister of the Interior, Makaroff, in trying to justify the slaughter of the miners by the gendarmes, laid before the Duma a most far-fetched and false report on the subject and concluded his speech with this hideous exclamation: "Thus has it ever been, thus will it ever be." Of course, one need not be a prophet to foretell that if it is true that such things

---

* having little or no money.

did happen (as in the case of Gapon, which was staged by Von Plehve), it is equally true that such a scheme of things cannot last forever. A régime under which such slaughters are possible cannot long exist, and October 17th is the beginning of the end.

After I had left the post of President of the Council of Ministers, some papers spread the rumour that I had received the chief leader of the Soviet and, with him, a delegation from the Soviet. Some of the Black Hundred leaders charged me with having entertained criminal relations with the Soviet and the revolutionists. Others went further and declared that I had set up the Soviet myself. *Novoye Fremya* is responsible for the silly joke to the effect that during my premiership there were two governments, Count Witte's and Nosar's, and it was for a while uncertain who was going to arrest whom: Witte Nosar or Nosar Witte.

I wish to declare here, in reply to all these fantastic rumours, that I have never in my life laid eyes on Nosar, and have never had any relations with either the Soviet or the revolutionists. Nor did I ever receive any members of the Soviet as such. Should they have come to me I would have dispatched them to the city governor. In general, I attributed no importance to this Soviet. It exerted an influence only on the workmen of the St. Petersburg district, and for that reason alone it seemed to me ridiculous to speak of its political significance. As soon as I judged it timely to arrest its members, I did so, without shedding a drop of blood. There were rumours that some compromising papers were in the hands of the Minister of the Interior relating to my alleged negotiations with the Soviet. I need not add that the rumours were entirely false.

The main centre of the revolutionary movement was, however, not St. Petersburg, but the ancient city of Moscow. Since the 'nineties of the last century Moscow had been the nest of opposition. More than bureaucratic St. Petersburg, Moscow was the laboratory of radical political and social ideas.

The régime of Grand Duke Sergey Alexandrovich and General Trepov, Governor-General and Governor, respectively, could not but drive all the classes of the population into the arms of that genuine, national opposition which springs from discouraged conservatism and prejudiced material interests. Moscow was the birthplace of the conventions of zemstvo and municipal leaders, who were destined to form the General Staff of the opposition forces.

After the assassination of Grand Duke Sergey Alexandrovich, the Government appointed General Kozlov, the former Chief of Police, to succeed him. Kozlov was a splendid man, respected by everybody, but, unfortunately, he was soon forced to resign, as he could not get along with General Trepov. Thereupon, P. P. Durnovo was chosen at the request of Count Solski, who before that had taken him into the Imperial Council. Very wealthy, a general, and ex-President of the St. Petersburg Municipal Duma, he was a peculiar combination of a liberal and an old-time despot, altogether disqualified for any serious business and wholly incapable of enlisting either the sympathy or the support of any social group or party in the city. In Moscow he was lost, did not have the least conception of what was going on, and finally became so bewildered that on one occasion he went out into the square, I was told, in the Adjutant-General's uniform, doffing his military cap, to talk things over with the revolutionary mob assembled under the red flag.

The whole of Moscow was in either open or secret opposition, including the representatives of the nobility and of the merchant class. Some of the Moscow millionaires contributed liberally not only to the cause of the constitutional movement, but even to the revolution. The industrial king Savva Morozov donated several millions to the revolutionists, through an actress who lived with Maxim Gorki and with whom Morozov was infatuated. Early in 1905, I remember, Morozov asked me over the telephone to receive him. I granted his desire, and he expressed to me the most extreme opinions to the effect that we must get rid of the autocracy, introduce a parliamentary system, etc., etc. Taking advantage of the fact that I had known him for many years and that I was many years his senior, I laid my hand on his shoulder and said to him: "As I wish you well, I shall give this advice: Attend to your business, and keep away from the revolution." Morozov was visibly taken aback, but my words sobered him and he thanked me for my advice. He was later caught red-handed in Moscow. To avoid a scandal, the police proposed to him that he leave the country. Abroad he became completely entangled in the revolutionary net and committed suicide.

Another leading spirit of the Moscow industrial world, Krestovnikov, chairman of the Stock Exchange Committee, if I remember rightly, came to see me soon after the publication of the constitutional manifesto. The purpose of his visit was to plead for a lowering of the rate at which the Imperial Bank discounted bills of exchange. In those days the country was passing through a severe financial crisis, and the safety of the gold standard of our currency depended upon my success in concluding a foreign loan. Without explaining to him our financial situation, I merely told him that I was unable to grant his desire. Krestovnikov clutched his head in despair, and exclaiming, "Give us the Duma, call it as soon as possible!" dashed out of my study like a crazed man. It is astonishing to what extent prominent public men misjudged the situation in those days. The Duma election law was already known at that time. Nevertheless, here was a notable representative of the moneyed class who imagined that, as soon as the Duma was convoked, I would proceed to enact measures furthering the interests of capital. But when the Duma failed to justify the hopes of the propertied classes, they backed out of the game of liberalism, and the stray sheep returned to the fold of autocracy.

The authorities were powerless to control the course of events in Moscow. Ill-informed and inefficient, they shirked their responsibilities, evaded personal dangers and shrunk from fighting the oncoming revolution. The story of the Moscow Peasant Congress is a fitting illustration of the state of affairs in the ancient Russian capital. I learned that the Congress was definitely committed to the policy of compulsory expropriation of private land property without compensation. In general, it was called for the open propaganda of most extreme revolutionary ideas. I did not for a moment doubt that the Governor-General would either prohibit the Congress or confer about the matter with the central government. Suddenly I learned from the newspapers that the Congress had opened. I telegraphed to the Governor-General warning him of the character of the Congress. For several days I received no answer. Finally, the convention was closed by the police, after it had held a number of sessions and succeeded in spreading broadcast a great many revolutionary ideas. This laxity of the authorities is largely accounted for by the terroristic activities of the revolutionaries.

Accidentally, I had a private source of information about the situation in Moscow. Once, when I was Director of the South-Western Railroads, a young woman, whom I had previously met at the house of a colleague, came to me and begged me, with tears in her eyes, to give her a chance to gain an honest living. I placed her in one of the numerous offices of the Railroad Management. Some years later I met her in St. Petersburg. Several weeks after the publication of the manifesto a lady came to see me and introduced herself as the wife of a well-known Moscow judge. I recognized in her the girl to whom I had done the little service many years before. She confided to me that a friend of hers was in love with a young man who occupied a prominent place in the revolutionary movement, and that through her she was *au courant* of the plans of the revolutionists. She told me that a regular insurrection with all its classical attributes, such as barricades, etc., was in the course of preparation in Moscow. The revolutionists being aware, she said, of the demoralization and panic of the administration and the troops, were seeking to deal the blow before the authorities came to themselves. She was prompted, she added, to disclose this to me by a desire to repay me for my kindness toward her and to save her friend.

Impressed by her words, I urged the Emperor to appoint a reliable Governor in Moscow. In the meantime, the revolutionary wave was rising higher in Moscow, and the intelligence which I received from my lady informant was growing more and more alarming. On November 9th (22), while His Majesty was leaving a session of the Council of Ministers, which took place under his presidency, I stopped him and declared that, unless a resolute and energetic man was appointed to take charge of Moscow, the city might fall into the hands of the revolutionists,—which event would be a signal for general anarchy in the country. I insisted that General Dubasov should be immediately appointed Governor-General of Moscow, and His Majesty granted my request. General Dubasov arrived in Moscow several days before the outbreak of the insurrection. Shortly afterwards, he requested me to assist him in getting more troops. The Minister of War informed me that a regiment sent from Poland was due in Moscow three days later. The regiment did not arrive in time, for the reason that the revolutionists made an attempt to wreck the train which carried a part of it. Before the regiment arrived General Dubasov asked again for troops from St. Petrograd. He informed me that he had barely enough men to guard the railway stations and that the city proper was altogether denuded of troops. I immediately telephoned to General Trepov asking him personally to tell His Majesty that I considered the immediate dispatch of troops an absolutely imperative measure, if we wanted to prevent the capture of the city by the revolutionists, with its numberless disastrous consequences. In the evening General Trepov informed me that His Majesty asked me to go to Grand Duke Nikolai Nikolaievich and persuade him to send troops to Moscow. I complied with His Majesty's request and went to see the Grand Duke. He realized that the troops at General Dubasov's disposal were few and demoralized, but he argued that his chief task at the time was to insure the personal safety of the Emperor and his august family and that, should he part with a portion of his forces, he would jeopardize His Majesty's person. As for Moscow, he was willing to let it go to the dogs. Was it not, he argued, the fountain head of revolution? On my part, I argued that St. Petersburg was practically safe while Moscow was in imminent danger. Our conversation lasted several hours, and it was well past midnight when a courier brought a note from His Majesty addressed to the Grand Duke. He read it and said: "His Majesty requests me to send troops to Moscow. I will do so." I urged him to make haste and left. The troops dispatched to Moscow included nearly the whole of the Semenov regiment and also some cavalry and artillery. I understand that the insurrection was suppressed unsystematically and with excessive cruelty on the part of the men of the Semenov regiment. The only ones to blame, however, are the civil authorities who did not take the necessary measures in due time and who did not prevent the demoralization of the local troops. General Dubasov was, no doubt, the only man in Moscow who did not lose his head and he saved the situation by his courage and good faith. As soon as the storm blew over, the St. Petersburg troops were withdrawn and General Dubasov wrote to the Emperor asking him to be magnaminous and not to try the arrested insurrectionists by court-martial. When consulted by His Majesty, I sided with the General, and as long as the two of us were in power the Moscow revolutionists were tried by civil courts, although the Minister of the Interior, Durnovo, advised court-martialing.

An unsuccessful attempt, as is known, was made on General Dubasov's life. The bomb which was hurled at his carriage killed his adjutant, Count Konovnitzyn, and also the driver, if I remember rightly, but left the General unharmed. He resigned from his post when I gave up mine. Though His Majesty did not persecute the General, he was cold to him, for the reason that on several occasions Dubasov expressed opinions which went against His Majesty's grain. In 1907 another totally unsuccessful attempt was made on Dubasov's life by a youthful revolutionist. I went to see him several hours after the attempt. He was perfectly composed. The only thing that deeply worried him was the fate of the youth who had shot at him. He feared that Stolypin's court-martial would make short shrift of his would-be assassin. "I cannot be calm," he told me; "I constantly see before me his boyish, kindly eyes, crazed with fear. It is ungodly to execute such irresponsible youths." He read me the letter he had written to the Emperor begging him to forgive the young terrorist. His Majesty replied the next day to the effect that he did not think he had the right to hinder the automatic and immutable course of justice, as administered by the newly established military courts. I scarcely know whether to qualify this reply as Jesuitic or puerile*. His Majesty did not find it at all impossible, however, to pardon men convicted of crimes against Jews and Liberals.

I need not say that all those who were arrested in connection with the attempt were immediately hanged. I might add, to complete the story, that the lady who, unwittingly, was the source of my information about the plans of the revolutionists succeeded in escaping abroad together with her lover.

Dmitry Feodorovich Trepov, (b. 1854-1906)

Chief of Police and Governor General of St Petersburg and later Commandant of the Imperial Palace, 1905.

Trepov distinguished himself by putting down rebellions but was unable to supress the revolution in 1905.

His brother Alexander, became Prime Minister (November 1916 to January 1917) and was unable to supress the revolution in 1917.

---

* Jesuitic - relating to the Jesuits, the trait of being crafty, subtle reasoning to conceal the truth or to avoid committing oneself.
Puerile - immature, petulant

CHAPTER XI

THE LOAN THAT SAVED RUSSIA

SHORTLY after my arrival from my peace mission in the United States, I had a heart-to-heart talk with Count Dimitry Solski, President of the Imperial Council, about Russian home affairs. "Count," he repeated, "you alone can save the situation." When I declared that it was my intention to keep aloof by all means, and to go abroad for a few months' rest, he burst into tears and reproached me for my egoism and lack of patriotism. "Go abroad!" he exclaimed. "In the meantime we shall all perish here!"

Unwilling to shirk the duty I owed to my Monarch and country, I did not go abroad. Although I had no illusions about the difficulty and thanklessness of the task, I assumed the burden of power and bore it for six months. My appointment as President took place immediately upon the publication of the historical manifesto of October 17th, which granted the Russian people civic liberties and a parliamentary régime.

In October, 1905, the Government had neither troops nor funds with which to fight the revolution. I soon perceived that only two things could save the dynasty and enable Russia to weather the revolutionary storm, namely, a large foreign loan and the return of the army from Transbaikalia and Manchuria to the European part of the country. These two measures, coupled with a determination on the part of the Government to carry out in good faith the promises of the constitutional manifesto, I was certain, would pacify the country.

At the time when I assumed the task of ruling the country, the bulk of the army, about a million men, was in far Manchuria. Those units which remained in Russia were largely depleted, both in their personnel and military equipment. As a matter of fact, the whole vast body of the Russian army was in a state of complete physical and moral prostration. Owing its existence, as it did, to universal military conscription, the army could not help being affected by the spirit of general discontent which prevailed in the country. Indeed, the most extreme subversive ideas found a fertile soil among the military, who felt more keenly than the civilian population the pain and disgrace of the disastrous war into which the country had been dragged by its irresponsible rulers. It should be noted that actual cases of mutinies in the army were rather infrequent, this being perhaps due to the energy Grand Duke Nikolai Nikolaievich displayed in dealing with the outbreaks.

Several days before my appointment I conferred with the Minister of War and General Trepov, then commander of the St. Petersburg garrison, for the purpose of ascertaining to what extent we could depend on the troops in case it should be decided to crush the revolution by armed force. The impression I gained from that conference was that the army was unreliable for two reasons, namely, because of its numerical weakness and its dangerous state of mind. This circumstance perhaps accounts for His Majesty's decision in preferring the road of reforms to the unstinted application of sheer force. I cannot explain His Majesty's choice otherwise, for like all weak people he believes most in physical force.

After the ratification of the Portsmouth treaty, in accordance with the letter of the law, it was necessary to discharge the reservists who had been called to the colours for the duration of the war. Since these soldiers were the most troublesome element of the army and had infected with revolutionary ideas both the Transbaikalian troops and the units stationed in European Russia, I had them demobilized immediately. As a result, the army at my disposal diminished in numbers, but it was purged of the troublesome element, which was at any moment liable to break out in uncontrollable mutinies. Thus, European Russia was practically denuded of troops. A sufficient number of them was available only in the St. Petersburg, Warsaw and Caucasian military districts, but as the situation in those regions was threatening the commanders there were extremely reluctant to part with their units for the benefit of other regions. Central Russia was almost completely deprived of troops. The disorganization was so great that the military authorities themselves did not know how many men were available and where they were stationed. Most of the units in the rear were far below their normal strength, but the military authorities were in many cases ignorant of the extent to which the units had been depleted. At the request of the local administration, a battalion would be dispatched, after long delay, to quell a peasant riot. We would next hear that, instead of a battalion no more than, say, a dozen men had arrived. We would then turn to the army authorities and learn that most of the personnel of the battalion in question was at the front. Such cases, I remember, were by no means exceptional. This chaotic condition, I later found out, was the result of General Kuropatkin's activity as Minister of War.

As we had at our disposal neither troops nor rural police, it was impossible to combat the agrarian disorders with any degree of efficiency. In the course of my premiership I succeeded in increasing and improving the police force, both municipal and rural. But at the height of the disturbances in some places there was no police at all, and even in Moscow the force was poorly armed. The policemen often reported for duty with empty revolver cases for all arms.

Since the local administration was in many places demoralized, I conceived the plan of sending His Majesty's Adjutant Generals to those districts where the situation was most alarming. Thus, Adjutant General Sakharov was sent to the government of Saratov, Adjutant General Strukov to the governments of Tambov and Voronezh, and Adjutant General Dubasov to the governments of Chernigov and Kursk. General Dubasov acted very energetically, but in such a way as not to arouse anyone's animosity. He was profoundly impressed by the extent and importance of the agrarian disturbances. He urged me, I recall, without waiting for the opening of the Duma to enact a law whereby the land forcefully seized by the peasants would be made their legitimate property. This, he argued, would pacify the peasants. As for the landowners, he said, it would be best for them, too, for otherwise the peasants would seize all the private estates and. leave nothing to their owners.

The peasant riots were caused by Russian conditions and also, to a certain extent, by the propaganda of the socialists.

In shaping the course of the revolution an exceedingly important rôle was played by the whole gamut of socialistic doctrines, from Tolstoy's Christian communism to "anarchistic socialism," which served as a disguise for plain robbery,—all these teachings having in common a denial of property rights as defined in Roman law. During the last fifty years the ideas of socialism have advanced with vigorous strides throughout the whole of Europe. They found a fertile soil in Russia, owing to the constant violation of every right, especially of property rights, on the part of the authorities, and also because of the lack of culture among the population. The revolutionists promised the factories to the workmen and the land of *pomieshchiki* (landowners) to the peasants, declaring that these commodities belong to the people by right, and had been unjustly taken away from them. The workers naturally responded with strikes, while the peasants began to practise what, in imitation of an orator of the French Revolution, Deputy Herzenstein in the First Duma called "the illumination" of the landowners' estates, i.e., they began to burn and loot the property of the landed gentry.

The Manchurian armies were naturally anxious to get home. Owing to the railroad strikes in European Russia and in Siberia, the Far East was oftentimes cut off from the rest of Russia for weeks together. As a result the most fantastic rumours spread among the troops like wildfire. Making his way home through Siberia, after the conclusion of the Portsmouth treaty, Prince Vasilchikov did not know, until he reached Cheliabinsk, whether the Emperor was still in Russia, for he had heard rumours to the effect that the Imperial family had escaped abroad and that my colleagues and myself had been strung up on lamp-posts on the Champ de Mars in St. Petersburg. This story I have from His Majesty himself.

I am under the impression that toward the end of 1905 the army at the front was thoroughly demoralized and revolutionary. If this was not a matter of common knowledge, it is because it was the policy of the military authorities to hide the plagues which were corroding the very heart of the army.

The first revolutionary wave, originating in the West, moved eastward and infected the Transbaikalian army. A movement in the opposite direction began toward the end of 1905, some of the discharged soldiers from the front bringing the revolutionary germ into the interior of the country. Alarming news of the state of mind of the Manchurian army had reached St. Petersburg in previous months. Under the influence of this news, the Minister of Agriculture, Schwanebach, laid before the Committee of Ministers a plan for allotting the crown lands in Siberia to the soldiers in active service who would consent to settle there. After a short discussion of this singular scheme, the committee declined to consider it further, and the whole matter came to nothing.

The strike on the Great Siberian Railroad, coupled with the eagerness of the troops to return home, completely disorganized the Eastern Chinese Railway, which circumstance added to the dissatisfaction of the army. The railroad strikes were responsible for the delay in assembling recruits and in transporting the Manchurian armies home. At one time the Siberian railroads were in the hands of self-constituted bands and organizations which refused to obey the governmental authorities. The revolutionists perceived that no sooner did the troops reach their homes than they lost all their revolutionary ardour and turned into a bulwark of law and order. For that reason they made every effort to keep up the railroad strikes in Siberia.

Traffic on the Siberian and Eastern Chinese Railways oftentimes ceased completely, and the troops indulged in rioting as they made their way westward. Then the strike of the telegraph operators came to increase the confusion. Day after day passed and the armies were still far away from Central Russia, their absence complicating both the internal and the international position of the country. I repeatedly pointed out the seriousness of the situation to Grand Duke Nikolai Nikolaievich, to the Minister of War, and to the Chief of the General Staff, General Palitzyn. They replied quite correctly that the matter was within the province of General Linevich, Commander-in-Chief of the armies in active service. The only official communication I received from the Commander-in-chief throughout the six months of my premiership was a dispatch informing me that fourteen (I remember that number very distinctly) anarchist-revolutionists had arrived at the front to stir up trouble in the army. I showed this telegram to His Majesty and he returned it to me with the following words written on the margin: "I hope they will be hanged."

At this juncture, I hit upon the idea of dispatching two military trains, one from Kharbin westward, the other from European Russia eastward, under the command of two firm and resolute generals, instructed to open up normal traffic on the Siberian roads and remove the causes which hindered the regular functioning of the roads. His Majesty was pleased by this idea and adopted my plan. General Meller-Zakomelski was placed at the head of the expedition which had Moscow as its starting-point, while the train dispatched from Kharbin was put under the command of General Rennenkampf. The two generals were ordered to reopen normal traffic and restore order along the Siberian railways *at any price*. They acquitted themselves of their task with eminent success, and the two trains effected a junction near Chita. Naturally enough, this extraordinary measure could not be carried into effect without severe repressions. On reaching Chita, which was entirely in the hands of revolutionists, General Rennenkampf proceeded to execute a number of people. While he was restoring order at Chita, my wife once came to me in alarm and showed me a telegram sent to her from Brussels, in the name of the Russian revolutionary group of that city. It read as follows: "If your husband does not immediately cancel Rennenkampf's death sentences, he and the following men (names follow) will be executed, your daughter and grandson will be killed on the same day." As a matter of fact, my daughter lived in Brussels with her husband, K. V. Naryshkin, who served at our Embassy, and they had a one-year old boy for whom both my wife and myself had an affection almost morbid in its intensity. Of course, I paid no heed to this threat, which, by the way, the revolutionists failed to carry out. This incident illustrates the perfection to which the revolutionists carried their system of underground communication, and also the difficult position in which we were in those days.

Simultaneously Commander-in-Chief Linevich was dismissed and General Grodekov appointed in his stead, at my recommenddation. He succeeded in restoring order in the army and transporting the Manchurian armies into the interior of the country. At my suggestion, the location of the troops was altered, with a view to the most effective suppression of local insurrections and riots. My principle was to oppose force to force and to take the most drastic measures against an open uprising, but at the same time I was against the practice of mass executions months and years after order had been restored.

My next great task was to secure a foreign loan. As early as 1904 the need for a foreign loan became apparent. At that time our financial system was already giving way under the pressure of the war expenditures. In concluding our second commercial treaty with Germany in 1904, I succeeded in securing Germany's permission to float our loan in that country. The next year I made an effort to prepare the ground for the loan in France and in the United States, where I went on the Portsmouth peace mission. My intention was to conclude the loan before the opening of the Imperial Duma. As I felt sure that the first Duma would be unbalanced and to a certain extent revengeful, I was afraid that its interference might thwart the loan negotiations and render the bankers less tractable. As a result, the Government, without funds, would lose the freedom of action which is so essential during a period of upheaval.

I had a keen personal interest in the loan. It must be borne in mind that I was responsible for the adoption by Russia (in 1896) of the gold standard of currency, and it was doubly painful for me to see this standard seriously threatened by the financial crisis brought about by the war, on the one hand, and by the nearsighted policy of the Minister of Finances, on the other. He waited for the end of the war to conclude a large loan, but he failed to foresee the outbreak of the revolution, with its disastrous effect on our credit.

France was willing to open its money market to us, but as a preliminary condition the French Government demanded the conclusion of peace with Japan. When the Portsmouth treaty was concluded, new obstacles presented themselves, notably the Franco-German conflict over Morocco, and the Paris Government made the conclusion of the loan contingent upon the peaceable settlement of that conflict. Elsewhere, in my remarks on the Kaiser, I tell the story of how I succeeded in having the clash arbitrated by an international conference at Algeciras. The conference lasted till the end of March, 1906, and until its termination the conclusion of the loan was out of the question.

The loan was to be an international one, but in view of its large amount the French group of bankers was to play the leading part. In 1905 I opened preliminary negotiations with Neutzlin, the head of the Banque de Paris et des Pays Bas. After the death of Germain, of the Credit Lyonnais, the Banque de Paris et des Pays Bas became the chief banking institution in the so-called Christian group of bankers' syndicates. The other group of banks, known as the Jewish group, was headed by the Rothschild firm. Old Baron Alphonse Rothschild, with whom I had been on very friendly terms, was already dead, and Lord Rothschild of London was now the head of the family. Consequently, I instructed Rafalovich, our financial agent in Paris, to go to London and find out what was the attitude of the Rothschilds toward our loan. Rafalovich's reply was to the effect that out of respect for Count Witte as a statesman they would willingly render full assistance to the loan, but that they would not be in a position to do so until the Russian Government had enacted legal measures tending to improve the conditions of the Jews in Russia. As I deemed it beneath our dignity to connect the solution of our Jewish question with the loan, I decided to give up my intention of securing the participation of the Rothschilds.

The Constitutional Democrats ("Cadets") were fully aware of the stabilizing effect the loan would have upon the Government. Consequently, they sought to defeat my efforts to conclude the loan before the opening of the Duma. Their representatives, chiefly Prince Dolgoruki and Maklakov, acted in Paris, trying to persuade the French Government that it was illegal for the Imperial Government to conclude the loan without the sanction of the Duma. It is not without shame, I am sure, that these public leaders, who were very decent men for all that, recall this activity of theirs, which could hardly be termed patriotic. Their only excuse lies in the fact that in those days the greater part of thinking Russia was in a state of intoxication. People were actually drunk with the old wine of freedom, which had been brewing for many generations.

As for our press, it did nothing to inspire the foreign investor with confidence. For instance, nearly all the papers printed the appeal of the revolutionists to the population enjoining it to withdraw their deposits from the banks and local treasuries, so as to force the Government to cease the exchange of credit bills and reduce the Treasury to a state of insolvency. On the other hand, the foreign press displayed a great deal of hostility toward us. Here is what Rafalovich wrote me from Paris on January 8, 1906: "The difficulties of the situation are clearly manifested in the attitude of the financial and economic press. While Mr. Paul Leroy Beaulieu (an authority on finance) is using all the prestige with which his special scientific competence invests him to reassure and enlighten the public, and while Mr. Kergall (editor of *La Revue Economique*) endeavours to act in the same direction, there are other publications whose utterances seem to be inspired by those feelings of hatred and joy which a savage may experience at the sight of the dead body of an enemy.... The English *Economist*, whose animosity is chronic, speaks of the collapse of the gold standard in Russia. Ill-informed, it announces that Russia is driven to resort to a forced rate of exchange and to the printing of paper money without the corresponding deposit of gold. Other papers repeat this yarn that a portion of Russia's gold resources has been absorbed by the purchase of Russian securities abroad made in order to stabilize the rates of exchange.... It is also said that. Russia is reduced to the necessity of issuing *billets escomptables* (notes at a discount).... It is the war cry of the enemies of Russian credit."

Already in November, 1905, our money circulation was in a very critical state and I found it necessary to keep the financial committee informed about the situation. With my approval, the committee appointed two of its members, V. N. Kokovtzev and Schwanebach, Minister of Agriculture, together with the Minister of Finances, I. P. Shipov, to watch the transactions of the Imperial Bank, but, of course, they were unable to suggest anything to improve matters. As the situation was rapidly growing worse and as some of the members of the financial committee thought it was possible to conclude a foreign loan immediately, I proposed to Kokovtzev that he go abroad with full powers to contract a loan. I knew very well that before the settlement of the Morocco conflict, this was out of the question, but I did not judge it possible to take the financial committee into my confidence with regard to the political aspect of the situation.

Kokovtzev went to Paris late in December, 1905, and was told, of course, by Rouvier that we could not conclude the loan before the peaceable termination of the Morocco affair. He also had an interview with President Loubet. Kokovtzev succeeded in getting an advance of 100 million rubles on account of the future loan. This sum was but a drop in the bucket, for the short-term bonds issued by Kokovtzev in Berlin were soon to fall due. Accordingly I asked Kokovtzev to stop in Berlin on his way back and try to obtain an extension of time for these bonds. This extension he secured, for the reason that the German Government was still undecided as to what course I would follow in matters pertaining to Russia's external policy. For, though I was instrumental in annulling the monstrous Björke agreement, I nevertheless made it clear that I was in favour of a coalition between Russia, Germany and France, which would dominate the whole of Europe, if not the world. If this plan, which was my chief political idea, was not realized, it was because of insufficient political farsightedness on our part and also on the part of Emperor William of Germany.

I have spoken elsewhere of the interplay of forces which determined the course of the Algeciras Conference, and how Germany endeavoured to drag out the negotiations so as to increase our difficulties and take revenge on me for the annulment of the Björke treaty. In January, 1906, I decided to push further the negotiations for the loan, which I had initiated in Paris on my way back from the United States. As I could not go abroad and as there was no one who could be entrusted with the task of conducting the negotiations,

I asked Neutzlin to come to Russia. It was a matter of extreme importance that his visit should be a secret to the public, for otherwise it would have had an undesirable effect upon the course of the Algeciras Conference and upon the Russian Stock Exchange. I may mention in passing that since I had left the post of Minister of Finances, in 1903, the Russian securities had fallen twenty per cent. Accordingly, Neutzlin came to Russia incognito and put up at the palace of Grand Duke Vladimir Alexandrovich, at Tsarskoye Selo. He arrived on February 2nd, and his visit lasted five days. In the course of that period I had several conferences with Neutzlin, and in the presence of the Minister of Finance, Shipov, we agreed upon the terms of the loan. At first, Neutzlin insisted that the loan should not be realized before the opening of the Duma, but I succeeded in convincing him of the undesirability of such an arrangement, and it was then agreed that the loan should be effected immediately upon the termination of the Algeciras Conference. It was also agreed that the amount of the loan should be made as large as possible, so as to enable us to get along for a considerable period of time without new loans and also in order to cancel the temporary loans contracted by Kokovtzev in France and in Germany. I insisted on 2,750,000,000 francs as the nominal amount of the loan. Anticipating upon the course of events, I may say that, owing to the treachery of Germany and of the American syndicate of bankers headed by Morgan, we had to reduce the amount to 2,250,000,000 francs—843,750,000 rubles. Neutzlin insisted on six and a quarter per cent., but I could not agree to that rate of interest, and it was fixed at six per cent., the loan certificates becoming convertible after ten years. The syndicate which was to handle the loan was to be made up, we agreed, of French, Dutch, English, German, American, and Russian banking firms. Austrian banks were also permitted to participate in the loan. The sums realized were to be left in the hands of the syndicate at one and a quarter per cent, and then transferred to the Russian Government in definite instalments in the course of one year. Not less than half of the amount of the loan the syndicate was to take upon itself. We also agreed upon the secondary details. Neutzlin returned home, conferred with the other members of the syndicate and they all indorsed the main terms of the agreement which was formulated at Tsarskoye Selo. I continued to advise him all the while, and until the very conclusion of the loan he turned to me personally for instructions.

In the meantime, Germany continued to obstruct the progress of the Algeciras Conference. Privately, I advised Rouvier to be more yielding, but our representative at the conference, the Spanish Ambassador Count Cassini, was instructed to vote for France in all cases. Germany's claims were so unfair that even the representatives of her Allies, Italy and Austria, in some cases voted for France. In my report to His Majesty upon the loan negotiations I spoke about the situation in the following terms:

I cannot get rid of certain, probably unfounded, suspicions regarding the conduct of the German Government. The international situation is at present such that Germany has an excellent opportunity to push France to the wall. Russia is not in a position at present to render any considerable military assistance to France. Austria and Italy will not stand in Germany's way. As for Great Britain, she is unable to help France on land, and there is no doubt but that from the military standpoint Germany is perfectly able to give France a sound beating. The temptation for Germany is great. Even granting that Germany is not thinking of war, she may still be bent, on the one hand, upon preventing her neighbor's, i.e., Russia's, speedy recovery from a disastrous war, and on the other, upon showing France that her salvation lies in a rapprochement with Germany. Consequently, I suspect, Germany must have ulterior motives in displaying so much interest in the Morocco question, which is, properly speaking, of little importance to her. I have noticed that Germany's civility and amiability is mere lip service.

About the same time Count Lamsdorff, Minister of Foreign Affairs, sent the following note to our German Ambassador, Count Osten-Sacken:

France has reached the limit of tractability in agreeing (at the Conference) to practically all the points of the latest Berlin proposal. The time has now come for Germany to give proof of that peace-loving spirit to which both the German Emperor and Prince Bülow have repeatedly referred in connection with the Morocco affair. In spite of their assurances, Germany, failing to see in the changes of the clauses relating to the police, which were suggested by France (at the Conference) a sufficient guarantee of the international character of the police, refused to agree to those changes in the hope that France would find another way out of the difficulties. It would be highly deplorable if, because of this comparatively insignificant police question, on which all the Powers are unanimous, the Algeciras Conference should be forced to interrupt its deliberations. We refuse to believe that Emperor William who, in the presence of our Most

August Monarch, advocated with firm conviction the preservation of peace in the interests of mankind and a rapprochement between Germany and France through Russia's instrumentality, that Emperor William should decide to disrupt the Conference and thus not only give up his political program but also arouse among the European Powers an alarm which in its manifold consequences would be no less pernicious than open warfare. The German Government is quite aware that certain financial operations of the highest importance to Russia are contingent upon the successful termination of the Algeciras Conference. Only the carrying out of those operations will enable the Imperial Russian Government to take the necessary measures for the final suppression of the revolutionary movement, which has already shown signs of spreading to the neighbouring monarchistic countries. The latter have recognized the necessity of concerted action against the international anarchist organizations. Despite the opinion, which is being spread abroad, that Jewish agitation prevents Russia from concluding the loan, we are in the possession of indisputable information to the effect that only the total uncertainty as to the outcome of the Algeciras Conference is forcing the French bankers to refrain from financial operations. Should Emperor William or the Chancellor in their conversations with you touch upon the Morocco affair, you may very frankly state your opinion in accordance with this dispatch.

The reference to Jewish agitation in this telegram is based on what His Majesty told Count Lamsdorff and myself. Emperor William had written him, he said, that we were unable to conclude the loan not because of the Algeciras Conference, but because the Jewish bankers refused to take part in the operation. On hearing that, I sent the following dispatch to Rafalovich, our agent in Paris:

Berlin insistently endeavours to convey the impression that the Algeciras Conference has absolutely nothing to do with the possibility of concluding the loan, that it is the Jews who are thwarting and will thwart it, and that the termination of the Conference would not in any way change the situation. It is very desirable that you should speak on that subject to Rouvier and that I should submit Rouvier's opinion to whom it may concern.

Rafalovich's reply, which I submitted to His Majesty, was as follows:

Rouvier replied: "Berlin views the situation in a false light, for, not the Hebrews, but all the people whose opinion carries weight consider the transaction impossible before the political horizon clears up, that is, before the Morocco affair is settled in a fashion guaranteeing European peace." I add: the papers create a pessimistic impression. It is my opinion that the German Emperor holds the key to our transaction.

In reply to Count Lamsdorff's telegram, our ambassador wired (on February 9th) that, in the opinion of Prince Bülow, the conclusion of the loan was impossible not because of the Algeciras Conference, but because of the revolutionary movement in Russia. As for the Conference, the prince believed that it was necessary for us to urge France to be more tractable. Count Lamsdorff's reply follows:

Prince Büllow's words convey the odd impression that his attention is chiefly concentrated on our loan and Russia's internal affairs. The two depend upon the outcome of the Algeciras Conference, and it seems to me that Germany as a monarchistic Power is considerably affected by the Russian revolutionary movement. In your conferences with the Chancellor it is necessary to emphasize Berlin's neglect of the conditions set by the French delegates for an understanding. Germany's intolerance was once more clearly manifested in the Chancellor's arguments presented to you. He entirely overlooked all the concessions made by the Paris Government. . . . Consequently, we hardly believe we could exert any pressure on France, which has given conclusive proofs of its conciliatory spirit. Should the Conference be disrupted, the opinion will no doubt prevail among all the Powers that the failure of the Conference was due exclusively to Germany's aggressive designs.

Seeing that Germany continued to make difficulties, I took advantage of the permission the German Emperor had given me to communicate with him through Count Eulenburg and I appealed to him directly, asking him to speed up the deliberations of the Algeciras Conference. My effort was labor lost. The Emperor informed me that he could not concede certain conditions without prejudicing Germany's prestige and ended with the usual advice to exert pressure upon France for the purpose of rendering her more tractable. I was indignant at Germany's conduct, and on one occasion I left no doubt in the German ambassador's mind as to my feelings in the matter. Under the impression of our conversation the German ambassador sent to von Bülow a dispatch, which, together with the Chancellor's reply, fell into my hands,—although neither document was intended for me by its author. "His Imperial Majesty's policy," said the ambassador among other things, "is directed as before toward peace, harmony and confidence. It does not follow, however, that we can sacrifice our firmly established rights and interests, when they are in danger. The failure of the Conference, with its numberless consequences, will be avoided if France agrees to terms which are sufficiently in keeping with international law." In his reply, the Chancellor pointed out that the removal of Delcassé was not a concession to Germany, as I insisted, but "an act of internal French policy."

Several days later Rouvier's Government fell, and was succeeded by a cabinet formed by Sarrien. It was in those days that a sensational polemic arose between the Paris *Temps* and the German newspapers about an article in *Temps* relating to an instruction given by us to Ambassador Cassini. The incident was started, Count Lamsdorff explained to me, through a false rumour spread by the Germans. For some time the German Chancellor had been setting on foot such rumours, intended to retard the proceedings of the Algeciras Conference and to set the Powers at variance.

As soon as Sarrien's cabinet was formed, I instructed Rafalovich to call on Minister of Finances Poincaré and report to him the state of the negotiations of the loan. Neutzlin, on his part, was also instructed by me to confer with Minister Poincaré on the subject of our loan. Early in March Rafalovich met first M. Henry, Director of the Commercial and Consular Division of the Ministry of Foreign Affairs, and then the Minister of Finances himself. After initiating these two statesmen into all the details of the situation, Rafalovich stated that, in my opinion, there existed a formal agreement between Rouvier and myself. According to that agreement, he said, I was to make every effort to regulate the Morocco problem, while the French Government, upon the successful termination of the Algeciras Conference, was to render us every possible assistance toward the conclusion of the loan, the basic terms of which were agreed upon between myself and Neutzlin.

The new cabinet, particularly Poincaré, assumed a favourable attitude toward the matter and spent some time in studying it, but they could not alter the essential fact, namely, that until the termination of the Algeciras Conference the conclusion of the loan was out of the question. Finally, in spite of Germany's efforts, the Conference came to a peaceable end. On March 16th, Count Lamsdorff wrote me: "From a very confidential source (Chancellor von Büllow's communication to Ambassador Schoen) I learn that Prince von Bülow considers the Algeciras Conference successfully terminated. He is now trying to convince Germany that he had achieved all she could desire." Shortly before, Neutzlin informed me that, in case of a successful outcome of the Conference, our representative would have to come to Paris about the 10th of April (new style) for the purpose of giving a final form to the agreement and signing the contract with the syndicate. In his letter Neutzlin pointed out that Poincaré was constantly raising the question of the legal right of the Imperial Government to contract a loan without the sanction of the Duma. I replied to the effect that when the moment for concluding the loan came I would prove our right to the satisfaction of all concerned. Thereupon, I asked Professor Martens, reputed in Europe as an authority on international law, and a member of the Council of the Ministry of the Interior, to look into the matter. Professor Martens composed a memorandum, in French, which proved conclusively the right of the Russian Government to carry out the transaction. This document I handed to our plenipotentiary, who was intrusted with the task of signing the contract with the syndicate of bankers. I also transmitted to Rafalovich Neutzlin's recommendations about the negotiations with the press, preliminary to the conclusion of the loan.

As it was clear that the Conference was drawing to a successful end, I asked His Majesty to appoint a special representative empowered to go to Paris, settle some of the secondary points of the agreement and sign the contract. His Majesty named Kokovtzev, although I recommended the Director of the Imperial Bank Timashev, who is now Minister of Commerce.

Neutzlin went to London to confer with Revelstock, the representative of the London banks, Fischel, German banker, of the Mendelssohn firm, and Morgan, senior, of the United States, and on March 22nd, he wired to me about the result of these negotiations. The representative of the German bankers, he informed me, was waiting for a permission from his Government to take part in the loan, and Morgan's attitude was less favourable. It will be remembered that I had secured the American banker's promise to participate in the loan during my stay in the United States. The next day Neutzlin telegraphed to me from London that the German Government, Fischel told him, had forbidden the German banking firms to take part in the loan. Thus, Germany first protracted the Algeciras Conference in the hope that, unable to contract a loan, we would cease the free exchange of credit notes for gold. Germany would have greatly profited thereby, for Russia would then be at the mercy of Berlin stock exchange speculation, as was the case before I introduced the gold standard. She failed, however, to reach her goal. Then at the last moment, on the very eve of the conclusion of the loan, she treacherously ordered her bankers to refrain from participation in that transaction. Morgan followed suit and also refused to participate in the loan. That American banker enjoyed the German Emperor's favour, and despite his democratic feelings as an American, highly valued the attention of that exalted crowned personage.

To Neutzlin's communication I replied as follows:

> I have given you warning of Germany's disposition. Berlin was waiting for a pretext to raise difficulties. Their latest step is essentially an act of vengeance for Algeciras and for our rapprochement with England. Under these circumstances there is no reason why the other countries should reduce their share; on the contrary, it would be logical for them to increase it. Likewise, there is no reason why the transaction should be postponed; rather should it be concluded in advance of the projected time.

I was nevertheless certain that the German money market would be thrown open to us privately, in spite of the fact that the Berlin banking firms would not be in the syndicate. I placed especial confidence in the Mendelssohn banking houses, which for nearly one hundred years had been faithful to Russia's financial interests and with whose head, Ernest Mendelssohn, I was on excellent terms. On the night of March 24th, I sent to Rafalovich the following dispatch:

> In revenge for Algeciras and in fear that the loan would unite us closer to France and lay the foundation for a rapprochement with Great Britain, the German Government at the last moment refused to authorize the participation of the German bankers in the inter-national syndicate. To find a plausible pretext, the German Government issued a loan unexpectedly. But two weeks ago, when Mendelssohn came to St. Petersburg with instructions, from his Government, there was no question of a refusal. The step was taken by the German Government on the spur of the moment, in order to upset the affair and as if to tell us: "All the while you have supported France, now you will see that you have made a blunder." Inform the French newspapers about this intrigue in proper form.

The refusal of the Germans and Americans to participate in the loan had no effect on the English. Neutzlin sent me a telegram to that effect immediately upon Fischel's declaration. The Algeciras affair was the first manifestation in many years of a growing rapprochement between Russia and England. At the Conference Russia and Great Britain showed the world an example of complete solidarity in giving their full support to France. Nor did the Austrian banks withdraw. Italy did refuse to participate, but for purely financial reasons. She had just succeeded in stabilizing her financial system. Several years ago the Italian king, while on a stay in Russia, presented me with an Italian gold coin, saying that he had brought me the first gold coin struck at the Italian mint, as a fitting gift to the man who introduced the gold standard in the great Russian empire.

On the 20th of March I received Kokovtzev and personally explained to him the loan situation in all its details. I also handed in to him a statement of the terms to which we agreed and gave him most definite instructions as to his official mission. On March 26th, if I remember rightly, he left for Paris, accompanied by Vyshnegradski, one of my former collaborators in the Ministry of Finances, who was an expert in credit transactions and whose presence was a guarantee that no blunder would be committed on our part. On the 3rd of April, the loan contract was signed by Kokovtzev, as the official Russian plenipotentiary, and by the representatives of the international syndicate of bankers. Several days later the envoys returned to Russia with the text of the contract in their hands. It was transmitted to me and subsequently laid before the financial committee by the Minister of Finances, Shipov. Having examined and ratified it, the committee submitted it to His Majesty for confirmation.

Ernest von Mendelssohn Bartoldi, head of the banking house of Mendelssohn & Company, the chief banking institution of Germany, dispatched to me, through Vyshnegradski, the following letter, dated April 5th (18th):

I avail myself of Mr. Vyshnegradski's passage here to send you these lines in order to congratulate you upon the achievement of the great undertaking and to tell you with what profound satisfaction we see this important transaction finally brought to a happy consummation. I should like very much to tell you with what feelings of regret we find ourselves out of action after all the pains we have taken and all the efforts we have made. But you know it all, and I need not resort to words to express our state of mind to you. The only thing which we could do and which we keep on doing, is to endeavor everywhere abroad to arouse and strengthen the interest in the new loan, and that not only in theory through correspondence and conferences with our various friends, but also in practice. In this connection I deem it necessary to tell you (but to you alone, since for reasons which you will readily understand it is absolutely necessary that all this be kept in strictest secrecy) that we have invested in the loan at Paris, London, Amsterdam, and St. Petersburg separately, so as to keep our transaction in each of these four places unknown to the others. Naturally, we have done so in order to produce the greatest possible effect on the respective houses and to nip in the bud the unpleasant impression which might be produced by Germany's withdrawal. In fact, I believe that this policy on our part has already borne fruit, and the uneasiness which had manifested itself here and there has been entirely eliminated. We are very nappy indeed to see matters take this turn! I am very glad to be able to tell you that we perceive tendencies very favorable to the transaction *in financial circles.*

It appears from this letter of the most prominent German banker that this time, too, the German Government had missed fire. In fact, as early as April 17th (30th) Neutzlin, the chief representative of the syndicate, wrote me as follows:

The international loan is an accomplished fact. The last stage was reached yesterday. This great financial victory is to-day the subject of general conversation, and Russian credit, for the first time since the beginning of the war, is in the process of striking root in a considerably enlarged territory. Having reported this triumph, to which, thanks to your Excellency, I have had the honor of contributing my share from first to last, I turn to your Excellency filled with profound gratefulness for the confidence you have shown me throughout the course of the negotiations. In abandoning, in the course of our conversation at Tsarskoye Selo, the plans prepared beforehand, your Excellency gave me the full measure of your approval, which alone sustained and encouraged me during the critical stages which the negotiations traversed.

The loan was indeed an achievement of the highest importance. It was the largest foreign loan in the history of the modern nations. After the Franco-Prussian War, Thiers succeeded in securing a somewhat greater loan, but it was largely an internal loan, while this one was almost exclusively subscribed abroad. By means of it Russia maintained intact its gold standard of currency, which I introduced in 1896. This, in its turn, served to sustain all the basic principles of our financial system, which were mostly inaugurated by myself, and which Kokovtzev preserved with laudable firmness. It was these principles that enabled Russia to recover after that ill-starred war and the subsequent senseless turmoil, known as the Russian revolution. This loan enabled the Imperial Government to weather all the vicissitudes of the period extending from 1906 to 1910 by providing it with funds, which together with the troops recalled from Transbaikalia restored consistency and assurance to the acts of the Government.

In view of all this, what was the Emperor's attitude toward the loan? His Majesty fully appreciated how important it was to conclude the loan and what a disaster failure to secure it would mean. In all financial matters throughout the time when I held the office of Minister of Finances he had full confidence in me and did not in the least thwart my activity. In this case, too, as on previous occasions, he granted me full liberty of action, as far as this financial operation depended upon political action. He stood there like a spectator, as it were, watching a great politico-financial game of chess, but a spectator fully cognizant of the momentous importance of the game's outcome for Russia and deeply engrossed in its course.

In the months of February and March I had already begun to lose patience with the reactionary attacks directed against the reform of October 17th. In certain circles people began to brand me as a traitor. At the same time, Durnovo, the Temporary Governors-General and others carried out many measures without my knowledge, although the responsibility for those measures fell upon me as the head of the Government. As a result I began to intimate that I had no objection to surrendering my post to a man enjoying more confidence. The invariable reply was to the effect that this was impossible before the conclusion of the loan. The Emperor was fully aware of the fact that I alone could negotiate it: first, because of my prestige in financial circles abroad; second, because of my vast experience in financial affairs. The following is from a letter written to me by His Majesty in his own hand and dated April 15th:

> The successful conclusion of the loan forms the best page in the history of your ministerial activity. It is for the Government a great moral triumph and a pledge of Russia's undisturbed and peaceful development in the future.

It is obvious that the Emperor fully appreciated the significance of the loan.

In concluding the story of the loan, I wish to return to Kokovtzev. On arriving from Paris, with the contract in his hands, he came to see me and congratulated me upon my success. I thanked him for having punctually acquitted himself of the mission with which he had been entrusted. Thereupon he asked me whether I could not obtain for him a gratuity in the form of 80,000 rubles, the sum to be drawn from the loan. This demand, at a time when our finances were in an extremely critical condition, put me out. Unable to collect my wits and find a suitable answer, I told him that I would take the matter up with the Minister of Finances, Shipov. I went to Shipov and retold him my conversation with Kokovtzev.

"Kokovtzev," I observed to Shipov, "apparently thinks that it is customary for Ministers of Finances and their collaborators to receive bonuses from the sum of a loan at its conclusion. He forgets," I added, "that the practice was abolished by Alexander III."

Kokovtzev's démarche surprised Shipov and aroused his indignation. I asked the latter to confer with Kokovtzev, with whom he was on good terms, and advise him not to raise that question again. It was then that Kokovtzev turned to the chairman of the Imperial Council, Count Solski, in an effort to procure for himself in connection with the loan a reward in another form. Count Solski spoke to me about the matter, and as I raised no objections, Kokovtzev was granted the Order of Alexander Nevski accompanied by an official announcement.

Finally, the Imperial Duma opened, I retired, and the Goremykin ministry was formed. The head of the cabinet offered the portfolio of Minister of Finances to Kokovtzev, who came to ask my opinion about the offer. I advised him to accept it. Later, to my surprise, he declared that Russia's financial situation had been saved by the 1906 loan. He also told, at some length, what an arduous task it had been for him to secure it and what an ordeal he underwent as director of the transaction. In a word, our most esteemed Vladimir Nikolaievich [i.e., Kokovtzev] intended to take advantage of the fact that no one in the Duma knew how the financial operation was actually carried out. He hoped to impose upon everyone the belief that he, Vladimir Nikolaievich, was the saviour of Russia. The whole man is in that gesture! ... Because of such statements on his part, I have collected all the documents relating to the loan of 1906, which had remained in my hands. Some of the documents I have utilized above.

Thus, I was upon the whole successful in dealing with the military and financial situation. But Russia was unable to reap the benefit of my triumph over our great difficulties, for, unfortunately, the ruling group was not enlightened and generous enough honestly to adhere to the principles announced in the constitutional manifesto of October 17, 1905.

The manifesto was drawn up hastily and until the last moment I did not know whether His Majesty would sign it. Had it not been for Grand Duke Nikolai Nikolaievich, he would not perhaps have done it. It is noteworthy that immediately upon the promulgation of the manifesto the Grand Duke embraced the creed of the Black Hundreds. Prince A. D. Obolensky, one of the authors of the manifesto, was in a state of neurasthenia at the time when he took part in its composition. Several days after the publication of the act this earnest advocate of the manifesto declared to me that his participation in the movement for the manifesto had been the greatest sin of his life. In the days immediately preceding the publication of the manifesto, His Majesty conducted two parallel sets of conferences. I participated in one, Goremykin in the other. This extreme duplicity at such a critical time greatly discouraged me.

As a matter of fact, I was rather opposed to the publication of a constitutional manifesto, and I gave much thought to the alternative plan of setting up a military dictatorship. The original text of the document was drafted against my will and behind my back. Seeing, however, that the high spheres were intent upon issuing the manifesto, I insisted that my own version of it should be adopted, if I was to be appointed Prime Minister.

The effect of the act of October 17th was in many respects salutary. Thus, for instance, the manifesto destroyed that unity of front which made the camp of the opposition so formidable. It sobered the country down, so that the voice of patriotism was heard in the land again, and the propertied people girt their loins* and arose in defence of their possessions. But it also had its serious drawbacks. The manifesto came as a bolt from the blue. Most of the provincial authorities did not understand what happened, and many were clearly out of sympathy with the new course of policy. As the

* to gird the loins is to prepare for something difficult or challenging. From Roman times it meant to pull up one's robe and tuck it in to the belt before commencing a physical activity.

manifesto came unexpectedly, the regions which had already been in a state of tension were thrown into a fever by its sudden appearance. Violent outbreaks, both revolutionary and counter-revolutionary, took place all over the country, the reactionary manifestations involving, of course, pogroms. The latter were organized or, at least, encouraged by the local authorities. Thus the manifesto actually stimulated disorder. That was what I feared, and that was why I opposed the idea of issuing a manifesto. Furthermore, it laid the imprint of undue haste upon all the other acts of the Government.

I did not for a moment doubt the necessity of a parliamentary régime for the country. In those days even the conservatives advocated a constitution. In fact, there were no conservatives in Russia on the eve of October 17, 1905. The manifesto cut Russia's past from her present as with a knife. The historical operation was surely necessary, but it should have been performed with greater care and more precautions. Yet, I thank the Lord that the constitution has been granted. It is far better that the past has been cut off, even though somewhat roughly and hurriedly, than if it had been slowly sawed off with a blunt saw wielded by a bungling surgeon.

Everybody understood that the act of October 17th marked an historical turning-point of great significance. The truly enlightened element, which had preserved its faith in the political decency of the ruling powers, perceived that the dream of several generations, to which, beginning with the Decembrists, so many noble lives were sacrificed, had come true. As for the embittered and the unbalanced, they felt that the chief representatives of the old order, above all the Monarch himself, should have gone into the scrapheap with the ancient régime. For did not Nicholas II actually ruin Russia and cast her off the pedestal on which she had stood? Many also suspected—and their suspicions proved eminently true—that the constitution had been granted by the Emperor in a fit of panic and that as soon as his position improved he would so manipulate the constitution as to annul it and turn it into a ghastly farce.

In October, 1905, a feeling of profound dejection reigned at the court. The following incident will plainly show how deep that feeling was. In those days we used to go to Peterhof by steamer to attend the official sessions, for the railway workers were on strike. Once, Adjutant General Count Benckendorf, a brother of our ambassador in London, happened to be with us on board the steamer. A sensible, educated man, very much devoted to the Emperor, he belongs to the few noblemen who lend the splendour of their culture to the throne. Count Benkendorf regretted, he said among other things to N. I. Vuich, who accompanied me, that their Majesties had five children (four princesses and the poor heir Alexis, a very nice boy, they say). Should the Imperial family have to leave Peterhof by steamer to seek shelter abroad, he explained, *the children would be a great hindrance.*

To show to what extent people, even intellectually prominent people, lost their heads in those days, I shall cite the following rather amusing and at the same time disconcerting incident. In 1906, at Vichy, where I had come for my health, after having resigned my office of president of the Council of Ministers, I was visited by the celebrated Professor Mechnikov. I had known Professor Mechnikov in my youth at the time when he taught zoology at the University of Odessa, from which I had graduated. In those days he was a liberal, a Red, while I held the conservative views to which I am still faithful. As a matter of fact, it was because of his liberal ideas that he was forced to leave the University of Odessa and go abroad, where he was welcomed at the Institut Pasteur.

The celebrated scientist came down all the way from Paris to consult me on a business matter. At the Institut Pasteur, he told me, he received the scanty salary of 3,000 francs a year, on which of course, he could not live. His main income, amounting to 8,000 rubles a year, he derived from his wife's landed property, situated in Russia. He had just been offered a chair at Oxford University, he continued, with a salary of 3,000, but he would not even think of leaving the Institut Pasteur, where he acquired a worldwide reputation, were it not for the fear that he might lose his Russian income, in view of the movement for the expropriation of landowners, which, he understood, was on foot in our country. Should the expropriation be effected, he concluded, he would be unable to live in Paris and would have to accept the chair at Oxford. I assured the alarmed scientist that should compulsory expropriation on a large scale take place,—which was unlikely—the owners would be duly compensated, and thereby allayed his fears.

In the course of our talk this great scientist actually found it possible to blame me for having killed too few people. He had a theory of his own with regard to the course of action which I should have followed when I stood at the helm. According to that scheme, I should have surrendered to the revolutionists Petrograd, or Moscow, or even a whole province. Then, several months later, I should have besieged and taken the revolutionary stronghold, shooting down several tens of thousands of men. According to the learned professor, that would have put an end to the revolution once and for all. In support of his theory, Mechnikov cited the example of Thiers in his dealings with the Communards. What ignorance and aberration! And to think that some Russians listened with bated breath to that plan of most brutal premeditated provocation! To begin with, Thiers did not create the Paris Commune by artificial means. Furthermore, in storming the Commune he was backed up by the Popular Assembly, elected by universal suffrage. He was doing the will of the whole of France. With regard to the repressions, he was in the position of one who had by every available means to restrain, not to goad, the Popular Assembly. If a popular assembly had been elected in Russia by universal suffrage, after the granting of the constitutional manifesto of October 17th, it would have demanded a complete cessation of all executions. Furthermore, it would no doubt have demanded the Emperor's abdication and the trial of all those responsible for the shame and horror of the Russo-Japanese War. As a result, there would have broken out a fratricidal civil war, ending in the secession of some of our border provinces and the occupation of a portion of our territory by foreign troops.

It soon became clear to everyone concerned that the position of the dynasty and of the régime generally was not as insecure as appeared at first. The revolutionary ardour of the educated proved to be but intellectual itching and the result of idleness. Then came repentance and, with it, a systematic attempt on the part of the ruling clique to nullify the act of October 17th. As a result, General Trepov, the Court Commandant, became the irresponsible head of the Government; while I, on whom rested the entire weight of responsibility, was reduced to the role of a figurehead. As early as January, 1906, I declared to Grand Duke Nikolai Nikolaievich that as soon as I contracted the loan and evacuated Manchuria I would resign my post, for the reason that I found it impossible to act the part of a screen for men and measures I opposed. I did not wish to be a cat's-paw* for General Trepov and Grand Duke Nicholas, and a shield for the Black Hundreds. I resigned in April.

* A person who carries out unlawful or dangerous work for another.

CHAPTER XII

MY PREMIERSHIP

AT the conference with His Majesty which preceded the publication of the constitutional manifesto, I was exceedingly cautious in the expression of my opinions. True, I stated my convictions, which were later embodied in my report to His Majesty, without the slightest equivocation. I did not hesitate to draw his attention to the fact that should, God forbid, anything fatal happen to him, the dynasty would be represented by the baby Emperor and the regent, Mikhail Alexandrovich, who is completely unprepared for the task of ruling the Empire,—a situation fraught with grave dangers for both the dynasty and the country, especially at a time of mighty revolutionary upheaval. It was therefore, necessary, I argued, to seek support for the political régime in the people, however deficient and unreliable the social consciousness of the uncultured masses may be. It was painful for me thus to speak to my Monarch, whom I had known since the days of his youth, whom I had served since the very beginning of his reign and who was the son of a man and ruler I had literally worshipped. Yet, had I failed to tell the Emperor the whole truth as I understood it, I would consider myself remiss of my direct moral duty.

While I was thus quite outspoken, nevertheless, I repeatedly told the Emperor that I might be in the wrong, and I urged him to take counsel with other statesmen in whom he had faith. It goes without saying that I did not advise him to do it on the sly, nor did I intimate that he should seek light from either such nonentities as Goremykin or from the court flunkeys. I did not conceal from His Majesty that, in my opinion, the situation was fraught with great difficulties and dangers. Seeing that he was bent upon placing the burden of power on my shoulders, I made use on one occasion of an allegory, in order to present to him the situation as I saw it. I likened His Majesty to a man who must cross a stretch of heavy sea. Several routes are urged upon him, I said, and several ships offered by different seamen. No matter what route is selected and what ship is boarded some danger and much injury is inevitable. I believed, I asserted, that both my route and my boat were the least dangerous and the most advisable from the standpoint of Russia's future. But should His Majesty accept my route and boat, this is what would happen. No sooner will he put to sea than the boat will begin to pitch and roll; later storms may come and probably damage the boat. It is then that wise counsellors could intimate that His Majesty ought to have chosen another route and trusted his own destiny and that of the country to another vessel. Hence doubts, hesitations, and plotting would arise and greatly endanger the public cause.

His Majesty protested and assured me of his unqualified confidence. I had, however, no illusions as to my Monarch's character. I knew that, devoid of either will or statesmanlike purpose, he was the plaything of all manner of evil influences, and that his personal peculiarities would add to the difficulties of the situation. I saw clearly that the near future held many bitter experiences in store for me and that in the end I would have to part with His Majesty without having accomplished my appointed task. The history of my brief premiership (October 20, 1905–April 20, 1906) fully bears out my predictions and justifies my apprehensions.

I found myself at the helm, essentially against my own will. His Majesty was forced to resort to me for the simple reason that his favourites, such as Goremykin, General Ignatyev and General Trepov, were scared by the revolutionary terrorists and lost themselves in the chaos of contradictory measures, for which they themselves were responsible.

Immediately upon my nomination as President of the Imperial Council I made it clear that the Procurator of the Holy Synod Pobiedonostzev, could not remain in office, for he definitely represented the past. His participation in my ministry, I argued, was incompatible with the inauguration of the new régime and out of keeping with the spirit of the times. As his successor I recommended Prince Alexey Dimitriyevich Obolenski. His Majesty at once agreed to my proposal and appointed Prince Obolensky to succeed Pobiedonostzev, who was nominated ordinary member of the Imperial Council. It was owing to my intercession that the venerable old statesman was granted certain privileges, such as the use of the apartments which he had occupied in his capacity of Procurator of the Holy Synod, and that His Majesty had the delicacy of himself announcing his decision to Pobiedonostzev, instead of informing him about it by means of an official rescript. The Emperor's behaviour in this matter is highly characteristic of the heartlessness and unceremoniousness with which he is accustomed to treat his old servants. Pobiedonostzev had known His Majesty since the latter's early childhood and for many years he had been the preceptor of the Czarevich. Since, however, the pupil was never called upon to recite, the teacher did not know whether or not the young Nicholas had profited by the instruction. Pobiedonostzev expressed himself to that effect on one occasion in the course of a conversation with me.

Simultaneously, it was decided to dismiss Minister of Instruction, General Glazov, who held his office by sheer misunderstanding, and also Bulygin, Minister of the Interior. The portfolio of Minister of Education I offered to Professor Tagantzev, a criminalist well known in the academic world, a member of the Imperial Council and of the Senate, and a man of moderately liberal views. The professor declared that he was in poor health and desired a day's space for consideration. In those days everyone was in poor health. The following day Tagantzev came to see me, accompanied by Postnikov, now director of St. Petersburg Polytechnic, whom I designed for the post of Assistant Minister of Instruction. The professor was in a state of visible excitement. He declared that he was not in a position to accept my offer and when I attempted to argue with him he clutched his head and ran out of my study shouting: "I cannot, I cannot." I followed him, but he had seized his coat and hat and was gone. In this connection I may observe that in those stormy days the thought of getting a bullet or a bomb kept many a man from accepting a ministerial portfolio.

My next candidate for the Minister of Instruction was Count Ivan Ivanovich Tolstoy, the Vice President of the Academy of Fine Arts. An alumnus of the University of St. Petersburg, the count had been for many years director of the Academy of Fine Arts. I expected that the Emperor would have no objection to this appointment.

I did not choose Count Tolstoy for his academic ability alone. In the time of a revolution the post of Minister of Education is a militant post and requires not only a technically competent official, but also a man of conservative views, who would be both respected and feared. During the strikes in our institutions of learning, when many of the authorities became mere toys in the hands of the students, Count Tolstoy proved that he was not a man to be trifled with. The students at the Academy, however, had a deep respect for the count. I felt certain that the count would not indulge in radicalism. At the time when the Emperor parted with the Minister of Education, Vannovski, because of his excessive liberalism, the Grand Duke recommended Count Tolstoy for this post. At that time, however, the Emperor doubted the wisdom of appointing the count, fearing that his conservatism would arouse the indignation of the students.

I invited the count to my study and asked him to accept the post of Minister of Education. Count Tolstoy at first declined. He explained, without affectation, that he did not think himself sufficiently competent to accept the portfolio. He advised me to invite someone more capable of bearing the responsibilities of this ministerial office. I explained to him that in these dangerous times few men could be found who were willing to accept this post, and that I could delay the formation of the cabinet no longer.

Then the count gave in, thinking it unpatriotic, as he told me, to refuse a post of responsibility at a time of crisis, and to decline to lend me his assistance in carrying out the principles proclaimed in the manifesto of October 17th. His Majesty confirmed the appointment without delay.

I now had to choose a Minister of the Interior.

Prior to the October revolution, Piotr Nikolaievich Durnovo, the Assistant Minister of the Interior, hinted to me on several occasions that he was the only official qualified for the post of Minister of the Interior.

His experience was really extensive. He began his career as a naval officer. During the change in the judicial system of Russia he became Assistant Attorney General in Kiev. Count Palen, the Minister of Justice, told me he knew Durnovo back in the '70's and valued him highly for his energy and competence. In the beginning of the '80's Durnovo was appointed director of the Department of Police. I knew very little about Durnovo's activities in the department. The reason, however, why Durnovo was forced to leave his post has not remained unknown to me.

Durnovo had gained notoriety at that time for his amorous exploits. As a matter of fact, while director of the Department of Police he used agents of the department for private purposes. At that time he had a love affair with a lady of rather lax morals. In order to reveal this woman's treachery he employed agents of the department to take letters which this woman had written to the Spanish Ambassador to Russia, out of the ambassador's desk.

A stormy scene of jealousy was followed by a reconciliation. As far as the lady was concerned, the matter would have ended then and there.

The Spanish Ambassador, however, wrote to Alexander III, stating the facts of the matter. The Emperor was indignant and made several insulting remarks about Durnovo. Durnovo was forced to resign.

Ivan Nikolaievich Durnovo, then Minister of the Interior (he was not a relative of Piotr Nikolaievich's) at last succeeded in persuading the Emperor to appoint Durnovo member of the Senate. Durnovo served in the Senate a considerable length of time. He was known for his sane, liberal ideas. Durnovo always defended the cause of the Jews, whenever new attempts were made to reduce their legal rights.

Durnovo served as assistant to two Ministers of the Interior, Sipyagin and Svyatapolk-Mirski. His work in this capacity was satisfactory and the views he expressed sane and liberal.

It was this man, besides Prince Urusov, that I selected as a candidate for the post of Minister of the Interior.

When I mentioned Durnovo's name at the Council of Ministers, most of the members opposed this appointment. They could not offer, however, a more satisfactory candidate. When I told the Emperor my plans, he seemed very much opposed to Durnovo, but said nothing about Urusov's candidacy. Trepov, too, spoke with animosity of both of my candidates.

I must admit that Trepov's dislike of Durnovo made me decide in favour of the latter. I already understood at that time that Trepov wanted to have indirect control of the Ministry of the Interior, or rather, of the Department of Police. He therefore desired the Minister of the Interior to be either a novice or a man absolutely ignorant of the intricacies of the Department of Police.

In the evening there was a conference. Shipov, Guchkov and Prince Tmbetzkoi declared they would not remain in the cabinet in case Durnovo was appointed. They insisted upon my taking the post. I explained to them that it was absolutely impossible for me to take it, as my time was limited. I could think of no one else who knew the workings of the ministry so thoroughly and who was not likely to fall under the influence of General Trepov and the Department of Police.

I requested the Emperor to appoint Durnovo Minister of the

Interior and also name him member of the Imperial Council.

The Emperor agreed to appoint Durnovo to the Imperial Council, but made him Manager of the Ministry instead of full-fledged minister. Durnovo's appointment was one of the greatest errors I made during my administration.

By making Durnovo Manager, the Emperor clearly indicated that should Durnovo succeed in pleasing him, he would forget about Durnovo's past,—even his liberalism in the Senate. On the other hand, should Durnovo fail to win the Emperor's favour, his administration would be a very short one.

When Durnovo became familiar with the state of affairs at the court and discovered that the Emperor considered my administration as a bitter necessity, forced upon him by the inexorable course of events, and would gladly replace me by someone whom he would find more convenient to use as a shield, Durnovo decided that it was far better to be a persona gratissima with the Emperor in Tsarskoye Selo than with me in St. Petersburg. To please the Emperor you had to please Trepov and the Grand Duke Nikolai Nikolaievich. Durnovo did not hesitate to curry favour with both these personages.

By January first, Durnovo was appointed Minister and became Privy Counsellor. The promotion came to me as a surprise. Generally speaking, Durnovo did not judge it necessary to keep me informed about the nature of his audiences with His Majesty, although I knew that they were numerous and oftentimes lengthy. Towards Easter time his daughter was made lady-in-waiting to the Empress.

Durnovo adored his daughter and it had long been his cherished dream to have her become lady-in-waiting. He had made many efforts before, but they proved futile. To create a lady-in-waiting it is necessary to secure the consent of both Empresses, and it seems that the old Empress stubbornly refused to give her sanction. It was only through great persistence that His Majesty broke her obstinacy.

Afterwards, when Durnovo was unexpectedly forced to leave his post of Minister of the Interior, after I resigned from the post of Premier, the Emperor rewarded Durnovo with 200,000 rubles (from the Government Treasury, of course) to console him for the loss of his position.

While Durnovo was deficient from the moral viewpoint, he was, no doubt, a man of great energy and competence. If the Emperor had made it clear to Durnovo at the very start that while I remained President of the Imperial Council, he, Durnovo, who had been appointed at my instance, could do nothing without my knowledge and approval, all would have gone on admirably. Durnovo would have become, in fact, the embodiment of what I desired the Minister of the Interior to be.

The portfolio of Commerce I entrusted to V. D. Timiryazev, although I had a rather low opinion about him. It was not a happy choice either. He held exceedingly liberal views, I soon found. He had been away from Russia for a long time and he must have imagined that we in Russia had entered the era of a democratic republic. I was compelled to dismiss him as a result of a scandalous incident in which were involved the notorious Father Gapon and a journalist who secured 30,000 rubles from Timiryazev for the purpose of restoring Gapon's labour organization and then attempted to embezzle the funds.

When he left my Cabinet, I learned that he used to receive reporters of radical papers almost daily and tell them about the Government's activities, posing as an ultra-liberal. The further course of his career, showed, however, that his liberalism was little more than a mask.

Timiryazev achieved nothing either under me or in Stolypin's premiership when he was again appointed Minister of Commerce and Industry. His predecessor had given up his post because, he refused to acquiesce in the unlawful doling out of petroleum fields. Timiryazev was more accommodating. The only thing he sought was to please and gratify the powers that be. When the Duma made an interpellation concerning the illegal dealings with oil-bearing fields, he delivered himself of a truly revolting speech in defence of his actions. On the one hand, he insinuated that he was but doing the Emperor's will; on the other, he observed, with admirable naïveté, that the Czar has the God-given right to dry the tears of the unhappy and that this prerogative is one of the best sides of monarchism. In commenting upon this utterance, which aroused universal indignation, someone observed that in this case His Majesty had confined himself to drying the tears of equerries and court masters of the hunt, exclusively.

I also chose to part with Prince Hilkov, Minister of Ways of Communication. A man of good character and of great experience in technical railroad matters, he was not administrator enough to be equal to his ministerial tasks. As his successor I recommended director of the South-Western Railroads Nemyeshayev, who had the reputation of an experienced railway administrator, and who, I knew, would be agreeable to His Majesty. The Emperor approved my choice. Nemyeshayev succeeded in restoring the railroads to their normal state.

I had nothing against the Minister of War Rediger and the Minister of the Navy Birilev, while the Minister of Justice Manukhin and Minister of Foreign Affairs Lamsdorff I highly valued. I did not particularly prize Kokovtzev and Schwanebach, Ministers of Finances and Agriculture, respectively, but I was willing to cooperate with them if they would stop intriguing.

Before proceeding with my task of forming a Cabinet of Ministers, I decided to call a conference of public leaders, including Shipov, a well-known zemstvo worker; Guchkov, now leader of the Octobrist Party in the Imperial Duma; M. A. Stakhovich, Prince Urusov, and Prince Trubetzkoi, Professor of the University of Moscow, later member of the Imperial Council. I had previously been authorized, as a matter of principle, to offer some of the portfolios to prominent public men, should I find that their prestige might help allay the unrest. The conference was a failure, and further acquaintance with these men convinced me that they were not fit for the responsible ministerial posts, in spite of the fact that some of them were persons of excellent character and eminent abilities. Thus, for several weeks after my appointment, I was unable to form a Cabinet which would be in sympathy with the principles set forth in the constitutional manifesto or which would at least recognize its historic inevitability. As a result, for some time I ruled the country, a huge Empire in a state of profound upheaval, single-handedly, with the vast and intricate machinery of government practically out of commission.

Some two weeks after my appointment, General Trepov, Governor-General of St. Petersburg, Commander of the garrison of that city, and Assistant Minister of the Interior, formally tendered his resignation. I informed him over the telephone that I accepted it. The next morning I met him on board the government ship which was taking me to Peterhof for my daily report to His Majesty. He informed me that he had been appointed Court Commandant. The news came to me as a complete surprise, just as it did to everybody else. His departure looked like a hurried escape from the capital. In the course of my audience with the Emperor I observed that I was glad to hear of General Trepov's new appointment. With all his secret service experience, I said, he was likely to be successful in his task of protecting His Majesty's life, the chief task of a Court Commandant. The Emperor was apparently displeased with the subject of the conversation, and hastened to change it.

Trepov was followed by Garin, director of Department of Police. The latter was immediately named Senator and eventually became General Trepov's unofficial secretary. It was he who penned for General Trepov the learned resolutions teeming with reference to law books, which resolutions were subsequently given out by His Majesty as his own productions. The Emperor himself has never in his life opened the Russian code of laws, and I am certain that he does not know the difference between the Department of Causation and the other departments of the Senate.

Trepov is a central figure in our revolution and must be dealt with at considerable length. Prince Urusov speaking before the first Duma characterized him as "a quartermaster by education and a pogrom maker by conviction." While it is impossible to squeeze a human being with all its complexities into a narrow word formula, nevertheless Prince Urusov's phrase succeeds in bringing out one essential feature of Trepov's personality. He was indeed "a quartermaster by education," and therein lay his own and Russia's misfortune. In his youth he attended a military school (the Corps of Pages), yet whatever education he had he received in the barracks of the Cavalry Guards, and in the Officers' Club. He probably never in his life read a single serious book. It cannot be denied, however, that he was a smart, thoroughly trained, and conscientious officer.

"Pogrom-maker by conviction,"—that is not altogether accurate. Trepov did not love the art of pogrom-making for its own sake. He merely did not hesitate to resort to pogroms whenever he considered them necessary for the protection of the vital interests of the State, as he saw them. Only his attitude toward anti-Jewish pogroms was rather light-hearted, but in this respect he resembled Plehve, Count Ignatyev, and many other high officials to whom the bloody game of pogrom-making was a mere political amusement. And did not the Emperor himself call on all of us to rally under the banners of the Union of Russians, which political party openly advocates the annihilation of the Jews?

I first noticed Trepov under rather odd circumstances. The

incident is to a certain extent characteristic of him. When the body of the deceased Emperor Alexander III arrived in St. Petersburg from Yalta, it was taken to the Cathedral of St. Peter and St. Paul. The streets along which the funeral procession passed were lined with troops. According to the ceremonial, the cortége was headed by the Ministers and members of the Imperial Council marching in double file. Then came the clergymen and the funeral carriage. In passing a line of Cavalry Guards on Nevski Prospect, I was amazed to hear a Guard officer give the following word of command: "Head to the right" (i.e., in the direction of the approaching funeral carriage); "look more cheerful!" Turning to a General who happened to be nearby, I inquired who was that fool. "Count Trepov, squadron commander, a smart officer," came the reply.

Trepov began his political career as Chief of Police of Moscow, under Grand Duke Sergey Alexandrovich, Governor-General of the same city. He owed his promotion to his superior's wife, Grand Duchess Elizabeth Fyodorovna, a worthy and very unhappy woman, who after the terrible death of her husband (he was assassinated by terrorists) was naturally inclined to be well disposed toward his close collaborator. The Grand Duchess succeeded in winning over to Trepov's side her sister, Empress Alexandra, which naturally meant also the Emperor. Trepov was also a protégé of Baron Frederich. In the simplicity of his mind, the Baron sincerely believed that a plucky Cavalry Guard like General Trepov was just the man to impose discipline not alone upon the actions but also the very thoughts of the Russian people. Besides, General Mosolov, married to Trepov's sister, was director of the Baron's chancery, and it must be said that he never failed to take advantage of an occasion to present Trepov's actions and intentions to his superior in the best light. As far as independent judgment goes, the Baron himself was altogether below criticism. He found it hard to grasp plain facts, let alone a chain of reasoning. His assistants used to coach him like a schoolboy each time he had to report to His Majesty. Trepov also had a powerful friend at the Court in the person of Prince Orlov, Her Majesty's intimate collaborator and favourite.

During the revolutionary days General Trepov became a house divided against itself, and exhibited a complete confusion of mind. Unassisted by either political education or vision, he expressed simultaneously the most opposed views and passed from one extreme to another. An advocate of absolute autocracy, he expressed the most radical opinions in discussing Bulygin's project of a consultative Duma. In October, 1905, he issued the famous order of the day instructing the troops "not to spare cartridges," i.e., in dealing with the revolutionists. Several days later he spoke in favour of a most liberal political amnesty. On one hand, in the Committee of Ministers he insisted on the most stringent measures against both the students and the teaching staff of the institutions of higher learning; on the other hand, he originated and carried the plan of granting to these institutions a broad and vaguely defined autonomy, a measure which was instrumental in precipitating the revolution.

It must be admitted, nevertheless, that whatever this sorry statesman did was done in good faith and in the spirit of absolute loyalty to the Emperor and the man in the monarch. It is noteworthy that toward the end of his life the General fell into disfavour with His Majesty, and the latter was going to get rid of Trepov when he died a natural death. I am certain that no one will suspect me of being partial to General Trepov. He was practically my archenemy, and it was he who, more than any one else, made my position as Prime Minister unbearable. I feel, therefore, at liberty to assert, that, when all is said, Trepov was a man of good faith and political decency.

While Trepov held the ostensibly modest and nonpolitical office of Court Commandant, in reality he was a cross between an irresponsible dictator and an Asiatic eunuch day and night attached to the person of his Master. A man of a resolute and martial air, he wielded an overwhelming influence over the weak-willed Emperor. It was in Trepov's hands that lay His Majesty's safety, inasmuch as he was in charge of both the open and secret defence of the Monarch's person. He was at liberty to advise His Majesty at all times, and he acted as a middleman between the Czar and the authors of various confidential memoirs and secret reports, which were addressed to the Emperor. He had the power to smother a document or bring it emphatically to the Monarch's attention. Naturally enough, the numerous people who in their efforts to rise rely on other means than sheer merit and who make their careers in society boudoirs, those people began to seek by hook or crook to gain access to Trepov's reception room in the palaces of Tsarskoye-Selo and Peterhof. It was also natural for the Court clique to choose Trepov as the instrument of reaction, which followed upon the confusion and panic of the revolution.

Trepov's influence over His Majesty was by far greater than

mine. In fact, he was the irresponsible head of the Government, while I wielded little power and bore all the responsibility. This circumstance greatly hindered my activities and was the chief reason why I gave up my post several days before the opening of the Imperial Duma. It is noteworthy that my successor Goremykin was on excellent terms with Trepov, which was, no doubt, one of the causes why he was appointed, for Goremykin had nothing except his huge whiskers to distinguish him from thousands of bureaucratic mediocrities. But Trepov could unmake a Prime Minister, just as he could make one, and as a matter of fact, Goremykin was dismissed at Trepov's suggestion. "It's Stolypin's luck," Goremykin told me on one occasion, in 1908, "that Trepov died a few weeks after his appointment."

It appears that on being appointed Court Commandant Trepov did not altogether sever his relations with the Department of Police. Rachkovski, head of the Secret Service under Trepov and formerly the leading spirit of the Department, was an assiduous habitué in the house of the Court Commandant. He had been removed by Durnovo from his high office and attached to the Minister of the Interior in the capacity of official charged with special functions. In January, or perhaps in February, 1906, Lopukhin, Director of the Police Department under Plehve, had a formal conference with me, in the course of which he imparted to me a piece of startling information. He knew it as a certainty, he declared, that there was at the Police Department a special section headed by Captain Komissarov, which was engaged in turning out proclamations inciting to anti-Jewish pogroms, and in disseminating them broadcast in the country. Only the other day, he said, large bales of this literature had been sent to Kursk, Wilna, and Moscow. He added that the section had originated under Trepov and had been directed by Rachkovski, who at the time was still connected with it.

Knowing Lopukhin's hostility toward both Trepov and Rachkovski, I assumed a skeptical attitude toward his tale, and asked him to submit proofs in support of his words. Several days later Lopukhin brought me samples of the proclamations he had spoken about. He warned me that, unless Komissarov were taken by surprise, he would be able easily to cover up his traces. The following day I summoned one of my secretaries and ordered him immediately to drive to the Police Department in my own carriage and from there to the place where Captain Komissarov was most likely to be found and bring me the man without the least delay and without allowing him the time necessary to change his clothes in case he was not in proper uniform.

A half hour later I beheld Captain Komissarov for the first time in my life. He wore citizen's clothes. I seated him and without mincing words asked him how he was getting on with the very important affair with which he had been entrusted and in which I took, I said, great interest. I went on mentioning such details that he was at once taken aback and made no effort to conceal his activities from me. He admitted that the proclamations were being disseminated, but he mentioned smaller figures than those given by Lopukhin. The printing, he confessed, was being done on presses seized during the raids on several revolutionary underground printing establishments and now housed in the basement of the Police Department building. When asked who was the organizer and head of the section, he hastened to assure me that he was acting on his own initiative, without the knowledge of either his former or his present superiors, merely because he believed the work to be highly useful. To press the point was to no purpose. "Give me your word," I said to him, "that immediately upon your return to the Police Department you will destroy the entire supply of pogrom literature and either demolish or throw into the Fontanka River all your printing presses; also that you will never engage in such activities. This sort of thing cannot go on. I shall not tolerate it. If I find out tomorrow morning that you have failed to comply with my order, I shall deal with you according to the letter of the law." Komissarov gave me his word of honour that he would literally carry out my instructions.

The next day I took up the matter with the Minister of the Interior. Durnovo, who apparently knew nothing of the activities of Komissarov's section, instituted an investigation. I have in my records Durnovo's report about its findings. While not denying the facts, the report naturally minimized them. The story then penetrated into the press and formed the subject of a speech delivered by Prince Urusov in the First Duma. In the course of my next interview with the Emperor I reported to him the whole matter. His Majesty was silent and appeared to be familiar with all the details of the matter. In conclusion, I asked him to refrain from punishing Komissarov. He remarked that he did not intend to punish the Captain anyway, in consideration of his services in obtaining secret military documents at the time of our war with Japan.

Speaking of Trepov and his influence upon the Czar, I cannot refrain from relating here one characteristic incident. On one occasion, towards the end of 1905, I met General Trepov in the Emperor's reception chamber. General Trepov told me that it would be desirable to have the Imperial Bank grant a loan to Skalon, an officer of the body-guards and son-in-law of Homiakov, now President of the Imperial Duma. I told him that the proper place to go to would be the Imperial Bank.

General Trepov informed me that the Imperial Bank refused to grant this loan, inasmuch as it did not belong to the types of loans provided for by the statutes of the Bank.

"If such is the case," I replied, "then Skalon will not receive the loan. Formerly loans were occasionally granted by orders of His Majesty, although not provided for by the statutes of the Bank. This is impossible now, however: first of all, because it would not harmonize with the spirit of the Manifesto of Oct. 17th, and secondly, because the country is going through a financial crisis. I know nothing about the substance of the case, but judging from the externals of the matter and my experiences with similar cases, I feel almost certain that the Bank will be the loser in this case. At all events, it will be a long-term loan."

Some time later Shipov, the Minister of Finances, came to inquire about my health. I had been in ill health since my return from America. He stated that he considered it his duty to share with me a confidential piece of information.

After Shipov had presented his last report, he told me, the Emperor instructed him to have the Imperial Bank grant a loan of two million rubles to Skalon. His Majesty added: "I request you to tell nothing about this matter to the President of the Council." I assured Shipov that in my official capacity I would act as if entirely ignorant of the matter, but that I was interested to know what he had done.

Upon his return to the Department, Shipov told me, he immediately wrote to the Emperor, telling him that he would obey His Majesty's orders, but that he judged it necessary to draw His Majesty's attention to those portions of the Bank's statutes, from which it appears clearly that the Bank has no right to grant this loan and that substantially the loan was unsound. His Majesty returned the report with a marginal remark: "Comply with my orders!" The Bank therefore granted this loan.

But Shipov paid dearly for the report he made to the Emperor. When I left the post of Premier, Shipov received no appointment in spite of my intercession. As for the loan, it is still unpaid.

To illustrate the workings of Trepov's mind and to exemplify the political reaction which set in in the wake of the country's pacification, I wish to relate also the story of Kutler's peasant bill.

I have not the slightest doubt but that the future phases of the Russian revolution will unfold in close connection with the land situation, especially since Stolypin has inaugurated the policy based on the axiom that Russia exists for a handful of landowners. During the first weeks which followed the publication of the constitutional manifesto, the peasantry seemed to have entirely gotten out of hand. It must be borne in mind that our peasants have always had but the vaguest notion of legality, normal justice and the institution of property as the basis of social order in a modern State. It was then that the landowners lost their heads. General Trepov was one of the first to fall into a complete confusion. Once, I remember, I had a remarkable talk with him at the Tsarskoye Selo Palace where I had come to report to His Majesty. The conversation turned to the peasant uprisings and Trepov declared that the only way to put an end to this disaster was to carry out an immediate and extensive expropriation of privately owned land for the benefit of the peasants. I expressed my doubts as to the advisability of adopting such a vastly important measure hastily and ill-advisedly, and that on the very eve of the opening of the Imperial Duma. He retorted that the landowners would welcome the measure: "I am a landed proprietor myself," he said, "and I would be very glad indeed to give away half of my land, provided I could be assured that on this condition I could safely keep the other half."

During the audience His Majesty handed me a document saying: "This is Professor Migulin's memoir. Take it up in the Council of Ministers." This memoir advocated the compulsory expropriation of land for the benefit of the peasantry, as a measure which should be immediately adopted and put into effect by Imperial decree. I understood at once who had laid the project before the Emperor. Professor Migulin, author of a great many clever and pretentious compilations entirely devoid of true scholarship, enjoyed some prestige among the middle class intellectuals and provincial lionesses. He had, therefore, no difficulty in gaining access to General

Trepov. After the audience, Trepov met me again and tried to persuade me that the measure advocated in the memorandum which had been handed to me should be adopted with all possible haste, before the peasants had taken away all the land from the gentry.

Migulin's project was examined by the Council of Ministers, and all its members, including Kutler, Minister of Agriculture, assumed a negative attitude toward the proposed measure. The unanimous opinion was that this measure, affecting as it did the vital nerve of the Russian body politic, needed a most thoroughgoing investigation and that, besides, it lay properly within the authority of the Imperial Duma and Imperial Council.

While rejecting Migulin's ill-advised suggestion, the Council of Ministers adopted two measures tending to better the peasants' condition, namely, the abolition of the redemption payments, i.e., payments for the land allotted to the peasants at their emancipation, and the extension of the land operations of the Peasant Bank. These two measures were immediately enacted by Imperial decree. The Council also decided to form a special commission under Kutler's presidency for the purpose of drafting bills relating to the peasant class, to be laid before the Imperial Duma. It is noteworthy that at one time Adjutant-General Dubasov, the man who suppressed the Moscow insurrection, held a view not unlike Trepov's regarding the method of dealing with the agrarian disorders. In the course of a conversation he had with me in December, 1905, he expressed himself to the effect that there was but one way to pacify the countryside, namely, to legalize the peasants' land seizures.

In the meantime, the revolutionary wave began to ebb, and in proportion as the general pacification of the country made progress, the ruling element began to repudiate more and more resolutely the views and opinions which were engendered by the panic of the revolution. Gradually the project of compulsory expropriation of landed estates ceased to be a subject of discussion and in the end it came to be considered a revolutionary, a criminal, and, indeed, a monstrous measure. Several weeks after the Council of Ministers had turned down Professor Migulin's project espoused by Trepov and after a commission had been formed for the preliminary work on peasant legislation, Kutler told me that the more he studied the problems of peasant landownership, the clearer he saw the inevitability of some form of compulsory expropriation of land for the benefit of the peasantry, and with compensation for the expropriated landowners.

Shortly afterwards, I found on my desk a package containing a number of mimeographed* copies of a preliminary project for the amelioration† of peasant landownership, drafted by Kutler's Commission. As His Majesty had asked me to rush all the measures relating to the peasant class, I immediately ordered copies of the project sent to the members of the Council of Ministers and also to some of the members of the Imperial Council. It was not before late in the evening that I found a free moment to look into Kutler's project. I found that it advocated compensated compulsory expropriation of a portion of privately owned land for the benefit of the peasants with insufficient holdings. The project providing for such a measure appeared to me untimely, to say the least. I had already noticed the reactionary change in the attitude of the high spheres toward the principle of compulsory expropriation. Consequently I had those of the copies of the project which had already gone out returned, and the following morning I told Kutler that I considered the moment inopportune for the discussion of the project of his Commission. The Minister did not insist, but asked me to take up the principles underlying the project at a private conference of the Ministers. I inquired whether he had taken the necessary measures to keep the project secret. I was afraid, I explained, that it might be used as a pretext for all manner of insinuations and intrigues. He had taken, he said, no such measures, for the idea had not even occurred to him.

The private session of the Council took place soon afterwards. The ministers, without exception, assumed a negative attitude toward the basic principle of Kutler's project. They advanced as chief argument the inviolability and sacrosanctitude of the institution of private property. I agreed with my colleagues, but I drew their attention to the fact that the historical act of the peasants' emancipation was in itself based on the principle of compulsory expropriation. I opposed the measure for the reason, I stated, that in my opinion it would complete the process of undermining Russia's fin-

---

* The *mimeograph* was a copy machine, the preluder to a photo copier. Mimeographs were copies of documents.

† *Amelioration* is the act of improving something or making it more tolerable. Witte is describing coming in to the possession of a copy relating to a project to improve the plight of the peasants.

ancial and economic resources, which was begun by the war and continued by the unrest. Kutler admitted that the measure he proposed might have a weakening effect on Russia's economic status, but that it was the only means of permanently pacifying the peasant masses. Upon the whole, he showed no persistence in defending his project. The Council of Ministers asked Kutler to alter the project, which he agreed to do. The Council also named several additional members for his commission, all of them staunch opponents of the principle of compulsory expropriation. After the session, Kutler thanked me for the opportunity I had given him for an exchange of opinions with his colleagues.

Several days later I received from His Majesty a note demanding a copy of Kutler's agrarian project. In reply I wrote to His Majesty that there was no such project in existence, that there was but a rough outline of certain legal measures (I enclosed it) which had been discussed at a private meeting of the Ministers and unanimously turned down just like Professor Migulin's project which had been laid before us some time ago by His Majesty himself, also that Kutler agreed with the judgment of the Council of Ministers, and that at present the commission presided over by this Minister, with its membership altered, was busy redrafting the project. Shortly afterwards I happened to be reporting to His Majesty. The conversation turned to Kutler's project and the Emperor remarked that everyone was aroused against Kutler and that it would be desirable to replace him. I asked His Majesty, in case of Kutler's dismissal, to appoint him member of the Imperial Council, to which the Emperor apparently assented.

No sooner, however, did I return home than I received from His Majesty an autographic note informing me that he considered it inappropriate to name Kutler member of the Imperial Council. Several days later I had another occasion to discuss the Minister's dismissal with His Majesty, and I secured his promise to appoint Kutler senator. But the Czar again changed his mind and refused to keep his promise. More correspondence followed, and finally, at His Majesty's suggestion, I summoned Kutler and told him that owing to the misunderstandings created by his project it would be best for him to send in his resignation, which he did (in February, 1906). At my instance, His Majesty granted the former Minister a pension of 7,000 rubles per annum. Thus, Kutler fell a victim to the reactionary zeal of Trepov and his like, who in their eagerness to retract their radicalism born of cowardice, needed a scapegoat upon which to lay their sins.

When it came to finding someone to take the place of the dismissed Minister of Agriculture, His Majesty pointed to Krivoshein, Kutler's assistant, as a desirable successor. I knew the man as Trepov's favourite and as an unscrupulous, self-seeking office-hunter. "Your Majesty," I said to the Emperor, "you are not personally acquainted with Krivoshein and you wish to appoint him at the recommendation of irresponsible advisors. As for me, I cannot admit to the Cabinet over which I preside men who are making their careers by crooked means. I should welcome a statesman of the most conservative views, provided his opinions are a matter of sincere conviction and not a means for self-aggrandizement." His Majesty yielded and asked me to let Krivoshein take charge of the Ministry temporarily, pending the appointment of a permanent Minister.

My own candidate for the Minister of Agriculture was Fiodor Samarin, a staunch Slavophile and a public worker of an immaculate reputation. He refused, however, to accept my offer, saying frankly that, on the one hand he could not enter my Cabinet for the reason that he was completely opposed to the act of October 17th, and that on the other hand, he was neither strong nor experienced enough to take such a responsible post. I named a number of other candidates, among them Yermolov, Minister of Agriculture under Alexander III, Prince Kochubei and Prince Urusov. Some of the men were rejected by His Majesty, others declined the portfolio themselves.

In the meantime intriguing against me and my policies was going on at full speed at the Court. All manner of denunciations and memoirs inveighing openly against my Cabinet were daily reaching His Majesty through Trepov, and the weight of these writings at the Court was constantly on the increase. In January, 1906, there was circulated among the large landowners a petition which accused some of the members of my Cabinet of revolutionary designs and demanded its dismissal. The petition was fairly long and contained, among others, the following passage:

It stands to reason that the men who have received the reins of power from the hand of your Majesty lack neither knowledge nor experience. Naturally enough, there are heard voices asserting that the Utopian legal measures of Count Witte's Cabinet are being elaborated with the hidden intention of transferring to the villages the revolution which had failed in the cities among the labouring classes.

The document concludes thus:

We deem it our sacred duty as loyal subjects of your Majesty to affirm that the present Government as represented by its head, Count Witte, does not enjoy the confidence of the country and that all Russia expects you to replace this all-powerful functionary by a man of firmer statesmanlike principles and more experience in the choice of reliable collaborators worthy of the people's confidence.

On the 10th of February I received from His Majesty a note informing me that he intended to appoint Krivoshein Minister of Agriculture and Rukhlov, Minister of Commerce. I was enraged and decided to tender my resignation, but before doing so I called my colleagues into session to announce to them my decision. They strenuously opposed my desire to resign and argued me into addressing the following letter to the Czar:

All the blame for the Government's actions and all the animosities aroused by them fall first of all upon me. This is a natural consequence of the law about the Council of Ministers, although that law is not strictly observed and I oftentimes learn from the papers about important measures taken in most cases by the provincial authorities. All this places me in a very difficult position, which for the time being I am enduring in spite of my fatigue and poor health, for I am sustained by the sense of duty I owe to your Imperial Majesty and inspired by a feeling of genuine patriotism.

Even now I am prevented from properly unifying the actions of the Government. Yet the Duma and the reformed Imperial Council will open shortly and I shall be forced to give account for actions in which I did not participate, for measures which I am unable to carry out, and for projects of which I do not approve.

Under the existing conditions a Government whose members lack solidarity in their mutual relationships, let alone homogeneity of convictions and views, is an impossibility. I do not think coöperation is at all possible between myself and either Krivoshein or Rukhlov. I had the honour of conferring with your Majesty regarding Krivoshein's case and your Majesty was pleased twice to assure me that he would be in charge of the Ministry but for a few days. On receiving your note to-day about your intentions with regard to Krivoshein and Rukhlov, I judged it advisable to verify my views on those two candidates through an exchange of opinions with the members of the Council. I called to-day a private conference of the Ministers, and we have come to a unanimous conclusion that neither Krivoshein nor Rukhlov is qualified for the posts in question and that their appointment would obstruct the activity of the Council and add to the difficulties of my position. Therefore, the Ministers have empowered me to report the matter to your Majesty and beg you to keep intact the homogeneity of the personnel of the Government and allow it to complete its difficult task of governing the country until the Imperial Duma is convened.

The Emperor yielded again, and at my recommendation A. P. Nikolsky, one of my collaborators in the Ministry of Finances, was appointed Director of the Ministry of Agriculture. I selected him because I knew that he was on good terms with Krivoshein and that His Majesty would, therefore, raise no objections.

In another connection I have spoken of the role played by Grand Duke Nikolai Nikolaievich in the critical days which preceded the publication of the constitutional manifesto. In his capacity of commander of the armies of the St. Petersburg District he complied with my request to keep the troops in readiness, should I find it necessary to proclaim military law in St. Petersburg and its vicinity. Several weeks after the interview in the course of which that subject was discussed, General Hasenkampf, shortly before appointed assistant to the Grand Duke, called on me and asked me, in the Grand Duke's name, in case of necessity to proclaim extraordinary instead of military law. "You see," he explained, "if extraordinary law is proclaimed the capital punishment cases will be within the jurisdiction of Durnovo (Min-ister of the Interior), while in case of military law the executions will depend on the Grand Duke, and he is likely to become a target of the terrorists."

No sooner did the Grand Duke perceive that the pacification was not likely to come at once than his relative judiciousness and restraint vanished. Before long I learned by chance that General Rauch, his nearest satellite, was conferring with Dr. Dubrovin, the notorious Black Hundred leader, who was then at the beginning of his career. Later the Grand Duke's relations with the Union of the Russian People (a Black Hundred organization, or more precisely, a band of mercenary hooligans) assumed a more direct character. At one time the St. Petersburg branch of the Union intended to elect the Grand Duke honorary president, but in the end the step was found to be a too risky one. It was only because Dubrovin relied upon the Grand Duke's, and also, I believe, Durnovo's protection, that he dared on one occasion to gather a gang of hooligans in the building of one of the riding-schools in St. Petersburg and to make incendiary speeches of such a nature that the crowd emerged from the building shouting: "Down with the cursed constitution and death to Count Witte!"

Among the most important problems with which my Cabinet had to cope was the modification of the electoral laws promulgated simultaneously with the decree of August 6, 1905, which created the purely advisory so-called Bulygin Duma. In pursuance of the manifesto of October 17th, it was necessary to change the electoral law, in the sense of liberalizing it, without, however, interfering with the elections for the Imperial Duma, which had already begun. One system of electoral laws was devised by a Moscow group of public leaders, headed by D. I. Shipov, Guchkov and Prince Trubetzkoi. In the course of the conference called to discuss the participation of these public men in my Cabinet, which participation, as I said, did not take place, they had taken upon themselves, or, rather, they succeeded by dint of sheer beggary, as it were, in securing the work of elaborating a franchise law. Another electoral law, the Government's, was drafted under my guidance and with my direct assistance, by Kryzhanowski, a functionary attached to the Ministry of the Interior, who is also responsible for the electoral law of the Bulygin Duma.

Kryzhanovsky's law did not attempt to alter the basic principles of the Bulygin franchise regulations, but merely extended them so as to include new categories of electors, while the law drafted by the public leaders aimed at approaching the realization of universal suffrage, the ideal of the Constitutional Democrats.

The two electoral law drafts were then examined at a special session of the Committee of Ministers under my presidency. The session was attended, in accordance with the law, by the chairmen of the departments of the Imperial Council (Count Solski, Frisch, and Golubyov), by some of the members of the Imperial Council, such as A. A. Saburov and Tagantzev, and also by the public leaders who took part in the formulation of the electoral law.

The public leaders except Count Bobrinski staunchly defended their project, but I succeeded in winning over a considerable majority of the members of the conference to the governmental version of the electoral law.

The two versions were then discussed at a special conference presided over by His Majesty and attended, besides the Ministers and some of the members of the Imperial Council, by several Grand Dukes and public leaders, including Count Bobrinski and Baron Korff. These two men, I felt certain, would support the Government's version, but I was mistaken. The Count afterwards told me that in the interval between the two conferences he had come to the conclusion, as a result of a trip in the country, that nothing short of an exceedingly democratic electoral law would satisfy the people. After the public leaders had spoken, His Majesty dismissed them and declared an intermission. The session was resumed, but we came to no decision. His Majesty was apparently in the throes of hesitation. The following day, at some Court function, I had an occasion to speak to the Empress. I told her that His Majesty would commit a mistake if he passed the democratic electoral law. This was the only time that I resorted to Her Majesty's influence in connection with State matters. Another conference followed and again the majority favoured the Government's, i.e., my project. Finally, the Emperor overcame his irresoluteness, and this version was adopted.

One of the most important bodies of statutes formulated during my administration was the group comprising the empire's fundamental laws, whose promulgation was deferred, however, until a few days after my withdrawal and the appointment of Goremykin to the premiership. The significance of these enactments rests in the vital protection they afforded the new governmental régime during the crucial period succeeding its creation on October 17th, and in the fact that they still constitute the basic law of the land, though in a form sadly distorted by Stolypin's unprincipled measures of June 3rd.

Although a committee of delegates to the famous council of zemstvo and town workers had already worked out, toward the end of 1904 or the beginning of 1905, a code of fundamental laws for the Russian Empire, which was extremely democratic, including, as it did, provisions for universal suffrage, single voting, secret ballot and direct representation, so that the power of the Emperor would be as limited as that of the President of the Swiss Republic, nevertheless, during the first two months of my premiership neither the Council of Members nor I myself, in my official capacity, had as yet considered the elaboration of the basic edicts necessitated by the manifesto of October 17th, with its mandate for the establishment of an Imperial Duma and the thoroughgoing revision of the imperial budget system; and, of course, we were still further away from a serious examination of the advisability of publishing these decrees before the Duma convened, in order that the new representative body might proceed at once to an intelligent discussion of legislative measures.

Early in 1906 Count Solski told me in a private conversation that under His Majesty's orders a fundamental code was then being worked out by the Imperial Secretary, Ikskul, a splendid man of wide administrative experience but of very few original ideas, and his assistant, Kharitonov. Adding that upon completion this draft was to be submitted for discussion to an unofficial conference, under his direct leadership, the Count urgently invited me to take part in the deliberations. Notwithstanding our cordial relations, I refused categorically, and, upon his continued pressure to accept, I explained that on account of my conspicuous position I was resolutely determined to abstain from participating in such committees, since by reason of my mere presence posterity would charge me with the responsibility for the serious defects with which, judging by past experience, systems evolved in this manner were bound to suffer, especially in such troubled times. Furthermore, I expressed it as my firm conviction that the formulation of fundamental laws, as well as ordinary statutes, should be left to the Council of Ministers, whose members, and I as Premier, would have to bear the onus. Solski was sorely displeased with my answer. Shortly afterwards he informed me that he had been commissioned by the Emperor to complete the draft of the proposed laws, which would then be sent to the Council of Ministers.

Toward the end of February I received from Solski the projected code in the form in which it was presented to His Majesty. The manner in which this plan reached me will be an illuminating commentary on the psychologically unsound condition of Russian society in general and of its representatives in particular at this juncture. Impelled by a motive unrevealed until afterwards, the prime mover in this enterprise of promulgating a system of fundamental law was General Trepov, at the time occupying a position much akin to that of a dictator, as I have described at some length elsewhere. His Majesty having approved of the idea, the work was assigned to the Imperial Secretary and his assistant. The hodge-podge of constitutional statutes which they concocted was turned over to a paragon of the aristocratic bureaucracy of St. Petersburg, a well-meaning liberal of exemplary gifts and education with a lifelong experience in the Imperial Council, in short, a perfect specimen of exalted officialdom. And so, finally, bearing this awe-inspiring stamp of approval, there comes to me, the head of the Government at this revolutionary crisis, a code of basic laws such as would, for the second time after October 17th, have reduced the Emperor's power of his own free will or, rather, unwittingly, and to such a marked extent that he would have become, not only incomparably less potent than the Mikado, but less than the President of the French Republic and in some respects even less than the President of the Swiss Republic. Shackled by such fundamental laws, the Empire and its government would have been at the mercy of the deranged people who made up such a large part of the first Imperial Duma. Of course, in the end, who would have been blamed for the resulting confusion worse confounded? Who, indeed, but Witte?

On this occasion I wrote to His Majesty as follows:

> The proposed code, in my opinion, suffers both from sins of commission and omission. It contains, on the one hand, a number of extremely dangerous provisions; and, on the other hand, it lacks provisions absolutely necessary in the new order of things. I would refer first of all to the need of distinguishing between laws and decrees. At present almost every measure may be regarded as a law, since, according to a strict interpretation of its functions, practically everything has to pass through the Imperial Council. Although such a mode of procedure may have been convenient for the Monarch while the Council was merely an advisory body, under the new conditions it would involve us in the most embarrassing difficulties. In spite of the fact that I have more than once adverted to this matter in discussing the regulations concerning the Imperial Council and the Imperial Duma, I find not a single word on the subject in the plan submitted to me by Count Solski. I would also call attention to defects in the basic laws concerning the succession and regency, which laws Your Majesty at one time desired to modify, according to information given me by K. P. Pobiedonostzev and N. B. Muraviov.

(The Emperor expressed this intention shortly after his serious illness with typhoid fever at Yalta, when, due to the pregnant condition of the Empress, a delicate question arose regarding the succession to the throne).

During all this time I received not the least statement from His

Majesty in reference to the fundamental laws. Apparently, throughout this affair, there was going on behind the scenes a game of which I was not fully cognizant until subsequently. As I have already remarked, the stage manager of the intrigue was Trepov, whose intention it was to omit me and the Council of Ministers from the cast altogether, or, rather, to have me play the rôle of *tété-de-ture*, i.e., scapegoat. Since I was too wary to fall into this trap, the project was transmitted to me through Solski without any instructions whatever. The Emperor certainly did not read the plan until I laid it before him in a revised form.

When the subject came up in the Council of Ministers, which devoted only a few hurried sessions to it despite its paramount importance, the first question discussed was whether or not the fundamental laws should be made public before the meeting of the Duma. It was clear to me that essentially the answer to this question would decide whether the régime ushered in on October 17th was to survive or be drowned in a deluge of blood. Evidently, if the laws were not promulgated before its convention, the Duma would resolve itself into a constituent assembly, thus provoking the use of military force with the consequent destruction of the new régime. Would this be for the best? Yes, provided a second Peter the Great were to appear. Having no faith at all, however, in such a miracle, I took a firm stand for the promulgation of the laws before the opening of the Duma. All the members of the Council took the same view with the solitary exception of A. D. Obolensky, who lost his bearings completely at this time and rushed distractedly from extreme liberalism to extreme conservatism. It was his opinion that the Duma should devise the fundamental laws. However, I, as well as all the rest of the members, had already ceased to take him seriously. My ideas were not fully revealed to the Council, and its members did not see as far ahead as I. The general view of the Council on this point is indicated by the following entry in the Council's journal, wherein the revised draft of the proposed laws was recorded:

> It is most unwise to postpone the promulgation of the basic statutes, in order to formulate them with the Duma's assistance, since this would mean that instead of beginning the constructive work of organization immediately, the newly elected representatives of the people would be drawn into dangerous and futile controversies about the extent of their

rights and the nature of their relation to the Supreme Power.

On beginning the examination of the project presented to us by Count Solski, I inquired of Count Lamsdorff, Minister of Foreign Affairs, and of Birilev and Rediger, Ministers of the Navy and War, respectively, whether they had any objections to those sections which related to the departments under their control. I was greatly astonished when they answered that they had no objections of any consequence to make. Thereupon I informed them that on my part I was unalterably opposed to the clauses relating to the conduct of foreign affairs and the control of the empire's military forces. I explained that in my estimation the direction of our foreign policy and the leadership of the army and navy belonged to the head of the Government, i.e., the Emperor, and that the Duma should deliberate upon these matters only from a financial standpoint, i.e., in connection with the budget. Influenced by my statements, the three ministers made suggestions which were discussed by the Council and led to changes and additions to the fundamental laws, so that His Majesty was confirmed as the dictator of foreign policies and the supreme commander of the army and navy. I believed, as I still do, that the Duma's meddling with these matters under existing conditions, which are not likely to change for a long time to come, would have resulted inevitably in undermining Russia's position among the great powers. Doubtless there will not be lacking opponents of this view, who will cite especially the gross blunder committed in bringing on the war with Japan. To this my reply will be that man is always prone to mistakes and insensate actions; but that one need merely glance at the changes in the map of Russia from the time of Ivan the Terrible and Peter the Great to the days of Nicholas II in order to realize that almost no other nation has, during so short a period, made such gigantic advances in the field of exterior intercourse and expansion. It is true, however, that during the reign of Nicholas II serious errors have been made in this respect. God forbid a repetition of them!

After this, turning to the problem which I had called to His Majesty's attention, I pointed out to the Council the necessity of differentiating between decrees and laws. In considering this question the Council concluded that, since legislative experience had demonstrated the impossibility of distinguishing between decrees and laws by their contents, it was necessary to detail more minutely in the fundamental laws those matters in which the supreme power exercised unlimited sovereignty. Accordingly the Council undertook to formulate a comprehensive definition of the Emperor's power, setting forth in particular his executive authority and his right to issue decrees for the establishment of certain administrative agencies of the government, for the maintenance of law and order and for the advancement of the general welfare of his people. In addition the Council deemed it advisable to record at greater length His Majesty's control over governmental employés and officials, particularly his prerogative of removing or dismissing any of them from office. About the last point, however, a controversy arose in connection with the Ministry of Justice. The majority, including myself, held that the Emperor's power of dismissal applied to the Department of Justice also, while the minority argued for an irremovable judiciary holding office under the law of Alexander II.

The Council of Ministers then proceeded to define the Emperor's exclusive privilege of minting coins, his power to proclaim martial law or a state of siege, to grant amnesty, to exempt from taxation, to define the areas of freedom of dwelling, and to condemn private property for public use. Furthermore, the Council considered it necessary to state that the Emperor possesses absolutely unlimited control over his estate and personal property, including securities, and over the management of the Department of the Imperial Court. In order to avoid misunderstanding, confirmation was also given to the fact that high government officials may not be subjected to criminal prosecution or sentenced by the properly instituted authorities without the Emperor's previous consent; likewise that members of the privileged classes may not be deprived of their rights without such consent.

Because the fundamental laws would, unlike ordinary statutes, be susceptible of revision only at the Emperor's command, it was deemed advantageous to include the most important provisions of the recent enactments regarding the imperial budget. For similar reasons a clause was incorporated to the effect that whenever the quota of recruits to be called out for military training during a given year was not fixed before May 1st, the same number as in the preceding year should be summoned. The particular object of this rule was to nullify possible obstructive tactics on the part of the legislative assembly in a matter of such vital moment.

Although the sections concerning the Council of Ministers were altered somewhat in order to effect coöperation between them and the representative body, the ministers remained responsible solely to the Emperor; and, of course, answerable to the courts in case they broke their oath of office.

Finally a clause guaranteeing liberty of conscience was inserted together with the decree of April 17, 1905, establishing religious tolerance.

On March 20th I presented the revised draft to His Majesty, who thereupon called a special conference to discuss the subject shortly after the Easter holidays. Besides the Ministers, many members of the Imperial Council were invited to the sessions, among them Count Palen, who was Minister of Justice during the reign of Alexander II; Goremykin, Count Ignatyev, and Grand Dukes Vladimir Alexandrovich, Nikolai Nikolaievich and Mikhail Alexandrovich, the latter accompanied by his counsellor, General Potozky.

During the discussions several heated controversies took place, the first one arising when Grand Duke Nikolai Nikolaievich recommmended that the number of recruits to be summoned to the colours yearly should be fixed in advance in the fundamental law, thus preventing the legislative body from meddling with this matter. He was vigorously opposed by Grand Duke Vladimir Alexandrovich, who asserted that, since the annual mobilization touched the well-being of the people at large so closely, it would be demoralizing to disregard the wishes of the popular delegates in such a question, evidently not a point of basic law, but a recurring measure of periodical effect. Stating that if we had no faith in the loyalty of the Russian people, we should not suffer them to have a Duma at all, but that if we believed in their patriotism we should allow their representative body to function naturally, he concluded: "For my part, I have abiding faith in Russia, I believe in the Russian people, and I believe that their Duma will be patriotic because it will be made up of public-spirited Russians. I have, therefore, no fear of the future." In consequence of this plea His Majesty refused to entertain further the proposal of Grand Duke Nikolai Nikolaievich.

There was also a sharp difference of opinion among the members of this special conference, as in the Council of Ministers, regarding judicial tenure of office. The Minister of Justice, Akimov, and myself spoke in favour of affirming the Emperor's right of dismissing judges. My contentions were, first, that the existing principle of the irremovability of magistrates restricted only the power of the

Minister of Justice and of the higher judiciary in general over subordinate officials, and could not apply to the Emperor himself, since the act had been promulgated at a time when the Monarch's sovereignty was not subject to limitation; second, that, due to the introduction of a new era on October 17th, with the concomitant abridgement of the ruler's authority, it now became necessary for the first time to decide whether or not the Emperor should surrender the prerogative in question; third, that if His Majesty reserved this privilege exclusively for himself, neither delegating it to subordinates nor granting it to the people, the result would be to encourage and safeguard the independence and impartiality of the administrators of justice. Count Palen strenuously opposed this view, apparently forgetting that while he was Minister of Justice, he had found it expedient in the case of examining judges to get around the legal prohibition of removal by discontinuing the appointment of regular magistrates and assigning to all vacancies substitutes, whose tenure is not fixed by law, so that at present our examining judges are all substitutes. Goremykin, too, warmly advocated a guarantee of judicial tenure. The Emperor concurred with this opinion in spite of the fact that it was held by a minority only. And now, what has become of this exalted principle of judicial inviolability under the régime of Messrs. Stolypin-Shcheglovitov? The members of the conference were led to believe that dismissal of judges would be an extraordinary measure, always dependent upon His Majesty's previous consent; but the Hon. Mr. Shcheglovitov, the law nothwithstanding, now discharges judges right and left according to his own sweet desire, so that the Department of Justice is rotten with crawling sycophants of the Minister of Justice, from whom all blessings flow, including the privilege of holding office.

During the discussion of the 31st chapter concerning the security of property, there occurred between myself and Goremykin a heated exchange which was fraught with the greatest significance, though I did not realize it at the time. In criticizing this section, Goremykin remarked, among other things, that the coming Duma should not be allowed to touch upon confiscation of private estates and that it should be dispersed forthwith in case of refusal to comply with this injunction. Although the chapter was finally left in, the form submitted by the Council of Ministers, this vehement expression of Goremykin's was favourably received by many of those present, and the Emperor, too, appeared to like it. On my part I declared my opposition to such a plan, observing that, whereas one might be unqualifiedly against forcible expropriation, it did not follow that the Duma should be prevented from discussing ways and means and planning laws in reference to this subject. On the contrary, the question, I added, is precisely one which the representative assembly should deem it important to consider; and, provided its proceedings are legally correct, I see no cause for dispersing the Duma, even though it does wish to deliberate upon the peasants' problem. In the event that the Duma should decide upon some irrational measure, the Council of Ministers is organized for the very purpose of forestalling the popular assembly's blunders and aberrations, I concluded. The debate ended there, but, as will be seen later, this controversy was one of the things that induced me to tender my resignation. Using this dispute as a stepping stone, Goremykin, with the assistance of Trepov, was enabled to take my place as Premier; and then he was constrained to disperse the First Duma when the peasants' question came up in that body, since having, so to speak, announced his platform at this conference, no other course was open to him.

When the discussion of the draft presented by the Council of Ministers was terminated, His Majesty stated that he accepted the projected code with the few minor changes, mainly editorial corrections, which were decided upon during the conference. The plan was signed in its final form, and I considered the matter closed.

By the time the fundamental laws were definitely approved April was well begun, and, having concluded the transaction of the loan shortly afterward, I wrote to the Emperor on the 14th, asking His Majesty to relieve me from my duties as President of the Council of Ministers. The following day the Emperor acceded to my request, and my withdrawal was officially announced on the 22nd.

Although it had previously been decided that my place would be taken by Goremykin, who had already formed a new ministry, the new code of basic laws was as yet unpublished. I had received intimations before this that the statutes would not be promulgated at all, but it was only upon leaving the Winter Palace for my home that I called General Trepov aside and spoke to him in the following strain: "It is clear to everybody that, being Premier no longer but simply a member of the Imperial Council, I am *not* responsible for ensuing developments. Nevertheless, I beg of you to see His Majesty at once and tell him that I, as his loyal subject, advise him most earnestly to promulgate the fundamental laws without any further delay, for, if the Duma convenes without a knowledge of the new code, it will begin to function without any predetermined course, so that serious confusion and perilous turmoil will result." Shortly afterward General Trepov informed me that he had given His Majesty an exact report of my recommendations. However, it was not till April 27th, the very day on which the new representative body assembled, that the laws were made public, with a few additional changes of no significance whatsoever.

In order to get at the causes of this delay and the supplementary alterations, it is necessary to take into account the following facts, which became known to me only in 1907 through Vladimir Ivanovitch Kovalevsky, who was my assistant when I was Minister of Finances. I was disinclined to put any stock in Kovalevsky's astonishing story until he presented documentary proofs, which, incidentally, are now in my archives. It appears that as soon as the Council of Ministers submitted the draft of the proposed fundamental laws to the Emperor, Trepov came into possession of the text and acquaintted Kovalevsky with it, requesting him to examine the project and draw up a detailed report on the subject. In carrying out this investigation, Kovalevsky invited the assistance of Muromtzev, who became President of the First Duma, Paul Miliukov and U. B. Hessen, all three "Cadets" [members of the Constitutional-Democratic party], in addition to M. M. Kovalevsky, a cultured scholar and liberal, at present a member of the Imperial Council. They prepared a statement which was transmitted by V. I. Kovalevsky to General Trepov, who presented it to His Majesty on the 18th of April.

The memorandum opens thus: "Under the cover of preserving the Imperial prerogatives, the formulators of this code have anxiously sought to perpetuate the existing unrestraint and irresponsibility of the ministers." After more stuff of the same sort, the note proceeds: "In order to avoid recasting the whole project, the plan is recommended for acceptance after the introduction of various changes of more or less importance, some, however, being merely editorial." Then follows a list of the suggested emendations, whose endorsement would not only have brought the Emperor's power down to that of M. Fallieres [President of French Republic] and introduced parliamentarism, but also committed the Government light-heartedly to the offhand decision of a chain of the most intricate problems bequeathed by Russian history. This report, it seems, undermined His Majesty's confidence, so that he could not bring himself to sanction the promulgation of the laws formulated by the Council of Ministers and reviewed by the special conference. Ultimately, however, under the influence of my telephone conversations, he did grant his authorization after the insertion of a few changes, mostly inconsequential, made in order to gratify the conceit of several back-stairs advisers and General Trepov himself, that man with the broad education of a military commander and the shallow opinions of an unsophisticated corporal.

The most important of the modifications introduced were the following: (1) The Emperor's power of issuing decrees was restricted, thus increasing the so-called executive function of the legislative body, which merely obstructs its legitimate law-making activities. During Stolypin's ascendency, however, this curb did not in the least prevent the publication of the Manifesto of June 3rd and the issue of decrees palpably in contravention of the fundamental laws. (2) The sanction of the Council of Ministers or of its President was prescribed for all Imperial orders before taking effect, thus adding a sort of parliamentary responsibility to the Ministers' accountability to the Emperor. (3) The scope of the section on religious toleration was considerably narrowed, probably at the instance of some of the hierarchs with the support of the Empress.

This account of the formulation and promulgation of the code of fundamental laws shows how unsettled conditions were during this period, how people were likely to rush from one extreme to the other under the pressure of some crisis, and how important a rôle was played by intriguers behind the scenes.

I wish to cite now the communications which I exchanged with His Majesty at the end of my administration. On April 14, 1906, I addressed the following letter to His Majesty:

Your Imperial Majesty,—

I had the honour of petitioning your Imperial Majesty most humbly for the good of the common cause to set me free from my duties as Chairman of the Council of Ministers, before the opening of the Imperial Duma, as soon as the loan is effected, and your Majesty was pleased to listen graciously to my considerations. I take the liberty of formulating most respectfully the motives which impel me to reiterate my aforementioned petition.

1. As a result of the general baiting whereof I am the object, I feel so

shattered in body and so nervous that I am not in a position to preserve the presence of mind which is imperative in my position, especially under the new conditions.

2. With all due respect to the firmness and energy of the Minister of the Interior, I have nevertheless, as is known to your Imperial Majesty, found his mode of action as well as the behaviour of some of the local administrators inappropriate, especially during the last two months, after the mass manifestations of the revolution have practically been wiped out. This mode of action, I believe, has irritated the majority of the population and resulted in the election of extreme elements to the Duma, as a protest against the policy of the Government.

3. My appearance in the Duma together with P. N. Durnovo will put both of us in a difficult position. I shall be forced to make no remarks in connection with all interpellations touching upon such actions of the Government as were carried out either without my knowledge or counter to my opinion. As for the Minister of the Interior, he will be embarrassed in my presence to offer explanations which I cannot countenance.

4. Regarding certain important political problems, such as the religious, the Jewish and the peasant problem, there is no unity either in the Council of Ministers or in the influential spheres. Generally speaking, I am unable to defend ideas which are out of keeping with my convictions, and I cannot share the extremely conservative views which have lately become the political credo of the Minister of the Interior.

5. At the last session of the committee on the Fundamental laws, Count Palen, member of the Imperial Council, and Chairman of the Peasant Conference Goremykin, who is considered by some an expert on the peasant problem, expressed their views not only on the substance of this problem but also on the future policy of the Government generally. The peasant problem will determine the character of the Duma's activity. If the views of these two statesmen are correct, they should be given an opportunity to carry them into effect.

6. For six months I have been the target of all those who write or shout and the object of systematic attacks on the part of those extremists who have access to your Imperial Majesty. The revolutionists anathematize me for having lent the entire weight of my authority to the most stringent measures directed against the revolution; liberals curse me because, in fulfilment of my oath and in obedience to my conscience, I have defended the prerogatives of the Imperial authority, as I will defend them till my dying hour; finally, the conservatives inveigh against me because they falsely ascribed to me those changes in the governmental régime, which had taken place since the appointment of Prince Svyatopolk-Mirski as Minister of the Interior.* So long as I am in power, I shall be the target of bitter attacks on all hands. The most harmful thing is the distrustful attitude toward the President of the Council on the part of conservative

noblemen and highest officials, who naturally have access to the Czar and who inevitably infect your Majesty with their own doubts and views.

7. Upon the opening of the Duma the Government must seek to work in harmony with it, or else it must be prepared to take the most extreme measures. In the first case, the change in the membership of the Cabinet is apt to facilitate the task of the Government, for it will eliminate the ground for violent attacks upon the head of the Cabinet and the individual Ministers, against whom much animosity has accumulated in late months. Thus all agreements are likely to be reached more easily. Should the Government, however, decide upon a policy of repression, its activity would need to centre around the Ministries of the Interior, of Justice, and of War. In that case I would be but a hindrance and no matter how I might act I would be the object of malignant criticism.

I could respectfully present additional, and in my judgment, well-grounded arguments in support of my petition to free me from my duties as Chairman of the Council of Ministers previous to the opening of the Duma, but it appears to me that the arguments cited are sufficient to decide Your Majesty graciously to grant my demand. I would have addressed you this petition earlier, as soon as I noticed that my position as President of the Council of Ministers became unstable, but I did not think I had the right to do it, as long as the country's financial position was in so precarious a state; I was aware of my obligation to make every effort to ward off Russia's financial collapse and to prevent conditions under which the Duma, taking advantage of the Government's financial straits, might force it to make concessions answering the purpose of the individual parties, and inimical to the interests of the State as a whole, with which interests your Imperial Majesty is inseparably identified. It is not for naught that all the revolutionary and anti-Governmental parties hold me to blame chiefly because of my participation in the negotiations for the loan. At this moment the loan is concluded and concluded successfully, so that your Imperial Majesty need no longer be anxious about the means for the liquidation of the debts incurred in connection with the war. At the same time, the unrest has to a certain extent died down. Under these conditions, when your Imperial Majesty is in a position to turn your attention to the internal organization of the Empire and to direct the activity of the Duma into an appropriate channel, I believe I have the moral right to renew my petition. Therefore, I take the liberty of laying at the feet of Your Imperial Majesty my most loyal solicitation for a discharge from the office of President of the Council of Ministers.

* (previous page) I welcomed that appointment and I have always had a feeling of friend-ship and respect for Prince Mirski, but he was nominated without my participation, for at that time I was in disfavor, holding the office of President of the Committee of Ministers.

On the evening of the same day (April 14th) I called the Council of Ministers into session and read them my petition to His Majesty. Ministers, including Durnovo, were apparently displeased with my step, for it rendered their own position insecure. Some of them expressed the desire immediately to send in their resignation, but I persuaded them to refrain from so doing. Only the Minister of Instruction, I. I. Tolstoy, was satisfied with my step. He knew, he said, what an intrigue was going on against me at the Court, and he felt certain that the Emperor would have gotten rid of me at the first opportunity, as soon as he felt that he could master the situation without my assistance.

Two days later I received from His Majesty the following autographic message:

Count Sergey Yulyevich:
Yesterday morning I received the letter in which you ask me to relieve you of the offices which you are now holding. I agree to grant your demand. The successful conclusion of the loan is the best page in the history of your activities. It is a great moral success for the Government and a guarantee of the future peaceful development of Russia. It appears that in Europe, too, the prestige of our country is high.* How things will shape themselves after the opening of the Duma, God alone knows. My view of the future is not as pessimistic as yours. It seems to me that the membership of the Duma has proved to be so radical not because of the Government's repressive measures, but owing to the excessive liberalism of the franchise law of December 11th, the inactivity of the conservative mass of the population and the complete non-interference with the election campaign on the part of the authorities, which is never practiced in other countries.† I thank you *sincerely*, Sergey Yulyevich, for your devotion to me and the zeal with which you have laboured at the responsible post you have occupied for the last six months under exceptionally trying circumstances. I wish you to take a rest and recover your health. Thankfully, Nicholas.

The following Imperial rescript was published on April 22nd:

Count Sergey Yulyevich:
The impairment of your health, brought on by your excessive labours, has compelled you to petition me for a release from the office of President of the Council of Ministers. In summoning you to this important post for the execution of my designs relating especially to the admission of my subjects to the legislative bodies, I was certain that your tried statesmanlike abilities would facilitate the inauguration of the new elective institutions

MY PREMIERSHIP

which have been created for the purpose of giving reality to the rights I have granted to the population. Owing to your persistent and enlightened labours, these institutions have now been shaped and are ready to be opened, in spite of the obstacles which were thrown in your way by the seditious elements, whom you combatted with your characteristic energy and resoluteness. Simultaneously, through your experience in financial matters, you have contributed to the stabilization of the country's financial resources by insuring the success of the recent foreign loan. In granting your most loyal request, I wish to express my most sincere and hearty gratitude to you for the numerous services you have rendered to the country. In recognition of these services I create you Knight of the Order of Saint Alexander Nevski with Diamonds [the last two words in the Emperor's own hand.] I remain unalterably well-disposed to you and sincerely grateful [the last three words autographed]. Nicholas.

The next day I presented myself officially at the Court to thank His Majesty for having accepted my resignation. I was also given the opportunity to take leave of Her Majesty. Both the Emperor and the Empress were very amiable, although Her Majesty has never been well disposed to me. It is said an interjection of relief was her only comment on the news of my resignation.

---

* (previous page) The Emperor must have thought that our prestige was especially high in Asia, after the disgraceful Russo-Japanese War. Several courtiers told me that His Majesty repeatedly expressed himself to the effect that the Russians had badly beaten the Japanese.

† (previous page) This sounds like reproaching me for not having manipulated the elections. As a matter of fact, on September 22nd, 1905, the Minister of the Interior issued a circular to the proper authorities, which contained the following passage: "The sacred will of His Imperial Majesty obligates all those charged with watching over the regularity of the elections, by every available means to guarantee to the population the possibility of electing the men who enjoy its confidence most, quietly and without any external interference. I, therefore, enjoin upon you to see that the Governmental officials and institutions should not permit themselves to exert the slightest pressure upon the election of deputies to the Imperial Duma." Upon the whole, these instructions were carried out, for the reason that I was in complete agreement with the spirit of Bulygin's circular. Stolypin's Government has, in fact, abandoned the policy of non-interference, and at present (1908) the elections are a mockery.

CHAPTER XIII

STOLYPIN'S REACTIONARY RÉGIME

IN the course of my audience with the Emperor which followed upon my withdrawal from the office of Prime Minister, His Majesty asked me to accept the first post of Ambassador to a European country which might become vacant, and ordered me to remind him of his promise as soon as such an opening presented itself. A year later I did so, but received no answer from the Emperor. He also asked me to return all the letters he had sent me throughout the period of my administration. I complied with his request, which later I greatly regretted. Those letters, reflecting as they did the Emperor's thoughts and opinions in all their unadorned directness, should have been preserved for the benefit of posterity.

Several weeks later I went abroad. In July, while sojourning at Aix-les-Bains, France, I received the following message from Baron Frederichs:

> I deem it necessary to share with you the impression made upon me by a conversation which I have just had with His Majesty. When your name was mentioned in connection with the present political situation, His Majesty expressed himself to the effect that your return at present to Russia would be highly undesirable. I have judged it advisable to inform you of this opinion of His Majesty in order that you may accordingly arrange the plan of your trip.

This was obviously equivalent to an order on the part of His Majesty forbidding my return to Russia. I immediately sent in an application asking to be relieved of the offices which I was still holding, including membership in the Imperial Council. Several days later I heard that the Duma had been dissolved. Unwilling to add to the difficulties of the Government, I had my petition held in St. Petersburg.

On August 20th, I wrote to Baron Frederichs as follows:

Having received your letter of July 17th, with the amiable advice not to return to my country at this time, I mailed a petition of resignation the following day. But becoming aware of the disastrous consequences which the dissolution of the Duma may have, and finding it unpatriotic to air personal grievances at such a time, I stopped the letter in St. Petersburg. Since that time upward of a month has passed, and at present I consider it possible to take up the matter again. When I left the post of President of the Council of Ministers, for reasons which I had the honour to report to His Majesty and which had been by no means new to him, I failed to notice any discrepancy between my step and the Emperor's views. In fact, His Imperial Majesty very graciously relieved me from my office and publicly recognized my services by means of a very favourable rescript and a suitable reward. Thereupon, a Cabinet was formed for whose members the Duma and the majority of the people could have no other feeling but that of contempt mingled with hostility. This Cabinet was to act the part of an impregnable "rock" (His Majesty's expression). And indeed it was a rock, in the sense that it sustained the blows of the waves without breathing a word and without being able to mould the course of events. . . . As a result of the subsequent dissolution of the Duma, the ministerial rock has practically crumbled away. . . .

No sooner did I retire from the office of President of the Council of Ministers than the official attitude toward me underwent an abrupt change. The semi-official paper of the Cabinet immediately opened a campaign of insinuations against me. The Ministers gave anonymous interviews to foreign correspondents, stating their political credo and making this an occasion for surreptitious attacks on me. . . . Finally, to-day, the newspapers carry a telegram sent to Kaiser Wilhelm by the monarchist party of the "true Russians" [Black Hundreds], which blames all of Russia's misfortunes upon me and brands me as a Jewish ruler. It has also come to my knowledge that some of the members of the Imperial family accuse me of being the cause of all that is now happening in our country. As a truly noble-hearted witness of the events which preceded and followed the publication of the Manifesto of October 17th, and as a member of my Cabinet, you know how little truth there is in these accusations. And now I hear that in St. Petersburg dissertations are being written to prove that it was Witte who brought about the disturbances and also the war. . . . And I, in my official capacity, must leave all these charges unanswered.

All this forces me to return to the original intention which I conceived on receiving your letter advising me not to return to Russia "at this time," although "at this time" even revolutionary emigrants and bombists have found in our country a shelter, either open or underground. As you know me, you do not doubt, I hope, that above all I hate to cause displeasure to His Majesty or even merely to discommode him. I grant that my complete withdrawal from State service may not be in keeping with His Majesty's desires or intentions. Nevertheless, the feeling of self-respect prompts me to petition His Majesty for complete retirement. As I do not possess the necessary means and as I do not wish to deprive my family of the comforts to which they are accustomed, I propose to offer my services to private institutions, thus earning sufficient means and indirectly benefiting society. Considering the spirit of these times, it may not be necessary to add that no change in my position will ever be able to shake my loyalty to my Sovereign and to those principles which His Majesty impersonates and which are bred in my bones. I trust that your chivalrous disposition will prompt you to see that this letter be answered without delay.

This message was, of course, brought to His Majesty's attention, but days passed and no answer came. On October 10th I dispatched to the Baron a letter which I shall quote in part:

Twenty days ago I informed you about the manner in which I reacted to your letter of July 17th, the insulting significance of which has been rendered more emphatic by the subsequent developments. . . . The fact that my letter has remained unanswered I interpret as an indication that the Emperor is entirely indifferent to the outcome of this affair. Therefore, I herewith request you to kindly present to His Imperial Majesty the enclosed petition. I urgently beg your assistance in obtaining a satisfactory reply with the least possible delay.

Thereupon I went to Brussels to visit my son-in-law, and it was there that I received the following letter from the Minister of the Court:

Upon the receipt of your letter, I did not fail to report it in substance to His Majesty, but I had to wait for an opportune moment to take up the matter of your return to Russia with the Emperor, which I did in the course of our trip to Norway. I can now tell you with assurance that in advising you not to return to Russia His Majesty had in mind exclusively the circumstances of that moment. He thought your presence here undesirable because he feared that ill-intentioned persons might use you as a pretext for adding to the difficulties of the Cabinet, but His Majesty was by no means actuated by personal enmity toward you. Acknowledging your desire to return to Russia to attend to your private affairs and believing that at the present moment your return will not cause any serious complications of a political character, His Majesty has commissioned me to inform you that he sees no obstacles to your return. I take pleasure in adding that on your return you will be cordially received by His Majesty and that it is the Emperor's absolute desire that you should not retire from State service.

I immediately wired to the Baron, letting him know that, if he saw fit, he might refrain from presenting my second letter to His Majesty. The Baron's reply came immediately. He informed me that he had not thought it proper to submit my letter together with the accompanying petition to the Emperor.

From Brussels I went back to Paris whence I intended to proceed to St. Petersburg. In Paris I received a telegram, in French, signed by Prince M. Andronikov, a cross between a spy *con amore* and a titled hanger-on. The text of the dispatch follows:

Having learned about your intention soon to return to Russia, and actuated by sincere devotion to you, I entreat you to prolong your stay abroad. The menace to your life here is more serious than you imagine. My last word is: "Come here if you wish to die."

Several days later (in October, 1906), I left for St. Petersburg. On arriving there, I went to see Prime Minister Stolypin and asked him to bring pressure to bear to the end that I might be completely relieved from State service. "If you insist on resigning," Stolypin said, "we will not keep you by main force, but let it be known to you that your withdrawal, especially at this time, will be equivalent to a successful bomb attack by anarchists." Naturally, I gave up my intention and since that time I have never raised that question again. Several days later I had an interview with the Emperor. He received me as if nothing had happened and did not say a word either about his prohibiting my return to Russia or about my attempt to resign.

I shall now turn to the political conditions as they have shaped themselves since I left the post of President of the Council of Ministers. There is but little to be said about my successor Goremykin. A bureaucratic nonentity, he had no definite program and achieved nothing. His cabinet did not outlast the first Duma, which existed some two months, and was succeeded by Stolypin's. This statesman was the embodiment of political immorality and the members of his Cabinet were not far superior to him. He ruled Russia by violating each and every law and he disdained no means, however reprehensible, to keep himself in power. Prior to the dissolution of the Second Duma he did not have the courage to reveal his true nature, which was that of an unprincipled, self-seeking office-hunter. In order to enlist the support of some of the elements of the population, he made Liberal speeches and adopted Liberal measures. But already early in his career he took under his protection "The Union of the Russian People," so-called. In his administration, this body, which consisted of plain thieves and hooligans, acquired great weight, for it was in every way assisted by the Government.

During the first two years after my return from abroad, now and then I exchanged official visits with Stolypin, but as time went on the intervals between the visits grew longer. The main cause of Stolypin's animosity toward me was the fact that in my speeches in the Imperial Council I did not hesitate to attack him when the occasion called for it. It should be noted that my word had always carried weight in the Council. A serious conflict occurred between us in connection with the problem of a Naval General Staff. I succeeded in showing that, to please the Duma majority, Stolypin intended to limit the Emperor's prerogatives, in contravention of the fundamental laws of the land. As a result, His Majesty refused to sanction Stolypin's bill, which had been approved by both the Duma and the Imperial Council. A second time we came to a grave clash over the problem of introducing the Zemstvo institutions in the Western provinces.

The outcome of this conflict was that Stolypin tendered his resignation. His Majesty refused to accept it, for he believed that Stolypin had put an end to the revolution and that his withdrawal would spell disaster for the régime. What methods Stolypin used to convince the world that he had pacified the country may be seen from the following two incidents.

Shortly after his attempt to resign, a district attorney was assassinated on board a train. The crime was obviously a terroristic revolutionary act, but the investigation was conducted so as to present it as a plain murder committed with the intention of robbing.

Finally, a man was arrested who declared that he had done the deed, acting under orders of the revolutionary committee. The man was put in jail at Sebastopol. Then the guards intimated to the prisoner that he would be allowed to escape, but when he made an attempt to flee the sentinels shot him dead, thus destroying the only proof that the crime was of a political nature.

This incident was related to me by Privy Councillor Przeradski, one of Stolypin's closest assistants. He also told me of a similar case which concerned him personally. In 1905, a relation of his, a naval officer by the name of Kurosh, bombarded the Finnish revolutionists who had hoisted the red flag over the fortress of Helsingfors. The revolutionists retaliated by killing, six years later, his seventeen-year-old son. The investigation was conducted with the intention of proving that the young man had committed suicide, although the boy was shot before the very eyes of both Przeradski and his wife by a man who appeared at the open window of the victim's room. To characterize the manner in which the investigation was conducted, my informant stated that in the witnesses' depositions some of the sheets were removed and substituted by forged testimonies corroborating the preconceived thesis of the examining magistrate, namely, that this was a case of suicide.

When I expressed my amazement at what might be the possible reason for these practices, Przeradski explained that after Stolypin's attempt to resign he issued instructions that all the political crimes should be presented as plain murders. It was apparently the Premier's intention to show that no terroristic acts were possible under his administration. "Why didn't you appeal," I said, "to the Minister of the Navy and the Minister of Justice?" Przeradski declared that he did speak to the Minister of the Navy and that the latter was indignant but could do nothing. As for Shcheglovitov, he was little more than Stolypin's valet, Przeradski said, so that it was quite useless to expect any independent action from him.

Stolypin disregarded the regulations relating to the budget, and under him the discussion of the report of the State Comptroller by the Duma became a mere formality. But it is Stolypin's treatment of Article 87 of the Fundamental Laws that illustrates best how unceremoniously he violated the laws he had been called to uphold. That celebrated article, of which I am the author, provides for the enactment of urgent and extraordinary measures by the Emperor's authority at the recommendation of the Council of Ministers during the time when the Duma is not in session. The article expressly stipulates that only such measures may thus be adopted as do not affect either the fundamental laws or the regulations relating to the Duma and Imperial Council. Furthermore, a regulation thus enacted ceases to be valid if it is not approved by the Duma within one month after its re-opening.

Now, Stolypin abused this provision in the most extraordinary fashion. By distorting the perfectly clear meaning of the article, he sought to mould the destinies of the country after his own will. In virtue of it he passed a great many laws of capital importance by his own authority, and in order to do so he purposely dissolved the legislative institutions, sometimes for as short a period as three days. It was on the strength of this clause that he promulgated a new election law, which was in itself a complete coup-d'état and which resulted in the submissive Third Duma. It was also on the strength of this article that Stolypin introduced court-martial in a form unknown in any country pretending to be civilized.

At the time when I assumed the burden of power, capital punishment in Russia was practised arbitrarily and without uniformity. Identical crimes were in some districts punished by death, while in others they were not. To impose order upon this chaos I introduced a bill which sought to define the criminal acts which were under the jurisdiction of the court-martial and could be punished by death. The project won an overwhelming majority in the Imperial Council, but when it was submitted for approval to the Emperor, he refused to sanction it. Thus the situation regarding capital punishment remained unchanged.

When Stolypin formed his Cabinet, after the Duma had been dissolved by Goremykin, he introduced field court-martial, which set the hands of the administration entirely free in the application of capital punishment. The new law went as far as demanding that the judges should be not military jurists, but plain officers of the line. The Second Duma refused to approve this law, whereupon Stolypin did not hesitate to modify several paragraphs in the military and naval regulations through the Army and Navy councils, thus safeguarding by his own authority the court-martial which he had created. The Government began to execute people right and left at the discretion of the administration. Capital punishment, in fact, has *become an act of assassination by the Governmental authorities.* Men and women, adults and mere youngsters are executed alike for a political assassination and for robbing a vodka shop of five rubles. Sometimes a prisoner is executed for a crime committed five or six years previously. And to think that this orgy of executions has been going on for six years after Stolypin declared "pacification" an accomplished fact!

Stolypin's treatment of the Duma was consistent with the general trend of his policy. I have already spoken, in another connection, of the history of the Duma election law. While nearly all the classes of the population sought, during the revolutionary days, to limit the Emperor's authority, the mass of the peasantry remained inarticulate. It was therefore imagined that the peasants would be loyal to the Czar, and the election law was so arranged as to grant the peasant class a proportionately larger representation than any other group. But a disappointment was in store for the Government. When the Duma opened, it was found that all the peasant deputies who had a definite platform were unanimous in demanding an additional allotment of land as a natural sequel to the abolition of serfdom, the great reform carried out by Emperor Alexander II. And so, when Goremykin appeared before the Duma and declared that private property was sacred, that the expropriation of the landowners for the benefit of the peasants was an impossible dream, etc., the peasant members abandoned the Government and pinned their faith to the Constitutional Democratic Party, which promised them land, and freedom into the bargain.

It was then that the landowning nobility, forgetting their newfangled liberalism, began to vociferate: "Treason is rampant in the land; the sacred right of property, the foundation of all modern civilized states, is endangered; the Czar's servants are betraying him either through lack of character or because of insidiousness; those who advocate distribution of land among the peasants must be severely punished." To make a long story short, the Duma was dispersed and a number of the delegates retired to the city of Vyborg, Finland, where they issued a vain appeal calling upon all Russian citizens not to pay taxes or furnish army recruits until the legislative body was reconvened.

The Duma members who signed the Vyborg Appeal were arraigned by Stolypin. His purpose was to deprive them of the right to be elected to the Imperial Duma. As the Minister of Justice was a mere plaything in his hands, Stolypin brought pressure to bear upon the judicial authorities, and the offenders were sentenced to imprisonment and deprivation of the right of election to the Duma. Competent jurists told me that the trial was both unlawful and unfair. The trial was not an act of justice, but a clever political move against the Cadet Party, for most of the convicted deputies were members of that organization.

The Second Duma differed but little from the First, although by a dexterous manipulation of the law Stolypin succeeded in barring from the elections a great many prominent public leaders, who as members of the First Duma had signed the celebrated Vyborg Appeal. Both Dumas owed their membership to the same election regulations and both stood for a régime based on the people's political consciousness as opposed to a régime founded on the selfish opinions and whims of a Court camarilla. As the character of the Second Duma immediately became clear to the Government, the legislative body was dissolved after it had been in session for a period of some three months, and, on the strength of Article 87, a new election law, known as the Law of June 3rd, was simultaneously promulgated. This law deprived several border provinces of the franchise and cut down the number of delegates from the rest of the border provinces. It drastically reduced the representation of the peasants and workmen and provided for the administration's direct influence upon the elections. In sum, the statute of June 3rd gave a decisive prevalence in the Duma to the propertied classes and especially to the large landowners. The purpose of this act was to obtain a Duma majority agreeable to the Government. When P. N. Durnovo in my presence once asked Kryzhanovsky, the author of that law, why certain regulations varied with the locality, the latter explained naïvely that all this was arranged with a view to securing "reliable" electors. This measure rendered the Duma both useless and unfaithful to its original purpose of voicing the wishes of the country. While the Imperial Council feared and, to a certain extent, reckoned with the First Duma, it neither fears nor reckons with the present (Third) Duma. It is noteworthy that the Government did not hesitate to use methods of coercion and bribery to influence the elections to the Third Duma. Thus, Stolypin put at the disposal of General Reinbot, Governor-General of Moscow, a special fund to buy votes for Guchkov, ostensibly the Octobrist candidate. The result was a legislative body not elected by the Russian people but *selected* by Stolypin.

Before the Law of June 3rd was passed, Baron Frederichs asked me what I thought of that measure. I do not know whether he did it on his own account or whether he was sent to me by people higher up. I pointed out to him that two ways were open to the Government. It could either wait patiently till the Duma became reasonable, or else a new election act, free from the failings of the existing one, must be elaborated with great care, taking advantage of the experience gained in applying the present regulations. Should the Government choose the first alternative, however, it would have to adhere in good faith to the letter and spirit of the Act of October 17, 1905. My advice was not heeded. The Second Duma was dissolved and there was promulgated the new election law, which had been concocted in great haste.

At my instance, the fundamental laws gave the Emperor very extensive prerogatives in matters pertaining to the defence of the country. When Stolypin enacted the election law of June 3rd, which resulted in an obedient Duma, with a majority belonging to the self-styled party of October 17th, so-called, a tacit agreement was made between the Government and the Duma. In virtue of it the Duma was allowed to criticize the military policy of the Government, but, in return, obligated itself not to touch upon Stolypin's régime of White Terror which was then at its worst. It was as if Stolypin spoke to the leaders of the Octobrist Duma majority in terms not unlike these: "You may play soldiers as long as you please; I shall not interfere with you, all the more so that I understand nothing of military matters. But you must not interfere with me, you must let me play the bloody game of executions and court-martial."

The Duma appointed a Committee on Defence, which began to discuss military matters with a comical air of competence. In the meantime the Octobrists' crack orators made long speeches, inveighing against the military budget of the Government, flaunting their patriotic ardour, and denouncing the Grand Dukes, to whom the Emperor was in a habit of addressing special rescripts of gratitude in recognition of their great services to the State. Such speeches were a novelty in Russia. Naturally enough, the general public admired the courage of these orators and expected much of them. But those who knew the speakers, and had also some familiarity with military matters could not be deceived as to the precise value of those performances. That the Grand Dukes often occupied important military posts for which they were not in the least qualified—was known to everyone. Such a favouritism was, no doubt, a great evil.

As for the rest, the speeches of the Octobrist leaders contained little except hearsay matter. Guchkov, the chief Duma orator on military matters, had a very limited and dubious knowledge of the subject he discoursed upon. He was in fact little more than a merchant by profession, with a weakness for military adventures. The utter incompetence of the Duma in military matters came to light especially in 1909, when it submitted to the Imperial Council a bill dealing with the General Staff of the Navy and providing for the complete control of both the budget and the technical organization of the General Staff by the Duma and the Imperial Council.

The Imperial Council, reformed in pursuance of the constitutional Manifesto, was intended to work in harmony with the Duma, the two legislative bodies completing each other. In reality, however, both subjected the legislative drafts laid before them to identical manipulations and were altogether out of harmony. If the Duma said "White," the conservative faction of the Imperial Council was sure to say "Black."

Stolypin's treatment of the thorny Jewish question is a striking illustration of his unprincipled policies and reckless methods. His views of this problem were almost diametrically opposed to mine. It has always been my conviction that the policy of restrictions cannot bring any results, for the reason that in the long run this policy cannot be followed out. The history of the Jewish people in western countries bears out this assertion with sufficient clearness. It is possible to assume various attitudes towards Jews. One may hate them, or be indifferent to them. That is a matter of personal feeling. But our emotional attitude cannot alter the natural course of events, in virtue of which the Jews, since they are human beings after all, acquire the full measure of civic rights. I believe, however, that the abolition of Jewish disabilities must be gradual and as slow as possible.

This view was held by both Nicholas I and Alexander II. Emperor Alexander III somewhat deviated from this tendency and entered upon the road of anti-Jewish restrictions. But like everything done by Alexander III, his anti-Jewish policy was firm but moderate and judicious.

Emperor Alexander III asked me on one occasion: "Is it true that you are in sympathy with the Jews?" "The only way I can answer this question," I replied to the Emperor, "is by asking Your Majesty whether you think it possible to drown all the Russian Jews in the Black Sea. To do so would, of course, be a radical solution of the problem. But if Your Majesty will recognize the right of the Jews to live, then conditions must be created which will enable them to carry on a human existence. In that case, gradual abolition of the disabilities is the only adequate solution of the Jewish problem."

His Majesty said nothing, but he never showed that he disapproved of my attitude toward the Russian Jews. It has remained substantially the same throughout my career. As Minister of Finance I vigorously opposed all measures intended to restrict the rights of the Jews, but it was not in my power to repeal the existing laws against the Jews. Many of these laws were unjust, and, upon the whole these laws did much harm to Russia and Russians. In dealing with the Jewish legislation, I did not consider primarily the advantages to be derived from a certain measure by the Jewish race. What was foremost in my mind was the effect of this or that measure upon Russia as a whole.

All the more important legal provisions relating to the Jews, which have become effective in the course of the last decade, were enacted as temporary measures. The decrees usually opened with the Pharisaic formula: "Pending the revision of the laws relating to the Jews, we order, etc.," the intimation being that such a revision would be favourable to the Jewish population. The truth of the matter is that the authors of the anti-Jewish laws did not have the courage to offer a radical and statesmanlike solution of the problem. As it was known that the Imperial Council was likely to oppose these restrictive measures, or, at least, tell the Ministers a few unpleasant truths, the anti-Jewish regulations were enacted either by the Committee of Ministers, by special commissions, or else by Imperial decrees.

Among the most implacable enemies of the Russian Jews was Grand Duke Sergey Alexandrovich, the man who, by his ultra-reactionary and near-sighted policy, drove Moscow into the arms of the revolutionists. The measures which the Grand Duke adopted against the Jews of Moscow the Committee of Ministers refused to sanction, so that they had to be passed either by special commissions or directly by Imperial decrees.

It will take decades or, more probably, centuries to do away altogether with the Jewish question. The racial peculiarities of the Jews will disappear only gradually and slowly. Had the Government followed Alexander II's policy toward the Jews, they would not have become one of the evil factors of our accursed revolution. The Jewish question would have lost its peculiar acuteness and would have assumed the form in which it exists at present in all those countries where Jews live in considerable numbers.

The whole mass of the legislation regarding the Jews consists of legal provisions of an extremely vague character. This circumstance led to a number of arbitrary and conflicting interpretations, which became a source of all manner of graft. No element of the population is so thoroughly mulcted* by the Administration as the Jews are. In some regions the graft has assumed the form of a veritable tax upon the Jews. Under these conditions, the whole burden of the anti-Jewish policy falls upon the poorer class of the Jews, for the more opulent a Jew is, the easier it is for him to smooth his way by means of graft and the less he feels the pressure of the restrictive measures. Not only do the wealthy Jews not feel the oppression of their legal disabilities, but they are, to a certain extent, in a domineering position, inasmuch as they exert influence upon the high local officials.

In the early '80's the Senate combatted this state of affairs, seeking to eliminate all arbitrary interpretations of the laws and all illegal restrictions upon the Jewish population. The result was that some of the Senators were denounced by the Minister of the Interior for interfering with the Administration. They were subjected to abuse and some of the more refractory were even removed and replaced by more obedient members. Consequently, the Senate, too, began to interpret the laws relating to the Jews in a manner distinctly anti-Jewish.

All this naturally rendered the Jewish masses revolutionary, especially the younger element, the process being furthered by the Russian schools. From the pusillanimous† people that the Jews were some thirty years ago there sprang men and women who threw bombs, committed political murders and sacrificed their lives for the revolution. Of course, all the Jews have not become revolutionists, but it is certain that no nationality in Russia has yielded such a large percentage of extreme radicals as the Jewish. Nearly the entire Jewish intellectual class, including graduates of the institutions of

---

* A word that means to take money or possessions from, as in taxation and other levies, and often by victimisation and oppression.

† * Showing weakness, a timidness or lack of courage.

higher learning, joined the "Party of the People's Freedom" (the Constitutional Democrats), which promised them equal rights. This political party owes much of its influence to the Jews, who lent it both intellectual and financial support.

I repeatedly warned the Jewish leaders, both in Russia and abroad, that they had entered upon a hazardous road and were likely to add to the acuteness of the Jewish problem in Russia. I told them that they must show an example of loyalty to the existing régime, and to seek to better their condition by appealing to the Czar's Government. I advised them, instead of dreaming of revolutionary freedom, to adopt the motto: "The only thing we beg is not to be discriminated against." But I pleaded in vain. Blinded by revolutionary ardour and deluded by the Cadet leaders, they disregarded my well-intentioned counsel.

Indeed, how could they heed the voice of prudence and loyalty to the Czar at the moment when, as they thought, they stood on the threshold of the triumph of the revolution, which meant also the triumph of the principle of equal rights for the Jews!

The outcome was a strong reaction. Many people who formerly either sympathized with the Jews or were indifferent to them, turned pronounced Jew-haters. Russian Jews never had as many enemies as they have now, nor was the outlook for the Jews ever more sombre than it is at the present. Such a state of affairs is highly unfavourable to the pacification of the country. It is my profound conviction that as long as the Jewish problem is handled in an unstatesmanlike, vindictive and non-humanitarian fashion, Russia will remain in a state of unrest and upheaval. On the other hand, I fear that the immediate granting of full rights to the Jews may lead to new disturbances and complications, thus defeating its purpose. I repeat, problems involving the historical prejudices of the masses which are based on race peculiarities, can be solved only by degrees and slowly. In these matters one should avoid disturbing the equilibrium, even though it should be a temporary and artificial equilibrium. A body politic is a living organism, and one must be exceedingly cautious in operating upon it.

The anti-Jewish legislation of 1882 is identified with the name of Count N. P. Ignatyev. He did much harm to the country by pursuing a ruthless anti-Jewish policy. Such an ultra-conservative but intelligent statesman as was Count Tolstoy, Minister of the Interior under Alexander III, would not have committed this mistake. He did not succeed in undoing Ignatyev's work, but he refrained from following in his footsteps. After Tolstoy's death, I. K. Durnovo resumed Ignatyev's policy, although he was on the best of terms with some of the Jewish millionaires. A man of very limited intelligence, he was prompted to take this course of action by his desire to please the Court camarilla, where the spirit of Jew-baiting was at that time predominant. But it is Plehve who was the leading spirit of the anti-Jewish policy and the author of all the anti-Jewish laws and administrative measures both under Ignatyev and Durnovo. Personally he had nothing against the Jews. This I know from my numerous talks with him on the subject of the Jewish question. He possessed enough intelligence to understand that he was following an essentially wrong policy. But it pleased Grand Duke Sergey Alexandrovich and apparently His Majesty. Consequently, Plehve exerted himself to the utmost.

The "pogroms," that peculiar feature of the Jewish question in Russia, raged with particular violence under Ignatyev. Count Tolstoy at once put an end to them. Under Plehve the tide of pogroms again rose high. Especially brutal and revolting was the anti-Jewish outbreak at Kishinev. I would not venture to say that Plehve personally and directly organized these pogroms, but he did not oppose these, in his opinion, counter-revolutionary outbreaks. When the Kishinev pogroms roused the public opinion of the whole civilized world, Plehve entered into negotiations with the Jewish leaders in Paris and also with the Russian rabbis. What he told them amounted to the following: "Make your people stop their revolutionary activity, and I will stop the pogroms and abolish the Jewish disabilities." "The situation is beyond our control," was the reply. "The young element, crazed by hunger, is out of hand. But should a policy of relieving the oppression of the Jews be inaugurated, we believe that the unrest among the people will subside." Plehve appears to have heeded these words and assumed a more liberal attitude toward the Jews, but he was soon assassinated.

I should like to say a word about the status of the Jews during my administration. It must be admitted that the Jews played a prominent part in leading the forces of unrest and in fanning the flame of discontent. Of course, this circumstance may be accounted for and, to a considerable extent, justified by the intolerable legal status of the Jews and the pogroms which the Government not only tolerated, but even organized itself. However that may be, the outstanding part of the Jews in the revolution is an indisputable fact.

Immediately after my appointment, a Jewish deputation headed by Baron Ginzburg, a very respectable and wealthy man, called upon me. I received them. I remember, besides Ginzburg, the deputation included: Vinaver, a lawyer, later a prominent delegate of the First Imperial Duma from the city of St. Petersburg, Sliozberg and Kulisher, also legal lights, and Varshawski, son of the celebrated railroad builder. They came to plead the cause of full rights for their people, and they begged me to lay the matter before the Emperor. I stated frankly my views on the subject, emphasizing the point that the removal of the legal disabilities must proceed by degrees, for otherwise in some rural localities genuine, not artificial, pogroms might break out. In order that I might be able to raise the question of granting substantial rights to the Jews, I told them, and that I might advance the principle of equalizing the Jews with the rest of the population, before the law, it was necessary for the Jews to change their mode of behaviour. They must publicly declare, I said, to the Monarch—and substantiate their declaration by actual deeds—that they beg of His Majesty nothing else than to be treated on an equal footing with his other subjects. "Of late years," I told the delegation, "the Jews have come to the fore as leaders of various political parties and advocates of the most extreme political ideas. Now, it is not your business to teach us. Leave that to Russians by birth and civil status, and mind your own affairs. I assure you that your present conduct is fraught with harmful consequences both to you and your children."

Baron Ginzburg declared that he completely shared my opinion. Sliozberg and Kulisher also agreed with me. The rest of the deputation, however, were not impressed by my arguments. Vinaver, for instance, declared that the moment had now come when the Russian people were going to obtain political freedom and full rights for all the citizens irrespective of race or faith, and that it was the duty of the Jews to offer every possible support to those Russians who were fighting for the political emancipation of the country. Thus the conference came to nothing.

When in the summer of 1907 I came to Frankfort-on-the-Main, the local Jewish leaders met me in the house of a wealthy citizen by the name of Askenazi, whom I had known for a long time. The chief representatives of the German Jewry, including the celebrated Dr. Nathan of Berlin, were present there. I reiterated to them substantially what I told the Jewish delegation in St. Petersburg. In this case Dr. Nathan played Vinaver's part. From Frankfort I went to Paris, where I had a conference with a number of prominent French Jews. I repeated to them the views which I had previously offered to their Russian and German co-religionists. The French Jews assured me that they agreed with me but that they were helpless to influence the Russian Jewry. At present, I think the Jews see clearly who was right, I or their tactless, to speak mildly, counsellors.

When Stolypin assumed power, narrow nationalism was predominant in the Court circles. Accordingly, he decided that it would be advantageous for him to adopt a policy of persecuting all the Russian subjects of non-Russian stock, i.e., one-third of the entire population of the Empire (about 60,000,000). New anti-Jewish restrictions followed. On September 16, 1908, His Majesty confirmed a bill drafted by the Council of Ministers "about the percentage of persons of Jewish faith admitted to educational institutions." This measure, being of a legislative character, should have passed through the Duma and the Imperial Council, but all that time Stolypin treated the Duma not as a legislative body but as a bureaucratic office subordinate to the Minister of the Interior. This act was the first shot in Stolypin's war against the Jews.

It is noteworthy that during my premiership the question of the percentage of Jewish students was raised by the Minister of Education, Count Tolstoy, but his purpose was to remove the measures which restricted the educational opportunities of the Jews. Count Tolstoy laid before the Council of Ministers a bill for the abolition of these restrictions. He argued from the premise, which to my mind is perfectly correct, that the most natural solution of the Jewish question is the assimilation of the race through Russian education. After a lengthy discussion the Council of Ministers decided in favour of the bill. But the Emperor refused to sanction it and returned it to the Council with a resolution that he would issue instructions on the subject at a later period. This case aptly illustrates the difference between the Jewish policy of my Cabinet and that of Stolypin's. It is true that at the beginning of his administration Stolypin was inclined to abolish some of the existing Jewish disabilities. He drafted a memorandum on the subject and submitted it to His Majesty, but the Emperor again postponed the matter. In 1907 the Council of Ministers under Stolypin's presidency took up the question of Jewish disabilities and adopted a resolution that it was necessary to enter upon the road of gradual abolition of the existing restrictions. The minutes of this session His Majesty refused to sign.

A year later Stolypin reversed his policy and gradually there arose in Russia an intense movement against the Jews, which is both un-Christian and politically indefensible. At present Jew-baiting is at its worst, and I believe that the baiters themselves hardly know whither they are headed and what they intend to achieve by this ruthless persecution. One may not sympathize with the Jews, one may consider them an accursed nation. Nevertheless, they are human beings and Russian subjects, and there is no other method of treating them than that which is adopted in all the civilized countries, i.e., the method of gradually making them full-fledged members of the communities where they reside.

In November, 1907, St. Petersburg was visited by Taft, then Secretary of War and now President of the United States. I remember having heard Roosevelt speak of him in friendly and commending terms. In fact, it was Roosevelt who has made him President in the hope that he would be faithful to him, but, as it often happens, the two men are now in opposite political camps, and right now the question is debated as to who of the two is to be elected President, should the Republican party gain the upper hand. On my part, I can say that, no doubt, Roosevelt is a much abler man than Taft. It is known that during the Spanish-American War Colonel Roosevelt commanded a military detachment in Porto Rico, although neither Roosevelt nor Taft are military men. It is said that during his stay in the capital Taft had an audience with the Emperor, in the course of which he took up the question of the right of American citizens of Jewish faith to enter Russia.

As early as April, 1905, Minister of the Interior Bulygin recommended that together with the introduction of new passport regulations all the restrictions upon the right of foreign Jews to enter the Empire should be removed. He pointed out that these restrictions served no purpose and merely complicated international relations. With the creation of the Duma, many of the legislative projects filling the dossiers of the Imperial Council were returned to the respective Ministers that they might be laid before the Duma. Such was also the fate of Bulygin's recommendation; it was returned to the Ministry of the Interior, and there it was permanently buried.

I have told elsewhere how President Roosevelt handed me a letter to His Majesty, asking him to remove the restrictions upon the right of American Jews to enter Russia. Five years passed, and the President's letter remained unanswered. I do not know whether any further negotiations took place, but the practice objectionable to the United States continued. As a result several months ago the American Government lost its patience and denounced its old commercial treaty with Russia. Our jingoists are naturally thundering against America. There is no doubt, however, that we ourselves have driven the United States Government to this step.

On the strength of Article 87 Stolypin also enacted a highly important agrarian law, which can be understood only in the light of the history of the land policies of the Russian Government for the last fifty years.

The men who emancipated the peasantry from serfdom favoured the peasant commune (*obshchina*), which meant the communal form of land ownership and tilling. This policy, which the Government adopted because it was easier for the Administration to deal with groups of peasants than with individuals, found support among the Slavophils and other antiquarians enamoured of the Russian past. It was declared that the *obshchina* was an ancient, peculiarly Russian institution, that it was in fact the very essence of Russian folk-life, and that to encroach upon it was to encroach upon the integrity of the Russian national spirit.

Prejudices die hard, and so there are still some people who cling to this view of the *obshchina*. But it is becoming a matter of common knowledge that communal landownership existed at one time or another practically everywhere, that it is merely a primitive phase in the socio-economic evolution of mankind. With the development of culture and statehood, the communistic forms give place to individualistic ones. In Russia the process has been artificially thwarted, with the result that both the people and the State have been greatly enfeebled.

The *obshchina* found also enthusiastic supporters among the Russian converts to socialism. They proclaimed the muzhik to be a born, if unconscious, communist. Socialism, be it mentioned in passing, inasmuch as it is a movement toward collectivistic forms of economic life, is bound to fail, at least in the near future. Thus far socialism has succeeded in pointing out, with great acumen and vigour, the foibles and failings of a social organization based on individualism, but it has failed to offer a rational and workable principle for the reconstruction of society along new lines.

During the period of reaction which followed the assassination of Alexander II, the *obshchina* continued to be the pet of the Minister of the Interior, but the civil rights of the peasants were considerably curtailed. The revolution found the peasants in a very lamentable state. The collective form of land ownership was still prevalent among them, and the burden of legal disabilities weighed down upon them heavily. Legally the peasant was not of age, so to speak. While no longer the landowner's serf, he was still the serf of the rural administration, and above all of the rural chief of police.

When I became Minister of Finances my acquaintance with the peasant problem was very superficial. For a time I was inclined to accept the Slavophils' view of the *obshchina*, for the teachings of those great idealists have always swayed my heart. Contact with reality and the influence of ex-Minister of Finances Bunge, who was a resolute enemy of the *obshchina*, increased my interest in the peasant problem and gave a different direction to my views on the subject. Before long, I perceived that the mediæval *obshchlna* was a serious hindrance to the economic development of the country. In order to raise the productivity of peasant labour it was necessary, I found, besides removing the legal disabilities of the peasant class, to make the product of labour the full and assured property of the toiler and his heirs. No efficiency or initiative can be developed as long as the peasant knows that the land he tills may be given away to another member of the commune; that the fruit of his labour will be divided not on the basis of common law, but in conformity with custom, which is often the synonym of arbitrary disposal; that he is responsible for the taxes unpaid by his neighbours, and, finally, that he is at the mercy of the rural chief of police.

The improvement of the legal and economic status of the peasant was one of my main preoccupations since the very beginning of the reign of Emperor Nicholas II. All my efforts to abolish the redemption payments during my administration of the Ministry of Finances proved unavailing ("Why indulge the muzhik?"), and it was only after the act of October 17th, 1905, that I succeeded in enacting this measure. A considerable extension of the operations of the Peasant Bank was another step toward a betterment of the peasant's condition, which was made by my Cabinet. We did not think it advisable to go further without placing the matter before the newly created legislative body, which was soon to convene. We also established a chain of local committees for the study of agrarian conditions and we elaborated a program of peasant reforms to be submitted to the Duma. Individual land ownership and full legal rights for the peasant class were the two basic principles of that program. The transition from communal to individual land ownership was to be gradual and free from all compulsion.

Stolypin's Cabinet and the third Duma took advantage of the legislative plan which we had laid, but in doing so they distorted them to such an extent that the land reform which is now being carried out may lead to grave revolutionary complications. Like myself, Stolypin intended to develop a class of small private landowners from among the peasants, but with his characteristic faith in the efficacy of coercion he inaugurated a policy of forcefully disrupting the time-hallowed institution of the *obshchina*. Besides, while forcing upon the peasant individual land ownership, the new law (Act of November 9, 1906) failed to grant him full civic rights, notably the right of inheritance. The reform is being carried out hastily and ill-advisedly, without paying due attention to the secondary problems raised by it, as if it were a mere police measure and not an act of overwhelming national importance. Its only outcome will be a chaotic condition in the village and rapid proletarization of the peasant masses.

By his arbitrary, deceitful and brutal actions Stolypin aroused against himself a considerable part of the population. No other statesman has ever succeeded in drawing upon himself the enmity of so many men and women. For instance, all the non-Russian national groups of the Empire were among his enemies. Furthermore, Stolypin lost the respect of all decent people. Through his double dealing he estranged the very Black Hundred leaders who were his main support during the first years of his premiership. Under these circumstances it was easy enough to foresee that he would come to grief. It was clear to me that since he stubbornly clung to his post, he would perish at it. To what extent my presentiment was definite may be seen from the following fact. When Dillon, the well-known English journalist, visited me at Biarritz and inquired about conditions in Russia, my reply was to the effect that some fatal catastrophe was bound to happen to Stolypin and produce a general change in the political situation.

My foreboding came true. On September 1, 1911, Stolypin was fatally wounded. The attempt took place at Kiev during a solemn theatrical performance attended by the Emperor, his daughters, all the Cabinet Ministers and a great many members of the high aristocracy. The shooting was done by a revolutionary terrorist who was at the same time a Secret Service agent. Several days later Stolypin died. The Emperor bestowed a number of favours upon the widow, while the jingoist papers mourned Stolypin's death as Russia's great loss, and opened subscription funds for the construction of a national chain of memorial statutes. Of course, this artificial agitation soon subsided and gave place to a sober estimate of the late Minister's historical rôle.

Some of Stolypin's friends blamed his death on the head of the Secret Service. They pointed out that the Director of the Police Department and the Chief of Gendarmes committed a number of unpardonable blunders. I agree that our police force, especially the Secret Service, was completely disorganized and demoralized under Stolypin. But, here again, Stolypin was at fault. As Minister of the Interior he appointed all the more important functionaries of the Police Department and was in fact its supreme head. The inevitable conclusion is that he fell a victim to his own mismanagement.

The murder of a human being is in itself a revolting act, but in considering Stolypin's assassination one should remember that hundreds of men and women were executed, or, rather murdered by Stolypin's Government for no reason whatsoever. Stolypin perished as many statesmen did who used the power vested in them, not for the benefit of the State and the people, but for purposes of self-aggrandizement. The great Napoleon said: "A statesman has his heart in his head." Unfortunately, Stolypin's heart was neither in his head nor in his breast. He possessed both temperament and courage, but he lacked moral stamina. As a result he demoralized and debased all the elements of Russian political life with which he came in contact.

From the standpoint of His Majesty, Stolypin may be said to have died in time. Several weeks before his assassination—I was at that time at Biarritz—I received a remarkable letter, signed by a Sazonov, whom I had known for a number of years. The career of this man is worth mention. In his youth Sazonov is said to have been intimate with Zhelyabov, the assassin of Alexander II. At one time he wrote for the radical press, but when the revolution came, he found it profitable to join the extreme reactionaries. He joined hands with Professor Migulin and later was befriended by such influential clergymen as Archbishop Hermogenes, Father Iliodor and *Staretz* [a saintly man] Rasputin. He became especially intimate with the latter. When visiting St. Petersburg, Rasputin stayed with Sazonov, who gradually assumed the rôle of a circus side-show manager demonstrating an outlandish prodigy to an avid public. High-born ladies who were among Rasputin's clientele would come to see him at Sazonov's house. Naturally enough, Sazonov became a personage of importance himself, for Rasputin wielded, and probably still wields, an enormous influence at the Court. Sazonov succeeded in obtaining from the Minister of Finance, Kokovtzev, direct and indirect subsidies for his weekly, *The Economist*. Then Kokovtzev granted to Sazonov and Professor Migulin a license to open a banking institution, which license the worthy pair sold for some 250,000 rubles. With a part of this sum, to which the directors of the bank, at Kokovtzev's suggestion, added 100,000 rubles, Sazonov founded a newspaper, where blackmailing by means of the printed word was practised under the guise of a fairly progressive tendency.

In his letter Sazonov informed me that Stolypin was done for and that the Emperor had formed a firm resolution to get rid of him immediately after the Kiev solemnities. His Majesty, Sazonov wrote, had chosen as Minister of the Interior, Khvostov, Governor of the Nizhni-Novgorod province. Sazonov further wrote that he and Rasputin were now going to Nizhni for a final conference with Khvostov. They were quite certain that he would be an admirable Minister of the Interior, but they had some doubts as to whether, on account of his youth, Khvostov would be a fitting substitute for Stolypin in his capacity of President of the Council of Ministers. Therefore, Sazonov wondered whether I would not be willing to accept the post of President of the Council in order to lend prestige to the new Cabinet.

Khvostov, I may remark, is one of the worst specimens of officialdom as it existed under Stolypin. In his contempt for the law he actually outdid all the other provincial governors. Shortly before, he had submitted to His Majesty a memorandum in which he asserted that Russia was in a state of latent unrest, that the revolution had been driven underground by Stolypin and might break out again, should the government fail to take proper measures. On his part he suggested that all suspects should be killed off in one way or another.

My answer to Sazonov was to the effect that I was in receipt of his letter and that their proposal made me wonder whether they themselves were out of their minds or whether they imagined me stark mad.

As a matter of fact, Stolypin was succeeded by Kokovtzev, while the portfolio of the Ministry of the Interior was given to Makarov. In late years Kokovtzev had been in opposition to Stolypin and so it was expected that he would inaugurate a liberal policy. This expectation was not realized. When Kokovtzev made his first appearance before the Duma, he delivered a long speech. Kokovtzev speaks well and likes to make long speeches, so that the Moscow merchants have dubbed him the "Gramophone". The substance of his speech was as follows: Policies do not change with Ministers, they are dictated from above; so long as he, Kokovtzev, was Minister of Finance he could disagree with the President of the Council, but now that he had become President himself he could follow no other policy than that of the late Stolypin.

Generally speaking, Stolypin's policy was to nullify the attempts to carry out the promises of the constitutional Manifesto, which were made under my administration. The Manifesto promised to grant the population the unshakable foundations of civic liberty, such as inviolability of person and freedom of conscience, of word, of assemblage, and of union. Our laws, as they were created by Emperor Alexander II, were in harmony with the legal consciousness prevalent among the civilized nations of the nineteenth century. Alexander III, under the influence of the assassination of his father, somewhat impaired them, chiefly by a set of temporary regulations, passed by the Committee of Ministers, including the "exceptional status" act, which practically outlaws the region where it is declared and gives it over to the tender mercies of the Administration or of the military authorities. The creation of two independent legislative institutions, the Duma and the Imperial Council, made it possible to hope that the flaws in our legislation would be eliminated and these two bodies would stand watch over the impartial and strict execution of the existing laws. The hope would not have been in vain, were it not for the fact that, on one hand, the Duma, politically speaking, lost its head and imagined that it was possible to introduce a democratic republic in Russia, and, and on the other, that the country's destiny was entrusted to a man like Stolypin.

The "exceptional status" regulations were a temporary law. Their terms having expired in 1906, Stolypin, by means of an Imperial decree, extended them for another three years, and the Duma, the

Third Duma, with a Government-picked membership, feigned not to have noticed the Government's lawless act. At present, the Administration declares "exceptional status" freely and at its own discretion. Furthermore, by arbitrary interpretation Stolypin rendered them more comprehensive than they were intended to be by their author (Plehve) and those who practised them for thirty years before Stolypin' advent to power. At present, we have reached a point when, without any semblance of legality, the police invades your home, searches it until there is not a whole piece of furniture left, seizes all the papers in which the gendarmes may evince an interest, arrests you for no earthly reason and even exiles you to some distant corner of our own country or to foreign lands.

The devotion of the present Government to the principle of the inviolability of person is aptly illustrated by the extent to which perlustration of private correspondence has grown under Stolypin. I remember, soon after my appointment to the office of President of the Council of Ministers, a functionary came to see me and in the name of the Minister of the Interior inquired whether I had any instruction to give regarding the perlustrated mail which was to be sent to me. Although I refused to give any instructions on the subject, Durnovo persisted in sending me daily a dossier with perlustrated mail. I looked these letters over, but, I confess, through-out the period of my Administration I did not come upon a single letter which presented any interest from the standpoint of the State or the police.

Some letters contained passages referring to me in abusive terms: I remember distinctly one curious case. Both my family and myself were on very good terms with Count S. D. Sheremetyev, now a member of the Imperial Council. He had become my ardent admirer after the conclusion of the Portsmouth treaty and gave vent to his enthusiasm in long epistles addressed to my wife. Now in the perlustrated mail which was submitted to me I repeatedly came upon letters with very uncomplimentary—to use a mild term—opinions about me, which were signed by Count Sheremetyev.

I believe that perlustration of private correspondence is essentially a harmful practice. It lays before the Administration intimate and purely confidential matters, thus giving the Minister of the Interior a means for settling personal accounts. I am certain that if Stolypin had not been given to the study of perlustrated mail he would have acted more properly with regard to many people, and would have had fewer enemies.

Speaking of Stolypin and his weakness for the practice of perlustration I recall a characteristic fact. In connection with a discussion of the Post Office in the Imperial Duma, the subject of perlustration of mail was touched upon. A representative of the Ministry of the Interior declared that perlustration was a myth, and that it was no longer practised. This was asserted at the time when perlustration was practised with unprecedented diligence. . . .

It may be observed in passing that the practice is still in existence. Only the other day I spoke about this matter to Kokovtsev and he told me frankly that he received daily a package of perlustrated letters. He added indignantly that this very day he happened upon an unfavourable report about himself, given by the Director of Agriculture, Krivoshein. In order to nonplus Krivoshein he called him up, he said, on the telephone and amicably advised him to be more careful in his correspondence.

In this connection I recall another trait characteristic of Stolypin. It often happens that Cabinet Ministers in a Parliament are pushed to the wall and are forced to give a definite answer to an interpellation. If for some reason or other the Minister is unable to tell the truth, he evades the question, but as a rule, does not tell a lie with noble gestures. As for Stolypin, he followed another rule. He told an outright lie in a most convincing manner. Here is an example:

When I became President of the Council I founded a Government newspaper under the title *The Russian State* (*Russkoye Gosudarstvo*). I was compelled to do it because the press had become revolutionized and it was necessary for the Government to have an organ for the purpose of issuing statements to the public, and refuting the fantastic stories with which the newspapers were overflowing. Stolypin found that *The Russian State* was unfit to exert a proper influence upon the public. He closed the newspaper down and took over the paper called *Russia*, which had already been in existence, in the belief that this newspaper would be more successful in moulding public opinion. But of course this naïve stratagem failed of its purpose and Russia knew very well that *Russia* was a Government organ, Government-subsidized and Government-directed.

When the Duma attempted to ascertain what *Russia* cost the country, Stolypin had the cheek to send his associate Kryzhanovsky with orders to declare before the Duma that the newspaper *Russia* was a private publication. Ever since then *Russia*, which is still in existence and which of course does not have the slightest effect upon public opinion, is usually referred to in the papers, as "a private publication." The constitutional Manifesto promised to grant the people freedom of the press. In pursuance of the Manifesto temporary regulations about the press were issued on November 14, 1905, in the form of an Imperial decree. It contained the following passage:

Before promulgating a general law regulating the functioning of the press, we have deemed it advisable to issue the temporary regulations regarding periodical publications, which were elaborated by the Council of Ministers on the basis of the data furnished by Kobeko and examined by the Imperial Council. These regulations do away with the control of the Administration over the periodical press and subject the criminal deeds committed by means of the printed word to the jurisdiction of the Courts of the land.

The application of these rules was materially obstructed by the failure of many newly established periodical publications to comply with the demands of the law. For this reason a set of additional regulations were published in March of the following year. Upon the whole, these new regulations did not violate the principles of freedom of the press and the principle of responsibility to the Courts for crimes committed through the printed word. Several days after my withdrawal from the post of President of the Council of Ministers, there were issued regulations relating to the non-periodical press.

Seven years have passed since the publication of the constitutional Manifesto and no definite law regarding the press had as yet been enacted. The press is still being regulated by the temporary rules issued in 1905. The important aspect of the situation is that these regulations were infringed upon by Stolypin, with the connivance of the Third Duma. While the first two Dumas were functioning, Stolypin did not dare to violate the law, but no sooner was the Second Duma dissolved than there began a general slaughter of the organs of the periodical press.

Stolypin found that the press laws issued during my Administration were far too liberal. Then Kokovtsev, supported by Kaufman, proposed that a new set of regulations should be elaborated and laid before the Duma. Stolypin, however, opposed this plan. He preferred to resort to the all-powerful "Exceptional Status" which empowered Governors to fine newspapers at their discretion, and, instead of passing new laws, to "interpret" existing regulations so as to render them more stringent. To do this was all the easier, since, owing to Shcheglovitov's efforts, the Courts had lost their independence. Although the other members of the Cabinet protested against such an unprecedented and in fact illegal policy Stolypin did not hesitate to carry out his intentions. As a result, the press is at present again at the mercy of the arbitrary power of the Administration. If a newspaper article happens to displease the authorities, the minister telephones to the Governor-General, or the Manager of his office, and instructs him to fine the guilty publication, which instruction is immediately carried out. Furthermore, if fining appears to be too mild a measure, the Governor-General, on the strength of the "Exceptional Status" puts the editor in prison for a number of months. . . .

A courtier, I forget his name, told me that once in speaking of Kobeko, the author of the temporary press regulations, His Majesty said: "I will never forgive him the general spirit of his press laws."

Under my Administration, the Council of Ministers drafted an elaborate set of laws regulating the right of union and assemblage. The fate of these laws is similar to that of the press regulations. Under Stolypin, especially after the coup d'état of June 3rd, these regulations were violated with even more effrontery than the press regulations. The law existed on paper only and failed to affect the practices of the Government. The Administration did what it pleased. This was indeed Stolypin's motto, and its demoralizing effect was so thorough-going that it will take the efforts of many years to purify the blood vessels of the Russian body politic.

Finally, as regards the freedom of conscience, the situation remains unchanged. Nothing has been added to the acts of December 4, 1905, and April 17, 1905, which latter decree affected only the status of the Old Believer. As for the promise to remove the other restrictions and discriminations based on religion, it has not been fulfilled. In fact, Stolypin made every effort to restrict the privileges granted by the above mentioned two decrees. It must be conceded that as regards the laws relating to religious freedom, the Third Duma acted commendably, but the bills were held up in the Imperial Council or else were so mutilated that they lost all value.

Thus my Cabinet upon the whole carried out that most vital article of the constitutional Manifesto which promised to grant civic liberty to the population. The legislative bodies were given control over the activity of the Administration. Laws were issued regulating the freedom of the press, union and assemblage. Since the opening of the Duma and of the new Imperial Council, the Exceptional Status seemingly could no longer be declared without the sanction of the legislative bodies. Finally, the principles of religious tolerance were legally established. Nevertheless at this writing, seven years after the act of October 17, 1905, civic liberty is still an unattained ideal. In fact, we enjoy now a lesser measure of civic liberty than that which existed prior to the publication of the constitutional Manifesto, and in the course of the past fifty years the *arbitrary* power of the administration has never been as unrestrained as it is now.

Several circumstances account for this state of affairs. On one hand, it is necessary to take into consideration the striking political tactlessness and nearsightedness not alone of our extreme revolutionaries, but also of nearly all the liberal parties. In those revolutionary days they were raving mad and instead of dealing with realities, they lost their senses and repudiated all the legislative acts of the Government as too conservative. On the other hand, the momentous upheaval of the vast Empire frightened many people. As a result, reaction took the upper hand. This movement found support among the Court circles. In its extreme wing, it was as insane as the extreme manifestations of the revolutionary movement. Then came Stolypin's Administration and with it the rule of men who had at heart nothing but their personal careers and to whom it did not matter whether Russia was a constitutional or an autocratic monarchy. Their loyalty to the principles of October 17th was lip service. In reality, they were for the arbitrary rule of the police.

What will be the outcome of it all? It is my firm belief that in the end Russia will have a constitutional régime and, as in other civilized States, the principles of civic freedom will take root in our country. The spirit of October 17th cannot be destroyed either by political stratagems or military force. The only problem is how the change will take place: whether it will come as a consummation of peaceful effort or out of torrents of blood. As a sincere monarchist, as a loyal servant of the reigning House of the Romanovs, as a firm and devoted collaborator of the Emperor Nicholas II, and as a man profoundly attached to the Emperor and full of compassion for him, I pray to God that the change may come about bloodlessly and peacefully.

CHAPTER XIV

MY EXPERIENCES WITH THE KAISER

IT was at Ems that for the first time I caught a glimpse of the man who was destined to become the present ruler of Germany. This was shortly before the death of his grandfather, William I, surnamed the Great. The young prince had been taken to Ems by the old Emperor, who used to go to that famous watering place periodically for his health. It was Emperor William's last trip to Ems. I, too, happened to be there for the sake of my health. The royal visitor stopped at the Kurhaus and, as was his wont, worked in his study by a large window which faced the square in front of the Kurhaus, so that everyone could see him at work. His grandson invariably stood by his armchair and, to my great surprise, acted as the Emperor's office boy. With an air of profound respect the young prince sealed and opened packages, sharpened his grandfather's pencils, handed him pens, and made himself useful in other small ways.

I caught another glimpse of the future German Emperor at the time when I served as Director of the South-Western Railroads, in the early days of the reign of Alexander III. One fine day, I recollect, His Majesty arrived at a small railway station situated between Brest-Litovsk and Bielostok. He was on his way to a military camp near Brest where he was to review a series of manoeuvres. Next morning Adjutant General Cherevin, chief of the Emperor's bodyguard, approached me and inquired how long it would take to bring one of His Majesty's uniforms from St. Petersburg. The old German Emperor, the general explained, had heard that Alexander III would be present at the Brest manoeuvres and dispatched his grandson, the present Kaiser, to greet him. His Majesty, General Cherevin continued, apparently did not relish the idea of having the youthful Hohenzollern about him at the manoeuvres and had decided to meet him at Brest at the end of them. It was for this meeting that His Majesty needed his Prussian uniform, which was at

St. Petersburg. I replied that special locomotives used in relays would cover the distance in forty-eight hours. The necessary orders were given, the uniform arrived in due time, and shortly afterwards His Majesty, accompanied by the Empress, left the castle close to the station, where he had been staying, and proceeded to Brest.

Naturally, I, too, was on board the Imperial train and the details of His Majesty's meeting with Prince William were engraved upon my memory. Our train rode into the Brest station several minutes before the arrival of the Warsaw train which carried the German prince. Emperor Alexander III alighted and paced the platform in front of his guard of honour. He wore his Prussian uniform underneath a Russian cloak. When Prince William's train drew up to the spot where His Majesty stood, he doffed his cloak and handed it over to his Cossack attendant who kept close to him. His Majesty greeted the grandson of William the Great and went through the ceremony of introducing him to the Imperial retinue and reviewing the guard of honour. All the while William behaved like His Majesty's aide-de-camp. The ceremony over, the Emperor turned to his Cossack, who had in the meantime withdrawn into the background, and said loudly: "My cloak!" William, who understood Russian to a certain extent, literally ran over to the Cossack, seized the cloak, and brought it to the Emperor and helped him into it. He was apparently awed by the Russian Czar. The behaviour of the prince greatly surprised me, for at the Russian court such manners were unheard of. Afterwards when I learned more about William's character, I perceived that his obsequiousness* in this case was in complete harmony with his convictions. He holds the view that an emperor is a superman. At present, Prince Henry, his brother, often kisses his hand at leave-taking in everybody's presence, without embarassing him. He accepts this sign of respect as his due. . . .

It is noteworthy that when William became Emperor of Germany (his father, as is known, died from a cancer in his throat after a few months' reign) the awe with which Alexander III inspired him at the time when he was young did not altogether vanish. I recall having heard Emperor William say that he had been deeply impressed by the personality of that great Russian Czar. "Yes," he told me on one occasion, "he was truly an autocrat and an emperor."

Indirectly I came in contact with Emperor William II in the course of our conflict with Germany which resulted in the conclusion of the

---

* The exaggerated servile act of overly trying to please an important person.

first Russo-German commercial treaty, in the year 1894. Briefly stated, the history of that clash is as follows: With a view to exploiting us economically, the German Government imposed prohibittive duties on goods imported from our country, especially raw materials, thus considerably affecting our agricultural industry. We retaliated by raising our duties on German exports. Our resistance, for which I am partly responsible, was so resolute and vigorous, that, after a veritable tariff war waged by the two countries, Germany had to surrender its scheme of encroachment and agree to a commercial treaty which was to a certain extent advantageous to us.

Emperor William's rôle in this matter was, upon the whole, conciliatory, especially since it became clear that we would not yield. It was with his support that Count Caprivi, Minister of Foreign Affairs, succeeded in putting the treaty through the Reichstag, in the face of stout opposition on the part of the large landowners and Junkers, whose interests were considerably prejudiced by the new tariffs.

Upon the signing of the treaty I had an audience with Emperor Alexander. In the course of it I called His Majesty's attention to the fact that Emperor William was instrumental in bringing about the ratification of the treaty by the Reichstag, and that he was, therefore, entitled to our gratitude. I had been informed, I said, that Emperor William was anxious to get the uniform of a Russian admiral and I would be glad, I added, if that distinction were bestowed upon him. I may say here, in passing, that William has a veritable passion for all manner of showy uniforms, especially military and naval. His Majesty smiled at my words, said he would gratify the German Emperor's ambition at the first opportunity, and asked me to remind him of the matter. Emperor Alexander died before such an opportunity presented itself, and it fell to his son to fulfill the promise. I found it necessary to report the matter to Emperor Nicholas, and at his first meeting with the German Emperor he presented the latter with the longed-for uniform.

In this connection I recall a similar incident which took place at the time when I held the office of President of the Committee of Ministers. It was again a case of craving for a Russian uniform, on the part of the German Emperor. This time the object of his ardent desire, I was told, was the uniform of an Adjutant General. I was at the time in disfavour with Emperor Nicholas, and so I could do nothing to satisfy the Kaiser's desire. I understand that he tried to work through Grand Duke Michael, but I do not know whether his efforts were crowned with success.

It may be properly mentioned here that in the early years of his reign Emperor Nicholas was by no means fond of the German Kaiser. In this respect he followed in the footsteps of his august father, who actually disliked the German ruler, with his weakness for stage effects and spectacular splurges. Emperor Nicholas' antipathy to William was further complicated by a feeling of personal rivalry. His Majesty could not help feeling that in the opinion of Russia and of the world the German ruler stood higher than himself. Even in appearance William was more of an emperor than he, Nicholas. Given His Majesty's somewhat excessive self-esteem, this could not but be a thorn in his flesh. After the first meeting of the two Emperors, I recall, there appeared picture postal cards which represented the two rulers in a friendly pose. William's arm rested on his Majesty's shoulder as if embracing him, and as Emperor Nicholas barely reached up to William's shoulder, the latter's arm stretched slightly downward. The cards were immediately confiscated.

Another circumstance which fed His Majesty's antipathy to Emperor William was the latter's attitude toward His Majesty's brother-in-law, the Duke of Darmstadt, and also toward the Empress. The Kaiser actually snubbed the Duke, and he treated Her Majesty not as the Empress of all the Russias, but as a petty German princess. In general, Emperor William does not stand on ceremony with his German relations. It is said that recently at the manoeuvres in the vicinity of Frankfort, he turned to the Duke of Darmstadt who happened to be nearby and remarked: "You are very anxious, I know, to get the Black Eagle of the first order. I will give it to you at once if you answer the following question: 'When a Hussar mounts his horse, which foot goes into the stirrup first?'"

In recent years, however, his attitude toward our Empress and her brother has undergone a subsantial change, for reasons which I shall presently point out. Some time before the outbreak of the Russo-Japanese War, the German Chancellor Bülow and Germany's Ambassador to St. Petersburg complained to me that Emperor Nicholas was not civil enough toward their Monarch, that he was slow in answering Emperor William's letters, that he did not requite the Kaiser's attentions, etc.,—which circumstances unfavourably affected the relations between the two countries. I pointed out to them that it was Emperor William who was largely responsible for this state of affairs. Let him, I said, show some attention to the Empress and her brother, and the relations between the two Emperors will be automatically improved. The German Emperor followed my advice and had no difficulty in winning the hearts of both Empress Alexandra and the Duke of Darmstadt. This circumstance, in its turn, affected His Majesty's attitude toward Emperor William, and an intimate correspondence sprang up between them. [Now famous as the "Willy-Nicky" letters.—EDITOR.]

At the beginning of their personal relations, the German ruler assumed a patronizing, mentor-like attitude toward our Emperor. Before long he perceived, however, that this was the surest way of arousing Nicholas' animosity. It was then that he abruptly faced about and began to treat Emperor Nicholas as his superior. His Majesty, it must be noted, hardly tolerates people whom he considers superior to himself either intellectually or morally. He is at ease only when dealing with men who are either actually his inferiors or whom he considers as such, or finally, those who, knowing His Majesty's weakness, find it expedient to feign inferiority. Count Lamsdorff, our Minister of Foreign Affairs, repeatedly assured me that ever since the beginning of the intimate correspondence between the two emperors, the Kaiser frequently had endeavoured to do an ill turn to his correspondent and to set him at variance with other powers, especially France, and that he, Lamsdorff, had to be constantly on the lookout. If the secret documents in his possession were ever published, the Count added, the world would be astonished. It was for this reason, perhaps, that Emperor William detested our Minister of Foreign Affairs.

His Majesty has exchanged a number of official and semi-official visits with Emperor William. One of the first visits paid by the German ruler to our Emperor was occasioned by the latter's coronation*. Emperor William, accompanied by the Empress, arrived in Peterhof on July 26th (Russian style), 1897, and remained there till the 30th. The arrival was, of course, marked by an official dinner in grand style, given in honour of the royal guests. As soon as I reached Peterhof—I was among those invited—one of the Kaiser's attendants informed me that the Emperor wished to make my acquaintance before the dinner and asked me to come to his apartment.

It was on that July afternoon, in one of the gorgeous rooms of the Great Palace, that I saw for the first time the German Emperor at

* The coronation in actuality took place in the preceding year, May 1896.

close quarters. I found him not fully attired, but ready with a little speech which he addressed to me after we went through the ceremony of greeting each other.

The substance of his speech was that he knew me to be a great and wise statesman and that, in recognition of my worth, he had decided to bestow upon me the order of the Black Eagle. Thereupon he handed me the decoration, adding that as a rule this mark of distinction was given only to persons of royal blood and to Ministers of Foreign Affairs. I hardly need say that I was greatly flattered.

The next day I met the Kaiser again at a luncheon given in his honour at the German Embassy in St. Petersburg. The invitation came, I was told, at His Majesty's express wish. The function was attended exclusively by diplomats, both German and Russian. When the luncheon was over and we retired to the drawing-room, the Emperor became very amiable toward everybody and behaved like a fop, gesticulating with his arms and legs, in a fashion not at all befitting an Emperor. After a while the Emperor drew me into the Ambassador's study, where we remained alone.

He opened the conversation by calling my attention to the dangers which were threatening Europe from beyond the seas. America, he said, is growing rich at Europe's expense, and it is necessary to build a high tariff wall around Europe so as to make it impossible for America to flood us with its products. The European countries must unite to shut out the transatlantic competitor, who is growing very dangerous, especially as regards agriculture, and thus to arrest the development of the United States of America. I took the liberty then of observing to the Emperor that the interests of continental Europe were not identical with those of Great Britain and that, therefore, she would have to be excluded from the contemplated European union. His Majesty retorted that England constituted no danger for the agriculture of Europe and that she could not be excluded, for the reason that it was his intention to establish the best of relations with her. The tariff wall should be erected against America alone, he reiterated.

Thereupon I pointed out that, whether or not England was included, an economic war against America was not practicable, because many European countries were not likely to agree to it. Speaking for Russia, I went on saying that we would be loath to embrace His Majesty's viewpoint, for the reason that ever since the

American Revolutionary War we had been on the best of terms with the United States of America and that we did not intend to quarrel with that country.

Having thus dismissed the Kaiser's scheme, I proceeded to expound my own views on the general political situation, as I saw it at the time and as I still see it. After referring to the unbreakable tie which exists between political prestige and economic power, I declared to His Majesty that, among the countries of the world, Europe seemed to me like a decrepit old woman. Unless a radical change is brought about, I went on, Europe will soon have to yield her dominating place in the world to the mighty empires which are rising beyond the seas. The time is not far off, I said, when this continent will be treated with that condescending respect which well-mannered people accord to venerable old age, and before the next few centuries are past, the greatness of Europe will be to the inhabitants of our planet what the grandeur of Rome, the glory of Greece, and the might of Carthage are to us.

The German Emperor was deeply impressed by my words and inquired how I proposed to deal with the disastrous situation I envisaged. "Your Majesty," I said, "picture a Europe which does not waste most of its blood and treasure on competition between individual countries, which does not maintain millions of soldiers for internecine* wars, which is not an armed camp with each country pitted against its neighbour, a Europe which is, in brief, one body politic, one large empire. Then, of course, we would be richer, and more vigorous, and more cultured, and Europe, instead of withering under the burden of strife, would become truly the mistress of the world. To achieve this ideal we must seek to create a solid union of Russia, Germany and France. Once these countries are firmly united, all the other States of the European continent will, no doubt, join the central alliance and thus form an all-embracing continental confederation, which will free Europe from the burden of internecine competition and establish its domination over the world for many years to come."

His Majesty listened to my remarks with great interest and graciously bade me farewell, saying that my views were original and interesting. Emperor Nicholas, in the course of my next audience with him, handed me a brief note the German Kaiser had given him

---

* Needless wars between related groups, such as the countries of Europe.

on leaving Peterhof. The note contained the statement of his opinion regarding the necessity of waging an economic war against the United States of America, which the German Emperor had expounded to me. I did not conceal from His Majesty that I had discussed the subject with the German Monarch, and I also stated my own ideas on the subject. His Majesty assured me that he shared my view and asked me to write a reply to the note from my standpoint,—which I did in the form of an unsigned memorandum. This, His Majesty said, he would send to Emperor William, together with a personal letter. It is noteworthy that when Theodore Roosevelt was elected President, Emperor William began to flirt with him, and the two rulers made a great show of their sudden friendship.

During the German Emperor's stay at Peterhof there occurred an incident which was destined to have the most far-reaching effects upon the course of Russian history. It was afterwards related to me by Grand Duke Alexey Alexandrovich. Once when the two emperors were driving alone out in the country, so our Emperor told the Grand Duke, the German Kaiser asked his host whether Russia had any use for the Chinese port of Kiao-Chow. He added that he would like to occupy that port and use it as a base for German shipping, but that he did not wish to take the step without his, Nicholas's, consent. His Majesty did not tell the Grand Duke whether or not he actually gave his consent to the occupation of Kiao-Chow. What he did say was that his guest had placed him in an awkward position and the whole incident was extremely distasteful to him. I have but little doubt that His Majesty, who is exceedingly well-mannered, found it impossible to refuse his guest's request point-blank and that the latter interpreted this attitude as indirect approval and implied consent.

Shortly afterwards German warships entered the harbour of Kiao-Chow. I noticed, not without amazement, that the news of the occupation did not come as a complete surprise to Count Muraviov, our Foreign Minister. This seizure of Kiao-Chow served as a signal for our occupation of Port Arthur and Ta-lieng-wan. It was, in fact, the first link in the chain of events which culminated in the disastrous Japanese war.

When I learned that, in spite of my desperate opposition, it had been definitely decided to occupy those two Chinese ports, in flagrant violation of all our pledges to China and counter to our traditional Far-Eastern policy, I went straight to the German Ambassador, Tschirsky, and asked him to wire to his Emperor that, in the interest of both my own country and of Germany, I earnestly entreated and advised him to withdraw from Kiao-Chow, after having meted out justice to the guilty and, if he saw fit, imposed an indemnity on China. Otherwise, I concluded, the step would eventually bring about most appalling results. Within a few days Tschirsky brought me the following dispatch written in the name of the Kaiser: "Tell Witte that, to judge by his dispatch, some very essential circumstances relating to the matter in question are unknown to him. Consequently, I cannot follow his advice."

It was then that I recalled Grand Duke Alexey Alexandrovich's story about the Kiao-Chow incident at Peterhof and also Count Muraviov's reception of the news of Germany's entrance into Kiao-Chow. Some time later Count Muraviov, in discussing with me my opposition to the occupation of Port Arthur, let the cat out of the bag. He admitted that we had, in his words, "rashly given our consent to the step which Germany had taken."

The subsequent course of events—I have described it at some length elsewhere in these memoirs—convinced me that it had been the intention of German diplomacy and of the German Emperor himself to drag us, by hook or crook, into Far-Eastern adventures, so as to divert our forces to the East and leave them a free hand in Europe. It may properly be mentioned here that Emperor William is also partly to blame for the Boer War. He ostentatiously encouraged President Krüger to refuse England's demands, sending him a most demonstrative and provocative telegram. Of course, when the war broke out, he discreetly withdrew into the background. As a result, the Republic of the Transvaal was destroyed and England considerably weakened for the time being. For those who worship nationalism in the extreme Emperor William is an ideal example of an eminent ruler. He stops at nothing to benefit the country and the people he governs.

Thinking of the methods which William used to influence the mind of our Emperor to his own advantage, I recollect an incident which marked the end of the manoeuvres at Reval, in the summer of the year 1902, attended by the two Emperors. In the course of the customary farewell signalling exchanged between the two Imperial yachts, the Emperor flashed the following phrase: "The Admiral of the Atlantic sends his greetings to the Admiral of the Pacific,"—which in plain language meant as much as this: "I seek to dominate the Atlantic; as for you, I advise you to try and become the master of the Pacific, and in that undertaking I am ready to help you." It is curious that the dispatches sent by His Majesty to Admiral Alexeyev in 1902, and, especially, in the following year, reveal an ill disguised desire on his part to reach a dominating position in the Pacific. There is no doubt in my mind that this disastrous orientation is partly due to William's influence on our Emperor.

I have reason to believe that His Majesty was to a certain extent aware of the fact that he was being hoodwinked by the German Emperor for the glory of the German cause. During the meeting of the two rulers at Potsdam in 1903, Emperor Nicholas surprised his host by studiously avoiding any discussion dealing with politics generally and Far-Eastern affairs in particular. It appears that the danger of a war with Japan was not brought home to His Majesty until the very last moment. Shortly before the beginning of the conflict, Emperor William warned His Majesty that Japan was feverishly preparing for war. His Majesty replied that there would be no war since he did not wish it.

Upon the outbreak of hostilities, Emperor William hastened to assure His Majesty of his devotion to Russia and of the security of our Western frontiers. Nevertheless, as if in compensation for his promise not to attack us, the German Emperor, in a private letter to His Majesty, requested his consent to a number of changes in the commercial treaty of 1894, which had just then expired. These changes were so ruinous to our industries that I resolutely opposed them and advocated the maintenance of the status quo in our economic relations with Germany, but, alas! the days of Alexander III were gone, and we had to yield. The matter was taken up by a special conference of statesmen under my presidency, and we arrived at the conclusion that, to avoid a break with Germany, we must submit to her demands. I was appointed to conduct the negotiations and instructed to secure access to Germany's money market in exchange for our concessions. By that time we had spent the funds I had accumulated as Minister of Finance and we were in sore need of foreign loans to finance the war and, later, to weather the revolutionary storm.

The negotiations were conducted at Norderney, Germany, Chancellor Bülow representing Germany. I spent two weeks on that island, most of the time in the Chancellor's company. His wife would sometimes join us after dinner. An admirer of Tolstoy, she was at that time reading a book on the Decembrists. Bülow was curious to know my opinion on the Japanese war, which was then in progress. I prophesied—alas! falsely—that on sea we would suffer reverses, but that on land we would eventually triumph. My host tried to impress me with the fact that the German Monarch was doing everything in his power to please the Russian Emperor and that he had shown himself to be a true friend of Russia. As for negotiations, I soon perceived, he felt sure that I would make all the concessions that were demanded of us. . . . He must have been informed from St. Petersburg that I had received instructions to bring the parley to a peaceful end at any price. We haggled a good deal, but finally came to terms. I cannot say that I acted freely. I could not for a single moment forget that we had on our hands a most unfortunate war and that our western frontiers were practically open.

Long before the end of the pourparlers, I broached to Bülow the subject of floating a Russian loan in Germany. Should we agree on the treaty, I said, we would expect Germany to throw open her money market to us. Personally he saw no obstacles, but he pointed out that the German Emperor's motto was: "German money for Germans only." To corroborate his statement, he showed me several telegrams he had received from the Emperor on that subject. When it came to signing the treaty—we went to Berlin for that purpose—I succeeded, by acting with determination, in securing the Kaiser's formal permission to float a loan on the German money market.

By dragging us into the war with Japan, Germany succeeded in weakening us and also, indirectly, our ally, France. Having achieved this result, she might have remained quiet for a long time, in spite of the Emperor's restlessness, had it not been for the rapprochement between France and England, which originated at that time. The two countries reached an understanding, embodied in a formal document, regarding their respective spheres of influence in Morocco. Germany seized upon this circumstance and declared that she had commercial interests of her own in Morocco, which she intended to defend and that, furthermore, neither England nor France could take any steps in Morocco without Germany's consent. A diplomatic wrangle ensued, in which Germany behaved so arrogantly that a break seemed probable. Since it was suggested from Berlin that as long as Delcassé, who had negotiated the Anglo-French Morocco agreement, remained Minister of Foreign Affairs, the German diplomats were likely to be intractable, Delcassé withdrew and his portfolio was entrusted to Prime Minister Rouvier.

That happened in 1905, shortly before my arrival in Paris on my way to the United States, where I was to negotiate peace with Japan. I found the French Government in a state of alarm. Everybody was anxious to see the war liquidated and our attention transferred from the fields of far Manchuria to the basin of the Vistula. The general apprehension was increased by the sudden meeting of the two Emperors at Björke. Count Lamsdorff did not mention this meeting to me at our last interview before my departure from St. Petersburg, for the simple reason that he knew nothing about it. His Majesty himself said nothing about it either, although he knew, of course, that it was going to take place. I assured all those who asked me that the interview had no political significance, but in the meantime I wired to Count Lamsdorff for an explanation. His reply—it came immediately—was to the effect that the meeting was a purely private affair. I showed the dispatch to Rouvier and thereby allayed his fears.

When President Roosevelt told me at Portsmouth that the whole world was anxious to see peace restored between Russia and Japan, I inquired of him whether the German Emperor was included. An emphatic "yes" was the reply. In fact, when peace was concluded, Emperor William sent enthusiastic congratulations to His Majesty. It was easy enough for him to be enthusiastic, for, in the meantime, did he not succeed, by the Björke agreement, in dragging Russia into a worse muddle than the war?

On my way back from the United States I stopped in Paris again, as I had important business to transact there. Already, during my previous visit, I had broached to Rouvier the subject of a Russian loan in France. He would help me contract it, Rouvier assured me, should I succeed in liquidating the war. Now that I came to take up the matter with him more definitely, he declared that, until the Morocco incident was peaceably settled, a loan was out of the question, and he earnestly begged me to use all my influence to render the German diplomats more tractable in their negotiations with France. In return for my services he promised to give me full assistance in the matter of the loan. I agreed to that arrangement and went straight from the Quai d'Orsay to see Prince Radolin, the German Ambassador in Paris, with whom I was on friendly terms. Without entering into a discussion of the Morocco affair, I pointed out to him that Germany should assume a less exacting attitude, for otherwise Rouvier's Cabinet was certain to fall and be succeeded by one that would be much less tractable. I also alluded to the fact that Russia was interested in seeing France, and Europe generally, at peace, for the reason that we intended to carry out a large financial transaction which would be thwarted if the unsettled condition of the European stock exchanges persisted. To my surprise, Prince Radolin confessed that he found Rouvier's demands perfectly just and that, personally, he saw no obstacles to an amicable settlement of the controversy. He added, however, that the negotiations were conducted, not by him, for he was considered a Gallophile in Berlin, but by a certain Kaufmann, a very bellicose and intractable person indeed. I was immediately introduced to the German plenipotentiary, and it did not take me long to find out that no concessions were to be expected from him.

The next day I visited Rouvier again. Personally, he confided to me, he attached little importance to the concessions in the Morocco affair on which Germany insisted, but the country, he said, was in such an ugly mood that, should he yield to those demands, his Cabinet would be forced to resign. I suggested then that he come to an agreement with his opponents regarding the secondary issues of the dispute and that he propose to Germany the arbitration of the main issues by an international conference, with the understanding that the decision of the conference was to be binding upon both sides. This, I added, would free the present Cabinet from the responsibility for the outcome of the Morocco affair. Rouvier remarked that this scheme had occurred to him, but that it had been rejected by the German plenipotentiary.

In the meantime, I had learned that King Edward of England desired to see me. A similar invitation was also received from Emperor William. I replied that, to my regret, I could not visit their Majesties before reporting to my Monarch. Afterwards, however, I was instructed to visit the German Emperor. Before leaving for Berlin, I paid a visit to the President of the Republic, Loubet, as a sop to French public opinion; and I also informed both Prince Radolin and Rouvier that I would try to convince Emperor William of the desirability of turning the Morocco conflict over to an international conference for arbitration.

I met the Emperor in his Prussian hunting castle at Rominten, which is situated near the Russian frontier, a short distance from

Verzhbolovo. I reached the railway station in the morning and was greeted in the Emperor's name by aged Count Eulenberg. He drove me in his car to the castle and told me that His Majesty entertained a very high opinion about me, that he admired my Portsmouth achievement, and that he was waiting for me with impatience.

The Emperor, accompanied by a small retinue, met me in front of the castle. He spoke to me very graciously and ordered the Minister of the Court to take me to the apartment assigned to me. Properly speaking, the castle of Rominten hardly deserves its high-sounding name. It consists of two plain, rustic, two-story houses, rising on a hill, with a number of cottages scattered below them. The two houses are joined by a roofed gallery, and one is of somewhat simpler construction than the other. They are occupied by the Emperor's family, his retinue and guests, the cottages accommodating the servants. A village lies at some distance, and all around there are woods, the Emperor's hunting grounds. The Emperor, his attendants, and the guests wear hunting costumes,—Emperor William, one must bear in mind, is very fond of all manner of uniforms. Life is very simple at the castle; the rooms are plainly furnished, but everywhere there are the customary German cleanliness and order.

Shortly after I found myself in my rooms, I was visited by Count Eulenburg, who is, by the way, one of the most intimate friends of the Emperor and a prominent member of the Court camarilla. Our talk turned about the general political situation, Russo-German relations and similar topics. The count told me, among other things, that His Majesty had not forgotten the conversation he had had with me at Peterhof some years ago, and I expressed my regret that my words had had no practical results. Count Eulenburg replied vaguely that my hopes were probably nearer realization than I thought.

At breakfast His Majesty introduced me to the Empress, whom I had already had the honour of meeting, and also the Princess, their only daughter, a homely but attractive girl whom her parents seemed to idolize. I was also introduced to the rest of the party, which included, besides Count Eulenburg, the Minister of the Navy, a general and two young adjutants. At table I sat next to the Empress and our talk was of a social nature. Her Majesty told me, among other things, that several years ago the Emperor had no liking for motor cars, but that recently he had grown so fond of them and drove at such a speed that she was sometimes actually worried. After breakfast His Majesty took me aside, and our talk assumed a serious aspect. Having referred briefly to my success at Portsmouth, he turned to the general political situation in Europe and reverted to our Peterhof conversation. I reiterated my profound belief in the desirability of a general rapprochement of the three main bodies politic of Europe: Russia, Germany, and France, this rapprochement tending to become a close union, which, of course, would be joined by other European powers. Delivered from the burden of military expenditures, Europe would be enabled to create a mighty naval force which would dominate the world. His Majesty assured me that he shared my views and then declared that my scheme had finally been carried into effect at his meeting with Emperor Nicholas at Björke. It was Emperor Nicholas himself who had authorized him to communicate to me this secret information, he added. Having imparted to me this extraordinary piece of news, His Majesty asked me whether I was satisfied with this development, and in my innocence I replied that his words had filled my heart with joy. We parted.

Later in the day, after His Majesty had returned from the hunt, we had another talk. I opened it by pointing out that French public opinion should be gradually prepared for the idea of a rapprochement with Germany by a series of well-thought-out and systematic measures. To my regret, I said, this has not been done, and in late years the two countries have been drifting apart, a circumstance which had thrown France into England's arms and finally resulted in the celebrated Morocco understanding. In the course of my recent visit to France, I added, I found that public opinion was greatly aroused against Germany and, while the market was seriously upset, I even heard talk of war. Apparently, I concluded, after the Björke compact, nothing had been done to bring about a rapprochement between the two countries. The Emperor admitted that nothing had been done up to that time, but stated that the necessary measures would be taken in due course. He was strangely reticent, I noticed, about the substance of the Björke understanding and clearly would not let me read the instrument. I thought he considered it proper to leave this to Emperor Nicholas.

In the course of our talk His Majesty strongly denounced the French Government, saying that it had always been hostile to Germany and to his person. He had repeatedly wanted, he said, to take the initiative in establishing harmonious relations with France, but the deplorable lack of good-will and tact on the part of the

Republic's representatives had invariably been a stumbling block. He was especially indignant at Delcassé's action in concluding the Morocco treaty with England. German diplomats had been aware, he said, of the negotiations, but they had not been alarmed because they had believed that once the treaty was concluded, they would be properly informed of its substance. Seeing, however, that not a word about the treaty came from either party, the Government concluded that the understanding did not affect Germany at all. But when the text of the treaty became known, His Majesty continued, it appeared that the agreement related to matters in which Germany was directly concerned, for she had vested commercial interests in Morocco. This forced us to show, His Majesty concluded, that no treaties regarding matters in which Germany's interests are involved can be made without her consent, let alone without her knowledge.

In reply to this tirade, I observed that France had given proof of her earnest desire to make up for that unfortunate incident. Had not Delcassé been forced to quit his post and had he not been succeeded by a man who was anxious to settle the matter amicably? I went on to quote Ambassador Radolin to the effect that Rouvier was willing to make all the concessions that could reasonably be expected of him and that, on the whole, the attitude of the French Government was very tactful. I also called His Majesty's attention to the fact that Rouvier was favourably disposed to the idea of a Franco-German entente and that, should the negotiations fail, his Cabinet was likely to be succeeded by one which might be disinclined to favour that idea. In my explanations I went into great detail, for I noticed that the Kaiser was not abreast of the negotiations which his plenipotentiary was conducting in Paris. I then repeated the arguments I had expounded to Ambassador Radolin in favour of having the matter arbitrated by an international conference, and I reported that both the German Ambassador and Rouvier approved of this plan. Should France reach an understanding with you as a result of the present parley, I added, some other country, for instance the United States of America, might object to that agreement and thereby place both parties to the treaty in a very awkward position. Under the circumstances, I concluded, an international arbitration conference is the best possible solution.

A pause ensued, at the end of which, His Majesty took a blank, penned a telegram to Chancellor Bülow and showed it to me, saying: "You have convinced me. The matter will be settled in accordance with your views."

Our conversation lingered on for a while. His Majesty spoke slightingly of our Ambassador to Great Britain, Count Benckendorff, whose chief diplomatic rôle was that of the King's partner at bridge. He asked me what I thought of Russia's internal situation, which, according to his information, was fraught with danger. I made no attempt to conceal from him the fact that, owing to our erroneous domestic policies and the unfortunate war, our country was seething with discontent and the Government had lost its prestige. I also ventured the opinion that in the end a constitution would have to be granted. Some of the reforms demanded by the people, the Emperor believed, should be yielded, but once the changes found necessary were introduced, no further concessions should be made under any circumstances. That opinion, His Majesty added, he had also expressed to Emperor Nicholas. The subject of our war with Japan the Kaiser studiously avoided. He had not forgotten, I should judge, the telegram I sent to him through Counsellor Tschirsky at the time of Germany's occupation of Kiao-Chow.

After we had parted and I returned to my quarters, the Minister of the Court brought me two presents from the Emperor. One was His Majesty's portrait in a gilt frame, bearing the following autograph inscription: "Portsmouth–Björke–Rominten. Wilhelm rex." The other was the chain of the Order of the Red Eagle. The inscription on the portrait summarized the course of policy which William had pursued ever since our decision to open peace negotiations. After his conversation with me, he apparently no longer doubted that, on one hand, Russia's defeat set his hands free in the East, and, on the other hand, that the Portsmouth and Björke agreements meant Germany's aggrandizement in the West with the help of Russia. And to think that all that was achieved without a drop of German blood shed or a German pfennig spent! But man proposes and God disposes.

As for the extraordinary decoration bestowed upon me by His Majesty—the chain of the Red Eagle is given only to sovereigns or members of their families—he could give me no other mark of distinction, for I had already the Order of the Black Eagle, which is the highest German decoration. This high honour must have been partly the reason why Emperor Nicholas was moved to bestow upon me the rank of Count.

I was told by the Court Minister that, if I wished to please His

Majesty, I should wear the chain at dinner. The request greatly embarrassed me, for I had taken along none of my uniforms, knowing that in America they would be useless to me. It was agreed that I should wear the chain on my dress coat and that the Minister would report to His Majesty why I appeared without my uniform and other decorations.

Having come down to dinner, I thanked the Emperor for his attentions to me. We dined in the circle which I have already described. After dinner the young Princess and the adjutants left and we passed into an adjacent room. Settled in comfortable arm-chairs, the company sipped coffee and beer, smoked, and generally behaved without any constraint or affectation. Later in the evening we took turns in telling anecdotes and humorous stories, this apparently being a customary feature of the gatherings in the castle of Rominten. The Emperor was the one to laugh and make merry more than anyone else. Most of the time he sat on the arm of the chair occupied by Count Eulenburg, embracing him, as it were, with his right arm. Of all those present it was precisely Count Eulenburg who looked and behaved like a sovereign. At about ten o'clock His Majesty bade us good-night and the party broke up.

The next day I again lunched with their Majesties. I was very favourably impressed by the remarkable simplicity of their life and the extreme amiability of their manners. In official life the Emperor is somewhat brusque in gesture and affects that fastidiousness which is characteristic of a well-born German officer of the Guards, but in private life he is charming. After the luncheon I took leave of the company and prepared to bid farewell to the Emperor, when, to my amazement, he declared that he would drive me to the railway station in his own motor car. His Majesty seated me at his side while the inevitable Count Eulenburg was in the front seat. The trip lasted some ten minutes and we could exchange but a few remarks. His Majesty advised me, I remember, to communicate with him, in case of need, through Count Eulenburg. "Writing to him," he said, "is the same as writing to me, and his replies are my replies." The Emperor accompanied me to the platform, where I took leave of him. Then I boarded the train. His Majesty stood on the platform till the moment when my train pulled out of the station.

As soon as I found myself alone, I penned on a scrap of paper a brief note to the French Ambassador in Berlin and dispatched it by the courier attached to the Berlin agent of our Ministry of Finance, who had accompanied me. In this note I asked the Ambassador immediately to inform Rouvier that I had arranged the Morocco affair and that the German Emperor had already given the necessary instructions to Chancellor Bülow. I have never been able to obtain the original of this note, in spite of its importance as documentary proof of the fact that in 1905 I prevented a clash between France and Germany. In 1907, however, I succeeded in getting for my files an official copy of my note in the form in which it was transmitted by telegraph to Minister Rouvier. The dispatch was sent from Berlin, in my name, on September 28 (new style), 1905, that is, immediately upon receipt of the original note by the French Ambassador. Its text follows: *J'ai eu l'honneur de présenter a l'Empereur d'Allemagne mes explications sur les questions marocaines et Sa Majesté a eu la bonté de me dire qu'Elle n'a pas l'intention de faire des difficultés au gouvernement français et qu'Elle donnera á ce sujet ses ordres impériaux.* ("I have had the honour of presenting to the German Emperor my explanations on the subject of the Morocco question, and His Majesty was good enough to tell me that he had no intention of causing any difficulties to the French Government and that he would issue the necessary instructions.")

On the day after my arrival in St. Petersburg I had an interview with Emperor Nicholas aboard the imperial yacht *Standard*, anchored off the coast of Finland. His Majesty received me in his stateroom and thanked me cordially for the successful achievement of the difficult task with which he had entrusted me [the Treaty of Portsmouth] and for the accuracy with which I had carried out his instructions, both in letter and spirit. Thereupon he bestowed upon me the rank of Count, in recognition of my services to himself and Russia. In the course of our subsequent talk, His Majesty told me that he had received a letter from Emperor William, in which the German sovereign spoke of me in admiring terms. He was glad, he added, that I shared the views which were the foundation of his agreement with Germany, concluded at Björke. I always have advocated, I interposed, an entente between France, Germany and Russia. His Majesty observed that he knew I had spoken about it to Emperor William several years before. The text of the mysterious agreement, however, His Majesty did not show me.

The next day I met Count Lamsdorff, our Minister of Foreign Affairs. After the customary greetings and congratulations, he asked me, his voice vibrant with ill-controlled indignation:

"Do you really approve of the Björke compact?"

I replied in the affirmative and proceeded to unfold my views on the desirability of an entente among Russia, Germany, and France, when he interrupted me, saying:

"But have you read the Bjorke treaty?"

I confessed that I had not, whereupon he handed me the text of the document, saying that he had received it only on the previous day and bidding me read it. The count looked profoundly excited and upset. As I read the document, I understood the cause of his excitement. The substance of the agreement was that Germany and Russia obligated themselves to defend each other in case of war with any other European power (including France, therefore). Russia pledged itself to make every effort to gain France over to this union (but whether or not this result was attained, the agreement between the two countries was, nevertheless, valid). The agreement was to become effective from the moment of the ratification of the Portsmouth Treaty (as much as to say: If the war keeps up, well and good; if the war stops, Russia will be dragged into a worse muddle). The instrument was signed by the two sovereigns and countersigned by a German official, whose name I was unable to make out and, on our side, by the Minister of the Navy, Birilev.

The agreement meant that we were to defend Germany in case she chose to wage war against France, and this in spite of the fact that since the beginning of the 'nineties we have had an understanding with France, in virtue of which we were pledged to defend her in case of a war with Germany. On the other hand, Germany obligated herself to defend European Russia in case of a war with any other European power, but this provision was practically worthless, inasmuch as in the Far East, our Achilles' heel, Germany left us to our own resources.

I declared to Count Lamsdorff that the agreement must be rescinded at any cost, and that I would rather go on fighting Japan than ratify the Portsmouth treaty and thus validate the Björke agreement.

"This is monstrous," I exclaimed. "The treaty dishonours us in the eyes of France. Is it possible that all this has been concocted without you and that you knew nothing about it?"

Count Lamsdorff repeated that until the preceding day he had been kept in complete ignorance of the matter.

"Does not His Majesty know that we have a treaty with France?" I asked.

"Of course His Majesty knows that," he replied, "but the fact must have slipped from his mind, or, what is more probable, his brain was befogged by William's verbiage and he failed to grasp the substance of the matter."

We put our heads together to find a way out of the difficulty. The hardest part of the task, in Count Lamsdorff's judgment, was to secure His Majesty's consent to the cancellation of the agreement. We could find some legal flaws in the agreement, on which to base a formal plea for its abolition. Finally, we agreed to advance the following arguments: first, that the treaty was not countersigned by the Minister of Foreign Affairs; second, that the treaty in question was in contradiction to our previous treaty with France; and, third, that the ratification of the Björke compact must be preceded by and depend upon a corresponding agreement with France. Should these arguments fail, we decided to declare that Russia would leave the Portsmouth treaty unratified rather than recognize the Björke agreement as it stood. This agreement, we determined, should be reduced to a simple statement on our part that we adhered to the principle of a Russo-Franco-German entente and were ready to obligate ourselves to carry that policy into effect.

In my capacity of President of the Committee of Ministers I had no official access to His Majesty. As for Count Lamsdorff, I did not set much store by his ability to influence His Majesty's mind in so weighty a matter. So I decided to turn for help to Grand Duke Nikolai Nikolaievich, who, I knew, exerted a strong influence upon His Majesty, owing both to his connection with occultism and to his devotion to Nicholas, not only as the Emperor, but also as a man. I have reason to believe that the Grand Duke was familiar with the substance of the treaty long before the Foreign Minister, but I did not find that out till later. He listened to me attentively and seemed to grasp the point that the agreement was essentially a dishonourable act on the part of His Majesty. Our task, I told him, was to secure His Majesty's consent to the abrogation of the agreement, and Count Lamsdorff would take care of the rest. He promised to discuss the matter with the Emperor.

The next man I happened upon was Minister Birilev, whose signature decorated the Björke compact.

"Do you know, Sir," I asked him, "what you signed at Björke?"

The Minister candidly confessed that he did not know. "I do not deny," he explained, "that I signed some apparently important document, but I haven"t the slightest notion what it was all about. This is how it all happened: His Majesty summoned me to his stateroom and asked me pointblank: 'Do you believe me, Alexey Alexeyevich?' Naturally, there could be but one answer. 'In that case,' His Majesty went on, 'sign this paper. It is signed, as you see, by the German Emperor and myself and countersigned, on Germany's side, by the proper official. Now, the German Emperor wants it to be countersigned by one of my Ministers.' Of course, I applied my signature to the paper."

Several days later I was summoned by the Emperor to Peterhof. I found there the Grand Duke Nicholas and Count Lamsdorff. His Majesty received us together, and at this improvised conference it was decided that the Björke agreement must be annulled. Though His Majesty keenly felt the awkwardness of his position, he consented, after some bickering, to the cancellation of the treaty and empowered Count Lamsdorff to take the necessary steps. The German reply to our first note was rather evasive, but its general tenor was: What's done is done and you cannot back out of the agreement. Then we dispatched a second note, wherein we did not mince words. Later, after I had assumed the task of governing the Empire in my capacity of Prime Minister, Count Lamsdorff told me in reply to my inquiry: "Rest assured, Sergey Yulyevich, the Björke agreement no longer exists." As a result of this incident, our Foreign Minister drew upon himself the enmity of Emperor William, and I was told that His Majesty had ceased admiring me and singing my praises. Ever since 1905 we have been drifting closer toward a union with England. In 1905, the two Emperors met again at Swinemünde; and I have been told by the Chief of our General Staff that, while no written agreement was concluded, the two Monarchs confirmed the intention to act *in the spirit* of the Björke understanding. This may have been a mere phrase, but it is my firm belief that if we fail to give Emperor William real satisfaction, he will constantly bear us a secret grudge.

Fortunately, the international conference for the settlement of the Morocco controversy met before the annulment of the Björke agreement. Had the conference been postponed, it would probably never have met, for, after the abrogation of that treaty, the German Emperor was in no mood to abide by the decisions of an assembly which owed its existence to my initiative. We were vitally concerned in the Algeciras game (the conference was held at Algeciras). I have mentioned already the fact that the conclusion of a loan in France was out of the question before the settlement of the Morocco affair. Consequently, our interest demanded the earliest possible termination of the conference. Germany, on the other hand, was inclined to prolong matters. She was guided by the time-hallowed principle of German diplomacy: "The longer you haggle, the more you gain." Besides, she was prompted by the desire, first, to increase our financial difficulties and, second, to retaliate on me for the annulment of the Björk agreement. As for Rouvier, he saw clearly our part of the game and grew less tractable, in order to force Kashin, our delegate at the conference, to side with France. In the meantime, our financial situation was rapidly deteriorating and a foreign loan was becoming more and more imperative.

In despair, I resorted to the good offices of Count Eulenburg and dispatched a letter to Emperor William, entreating him to speed up the proceedings of the Algeciras Conference, thus enabling us to contract the sorely needed loan. I pointed out to him that it was essential for us to conclude the loan before the meeting of the First Imperial Duma, so as not to become totally dependent upon that newly created institution. Emperor William's reply was amiable but negative. It was clear that I could expect no assistance from that quarter. Some time later, the German Emperor wrote me, through Count Eulenburg, asking me to bring pressure to bear for the purpose of rendering the Frenchmen more tractable. At the same time he wrote to Emperor Nicholas that I would fail in my efforts to contract a loan, for the reason that the Jewish bankers would not participate in it. As for Rouvier, he reiterated his readiness to render me every assistance in floating the loan, but not before the end of that accursed conference. Under these circumstances, I went forward hurriedly with my extensive preparations for the loan, so as to effect it without unnecessary delay as soon as the conference was terminated.

In proportion as Germany grew more exacting and dilatory, our representative at the conference sided more and more strongly with France. Finally the conference ended, France having scored a complete triumph, owing to our support and that of England. To retaliate for this outcome of the conference, the Berlin Government forbade the German bankers to participate in our loan. The Germans even went further in their resentment. During my visit to the United

States I arranged for the American group of bankers, headed by Morgan, to take part in the loan. Now, Morgan is on very good personal terms with the German Emperor. His banking firm took part in the preliminary negotiations for the loan, but at the last moment, when the German Government forced its bankers to refrain from participation in the loan, Morgan's group, too, withdrew. There's German friendship for you! ... Nevertheless, I foiled the efforts of Emperor William's Government and succeeded in floating the largest foreign loan in the history of modern European nations, a loan the importance of which for Russia could hardly be exaggerated. The full story of that loan, with all its remarkable incidents, is told elsewhere in these memoirs.

Goremykin's Government, which succeeded mine in April, 1906, is fairly to be charged with an effort deliberately to sully my political reputation in the eyes of the world, and particularly in the eyes of Emperor William. They must have feared my political resurrection, I should judge. An indictment of me and my policies was drawn up in the form of a memoir, and Baron Ehrenthal, formerly Austrian Ambassador to Russia, was entrusted with the task of presenting it to the German Emperor, which he did. A year later the memoir was published, if I remember rightly, in *La Revue des Revues*. The document, I have reason to believe, made no impression on the German sovereign. Nevertheless, this memoir, coupled with a missive he had received from a Black Hundred Chief of Kiev and, perhaps, with a gentle hint or two from high sources, made it clear to him that further attentions to me might displease His Majesty, Emperor Nicholas. It is true that long before the appearance of that memoir I had ceased to be *persona grata* in Berlin. In fact, I believe that His Majesty's critical attitude toward my policies, in the second phase of my premiership, was partly due to Emperor William's influence. At any rate, I have not seen Emperor William since our memorable interview at Rominten, and the last New Year's card he sent me is dated 1906. I am told, however, that whenever he happens to speak about my activities, he mentions my name with great respect and calls me the most intelligent man in Russia. Early in May, 1911, the German Kronprinz Friedrich and his wife visited Tsarskoye Selo. On a previous occasion I had been introduced to him in St. Petersburg. The two of us attended a reception and concert given by the German Ambassador, but he did not approach me in the hall, which was rather crowded. Whether or not this happened by mere chance, I cannot tell.

In September, 1907, Russia and Great Britain concluded a treaty relating to Persia, Afghanistan and Tibet. The agreement inaugurated the policy of philandering with England. Since we did not give up our traditional flirting with Germany, the situation became rather ambiguous. At present we are trying to adjust ourselves to it by assuring Germany that, of course, we love her best and that we are flirting with England merely for appearance's sake, while to England we say the reverse. I believe we shall soon have to pay for this duplicity.

The rapprochement with England, the ally of France, who is our own ally, has resulted in the formation of a triple Entente, as opposed to the triple Alliance of Germany, Austria-Hungary, and Italy. The history of the Entente is as follows: On my way from Portsmouth I stopped in Paris and met there, among other people, Kozell-Poklevski, first secretary to our Embassy in London. He brought me an invitation from King Edward to pay him a visit, but I could not accept it without my Monarch's express permission, which I failed to obtain. At the same time our Ambassador in Paris, Izvolsky, submitted to me a project of an agreement with Great Britain, substantially identical with the one which was later actually concluded. I asked Kozell-Poklevski to inform the King that should I on my return to Russia assume the governmental power I would use all my influence to establish friendly relations with Great Britain. I added, however, that I was decidedly opposed to the idea of concluding the treaty sketched to me by Izvolsky, for the reason that it was best for us not to tie ourselves down by treaties. I feared that an agreement with Great Britain would arouse the jealousy of Germany. As a result, we would perhaps be forced into making an agreement with that country, too, and be cheated in the end. It was owing to my opposition that the agreement was not concluded before 1907.

The agreement was a triumph of British diplomacy. It dealt chiefly with Persia. The Northern part of that country, which includes its most fertile and thickly populated sections, had from times immemorial been within our sphere of influence. With the conquest of the Southern parts of the Caucasus, formerly provinces of Persia and Turkey, the Northern part of Persia was naturally destined, so to speak, to become a part of the Russian Empire. To prepare that eventuality we sacrificed a great deal of our blood and treasure. The agreement set all these sacrifices at naught. According to it, Southern Persia was to be under the economic influence of Great Britain, while the North was left to us. As for Persia's central Government, it was to be controlled by Russia and Great Britain acting jointly. Since Teheran, the seat of the central Government, is situated in the North, this meant British influence in the North as well as in the South.

Russia has no annexationist designs upon Afghanistan. We are merely interested in preserving its status quo as a buffer State between Russia and British India. True, the agreement provided for the preservation of this status quo, but stipulated that the country should be under the exclusive influence and protection of Great Britain, so that we were not even allowed to have our diplomatic representative there. This meant that all our negotiations with the Government of Afghanistan were to be conducted through the British authorities. Under these circumstances the buffer became something in the nature of a loaded gun pointed at us. In Tibet the contracting parties obligated themselves not to introduce any missions or troops. We also renounced all claims to the Southern Persian ports.

The agreement was concluded without regard to the claims of the other Powers upon Persia. For that reason the division of Persia was rather futile. No sooner was the treaty published than Germany began to seek to safeguard its economic interests in Persia. As early as 1904 the German Government in the person of von Buelow complained to me that we were hindering the freedom of importing German goods to Persia. In 1911 we concluded an agreement with Germany, agreeing to connect the railroads of Northern Persia with the German Bagdad line and also to give her a free hand in Northern Persia with regard to her imports. In sum, what have we achieved? By signing the agreement with Great Britain we made it impossible for us to annex Persia politically, and by entering into an agreement with Germany we lost Persia economically, for economic competition with Germany under equal conditions means certain defeat for us. In a word, Persia has slipped out of our hands. At present [1912] we can play there merely the part of a policeman, until the native Government grows strong enough to restore order.

END

INDEX

Afghanistan, agreement with Great Britain in respect to, 367

Agrarian law of Stolypin, 332

Agricultural Conference, formation of, 199

Agricultural Experiment Station at Murgab, 58

Alexander II, policy adds to ranks of revolutionists, 60; killed by terrorists, 61; visit to Kiev, 52; unsafe speed of Imperial train, 53; in railroad wreck at Borki, 54; desires that W. accept post of Director of Department of Railroad Affairs, 55; interested in reducing diets, 56; memories of, 60; service in war with turkey, 60; of limited education, 60, 61; personal thrift, 61; led unimpeachable life, 62; importance as ruler, 63; attitude towards peasantry, 64; attitude towards war, 64; "the peacemaker," 65; favorable treatment of Poland, 65; in failing health, 66; dies at Yalta, 67; efforts to curtail vodka traffic, 74, 75; endorses retaliatory tariff against Germany, 83; prefers Yekaterina Harbour to Libau as naval base, 171; Jewish policy of, 324; meets future German Kaiser at Brest-Litovsk, 343

Alexander Mikhailovich, Grand Duke, warned of danger of Port Arthur seizure, 109; efforts in extending Russian influence in Korea, 121

Alexandra, Empress, enmity toward W., 181; as Princess Alix, sought as wife for Nicholas II, 183; their marriage, 185; gratified at W.'s resignation, 313

Alexey Alexandrovich, Grand Duke, presides at conference on Sino-Japanese situation, 95; responsible for Alexeyev's rise to power, 129; forces Nicholas II to sign decree constituting Libau the naval base, 171

Alexeyev, Admiral, appointed Viceroy in the Far East, 126; appointed commander-in-chief of fighting forces, 129; difficulties with Kuropatkin and his dismissal, 132; decorated on arrival home, 133

Algericas Conference, effect on proposed Russian loan, 260, 261, 263; a German defeat, 365

Amur Railroad, a military project, 168

Anastasia, Princes, divorces Prince Yuri of Leuchtenberg, and marries his cousin Grand Duke Nicholas, 186, 187, 188

Andreyevski, succeeded by W. as Director of South Western Railroad, 49

Andronikov, Prince M., telegraphs W., of danger in returning to Russia, 317

Arctic sea route to Far East, search for, 112

Armenians massacred in Constantinople and in Asia Minor, 176

Army, number recruits mobilized yearly left to Duma, 305

Arsenyev, in delegation asking W. to induce Emperor to receive workmen's petition, 227

Austria, preparations for war with, 126

Badmayev, contends for Peking as terminus for Trans-Siberian Railway, 98

Benckendorf, Count, fearful for safety of royal family, 274; comment of William II on, 358

Bezobrazov, militaristic plots of, 93; efforts in extending Russian influence in Korea, 122; influences Nicholas II in Manchurian aggression, 122; appointed Secretary of State, 123; attends conference at Port Arthur, 124; Manchurian enterprises a failure, 127

Bieberstein, Marschall von, acting for Germany in drawing up commercial treaty, 85

Birilev, ignorant of text of document signed at Björke, 363

Bismarck, protests against Russian customs duties, 80; protests to Giers against protective tariff, 80; expresses high opinion of W., 87

Björke, agreement between German and Russian Emperors at, 354, 355, 357, 361

Black Hundreds, "anarchists of the Right," 179; instigate pogrom against the Jews, 244

Blavatski, Yelena Petrovna, career of the celebrated theosophist, 36

Blioch, head of railroad corporation, 48

Bloody Sunday, of the revolution, 226

Bobrikov, appointed Governor-General of Finland, 232; assassinated, 233

Bobrinski, Count Vladimir, induces W. to enter railway service, 44; at parliamentary conference, 209; contends for democratic election law, 298

Bokhara, Emir of, calls on Li Hung-Chang, 104

INDEX

Borki, accident to Imperial train at, 54

Boxer Rebellion, outbreak of, 113

Bryanchaninov, journalist with Peace Mission, 136

Budberg, formulates plan for the manifesto, 220, 223; urges military rule in Baltic provinces, 232

Budget, juggling with the, 180

Bülow (ed. Aka Bülow), Prince, attitude toward Russian loan, 265; negotiations with at Norderney, 352

Bulygin, appointed Minister of Interior, 206; a dummy official, 207; only serious reform, 207; removed as Minister of the Interior, 279

Bunge, Ex-Minister of Finances, protests against issue of paper money, 69; tutor to Czarevitch Nicholas, 73; resolute enemy of the *obshchina*, 333

Caprivi, Count, acting for Germany, in drawing up commercial treaty, 85; puts through Russo-German commercial treaty, 345

Cassini, Count, instructed to vote for France at Algeciras Conference, 263; sensational *Temps* article on instructions to, 266

Censorship regulations, committee for revising, 204

Chang Ing Huan, signs lease of Kwantung Penintula, 101; exiled and murdered in consequence, 113

Cherevin, Adjutant-General, expresses Emperor's displeasure at slowness of trains, 54; responsible for wreck of Imperial train at Borki, 55

Chikhachev, Admiral, N. M, head of Odessa Railroad, 44; scapegoat after Telegul catastrophe, 45, 46; responsible for selection of Libau as naval base, 171; dismissed from his post, 171; member of conference on needs of agricultural industry, 199

China: Russia prevents Japan from occupying Liaotung peninsula, 97; secret treaty signed with, 102; grants railroad concession, 104; signs lease of Kwantung Peninsula, 111; Wei-Hai-Wei seized by Great Britain, 113; French occupation of South China, 113; agreement with, for evacuation of Manchuria, 122; Germany plans for conquests in, 350; Kiao-Chow seized by Germany, and Port Arthur by Russia, 351

Chino-Japanese War, effects on Russia, 95

Cholera, investigations of epidemic, 59

Columbia University, bestows degree upon W., 163

Concessions, court traffic in, 60, 72, 89

Congress of Berlin, robs Russia of fruits of victory, 61

Constitutional manifesto, publication of, 212

Cotton experiments in growing, 58

Council of Ministers, establishment of, 218

Currency reform, gold standard adopted, 77

Curtin, Jeremiah, visits W. at Portsmouth, 158

Darmstadt, Princess of, bride of Nicholas II, 67

Delcassé, considers war between Japan and Russia impossible, 127; urges Russia to construct Orenburg-Tashkent Railway to threaten India, 169; forced to retire by pressure from Berlin, 354

Delyanov, Minister of Public Education, removes prominent professors of liberal tendencies, 64

Derviz, railroad king, 48

Dillon, Dr., English journalist accompanying Peace Mission, 136; sends first wireless interview from ship, 138; visit at Biarritz, 334

Dolgorukov, Prince, member of conference on needs of agricultural industry, 199; discharged as Chairman of District Board of Kursk, 200; in Paris opposes loan to Russia, 260

Drenteln, Governor-General, in Poland, 66

Dubasov, General, appointed Governor-General of Moscow, 250; attempt on his life, 251

Dubrovin, Dr., actions approved by Nicholas II, 180; a leader of the Black Hundreds, 297

Duma, decree providing for, 209; formation of, 298; difficulties with Stolypin, 320

Dundukov-Korsakov, Prince, Governor-General of Kiev, 38

Durnovo, Ivan Nikolaievich, against importing foreign capital, 88; his opinion of Nichlas II at time of accession to throne, 170; at head of conference for study of needs of land gentry, 193; opposes formation of conference for study of peasant problems, 295, 297; anti-Jewish policy, 327

Durnovo, Piotr Nikolaievich, explains Grand Duke Nikolai's attitude toward dictatorship, 224; unfortunate appointment as Minister of the Interior, 280; reports on Komissarov's anti-Jewish activities, 289

Durnovo, P. P., becomes Governor-General, 248

INDEX

Duties, differential, with America, abolished, 159

Economist, The, on collapse of gold standard in Russia, 260; subsidies obtained by, 336
Electoral laws, drafting of, 298; discussions on, 298
Employers' Liability Bill favoured by Nicholas II, 76
Entente, Triple, history of, 367
Eulenberg, Count. at Rominten, 356
"Exceptional status" regulations, 337, 340
Exploration of land for peasantry, bills proposed for, 291

Fadeyev, Gen. Audrey Mikhailovich, grandfather of W., 35; influence in deciding career, 44; result of letter to, against revolutionists, 49
Fashoda incident, the, 169
Finances, condition of, during
Finland, Russification of, 233; revolution in, 233
France, occupies territory in China, 113; attitude toward Russo-Japanese Peace Treaty, 156; supported by Russia in Moroccan controversy, 263
Frederichs, Baron, Nicholas II answers W.'s memorandum orally through, 175; succeeds Count Vorontzov-Daskov as Minister of the Court, 181; at conference discussing successor in case of death of Nicholas II, 182; draft of Manifesto read to, 219; visits W. to discuss manifesto, 220; letter advising W. not to return to Russia, 314; the reply, 364; second message to, 316
Freedom of the press granted by Constitutional Manifesto, 340; throttled by Stolypin, 341
French intrigue against adoption of gold standard by Russia, 78
Fundamental code, drafting of, 299

Galitzin, Prince, in the public workers' union, 230
Gapon, Father, organizer of police socialism in St. Petersburg, 226; exiled, 228; offers to betray revolutionary committee to Government, 229; assassinated, 229
Garin, named Senator, 285
Germany, commercial treaty concluded with, 80; preparations for war with, 126; opposed by Russia, in Moroccan contention, 263; forbids participation in Russian loan in resentment for Russia's part in Algeciras settlement, 366
Gerard, member conference on needs of agricultural industry, 199; appointed Governor-General of Finland, 233
Giers, Bismarck protests to against protective tariff, 80; objection of, to retaliatory measures, 82
Ginzburg Baron, in deputation to plead cause of Jews, 329
Glazov, General, attitude during revolution, 231; dismissed as Minister of Instruction, 279
Gold standard, introduction of, 77, 259
Golitzyn-Muravlin, appointed to committee on revision of censorship regulations, 204
Goremykin, at head of futile agricultural conference, 201; formulates plan for the manifesto, 220, 223; at conference discussing fundamental laws, 305; dissolves Duma, 307; succeeds W. as President of Council of Ministers, 307; a failure in office, 318
Gorki, Maxim, in delegation asking W. to induce Emperor to receive workmen's petition, 227
Great Britain seizes Wei-Hai-Wei, 113; attitude toward Russo-Japanese Peace Treaty, 162; signs Treaty with Russia relating to Persia, Afghanistan, and Tibet, 367
Gredeskul, in the Union of Zemstvos and Town Delegates, 230
Grodekov, General, appointed commander-in-Chief, 258
Gübbenet, inefficient Minister of Ways of Communication, 57
Gubonin, railroad king, 48
Guchkov, in the Union of Zemstvos and Town Delegates, 230; at conference of public leaders, 284; chief Duma orator on military matters, 324
Gurko, Governor-General, in Poland, 66

Hadémant, journalist, accompanies Peace Mission, 137
Harden, Maximilian, calls on W. at Bismarck's suggestion, 86, 87
Hartman, revolutionist, plot to kill, 50
Harvard University, visit to, 144
Hesse, General, connection with destruction of Sipyagin diary, 173; asks Rachkovsky for report on the charletan Philippe, 187
Hessen, I. V., in the Union of Zemstvos and

INDEX

Town Delegates, 230; assists in statement to Emperor criticizing draft of fundamental laws, 308

Heyden, Count, in the Union of Zemstvos and Town Delegates, 230

Hilkov, Prince, emotion at signing of rescript providing for parliamentary legislation, 283; at conference on revolt of 1905, 218; defends Union of Railway Workers, 231; relieved as Minister of Ways of Communication, 283

Hirsch, court physician, 181

Hirshman, on Manchurian military policy, 117

Holy Brotherhood, The, formation of the society, 49

Hume, spiritualistic medium, 37, 38

Ignatyev, Count N. P., a Jew-hater, 179; at parliamentary conference, 209; at conference discussing fundamental laws, 305; anti-Jewish policy, 327

Industry and commerce, development of, 90

Insurance, obligatory workers', 205

Irrigation opposed by people of Transcaspia, 58

Italy, demands cession of Sang-Ming by China, 113

Japan, War with. 93; prevented from occupying Manchuria after Sino-Japanese War, 96; treaty signed with, regarding Korea, 107; appeals to Great Britain and the United States regarding Russian activities in Yalu district, 124; renews negotiations regarding spheres of influence in Manchuria and Korea, 126

Jews, Kiev and Odessa riots against, 51; attitude of Nicholas II toward, 178, 179; the pogrom at Homel, 179; attitude of high officials against, 285. 288; uprising in Odessa. 236; pogrom instigated by Black Hundreds, 244; difficulties under Stolypin, 324, 330; attitude of Alexander III toward, 324; evil factors of the revolution, 325; anti-Jewish legislation and pogroms, 327

Jews, in America, attitude toward Russia, 145; give support to W. at Peace Conference, 156; deputation at Portsmouth asks alleviation of abuse of Jews in Russia. 158

Jewish opposition to Russian loan, 259, 264

Jewish problem, discussed by Committee of Ministers, 206

Judges, tenure of office, 304, 306

Katkov, famous journalist, 39

Kaufmann, German plenipotentiary in Moroccan controversy, 354

Kerbedz, associated with W. on South-Western Railoads, 48

Khvostov, proposed for Minister of the Interior, 336

Khodynka disaster, 172

Kiao-Chow, William II plans for occupation of, 350 seizure of, 107, 350

Kiev, anti-Jewish riots. 51

Kishinev, anti-Jewish outbreak, 328

Kleigels, abandons post as Governor-General of Kiev, 236

Kobeko, author of temporary press regulations, 341

Kokovtzev, N. assistant to Minister of Finances, 71; wrongful use of vodka monopoly, 75; becomes Minister of Finance, 128; as Minister of Finances objects to projected abolition of redemption payments, 200; opposed to a Cabinet of Ministers, 210; attitude during revolution, 231; on committee to watch transactions of Imperial Bank, 261; efforts to obtain loan, 261; sent to Paris to conclude loan negotiations, 267; asks for bonus on conclusion of loan, 272; claims entire credit. 272; succeeds Stolypin, 337; continues perlustration of private correspondence, 339; proposes new regulations for control of press, 340

Komissarov, anti-Jewish activities, 288

Komura. attitude in America, 139; meets Russian envoys on President Roosevelt's yacht, 143; compared to other Japanese statesmen, 147; at the Peace Conference, 148

Konovnitzyn, Count, assassinated, 251

Korea, treaty signed with Japan demarcating spheres of influence, 107; Japan's dominating position recognized, 113

Korostovetz, with Peace Mission, 136

Kotzebue, Gount. Governor-General of Odessa, 44; efforts against anti-Jewish rioters, 51

Kovalevsky, M. M., assists in statement to Emperor of criticizing draft of fundamental laws, 308

Kovalevsky, Vladimir Ivanovitch, delegated by Trepov to report on test of fundamental laws, 308

Kozell-Poklevki, brings invitation to W. to visit King Edward, 367

Kozlov, General, becomes Governor-General but forced to resign. 248

372

INDEX

Krasovsky, in the union of Zemstvos and Town Delegates, 230

Krestovnikov, favours the Duma, 249

Krivoshein, in plot against Agricultural Conference, 201; controversy with Emperor over appointment of, 295-296

Kronstadt, revolutionary riots break out, 243

Krüger, President, encouraged by William II, in contest with Great Britain, 351

Kryzhanowski, drafts electoral law, 298

Kulisher, in deputation to plead cause of Jews, 329

Kurino, insists on answer to Japanese note, 128

Kuropatkin, General, Alexey Nikolaievich insists on building of strategic railroads, 89; opposes appeal to Powers for partial disarmament, 106; sees in Boxer Rebellion an opportunity to seize Manchuria, 114; dispatches troops to Manchuria, 116; self-seeking efforts with the Emperor and Empress, 120; insists on holding of Manchuria, 122; submits report on activities in Korea, 124; to command troops on Austrian front in case of war, 126; appointed commander of armies in Far East, 129; asks advice of W., 130; difficulties with Alexeyev, 132; succeeds him but is in turn succeeded by General Linevich, 132; reproaches Plehve with being only Minister to desire Russo-Japanese War, 226; in Russification of Finland, 233; responsible for demoralization in Army, 254

Kutaisov, inefficient Governor-General of Siberia, 237

Kutler, project for expropriation of land for peasantry, 291; made scapegoat, 294

Lamsdorff, Count, contends for handling of Far Eastern affairs by diplomatic, not military service, 123; ignored in treating with Japan, 127, 128; asks W. if he will accept post of peace plenipotentiary, 134; at conference discussing successor in case of death of Nicholas II, 182; note to Count Osten-Sacken on Algeciras Conference, 263; enlightens W. on real Björke compact, 362

Leiden, Dr., treats Alexander III, 66

Li Hung Chang, Ambassador Extraordinary to Russia, 97; reduced in power, 113; signs lease of Kwantung Peninsula, 111; remarks on attitude of Nicholas II on Khodynka disaster, 172

Libau, selected as naval base, 171

Likhachov, Adjutant-General, desire to crush revolt of 1905, 217

Linevich, General, succeeds Kuropatkin as Commander-in-Chief, 131; slowness in returning troops from Manchuria, 257; dismissed as Commander-in-Chief, 258

Lisanevich, Madame, becomes wife of W., 59

List, Frederick, German economist, 80

Litvinoff-Falinski, argues against arrest of Nosar, 245

Lobanov-Rostovski, Prince, at conferences on Sino-Japanese affairs, 96; at signing of secret treaty with Li Hung Chang, 103

Lopukhin, gives information of anti-Jewish plot, 288

Lvov, in the Union of Zemstvos and Town Delegates, 230

Makarov, Admiral, killed at Port Arthur, 112; Commander Post of Kronstadt, 113; appointed Commander-in-Chief of Far-Eastern Navy, 113; goes down with his ship, 132

Makaroff, tries to justify shooting of Lena miners, 246

Maklakov, in Paris opposes loan to Russia, 260

Malishevski, Director of the Credit Chancery, 71

Manchuria, native opposition to building of railway, 115; agreement with China for evacuation of, 122

Manifesto of October 17, 1905, text of W.'s memorandum on, 216; nullified by Stolypin, 336

Manuilov-Manusevich, intercedes for Father Gapon, 229

Manukhin, Minister of Justice, publishes manifesto against parliamentary reforms, 208

Marchand, Colonel, at Fashoda, 169

Maria Fyodorovna, influence of, on her son Nicholas II, 182, 183

Martens, Professor, member of Peace Mission, 135

Martino, demands cession by China of Sang-Ming to Italy, 133

Maximovich, General, removed as Governor-General of Poland, 234

Mechnikov, Professor, in University of Odessa, 43; displaced, 64; fearful of confiscation of his property, 275; brutal scheme for suppression of the revolution, 276

Meller-Zakomelski, succeeds Sologub as Governor-General of Baltic provinces, 232; General, success in reopening Siberian railway, 257

Méline, intrigues against adoption of gold standard by Russia, 78
Mendeleyev, Director of Chamber of Measures and Weights, 71; advocates Polar route to Far East, 112
Mendelssohn, banking house, participation in loan, 267, 268, 269
Meshchersky, Prince, asked to warn Nicholas II of danger in Manchurian policy, 123
Migulin, Professor, project for expropriation of land for peasantry, 291; connections with Sazonov, 335
Mikhail Alexandrovich, Grand Duke, selected to succeed to throne in case of death of Nicholas II, 182; at conference discussing fundamental laws, 305
Mikhail Nikolaievich, Grand Duke, his father's favourite, 62; President of Imperial Council passing gold standard bill, 79; at conference discussing successor in case of death of Nicholls II, 182
Militza, Princess, Montenegrin wife of Grand Duke Peter, 186, 187
Miliukov, in the Union of Zemstvos and Town Delegates, 230; assists in statement to Emperor criticizing draft of fundamental laws, 308
Mirski, Prince, *See* Svyatopolk-Mirski
Mitrovich, paramour of Mme. Blavatski, 37, 38
Moksovskiya Vedomosti, articles written for, 52
Montenegrin Princesses, baleful influence upon Russian Court, 186, 187
Morgan, J. P., negotiations with, 162; the famous nose, 163; refuses participation in Russian loan, 262, 267
Moroccan Controversy, France favoured over Germany in Algeciras Conference, 263; attitude, 353
Morozov, Savva, enmeshed in revolutionary net, commits suicide, 248
Moscow, insurrection in, 250
Moscow Peasant Congress, closed by police, 249
Mosolov, General, on impossibility of dictatorship, 224
Mount Vernon, visit to, 164
Mukden, defeat at, 132
Mukden, Governor of, issues proclamation accusing Russia, 116
Muraviov, Count Mikhail Nicolayevich, appeals to Powers for partial disarmament, 105; proposes seizure of Port Arthur, 108; appointed plenipotentiary to conduct peace negotiations with Japan, but refuses post, 134; admits Russia gave consent to German occupation of Kiao-Chow, 351
Muraviov-Amursky, Count. under the spell of "Dr." Philippe, 186
Murgab, visit to, 58; people oppose irrigation, 58
Muromtzev, assists in statement to Emperor criticizing draft of fundamental laws, 308

Nabokov, with Peace Mission, 136; in the union of Zemstvos and Town Delegates, 230
Naryshkin, at parliamentary conference, 209
Naryshkin, K. V., revolutionists threaten to kill wife and daughter of, 258
Neidhart, brutality in Odessa, 236
Nelidov, nearly causes war with Turkey, 176
Nemyeshayev, appointed Minister of Ways and Communications, 284
Neutzlin, negotiations with for loan, 259; asked to come to Russia and arrange terms of loan, 262; instructions as to final procedure, 266; goes to London to confer with bankers on loan, 267; advises that loan is accomplished fact, 270
Newspapers unite against Government 230
Newport, visit to, 144
Nicholas II, boyish pranks, 52; incapable of appreciation. 63; marriage with Princess of Darmstadt, 67; personal interest in railroad building, 73; favours Employers' Liability bill, 76; mainly instrumental in adoption of gold standard, 79; presents uniform of Russian admiral to Wilhelm II, 86; expresses appreciation of W.'s services in Imperial rescript, 92; appoints W. President of Committee of Ministers, 93; ambitious for Eastern conquest, 95; sends ultimatum to Japan preventing occupation of Liaotung peninsula, 96; receives Li Hung Chang, 100; appeal to Powers for partial disarmament, 105; resolves to seize Port Arthur, 108; goes to Darmstadt, 127; reviews all army contingents before departure to the Manchurian front, 131; asks W. to accept post of peace plenipotentiary, 135; insistence on no indemnities or cession of land to Japan, 150; instructions to break off peace negotiations, 153; accession and coronation, 171; unscrupulous tendencies, 173; his early desire for war, 175; vacillating policy during Russo-Japanese War, 175; plans for war with

Turkey, 177; hostility toward Great Britain, 178; attitude toward illegal executions, 178; attitude toward the Jews, 179; serious illness at Yalta, 181; under influence of his mother, 182, 183; effort to find wife for, 183; marries Princess Alix of Hessen-Darmstadt, 184; belief in holiness and miracles of Saint Seraphim, 190; orders canonization of Father Seraphim, 190; his attempts at reforms, 192; signs decree for liberal reforms, 204; signs rescript providing for parliamentary legislation, 209; manifesto of October 17, 1905, 216, attitude toward pogrom against Jews, 244; attitude toward the Russian loan, 271; insists that Skalon be granted large loan from Imperial Bank, 290; controversy with, over appointment of Krivoshein, 295; powers restricted, 308; message to W., accepting resignation. 312; the Imperial rescript, 313; attitude toward Jews, 330; antipathy to German Kaiser, 346; bestows rank of Count on W., 361; induced to annul Björke agreement, 364

Nicholas, Prince, of Montenegro, seeks favour of Alexander III, 186

Nikolai Nikolaievich, Sr., Grand Duke, 46, 47

Nikolai Nikolaievich, Jr., Grand Duke, Commander-in-Chief of proposed Army to face Germany, 126; influence over Nicholas II, 182; belief in the divinity of the Emperor, 183; at conference submitting draft of manifesto to Emperor, 219; in favour of manifesto, 221; indifferent to fate of the country, 222; induces Emperor to sign manifesto, 224, 273; attitude toward constitution, 225; persuaded to send troops to Moscow, 251; attitude when revolution threatened, 297; at conference discussing fundamental laws, 305

Nikolsky, A. P., appointed Director of Ministry of Agriculture, 297

Noblemen's Conference, discussions at, 193

Nolde, Baron, drafts decree for projected reforms, 203

Norderney, negotiations with Chancellor Bülow, at, 352

Nosar, president of first soviet, 241; arrested, 245

Novoye Vremya preaches doctrine of *revannche* against Japan, 168; in league with other newspapers against the Government, 229; influenced by Workmen's Soviet, 242, 245, 247

Obolenski, Prince Alexey Dimitriyevich, not favoured by Count Lamsdorff for peace mission, 134; delivers oral answer of Nicholas II to W.'s memorandum, 175; complains of Court interference in affairs of Holy Synod, 190; asked by W. to draw up plan of Manifesto, 219; memoir by, 222; resigns as Governor-General of Finland, 233; regret at participation in movement for constitutional manifesto, 273; appointed Procurator of the Holy Synod, 278; tends to extreme conservatism, 302

Obruchev, Chief of Staff, obsessed with idea of strategic railroads, 89; indifferent on Eastern policy, 96

Obshchina, the peasant commune, 332

Occultism in Court of Nicholas II, 182, 185

Odessa, anti-Jewish riots, 51

Orlov, Attorney-General, draws up indictment against W. and other students, 43

Orlov, Prince, asks W. to attend conference with Emperor on revolt of 1905, 219

Osten-Sacken, Count, his opinion of Princess Alix, 184; note from Count Lamsdorff on Algeciras Conference. 263

Ott, Professor, physician to the Empress, 189

Palen, Count, advocates force to crush revolt of 1905. 217; at conference discussing fundamental laws, 305

Parliamentary body, attempt to create, 207

Passport regulations, mitigation of, 198

Pauker, inefficient as Minister of Ways of Communication, 57

Peace Mission, personnel of, 136

Peking, looting of, 114, 132

Perlustration of private correspondence, evils of, 338

Persia, agreement with Great Britain in respect to, 367; economic treaty with Germany, 368

Peter Nikolaievich, Grand Duke, marries one of the Montenegrin Princesses, 187; indifferent to fate of country, 222

Petropavlovsk, Admiral Makarov's flagship, sunk. 132

Philippe. "Dr.", influence at Russian Court, 184, 185; previous history of, 186; attains great influence at Court and with the Empress. 188; death of; 191

Planson, member of Peace Mission, 135

Plehve, Vyacheslav Konstantinovich, against use of foreign capital, 88; militaristic plots of,

93; influence on Nicholas II in Korean affairs, 127; a Jew-hater, 179; forced to dismiss Rachkovsky, 188; champion of ultra-feudal tendencies, 193; opposes formation of conference to study peasant problem, 195, 197; appointed Minister of the Interior, 200; assassinated, 200; favours a foreign war to stem tide of revolution at home, 226; extends police socialism to St. Petersburg, 227; leading spirit of anti-Jewish policy, 328; assumes more liberal attitude, 328

Pleske, appointed Minister of Finance, 93; becoming ill, succeeded by Romanov, 128

Pobiedonostzev, K. P., influence on policy of Alexander III, 60; against University Code, 64; against Employers' Liability bill, 76; fearful of misrule of Nicholas II, 171; informed by W. of impending attack on Turkey, 177; protests the canonization of Seraphim of Sarov, 189; obstacle to reform, 202, 204, 208, 209; attitude during revolution, 231; removed as Procurator of the Holy Synod, 278

Podgorichani, Count, organizes anti-Jewish riots at Homel, 179

Poincaré, favorable to loan, 266

Pokotilov, member of Peace Mission, 135

Poland, on verge of revolt, 234

Polovtzev, against Employers' Liability bill, 76

Polyakov, railroad king, 48

Polyanski, of "The Holy Brotherhood," 50

Port Arthur, seizure of, 108, 350; captured by Japan, 132

Portsmouth Peace Conference, arrival of diplomats, 145; signing of treaty, 154; church celebration on signing of peace treaty, 155

Postnikov, Professor, Assistant Minister of Education, 279

Posyet, forced to resign as Minister of Ways of Communication, 55; why appointed, 57

Potozky, General, at conference discussing fundamental laws, 305

Propper, editor of *Birzheviya Viedomosti*, demands from the Government, 230

Przeradski, Privy-Councillor, exposes Stolypin's practices, 318, 319

Rachkovsky, report on the charlatan Philippe, brings him into disfavour at Court, 187, 188; anti-Jewish activities, 288

Radolin, Prince, conversation with on Port Arthur occupation, 111; conversation with over Moroccan controversy, 354

Rafalovich, interviews Rothschilds as to loan, 259; writes from Paris explaining difficulties, 260, 264; dispatch to, on Germany's refusal to participate in loan, 268

Railroad building for strategic considerations a fantasy, 89

Railroad concessions and exploitation, 45, 48

Railroads, State ownership, 72

Railway strikes, revolutionary, 241

Rasputin, friendship for Sazonov, 335

Rediger, General, confident of disaster in Russo-Japanese war, 132; at conferences on revolt of 1905, 218, 219; attitude during revolution, 231

Reitern, Minister of Finance, efforts to establish gold standard, 61

Religion, conference on religious toleration, 205; necessity of, 205; freedom of conscience, privileges restricted, 341

Rennenkampf, General, success in reopening Siberian railway, 257

Revolution of 1905-1906, 277

Richter, Captain, indiscriminate execution in Reval district, 178; urges military rule in Baltic provinces, 232

Romanov, Piotr Mikhailovich, draws up agreement with China for railroad concession, 104; becomes Minister of Finances, 128

Roosevelt, President, displeased at Witte's attitude toward Japan, 142; ambition to be president of Harvard University, 145; at Peace Conference, 149; letter to Baron Kaneko at Peace Conference advising against insistence on indemnity, 151; farewell visit to, 159; on peace questions deals direct with Mikado, 149; with Nicholas II, 160; sends message to Nicholas II asking free entrance of Jews of American citizenship, 166; compared with Taft, 331; fate of letter to Emperor on behalf of American Jews, 331; assures W. at Portsmouth that German Emperor favoured peace, 354

Rosen, Baron, member of Peace Mission, 135; meets Peace Mission on arrival, 141

Rothschild and the Russian loan, 71; advocate of bi-metallism, 78

Rothschild, Baron Alphonse, discusses prevalence of occultism at Russian Court, 185

Rothstein, negotiates loan with Rothschilds, 71

Rouvier, postpones question of Russian loan until settlement of Moroccan question, 261, 264; fall of his cabinet, 266; succeeds

INDEX

Delcassé, 354; assures of help in obtaining loan, 354

Rozhdestvensky, Admiral, fleet destroyed, 133

Russia, a government organ, 339

Rus, articles written for, 52

Russian State, The, founded by W., closed down by Stolypin, 339

Rusin, Captain, member of Peace Mission, 136

Russo-Chinese Bank, founded, 97

Russo-Japanese War, origins and course, 112; Japan attacks warships off Port Arthur—Russia declares war, 129; Japanese underrated, 131; principal events of the war, 131; destruction of Rozhdestvensky's fleet, 133; Peace of Portsmouth, 134; signing of Peace of Portsmouth, 154; effect on international situation, 169

Samarkand, visit to, 58

Samoylov, Colonel, member of Peace Mission, 135

Sang-Ming, cession demanded by Italy from China, 113

San Stefano Treaty, nullified by Congress of Berlin, 61

Sarrien, formation of cabinet, 266

Sazonov, career of, 335

Schiff, Jacob, at Portsmouth, 157

Schwanebach, attitude during revolution, 231; plans for allotment of lands to soldiers, 256; on committee to watch transactions of Imperial Bank, 261

Sechenov, in University of Odessa, 43

Seligman, — at Portsmouth, 157

Seraphim of Sarov, canonization of, 189

Sergey Alexandrovich, Grand Duke, favours scheme of police socialism, 266; assassinated, 248; implacable enemy of Jews, 325, 328

Shakhmatov, in delegation asking W. to induce Emperor to receive workmen's petition, 227; in the Union of Zemstvos and Town Delegates, 230

Shcheglovitov, controls judiciary, 306

Shcherbina, exiled from Voronezh, 200

Sheremetyev, Count, efforts to recover Sipyagin diary from Nicholas II, 174; member of conference on needs of agricultural industry, 199

Sherval, Baron, responsibility in wreck of Imperial train, 54, 55

Shipov, member of Peace Mission, 135; in the union of Zemstvos and Town Delegates, 230; on committee to watch transactions of Imperial Bank, 261; at conference of public leaders, 284; informs W. of the Skalon loan, 291; vain protests to the Emperor, 291

Shirinski-Shakhmatov, Prince, career due to Saint Seraphim incident, 190

Shishkin, draws up minutes of Conference on war with Turkey, 177

Shuvalof, Count Pavel, initiates W. into "The Holy Brotherhood," 49; Russian Minister in Berlin, 65; objects to retaliatory tariff, 82; acknowledges he was wrong, 85

Siberian Railway, construction of, 72

Shimonoseki, Peace of, 95

Sipyagin, letter to on Manchurian occupation, 118; diary of, destroyed by Nicholas II, 173; at conference discussing successor in case of death of Nicholas II, 181; appointed Minister of the Interior, 199; assassinated, 200; opposes scheme of police socialism, 277

Sipyagin, Mme., efforts to recover her husband's diary, 174

Skalon, Governor-General of Poland, 234; obtains personal loan from Imperial Bank, 290

Sliosberg, in deputation to plead cause of Jews, 329

Sologub, Governor-General, protests against illegal military executions in Rival district, 178; appointed Governor-General of Baltic provinces, 232

Solski, Count, Dimitry, delegated by Emperor to call council of Ministers in his stead, 207, 211; efforts in obtaining parliamentary legislation, 209; desire to retire, 211; appeals to W. to remain in harness, 253; asks that order be conferred on Kokovtzev, 272; informs W. that a fundamental code was being drafted, 300

Solski Conference, reforms inaugurated by, 207, 210

Soviet of Workmen's Deputies, organization, 241; members arrested, 245

Spiridonov, Madame, becomes wife of W., 47

Stakbovich, M. A., in the Union of Zemstvos and Town Delegates, 230; at conference of public leaders, 284

Stambulov, Stephen, 47

Stolypin, plans building of Amur Railroad, 169; inaugurates repressive measures, 243; requests W. not to resign from state service, 317; conflict with, 318; attempts to show political crimes as ordinary murders, 318,

INDEX

319; flagrantly violates laws, 319; treatment of the Duma, 321; handling of Jewish question, 324; enacts important agrarian law, 332; assassinated at Kiev 334; weakens for perlustration of private correspondence, 338; throttles freedom of the press, 340

Straus, Oscar, at Portsmouth, 157

Strikes on railroads and in mills and factories. 240

Strikes, railroad, effect on returning of troops from Manchuria, 256

Student life in America, impressions of, 163

Subotich, General, defeats Boxer force in Manchuria, 116

Sukhotin, Governor-General at Omsk, 237

Suvorin, journalist with Peace Mission, 136

Suvorin, A. S., favours constitution for noblemen only, 240; dies a millionaire, 242

Svyatopolk-Mirski, remarks on strength of intellectuals, 178; displeases emperor in retiring Prince Shirinski-Shakhmatov, 190; succeeds Plehve as Minister of the Interior, 200; liberal ministry of, 202; retired by the Emperor, 206; at Conference deciding attitude of Government on receiving workmen's petition, 228

Taft, William H., in audience with Emperor, brings up question of American Jews entering Russia, 332

Tagantzev, Professor, declines portfolio of Minister of Education 279

Ta-lieng-wan, seizure of, 108, 350

Tarle, Professor, wounded in street fighting, 243

Taxes, reforms introduced in levying, 198

Telegul catastrophe, the, 45

Temps, article on Cassini instructions, 266

Tereshehenko, causes shooting of miners at Lena, 246

Timiryazev, Vasili Ivanovich, sent to negotiate commercial treaty with Germany, 82, 85; appointed and dismissed as Minister of Commerce, 283

Tolstoy, Count A. D., instrumental in changing university code, 64; policy toward the Jews, 327

Tolstoy, Count Leo, intercedes for exiled peasant. 200; influence of doctrines on revolution, 255

Tolstoy, Count Ivan Ivanovich, appointed Minister of Instruction, 279; in sympathy with W.'s policy in resigning, 312; policy toward the Jews, 330

Trepov, General, a Jew-hater, 179; in plot against Agricultural Conference, 201; appointed Governor-General of St. Petersburg, 206; associate Minister of the Interior and veritable dictator, 207; anxious to retire from dictatorship, 231; at conference on revolt of 1905, 218; advised of plans for the manifesto of October 17, 1905, 220; takes "delegation" of workmen to the Emperor, 228; régime causes national opposition, 247; resigns as Asst. Minister of the interior and is appointed Court Commandant, 285; incident at funeral of Alexander III, 285; powerful friends at court, 286; interests himself in Skalon loan affair, 291; incident of Kutler's peasant bill, 291; prime mover in promulgating fundamental code, 300; presents statement to Emperor on fundamental laws, 307

Trubetzkoi, Prince, at conference of public leaders, 284

Tschirsky, asked to entreat German Emperor to withdraw from Kiao-Chow, 109

Turkestan, visit to, 58

Turkey, war with, 46, 47, 60; pretexts for war with, 176

Tyrtov, at conference on seizure of Port Arthur, 108

Tzerpitzky, General, loots town of Kulo, 117

Tzion, falsely accuses Vyshnegradski of accepting graft, 70

Ukhtomski, Prince, escorts Li Hung Chang to St. Petersburg. 98

Ungern-Sternberg, Baron, 45

Unions, organization of, 230

United States, denounces commercial treaty with Russia, 331; William II, proposes economic war against, 350

Universities, granted autonomy, 210

University Code of 1884, unpopularity of, 64

Urusov, Prince, at conference of public leaders, 284; speech in Duma on pogrom literature, 289

Ushakov, influence on Grand Duke Nikolai, 225

Vannovski, Piotr Semyonovich, favours retaliatory tariff, 84; supports W. in principle of maintaining integrity of Chinese Empire, 96; at conference on seizure of Port Arthur, 108

Varshawski, in deputation to plead cause of Jews, 329

INDEX

Vasilchikov, Prince, misled by rumours of revolution, 256

Vinaver, in deputation to plead cause of Jews, 329

Vladimir Alexandrovich, Grand Duke, fearful of results of vodka monopoly, 75; informed by W. of impending attack on Turkey, 177; at conference discussing fundamental laws, 305

Vodka, efforts to restrict use, 73; state monopoly, 74

Vogak, appointed General of His Majesty's retinue, 123

Von Meck, railroad king, 48

Vonlyarlyarski, Colonel, resells mining concession, 89

Vorontzov-Dashkov, Count, letter to, 51; displeased at slow speed of Imperial train, 53; originator of phrase "the Peacemaker," as applied to Alexander III, 65; efforts in extending Russian influence in Korea, 121; remonstrated with for increasing expenses of Ministry, 181; member of conference on needs of agricultural industry, 199; a failure in the Caucasus, 237

Vuich, N. I., examines draft of manifesto of October 17, 1905, 217; memoir by, 222

Vyshnegradski, Ivan Alexyevich, head of management, South-Western Railroads, 48; offers W. post of Director of Department of Railroad Affairs, 55; accompanied on trip to Turkestan, 58; resigns as Minister of Finances and appointed member of Imperial Council, 69; death, 70; accused of accepting graft but proved guiltless, 70, 71; accompanies Kokovtzev to Paris to conclude loan negotiations, 269

Wallace, Mackenzie, accompanies Peace Mission, 137

Wei-Hai-Wei, seized by Great Britain, 113

Wendrich, Colonel, removal from railroad service, 57

Werder, General, German Ambassador to Court of St. Petersburg, 82

West Point, visit to, 161

Wilhelm der Grosse, Peace Mission embarks on, 136

William I, at Ems, 343

Wilhelm II, desires uniform of Russian admiral, 86; efforts to entangle Russia in Far East, 112; directly appealed to speed up work of Algeciras Conference, 265; with his grandfather at Ems, 343; at manoeuvres at Brest-Litovsk, 343; clash with, over tariff war, 344; craving for Russian uniform, 345; disliked by Nicholas II, 346; discourtesy toward Russian Empress, 346, 347; attitude toward Nicholas II, 347; cordiality toward W. at Peterhof, 347; suggests tariff wall against American products, 348; plans for conquests in China, 350; appealed to by W. to withdraw from China, 351; encouragement to President Krüger partly responsible for Boer War, 351; at naval manoeuvres at Revel, 351; takes advantage of Russia when at war with Japan in exacting ruinous commercial concessions, 352; visit to, at Rominten, 356

Witte, family history, 35; early training, 40; enters Odessa University, 41; from opulence to poverty, 43; enters railway service, 44; scapegoat after Telegal catastrophe, 45; valuable services in war with Turkey, 46, 47; adherent of "Slav idea," 47; marries Madame Spiridonov, 47; member of Railroad Commission, 48; Director of South-Western Railroads, 49; in "The Holy Brotherhood," 49; literary work, 52; contention against high speed of Imperial train, 53; accepts post of Director of Department of Railroad Affairs, 55; appointed Minister of Ways of Communication, 57; officially visits Turkestan, 58; his wife's death, 59; marries Madame Lisanevich, 59; investigates cholera epidemic, 59; appointed Minister of Finances, 59; efforts in construction of Trans-Siberian Railway, 72, 98; transfers vodka traffic into hands of the Government, 74; prophesies that no parliament will ever curb liquor traffic, 76; introduces gold standard, 77; concludes commercial treaty with Germany, 80; promotes commercial and Industrial education, 91; highly commended by Nicholas II in Imperial rescript, 92; appointed President of Committee of Ministers, 93; dealing with Li Hung Chang, 95; advocates principle of maintaining integrity of Chinese Empire, 96; opposes seizure of Port Arthur, 108; and tenders resignation to Emperor, 110; protests against Manchurian policy, 118; against schemes for extending influence in Korea, 121, 123; submits report on Far Eastern problem, 125; advice to Kuropatkin on departure to war, 130; appointed chief

INDEX

plenipotentiary for purpose of conducting peace negotiations with Japan, 134; attitude in America, 138; impressions in New York, 141; visits President Roosevelt at Oyster Bay, 142; visits Harvard University, 144; the Peace Conference, 147; signing of Peace Treaty, 155; rewarded by title of Count, 156, 167, 361; jealousy at Russian Court, 159; degree bestowed by Columbia University, 163; visit to Washington, D. C., and Mount Vernon, 164; random impressions, 165; argues that war with Turkey would precipitate general European war, 176; object of Alexandra's enmity, 181; at conference discussing succession in case of death of Nicholas II, 182; opposes granting further privileges to nobility, 193; proposes conference for study of peasant problems, 195; addresses letter to Nicholas II imploring him not to give up formation of this conference, 195; succeeds in carrying out tax reforms and mitigation of passport regulations, 198; commissioned to form "Special Conference on the Needs of the Agricultural Industry," 199; at conference on liberal reforms, 202; first president of Council of Ministers, 211; text of report to His Majesty. 212; text of memorandum on the Manifesto of October 17, 1905, 216; not in favour of the Manifesto, 222; opposes police socialism scheme, 226; exiles Father Gapon, 228; opposes establishment of military rule in Baltic provinces, 231; handling of Polish situation, 234; difficulties during premiership, 243; falsely charged with collusion with Soviet, 247; President of Imperial Council, 253; difficulties in securing foreign loan, 258; in report to Nicholas II accuses Germany of ulterior motives in Moroccan controversy, 263; appeals direct to William II, to speed up work of Algeciras Conference, 265; resignation, 276, 307; account of his premiership, 277; formation of cabinet, 278; intrigues against, at Court, 295; letter to Emperor explaining resignation, 309; the Emperor's reply, 312; Imperial rescript 313; practically banished, 314; attitude to Jews, 324, 328; handling of peasant problem, 333; experiences with the Kaiser. 343; negotiations with Germany at, Norderney, 352; efforts in obtaining loan in France, 354; part in settlement of Moroccan controversy between France and Germany, 354, 365; visit to William II at Rominten, 356; efforts to nullify Björke compact, 362

Wittgenstein, Adjutant-General, activities in the "Holy Brotherhood," 51

Workmen's insurance law enacted, 246

Yekaterina Harbour favoured as naval base by Alexander III, 171

Yermolov, General, member of Peace Mission, 135

Yuri, Prince, of Leuchtenberg, marries one of the Montenegrin princesses, 187

Yuryevski, Princess, implicated in concession scandal, 60

Yuzefovich, appointed to committee on revision of censorship regulations, 204

Zakharin, Professor, summoned to attend Alexander III, 66

Zemski Nachalnik, Rural Chief of Police, instituted by Alexander III, 64

Zemstvos and Town Delegates, Union of, 230

Zograf, activities in the "Holy Brotherhood," 51

Zubatov, Sergey, counter-revolutionary tactics, 226

THE COUNTRY LIFE PRESS
GARDEN CITY, N. Y.

COPYRIGHT 1920, 1921, BY DOUBLEDAY, PAGE & COMPANY
ALL RIGHTS RESERVED, INCLUDING THAT OF TRANSLATION
INTO FOREIGN LANGUAGES, INCLUDING THE SCANDINAVIAN

BOOK TWO

Verestchagin Sculps.

M. V. RODZIANKO.

First Published   April, 1927
Second Impression   May, 1927

Made end Printed in Great Britain by C. Tinling & Co. Ltd.
Liverpool, London, and Prescot.

THE REIGN OF RASPUTIN:
An Empire's Collapse

MEMOIRS OF
M. V. RODZIANKO
President of the Russian State Duma

Translated by
CATHERINE ZVEGINTZOFF

Introduction by
Sir BERNARD PARES

LONDON:
A. M. PHILPOT LTD.
69 Great Russell Street, W.C.1.
1927.

INTRODUCTION

M. V. Rodzianko was born in 1859 of an old noble family. He was educated in the aristocratic Corps des Pages, served in Her Majesty's Regiment of the Cavalry of the Guard, and was appointed Kammerherr of the Imperial Court. Later he served as Marshal of the Gentry and as President of the Provincial Zemstvo Executive.

When the Duma was created, and the Council of State was turned into an Upper House supplemented by elected members, M. V. Rodzianko served in it as an elected representative of the province of Ekaterinoslav. Elected to the Third Duma in 1907, he became a prominent figure in the Union of 30th October (the Octobrists). The Octobrists included a number of enlightened gentry who held high offices in the central administration; they were committed to a programme of gradual and detailed reform, and they were personally pledged not to accept office until their programme should be accepted by the Emperor. After Gutchkoff resigned the presidency of the Duma he was succeeded by Rodzianko, who continued to hold this office until the March Revolution of 1917.

Rodzianko made a good President, and his striking personality and voice helped materially to uphold the dignity of the discussions. The President of the Duma was allowed to report personally to the Emperor at more or less regular intervals, and Rodzianko, with his Court connections and the sturdiness with which he put his views, was able to add to the consequence of the House which he represented. His views were those of English country Toryism. He was entirely opposed to the reactionary group and wished to make the national voice independent of the bureaucracy.

His tenure of office covered most of the period of the intimate though informal entente between Russia and England. Rodzianko, who could speak English, threw himself wholeheartedly into the development of this entente. I can recall that in his room at the Duma the creation of social ties with England was represented on a list of some twelve subjects in which the President wished to remain personally and directly interested. When in January, 1912, a representative party of Englishmen, including some eighteen members of both Houses of Parliament, visited Russia on an invitation which was initiated by the Duma, Rodzianko was one of the principal hosts of the visiting party, and he presided at an inter-parliamentary dinner, the first of the kind which could ever have been held in Russia.

During the war Rodzianko was necessarily always to the fore in the thousand and one activities which helped to knit closer the intimacy of the Allies. He was the personal friend of Sir George Buchanan. After the gross munition scandals of the early summer of 1915, co-operation between the Allies became even more intimate and far-reaching, and had the entire backing of the Duma. It was the principal support of the Central Munitions Committee created at its request, and on that Committee Rodzianko was the most authoritative representative of public opinion. This task he performed with success. His antecedents, his official position and his personal courage forced the incompetent Government to pay a greater attention to the pressing needs of the army. It was precisely in this field that the Duma was extending its moral influence, and it was precisely here that the Duma as such was directly challenged by the Empress, who, while entirely loyal to the Alliance, resented any public initiative other than that of the Emperor, The letters of this unhappy lady contain many references to Rodzianko, and her complete blindness to the situation was such that an ignorant reader might almost take this solid Tory gentleman for a revolutionary conspirator.

Rodzianko, however, though an honest and courageous man, was not a strong one; and the outbreak of revolution in March, 1917, put him to a test which might easily have been too much for the soundest political judgment and the greatest political courage. When the Duma reassembled in Petrograd, it was known that the Emperor would dissolve it, and the members were determined not to disperse. Further than that they did not see. It was precisely owing to the loyalty of the Duma, and more than anyone else of Rodzianko, that the outbreak in the streets of Petrograd, which the Ministers were entirely incapable of combating, was left to develop of itself without any lead from the Duma, while Rodzianko sent telegram after telegram to the Emperor urging that the last hour had come and that the dynasty was in danger, without receiving any reply.

Finally, Rodzianko acceded to the constitution of a Provisional Government. He remained a member of the Provisional Committee of the Duma, as such, which had already been formed, but he accepted no office in the new Government. His position was still one of great moral authority, for though the Duma had lost its legal basis in the March Revolution, its President as such still possessed a public significance in Russian eyes. With the failures of the Provisional Government Rodzianko cannot personally be credited, but he may be blamed for not having put the consideration which he enjoyed to more use during the period. He was completely prostrated by what had happened and felt himself in an entirely false position. "The most unhappy man in Russia," he said to the writer at that time, "is the President of the Imperial Duma." M. V. Rodzianko was later with Denikin in South Russia, but took no part in the Civil War. He was evacuated with the retreating troops of Wrangel, making the journey in the greatest discomfort. Thenceforward he resided in Serbia and was bitterly attacked by the ultra-monarchists.

At the time of his influence the predominating issue was the government of Russia by the infamous Rasputin. It is apparent from the Empress's letters that the head and front of Rodzianko's offending was the warning that he had the courage to give the Emperor long before the Revolution, for which the Empress hysterically insisted that he should be deprived of his Court rank. For his ultra-monarchist critics Rodzianko's offence was that he treated his Sovereign as a Sovereign and not as a mere *Eigentums-Besitzer*,* and that he regarded Rasputin as an unsuitable steward for the Russian Empire.

Rodzianko was no great man; but he was a true and warm friend of this country and an unflinching supporter of the Alliance. In the home politics of Russia Rodzianko failed at a time when everyone else failed, and committed mistakes which were less errors of judgment than defaults of judgment; and his actions were throughout ruled by the highest instincts of Russian patriotism.

He died in great poverty in Serbia in 1924.

BERNARD PARES.

CONTENTS

CHAPTER	PAGE

INTRODUCTION 383

AUTHOR'S NOTE 389

CHAPTER I 391
    Mysticism of the Empress and " Prophets " from the West—Bishop Feofan and the appearance of Rasputin—Secret of his influence on the Empress—Conflict between Bishop Hermogen and the Monk Iliodor and the High Procurator of the Synod, Sabler

CHAPTER II 407
    P. A. Stolypin and Rasputin—Case of the Imperial Children's Nurse—Disgrace of the Metropolitan Anthony—Questions about Rasputin in the Duma—Conversation with the Dowager Empress

CHAPTER III 419
    Audience of the Emperor concerning Rasputin—Documents on the Case—Interview with the Emperor's Confessor—The Emperor's Refusal to grant an Audience

CHAPTER IV 436
    Imperial *Levée* for Members of the Duma—The Emperor's Displeasure—Effects of the Reception—Borodino Anniversary Celebrations—The Fourth Duma Election Campaign—M. V. Rodzianko's Re-election—Audience of the Emperor

CHAPTER V 443
    The Tercentenary of the Romanoff Dynasty—Rasputin's Expulsion from the Cathedral—Radko Dmitrieff's visit to St. Petersburg

CHAPTER VI 452
    The Intrigues of the Right—Boycott of the Duma—Unveiling of the Stolypin Memorial—Bishop Agapit—A. I. Gutchkoff's Warnings.

CONTENTS

| CHAPTER | PAGE |

CHAPTER VII 461
    The Audience of December 22, 1913—Dispute over the Purchase of Dreadnoughts—Admiral Beatty's Squadron off Reval—Port Hangö

CHAPTER VIII 469
    Declaration of War—Disorganization in the Red Cross —At the Warsaw-Vienna Station—General Rennenkampf—Army Boots and the Minister N. A. Maklakoff—The Emperor at Lvoff (Lemberg)

CHAPTER IX 485
    The Stavka after the Retreat—Scheme of a Special Council of Defence—The Industrialists' Congress—Nicholas II and N. A. Maklakoff—The Port of Archangel—The Grand Duke Sergei Mikhailovitch

CHAPTER X 499
    The Emperor as Commander-in-Chief—Increasing Influence of the Empress—Goremykin dissolves the Duma—A. D. Samarin's Dismissal—The Putiloff Works—The British and our Mercantile Marine

CHAPTER XI 512
    Strikes—The Inventor Bratoliuboff and Mme. Brasova—Letter to Goremykin—The Maid of Honour M. A. Vasilchikova

CHAPTER XII 517
    The Metropolitan Pitirim and Sturmer—The Emperor in the Duma—Bad Meat and Food Shortage—Arrival of MM. Viviani and Thomas—The Prime Minister's Dinner—Russian Parliamentary Delegation—A Dictatorship Scheme

CHAPTER XIII 538
    Dismissal of Sazonoff—Sturmer as Dictator—The Guards on the Stokhod—Aircraft from Abroad

CHAPTER XIV 547
    Protopopoff becomes Minister—The President of the Duma states his Terms—A Greek Prince—Refusal of an Audience—A Visit to Sturmer

CONTENTS

CHAPTER	PAGE

CHAPTER XV 557
    The " Junge Zarin " ; Miliukoff's Speech and its Consequences—Stunner and Protopopoff demand the Dissolution of the Duma—Markoff II makes a Scene —After Rasputin's Murder—Protopopoff as Spiritualist

CHAPTER XVI 571
    Disruption in the Rear—Krymoff urges a *Coup d'État*—Luncheon with the Grand Duchess Marie Pavlovna—Visit of the Grand Duke Mikhail Alexandrovitch—Audience of January 7

CHAPTER XVII 582
    Entente Delegates in Petrograd—Police and Machine Guns—The Last Audience—Labour Arrests—The Emperor agrees to a Responsible Ministry—His Sudden Departure—Adrift

APPENDIX I 588
    M. V. Rodzianko's Speech at the Celebration of the Tercentenary Anniversary of the House of Romanoff, 1913

APPENDIX II 589
    M. V. Rodzianko's Speech at the Opening of the Imperial Duma on July 26 (O.S.), 1914

APPENDIX III 590
    Letter from General Alexeieff to M. V. Rodzianko

APPENDIX IV 591
    M. V. Rodziamko's Speech at the Industrialists' Congress, 1915

INDEX 592

AUTHOR'S NOTE.

In my attempt to narrate the course of events which preceded the Russian Revolution, and to describe the conditions under, or rather because of which Gregory Rasputin appeared at the Court of the Emperor Nicholas II and exercised so fatal an influence on State policy, nothing was further from my mind than to cast any aspersion on the person of the Tsar who has since died a martyr's death.

There can be no doubt that throughout his life he was filled with the most genuine desire for the good and happiness of his people. Nevertheless, through lack of will power, softness of disposition and easy submission to evil and obscure influences, he not only failed to achieve anything, but brought his country to the present state of anarchy, in which he himself and all his family perished.

I felt that, because of my close association with the rulers of Russia, I had no right to conceal those dark pages of the history of the Russian Empire that were revealed during the world war, which proved so disastrous for us.

Our descendants, for their own education, ought to know the history of their nation in all its details, and from the errors of the past gain experience for the present and future. No one has the right to withhold any intimate details of historical interest or political value which he possesses, but must unhesitatingly bequeath to posterity his knowledge and experience. It is in this spirit that I beg my readers to treat these memoirs. I have set myself to be as objective as possible, and strenuously endeavoured to avoid framing a harsh and biassed judgment of the period I describe.

Whatever may be said, the appearance at Court of Gregory Rasputin, and the influence he exercised there, mark the beginning of the decay of Russian society and the loss of prestige of the Throne and of the person of the Tsar himself. Nicholas II, however, cannot alone be held responsible for the fatal consequences for the State of the influence wielded by Rasputin. There is no doubt that the main burden of responsibility rests on the shoulders of those statesmen and courtiers who, in the selfish pursuit of their own interests, could not, or would not, realize the depth of the abyss which might engulf not only the Imperial Family, but Russia herself.

The presence so close to the Throne of an immoral and dirty adventurer cast a shadow on its lustre. It was, then, the duty of all who put the destiny of the State above their personal aims and interests to unite, with no thought of themselves, in the name of the Motherland and save her from, it might be, terrible convulsions. But this did not happen. Those very men who should have steadfastly resisted the growing evil failed in their duty to their Motherland. More than this, in pursuit of their selfish aims, they supported the blighting influence of Rasputin on the Imperial Family, as they saw in him a sure means of attaining their vain and greedy ends.

I most emphatically and definitely reject all those worthless and base insinuations which were levelled against the Imperial pair during the last years of Nicholas II's reign, as well as all the street-corner pamphlets which the excited mind of a credulous public readily accepted. My conscience urges me to declare that the causes of Rasputin's influence lay deeper. They are related to the unhealthy mysticism of the Empress Alexandra Feodorovna, which was continually and artificially maintained by Rasputin and his accomplices, and was in no way founded on intimate relations,

I base my narrative on numerous documents now in my possession, as well as on the private diaries which I have kept. I shall be obliged, however, occasionally to cite rumours and stories which were current in Russian society, and which directly reflect the state of men's minds during the period I am about to describe.

M. V. RODZIANKO

CHAPTER I

Mysticism of the Empress and "Prophets" from the West—Bishop Feofan and the appearance of Rasputin—Secret of his influence on the Empress—Conflict between Bishop Hermogen and the Monk Iliodor and the High Procurator of the Synod, Sabler.

My more or less intimate acquaintance with Russia's high governing circles dates back to the time when, after the Japanese War, I was elected a member of the Council of the Empire by the Zemstvo of the province of Ekaterinoslav. Thus many details of official life became familiar to me of which the general public knew nothing.

There existed a widespread opinion in society, undoubtedly correct, that the Empress Alexandra Feodorovna had had from her childhood a strong tendency towards mysticism. This disposition, in the opinion of many hereditary, increased with advancing years till, at the time I am speaking of, it had attained a state of religious mania; nay, more—of religious ecstacy—a firm belief in the possibility of foretelling the future, plus a considerable dose of superstition.

The causes of this psychological phenomenon cannot, of course, be easily explained. Whether it was the effect of frequent childbirth and of the passionate desire for an heir, when she always gave birth to daughters, or whether this state of mind was purely temperamental, it is not for me to say. But the fact of her mysticism, with its attendant tendency towards the supernatural and even the occult, remained beyond doubt.

The far-sighted politicians of Western Europe, who always made a closer study of the Imperial Court than we Russians, lost no time in turning this phenomenon to account. Desirous of obtaining a strong hand at the Russian Court, and having, as it were, rapidly taken their bearings, they determined to take advantage of this temperamental peculiarity of the young Empress.

Towards the beginning of 1900, various mysterious apostles of mysticism, hypnotizers and prophets of the future began to appear at the Imperial Russian Court, and gained considerable influence over the mystically inclined mind of the Empress Alexandra Feodorovna. Owing to the confidence these adventurers inspired in the Imperial pair, they soon became the centre of small groups of courtiers, who thus assumed a certain importance in the life of the Imperial Court. There is no doubt that agents of certain foreign Embassies had secret access to these circles, which enabled them to gain detailed information concerning Russian social and public life.

It was at this time, for instance, that a certain Philippe made his appearance at Court. He was exactly the type of man to place his influence over the minds of the Imperial pair at the service of any cause or person from whom he could expect a suitable remuneration for his "work."

This gentleman was introduced at Court by two of the Grand Duchesses. Shortly after his arrival, however, Ratchkovsky, the agent of the Russian Secret Service in Paris, reported to St. Petersburg that Philippe was a shady and suspicious character of Jewish nationality, and had some sort of connection with masonic organizations and the society called the "Grande Alliance Israelite." Philippe, meanwhile, was acquiring an ever-increasing influence. He held meetings, performed various spiritualist "passes," foretold the future and persuaded the Empress that she would soon give birth to a son. Philippe gained such power at Court that the agent Ratchkovsky was dismissed for denouncing him. Shortly after this, however, Philippe himself disappeared mysteriously during a visit to Paris.

No sooner had he made his exit than another adventurer, a certain Papus, claiming to be his disciple, arrived in St. Petersburg, and was in a similar manner introduced at Court.

I cannot but render justice to the leading Russian statesmen of the time and to the prelates of the Russian Church. They were all profoundly perturbed by the growing influence of these mysterious arrivals, who might easily have been emissaries sent for unknown purposes. On the one hand, the civil authorities feared the possibility of political complications and intrigues arising from the confidence these men enjoyed at Court, where they became the centre of cliques of courtiers bent, it is true, on the pursuit of their own private ends, but capable of much worse things. The ecclesiastical authorities, in their turn, feared that sectarianism emanating from the Court might spread among the upper circles of society and injure the Russian Orthodox Church. Such instances had already occurred in the history of Russia, during the reign of Alexander I.

CHAPTER I

Whether by the united efforts of the civil and ecclesiastical authorities, or owing to other circumstances or possible intrigues, Papus was soon dismissed. His place was taken by Bishop Feofan, the Principal of the Theological Academy of St. Petersburg, who was also appointed their Majesties' confessor. According to rumours circulated at the time in St. Petersburg society, of the truth of which I have no documentary evidence, it was decided at a secret conference of Church prelates that it was necessary for the Church, as the guardian and defender of the Orthodox faith, to exercise her wise and moderating influence on the mystically inclined spirit of the young Empress, so as to combat the pernicious activities of base foreigners obviously in pursuit of totally different aims.

The high moral qualities of Mgr. Feofan won universal respect. A man of absolute purity of soul and a firm Christian, he was imbued with the true Orthodox spirit of faith and humility. In this respect all were agreed. Alien alike to politics and personal ambition, he was a true and faithful servant of the Church, and so could not become the centre of any base scheming or intrigues. It appears, therefore, all the more incomprehensible that it was through him that Rasputin was introduced to the Imperial Court. One can only suppose that Mgr. Feofan was profoundly mistaken in his estimate of Rasputin's moral character and personality. The meek, gentle and confiding bishop was cunningly duped by this clever and astute, though almost illiterate, *mouzhik*; his pure soul was incapable of fathoming all the depths of immorality and licentiousness in such a man as Gregory Rasputin. Presumably Bishop Feofan hoped that the simple and unsophisticated spiritual outlook of a plain God-fearing and believing Orthodox Russian peasant would be most likely to appeal to the harassed soul of the young Empress. He naturally thought that this God-fearing *starets*, as he pictured Rasputin, would by virtue of his serene simplicity be better able than anyone else to provide an answer to her questionings and disperse the clouds of mysticism which darkened her soul. But fate decreed that the honest bishop should be cruelly deceived by the cunning charlatan and should pay dearly for his mistake.

Who, then, was Gregory Rasputin? His *curriculum vitae* prior to his appearance in Russian politics has been definitely established.

A native of the village of Pokrovskoe in the province of Tobolsk, he was an ordinary peasant of average means, hardly differing from any of his fellow villagers. The evidence in his case disclosed that from his youth he had strong leanings towards sectarianism, his keenly inquiring intellect driving him to seek new paths of religious experience. It is clear that the principles of Orthodox Christianity had never been implanted in his soul, and consequently it lacked the corresponding moral qualities. Even before his appearance in St. Petersburg he was a man devoid of ethical code or conscience, greedy for material gain, of a boldness verging on insolence, utterly unscrupulous in the pursuit of his aims.

Such was the morality of Gregory Rasputin, revealed by the legal evidence which came into my possession. I have been able to gather from the same source the following details concerning his career.

Certain strange doings in and around Rasputin's house attracted the attention of the parish priest of Pokrovskoe. A building without windows, supposed to be a bath house, had been erected in a remote corner of the yard, and in it mysterious meetings were held after dusk. Rasputin himself began frequently to absent himself on visits to the Abalaksky monastery, in which persons exiled for belonging to various religious sects were confined. While the local priest was endeavouring to unravel the secret of the mysterious doings which took place in Rasputin's house, the latter decided to try his luck outside his native village and slipped away to St. Petersburg. I was unable to obtain any exact information as to how Rasputin contrived to worm himself into the confidence of Bishop Feofan. Rumours on the subject were so numerous and varied that to credit them all was impossible. According to the most current version, Rasputin was introduced to the bishop by a certain priest named Yaroslav Medvied, the confessor of one of the Grand Duchesses. This man either visited or was exiled to the Abalaksky monastery, where he was alleged to have met Rasputin and brought him to St. Petersburg. This story seems to be the most plausible, but there were many others. In any case, Rasputin was, as early as 1900 and before the Chinese (Boxer) war, on intimate terms with their Majesties' confessor, Mgr. Feofan. That short-sighted prelate introduced him at Court as a *starets* and *natchetchik**

At first Rasputin behaved with the utmost caution, never revealing his actual intentions. It was natural that he should take his bear-

---

* A *starets* was a man, not necessarily a monk or in holy orders, who for his high moral qualities and holy life was recognized as a spiritual teacher. A *natchetchik* was a man versed in the Scriptures, an expert reader.

CHAPTER I

ings, study the personalities, life and customs of the Court. Thus, not only did he strengthen Bishop Feofan's confidence in him, but he acquired another influential champion in the person of Bishop Hermogen of Saratoff, later a member of the Holy Synod, who subsequently realized his error and suffered heavily for it. Another of Rasputin's partisans was the notorious monk Iliodor. The latter, however, was definitely accused of being an *agent provocateur* out to make a career, though his passionate temperament and fiery eloquence made him at one time the idol of the Saratoff crowd. Certainly his influence over the populace was enormous, and, moreover, he enjoyed the powerful patronage of Bishop Hermogen.

During this period Rasputin never abandoned the role of a pious and God-fearing *starets* and zealous intercessor for the Orthodox Church of Christ. During the troubled years of the Japanese war and the Revolution of 1905, he ministered to the spiritual needs of the Imperial Family, praying devoutly in their presence and assuring them that while he was there to intercede for them, no harm would befall either them or the little Tsarevitch. Apparently unnoticed, his influence steadily grew, so that finally he was entrusted with the office of the "Emperor's lampkeeper," whose duty it was to tend the lamps burning day and night before the holy ikons.

He thus obtained free access to the Imperial palace, and in virtue of his office came daily to the Tsar's apartments, which he had hitherto entered only by special invitation. It should be remembered that the Emperor Nicholas II was a great lover and connoisseur of ancient ikons, and possessed a rare and extremely valuable collection which he greatly treasured. It must be supposed that since the Tsar entrusted this precious collection to Rasputin's care, he must have felt a certain amount of confidence in his newly-appointed lampkeeper, and, believing his piety to be genuine, deemed him worthy to become the custodian of these holy images.

Having thus obtained a firm foothold in the palace, Rasputin began gradually to change his tactics and to give a freer vent to his depraved instincts and sectarian impulses.

With the gradual subsidence of revolutionary turmoil and resumption of normal life, rumours, at first vague and indefinite, began to circulate concerning the doings of this knave. Soon, how-ever, these rumours became more precise. It began to be said more and more definitely that Rasputin was engaged in founding "*khlysty ships*"*, which consisted mainly of young women and girls; also that he was frequently to be met in the private cabins of the St. Petersburg public baths, where he indulged in the most unrestrained immorality. Names of ladies belonging to the highest circles of St. Petersburg society were mentioned as having become adherents of his sectarian doctrine. These rumours gradually grew and gained publicity. People began to say openly that so and so had been seduced by Rasputin; that two sisters, both of them young girls, had been dishonoured by him; that secret orgies and promiscuous immorality were practised in certain flats.

I had in my possession scores of letters from mothers whose daughters had been seduced by Rasputin. I had also in my possession photographs of a *"khlysty ship."* In the centre sat Rasputin, surrounded by about a hundred of his followers, all of them young men and women. Two of them held in front of him a large placard inscribed with *khlysty* texts. Another photograph taken in Rasputin's drawing-room showed him in the midst of the society women who were his followers; to my amazement I recognized many of them. I was also given two photographs of Rasputin himself. In one of these he was wearing his peasant's dress with a pectoral cross, his right hand raised with fingers clasped as though giving a blessing. In the other he was in a monk's habit and cowl and again wearing a pectoral cross.

I had soon collected a whole volume of incriminating evidence. If only a tenth part of the material submitted to me were genuine, it would have amply sufficed for the institution of criminal proceedings against Rasputin. As President of the Duma I received from all sides complaints and disclosures concerning the criminal activities and debauchery of this man. Finally, the matter was taken up by the daily Press. The Censorship Committee and the Minister of the Interior became seriously alarmed, especially as they undoubtedly possessed, through the medium of the Secret Service, far more precise information and much more irrefutable evidence of the truth of the rumours which were circulated in public. The State authorities were faced with a situation of exceptional difficulty. They could not but realize the depth of the abyss into which Rasputin was drawing the Imperial couple, while on the other hand the growth of the influence of this disgusting libertine over them was daily becom-

* (on previous page) The khlysty belonged to a sect whose religious practices were of a most obscene and erotic nature. Each community was called a " ship," with a " helmsman " at its head.

CHAPTER I

ing more apparent.

What was the secret of this fatal influence, which undoubtedly led to the commencement of the Russian Revolution, inasmuch as it weakened the Tsar's prestige?

There is no doubt that Gregory Rasputin, apart from being a man of more than average intelligence, extraordinary astuteness, and possessing a will unchecked by any moral scruples, was further gifted with great hypnotic power. I should think that he would have been a subject of extraordinary interest to a scientist. The opinion of all those who came in contact with him was unanimous on that point, while I myself, as will be seen later, experienced the force of his power of suggestion. It goes, therefore, without saying that the neurotic and mystically inclined Empress, whose tortured soul suffered continual agonies of fear for the fate of her son, the Heir to the Throne, and for that of her exalted husband, fell under the influence of Rasputin's hypnotism to an extraordinary degree. I can confidently assert that by this force of suggestion he gained absolute control over the will of the young Empress. By that same force he impressed upon her that while he remained at Court no harm could befall the dynasty. He impressed her with the idea that, as he was a son of the common people, he was best fitted to know their needs and the way to be followed to make Russia prosperous and happy. By his hypnotic power he implanted in the Empress a firm and unshakable faith in himself as the man chosen by God for Russia's salvation.

Besides this the Empress, who according to medical opinion was of a very highly strung and neurotic disposition, was subject to frequent attacks of mild hysteria which caused her acute suffering. These Rasputin was able to alleviate by using his powers of hypnotic suggestion, and herein alone lay the secret of his influence. It was a purely pathological phenomenon and nothing more. I remember speaking of it to I. L. Goremykin, then Premier, who unhesitatingly replied, "*C'est une question clinique.*" It was, therefore, all the more odious to me constantly to hear disgraceful insinuations and stories of alleged intimacy between Rasputin and the Empress. The blameless nature of the family life of the Imperial couple was patent to all, while to those who, like myself, became acquainted with their private correspondence during the war it was proved by documentary evidence. Nevertheless, Gregory Rasputin became the Empress Alexandra Feodorovna's oracle, and for her his opinion was law. On the other hand she, herself strong-willed, almost despotic by nature, exercised over her august consort, who lacked all traces of will or character, an unlimited, almost overwhelming influence. She contrived to make him amiably disposed towards, and even to confide in, Rasputin, though from my own personal experience I can positively assert that to the very end of his reign Nicholas II was, in his inmost soul, assailed by painful doubts. In spite of this Rasputin had free access to him and dominated him absolutely.

My old schoolfellow at the Corps des Pages and personal friend, General V. N. Dediulin, then A.D.C. to the Emperor and Palace commandant, told me the following story. "I studiously avoided," he said, "making Rasputin's acquaintance, and even went out of my way to do so, because the dirty *mouzhik* physically repelled me. One day after dinner the Emperor said to me: 'Why is it, V.N., that you so persistently avoid meeting Gregory Efimovitch?' I replied frankly that I disliked him intensely, that he had more than a tarnished reputation, and that it pained me as a loyal subject to see this rascal so close to the sacred person of my Sovereign. 'You are wrong in thinking so,' replied the Emperor, 'he is just a good, religious, simple-minded Russian. When in trouble or assailed with doubts I like to have a talk with him, and invariably feel at peace with myself afterwards.'"

Such was the influence which, by means of the Empress, Rasputin had gained over Nicholas II. Small wonder, then, that all manner of ambitious climbers, careerists and shady characters clustered around Rasputin, in whom they found a suitable instrument for attaining their personal ends. This was a source of trouble for the State authorities, whose duty it was to safeguard and maintain untarnished the prestige of the Imperial Crown. It should also be remembered that Rasputin numbered among his circle certain highly influential personages, as, for instance, Sturmer, Sabler, the High Procurator of the Holy Synod, and the Metropolitan Pitirim.

As I have said, stories of Rasputin's exploits began to appear in the Press. So far this had been confined to the St. Petersburg and Moscow papers and had not penetrated to the provinces, so that it was not yet too late: the conflagration could easily be suppressed.

Instead, however, of fully realizing the full horror of the situation, and of uniting in their efforts to strike at the very root of the evil which menaced the Throne, and of which the Emperor and Empress were obviously unconscious, the highest officials in the State were themselves divided in two hostile camps—pro- and anti-Rasputinites. There was too, unfortunately, yet a third group—the neutrals. These, while fully realizing and deploring the existing state of affairs and capable of fighting the danger, yet, either from lack of courage or, perhaps, personal motives, obstinately remained silent and passive. The group of Rasputin's active supporters included the High Procurator of the Holy Synod Sabler, his assistant Damansky, the Archpriest Vasilieff, religious teacher of the Imperial children, General Voeikoff, the Metropolitan Pitirim, A. S. Taneieff, Gentleman Usher to the Emperor, his daughter Madame Vyrubova, B.V. Sturmer, and many others of the same stamp. Among the leaders of the second group were: P. A. Stolypin (until his death), with all his fellow-Ministers, the Metropolitan of St. Petersburg, Mgr. Anthony, and the Bishops Hermogen and Feofan, both of whom had now realized their error.

It is obvious that such a cleavage among the leading statesmen only played into the hands of Rasputin's adherents. The latter, availing themselves of his influence at Court, removed their enemies from their path by calumny and intrigue, thus both clearing the way for themselves and incidentally enhancing the importance of their patron. It should be noted, too, that the spectacle of the successful careers of Rasputin's followers lowered the *moral* of his opponents, and secessions from the ranks of the anti-Rasputinites became more frequent. Even the neutral group appeared to be vacillating. If the upper strata of Russian society could have presented a united front and could have offered a steadfast resistance to this abnormal state of affairs; if the Crown could have clearly seen that there was but one opinion about Rasputin, and that it had no one to rely on for support, it is absolutely certain that both Rasputin and his clique would have been completely destroyed.

The Rasputinites, together with the parties of the Extreme Right, laid the foundations of the Russian Revolution, for they estranged the Emperor from his people and allowed a shadow to be cast on the lustre of the Crown. Faced with this cleavage of opinions in his immediate entourage, being completely under the influence of the Empress, and certain of no other support, Nicholas II was organically incapable of adopting any anti-Rasputin policy. I venture therefore definitely to assert that the blame for the process of disruption which began to manifest itself at this time cannot be laid upon the Emperor Nicholas II alone. The burden of responsibility rests fully on those members of the ruling classes who, blinded by their ambition, cupidity and desire for advancement, forgot the terrible danger which was threatening their Emperor and Russia.

As soon as Rasputin felt that he was standing on firm ground he gradually altered his passive tactics, became aggressive and, encounterring no obstacles to his fanatical outbursts, grew daily more insolent. Nevertheless, the rapidity with which he acquired followers and disciples was amazing, especially in society, where their number was considerable, particularly among the women. They clung to him like flies to a honey-pot.

I was told the following story, which I know to be perfectly true, of Rasputin's power of suggestion. A lady who lived in the provinces, having heard of Rasputin's influence at Court, determined to try and obtain through him promotion for her husband. This lady was a happy and model wife and mother. On her arrival in St. Petersburg she managed to obtain an interview with Rasputin, who, on hearing her petition, assumed a stern and authoritative air and replied, addressing her as "thou":

"Very well, I'll try. Only to-morrow you must come to me in a low-necked dress with bare shoulders. And don't you dare come to me otherwise."

When he spoke to her his eyes seemed to pierce her through and through, and his whole behaviour was more than familiar. The lady, outraged by Rasputin's words and manner, went away, firmly resolved not to pursue her plea. On her return home, however, she was seized with an unaccountable yearning; she became obsessed with the idea that she had to do something. Next day, having procured a *décolletée* dress, she presented herself at the appointed hour at Rasputin's flat. Shortly afterwards her husband received his promotion.

It can easily be imagined what a repulsive impression the orgies of Rasputin and his women followers made, not only on the servants, from whom nothing ever remains a secret, but also on simple folk in general. How great must have been their contempt for the "gentry" who so cynically indulged in shameful immorality! What religious considerations or what quest of higher truths could justify such conduct? It was clear to all that those who sought Rasputin's patronage were guided solely by the lowest of instincts and nothing else. It is worthy of note that all the common people who ministered to the freaks of this libertine, such as the cabmen

CHAPTER I

who drove him and his women to the baths; the bath attendants who showed him to his private room; the waiters who served him during his drunken orgies; the policemen and Secret Service agents who stood freezing at street corners all to protect his precious life—all these people were not in the least imposed upon by Rasputin's sanctity, because his everyday life, which lay open to them, told them quite a different tale. Their comments were pithy and to the point: "The gentry are out for fun." Yet Rasputin was intimate with, and under the patronage of, the most exalted persons. What conclusions were drawn from this my readers can judge for themselves!

Rasputin's increasing immorality and cynicism at last opened Bishop Feofan's eyes to the true nature of his former protégé. The Bishop overtly joined the camp of Rasputin's opponents and endeavoured to persuade the Empress that the pseudo-righteous *starets* was quite unworthy of the honour and attention bestowed on him, and that he ought to be banished from the Court, which he discredited by his presence. The unworthy *starets* proved more powerful than the righteous prelate. The combat was unequal. Bishop Feofan was soon relieved of his office as the Emperor's confessor and from the post of Principal of the St. Petersburg Theological Academy, and was transferred to the see of Simferopol, in the Crimea.

Rasputin was victorious. The ease with which this victory had been carried off made him fully realize the extent of his power. He straightway proceeded, first, to sweep from his path all those who opposed him at the Imperial Court, next to apply these tactics to the ranks of the higher clergy, and finally turned his attention to the statesmen and dignitaries of the realm. The fate of Bishop Feofan was shared by Rasputin's other patron, Mgr. Hermogen, who also came at last to realize the true nature of the holiness of the *starets* whom he had so rashly recommended. The removal, or rather the downfall, of Bishop Hermogen was, however, the occasion of a public scandal. Since he had no access to the Court, Mgr. Hermogen decided on another course. Having become convinced of Rasputin's immorality and of the danger that threatened the Imperial Family through their association with him, Mgr. Hermogen summoned him to his house. He then, in the presence of the monk Iliodor, a Cossack officer named Rodionoff (author of a fairly well-known book, "Our Crime"), a lay brother in the bishop's service and a pilgrim named Mitia, arraigned Rasputin for all his disgusting behaviour and admonished him to repent and voluntarily to leave the Emperor's house.

"You are an impostor and a hypocrite," Mgr. Hermogen said to Rasputin (I repeat here the story told me by Rodionoff). "You pose as a holy *starets*, while leading a shameful and unclean life. You duped me in the past, but now I see what you really are and feel that I have sinned in introducing you to the Emperor's family. You disgrace it by your presence, while by your behaviour and conversation you cast a slur on the name of the Empress, whose sacred person you dare to touch with your unclean hands. This can no longer be tolerated. I adjure you in the Name of the living God to depart and to cease from troubling the Russian people by your presence at the Imperial Court."

Rasputin's answers to the indignant bishop were insolent, and a violent scene followed, in the course of which Rasputin, after abusing Mgr. Hermogen in vulgar language, flatly refused to submit to his command and threatened to "make short work of him." At this Bishop Hermogen, losing his self-control, exclaimed: "So, you dirty scoundrel, you refuse to submit to my episcopal command, and dare to threaten me. Then know that I, as a bishop, anathematize you!"

Rasputin, as if possessed, clenched his fists and flung himself on the prelate, his face, said Rodionoff, losing every trace of humanity. Afraid lest, in his access of fury, Rasputin should murder the bishop, Rodionoff drew his sword and, with the others, hastened to the rescue. With difficulty they managed to drag Rasputin away. His bodily strength was such that he managed to wrench himself from their grasp and take to his heels. He was, however, overtaken by the lay brother and the pilgrim Mitia and roughly handled. Still he managed to escape and ran out into the street shouting: "You wait a bit. I'll pay you out." This threat, taking advantage of the following circumstances, he carried out to the letter.

A bishop, one of the members of the Holy Synod, told me that at a secret conclave of the latter the High Procurator Sabler, one of Rasputin's most influential patrons, recommended Rasputin as a candidate for the priesthood. The Holy Synod rejected this proposal with righteous indignation. In vain Sabler insisted, and intimated that the suggestion emanated from high quarters. The Synod could not be persuaded to yield. Bishop Hermogen on this occasion delivered a fulminating speech exposing the immoral life

CHAPTER I

and activities of the pseudo-holy *starets*. The latter, of course, heard of all that took place from Sabler himself.

Almost simultaneously the following episode occurred. The Empress's sister, the Grand Duchess Elizabeth, presented to the Synod a request stating her desire to found, or rather restore, the ancient Order of Deaconesses. In the early days of the Christian era these semi-monastic communities did many works of charity; they organized prayer meetings, founded hostels and asylums, children's homes and almshouses for aged people, and ministered to the sick and the infirm. The discussion of this question in the Synod almost coincided with the incident concerning Rasputin's ordination. The debate was an extremely heated one. The moving spirit of the opposition to the Grand Duchess's request was again Bishop Hermogen. In opposing the scheme he argued that the foundation of such communities would be contrary to the canons of the Church, for the Order of Deaconesses had been abolished by a decree of one of the Œcumenic* Councils.

Meanwhile Sabler, seeing that the Synod remained unyielding on the point of Rasputin's ordination, devised another scheme, which he presented to the Synod at the same time as the Grand Duchess's request. He suggested that a certain Archimandrite† Barnabas, an adherent of himself and of Rasputin, an ignorant monk, who before taking the vows had been a common market gardener, should be consecrated Suffragan Bishop of Kargopol. The High Procurator hoped that this bishop would prove an obedient tool in his hands and would ordain Rasputin. In all justice to the Synod, it must be stated that this proposal also met with unanimous opposition and rejection. Nothing daunted, Sabler declared that it was no concern of his personally, but that it was the will of persons more highly placed than himself. The Synod began to waver. The presiding member, Mgr. Anthony, Metropolitan of St. Petersburg, was so profoundly shocked by this intrigue that he fell seriously ill after the meeting and remained confined to his bed all through the winter, taking no part in the deliberations of the Synod. Sabler finally succeeded in cajoling the majority of the members of the Synod into

---

* Œ is a grapheme of Latin and Greek alphabet origins, known as an ethel or œthel. It would be fair to treat it as the common letter 'E'

† An honorary tile given to the superior of a large monastic complex by the Russian Orthodox Church - equivalent to an Abbot.

acquiescence. At a conclave presided over by Bishop Sergius of Finland, acting as deputy for the Metropolitan Anthony, the motion for Barnabas' consecration was put to the vote and carried.

Bishop Hermogen remained true to himself. Refusing to give in, he inveighed against the High Procurator and the weakness of the members of the Synod, and finally created a demonstration by quitting the assembly, declaring that he would not be a party to such wickedness and threatening to excommunicate its participants for their lack of zeal for the honour and purity of the Orthodox Church. By some strange freak of fate all these intrigues happened to coincide. The result of Bishop Hermogen's denunciatory speech was quite unexpected. By an Imperial ukase he was deprived of his membership of the Synod and ordered to return immediately to his diocese. At the same time Iliodor, who had nothing whatever to do with the Synod's decision, was also banished from St. Petersburg.

Such drastic treatment of the two most avowed enemies of the *starets* showed plainly who was the instigator of these proceedings, and who was taking his revenge by sweeping them from his path. Mgr. Hermogen, however, would not accept his disgrace. In a sincere and impassioned letter he implored the Emperor to eradicate the tares* which had sprung up around the Throne, and brought irrefutable evidence to prove how cowardly the Synod had been and how morally wrong and disgraceful the whole affair was. He used all the strength of his fiery eloquence in praying the Emperor to take heed of the danger, to guard himself, the Heir to the Throne and the whole Imperial Family from the terrible evil with which they were menaced. He claimed for himself the right to be tried before a court of bishops, which alone, according to the canons of the Church, could deprive him of his membership of the Synod. The letter remained unanswered, and Hermogen himself was informed by the High Procurator Sabler that, as a punishment for his disobedience to the Emperor's command, he was to be exiled to the distant Zhirovetsky monastery, wither he would be conveyed forcibly should he refuse to go of his own free will. The bishop was taken seriously ill, but on his recovery humbly submitted to the order and went voluntarily into exile.

The monk Iliodor, however, took advantage of his own banish-

---

* Originating from biblical use (Matt. 13:24–30), an injurious weed, thereby causing or likely to cause harm.

CHAPTER I

ment to create a sensation. Wherever possible, he gave interviews in which he openly pointed to Rasputin as the principal cause and instigator of all that had occurred. Later he disappeared mysteriously, having set off to Saratoff on foot. He was closely pursued by reporters, who described every detail of his pilgrimage, which assumed the character of a triumphant progress. Finally, Iliodor was arrested and domiciled in the place appointed for his exile. All this caused considerable public scandal. Indignation was widespread, and Bishop Hermogen received messages of sympathy from all quarters. I well remember how one day V. M. Purishkevitch*, a member of the Duma, entered my study in a violent state of agitation and, in a voice trembling with horror and grief, said to me: "Where are we going? Our last mainstay, the Holy Orthodox Church, is being destroyed. There was a revolution which attempted to undermine the Crown; it failed. The army remained loyal to its duty; it is now being openly subverted. As a climax, the powers of darkness are now attacking Russia's last hope—the Church. And the most terrible part of it all is that this seems to emanate from the Throne itself. A charlatan, a *khlyst*, a filthy, illiterate peasant is playing his dirty tricks on our prelates. Into what abyss are we being driven? Oh, my God! I want to sacrifice myself and kill this vermin, Rasputin!"

And yet Purishkevitch belonged to the Extreme Right wing of the Duma. But he was a sincere and honest man, a warm-hearted patriot, who did not think of himself or his career. I had the greatest difficulty in calming his agitation and persuading him that all was not yet lost, that the Duma might still have a word to say in the matter, and that perhaps the Emperor might listen to the voice of the chosen representatives of the people.

It is characteristic of the Emperor Nicholas II that personally he had nothing against the exiled bishop. On his arrival at his new abode Mgr. Hermogen sent his secretary to me with a letter, in which he exhorted me to do my duty by revealing to the Emperor the whole truth and warning him of the approaching danger.

When next I waited on the Emperor to present my customary report, I laid before him the whole inner history of the incident which had taken place in the Holy Synod, and petitioned for leniency for the bishop, who had been made to suffer for no offence

*One of those who murdered Rasputin in 1917.

at all. The following were the Emperor's very words:

"I have nothing against Bishop Hermogen. I consider him to be an upright and truthful pastor, straightforward man capable of fearlessly and firmly defending the truth, steadfast in his service of upholding the purity and honour of the Orthodox Church. He will soon be allowed to return. But I was obliged to inflict a punishment on him for openly refusing to submit to my command."

Forgiveness, however, did not follow. Probably other influences proved stronger, and overruled the Emperor's feeble will.

The Emperor sent his A.D.C., Mandryka, to Tsaritsin to investigate Iliodor's case. In the course of the inquiry, Mandryka obtained a great deal of information concerning the criminal activities of Rasputin, and, being an honest man, decided on his return to St. Petersburg to acquaint the Emperor with all the facts. At an audience with the Emperor, at which the Empress was present, Mandryka, in a state of the most violent agitation (he actually fainted, and the Emperor himself brought him a glass of water), told the Emperor all he had learned at Tsaritsin of Rasputin's dealings with the *khlysty*. This affords further proof that the Emperor was not left in ignorance concerning Rasputin.

The public conscience was roused and clamoured for the truth. The whole case, with all the minutest details, appeared in the Press. Editors paid heavy fines to the censor, but continued to publish the articles. From whatever standpoint the affair was regarded, truth and justice remained on the side of Mgr. Hermogen.

Such was the powerful influence exercised by Rasputin and his circle even so far back as the end of 1911. How could the Russian public remain an indifferent spectator of all that was taking place? But who did anything to combat the growing and spreading evil?

CHAPTER II

P. A. Siolypin and Rasputin—Case of the Imperial Children's Nurse—Disgrace of the Metropolitan Anthony—Questions about Rasputin in the Duma—Conversation with the Dowager Empress.

I MUST here go back to an earlier date, namely, to the period between 1908 and 1910. I am bound to state that Rasputin's unexpected and steadily growing influence was viewed with considerable apprehendsion by P. A. Stolypin, who then held the posts of Prime Minister and Minister of the Interior. His anxiety was shared by P. P. Izvolsky and Lukianoff, both of whom consecutively occupied the post of High Procurator of the Holy Synod during Stolypin's Premiership. Stolypin had more than once drawn the attention of the Emperor to the disastrous consequences which might result from the proximity to the Imperial pair of an avowed sectarian. During the period between 1905 and 1909, however, Rasputin remained comparatively in the background, though slowly and surely paving the way for his future activities. Little by little, as he realized his growing power, this fanatic let himself go. His amorous exploits became more cynical and overt; the number of his victims increased, as also did the circle of disciples and women followers. In view of these circumstances the then Procurator of the Holy Synod, Lukianoff, with the approval of Stolypin, proceeded to investigate all the existing documentary evidence concerning Rasputin in order to cast a light on the hitherto mysterious and obscure personality of this adventurer. The truth was soon revealed in all its unattractive nakedness.

Lukianoff, who had all the secret archives of the Synod at his disposal, found no difficulty in deciphering the actual personality of the "great *starets*." These documents which the investigation brought to light were later studied by me. The results of the inquiry were sufficiently convincing.

Stolypin, on the strength of these documents, drew up a comprehensive report, which he presented to the Emperor. This step led to a somewhat unexpected result. Nicholas II listened attentively to the Premier, but came to no definite decision, and desired Stolypin to interview Rasputin and form his own judgment of the man. A statement to that effect was made to me by the Emperor himself on the occasion of my own report to him on the subject. Stolypin, too, told me of his interview with Rasputin. On entering the Premier's study, the *starets* immediately attempted to hypnotize him.

"He ran his pale eyes over me," said Stolypin, "mumbled mysterious and inarticulate words from the Scriptures, made strange movements with his hands, and I began to feel an indescribable loathing for this vermin sitting opposite me. Still, I did realize that the man possessed great hypnotic power, which was beginning to produce a fairly strong moral impression on me, though certainly one of repulsion. I pulled myself together and, addressing him roughly, told him that on the strength of the evidence in my possession I could annihilate him by prosecuting him as a sectarian. I then ordered him to leave St. Petersburg immediately of his own free will for his native village and never show his face here again."

This happened at the beginning of 1911. The Premier proved to be more powerful than the hypnotizer, who, realizing that matters were assuming a bad turn, suddenly disappeared from St. Petersburg and was not seen there for some time. Nevertheless, it is worthy of comment that by his hypnotic power Rasputin had been capable of producing an impression even on a man of such iron will as Stolypin. How much greater, then, would his ascendancy be over natures endowed with weaker nerves and less self-control!

In spite, however, of the Emperor's seeming acquiescence to Rasputin's exile, on which Stolypin had insisted, matters soon took a different turn. Soon after the departure of the *starets* to his native village, he was followed by A. A. Vyrubova, one of the ladies attached to the person of the Empress Alexandra Feodorovna*. Rasputin returned with her, not to St. Petersburg, but to Kieff, where the Imperial Family had arrived for the inauguration of the Zemstvo institutions in South-Western Russia. It should be remembered that Stolypin's position at Court was by now seriously compromised. The bill for the introduction of Zemstvos in South-Western Russia, which was passed by the Imperial Duma, was thrown out by the

---

* Mme. Vyrubova never occupied the official post of lady-in-waiting to the Empress. Her position at Court was that of an "intimate friend" of her Majesty.

CHAPTER II

Council of the Empire. Stolypin offered his resignation to the Emperor. A compromise was reached by which both the legislative chambers were prorogued for three days. The South-Western Provinces Zemstvos Act, as passed by the Imperial Duma, was passed by decree on the strength of Article 87 of the Fundamental Laws, and Stolypin withdrew his resignation. The anger of the members of the Council of the Empire knew no bounds, and a violent agitation against the Premier was started in Court circles. It was rumoured that the Rasputin faction, which was already in existence, took an active part in this campaign. Whether these rumours were true or not, the fact of Madame Vyrubova's journey to Pokrovskoe with the obvious purpose of bringing back Rasputin appeared to corroborate them. It was definitely asserted at the time that Rasputin had already succeeded in persuading the Imperial pair of the beneficent effect of his presence at Court, which would preserve them, and especially the little Tsarevitch, from any possible harm. The mystically inclined Empress, whose love and constant fear for her son almost bordered on distraction, was completely subjugated by the suggestions of the astute hypnotizer. She was firmly persuaded that it was her duty to take every precaution for guarding the safety and welfare of her adored son, and became convinced of the necessity of Rasputin's constant presence in Kieff during the numerous ceremonies and public functions at which the Imperial pair were to appear. At all events Rasputin was brought to Kieff by Madame Vyrubova, and later followed the Imperial Family to Livadia, in the Crimea. He did not live at Livadia itself, but at the Hotel Edinburgh at Yalta, under the assumed name of Nikonoff. As soon as the Prefect of Yalta, General Dumbadze, a bluff and honest soldier, heard of this, he immediately expelled Nikonoff-Rasputin from the town, without considering the danger to his own career. When the Imperial Family returned to St. Petersburg Rasputin was already there, and was very, soon reinstated in his former position at Court. The apparent victory won by Stolypin and the Procurator Lukianoff had been nothing but a temporary concession to public opinion, and things soon resumed their ordinary course.

In the midst of the Kieff celebrations Stolypin was treacherously assassinated during a gala performance at the theatre. V. N. Kokovtzeff was appointed Prime Minister. Lukianoff, realizing that he would never retain his post without Stolypin, resigned, and was replaced by V. K. Sabler, a staunch supporter of Rasputin. It was during his tenure of office that the incidents described in the previous chapter, which resulted in the disgrace of Bishop Hermogen and the monk Iliodor, occurred in the Holy Synod.

Emboldened by such a series of political victories, Rasputin gave vent to his instincts.

It became known that he had seduced the nurse of the Imperial children, formerly an inmate of the Imperial Home for Foundlings. It came to my knowledge that the girl disclosed her secret to her confessor, and told him she had accompanied her seducer to the baths; later, realizing the gravity of her sin, she had confessed everything to the Empress, imploring her to renounce her faith in Rasputin and guard the children from the terrible influence of this "devil," as she called him. This nurse was shortly after pronounced to be suffering from nervous disorder, and sent to the Caucasus for treatment. She there visited the Metropolitan Anthony, who was taking a water cure at Kislovodsk, told him all, and after describing in detail Rasputin's criminal doings in the Palace, entreated the Metropolitan to save the little Tsarevitch from the "clutches of the devil."

On his return to St. Petersburg at the beginning of 1911, Mgr. Anthony requested an audience of the Emperor, and presented him with a detailed account of the events which had come to his knowledge. The Emperor heard him with obvious displeasure, and remarked that the Imperial Family's private affairs did not concern the Metropolitan. Mgr. Anthony possessed sufficient strength of character to reply; "No, Sire, this is not merely a family affair, but the affair of all Russia. The Tsarevitch is not only your son, but our future Sovereign, and belongs to all Russia." And when the Emperor silenced him a second time by declaring he would permit no one to interfere with what was going on within the Palace, Mgr. Anthony, overcome by emotion, replied: "Sire, I obey your command; but I may be permitted to think that the Tsar of Russia ought to live in a palace of crystal, where his subjects can see him."

The Emperor bade the Metropolitan a curt farewell. Soon after Mgr, Anthony had a nervous stroke, from the effects of which he never recovered.

Meanwhile, Rasputin's influence was visibly increasing, as was also the number of his adherents. Appeals and applications for help

CHAPTER II

were addressed to him from all sides. He now had a staff of secretaries; like a person of high rank he received at certain hours and was even difficult of access. Nevertheless, people came to him from far and near, even from the provinces, with all manner of possible and impossible requests, with a firm belief in the power of the "holy *starets*." Rasputin himself apparently shared this belief. At any rate, Stolypin, and after him other leading statesmen, began to receive from Rasputin illiterately written notes, couched in peremptory terms, and addressing his correspondent as "thou," with orders to "help so and so," or "grant so and so's request," because "I know him, he is a good man."

These importunities, I regret to say, seldom met with a refusal. I myself once received a similar note, which of course I ignored, and after certain drastic steps on my part the attempt was never repeated.

Owing to the privileged position which he enjoyed, Rasputin soon became the centre of groups of business men of shady character and doubtful reputation, who hoped to "do good business" with the help of the *starets*. And what is more, there was sufficient evidence that they succeeded. The Imperial Duma, of course, could not remain indifferent to all that was said about the political significance of the growing scandal. There was a feeling of great apprehension among its members. But of its very nature the Duma was, to a certain extent, powerless to take any steps to calm public opinion. Many members feared an open avowal on the part of the Duma of the fact that an adventurer and a *khlyst* had assumed the exclusive role of the Emperor's counsellor and wielded such power as to necessitate the intervention of the legislative assembly. Unfortunately, such intervention could not in the end be avoided. As yet the members of the Duma refrained from direct action in the matter.

There would have been no particular cause for alarm if it had only been a question of the Empress Alexandra Feodorovna's infatuation for this man's imaginary gift of prophecy and hypnotic power, which alleviated her nervous complaint and allayed her fears for the safety of her family, particularly for the life of the Tsarevitch. But once Rasputin had gained the complete confidence of the Imperial Family, he proceeded to organize a closely united group of confederates—or rather, it was organized for him by others. This intimate circle, which began by pursuing its own private interests, soon transferred its activities to wider spheres, first interfering in

Church matters and finally in affairs of State, removing popular statesmen and replacing them by its own nominees. The Heir Apparent, too, was growing up. Rasputin's interference in the private family life of the Emperor was common knowledge, and the fear that Rasputin's sectarian teachings might have a profound impression on the child's receptive mind, and that the young Heir to the Throne would be alienated from the Orthodox Church, was, therefore, not without foundation. Moreover, the fanatical ideas of this pervert might gradually cloud the boy's spiritual outlook with an unhealthy mysticism, so that he would grow up nervously high-strung and devoid of will-power and self-control. Lastly, the mere fact of the close proximity to the Emperor's Throne of a debauched, illiterate and immoral peasant, the fame of whose disgusting adventures had spread far and wide, was in itself sufficient to undermine and uproot all the respect and reverence due to the Crown.

Dark rumours were current that this was actually the plan of those who inspired Rasputin's group of followers, some of whom were alleged to be acting on directions emanating from foreign countries. At any rate, when I was collecting material for an impending report to the Emperor, I received some foreign Press cuttings. According to these, the Masonic Congress held in Brussels in 1909 or 1910 had, among other things, discussed the question whether Rasputin was a convenient tool for spreading in Russia the slogans of the Order, and whether under his destructive influence the dynasty could last for more than two years. I fully realized, therefore, that taking into account the general state of public opinion, I, as President of the Imperial Duma, would not be in a position to avoid presenting to the Emperor a detailed report on the situation. Events, however, moved quicker than I had anticipated.

At the time of the sensational affair of Bishop Hermogen and the monk Iliodor, which occurred towards the end of 1910, a M. Novoseloff, a lecturer at the Moscow Theological Academy and an expert on sectarianism, published a pamphlet containing detailed and documentary evidence exposing Rasputin as belonging to the sect of the *khlysty*. In this pamphlet Novoseloff accused the highest dignitaries of the Church of tolerating sectarianism. The pamphlet was immediately withdrawn from sale and confiscated by the police. The daily paper *Golos Moskvy*, in which a spirited article by the same author appeared, together with excerpts from the pamphlet,

CHAPTER II

was heavily fined by the censor, and copies containing the article were seized by the police. These measures of suppression, of course, produced exactly the opposite effect. There was a general rush for the pamphlet and the remaining copies of the *Golos Moskvy*, which fetched fabulous prices, and articles on Rasputin and the illegal confiscation of Novoseloff's book appeared in all the daily papers. Letters from Rasputin's former victims were openly published, as well as photographs of himself surrounded by his followers. The greater the zeal displayed by the police and the censor's committee, the more numerous became the articles, notwithstanding the heavy fines paid by the editors. The case of Bishop Hermogen had already aroused great excitement and apprehension in the Duma; the publication of the Novoseloff pamphlet, with the attendant scandal of its seizure by the police, merely added fuel to the fire. In view of these circumstances I resolved no longer to delay my request for an audience with the Emperor.

Quite unexpectedly, however, and without previously consulting me, a group of members of the Duma presented a written interpellation on the illegal action of the Government in confiscating the Novoseloff pamphlet and the number of the *Golos Moskvy*. By the order of procedure of the Imperial Duma I had not the right to disallow a debate on a question raised as urgent. As, however, the debate on the urgency of the interpellation would itself probably lead to an outburst in the Duma, I invited the various party leaders to a private conference on the subject, and endeavoured to persuade Gutchkoff, who was the first signatory of the interpellation, to postpone the motion in order to save the Crown from becoming the subject of a heated debate in the Duma. I felt that the time had not yet come for exposing all these events to the judgment of the nation, and considered such publicity to be premature. I urged that a wiser course would be to attempt, by means of a report by the President of the Duma, to demonstrate to the Tsar, on the strength of irrefutable evidence, the dangerous trend of events, and secure the banishment of the pernicious false teacher from the Court.

A. I. Gutchkoff replied that public feeling was running so high that, if the interpellation were dropped by the moderate parties, it would be taken up by the Socialists, whose tactics would only thicken the atmosphere instead of clearing it. On the other hand, if the interpellation were moved by the moderate parties, a compromise might be arrived at, and a scandal averted. Gutchkoff was of opinion that a debate on the present interpellation could be confined to the subject of Bishop Hermogen and the Novoseloff pamphlet, whereas otherwise the whole question would be brought up during the debate on the Synod Budget Estimates. Gutchkoff's opinion carried the day, and the question of the urgency of the interpellation was submitted to debate.

In justice to the Duma it should be said that the attitude of all the members was perfectly correct during the debate, which passed off without any unseemly demonstration. A. I. Gutchkoff and V. N. Lvoff spoke in favour of urgency, and the motion to that effect was carried unanimously.

The attitude of the Government towards this incident is worth mentioning. The post of Minister of the Interior was then occupied by A. A. Makaroff. When the interpellation on the seizure of the Novoseloff pamphlet was laid before the Duma, I wrote him a letter requesting that a copy of this pamphlet should be forwarded to me for perusal, to enable me to control the debate. Makaroff replied that he had no copies of the pamphlet at his disposal, neither did he see any reason, for circulating it. This reply made me exceedingly angry, and I resolved to call on the Minister myself. My visit obviously came as a surprise, for on being ushered into his study, I observed to my astonishment that several copies of the notorious pamphlet were lying on the Minister's desk. This proved that even such a perfectly honest man as Makaroff undoubtedly was nevertheless not entirely free from servility when it came to shielding Rasputin. After a stormy scene, I succeeded in securing a copy of the pamphlet. Here was another clear example of Rasputin's power: Government officials thought it necessary to shield him instead of devoting their energies to more important affairs of State.

Thanks to the interpellation in the Duma, the whole affair was brought to the public notice. The article from the *Golos Moskvy*, which led to the seizure of the paper, figured in the stenographic reports of the debate and was therefore reprinted in all the papers. This article, entitled "The Voice of an Orthodox Layman," and signed by Mikhail Novoseloff, editor and publisher of the review, the *Religious and Philosophical Library*, had appeared in No. 19 of the *Golos Moskvy* in the form of a "Letter to the Editor," and began with the words:

> "*Quo usque tandem!*". . . . Such is the cry of indignation escaping from the lips of all Orthodox men and women against that cunning

CHAPTER II

conspirator against our Holy Church, that fornicator of human souls and bodies—Gregory Rasputin, acting under the holy cover of that Church. "*Quo usque!*" —such are the words which, in anguish and bitterness of spirit, the sons of the Orthodox Church are compelled to address to the Synod, in view of the unheard-of tolerance exhibited towards the said Gregory Rasputin by the highest dignitaries of the Church. . . . How much longer will the Synod remain silent and inactive in the face of this shameful comedy, enacted for years before its very eyes? . . .

The letter ended with an "apology for its author's boldness," and the " respectful request to be allowed to produce before a supreme ecclesiastical court conclusive evidence proving the justice of the charge laid against the heretic seducer—Rasputin."

The appearance in the Press of the Novoseloff pamphlet, together with the interpellation to the Government concerning its confiscation, placed the whole case of Gregory Rasputin's activities and influence at Court on a documentary footing. No doubt whatever could now be entertained as to the truth of all the rumours and stories that were circulated about him. Now that an interpellation on the subject of Rasputin, based on circumstantial evidence, had been moved in the Duma, the Crown was faced with the necessity of deciding once and for all whether Rasputin was or was not to be. Everyone realized that the combat between Rasputin and Russia must be decided by the victory or the defeat of one of the opposing sides. But the forces were too unequal. On Rasputin's side was the Empress Alexandra Feodorovna, strong-willed, despotic, and exercising unbounded influence over the Emperor. She was supported by the Court clique, who knew what they wanted. On the other hand, indecision and fear of incurring the displeasure of highly-placed personages reigned in the opposing camp. Solidarity and singleness of purpose were lacking there, because none really cared for what ought to have been paramount in their thoughts—the good of Russia.

The Emperor was vacillating between the two and waiting for events which would force him to dismiss Rasputin, for in those days he was still dimly conscious of the true significance of what was passing, but he was entirely dominated by the stronger will of his consort. The whole burden of the struggle, therefore, fell upon the Imperial Duma. This gave certain circles an opportunity of accusing the Duma of revolutionary tendencies, while, as a matter of fact, the

Duma was fighting for the inviolability of the Emperor's prestige.

After the interpellation in the Duma, the Prime Minister, Kokovtzeff, was summoned to the Emperor. He told me afterwards that the Empress had insisted on the dissolution of the Duma. If before the interpellation I had entertained any doubts as to the expediency of presenting a report to the Emperor, my mind was now firmly made up, and I resolved to request an audience, in the course of which I determined that I would speak to the Emperor about Rasputin.

A whole month was spent in collecting evidence. I was assisted by Gutchkoff, Badmaieff, Rodionoff and Count Sumarokoff, who was in touch with agents abroad. Prince Yusupoff kept us informed of what was going on at the Palace. Badmaieff supplied us with data concerning Mgr. Hermogen and Iliodor and their connection with Rasputin. Rodionoff produced the original letter of the Empress Alexandra Feodorovna to Rasputin, which had been wrested from him by Iliodor during the scuffle in the corridor of Bishop Hermogen's house, when the *starets* had been roughly handled by Iliodor and the lay brother. Rodionoff also produced letters written by the Grand Duchesses Olga, Tatiana and Marie.

In February, 1912, I learnt through Prince Yusupoff that the Dowager Empress Marie Feodorovna was greatly perturbed by all she had heard of Rasputin. Prince Yusupoff was of opinion that I ought to wait on her and acquaint her with the details of the case.

Soon afterwards I received a call from General Oseroff, general in waiting on her Majesty, who transmitted to me the desire of the Dowager Empress to see me and learn from me all there was to hear. Before this, the Empress had summoned Prince Yusupoff, questioned him about me as a man, and asked him whether the President of the Duma was in a position to tell her all there was to know. Prince Yusupoff replied: "He is the only man, thoroughly informed, on whom you may rely to tell you nothing but the absolute truth."

The whole Imperial Family awaited my audience with the Emperor in a state of keen excitement: would I dare speak of Rasputin? and what would be the impression produced by my report? The Grand Duchess Olga Alexandrovna told Prince V. M. Volkonsky that she very much hoped the President of the Duma would speak to the Emperor about Rasputin.

A few days before the date fixed for my audience with the Em-

CHAPTER II

peror, I received a telephone message bidding me wait on the Empress Marie Feodorovna next morning at eleven o'clock. Collecting all the documents in my possession I started for the Dowager Empress's Palace. I was immediately introduced into her boudoir, where the Empress was awaiting me. She received me with the words: "You are of course aware of the object of our interview? First of all, however, I wish you to explain to me the cause and meaning of the interpellation. Were not its actual motives of a revolutionary character, and, if so, why did you not prevent it?"

I explained to the Empress that though I was myself opposed to the interpellation, I nevertheless resolutely denied its having been inspired by revolutionary motives. On the contrary, it had been a necessary step for the calming of public opinion; the rumours had gone too far, and the attitude of the Government merely served to increase the general irritation.

The Empress then desired to see all the documents in my possession, I read her extracts from the Novoseloff pamphlet and told her all I knew. She informed me that she herself had only recently learnt the whole story. She had certainly heard of Rasputin before, but had never attached much importance to his existence.

"I only learnt all these details a few days ago from a person of my acquaintance, and I was absolutely aghast. It is terrible, terrible," she repeated. "I know, too, that there is a letter from Iliodor to Hermogen"—(a copy of this denunciatory letter was actually in my possession)—"and a letter from the Empress to that dreadful man. Show it me," she added.

I replied that I was unable to do so. At first she insisted on having it, but finally, laying her hand on mine, said:

"You will destroy it, will you not?"

"Yes, your Majesty, I will destroy it."

"That is good."

This letter is still in my possession. I soon learnt that distorted copies of it were being circulated and deemed it wiser to preserve the original.

The Dowager Empress said to me:

"I hear that you intend to speak to the Emperor about Rasputin. Do not do so. Unfortunately he will not believe you, and it will cause him much pain. He is so pure of heart that he does not believe in evil."

I replied that to my great sorrow I could not leave such an important matter unmentioned in my report. It was my duty to speak and inform my Sovereign. The affair was too serious, and the consequences might be too dangerous.

"Have matters gone so far then?"

"Madam, it is a question of the dynasty. We Monarchists can no longer keep silent. It is a great joy to me, your Majesty, that you have given me the pleasure of seeing you and speaking frankly on the subject. You see me now profoundly perturbed by the thought of the responsibility which rests upon me. I most humbly ask you to give me your blessing."

She raised her gentle eyes to my face, and laying her hand on mine, said in a voice trembling with emotion':

"God bless you."

I was on the point of leaving the room, when the Empress made a few steps forward and added Softly:

"Do not hurt him too much."

I subsequently heard from Prince Yusupoff that after my audience the Empress Marie Feodorovna visited the Emperor and declared to him, "Either I am here or Rasputin," intimating her intention of departing if Rasputin remained.

On my return home I had calls from Prince V. M. Volkonsky, and Prince F. F. and Princess Z. N. Yusupoff. The Prince said to me: "We have overcome a big intrigue."

It appeared that the Court clique had endeavoured to prevent my interview with the Dowager Empress, and when this failed, V. N. Kokovtzeff (the Prime Minister) visited the Empress Marie Feodorovna in order to ask her to dissuade me from speaking of Rasputin to the Emperor. Meanwhile, everything was ready for the report, and I presented m y request for an audience to the Emperor.

CHAPTER III

Audience of the Emperor concerning Rasputin—Documents on the Case—Interview with the Emperor's Confessor—The Emperor's Refusal to grant an Audience.

I PERFECTLY realized the relative uselessness of a report presented solely by the President of the Duma, for it could not possess sufficient weight for the Emperor to adopt, on the strength of it, an irreconcilable attitude towards Rasputin, and defy any efforts made in defence of the favourite. My idea was to prevail on the Prime Minister and the Metropolitan presiding in the Holy Synod to present with me a joint report to the Emperor. Such a step would surely demonstrate to him that it was not the Duma alone, but all sections of the nation, that realized and feared the depth of the abyss into which Russia and the Emperor were being precipitated through Rasputin's influence.

Unfortunately my efforts were not successful. For one reason or another the persons mentioned above demurred from supporting me, and I was therefore compelled to act alone, thus taking upon myself the full responsibility for the ultimate consequences of my decision.

The Emperor sent for me at six o'clock on February 26. That morning my wife and I drove to the Kazan Cathedral, where we heard a special service of intercession. My report to the Emperor lasted nearly two hours. I first spoke of current affairs, touching also on conditions in the Artillery Department, administered by the Grand Duke Sergei Mikhailovitch[*], and referring to the doubtful safety of the Caucasus under the equally doubtful administration of Count Vorontzoff-Dashkoff. I then broached the principal subject of my report.

I said:

"Your Majesty, my report to-day extends to matters far beyond its usual scope. Granted the gracious permission of your Majesty, I in-

[*] Second cousin to the Emperor.

tend to lay before you the detailed and documentary evidence concerning a process of destruction which has begun, pregnant with the most disastrous consequences to all concerned . . ."

The Tsar glanced at me in some astonishment.

I continued:

"I refer to the *starets* Rasputin and to the inadmissible fact of his presence at your Majesty's Court. I beseech you, Sire, as your Majesty's most loyal subject—will it be your pleasure to hear me to the end?—if not, say but one word, and I will remain silent."

With bowed head and averted gaze the Tsar murmured in a low voice:

"Speak."

"Your Majesty, the presence of this man of more than tarnished reputation in the most intimate Court circles is an event unparalleled in the history of the Russian Monarchy. The entire nation, all circles of the community, view with profound apprehension the influence this man exercises on the affairs of Church and State. The whole machinery of government, from Ministers to the inferior ranks of the secret police, is mobilized for the purpose of shielding this adventurer. Rasputin is a tool in the hands of Russia's enemies; he is their instrument for undermining the Church and the Monarchy itself. No revolutionary propaganda could achieve as much as Rasputin's mere presence at Court. Everyone fears his intimacy with the Imperial Family. Public feeling is running very high."

"But why such attacks on Rasputin.?" interrupted the Tsar; "why is he considered so harmful?"

"Your Majesty, the fact that Rasputin has created a split in the Synod has become common knowledge, both by hearsay and through the Press. Everyone knows that bishops are being transferred from their posts owing to his intrigues."

"Which bishops?" asked the Tsar.

"The case of Mgr. Hermogen aroused universal indignation, as being an undeserved insult to a prelate. Mgr. Hermogen has many supporters. I have received a petition signed by ten thousand people, begging me to intercede on his behalf before your Majesty."

"I think Mgr. Hermogen is a good man," said the Tsar; "he will soon be permitted to return. Still, I could not allow him to remain unpunished for his flagrant disobedience to my Imperial order."

"Your Majesty, according to the canons of the Church, an episcopal court can alone sit in judgment on a bishop. Mgr. Hermogen

CHAPTER III

was sentenced to banishment on the sole charge of the High Procurator and on the strength of his personal report. It was an infringement of the canons of the Church."

The Tsar listened in silence.

"The case of Iliodor, too, has made a most painful impression on the people. After the inquiry held by order of your Majesty, his trial was cancelled a year ago. Now, without trial, he is confined in the Floristchevo hermitage—and this was done after he had dared to speak openly against Rasputin. These two were not the only ones to suffer. Bishop Feofan was deprived of his office of the Empress's confessor and removed to Simferopol. Bishop Anthony of Tobolsk, who was the first to inform the Synod of Rasputin's adherence to the *khlysty* sect and to demand his trial, was transferred to Tver. Anyone who dares utter a word against Rasputin is persecuted by the Synod. Such a state of affairs cannot be tolerated, your Majesty. How can Orthodox Christians stand by in silence, when Orthodoxy is being defiled and destroyed by the pernicious activities of this rogue? One may well understand the general outburst of indignation which followed the disclosure that Rasputin was a *khlyst.*"

"What proofs have you?"

"The police discovered that he went to the baths with women. That is one of the peculiarities of their religious practices."

"What of that? It is merely a custom among common people."

"No, your Majesty, there is no such custom. Perhaps husbands and wives go together, but what we have here is sheer debauchery. Permit me, in the first place, to read you letters from those of his victims who fell into the trap and repented afterwards. Here is a letter from a priest in Siberia, addressed to several members of the Duma [I did not like to mention Gutchkoff by name], and imploring them to inform the authorities of Rasputin's exploits, his immoral conduct and the rumours he circulated concerning his position and influence at the Imperial Court." (This letter I read out from end to end.)

"Here is another letter written by a lady confessing having been seduced and morally corrupted by Rasputin. She afterwards recoiled from him and repented of her fall . . . and met him one evening coming out of the baths in the company of her two daughters. . . The wife of an engineer, Mme. L., also fell a victim to Rasputin's teachings. She became insane and is now in a lunatic asylum. Will your Majesty order this evidence to be verified?"

"I believe you," said the Tsar.

I read him other letters and extracts from Novoseloff's pamphlet; I laid stress on the painful impression which the prohibition of any publication in the Press concerning Rasputin had made on the public mind. He did not belong to the category of persons of whom it was forbidden to write. He occupied no exalted position, neither was he a member of the Imperial Family. Ministers of the Crown, the presidents of the Imperial Duma or of the Council of the Empire were freely criticized in the Press. Why, then, this enforced silence concerning Rasputin? Such a policy naturally led the public to suppose him to be intimately connected with the Imperial Family.

"But why do you assume him to be a Khlyst?"

"Your Majesty should read Novoseloff's pamphlet. He made a special investigation of the case. He states that Rasputin was prosecuted on the charge of belonging to that sect, but that for some reason or other the prosecution was stopped. Moreover, as has been ascertained, meetings of Rasputin's followers were held at Sazonoff's flat, where Rasputin himself was staying at the time. Permit me to show you a foreign newspaper cutting, in which it is said that at the Masonic Congress in Brussels Rasputin was mentioned as being a useful instrument for carrying out the freemasons' policy in Russia. The whole intrigue, with all its subsequent developments, is as clear as daylight. It is not the fate of the dynasty and the prestige of the Imperial Family alone which are involved,"

"How?" inquired the Tsar, greatly agitated.

"Your Majesty, there is no serious or responsible person in charge of the Tsarevitch; he is entrusted to the care of a country yokel, Derevenko, who may be a very good man, but is a simple peasant. Ignorant folk are naturally inclined towards mysticism. What if anything were to happen to the Heir Apparent? This is a subject of profound anxiety to all. . . . Such a charming child, so universally beloved."

The Tsar was evidently struggling to overcome his emotion. He nervously lit one cigarette after another, then threw them down again.

I here decided to approach the subject from another side and to persuade the Emperor that Rasputin was a sycophant. I produced a photograph of the *starets* wearing a pectoral cross.

"Your Majesty knows Rasputin is not in holy orders; yet here he is depicted as a priest."

CHAPTER III

The Tsar replied:

"Yes, this is really going too far. He has no right to wear a pectoral cross."

"It is blasphemy, your Majesty. He is an illiterate peasant and not entitled to wear a cowl, which appertains to the priesthood. Here is another photograph. It is a '*khlysty* ship.' This was reproduced in the *Ogonek** and circulated throughout the country. Here is Rasputin surrounded by young girls; there are also boys with him in their midst. Here he is with two young men. They are carrying a placard inscribed with *khlysty* texts, and he is holding a *khlysty* ikon of Our Lady in his hands. It is a 'ship' bearing its inmates towards fornication."

"What is that?" asked the Tsar.

"Read Novoseloff's pamphlet, which I will submit to you. Here is another photograph of Rasputin with two women, and inscribed: 'The Way to Salvation.' . . ."

"The suppression of any mention of Rasputin in the Press encourages the idea that the *khlysty* enjoy the patronage of the Tsar. What if a war broke out? Where is the prestige of the Tsar's name and authority? A number of persons closely connected with the Court are openly designated as Rasputin's followers. Rumours are current that the highest society is contaminated with his sectarian teachings. Thus a slur is cast on society and on the Court. In defiance of the censorship all the rumours and stories about Rasputin are being feverishly seized upon and reproduced by the provincial Press."

"Have you read Stolypin's report?" asked the Emperor.

"No, I have heard it spoken of, but never read it."

"I rejected it," said the Tsar.

"It is a pity," I replied, "for all this would not have happened. Your Majesty, you witness my profound emotion. It pains me exceedingly to be obliged to speak the cruel truth. But I dared not keep silent, I had no right to conceal from my Sovereign the menacing state of affairs with their possible terrible consequences. I believe that God has placed me as a mediator between the Tsar and the representatives of the people summoned together by his august command. It is my duty, Sire, as a Russian and as your Majesty's loyal subject to warn you that our enemies are striving to undermine the Throne and the Church and to cast a shadow on the beloved

* An illustrated weekly.

name of the Tsar. I always bear in mind the text of the oath of allegiance. In the name of all you hold sacred, in the name of Russia, and for the sake of the welfare and happiness of your successors—I implore you to banish this villainous rogue, and so dispel the fears which assail those who are loyal to the Throne."

"He is not here now," replied the Tsar in a low voice.

"Will you authorize me to tell everyone that he will not return?"

The Tsar remained silent for a while, then said:

"No, I cannot promise you that. Nevertheless, I fully believe all you have told me."

"Do you believe, Sire, in the absolute loyalty and trustworthiness of all those who raised the question in the Duma. Will you believe that they were inspired by the same motives which prompted my coming to lay the whole case before you?"

"I felt the sincerity of your report, and I trust the Duma because I trust you."

I was anxious to learn whether the Emperor was pleased with my report. I continued:

"Your Majesty, I came here fully prepared to pay the penalty if I had the misfortune to incur your Majesty's displeasure. If I have overstepped my rights, you have but to say a word, and I will resign my office of President of the Imperial Duma. I sought but to do my duty in laying the whole matter before you. In view of the excitement raised by this affair in the Duma, I did not think it right to conceal it from my Sovereign."

"I thank you. You acted as an honourable man and a loyal subject."

"Your Majesty, may I, as a special favour, be granted the happiness of being presented to his Imperial Highness the Tsarevitch?"

"Do you not know him?"

"I have never seen him."

The Tsar sent for the Tsarevitch, to whom I introduced myself as "the biggest and fattest man in Russia," at which the boy broke out into a merry laugh. On my asking him whether yesterday's collection on behalf of an "Ear of Corn" had been successful, the child's singularly attractive face lit up with pleasure, as he answered quickly: "Oh yes! I alone collected fifty roubles. That is a lot, you know."

The Tsar added, smiling tenderly at his son: "He would not part with his collecting box all day."

Then the Tsar rose from his chair, and holding out his hand to

CHAPTER III

me, said: "*Do svidaniya*, Mikhail Vladimirovitch."*

As I left the room I heard the Tsarevitch's loud whisper: "Who's that?" and the Tsar's answer: "The President of the Duma."

The little Tsarevitch ran after me into the hall, and all the time stood peeping at me through the glass door.

"Don't catch cold," I said to him; "it is draughty here."

"No, no, it's all right!" he shouted back.

The smiling Derevenko† appeared on the scene. I scrutinized the faces of the footmen, soldiers and Cossacks standing at attention in the hall. How lovingly they all looked at the Tsarevitch!

A typical glimpse into the state of mind prevailing among the Court servants was given me at my departure. On seeing me to the door the Emperor's head valet, Tchemoduroff, said to me: "Come more often, your Excellency. So few people visit us, and we never hear any news."

I was deeply moved by the Emperor's mark of confidence in me and the patience with which he had heard me to the end. And this was in spite of the warnings received by me from all sides: he will not listen to you, he will be angry, he will assume his stubborn mood, etc.

That same evening I had a curious conversation by telephone with A. S. Taneieff‡, who was at the head of his Majesty's Private Chancellery. He called me up at my flat.

"Mikhail Vladimirovitch, would you mind telling me what was it two members of the Duma wished to see me about?"

"I can't tell you, because I know nothing about it."

"I am afraid it might have something to do with Gregory."

"What Gregory?"

"Oh, you know... Gregory .."—stammer—" Rasputin..."

"What connection is there between you and Rasputin?"

"Well, you know... I thought..."

"I am glad you admit there is a reason for speaking to you about this disgusting sectarian. Let me tell you that if you are an honourable man you ought to turn him out of Tsarskoe... And you know how."

"I know nothing at all."

"Yes, you do. And if you fail in your duty as an honest man, all

---
* (from previous page) *Au revoir.*
† The sailor attached to the Heir Apparent.
‡ Mme. Vyrubova's father.

Russia will hate you for it. As it is, your name is everywhere coupled with that of Russia's curse—Rasputin."

(Inarticulate murmurs) . . . "*Au revoir.*"

That same evening I drove to the Duma, where I was immediately surrounded by groups of deputies. I gave them a brief account of the interview and of the gracious reception accorded me by the Emperor. My narrative produced a most excellent impression on all. I gave a verbatim account of the whole interview to my most intimate associates.

On the morning of February 28, General V. N. Dediulin, Commandant of the Imperial Palace and A.D.C. to the Emperor, telephoned to me from Tsarskoe Selo, asking me to call on him at his flat in town. General Dediulin was an old schoolfellow of mine and a personal friend; hence the conversation which ensued was of an intimate nature. Dediulin imparted to me the following news.

"After your visit to Tsarskoe Selo," he said to me, "it became known that the Tsar had scarcely touched his dinner and remained all the time extremely taciturn and thoughtful. When I reported to him next morning I took the liberty of saying to him: 'Your Majesty, you have received Rodzianko. It appears he has fatigued you very much.' "

The Tsar replied: "No, I am not in the least tired. I see that Rodzianko is a loyal subject who is not afraid of speaking the truth. He told me much that I knew nothing about. You are an old schoolfellow of his. Tell him, from me, to investigate Rasputin's case. Let him take from the Synod all the secret documents concerning Rasputin, thoroughly examine them and report the results to me. But tell him to keep the whole affair secret for the time being."

I was astounded by the news. That same evening I invited V. I. Karpoff, a member of the Council of the Empire, and the members of the Duma Kamensky, Shubinsky and Gutchkoff, to come to see me. We discussed far into the night the best means for proceeding with the mission entrusted to me by the Tsar. Next day I asked M. Damansky, Assistant High Procurator of the Synod, to come to the Duma and bring me the secret *dossier* on Rasputin's case. Damansky arrived. In order the better to draw him out, I decided to feign complete ignorance. This manoeuvre met with complete success. My informant divulged all I wished to know. In his endeavours to persuade me of Gregory's holiness and purity, he declared that the

CHAPTER III

starets was honoured and respected by many highly placed persons, who enjoyed and found edification in his conversations. Damansky revealed many names and confirmed much evidence already familiar to me through other channels. He said that Rasputin lodged with the Sazonoffs, a very respectable family with whom he, Damansky, was on intimate terms; that the house was visited by M. Taneieff, Gentleman Usher to the Emperor, by the wife of General Orloff, Countess Witte[*], "such a universally respected man" as Bishop Barnabas, and many others. I expressed my astonishment at all this, and nodded in assent.

All this time Damansky kept a firm hold on the file of documents in his hands, and kept repeatedly assuring me the case was in itself too trivial to be worth looking into. While dwelling on the virtues of the *starets*, Damansky professed profound indignation at the gossip and calumny of which he was the subject. "He is accused of being a *khlyst* and a libertine. Some people go so far as to allege an intimacy between him and the Empress Alexandra Feodorovna . . ."

Here I dropped the mask, struck the table with my fist, drew myself up to my full height[†], and looking as ferocious as I could, shouted at the top of my voice so as to be heard in the adjoining room:

"Are you mad, sir? How dare you utter such abominations in my presence? You forget of whom and to whom you are speaking! I refuse to listen to you any further."

My outburst was so unexpected that he turned pale, cowered and hastened to excuse himself. The object of his mean behaviour was obvious. He imagined me to be his dupe, and hoped to lead me on to talk scandal with the intention of reporting it in certain quarters afterwards. He expected to convince me by his explanations, and prevent my claiming the documents. He was, therefore, completely taken aback when I wrenched the file from his grasp, locked it up in my desk and, placing the key in my pocket, declared: "By order of his Majesty the Emperor, I shall examine these documents, and inform you later of the results."

Having obtained possession of these important documents, I at once ordered the clerical staff of the Duma and the sworn-in lady typists to make complete copies of them. With the aid of J. V. Glinka,

[*] Wife of the ex Prime Minister.
[†] M. Rodzianko was an exceptionally tall and powerful man.

the head of the Duma clerks' office, I myself proceeded to draft a plan of procedure for the task in hand—a task demanding great circumspection in view of the extremely delicate nature of the case.

The very next day Damansky telephoned asking for a private interview at my flat. Suspecting a trap, I replied that I did not give private interviews on matters of State; I therefore requested his presence in my room at the Duma at three o'clock that afternoon, and to avoid any further explanations I immediately hung up the receiver.

On my arrival at the Duma I found Damansky waiting for me. To my astonishment he was accompanied by the Archpriest Alexander Vasilieff, the religious teacher of the Imperial children. The reverend father's presence at the Duma was rather surprising. I at once realized that some plan for putting pressure on me was afoot, and decided to separate them. They were, therefore, shown into different rooms.

First I tackled Damansky. He explained that he was entrusted with a mission to reclaim from me the file containing the documents on Rasputin. I expressed surprise at this request, and replied that the documents had been placed in my keeping by the Emperor's orders, and that their surrender could only be claimed by a similar act, i.e., by an Imperial order transmitted either verbally through an adjutant-general or a Secretary of State, or by written decree. At this juncture, looking somewhat perturbed and agitated, and lowering his voice, Damansky explained that though he did not bear an order from the Emperor, the demand came from a very exalted person.

"Who was it?" I asked. "Sabler?"

Damansky made a deprecating gesture.

"No, someone much more highly placed," he replied.

"Who was it, then?" I repeated, putting on an expression of astonishment.

"The Empress Alexandra Feodorovna."

"If that is the case, will you kindly inform her Majesty that she is as much a subject of her August Consort as myself, and that it is the duty of us both to obey his commands. I am, therefore, not in a position to comply with her wishes."

"What!" exclaimed Damansky, "must I really tell her that? But it is her desire."

"I am very sorry," I replied, "but nevertheless I am unable to accede to it." And to prevent further insistence on Damansky's part,

CHAPTER III

I ended the interview.

I then passed on to Father Vasilieff. He was instructed by the Empress Alexandra Feodorovna, he said, to communicate to me his opinion on the *starets*.

"He really is a God-fearing and pious man, absolutely harmless and even rather useful to the Imperial Family," said Father Vasilieff.

"What part does he play in the intimate life of the Imperial Family, particularly in relation to the children?"

"He has talks with them about God and about religion . . ."

At these words I flew into a passion.

"You dare tell me that! You, an Orthodox priest and the religious teacher of the Tsar's children! You tolerate that a stupid, ignorant *mouzhik* should speak to them on matters of faith; you tolerate his pernicious hypnotic influence on their pure childish souls? You are a witness to the part played by this sectarian *khlyst* in the family life of the Tsar, and yet you keep silent. By countenancing this man's criminal activities you betray your holy office and your oath of allegiance. You know everything that is going on, and yet out of cowardice and servility you prefer to hold your tongue when, as a servant of the Church of God, your duty bids you raise your voice in defence of our faith. By your criminal connivance you, too, become a sectarian and a participator in the devilish conspiracy engineered by the enemies of Russia and of the Tsar, who aim at defiling the Throne and the Orthodox Church."

The unfortunate priest, completely taken aback by my vehemence, grew pale and murmured tremulously:

"No one has ever spoken to me like this before. You have opened my eyes. Tell me what I am to do."

"Go and tell the Empress from me, that if she does not want to see the ruin of her husband and son and the collapse of the Throne, she must dismiss this obscene *khlyst* from her presence for ever. The position is serious. No revolutionary propaganda could inflict greater injury on the Monarchy nor degrade the prestige of the Imperial House as does Rasputin's presence at the Palace. If you continue to be silent and fail to disclose the truth—then the cross you wear upon your breast will brand your very heart and soul."

He told Prince Volkonsky afterwards: "When I left the President I was trembling all over, and fully realized the force and truth of his arguments."

Father Vasilieff, however, as I was subsequently informed, gave a completely distorted account of our interview to the Empress, thereby merely strengthening the disfavour in which she already held me. He continued to encourage her infatuation for Rasputin, and persevered in his ambiguous behaviour.

From Gutchkoff I learnt that my prolonged interview with the Tsar had seriously agitated all Rasputin's followers, and that they had decided to recall him to St. Petersburg.

Princess Z. N. Yusupoff informed us by telephone that the Empress was so distressed by Rasputin's dismissal that she took to her bed. It is interesting to recall that after the questions on Rasputin in the Duma, the Empress wrote a despairing letter of eight pages to Princess Yusupoff complaining of the unjust attacks and calumnies of which they were the object. "No one loves us," wrote the Empress; "everyone is trying to do us harm. This interpellation was a revolutionary act."

The Empress's complaints of their tragic position were so bitter that Princess Yusupoff felt sorry for her and sent a telephone message that she would come to see her next day. Owing, however, in all probability to some intrigue on the part of Mme. Vyrubova, Princess Yusupoff was informed that the Empress was indisposed and unable to receive her.

It was not till March 9, 1912, that Princess Yusupoff was admitted to see the Empress. Her visit took place after Gutchkoff's speech in the Duma on the Synod estimates, in which he made a further allusion to Rasputin. Princess Yusupoff spoke very gravely on the subject and tried to impress the Empress with the same arguments I had submitted to the Tsar, but in vain. The Empress remained obdurate, working herself into a state of great indignation and excitement. She expressed her displeasure at the tenor of my report to the Tsar, and was particularly angry at my refusal to return the Rasputin documents.

"What right had he to keep them and refuse their surrender?" the Empress repeated.

Princess Yusupoff tried to persuade her to believe the word of the President of the Duma.

"He is an honest and truthful man," she said.

"No, no! You don't know what he told Father Vasilieff! Hanging is too good for men like Rodzianko and Gutchkoff!"

"How can you say such things?" the Princess exclaimed indignantly. "You ought to thank God for sending you honest men who

CHAPTER III

speak the truth to the Tsar. Rasputin must be turned out. He is a *khlyst* who abuses your confidence."

"No, no, that is a calumny. He is a holy man."

A thorough examination of the documents produced by Damansky revealed the history of Rasputin in all its sordid reality.

The first time that Rasputin was arraigned as a *khlyst* was as far back as 1902, when, on the strength of an official intimation from the parish priest of Pokrovskoe, the head of the district police denounced him to the Governor of Tobolsk. The Governor handed over the case to the local bishop, Mgr. Anthony, who ordered one of the diocesan missionaries to carry out a detailed investigation. The latter, being an energetic man, made a domiciliary search in Rasputin's house, carried off various material proofs, and brought to light numerous obscure facts all tending to prove irrefutably Rasputin's adherence to the *khlysty* sect. A detailed report on the case, supported by important circumstantial evidence, was presented to the bishop. Some of the details mentioned in the report were of so obscene and revolting a nature, that it was impossible to read them without a feeling of repulsion.

On receiving the report Mgr. Anthony handed it over for study to an expert on sectarianism, a M. Berezkin, inspector of the Theological Seminary at Tobolsk. The affair dragged on indefinitely. Rasputin, meanwhile, had made his way to St. Petersburg, where, as I have previously described, he gradually wormed himself into the confidence of highly-placed persons and was introduced at the Palace.

A survey of the very thorough and conscientious investigation carried out by Berezkin, confirmed, moreover, by the evidence of numerous witnesses, letters and references to the teachings of the *khlysty*, revealed beyond the shadow of a doubt Rasputin's adherence to that disgusting sect. He was, moreover, a *khlyst* of a superior order, a clever propagandist and a pernicious corrupter of souls of simple-minded Orthodox folk. The evidence in hand established beyond doubt his connection with many of the *khlysty* "prophets," among whom he occupied a more or less important position.

In his report to the Bishop of Tobolsk, M. Berezkin declared that he had no doubt whatever that Rasputin belonged to the *khlysty*, and recommended that the whole case should be referred to the civil authorities in order that Rasputin might be prosecuted.

Before doing so, however, M. Berezkin advised the Bishop to collect certain additional evidence on the case. Acting on the strength of this report Bishop Anthony ordered the consistory of Tobolsk to carry out M. Berezkin's injunctions and hand over the case of Gregory Efimoff Rasputin to the judicial authorities.

While this inter-departmental procedure was going on, Rasputin returned from St. Petersburg to his native village. He brought with him considerable sums of money and proceeded to build himself a large, well-furnished house. He openly boasted of favours received from members of the Imperial Family, and exhibited to everyone the presents they had given him—for instance, a richly ornamented gold cross on a golden chain, a medallion containing a portrait of the Empress Alexandra Feodorovna, and photographs of exalted personages with appropriate inscriptions. He flaunted about in expensive sable-lined coats. In a word, the prosecuted sectarian was transformed into an influential personage, whose patronage was already beginning to be sought by many.

After Bishop Anthony's resolution recommending Rasputin's prosecution, the affair was brought to an end by an ukase of the Holy Synod appointing, by Imperial warrant, Bishop Anthony of Tobolsk to the archbishopric of Tver and Kashin, i.e., the removal of Mgr. Anthony from his former diocese. As I learnt afterwards from competent sources, to avoid a public scandal over the Rasputin case, Bishop Anthony was given the choice of two alternatives: either to withdraw his charge against Rasputin and receive promotion to the see of Tver, or to retire to a monastery. He chose the former, and Rasputin's prosecution was suppressed.

Having completed a thorough and all-round examination of the documents submitted to my investigation, I drew up a comprehensive and concise summary of the case, and on March 8, 1912, presented a request for an audience with the Emperor for the purpose of reporting on the result of the mission entrusted to me by his Majesty.

For a long time my petition remained unanswered. The Empress Alexandra Feodorovna, I learnt, was absolutely opposed to my having a second interview with the Emperor, particularly as I should confront him armed with official and incriminating evidence against Rasputin.

A few days prior to the Imperial Family's departure for the Crimea, my petition for an audience was at last returned, not to me, but to the Prime Minister, V. N. Kokovtzeff. The Tsar had written on it the following note: "I request V N. to inform the President of the Duma that I am unable to receive him, nor do I see any necessity for so doing, as I received him a week and a half ago. The Duma debates on the Synod's budget estimates have taken a turn of which I disapprove. I desire you and the President of the Duma to take steps to prevent a recurrence of this in the future."

We were both dumbfounded on reading these lines, which contained a direct affront to the Duma and a slight on its president. According to the Fundamental Laws of the country the presidents of the legislative chambers enjoyed the right of direct communication with the Sovereign. Now the Premier was charged with a mission he was not entitled to execute, as he did not possess the right to act as intermediary between the Crown and the president of one of the legislative chambers. I declared to Kokovtzeff that as the dignity of the Duma had been slighted, I should be obliged to tender my resignation and divest myself of my Court rank*.

Such a step would inevitably create a state of conflict between the Duma and the Crown, and give colour to the charge of revolutionary tendencies already made against the Duma, thus further complicating a sufficiently unpleasant situation.

We finally arrived at the following decision. Kokovtzeff would go to Tsarskoe Selo on the very next day, point out his blunder to the Tsar, and insist that he should either grant an audience or send a personal letter to the President of the Duma. This plan was carried out to the letter. Kokovtzeff discharged his mission exceedingly well. He repeated my words to the Tsar and emphasized my intention of resigning and giving up my Court rank. To this the Tsar replied:

"I did not mean to hurt his feelings; on the contrary, I am very well satisfied with him. The Duma under him is quite changed; they have voted credits for the Navy and the Artillery Department. ... What is to be done?"

Kokovtzeff advised the Tsar to write an autograph letter, which I received next day. It ran as follows; "Being pressed for time and un-

* Honorary Court ranks were given for distinguished service.

able to receive you before my departure for the Crimea, I request you to forward me a written report."

This letter I have kept.

I did not consider it necessary to inform the Duma of this incident, merely stating that I had received an autograph letter requesting me to forward a written report.

This of itself aroused considerable displeasure, many of the members expressing their indignation at the Tsar's having found time to receive Balashoff, a delegation of students, and various other people, and refused to see the President of the Duma.

I immediately proceeded to draw up a written report, in which task I was rendered valuable assistance by V. I. Karpoff and the head of the Duma office, J. V. Glinka.

The report was very convincing, particularly the latter part of it, which dealt with the measures to be taken to pacify public opinion and reform the Church. Mgr. Hermogen must be recalled, Rasputin banished, and a Church Convocation summoned. While engaged in this task I had a visit from Rodionoff, who brought me a message from Bishop Hermogen saying he knew of my conversation with the Tsar in defence of the Orthodox faith. The bishop sent me his blessing, said he remembered me in his prayers, and bade me stand firm.

In the meantime Rasputin again made his appearance at St. Petersburg and, according to the papers, received a great welcome from his admirers assembled at the flat of Mme. Golovina. This time he was closely tracked both by the police and by pressmen. Rasputin was brought by his friends to Tsarskoe Selo, but their attempts to gain him admittance to the Empress suffered a defeat.

In the sixth week of Lent the Imperial Family left for the Crimea. Mme. Vyrubova succeeded in smuggling Rasputin on to the suite's train, where he was concealed in Prince Tumanoff's compartment. Someone informed the Emperor, who was exceedingly angry at such flagrant disobedience to his command and ordered the train to be stopped at Tosno.* Rasputin was removed from the train and, under surveillance of a secret service official, conveyed to the province of Tobolsk.

My words had struck home. After that Rasputin ceased for some time to appear at Court. Now and again he returned to St. Petersburg, never daring to remain for more than two or three days. The chief of the police department used to complain to me: "I am utterly sick of him. He has to be watched. Directly he arrives, off he goes, straight from the station to the baths; with two ladies."

The Empress, I feel sure, never forgave me for my interference.

---

*A station on the Nicholas railway between St. Petersburg and Moscow.

CHAPTER III

No news reached me concerning the fate of my report; I received neither reply nor reproof. Had the Tsar read it? I did not know. A rumour was current that he read it in the Crimea with his brother-in-law, the Duke of Hesse.

Princess Zinaida Nikolaevna Yusupoff (b. 1861-1939)

Princess Yusupoff was the daughter of a Court Marshall and Lady in waiting at the court of Nicholas I. After her father died, Alexnader III granted her husband Felix the title of Prince and on his death she inherited the largest fortune in the Russian nobility.

She remained a widow, the sole head of the House of Yusupoff, and a lady in waiting to Tsarina Alexandra Feodorovna and was considered one of the most conversant, intelligent, and beautiful women in Russia.

CHAPTER IV

Imperial Levée for Members of the Duma—The Emperor's Displeasure—Effects of the Reception—Borodino Anniversary Celebrations—The Fourth Duma Election Campaign—M. V. Rodzianko's Re-election—Audience of the Emperor.

IN May, 1912, I was present in Moscow at the unveiling of the memorial to the Emperor Alexander III in the presence of the Imperial Family. The Emperor's attitude towards me was cool; the rest of the Imperial Family, on the contrary, treated me with particular cordiality.

Many members of the Duma belonging to the parties of the Right and the Octobrists, and especially the peasants of all parties, expressed their wish to be presented to the Emperor before the end of the spring session. Such a desire, in my opinion, was inspired by a feeling of sincere patriotism and loyalty to the Throne. I therefore began to work hard, through Kokovtzeff, to secure the granting of this request. The Emperor treated it somewhat suspiciously and—probably influenced by the Empress, who was present at the interview with Kokovtzeff and kept repeating all the time that it was absolutely unnecessary—at first flatly refused to receive the members of the Duma. Meanwhile pressure in favour of their being received was being applied from other quarters through the intermediary of Baron Fredericks, Minister of the Imperial Court. Only when both Kokovtzeff and Baron Fredericks declared that they would resign if the Duma were not received, did the Emperor give a grudging consent.

The news of the coming reception was received with acclamation by the Duma, and the members started for Tsarskoe Selo in high spirits. Great was their disappointment and mortification at the Emperor's words of displeasure and criticism concerning "the impassioned and immoderate tone of the debates on certain questions." That was all. No allusion whatever was made to the patriotic work of the Duma—the credits for the Navy, the progress of the agrarian

CHAPTER IV

reform, the legislation concerning the province of Kholm or the Zemstvos in Western Russia, the question of Finland—all this work was ignored by the Emperor. The impression created by the reception was that the Emperor was dissatisfied—indeed, angry with the Duma. Everybody understood that the cause of this was the Rasputin case and the influence of the Empress. In the official statement to the Press, the text of the Emperor's address to the Duma was much toned down. But those of us who listened to it well remember how bitterly we all felt the undeserved affront.

The Emperor's final words contained a reminder concerning the bill for the provision of funds for the parish elementary schools. He expressed the hope that the credits for the development of institutions particularly dear to the heart of his late father would be passed by the Duma. Next day a gloom seemed to pervade the Duma. On my questioning the various party leaders and influential members as to the probable results of the vote on the Parish Schools' Credits Bill, they all (with the exception of a few belonging to the Extreme Right) emphatically declared that the bill would be rejected. Even the Nationalists openly said that the Emperor had no esteem for us. "God knows how he treats us. He thinks more of Rasputin and Sabler . . ." and so on. My own position was a most delicate one. It was impossible to place on the agenda a bill in which the Emperor took an interest, knowing that it would be immediately thrown out. By so doing I should be creating a conflict between the Crown and the Duma, and the session would close, as it were, with a demonstration against his wishes. I resolved to strike the bill off the agenda. By so doing I took all the blame for the incident on myself and shielded the Duma. My decision aroused great resentment among members of the Right wing, especially the clergy. Without troubling to go into the matter they raised an uproar, and declared that they would make a disturbance at the close of the session. As I walked through the Duma to take the chair, I had to be escorted by a bodyguard of Duma serjeants-at-arms to avoid the possibility of an unpleasant demonstration on the part of the clerical members. In the interval of the sitting I sent for Bishop Eulogius to my room and explained the motive of my action. He realized his error and apologized, as did many of the Conservative members who had previously expressed their resentment.

During my stay at Nauheim that summer (I was there taking a cure), I learnt from the papers as well as from a letter written to me by a member of the Duma, Kovzan, that the Government intended to dissolve the Duma three days before the centenary anniversary of the Battle of Borodino on August 26, so that the representatives of the people would not take part in the festivities. Knowing what an unfavourable impression such a step would be bound to create, I wrote at once to Kokovtzeff urging him at all costs to persuade the Emperor to postpone the dissolution of the Duma until after August 26. I received a reply a few days later to the effect that the Duma would be dissolved on the 30th.

On my return to St. Petersburg I at once went to the Duma, where I found about twenty deputies, among them several who had arrived in the hope of obtaining tickets for the celebrations. They were keenly disappointed when, on reading the programme of the ceremony, they saw that no places had been reserved for the members of the Duma either on the battlefield of Borodino or in Moscow. After studying the arrangements for the ceremony I noted that, although the President of the Duma was everywhere placed on an equal footing with the President of the Council of the Empire, the members of the two houses were not treated as equals. Such an attitude towards the representatives of the people made me extremely angry, and my first impulse was to refuse to take part in the celebrations. The members of the Duma, however, especially the peasants, persuaded me to revoke my decision. "If we are not there," they said, "then at least let the President of the Duma be present at this great anniversary of our national glory."

After some hesitation I decided to attend the unveiling of the memorial at Borodino, while avoiding the rest of the celebrations. I explained the cause of my absence from Moscow to Kokovtzeff and to the Master of Ceremonies, Baron Korff. The latter's reply was characteristic: "Members of the Duma do not enjoy the right of access to the Court," to which I retorted: "This is not a Court, but a national celebration. Besides, Russia was saved, not by masters of ceremonies, but by her people."

The Emperor, who passed quite close to me on the field of Borodino, looked askance at me and did not acknowledge my salutation. I understood that the causes of his dissatisfaction with me were the elimination of the Church Schools' Bill from the agenda of the Duma and my report on the Rasputin case.

After the Borodino celebrations, the Government apparently decided on a most drastic course of action to ensure, during the

CHAPTER IV

coming electoral campaign for the fourth Duma, the election of such candidates as would be willing blindly to support the Government's policy. No stone was left unturned to discover some point of law which could be utilized to eliminate candidates of "undesirable" or independent views.

I was re-elected President of the Imperial Duma. The Extreme Right and the Nationalist parties found themselves in a quandary. They left the assembly in a body as a protest against my election, and in order to demonstrate their unwillingness to hear the inaugural speech of a President who had been elected by the votes of the Left (I obtained a majority by the vote of the Cadets; the Socialists and Labourists, as usual, abstained from voting). A number of members of the Right, however, did not obey their leaders, but crowded at the door, where they stood silently watching the "revolutionary" (as they called it) Duma cheering the President's statement on the recovery of the Tsarevitch from his illness. Even the deputies of the Extreme Left, on purpose, applauded and cheered their loudest. The discomfited Conservatives said afterwards that had they known the contents of my speech beforehand, they would certainly have remained in the hall.

This incident was taken up by the Press; only papers of the Right said nothing about it.

Immediately after my election I solicited an audience with the Emperor. On receiving me the Emperor appeared somewhat agitated and, contrary to his usual custom, remained standing throughout the interview, which only lasted twenty minutes.

I said:

"I have the honour to present myself as the newly-elected President of the Duma."

" Yes, fancy . . . how quickly it has all happened," the Emperor began, seemingly ill at ease, and added: "I learnt with pleasure of your re-election, Mikhail Vladimirovitch. I thank you for your splendid speech. Every Russian ought to think and feel like that. But why do you call our form of government constitutional?"

"Sire, it was your Majesty's magnanimous desire to summon the representatives of the people to take part in the work of legislation. Such participation means constitutional government, and I therefore deemed it impossible to oppose even by a single word your Majesty's sovereign will."

"Yes, yes, now I understand you. But tell me, why, then, did the members of the Right and Nationalist parties leave the hall during your speech? How very tactless and out of place that was, while you were delivering your highly patriotic speech!"

"Sire, they were expecting a different speech, and had decided to protest in advance, and not to take part in revolutionary manifestations. Yet I dare assure you, that in spite of the numerous acts of injustice which your Government committed during the election campaign, the Imperial Duma, or at any rate the majority of it, is not revolutionarily inclined. My speech was a true reflection of the feelings actually animating the members of the Duma. As a matter of fact, by absenting themselves from the hall during my address, the Nationalists and the Right wing placed themselves in opposition. They took no part in the loyal demonstration made by the Duma in response to my motion for expressing to your Majesty our joy at the recovery of the Tsarevitch, and were thus punished for their tactlessness."

"The Empress and I were deeply touched by your words, and I beg you to convey our thanks to the Duma."

Two days after the audience I received the following intimation from the Minister of the Imperial Court:

"DEAR MIKHAIL VLADIMIROVITCH,
In reply to the petition presented by the member of the Duma, Jägermeister Balashoff, on behalf of a group of deputies, soliciting the honour of being presented to his Majesty the Emperor, his Imperial Majesty has graciously pleased to accord in principle his consent to receive the members of the fourth Duma in accordance with the precedents of 1907 and 1908.

In informing your Excellency of this his Majesty's pleasure, I beg you to forward me the list of those members of the Imperial Duma who have signified their desire to have the pleasure of being received by his Imperial Majesty.

Believe me,
    Yours respectfully and sincerely,
      BARON FREDERICKS,
        November 27, 1912."

It transpired that the Nationalists and members of the Right, desirous of justifying their strange behaviour, had decided as a group

CHAPTER IV

of "loyal Conservatives" to petition for an audience from the Emperor, without the knowledge of the President of the Duma. This step apparently displeased the Emperor, and without replying to Balashoff, he addressed an answer direct to the President.

The deputies proceeded to register their names for the reception. I called on Baron Fredericks to inquire whether it would be the Emperor's pleasure to receive members of the Cadet party. The Baron replied that the Emperor was willing to receive anyone desirous of being presented, even the Socialists. A large number of Cadets signified their wish to go, and at a meeting of the party it was decided to give individual members liberty to act as they pleased in the matter. I took great pains to induce as many members as possible to go to the reception. For a long time I tried to persuade Miliukoff. Our conversation took place in the corridor of the Marie Opera House, during the performance of "Judith" with Shaliapin in the leading part. Miliukoff brushed my arguments aside. "I am afraid the mere sight of me will recall too many unpleasant recollections in the Emperor's mind," he finally said, evidently hinting at the Viborg manifesto.*

Miliukoff did not go, but the members of the Opposition who did attend numbered 26 Cadets, 44 Progressives, the Poles, the Lithuanian and White Russian group, the Mussulmans and the non-party members—87 in all, while the number of deputies who attended the reception was 374 out of the total of 440. This was a momentous event, as it was the largest attendance at a reception ever recorded, and the Cadets had never before taken part in one at all.

The Emperor gave us a most cordial welcome. He shook hands with the President and made a tour of the deputies, who were grouped according to their constituencies. The Master of the Ceremonies, Baron Korff, began to present them by name, but the Emperor waved him aside, saying:

"Do not trouble, Baron, the President of the Duma will present the deputies to me." The Emperor found a word to say to each member, and appeared to treat the Conservatives more coolly than the rest.

*After the dissolution of the first Imperial Duma in 1906, a group of members of the Constitutional Democratic Party assembled at Viborg, in Finland, and issued a manifesto to the people urging them to refuse to pay taxes and supply recruits to the army, as a protest against the action of the Government. This appeal produced no impression whatever.

One of the deputies, Khvostoff, appeared decorated with a large badge of the Union of the Russian People.* This was a breach of etiquette, because no fancy orders or decorations might be worn with uniform. The Emperor asked him: "What is this badge?" Khvostoff replied: "It is a sign of membership of the Union of the Russian People." The Emperor passed on, shrugging his shoulders with a murmured: "Strange,"—after which Khvostoff removed his badge.

After the Emperor had made a tour of the assembly, the members of the Right moved forward as if to encircle him, but the Emperor walked into the centre, said a few words conveying his wishes for our united and fruitful labours, and wished everyone a happy Christmas.

Pavel Nikolayevich Milyukov (1859-1943) Member of the Russian Constituent Assembly

Founder of the Constitutional Democratic party (Cadets). He helped to draft the Vyborg Manifesto, calling for reforms and political freedoms.

Milyukov was elected to the Fourth Duma, and like chairman Rodzianko, he confirmed that leading up to World War One, Rasputin had developed considerable influence in Russian politics.

* A patriotic and extremely reactionary society.

CHAPTER V

The Tercentenary of the Romanoff Dynasty—Rasputin's Expulsion from the Cathedral—Radko Dmitrieff's Visit to St. Petersburg.

FRESH rumours of Rasputin's reappearance in St. Petersburg began to be persistently circulated in the Duma. I received a letter from Tsaritsin, confirmed by numerous signatures, informing me that to the certain knowledge of the inhabitants, Rasputin was staying at the house of V. K. Sabler, and had been re-admitted at Court. I forwarded this document to Sabler, accompanied by a letter requesting him to give these people a conclusive reply. Sabler wrote me a somewhat unpleasant note to the effect that he had never met Rasputin or had anything to do with him.

Shortly after I had received this letter, the new Minister of the Interior, Maklakoff, paid me an official call and stated that the Emperor had received information that the Duma was preparing a fresh interpellation on the question of Rasputin, and that this step had the support of the President. Maklakoff had been commissioned by the Emperor to express his Majesty's disapproval and his wish that the question of Rasputin should not again be raised in the Duma. I replied that nothing of the sort had happened, that this was probably an intrigue of Sabler's, and acquainted him with the contents of the letter from Tsaritsin. Soon after I met Sabler at a dinner party at Kokovtzeff's, and expressed to him my indignation at his having thus misrepresented the complaint of the citizens of Tsaritsin concerning Rasputin's presence in the High Procurator's house. Sabler was exceedingly abashed and assured me that I had misunderstood him. I, for my own part, warned Sabler that I should report the affair to the Emperor. And at my first audience I presented the following version of the incident.

"I take the liberty," I said, "to lodge a complaint to your Majesty against the High Procurator of the Holy Synod in that he intentionally misinformed your Majesty concerning the petition of the citizens of Tsaritsin, to which were affixed nearly 500 signatures. As the petition was directed against the activities of the High Procurator, the normal course would have been to refer the case for investigation at its source, that is to say, to the High Procurator himself. He therefore had no business to trouble your Majesty. With regard to the second part of the question transmitted to me by your Imperial command through the medium of N. A. Maklakoff—it is all absolutely untrue. The spirit which animates the Duma is wrongly interpreted; all mention of Rasputin has died down, there is no question of any interpellation, and I am therefore of opinion that the High Procurator of the Holy Synod has simply slandered me, for reasons of which I am, of course, in ignorance."

After listening attentively to my report, the Emperor admitted the validity of all my arguments.

Seeing the Emperor was graciously disposed towards me, I took advantage of the opportunity offered to plead the cause of the priest Dmitrieff. The priest Dmitrieff, a member of the third Duma, was, after its dissolution, subjected to persecution by Bishop Agapit of Ekaterinoslav for belonging to the Octobrist party. The bishop deprived him of his parish, and dismissed him from the post of divinity teacher at the high school. The unfortunate priest was left without any means of livelihood, was dependent on the charity of his former parishioners, and suffered a regular persecution. I pleaded that complete restitution should be made to Dmitrieff. The Emperor wrote down the whole case in his note-book and promised to accede to my request, which, in fact, he did.

In spite of my having been obliged to touch upon the delicate topic of Rasputin, the audience terminated graciously. My request for permission to deliver a congratulatory address at the forthcoming Romanoff jubilee celebrations was graciously granted by his Majesty.*

These celebrations were fixed for February. A rumour that the members of the Council of the Empire intended to present the Imperial Family with an ikon became current in the Duma. Having verified this report, the members of the Duma determined not to be outdone by the Council.

I convened the Senioren-convent, at which it was decided to present an ikon to the Imperial Family from the Duma. The President's secretary, Stchepkin, was dispatched to Moscow to consult Professor Ostroukhoff, who advised the purchase of a beautiful

* According to the programme, there were to be no speeches at the celebrations.

CHAPTER V

ikon of rare antiquity. Professor Ostroukhoff also proposed to buy an antique tapestry on which was depicted Mikhail Feodorovitch Romanoff (the first Tsar of the Romanoff dynasty) welcoming his father Filaret Nikititch on his arrival in Moscow. This tapestry was made of white linen cloth, twenty yards long, on which were embroidered processions of boyars and their wives in multi-coloured garments, armed *ryndys* (guards), Filaret descending from his coach, peasants offering the bread and salt, and Mikhail Feodorovitch prostrating himself before his father. In the background rose the golden cupolas of the Moscow Kremlin, and above was an image of the Holy Trinity surrounded by angels blowing trumps of glory. A cloth of gold of antique design was bought, out of which two cases were made tied by long gold cords; on their ends were suspended gold tassels and antique eagles ornamented with precious stones. The effect of the whole was beautiful and most appropriate.

The Duma approved and consented to make good the overdraft on the sum originally intended.

The Romanoff tercentenary celebrations were to be inaugurated by a liturgy and special thanksgiving service in the Cathedral of Our Lady of Kazan, which were to be celebrated by the Patriarch of Antioch, clad in the vestments presented to him by the Emperor. That very morning I learnt that the places reserved in the Cathedral for members of the Duma were not in accordance with the dignity of that institution. As a matter of fact the space reserved for the Duma was not only far in the rear of that set apart for members of the Council of the Empire, but also of that reserved for the Senate. If the Romanoff jubilee was intended to be a national rejoicing, it should not be overlooked that in 1613 it was an assembly of the people and not a group of officials that elected Mikhail Feodorovitch Romanoff Tsar of Russia.

I pointed this out to Baron Korff and Count Tolstoy, the Masters of the Ceremonies, and, after an unpleasant argument, insisted that the members of the Duma should occupy the places reserved for the Senate, the latter being removed to the far end of the Cathedral. Having achieved my object, I walked out into the Cathedral porch for a rest, as there was still plenty of time before the arrival of the members of the Duma. I must add that in order to "fortify" our newly occupied "positions," I surrounded them by a cordon of the available Duma serjeants-at-arms. I had not been in the porch ten minutes when Baron Fersen, the senior serjeant-at-arms, rushed out of the Cathedral, looking very excited, and told me that an unknown man, in peasant's dress and wearing a pectoral cross, had placed himself in front of the space reserved for the Imperial Duma and refused to move. I guessed at once who it was, and hastening to our places found there the individual described by Baron Fersen. Sure enough, it was Rasputin. He was dressed in a magnificent Russian tunic of crimson silk, patent-leather top boots, black cloth full trousers and peasant's overcoat. Over his dress he wore a pectoral cross on a finely-wrought gold chain.

I drew quite close to him and said in an impressive whisper: "What are you doing here?"

He shot an insolent look at me and replied: "What's that to do with you?"

"If you address me as ' thou,'* I will drag you from the Cathedral by the beard. Don't you know I am the President of the Duma?"

Rasputin faced me, and seemed to run me over with his eyes; first my face, then in the region of the heart, then again he stared me in the eyes. This lasted for several moments.

Personally I had never yielded to hypnotic suggestion, of which I had had frequent experience. Yet here I felt myself confronted by an unknown power of tremendous force. I suddenly became possessed of an almost animal fury, the blood rushed to my heart, and I realized I was working myself into a state of absolute frenzy.

I, too, stared straight into Rasputin's eyes, and, speaking literally, felt my own starting out of my head. Probably I must have looked rather formidable, for Rasputin suddenly began to squirm and asked: "What do you want with me?"

"Clear out at once, you vile heretic, there is no place for you in this sacred house!"

"I was invited here at the wish of persons more highly placed than you," Rasputin answered insolently, and pulled out an invitation card.

"You are a notorious swindler," I replied, "no one can believe your words. Clear out at once, this is no place for you."

Rasputin shot a sidelong glance at me, fell heavily on his knees and began to pray, bowing down to the ground. Outraged by such insolence, I nudged him in the side and said: "Enough of this tomfoolery. If you don't clear out at once, I'll order my serjeants-at

---

* The conversation was carried on in the second person singular.

CHAPTER V

arms to carry you out."

With a heavy groan and a murmured: "O Lord, forgive him such sin!" Rasputin rose slowly to his feet and, shooting a parting look of anger at me, slunk away. I followed him to the western doors of the Cathedral. There a Court Cossack helped him on with his magnificent sable-lined coat and placed him in a car, and Rasputin drove away.

Much later, Rasputin himself recounted this episode to a member of the Duma, Kovalevsky, whom he accidentally met in a train in the summer of 1913. Rasputin began by abusing me, asked why the President of the Duma was so popular among the members, and finally declared: "He is not a good man. Do you know what he did at the celebration? He actually turned me out of the Kazan Cathedral, and never even gave me a chance of telling him that the Tsar himself had asked me to be there."

In repeating this to me Kovalevsky had added: "To tell you the truth, till now I always thought your story of how you turned him out of the church was a bit of brag!"

The whole Duma was present at the levée at the Palace. I delivered my address and presented the ikon and tapestry, which was held unfolded by the deputy-presidents. The fact that the President of the Duma was the only one to deliver an address, when it was officially declared there were to be no speeches, was particularly significant.

The Balkan war with Turkey was by that time nearing a climax. The heroic struggle for liberty of the Slav peoples was watched with attentive enthusiasm by the Duma. Sympathy with their cause was whole-hearted. This feeling increased in proportion to the growth of indignation against the blunders of our diplomacy, particularly against the Minister for Foreign Affairs, Sazonoff. The Duma held him responsible for the insignificant part played by Russia in the crisis. Outside the Duma, this feeling of general resentment and national humiliation found expression in the Press of all shades of opinion.

In March, 1913, the Bulgarian General, Radko Dmitrieff, the national hero of the war, with the President of the Bulgarian National Assembly, arrived in St. Petersburg. They were met at the station by Slavonic associations, crowds of young men and women and many members of the Duma, and received an enthusiastic ovation. The day after their arrival, I believe, there came the news of the fall of Adrianople. This event made a tremendous impression in the Duma. The sitting was interrupted, there were enthusiastic cheers and demands for a Te Deum.

Several deputies were dispatched to fetch Radko Dmitrieff, Daneff and the Bulgarian Minister Bobcheff. On their arrival they were borne shoulder high amid wild cheering, embraced and kissed. The enthusiasm was general. Party and personal quarrels were forgotten, all shook hands and congratulated one another on this pan-Slavonic triumph. The Slavs were moved to tears. The Te Deum was celebrated in the Catherine hall by the priests who were members of the Duma. The deputies formed a choir, which I conducted. The Russian and Bulgarian national anthems were sung.

At the height of this outburst of enthusiasm I was called up on the telephone by the Prime Minister, Kokovtzeff.

"What is going on in the Duma? Couldn't these demonstrations be stopped?"

I replied: "It is impossible. Popular enthusiasm cannot be stifled. Besides, why should it?"

"Look here, Mikhail Vladimirovitch, this may provoke Austria and give rise to unpleasant complications."

"Try yourself. Come here and try to quell this enthusiasm! I can't!"

It turned out that news of this demonstration had reached the Austrian Embassy, and representations had been made to the Prime Minister.

Next day I gave a large dinner party in honour of our Bulgarian guests Bobcheff, Daneff and Radko Dmitrieff, and later a reception, at which over sixty members of the Duma, all the party leaders, the members of the Committee of the Octobrist party in the Duma and prominent Octobrists were present. The reception was extremely animated. Everyone clustered round Radko Dmitrieff to hear his accounts of the war and the general situation in the Balkans. The Slavs behaved with great tact and calmness. They never so much as hinted at our diplomatic policy, nor did they even show much resentment against Austria, though they did not conceal their distrust of that country.

In proposing the toast of "the heroic Slavonic peoples" I said: "We all watch with tense admiration their glorious advance in the

CHAPTER V

name of the Cross and liberty." We never doubted, I said, the victorious termination of the war, but the fruits of every campaign were judged by the success of the peace treaty following on war. "Permit me I continued, "to offer you good advice in the name of Russia, the elder sister of the Slavonic nations: keep peace among yourselves, as allies and fellow fighters. Beware of dangerous and ill-advised jealousies and rivalries, and we, your brothers, now rejoicing at your military prowess, implore you to strain every nerve to preserve your unity of purpose in the days of coming peace . . . I drink to the success of our victorious brother Slavs, and to the unity and welding together of the Slavonic family. . . ."

After exchanging looks with his companions, Radko Dmitrieff rose to reply. We were right, he said, in calling them our younger brothers, because the Slavonic peoples had of old been accustomed to look up to Russia with love and reverence. The Slavonic nations would never forget that they owed their new life and freedom to the sacrifices and magnanimity of the Russian people. . . . In their first independent fight against their age-long foe, they still looked to their elder brother and asked him to remove all pernicious alien influences. It was for Russia to avert or suppress any misunderstandings which might arise between the Slavonic nations. Great Russia alone had the right to intervene in their domestic quarrels, and the Slavonic peoples would submit them to her alone. His voice quivered with emotion as he said this.

During the after-dinner talk the Slavs said to us: "You have no idea of the extent of Russia's prestige in the Balkans; with what hope and trust we all look towards her, how she is feared in Europe. Now or never, Russia must say the word." Our only answer to this could be; "You have seen the expression of public opinion and of the Press, you witnessed the enthusiasm of the representatives of the people. We can say nothing more, nor guarantee you anything."

Radko Dmitrieff led me off to my room and said: "I have come on a secret mission to lay Constantinople at his Majesty's feet. What am I to do—how shall I speak of it to the Tsar?"

I replied: "Be frank. He loves the truth, and in any case, this would be much the safer course. For my part, I think it would be better, before your interview with the Emperor, for me to ask for a special audience."

Radko Dmitrieff thanked me and asked me to do so. One longed to believe, and did believe, that Russia would utter the decisive word, advance victoriously southward and support the Slavs. As events soon proved, these were but empty hopes.

On March 16 there were popular street demonstrations in honour of the fall of Adrianople. The Slavonic Society celebrated the event by a Te Deum in the Church of the Resurrection.* On leaving the church Radko Dmitrieff was carried shoulder high amid deafening cheers. A huge crowd of people poured into the Nevsky Prospect singing "God save the Tsar" and "Shumi Maritsa,"† and marched to the Bulgarian Legation. Bobcheff came out on the balcony and made a speech ending with: "Long live Great Russia!" The crowd answered by singing the Bulgarian and Russian national anthems. Then, swelled by fresh numbers, it marched to the Serbian Legation. The Serbian Minister, too, stepped out on the balcony, but no sooner had he uttered a few words than up came a squad of mounted police, dealing blows to right and left. Remonstrances to the effect that the crowds were perfectly peaceful and singing "God save the Tsar" were of no avail. The police, having apparently received definite instructions, worked with a will. They were particularly careful to guard the Foreign Minister Sazonoff, whose house was surrounded by two squadrons of mounted gendarmes, and the Austrian Embassy, whither the crowds had not the slightest intention of going. Besides, the crowd consisted of serious, well-conducted people—officers, society ladies, senators, Government officials, etc. It was even said that one senator was badly bruised in the *mêlée*.

That same night Sazonoff had a dinner-party, to which I was invited.

"I had a pleasant surprise on entering your house," I said to him. "I rejoice to see that at last our diplomacy is following the right course."

"What do you mean?" inquired Sazonoff in astonishment.

"I see you are arming to help the Slavs; there are two squadrons of soldiers in your courtyard."

Next day there was an interpellation in the Duma on the subject of the police attack on the demonstrators. The Minister of the Interior, Maklakoff, gave absolutely unsatisfactory explanations in

---

* Erected on the site of the assassination of the Emperor Alexander II (1881), who fought for the liberation of the Balkan Slavs in the Turkish War of 1877-1878.
† The Bulgarian national anthem

CHAPTER V

excuse of the action of the police. Similar incidents were repeated during the next two days. The Prefect of the city, Drachevsky, himself drove up in a car to disperse the crowds who were singing "God save the Tsar." Shouts arose of: "We're singing the national anthem; please stand up!" He rose reluctantly and stood at attention. The Government was, nevertheless, perturbed by this popular effervescence, and Sazonoff determined to offer some explanations. He invited the members of the Duma to "a cup of tea," but divided them into two groups. Right and Left, and received them on different days.

As a matter of fact Sazonoff gave no explanations at all. The Cadets alone were satisfied, and sang his praises in their party organ, the *Retch*.

Sergey Dmitrievich Sazonov (b.1860-1927)
Russian Minister of Foreign Affairs (1910-1916)

Sazonov was brother-in-law to Pyotr Stolypin, the Prime Minister from 1906 to 1911. He was previously ambassador to American and the UK.

CHAPTER VI

The Intrigues of the Right—Boycott of the Duma—Unveiling of the Stolypin Memorial—Bishop Agapit—A. I. Gutchkoff's Warnings.

FROM the very beginning of the new session a feeling of unrest pervaded the Duma. The Government was disappointed that in spite of all the pressure exercised during the election, the spirit of the Duma was different from what they had anticipated. They had reckoned on a majority of the Right, which did not materialize, and moreover, the presidential body was elected by a majority of the Left. As time wore on the Government's hostility to the Duma increased. The pro-Slavonic demonstrations, the criticisms of the Government's policy, the stern rebuke given by the Duma to General Sukhomlinoff* for the illegal modification of the Statutes of the Military Medical Academy, which even the Senate refused to publish—all these irritated the Government. Rumours of the Government's desire to "disperse" the Duma cropped up persistently. Prince Mestchersky, editor of a journal of the Extreme Right, the *Grazhdanin* ("The Citizen"), wrote denunciatory articles against the Duma and its President. Everyone knew that the *Grazhdanin* was the only paper read by the Emperor, and it seemed almost as if the Government's policy depended on the influence exercised by this subsidized publicist. All this was most disheartening.

There was an obvious desire on the part of the Government to do away with the Duma by passive if not by active methods. In spite of blatant promises to introduce new reform bills the Government stubbornly refused to do anything, and nothing was left to the Duma except the Budget Estimates and interpellations. Even the data necessary for the work of the Budget Commission was withheld by the Ministries. The members of the Extreme Right, who resented being in a minority, launched, with the support of the Government, an intrigue against the majority in the Duma. They called a joint

* The Minister for War.

CHAPTER VI

conference of all the Monarchist organizations, the first point on the agenda being a discussion on the necessity for dissolving the fourth Duma. They tried to keep this a secret, but of course it all came out at once, while the full text of the agenda appeared in the *Vechernie Vremia* and other papers. The absence in the Duma of a solid majority, the uncertainty and constant expectation of a speedy dissolution, the absolutely fruitless work—all the most important interpellations and bills brought no response from the Government—could not but affect the general spirit.

During Holy Week I presented my report to the Emperor. He greeted me graciously, as usual. Nevertheless, I was obliged to tell him many unpleasant facts. Referring to the Statutes of the Military Medical Academy and the Duma interpellation, I pointed out the illegality of the proceedings of the War Minister Sukhomlinoff, who had thrown the responsibility for his action on to the Crown.

I said: "Your Majesty was misinformed and given to ratify a statute passed by Order in Council, whereas, according to the law, it should first have been submitted to the legislative chambers."

The Emperor said nothing to this.

With regard to the activities of the police during the street demonstrations, I remarked that the feeling of resentment and wounded national pride would rankle for a long time. The Emperor appeared to agree with me, and commented on the Minister of the Interior's want of tact. I urged decisive action. Troops could be moved against Erzerum from the one side, and against Constantinople from the other. I repeated several times:

"Your Majesty, there is still time. We must take advantage of the popular enthusiasm. The Straits must become ours. A war will be joyfully welcomed, and will raise the Government's prestige."

The Emperor maintained a stony silence.

I spoke of administrative tyranny, and recounted how the chairman of the Zemstvo Board of the province of Tchernigoff, Savitsky, a popular and respected public servant, was prosecuted for the escape of a political prisoner. His prosecution was engineered by N. A. Maklakoff, then Governor of the Tchernigoff province. Its object was perfectly clear. Persons who were the subject of preliminary legal proceedings, or had been committed for trial, were deprived by law of both active and passive electoral rights. N. A. Maklakoff, who at that time was Governor of Tchernigoff, was ill-disposed towards Savitsky. The mere fact of a political prisoner's escape from the Zemstvo hospital was not in itself sufficient ground for a prosecution. If responsibility for what occurred at the hospital was thus shifted from the senior medical officer to the chairman of the Zemstvo Board, then, in ascending order, first the Governor, and finally the Minister of the Interior, must be held to blame, especially as the latter was now that same Maklakoff who was then Governor of Tchernigoff.

To this the Emperor remarked: "Yes, you are right."

Towards the close of the session there occurred an incident trivial in itself, but pregnant with far-reaching effects. During a debate on the Budget Estimates of the Ministry of Finance, Markoff II rapped out: "No stealing allowed." Prince Volkonsky, who was presiding, failed to call him to order, and the Minister of Finance, Kokovtzeff, treated this sally as a personal insult. He declared that the whole Duma was in fault for not having censured the deputy, and that it ought, therefore, to apologize to the Government. "Until this is done by the President of the Duma," added Kokovtzeff, "the Cabinet Ministers will abstain from attending the Duma."

The Duma refused to consider itself responsible for a remark made by an individual member, and I had no intention of tendering any apologies. The whole incident—both the sharp words used against the Government by a deputy of the Extreme Right, and the unexpected touchiness of the Ministers, rather savoured of a deliberate provocation. At first it was treated as a joke, but the situation soon became impossible. Owing to the Ministerial boycott work in the commissions practically came to a standstill. Explanations of the estimates of the various Ministries were given, not even by the Assistant Ministers, but by secretaries of departments, with whom the Chairman of the Budget Commission, Alexeyenko, finally refused to deal.

In a report presented by me to the Emperor in June, 1913, after the close of the session, I again spoke on questions of foreign policy and urged decisive action. Then I mentioned the Ministers.

"Your Majesty, the Ministers no longer come to the Duma, they refuse to take part in legislative work. This may inspire the nation with rather a bold idea."

"What idea?"

"Well, that they could be dispensed with,"

To which the Emperor replied: "They will have thought better of it by the autumn."

CHAPTER VI

In the autumn of 1913 we went to Kieff for the unveiling of the memorial to P. A. Stolypin. It was characteristic that the elements which were hostile or unfriendly to the Duma in general and its President in particular took advantage of the occasion to emphasize their disdain. Thus the most uncomfortable compartment was reserved for me on the official train. No one came to meet me on my arrival, no accommodation was reserved, and the Governor permitted himself a somewhat incorrect and even rude behaviour towards us. The public, on the other hand, vied with one another in their endeavours to express due regard for the Duma delegation.

At the laying of the foundation stone of the Zemstvo council building I had the following conversation with the Prime Minister. I approached Kokovtzeff, who was standing slightly apart, and said to him:

"Well, Vladimir Nicolaevitch, are you going to stop the boycott of the Duma? Is there any hope of seeing you there in the autumn?"

"Until the Duma apologizes we have all decided not to go there."

"I must tell you that the Emperor, at my last audience, expressed the hope that you would think better of it by the autumn."

A few days later this conversation, with a strong tendency to caricature my part in it, appeared in the newspaper *Russkoe Slovo*. A paragraph was added announcing Kokovtzeff's forthcoming departure to Livadia with a report to the Emperor. As no one was present during our conversation with Kokovtzeff, I realized that he himself was the author of this paragraph. His object was probably to show a cutting to his Majesty and point out how lightly the Sovereign's words were treated by the President of the Duma, who even permitted himself to print them in a more or less Opposition newspaper.

Having read this paragraph, I published a refutation stating that the conversation referred to had taken place in *tête-á-tête* and in quite a different form, and that therefore no doubt was possible as to who was the actual author of the newspaper report.

On my arrival at Kieff I was shown the list of speakers. Balashoff was the only one chosen from the Duma. The desire to prevent me or any other member from speaking was obvious from the haste with which the list was submitted to me. The Octobrists were deeply offended and determined to refrain from making any speeches, and Gutchkoff, who laid a wreath at the foot of the memorial, merely bowed to the ground in silence. This silent homage expressed more eloquently than words the profound sorrow caused by Stolypin's death.

After the Kieff celebrations I joined a party of members of the Duma who were going to visit the Dnieper rapids in connection with the proposed credits for sluicing the river. We arrived at Ekaterinoslav by steamer.

Everywhere the population came out to welcome its chosen representatives, the members of the Imperial Duma. At Kremenchug, for instance, almost the whole town assembled on the pier. The mayor presented the bread and salt* and delivered a moving address. Ceremonies like this took place even in the villages, and the elders of the communes greeted the travellers in artless but touching words.

At a reception given by the Ekaterinoslav marshal of the nobility, Prince Ourussoff, I had a curious talk with Archbishop Agapit.†

Mgr. Agapit had taken an active part in the election campaign, agitating against the Octobrist party, and after the elections had preached a sermon from the pulpit in which he said: "Whom have you elected? Octobrists who sold Christ!"

I naturally avoided him at the reception, but Mgr. Agapit himself came up to me saying, "Allow me, Mikhail Vladimirovitch, in token of reconciliation to give you my blessing. I know you are angry with me."

"No, Vladiko, I will not accept your blessing. You insulted me profoundly during the elections, and afterwards you said that we had 'sold Christ.'"

"Not you personally, Mikhail Vladimirovitch, not you," interrupted the archbishop, clasping his hands to his breast.

"It makes no difference whether it referred to me or to those I stand for. In insulting the Octobrists you insulted me. Though perhaps I am much more Orthodox than many of your priests, particularly those ignoramuses who receive parishes so liberally at your hands. Remember that when I came to Ekaterinoslav last year, I called on you at once out of respect for your rank. Really, it would be much better if you kept away from politics. Your place is the church; you ought, like a good shepherd, to draw your flock to-

---

* An old Russian custom signifying welcome.

† This prelate, after the Revolution, delivered an address of welcome to Petliura when the latter occupied Kieff before the arrival of the Bolsheviks.

CHAPTER VI

gether by love and charity, instead of sowing discord by denunciatory sermons and instructing your priests how to vote. Let the priests remain pastors of the Church. What have you gained by it all? You have destroyed the last vestige of respect which still existed for the office of priest."

"Forgive me, Mikhail Vladimirovitch," murmured Mgr. Agapit, in consternation.

"You may well say 'forgive,' but forget I cannot. I did not seek this interview; you came up to me yourself. I suppressed my feelings, but now I can remain silent no longer. I must speak out and let you feel my indignation. Remember what you told me when I called on you. I did not ask for your support; you yourself assured me that you considered the Octobrists trustworthy Orthodox men. You repeatedly told me and others that I was your candidate. And what happened during the elections? You cannot deny that the clergy were mobilized to work against us."

"Pardon me, Mikhail Vladimirovitch," the archbishop said, trying to interrupt me. But I was too excited to let him speak.

"No one forced you to express your opinions. Why did you act against your conscience? Why profess one thing before the elections and practise another? What is the result? You have merely dishonoured your high calling and demeaned the clergy in the eyes of the electors."

Champagne being brought in at this juncture. Mgr. Agapit took a glass, saying: "Your health, Mikhail Vladimirovitch, and may our next meeting be more friendly."

"I am willing to drink your health," I replied. "As for our next meeting, it will probably occur in the world to come. And I may confidently assert that I shall not be called upon to answer before God for what I have said to you to-day."

We touched our glasses, and I moved away. All through this conversation Mgr. Agapit gave one the impression of a schoolboy in disgrace trying to excuse himself before his seniors. Our talk soon became public property in Ekaterinoslav. Most people were pleased that the archbishop had received a "drubbing" for his disgraceful role at the elections; others criticized me.

Next day I called on Prince Ourussoff to apologize for my curt behaviour in his house to a guest of his. Great was my surprise when I learnt from him that on taking leave, Mgr. Agapit had particularly thanked him for the opportunity of having "such a good talk with

Mikhail Vladimirovitch."

The result of this conversation was that appointments of semi-illiterate priests ceased entirely, and Mgr. Agapit's general behaviour became much subdued.

With the opening of the new session of the Duma the question of the "Ministerial strike" was again brought into the foreground. Before the opening I called on the State Comptroller Kharitonoff, who advised me not to invite the Cabinet for the opening ceremony, as the Ministers would decline to come, thus merely creating a fresh pretext for misunderstandings. This advice was followed, and the Ministerial box was conspicuous by its emptiness. Such a state of affairs went on for about a fortnight. The Government at last realized the disadvantages of its policy and made a move towards reconciliation. The Ministers decided that they would be satisfied by an apology from Markoff alone. This was conveyed to Markoff; at the sitting of November 1 he read out an abridged formula of apology and the incident was closed. The Duma preserved its dignity, while the Ministers became still more unpopular. This victory of the Duma was particularly gratifying, as rumours were still current of the Government's intention to "disperse" it. Frequent remarks to that effect in the *Grazhdanin* made one think such an event to be within the range of possibility.

Shortly before this, the Prime Minister Kokovtzeff had returned from abroad, where, in an interview with a French reporter, he had complacently affirmed that "no one in Russia within a hundred versts' radius from the capital and thirty from the district towns gave a thought to politics." This statement was ridiculed by the Press. As a counterpart to Kokovtzeff's statement Gutchkoff made a brilliant survey of the internal and international situation of Russia in a speech delivered on November 8 at a Congress of the Octobrist party in St. Petersburg. The Government, he said, were heading towards Russia's ruin; the country was on the eve of a second revolution, and the time had come to turn over a new leaf. As a matter of fact, Gutchkoff's speech was anti-dynastic, and the Octobrists as a loyalist party ought not to have followed the course urged on them by their leader.

The Congress passed the following resolution regarding the policy of the party in the Duma: "It behoves the parliamentary

CHAPTER VI

faction of the Union of October 17, as an organ of the party best equipped with the means of influencing the Government, to assume the duty of combating the dangerous and pernicious tendencies of the policy of the Government, as well as all the instances of abuse and violation of the law from which the country is continuously and grievously suffering. The parliamentary faction should resort in full measure to all legal forms of parliamentary combat, such as the freedom of the tribune, the right of interpellation, the rejection of bills and the refusal of credits."

The impression made on the Government by this resolution was instantaneous, almost ludicrous. The very next day all the information and data withheld for a year were presented by the Ministers concerned.

The time for the elections to the presidential body approached. My more intimate friends tried to dissuade me from standing for the presidency.

"The Tsar will not listen to you. There is no majority in the Duma, the situation is uncertain; it will only mean endless nerve-racking."

Unfortunately events admitted of no refusal. No other candidate was even nominated. Moreover, the political situation was such that after my inaugural address a refusal would have been tantamount to a repudiation of our programme, a surrender of our positions without a fight. The initiator and promoter of a definite political course would be likened to a captain abandoning his ship. I was therefore compelled by sheer force of circumstances to accept, and was elected by an enormous majority of 272 against 70 votes, larger than on any previous occasion. I delivered a speech, which, though applauded, was less appreciated than that of the year before. I myself thought it inferior, weaker and, above all, more colourless than the former. I had been uncertain whether I ought to make a speech at all, and whether I should repeat what had been said a year ago.

After the elections, disaccord set in in the parliamentary group of the Octobrist party. At their very first meeting the Right wing, under pressure from the Government, contested and even condemned the resolution passed by the Octobrist Congress. The Centre decided to "take note of it," while the Left wing insisted on its being laid down as the basis of the group's policy in the Duma. The deputies of the Left, led by Gutchkoff, held meetings in which the Centre took no part. The Centre declared that they refused their adherence to the Right wing, but, at the same time, declined to submit themselves blindly to Gutchkoff's orders.

A split occurred. I summoned a conference and endeavoured to patch up the party, but failed. Twenty-two members of the Left seceded from the group. The chief among them were Sergei Shidlovsky, Khomiakoff, Zvegintzoff, Godneff and others. A second conference met at my flat to try and save the situation. Savitch, Nicholas Shidlovsky, Alexeyenko and myself resolved to form a new party—the "Zemstvo-Octobrists." The party determined to be distinct from the Right wing. When this became known in the Duma a great many members wanted to join our group, which soon numbered fifty members, and rose to seventy during the Christmas recess.

Thanks to this successful move the party again obtained a majority. On the other hand the need arose of providing it with an energetic leader. The former chairman of the parliamentary group (Gutchkoff) had failed to weld it together during a split, and when matters came to a climax hastened to withdraw. I began to contemplate resigning the presidency of the Duma and putting myself at the head of the new party.

Vladimir Nikolayevich Kokovtzeff
4th Prime Minister of Russia (1911-1914)
Minister of Finances (1904-1905 and 1906-1914)

CHAPTER VII

The Audience of December 22, 1913—Dispute over the Purchase of Dreadnoughts—Admiral Beatty's Squadron off Reval—Port Hangö.

ON the Tsar's return from the Crimea I asked for an audience, and on December 22, 1913, was received by his Majesty. It was of urgent importance that the Emperor should be informed of the absence of co-ordination in the Government's policy. Quite recently, the Prime Minister, Kokovtzeff, had defended in the Council of the Empire a bill which Maklakoff had secretly ordered the members to reject. The majority of the members of the Council nominated by the Crown did not attend the sitting, the others voted against the bill and, to the amazement of the unsuspecting Kokovtzeff, it was rejected. It was essential that the Emperor should know of these proceedings. At my next audience I said to him:

"Your Majesty, permit me to inform you that we have no Government."

"What do you mean—no Government?"

"We have been accustomed to think that part of the executive power of the Crown was delegated to the Ministers and to the nominated members of the Council of the Empire. These latter execute the will of the Government and are its dependents in the legislative assembly. We, the members of the lower chamber, have been accustomed to think so. What happens now? During the last session we debated the bill for the admittance of the Polish language in the schools of the Vistula provinces*. It was your Imperial Majesty's wish that the language should be admitted in order to improve the position of the Poles and make it comparable to their position in Austria, and so enlist their sympathies on behalf of Russia."

"Yes," replied the Tsar, "that is just what I had in view."

"So we understood it, and the bill was worked out in the Duma

---

* Ten Polish provinces in the basin of the river Vistula.

in that sense. Now this bill is being debated in the Council of the Empire, and its leading principle is defended by a representative of the Government. Meanwhile, some of the nominated members of the Council are absent, others vote against it, and the bill is rejected. Your Majesty will agree that members of the Government either do not wish to carry out your will, or do not take the trouble to understand it. The nation feels bewildered. Each Minister has his own opinion. The Cabinet is generally split into two parties, the Council of the Empire forms a third, the Duma a fourth, and your own will is unknown to the nation. This cannot go on, your Majesty; this is not a Government, it is anarchy."

"But what am I to do? I cannot influence the freedom of opinion of members of the Council of the Empire."

"The list of the nominated members of the Council is in your Majesty's possession. Revise it, appoint more liberal members, who agree with your views. Compel the Ministers to obey you."

This conversation had no effect. The list of members of the Council of the Empire remained practically the same, or, if revised, in exactly the opposite way to that which I recommended.

During the same interview I showed the Emperor two Press cuttings: one from the *Kolokol* ("The Bell"), the official Synod review, the other from the *Vechernie Vremia*. The passage from the *Kolokol* ran approximately as follows: "That we escaped a war last year is due to the influence of the holy *startsy* who direct our foreign policy, for which we should be profoundly grateful. The appointment of new hierarchs is also due to them. Let us trust that in this sphere their influence will be equally beneficent."

The *Vechernie Vremia* retaliated by pointing out to the *Kolokol* that the direction of foreign policy was a prerogative of the Crown, "and we remind the *Kolokol* that there can be no question of *startsy*. The direction of foreign policy is an attribute of the Crown, and bishops likewise are appointed by the Emperor."

Having read this, the Emperor said: "What *startsy*? Who are the *startsy* alluded to?"

"Your Majesty," I replied, "there is but one *starets* in Russia, and you know who he is. He is the sorrow and despair of all Russia."

The Emperor was silent.

"Your Majesty," I continued, "I have one more question to submit to you. It is of vital importance to the State, and though not directly concerned with my report, one which I should very much

CHAPTER VII

like to bring to your notice."

"Please tell me."

The Duma Commission on Military and Naval Affairs, I told the Tsar, was informed that in the yards of Vickers and Armstrong there were five super-Dreadnoughts, which were for sale for the total sum of 120,000,000 roubles. The cost of each was ten million less than the estimates submitted in Russia. By purchasing them we should save 50,000,000 roubles. They were all first-class ships and already finished or nearly so, whereas the building of similar ships in Russia would take years. For some reason or other the Ministry was very averse to purchasing them. The Duma was taking this matter very much to heart, and had built high hopes on my report to his Majesty.

The Emperor said: "Yes, but what would be the use of buying ships for the Baltic, when we need to strengthen the Black Sea? We cannot transfer them there."

"If the Germans trouble us in the Black Sea, we can trouble them from the north, and in diplomatic conversations we shall always be able to remind them that we are stronger than they are in the Baltic."

"Yes, you are right," said the Emperor. " Do you remember what you said to me a year ago about the Balkan problem? You were right then, too. Had we then acted with greater energy, the Straits would now be ours."

"Your Majesty, it is not too late even now. If we buy those Dreadnoughts we shall be stronger than Germany; then our building can go on without being accelerated, we shall improve our old ships, and by 1915 we shall possess a powerful fleet."

The Emperor appeared greatly interested, thanked me for my information, and expressed his desire to purchase the ships at once.

"Only, do not allow the matter to be discussed in the Ministry of Marine," I said on taking my leave. "Simply order the ships to be bought, your Majesty; for the Ministry will oppose it."

"Why?"

"Because, your Majesty, they will gain nothing from the transaction."

"What do you mean by that?"

"It is not for me to explain, your Majesty. You know better than I do."

"Yes, they were inclined that way, I remember. But what about the Duma? It has risen. The purchase will have to be carried through by means of Article 87, and there will be unpleasantness with the Duma."

"Your Majesty, I give you my word that the Duma will only applaud you."

Next day the Minister of Marine rang me up on the telephone.

"What did you tell the Emperor? Why am I urgently summoned to Tsarskoe?"

I declined to pursue the conversation by telephone and went to see Grigorovitch* myself. For two hours we shouted at one another, each defending his particular point of view and paying no heed to the orderly who was serving tea.

Soon after a special conference, consisting of Ministers and higher Admiralty officials, was called by order of the Emperor to discuss the purchase. The conference was opposed to it, and the matter was adjourned. Meanwhile Turkey, subsidized by Germany, bought the most powerful Dreadnought out of the five, the one which was most similar in type to ours. Two others, also through German efforts, were withdrawn from sale, while the price of the remaining two was raised. While the higher Admiralty officials were opposing the transaction, the rank and file of naval officers were continually asking: "Will the purchase be arranged soon?" Some said: "Our grandpapa (the Minister of Marine) is making a fool of himself. You must persuade him in the Duma."

In the Commission on Military and Naval Affairs feeling ran high, and on Grigorovitch's arrival he was met in battle array. I purposely refrained from attending the sitting to prevent his thinking that the Commission was acting under pressure from the President. I was kept informed of the progress of the debate by the Duma serjeants-at-arms. Representatives of all parties were unanimous, and all Grigorovitch's arguments were refuted by actual statistics. He was especially nonplussed by the attitude of the Socialists and Labourists, who insisted on the advantages of the transaction. "If we must spend money on armaments," they said, "better save ten millions on each ship."

No alternative was left to Grigorovitch but to state that in his next report to the Emperor he would back the desire of the Commission. This statement was received with tumultuous applause. He kept his word. Before my departure for the Easter vacation I was again rec-

* The Minister of Marine.

CHAPTER VII

eived by the Emperor, who said to me :

"Is it not strange?—the Minister of Marine at first opposed this purchase, saying it would create ill feeling in the Duma, Now, it appears, the Duma is in favour of it, and he himself supports this view,"

Grigorovitch sent me the following message: "Tell the President of the Duma that the two Dreadnoughts will be bought; and tell him also that the Minister of Marine will have nothing to gain personally from the transaction."

Admiral Stetsenko, known for his sterling integrity, was, by the desire of the Duma, appointed to transact the business.

On meeting me at the wedding of Prince Felix Yusupoff, Grigorovitch said: "I trust we now have your approval."

The general impression during the winter of 1913-14 was as if the higher society of St. Petersburg had suddenly had its eyes opened. Everyone spoke of Rasputin with the greatest apprehension. What had stirred the Duma two years ago had only now reached Court circles. People who so far had kept strictly silent on matters concerning the Imperial Family, whether from a feeling of decency or simply out of respect for their Sovereign, now spoke of this man, some with fear, others with disgust or with an ironical smile.

I will here mention a characteristic incident illustrating the unbounded influence exercised by Rasputin. The little Tsarevitch had to undergo a slight operation. The Court surgeon Fedoroff, after preparing everything in the operating room, went out to call the Tsarevitch. Imagine his horror, when on his return he found all the requisites—bandages, muslin, etc.—which he had thoroughly sterilized, covered with a dirty nondescript article of clothing. On questioning his assistant he was told that "Gregory Efimovitch had just been in the room, had prayed over the requisites prepared for the operation, and covered them with a garment of his own. Fedoroff went to complain to the Emperor, but the latter treated the matter lightly.

The whole of the spring session was devoted to conflicts between the Duma and the Minister of the Interior Maklakoff, who was issuing illegal orders and had appointed as governors in the provinces men unfit for their posts. His influence, however, grew at Tsarskoe Selo. According to information from Court sources, he had assumed the role of Court jester. He told funny stories, mimicked various people, birds and animals, amused the young Grand Duchesses by acting "the love-sick panther," and generally posed as the "funny man" on an intimate footing at the Palace. As a member of the Government, however, he was universally despised.

The Duma session was very long and lasted well into the summer. Progress was considerably hampered by the continued boycott on the part of the Government.

In May, members of the Commission of Defence paid a visit to Reval, there to inspect the docks and fortifications. This trip coincided with the arrival at St. Petersburg of the British squadron under command of Admiral Beatty. As this would inevitably entail a visit of the members of the Duma to the British squadron then anchored off Reval, which would have the character of an official greeting to the British guests before their arrival in the capital, I solicited a special audience of the Emperor to ascertain his views on the matter.

The Emperor considered it right for us to meet the squadron, and gave his approval to the most cordial speeches of welcome possible. Armed with the Imperial sanction, a large party of members of the Duma, including the whole presidential body, started for Reval on board the cruiser *Bogatyr*, escorted by the torpedo boat *General Kondratenko*.

We were greeted by a combined salute from the Russian and British squadrons. Admiral Beatty's flagship, the *Lion*, flying the Russian national flag in honour of the Duma. The British Admiral's flag-captain immediately arrived on board the *Bogatyr* with an invitation to us all to lunch on board the *Lion*. I decided to deliver my address of welcome in Russian, and asked a member of the Duma, Zvegintzoff, to act as interpreter.

At the close of my speech Admiral Beatty turned to Zvegintzoff and asked him to translate his reply. As previously agreed, Zvegintzoff replied: "There is no need, as the President of the Duma both understands and speaks English."

To this Admiral Beatty and all the commanders and officers assembled from the ships uttered a long-drawn "Oh—oh," and afterwards signified their appreciation of the motives which prompted the President of the Duma to greet the British guests in

CHAPTER VII

his own tongue. Later, the officers who showed us round their splendid ship told us they realized the necessity of studying Russian in view of the inevitable future alliance between the two countries. After the festivities attending the visit of the British squadron and an inspection of the Reval fortifications, the members of the Duma made a cruise among the Finnish skerries, calling at Hangö, while the British squadron sailed for St. Petersburg.

The British were greatly impressed by the presence at Reval of a delegation from the Imperial Duma headed by its President. They regarded this as a mark of special courtesy. All the papers were full of it. The incident created a great commotion in Germany. German politicians were disturbed by the British visit and still more by the presence at Reval of the Duma delegates. It may be that this event, or the visit of the French President, hastened the war. It was rumoured that the Kaiser had declared: *Jetzt oder niemals* ("now or never").

On June 4, 1914, news appeared in the Press that Rasputin had been murdered in his native village of Pokrovskoe, in the province of Tobolsk. An ugly, noseless woman had come up to him and "stuck" a knife into his abdomen. Rasputin telegraphed to Tsarskoe Selo a message which may be rendered: "Hussy stuck knife in my belly." The woman proved to be one of his former mistresses. She declared that she wanted to kill him because he was an impostor and a false prophet. She denied having any accomplices. The papers said that she had received Iliodor's blessing for the attempt, but this she also denied. During her examination the woman was in violent hysterics. The Press, glad of the opportunity, again took up all the old and forgotten stories of Rasputin's exploits. News appeared to the effect that the Court surgeon Fedoroff had been despatched to Pokrovskoe; that Rasputin's women admirers, including Mme. Vyrubova, had left St. Petersburg and were on the way to Siberia; that Rasputin was at the point of death. All this rejoicing, however, proved to be premature. The next news was that Rasputin kept on repeating: "I'll pull through. I'll pull through." His condition soon improved, and the Press ceased to trouble about him. Eventually he did "pull through" and recovered.

Public attention was diverted by the visit of foreign guests from friendly countries—the British and French sailors. They were warmly welcomed in St. Petersburg. While officers and men were being entertained at dinners and receptions the diplomatists were busily at work, and the Triple Entente was apparently transformed into an Alliance.

On the return voyage from Reval a group of members of the Duma, at the insistent request of Admiral Essen, visited the port of Hangö, in Finland, opposite Reval. There a harbour had been built, splendidly equipped to facilitate a landing of large German forces. The Finnish authorities explained the construction as being intended for merchant ships, and said it had cost them ten million marks. An inspection proved, however, that all these constructions were designed for a military landing. Meanwhile the promontories on the surrounding coast, on which Peter the Great had ordered forts to be built, remained unfortified.

Essen asked that this fact should be reported to the Emperor. I did this at my audience after the close of the session. The Emperor knew nothing of it. Essen had declared that if war broke out he would cause all these constructions to be blown up. This he did on the very first day of the war.

Nikolay Alexeyevich Maklakoff (b. 1871-1918) Minister of Interior (Dec 1912-Jun 1915)

Maklakoff was a member of the Union of the Russian People, (Black Hundred).

He resigned amid allegations that he supported a peace with Germany.

On the final day of the February Revolution 1917, Maklakoff was arrested and imprisoned, and a year later taken to Petrovsky Park in Moscow and executed.

Maklakoff's elder brother Vasily, served in the Second, Third and Fourth Dumas. In October 1917 he became ambassador to France and so was already out of Russia when Leon Trotsky rescinded his position.

CHAPTER VIII

Declaration of War—Disorganization in the Red Cross—At the Warsaw-Vienna Station—General Rennenkampf—Army Boots and the Minister N. A. Maklakoff—The Emperor at Lvoff (Lemberg)

THE heir to the Austrian Throne, leader of the war party and oppressor of the Slavonic people of Bosnia and Herzegovina, was assassinnated at Serajevo, with his wife, on June 15 (old style) by a Slav patriot. The blame for the crime was laid by Austria on the Serbian Government. An exchange of diplomatic notes was followed by an ultimatum and finally by the declaration of war. The Austrians crossed the Danube. The Serbs abandoned their capital and retired into the interior of the country.

The days that preceded the outbreak of war found me at Nauheim, where I was taking a cure.

On my return to St. Petersburg from abroad I learnt that the day before I had been repeatedly called up on the telephone by General Sukhomlinoff, the Minister for War. On hearing that I was expected home at any moment, he left a message asking me to telephone to him directly I arrived. I did so, and received a pressing request to call on him at once on a matter of urgent importance, as he himself was unable to come on account of pressure of work. I went at once, and the following conversation took place.

"I asked you to come and see me," said Sukhomlinoff, "because I am in a very awkward situation. Imagine what an awful thing has happened. The Emperor is suddenly vacillating in his decision, and has ordered the mobilization in the military districts intended for action against the Austrians to be stopped. I am utterly at a loss how to explain this sudden decision. If he insists on this order being carried out, the result may be a catastrophe. All the mobilization notices and orders have already been sent out. It is impossible to recall them, and any delay in the matter will be fatal. What am I to do? Give me your advice."

"I must tell you," I replied to the Minister, "that the declaration of war by Germany is absolutely imminent; if there is the slightest delay, the Germans will cross the frontier unopposed. Passing through Wirballen I saw a cordon of German cavalry stationed along the frontier, in full war kit and ready for action. You must tell the Emperor of all this at once."

"On the contrary, Mikhail Vladimirovitch, I beg you yourself immediately to request an audience at Peterhof and inform his Majesty of these circumstances personally."

"I should be pleased to do so, but time is short. There is not a minute to lose, and the procedure of requesting an audience is long. No, it is you who must go, and at once."

"But I have said it all several times, both by telephone and in conversation. It is obvious that the Emperor does not believe me. I am absolutely at a loss what to do."

I advised him to call immediately on the Minister for Foreign Affairs, Sazonoff. We found him on the point of starting for Peterhof. Apparently he was ignorant of the Emperor's altered state of mind. We informed him of the actual state of affairs. Moreover, I requested Sazonoff officially to transmit to the Emperor that I, as the head of the representatives of the people, solemnly declared that the Russian people would never forgive a delay which might precipitate the country into fatal confusion. Apparently the report of the Minister for Foreign Affairs, backed by the weighty evidence of the Minister for War and of the President of the Duma, obtained the desired effect. The Emperor overcame his scruples; the mobilization was not cancelled and followed its normal course.

Characteristically enough, the rumour of the postponement of the mobilization made the most painful impression on the troops of the St. Petersburg military district. A great number of officers visited me, demanding a definite answer as to whether the mobilization had been postponed. Their attitude to the ruling powers was by no means a friendly one, and had the mobilization been cancelled dangerous complications would undoubtedly have arisen.

St. Petersburg was the scene of ceaseless popular demonstrations, which took place mainly in front of the Serbian Legation, opposite my house. Every day the crowd approached our house and clamoured to see me. I came out on the balcony, and one evening, the clamour having become particularly insistent, I had come down into the street with some other members of the Duma. I was asked to

CHAPTER VIII

stand up in a motor car and address the crowd.

On the day that the Emperor issued the manifesto announcing a state of war with Germany, huge crowds assembled in front of the Winter Palace. After a special service in the chapel, the Emperor spoke a few words to the assembly in the Palace, concluding with the solemn promise not to lay down arms while a single span of Russian land remained in the enemy's hand. Thundering cheers resounded through the Palace and were taken up by the crowds outside. The Emperor came out on to the balcony, followed by the Empress. A vast crowd filled the whole square and all the adjacent streets. At the sight of the Emperor, an electric current seemed to pass through the mass of people; a mighty "hurrah" filled the air. Banners and placards, on which were inscribed the words "Long live Russia and the Slavonic cause," were lowered to the ground, and the whole crowd, as one man, fell on their knees before the Emperor. He tried to speak, raised his hand: the front rows endeavoured to silence the rest, but nothing could be heard amid the deafening cheers and roaring of the crowd. The Emperor stood for a while with bowed head, overpowered by the solemnity of the moment, when Tsar and people became one. Then he turned slowly, and withdrew into his apartments.

On leaving the Palace we mingled with the crowd of demonstrators, and came across some factory workers. I stopped them and asked how they came to be here, when they had been on strike, and almost on the point of an armed rising a short time ago. The workmen replied: "That was our own family dispute. We thought reforms came too slowly through the Duma. But now all Russia is involved. We have rallied to our Tsar as to our emblem, and we shall follow him for the sake of victory over the Germans."

The Imperial Duma and the Council of the Empire were convened on July 26 (Old style), 1914. Before the session the members of both Chambers were received at the Winter Palace by the Emperor. All the members attended the reception, even the Labourists. Everyone was stirred to patriotic enthusiasm, and party differences were forgotten. All the Ministers of the Crown, the highest dignitaries of the Court, the whole Council of the Empire, and the Imperial Duma were assembled in the great Nicolaevsky Hall.

The Emperor entered accompanied by the Commander-in-Chief, the Grand Duke Nicolai Nicolaevitch, and addressed the assembly in the following words:

" I welcome you in these solemn and anxious days through which all Russia is passing. Germany, followed by Austria, has declared, war on Russia. The great wave of patriotism and loyalty to the Throne which has swept our native land is to me, and presumably also to you, a token that our great Mother Russia will carry on that war, sent as a visitation by God, to its desired consummation. This unanimous impulse of love on the part of my people and their readiness to sacrifice everything, even life itself, give me the necessary strength, calmly and steadfastly to anticipate the future. We are not merely defending our honour and dignity within the confines of our own country, but are fighting for our congenital brother-Slavs. I rejoice to see that at this solemn moment the Slavs are being so closely and indissolubly united with Russia. I am certain that each of you, at your respective posts, will help me to bear the trials which are sent us, and that we all, beginning with myself, will do our duty to the end. Great is the God of the Russian land."

Ringing cheers resounded through the hall. The following speech was delivered by the Deputy-President of the Council of the Empire, Golubeff (the President, Akimoff, was ill and died soon after). The next speaker was myself. I said:

"Your Imperial Majesty: It was with a feeling of profound emotion and pride that Russia heard the call of the Russian Tsar summoning his people to be one with him in the solemn hour of trial sent to our Motherland. . . .

The representatives of the people, called into political being by the will of your Majesty, now stand before you. The Imperial Duma, which embodies in itself the unanimous impulse of all Russia's component parts and united in a singleness of purpose, has empowered me to tell you, Sire, that your people are ready to take up arms for the honour and glory of the Motherland. Without differences of opinion, views and convictions, the Imperial Duma, speaking in the name of the whole Russian nation, says calmly and firmly to her Tsar: 'Sire, be of good cheer, the Russian people are with you. With a firm belief in the grace of God, they will grudge no sacrifice until the foe is vanquished and Russia's honour vindicated.' "

The Emperor's eyes were full of tears. He replied:

"I thank you from my heart, I thank you, gentlemen, for your

CHAPTER VIII

patriotic spirit, which I never doubted, and of which you have now given me actual proof. With all my heart I wish you every success. God is with us."

The Emperor made the sign of the Cross; so did we all, and sang: "Lord, save thy people."

The general enthusiasm was unbounded. Coming up to me, the Grand Duke Nicolai Nicolaevitch embraced me and said: "Now, Rodzianko, I am your friend till death. I'll do anything for the Duma. Tell me what you want."

Taking advantage of this, I asked that the embargo should be removed from the daily paper *Retch**, which the Grand Duke had ordered to be suppressed for anti-patriotic articles against Serbia.

"Miliukoff has made a mistake," I said, "and himself repents of it. Make him promise to alter his policy. We shall now need all the support of the Press."

The embargo was removed, the *Retch* reappeared next day, and Miliukoff maintained a national policy throughout the war.

After the reception in the Palace, the deputies adjourned to the Taurida Palace, where the Duma sat. There was first a special service of intercession. The Cabinet was present in a body, as were the diplomatic representatives of the friendly Powers. Spectators crowded the galleries. The opening speech was delivered by the President of the Duma, who was followed by the Prime Minister Goremykin and the Minister for Foreign Affairs Sazonoff. The latter was loudly acclaimed by the Duma; he appeared to be deeply moved. It was some time before he could commence his magnificent speech. It was said that it had been written by Prince G. N. Trubetzkoy. Sazonoff was followed by the Minister of Finance, Bark.

After the Cabinet Ministers came the turn of the deputies from all parties and nationalities. All united in the cry—the integrity and honour of the Motherland must be defended. The speech of the Lettish representative was particularly pithy. "In every one of our huts the enemy will meet a deadly foe, whom he may perhaps behead, but even from the dying he will hear the cry: 'Long live Russia!' "

After the historic session of July 26 the Duma was prorogued.

* * *

* A Liberal paper voicing the opinions of the Constitutional Democratic (Cadet) Party.

After the very first battles, news of the highly unsatisfactory state of the medical transport service spread from the front. Chaos reigned supreme. Goods trains arrived in Moscow packed with wounded, who lay on the bare floor of the trucks without straw litter, themselves often without clothes, with badly dressed wounds and having had no food for several days. At the same time my wife, who was patroness of the Elizabeth community of sisters of mercy, received letters from the nurses at the front telling her that their unit was left without work and was constrained to remain an inactive spectator of the disorder, the nurses not even being allowed to enter the trains at the railway station. This state of affairs was the result of rivalry between the Ministry for War and the Red Cross. Instead of co-ordinating their work, each department acted independently.

The first aid organization on the military side was worst of all. There were no vehicles, no horses, and no medical appliances. In spite of this, no other organizations were allowed at the front. The only possible solution was to lay the matter before the Grand Duke Nicolai Nicolaevitch. I wrote him a letter, in which I pointed out that the general patriotic enthusiasm had caused numerous voluntary sanitary organizations to spring up, but that all these bodies, which were far better organized and efficient than the corresponding military service, were looked at askance by M. Evdokimoff, the head of the Army Medical Department, who placed difficulties and obstacles in the way of their work wherever he could. Meantime the wounded could not wait. They had to be doctored and looked after, while the advancing troops in the firing line had to be provided with properly equipped flying units. No time could be lost. As co-operation between the Army Medical Department and the volunteer organizations was apparently out of the question, it was necessary to place a dictator at the head of the whole medical and sanitary service, who could be entrusted with the task of bringing order out of chaos.

Having despatched this letter, I called at once on the Empress Marie Feodorovna, who was residing at the Elagin Island Palace, and told her everything. She was horrified.

"Tell me what you think ought to be done," said the Empress.

I advised her to send a telegram to the Grand Duke Nicolai Nicolaevitch, requesting him to order the head of the Army Medical Department, Evdokimoff, to improve the existing conditions and permit the volunteer Red Cross organizations, which he was deli-

CHAPTER VIII

berately preventing from working at the front, to take part in the work. The Empress immediately asked me to write out a telegram in her name. The result of our efforts was first a telegram and then a letter from the Grand Duke Nicolai Nicolaevitch, saying that he was in complete agreement with the President of the Duma, and promising to take the necessary steps. Soon afterwards Evdokimoff was summoned to the Stavka (General Headquarters) and Prince Alexander Petrovitch of Oldenburg was appointed supreme head of the Medical and Evacuation Department with a dictator's powers.

The Grand Duke Nicolai Nicolaevitch wrote to me that he had long ago insisted on Evdokimoff's dismissal. It was not carried out because he was in high favour with Sukhomlinoff and the Empress Alexandra Feodorovna, who persuaded the Emperor to keep him at his post. The reason for this, it was rumoured, was the Empress Alexandra's desire to oppose the wishes of the Empress Marie Feodorovna.

Soon after the opening of military operations it became apparent that the young Empress had nothing to do. In order to give Alexandra Feodorovna a prominent position in the public war work, a Supreme Council was established under her nominal presidency. The composition of this Council was exceedingly cumbersome. Though the Empress was nominally president, the Prime Minister, I. L. Goremykin, presided at the meetings, thus introducing an undesirable dual control in the management of affairs. Goremykin endeavoured to anticipate the wishes of the Empress, while she herself did not know what she was expected to do. The main source of the Council's activities—the financial side—hung, so to speak, in mid-air, as it had no legal funds at its disposal, and grants were expected to be forthcoming from the war fund, which itself was placed under the control of the Council of Ministers.

The members of the Council realized from the outset that debates would be purely academic and that all decisions would depend on other organizations, whose views on the subject were absolutely unknown and undefined. The sittings were purely formal and bored everybody, and the presence of the Empress created an icy atmosphere.

Soon after my arrival in Warsaw in the autumn of 1914, the

plenipotentiary delegate of the Zemstvo Union, Vyruboff, called on me and proposed that I should visit the Warsaw-Vienna railway station, at which 17,000 wounded from the battles of Lodz and the Beresina were collected. There we found a heartrending scene: the platforms were strewn with countless numbers of wounded, who lay in the cold rain and mud without so much as straw litter. The air was filled with their piteous cries: "For God's sake, have our wounds dressed, we've been without dressings for five days." It should be noted that after fierce fighting these wounded were removed from the front in goods trucks in complete disorder, and abandoned without help at the Warsaw-Vienna railway station. The only medical staff in attendance on these poor creatures were the Warsaw doctors, assisted by volunteer nurses. This was a Polish society unit numbering about fifteen members. One cannot speak too highly of the indefatigable devotion and self-sacrifice of these true friends of humanity. I do not remember their names, but heartily wish my earnest gratitude to reach them as a token of a Russian's heartfelt admiration. At the time of my arrival at the station these splendid people were working the third day at a stretch without rest or respite.

Such treatment of the wounded roused my profound indignation, and I immediately summoned by telephone the chief of the Medical Department, Daniloff, and the Red Cross delegate, General Wolkoff. As soon as they arrived we, with Vyruboff, discussed some means of coping with this horrible and tragic situation. Both General Daniloff and General Wolkoff declared emphatically that they had no medical staffs at their disposal; yet, on visiting a Red Cross hospital a short time before, I had found six doctors and about thirty nurses doing nothing. On my pointing out that they ought at once to be turned on to work, General Daniloff replied decidedly that he was unable to do this, as they were for staffing hospital trains now in formation. And this was said when 18,000 sufferers were lying unaided on the station platforms.

I demanded that General Daniloff should immediately proceed to organize special trains with heated trucks for the removal of the wounded from the station. Daniloff declared that this, too, he was unable to do, as by orders received from the supreme head of the Medical Department, the wounded were to be evacuated into the interior in hospital trains only, and he had only eight of these at his disposal. Outraged by such heartless indifference to the fate of these

CHAPTER VIII

suffering men, I threatened to telegraph to the Prince of Oldenburg and inform him of the disgraceful state of affairs and demand that those in authority should be brought to trial and dismissed for criminal inaction. The fear of the Prince was so great that my menace took effect, and they went energetically to work. Available doctors and nurses were found, and during the next two or three days all the wounded were attended to and removed to the rear.

Such was the state of the Army Medical Department during military operations.

While at Warsaw I visited General Russky. The Commander-in-Chief* made an excellent impression. As a man he was exceptionally modest, almost shy. I alluded to him as a national hero, and said I considered it my duty to call on him on my arrival in Warsaw. He looked terribly uncomfortable, and waved his hands in protest. "Oh no—I've nothing to do with it," he said.

While in Warsaw I asked the Grand Duke Nicolai Nicolaevitch's permission to visit the Stavka. I wanted to acquaint him with all I had seen and heard in Warsaw. In his conversation with me General Russky had complained of the shortage of munitions and kit, in particular the lack of boots. The soldiers in the Carpathians were fighting barefoot, and the delegate of the Zemstvo Union asked me to see to that. Russky said that the lack of munitions made the situation very difficult; elaborate manoeuvres were necessary to enable the troops to hold their ground.

The Red Cross hospitals and units I came across were all up to the standard. Conditions were bad only in the military hospitals: there carelessness, lack of requisites, and absence of co-ordination between the various departments were very marked. To get from the military clearing stations at the front to the Red Cross hospitals, one was sometimes obliged to walk ten miles or more with no chance of even hiring a waggon, as all the population had either fled or been completely ruined.

The Grand Duke greeted me very cordially, told me he was going to a conference of army commanders at Brest Litovsk, and asked me to accompany him. My proposal to use waggons loaded with hay for transporting the wounded met with his approval, and a few days later the Government was commandeering them in our province, and horses and waggons were being despatched to the front.

* Of the Western Front

In general the Grand Duke listened willingly to all I had to tell him, and invited me to come oftener and inform him of what was going on. At the mention of Rasputin I repeated to him the latest Petrograd gossip. The story ran that Rasputin had wanted to go to the Stavka and sent a telegram to that effect, but that Nicolai Nicolaevitch had replied; "Come—and be hanged." On my asking whether this was true, the Grand Duke laughed and said, "Well, not exactly." It was clear from his answer that something of the sort had actually taken place.

The Grand Duke complained of the fatal influence of the Empress Alexandra Feodorovna. He said frankly that she was a great hindrance to everybody. When at the Stavka the Emperor agreed to everything, but on rejoining her he altered all his decisions. The Grand Duke realized that the Empress hated him and desired his dismissal. He spoke of Sukhomlinoff, in whom he had no confidence and who was trying to gain an influence over the Emperor. He said that he had been compelled temporarily to suspend operations owing to the lack of munitions and the shortage of boots.

"You have influence," the Grand Duke added, "and you are trusted. Do organize the supply of footwear for the army as soon as possible."

I replied that this could be done by inviting the co-operation of the Zemstvos and other public organizations, particularly the former. Plenty of material could be found in Russia; labour, too, was plentiful, but one province produced leather, others nails, soles and so forth, while the cheap labour, the bootmakers who worked at home, lived in yet another region. The best way to bring all these together was to call a conference of presidents of the provincial Zemstvo Boards and organize the business with their assistance. The Grand Duke entirely approved of my scheme.

On my return to Petrograd I went to the Duma Organization Committee and asked the advice of the members of the Duma as to the best way of organizing the supply of footwear. We decided to send a circular of questions to all the presidents of the Zemstvo Boards and mayors of the towns. This was soon done, and favourable answers came pouring in. As there was reason to expect that this scheme would be opposed by the Government, I decided to call on some of the Ministers separately and talk it over with them. Krivoshein, Sukhomlinoff and Goremykin approved of the idea of a conference and promised to support my proposal before the

Cabinet. The interview with the Minister Maklakoff took rather a peculiar turn. On my statement that I was entrusted by the Commander-in-Chief with the urgent task of organizing the supply of boots for the army and of summoning a conference of presidents of the Zemstvo and Municipal Boards in Petrograd, Maklakoff said: "Yes, yes, what you say tallies exactly with the information we have received through our agents."

"What information?"

"According to my secret information, this conference, under cover of the needs of the army, will discuss the political situation and demand a constitution."

The Minister's declaration was so unexpected and grotesque that it made me actually jump in my chair, and I replied sharply:

"You have gone out of your mind. What right have you to insult me like this? To suppose that I, the President of the Duma, should, at such a time and under pretence of war needs, summon a conference for promoting revolutionary manifestations! Besides that, you are completely wrong, because we have a constitution already."

Maklakoff was visibly abashed and endeavoured to smooth matters over.

"Please, Mikhail Vladimirovitch, don't take my words as a personal offence. In any case I cannot authorize such a conference without the consent of the Council of Ministers, and I will raise this question at our very first meeting."

I informed Maklakoff that some of the Ministers had promised their support, and left him, feeling very indignant and upset.

The proposed conference was spoken of among the members of the Duma, and many presidents of the Zemstvo Boards were unofficially informed of the Commander-in-Chief's desire to enlist the Zemstvos' assistance for war work. The response was widespread. Some sent the necessary information; others, without waiting for an invitation, arrived personally in Petrograd. Then came letters from the Zemstvos reporting that orders had already been placed with the home-working bootmakers and the small workshops, that leather was being bought up and work was in full swing. One Zemstvo, in view of the shortage of tanning materials, despatched its agent to the Argentine. Even some of the governors responded to the call and expressed their approval of the idea of getting the Zemstvos to supply the army.

Here, too, the Minister Maklakoff did his best to hinder the work. He insisted that all orders should be transmitted through the medium of the governors. The public felt slighted and the work was hampered. Simultaneously Maklakoff issued the famous order prohibiting the transport of supplies from one province to another. This completely disorganized and cramped the plan for utilizing the products and possibilities of the various provinces. A few days later I received a letter from Maklakoff informing the President of the Duma that the latter's scheme for summoning a conference was disapproved of by the Council of Ministers, and that the task of supplying boots for the army was entrusted to the head of the War Commissariat, Shuvaeff, whose business it was to get in touch with the Zemstvos and municipalities. The very next day Shuvaeff came to see me and declared frankly that he was unable to take up the business, and was of opinion that the Zemstvos did not trust the Commissariat and would probably refuse to deal with it direct. Shuvaeff asked for our help. I replied that as the Council of Ministers considered I could not be trusted with the task, there was nothing left for me but to refuse to take any part in it.

Soon after this Goremykin called on me to discuss the summoning of the Duma. I reminded him of his promise to support the proposal in favour of a Zemstvo conference.

"What conference?" asked Goremykin in astonishment. "We never discussed anything of the kind in the Council of Ministers."

I showed Goremykin Maklakoff's letter. He read it with great surprise, repeated that no such question had been discussed in the Council of Ministers, and, referring to Maklakoff, remarked: "*Il a menti comme toujours.*"

In spite of opposition from the Government the Zemstvos continued to work. Shuvaeff received consignments of boots, while Maklakoff's orders were treated with contempt and indignation. The prohibition to transport produce from one province to another was particularly irritating. Owing to this there was a superfluity of produce in some provinces and a shortage in others, and sometimes it happened that landowners who possessed estates in different provinces were unable to transport their own seeds for sowing their fields.

When I reported all these matters to the Emperor he listened to me, but did not pay particular attention. I asked the Emperor his opinion of my visits to the Stavka, whether he did not consider them inopportune. The Emperor replied that he knew the Grand Duke thought highly of me, and that he personally would be pleased if I

CHAPTER VIII

went there oftener. This time the Emperor behaved most graciously towards me. I asked that the Duma should be summoned as soon as possible, and recounted to the Emperor the contents of Maklakoff's letter and his unfounded suspicion of the Zemstvos.

The Duma was summoned to debate the Budget Estimates, but the very first sitting developed into a patriotic demonstration, as in the early days of the war. Only the Extreme Left took no part in the manifestation, and the Balts and other Duma Germans maintained a strange silence. It was discovered that they had been conducting an antiwar propaganda, and documents were found proving one of them to have openly written that Germany's victory would benefit Russia. The Social Democratic Party intended to present an interpellation to the Government on the subject. Had this been done, the atmosphere of unanimity of the sitting would be broken, and the whole business would have made an unfavourable impression. An interpellation (to be valid) needed thirty signatures; the Left wing did not number as many members, and the motion depended on whether the Cadets would add their signature, as they had done on many previous occasions. This time, however, they refused, and everything passed off well. Miliukoff delivered an excellent and patriotic speech, mentioning a member of their party, Koliubakin, who had just been killed at the front, and said it with such feeling that not only the whole House, but members of the Government, rose to do honour to his memory.

The speech of the President of the Duma was followed by speeches from Goremykin and Sazonoff. They both pointed out that the hopes of victory were merging into certainty, that we stood firm in Galicia, and that from a military point of view we were well prepared for war. Goremykin mentioned that many new problems of internal policy had arisen out of the current events, which, however, would have to be dealt with after the war. The Minister for War, Sukhomlinoff, stated that the army was fully provided for, and that by March there would be more munitions and rifles than were actually required. As news was coming from the front of a shortage of munitions, the War Minister's words and categorical assertions had a calming effect on many people.

Soon after this sitting, in February, there appeared the Commander-in-Chief's statement that Colonel Miasoiedoff and his accomplices had been hanged. Colonel Miasoiedoff's friendship and frequent intercourse with the War Minister were common knowledge. After this episode many people became inclined to attribute our first defeat at Soldau to Miasoiedoff's activities. Confidence in Sukhomlinoff was being finally undermined; even rumours of treason became current. Faith in the generalissimo, the Grand Duke Nicolai Nicolaevitch, alone remained unshaken. In connection with Miasoiedoff's execution, many recalled the disclosures made by Gutchkoff as long ago as the time of the third Duma, when he had made charges against Sukhomlinoff and Miasoiedoff. Gutchkoff had then pointed out the undoubted connection between Sukhomlinoff and Miasoiedoff and a certain Altshuller, who, with Miasoiedoff, stood at the head of a firm which provided artillery supplies for the army through the medium of Sukhomlinoff. The activities of Altshuller and Miasoiedoff were exposed by General N. I. Ivanoff. At that time Gutchkoff charged Sukhomlinoff with having organized a secret surveillance over the officers' corps, which he had entrusted to Miasoiedoff. In spite of the growing public indignation against Sukhomlinoff, the Emperor continued to hold him in high favour.

At the front, during the winter, we continued our advance in Galicia. Amid untold hardships the troops pushed on over the Carpathians and descended into the plains of Hungary. Przmysl, on the 9th March, fell almost without resistance. Selivanoff, despairing of ever taking Przmysl, was on the point of raising the siege, when almost on the day fixed for the withdrawal the fortress surrendered. We captured 117,000 prisoners. After the fall of Przmysl, the Grand Duke Nicolai Nicolaevitch received a diamond sword with the inscription; "For the conquest of Chervonnaia Russ."*

In order to test the accuracy of various reports which had reached members of the Duma from the front, I made a journey to Galicia at the beginning of April. I was able to visit the front up to the river Dunajetz along the lines occupied by the armies of Radko Dmitrieff, Letchitsky and Brusiloff. Everywhere I heard the same thing: the armies lacked munitions. General Russky had complained of this as far back as the autumn of 1914. When I repeated my conversation with Russky to the Grand Duke at the Stavka, the latter assured me that it was only a temporary hitch, and that quantities of munitions would be forthcoming in a fortnight. Now the same com-

---

* "Chervonnaia (or Red) Russia" was the name of that part of Galicia which had of old formed part of the Russian dominions.

CHAPTER VIII

plaints were repeated from all sides. The generals were in des pair and implored our help. I was accompanied on this trip by my wife, her sister, and J. V. Glinka, who took down notes during our tour of the front. The Grand Duchess Xenia Alexandrovna travelled on the same train with us.

At the railway station at Lvoff (Lemberg) we caught sight of a group of civilians, who appeared to be expecting someone. The Grand Duke Alexander Mikhailovitch, who was meeting his wife, was also standing near them. We alighted from the carriage, and when the group of civilians approached us, we naturally made way for the Grand Duke and his wife, thinking it was they who were being met. A slight delay ensued. Then an old gentleman left the group of civilians and approached me with a greeting. It appeared that these were Galician public men, with Dudykevitch at their head, who had come to welcome the President of the Russian Imperial Duma. (I mention this episode because the Minister N. A. Maklakoff contrived to give the Emperor a totally erroneous account of this modest demonstration and of my whole stay in Galicia.)

Beautiful, gay Lvoff, all in green, made a most pleasing impression. The clean streets, the lively crowds, Russian soldiers, and even policemen at the street corners—there was nothing to remind one of a conquered city. One might suppose we were at home in the midst of friends, with no trace of hostilities; even the peasants, by their dress and manner of speech, reminded one of our Little Russians.

On our return to Lvoff after a visit to Przmysl, we learned that the Emperor and the Grand Duke Nicolai Nicolaevitch were expected to arrive in two days' time. Preparations were afoot for a triumphant welcome; arches were being built and the town decorated with garlands, flags and bunting I did not consider this visit very opportune, and in my heart of hearts criticized the Grand Duke Nicolai Nicolaevitch.

On the day of the Emperor's arrival everyone assembled in the temporary cathedral. Troops were lined up in the streets, crowded with people and the "hurrahs" rolled and swelled as the Imperial cortege drew nearer. After a Te Deum Archbishop Eulogius gave a moving address; everyone was affected and believed in our final victory. That same day there was a big dinner. The Emperor came up to me after dinner and said:

"Did you ever think we should meet at Lvoff?"

"No, your Majesty, I did not; and under the circumstances, Sire, I greatly regret that you have decided to pay this visit to Galicia."

"Why?"

"Because in three weeks' time Lvoff will probably be retaken by the Germans, and our army forced to abandon the positions it now holds."

"You always try to frighten me, Mikhail Vladimirovitch, and tell me unpleasant things."

"Your Majesty, I should not dare to tell an untruth. I have been to the front, and I am surprised that the Commander-in-Chief has allowed you to come here under existing conditions. The soil on which the Russian monarch has once set foot cannot be lightly surrendered: torrents of blood will be shed upon it, but nevertheless we shall not be able to hold it."

After dinner the Emperor stepped out on the balcony and spoke to the people, mentioning the ancient Russian territories. The crowd cheered; ladies waved their handkerchiefs. Next day the Emperor, with the Grand Duke, left for Przmysl.

A week later my wife and her sister returned to Petrograd, and I and my son went to the front to inspect the Red Cross organizations. We only just had time to return to Lvoff before our catastrophic retreat began. The warnings of my son and all serious military experts were realized; all our victories and the blood so freely shed were brought to nought by the shortage of munitions.

My son Nicholas, whose unit was attached to Korniloff's division, was surrounded, but thanks to his knowledge of the country managed to escape and brought safely back to the river San, not only his unit and the wounded, but part of the baggage and munitions. For this he received the order of St. Vladimir with swords. General Korniloff refused to abandon his division, which was spread over twenty-five miles. He insisted that the medical unit should depart, while he himself returned to the regiments which lagged in the rear. He was wounded, surrounded and made prisoner, with part of his division.

CHAPTER IX

The Stavka after the Retreat—Scheme of a Special Council of Defence—The Industrialists' Congress— Nicholas II and N. A. Maklakoff—The Port of Archangel— The Grand Duke Sergei Mikhailovitch.

ON my return from Galicia I called at the Stavka to recount my impressions to the Commander-in-Chief. The Grand Duke seemed greatly altered. During his tour he had appeared so gratified by the spirit of the troops, the organization of the rear and the medical conditions and supplies, and by the general confidence in victory, but now he was oppressed by the incompetence of the commanding staff, the want of talent in General Ivanoff's plan of campaign, and particularly by the deficiency in ammunition, rifles and shells. The atmosphere at the Stavka was depressing. The Grand Duke realized that Ivanoff's plans in the Carpathians had failed. Radko Dmitrieff was placed in an impossible situation. No fortified posts had been prepared along his line of retreat, and the refusal to send him reinforcements (general opinion laid the blame for this on Vladimir Dragomiroff, who was at loggerheads with Radko), together with the long drawn-out front line occupied by his army, too weak numerically and lacking the necessary amount of munitions, rendered his position desperate. The Third Army was forced to retreat beyond the San and abandon the whole of Western Galicia, which had been conquered at the cost of such heavy sacrifices.

This was not a time to stand on ceremony, and I considered it my duty to tell the Grand Duke the whole truth:

"Your Highness, you are sacrificing the men in vain, you must demand from the Artillery Department an absolutely precise account of what they have in readiness and the exact amount of the artillery supplies they are able to deliver. So far they have not kept their promises."

To this the Grand Duke replied:

"I cannot get anything out of the Artillery Department. My position in general is very difficult; the Emperor is being influenced against me."

The Grand Duke complained of the Minister Maklakoff, through whose influence he was prevented from finding out what the State munition factories were doing. The Grand Duke had persuaded the Emperor to appoint Litvinoff-Falinsky (the head of the Department of Industry and senior factory inspector) to carry out an investigation of all the factories working for the army. The Emperor, when at the Stavka, had given his consent and signed the appointment, but on returning to Petrograd, had changed his mind. Litvinoff- Falinsky was dismissed without any explanations.

My interview with the Grand Duke lasted some time. I insisted that in view of the existing conditions at the front it was impossible to be silent and to give way to compromise; that he must speak out and tell the Emperor the truth, and insist on his proposals being accepted. Who but the Commander-in-Chief had the right, not only to speak, but to demand?

To this the Grand Duke remarked:

"Oho, you express yourself pretty strongly."

"Not too strongly, your Highness," I replied; "the whole nation is fighting, and the whole people will revolt in the event of an unsuccessful war, if once they see that all their sacrifices and the blood they shed were in vain. The nation has shown itself worthy of its great mother country, but the Tsarist Government is utterly unworthy of Russia. First of all, it is absolutely necessary to insist on the resignation of Maklakoff and of the Grand Duke Sergei Mikhailovitch; the thieving gang operating under cover of the Grand Duke's name must be got rid of."

In speaking of his powerlessness to cope with the Artillery Department, the Commander-in-Chief mentioned that he was aware of the part taken, and the influence exercised, in questions of artillery supplies by the dancer Kshesinskaia, who acted as an intermediary for the placing of orders with different firms. When I suggested that it was high time Sukhomlinoff was removed, the Grand Duke replied;

"Here, too, I am powerless: Sukhomlinoff of late has enjoyed particular favour with the Emperor."

This conversation left an extremely painful impression. The Grand Duke did not possess sufficient energy.

As I took my leave, the Grand Duke asked me what could be

CHAPTER IX

done to save the situation. I proposed my old scheme, which I had long kept in my mind—to form a committee of members of the Duma, delegates from the various industries, from the Artillery and other military departments, with wide powers to deal with all matters of war supplies. The Grand Duke joyfully caught hold of the idea and promised to speak to the Emperor, who was expected at the Stavka. After my interview with the Grand Duke I had a long talk with his chief subordinates at Headquarters, Yanushkevitch and Daniloff. They both left an impression of mournful helplessness; both realized the horror of the situation and repeated over and over again, "You alone can save the situation." Yanushkevitch even spoke with tears in his eyes of the mental tortures he was going through, not being able to obtain the necessary supplies from the Artillery Department, and knowing in what dishonest hands it was.

On my return to Petrograd I invited Litvinoff-Falinsky to my house, and together with the deputies Savitch, Protopopoff and Dmitriukoff, we discussed the forming of a committee. Litvinoff and Savitch informed us of numerous cases when the Artillery Department had refused offers of factories to take orders for shells, shrapnel and so forth. The department refused to deal with private firms, while the output of the State factories, owing to their atrocious organization, amounted to about one-fifth of the normal. The dishonesty and cupidity of the Artillery Department was a common topic of conversation in Petrograd. Their methods struck the eye of even the man in the street. The munitions factory on the Liteiny was not even guarded; it was the same at all the other factories, and the explosion at the powder factory destroyed the last remnant of public confidence in those in control of the Department. German subjects still remained at the head of many State factories. They enjoyed the patronage of the Minister Maklakoff, several Grand Duchesses and a clique of courtiers, and it was impossible to obtain an order for their deportation. Treason was in the air. No other explanation could be found for the stupendous phenomena happening under the very eyes of the public. The climax was reached by the publication of the Miasoiedoff case*.

---

* Colonel Sergei A. Miasoiedoff (alt. Myasoedov) was a gendarme officer executed by a military court for espionage, on 20 March 1915. It caused a scandal because it happened just before a series of major losses that began the Great Retreat from Poland and Lithuania. For the military, it offered a convenient scapegoat for the atrocious number of casualties.

After collecting detailed data I sent a letter to the Grand Duke at the Stavka in which I reiterated all my former statements, supported by references to facts and documents. I also recounted the horrors which were taking place in the army as a result of the lack of munitions and the inefficiency of the higher military authorities, particularly of Sukhomlinoff. The Emperor arrived at the Stavka, and I received the following telegram from the Grand Duke Nicolai Nicolaevitch: "Your scheme must wait."

Next day, however, another telegram arrived summoning me to the Stavka, and bidding me bring those whom I considered useful. Litvinoff-Falinsky, Vyshnegradsky, and Putiloff accompanied me. At the Stavka I was received by the Emperor, and with perfect frankness urged him to recognize the necessity of convening a special committee in which public workers should participate. I told him of the general unrest in the rear, of the army's distrust in the military authorities at home, and of the inevitable increase of this lack of confidence while the army continued its retreat.

The Emperor looked extremely pale and worried; his hands trembled. He seemed particularly impressed when, myself deeply affected and scarcely able to restrain my tears, I spoke to him of the troops' unswerving devotion and love for their Tsar and Motherland, their readiness to sacrifice themselves, and their simple unaffected response to the call of duty. After describing the situation at the front and at home, I entreated the Emperor to remove Maklakoff, Sabler, Stcheglovitoff* and Sukhomlinoff. When the blood of so many men was being shed so freely, it was impossible to tolerate at the head of affairs the presence of persons who irritated public opinion —"which, after all, your Majesty should reckon with," I added.

The Emperor seemed pleased with my idea of creating a Special Council, and the outlines of the organization were immediately drafted. The Council was to include representatives from the banks which subsidized the war industries, delegates from the industries themselves, public men, members of the legislative chambers and representatives from the Ministry for War. The first to be summoned were Litvinoff-Falinsky, Putiloff, Vyshnegradsky, the banker Utine, Gutchkoff, and others. The Emperor asked:

"Who will preside over the Special Council?"

I replied that the chairman ought to be the Minister for War, as

* Minister of Justice.

CHAPTER IX

the Council would deal with war supplies. There was no other alternative, as, were another chairman appointed, Sukhomlinoff would at every turn endeavour to impede the work of the Council.

When rumours of the projected Council, which had not yet received official sanction, reached the War Ministry, they created great consternation. Attempts were made to persuade the Emperor that the Council was illegal, that it was actually a new Ministry, the formation of which necessitated a new law and the execution of a whole series of formalities which demanded a certain lapse of time. Fortunately these intrigues failed; the Emperor disagreed with the arguments put forward. Attempts were next made to prove that during the interim between the sessions of the legislative chambers the President of the Duma did not exist, and his presence in the Council would be illegal. The Emperor paid no heed to this either. The appointment of the Special Council was to be passed by the Council of Ministers and presented to the Emperor for sanction on the strength of Clause 87 of the Fundamental Code of Laws. The Ministers Maklakoff and Stcheglovitoff were particularly opposed to this Council. The former approached all the Emperor's entourage in order to obtain an audience, but the Emperor refused to see him. Before the meeting, when the question of the Council was to be decided, the Emperor summoned Sukhomlinoff and said to him:

"Tell the Council of Ministers that I greatly approve of the formation of this Special Council, and welcome the idea of the participation of the members of the legislative chambers."

Sukhom-linoff delivered the Emperor's message during the debates, and Goremykin took advantage of it to say: "I think that this is not an occasion for prolonged debate: we have but to conform to the will of our gracious Sovereign."

When it came to the vote, Sabler and Stcheglovitoff, after a private consultation, voted for the scheme; Maklakoff alone voted against it. (This, it was said, displeased the Emperor very much.) The scheme received the Imperial sanction, and the Council began its work.

Before the final settlement of the Council question by legislation, I considered my duty to acquaint the members of the Duma with the whole scheme. At the end of May I assembled the Senioren-Convent and laid before them the whole course of events which brought about the idea of this Council. The attitude of the various parties was characteristic. As might be expected, the members of the Right maintained a stony silence, the Nationalists and Octobrists fervently approved of all the steps I had taken. The Cadets, through their leader P. N. Miliukoff, quite unexpectedly declared themselves against my idea on the plea that all co-operation and intercourse with the Ministry for War under Sukhomlinoff would discredit the Duma, and that therefore they, the Cadets, would not on any account take part in the newly-formed Council.

To my still greater astonishment this view was hotly challenged by Kerensky. With his customary verve and impetuosity he attacked Miliukoff in an impassioned speech, proving the absurdity of his standpoint. "The Cadets," said he, "always take theoretical considerations as their starting point, and diverge into the abstract, repudiating everything, however useful in itself, which does not tally with their theory. I am a political opponent of the President of the Imperial Duma, but I see that he is suffering from our continual discords and is painfully seeking a remedy for the appalling defects of our military organization. We Labourists fully sympathize with his endeavours, approve of them and assure him of our support."

After hearing the opinion of my fellow-deputies I moved a vote of confidence which was carried unanimously. It was with great difficulty that the Cadets were subsequently persuaded to take part in the Council. The Extreme Left wing refused to participate, the sole motive of their refusal being that as members of the Left they would be treated with prejudice and suspicion by the representatives of the Government.

In the same month of May, 1915, a congress of industrialists was held in Petrograd. I heard from all sides that feeling ran very high amongst all the delegates and that revolutionary speeches might be expected. This would exactly suit Maklakoff; he was on the look-out for something to justify his constant denunciations to the Emperor, and would not miss an opportunity of closing the congress and arresting its chief promoters. Well-informed persons said that the Moscow business men had drafted a resolution for the Petrograd congress containing a demand for a Constituent Assembly.

On the morning of the opening day Prince G. E. Lvoff and the member of the Duma, B. Maklakoff (not to be confused with the Minister), called at my flat. Both were exceedingly perturbed and excited; they spoke of what might be expected at the congress, particularly of the Moscow resolution. They advised me not to attend the congress, and tried to intimidate me by pointing out the responsibility I would incur in the event of revolutionary speeches.

CHAPTER IX

"Think of the responsibility you are taking on yourself," they said.

"If one was afraid of responsibility," I said, "one could never do anything. I am determined to go to the congress; it must be saved, and calm restored."

They then endeavoured to persuade my wife to exert her influence on me and prevent my going. My wife replied that she could not interfere in my affairs, but was sure everything would turn out well.

I went to the congress with Protopopoff, was greeted with applause, and made an impromptu speech, in which I welcomed the delegates and appealed to them to unite their efforts, irrespective of party views and dissensions, to those of the Imperial Duma and other public bodies, in order to ensure to our gallant armies all that was necessary for victory. "Our troops," I said, "who are willingly sacrificing their lives for their country, must rest assured that the people at home are at one with them in the fulfilment of our common duty."

When the congress learnt that the Government's attitude towards the public was one of confidence and that something might still be done to improve the situation, the irritation against the Government subsided, and the members turned to a business discussion of the agenda. At the very first sitting a resolution was carried, differing totally from the one originally drafted.

Towards the end of May I sent in a request for an audience to the Emperor. No reply was forthcoming for four or five days. Instead, I learnt that the Minister Maklakoff was prejudicing the Emperor against the Duma and assuring him that the President of the Duma was going to present extraordinary demands, almost an ultimatum. These rumours spread to Moscow, and young Yusupoff, who had just arrived from that city, repeated stories current there according to which the President of the Duma had placed himself at the head of the revolutionary movement and had formed, against the Government's wish, a Special Committee, *Comité du Salut public*, on the model of the French Revolution (such, apparently, was the interpretation given to the Special Council).

At last the Emperor fixed a day for my audience; it was May 30. On entering the study I found the Emperor looking very pale and upset, and the stories I had heard of Maklakoff's intrigues came involuntarily to my mind. It was necessary at once to dispel all suspicions.

"Your Majesty," I began, "I have not come to you with any demands or an ultimatum . . . "

"Why do you speak of an ultimatum.? . . . What ultimatum?"

"Your Majesty, I am told that I have been described to you as a very dangerous man; you were told I should come not with a report, but with demands. You were even advised not to receive me at all."

"Who told you that, and whom are you hinting at as having prejudiced me against you?"

"Your Majesty, all this may be gossip, but these rumours are well-founded and emanate from such trustworthy sources that I made up my mind to lay them before you. The Minister of the Interior Maklakoff spoke against me to you. Sire, I have no report to make to you about the Duma. I have come to speak on general matters, to confess to you as a son to his father, to tell you the whole truth, as I know it. Do you command me to speak?"

"Speak."

The Emperor turned towards me, and all through my report looked me straight in the eyes, evidently testing my sincerity. I, too, never took my eyes off his face. I spoke of all the painful and harassing details of the past weeks; of the state of the Artillery Department; of the insignificant output of the munition factories ; of the fact that Germans stood at the head of most of them; of the Moscow disorders; of the troops, dying heroically at the front and betrayed in the rear by those who managed the supplies; of the baseness and intrigues of the Minister Maklakoff, and of much else. I said how, in connection with the Miasoiedoff affair, public indignation was growing against Sukhomlinoff, who was hated both at the front and in the rear and looked upon as Miasoiedoff's accomplice. I endeavoured to explain and prove that Sukhomlinoff, Maklakoff, Sabler and Stcheglovitoff could no longer be endured, that the Grand Duke Sergei Mikhailovitch ought to resign, as otherwise the resentment against the Artillery Department would fall on the head of a member of the Imperial Family, and indirectly on the Imperial Family itself: in a word, I spoke of all that I knew and that should be known by the Emperor.

My report lasted for over an hour, and all this time the Emperor did not smoke a single cigarette, which with him was always a sign of attention. At the end he leaned his elbows on the table and sat with his face buried in his hands. I finished, but he still sat in the same posture. At last I rose.

CHAPTER IX

"Why did you get up?"

"Your Majesty, I have finished, I have told you all."

The Emperor also rose, took my hand in both his, and looking me straight in the face with his kind, moist eyes, held my hand tightly and said:

"Thank you for your straightforward, frank and courageous report."

I bowed low and felt the tears welling up in my throat. The Emperor, too, was visibly affected and, after uttering his last words, pressed my hand once more and passed quickly out through another door, unable to conceal his emotion.

I learned much later what had been the real cause of the Emperor's emotion during this audience. After the Revolution I was summoned to give evidence before the Supreme Commission which at all costs was endeavouring to discover criminal intention in the acts of the ex-Emperor. I spoke for five hours at a stretch, trying to prove the absence of a criminal element in the Emperor's acts, which were dictated by a mistaken policy fatal to the country's interests but in no way by a premeditated desire to harm the country.

After I had finished. Senator Tagantzeff came up to me and said: "Now that you have finished, read this document."

The document was dated May, 1915 (I forget the exact date), and corresponded to the time when I was summoned to the Stavka after the Lvoff celebrations. It was a report from the Minister Maklakoff, who wrote:

"I have the honour most loyally to report to your Imperial Majesty that I have more than once had the pleasure to point out to your Majesty that the Imperial Duma and its President, wherever possible, to increase their power and importance within the State, and in their pursuit of popularity, are seeking to degrade the powers of your Imperial Majesty. I have the honour to draw your attention to the behaviour of the President of the Duma after your departure from the city of Lvoff. The President of the Duma accepted a festival organized in his honour by the Galicians, and, taking advantage of your Majesty's departure, comported himself as if he were the head of the Russian State.

"In drawing your Majesty's attention to the above, I beg to remind you of my not infrequent reports to your Majesty on the necessity of limiting the powers of the Imperial Duma and of reducing it to the status of a consultative institution." (I am quoting from memory, not verbatim.)

After reading the document, I handed it to Tagantzeff with the words: "What is there surprising in that? Only the Minister of the Interior's usual libel."

"Read what is written overleaf," said Tagantzeff.

On the back of the sheet stood the following words written in the Emperor's own hand:

"It is indeed high time to reduce the powers of the Imperial Duma. It will be interesting to see how Messrs. Rodzianko & Co. will take it."

The date of this annotation coincided with the time when the Emperor seemed favourably inclined towards the Duma, and was discussing with me the scheme for creating a Special Council of Defence.

Soon after my report Maklakoff was dismissed. This step met with general satisfaction. His successor was Prince N. B. Scherbatoff, an absolutely straight and honest man.

In addition to my report I sent the Emperor a letter in which once again I emphasized the necessity of removing Sukhomlinoff and accelerating the summoning of the Duma. I did not conceal that the debates would be tempestuous and criticism of the Government scathing, but it would be better for this to take place within the walls of the Duma than out in the streets.

It may have been this letter, or it may have been something else, that was the final straw, but at last Sukhomlinoff was removed and soon afterwards replaced by General Polivanoff, who enjoyed popularity in the Duma and among the general public. Shortly after Sukhomlinoff's dismissal, a Supreme Commission of Inquiry was set up, presided over by Petroff, a member of the Council of the Empire, and including two members of the Duma (Bobrinsky and Varun-Secret) and two members of the Council of the Empire.

After months of investigation and inquiry the Commission found Sukhomlinoff guilty of peculation and of State treason. In spite of this, Sukhomlinoff was not brought to trial for a long time, and not only did he remain at liberty, but he continued to wear his adjutant-general's epaulettes and retained the right of attending the sittings of the Council of the Empire.

The Emperor left for the Stavka on June 11, and on the 14th all

CHAPTER IX

the Ministers, except Sabler and Stcheglovitoff, were summoned thither. Of the new Ministers, Polivanoff and Scherbatoff were also present. The summoning of the Duma and the organization of war supplies were the questions discussed. The result was an Imperial rescript addressed to Goremykin, in which the Emperor for the first time publicly announced the summoning of a Special Council, and spoke of appealing to the public and to the industrialists, and promised that the Duma should be speedily summoned. The rescript made a favourable impression: the statement of confidence in the nation was clear and precise, and there was reason to hope that this attitude would remain unaltered. After this conference at the Stavka, Sabler and Stcheglovitoff were dismissed, and A. D. Samarin was appointed High Procurator of the Synod. He accepted this post on the condition that Rasputin should be banished. Stories (attributed to Goremykin himself) were current in society that the Empress had demanded that he should oppose Sabler's dismissal and Samarin's appointment, but that Goremykin had refused to interfere in the matter and said that the Emperor's will must be obeyed. The Empress would not submit, and spared no effort to regain her influence over the Emperor's decisions. Unfortunately she succeeded, and Rasputin, who had been banished to Siberia, soon returned to Petrograd.

The Special Commission was already at work. At its first sittings it began to investigate the affairs of the Artillery Department and discovered many dishonest transactions. Senior officials had to be dismissed one after another, and General Manikovsky was placed at the head of the Department. I called personally on the Grand Duke Sergei Mikhailovitch and told him frankly that it would be better for him to resign on the plea of ill-health; so far the accusations were directed against his subordinates, but as they might also be levelled against the Grand Duke himself, this would reflect on the Imperial Family. The Grand Duke soon resigned his post as head of the Artillery Department, but was simultaneously appointed inspector-general at the Stavka.

Scandalous abuses were discovered by the Council in the port of Archangel. As far back as the beginning of the war, the Duma had received information that the transport of supplies from Archangel over the narrow-gauge railway was very difficult, and that the port was crammed with stores. Supplies from America, England and France were piled up mountain high and could not be transported to the interior. At the very outset of the war Litvinoff-Falinsky had warned the Government of the appalling state of Archangel harbour. A large consignment of British coal was expected for the Petrograd factories, but there was no room even to store it. In spite of the fact that Archangel was the only military port which linked us up with our Allies, no special attention was paid to its proper equipment. The subject was raised at one of the very first meetings of the Special Council, and the question was put to the Government what they intended to do. The Government, in the person of the Ministers Sukhomlinoff, Rukhloff, and Shakhovsky, either wrote non - committal answers or made verbal promises which came to nothing. Towards the end, the accumulation of goods was such that packing cases lying on the ground were liberally sinking into the soil owing to the sheer weight of the stores piled up on top of them.

The Artillery Department declared to the Council that it was impossible to increase the output of shells, as there was no plant for the manufacture of time fuses. Members of the Duma urged that plant could be provided, if there was the will to look for it. The Council got into touch with technical and craft schools, some members undertook a tour of Russia, and soon telegrams began to pour in to the effect that thousands of apparatus had been found in various places. Factory plant evacuated from districts in enemy occupation could also be utilized, but here, too, no one wished to take the trouble to do it. The Special Council stirred up dormant energies. Textile and other factory directors, on being questioned by the Council, offered their premises for munition work; they added that they had already offered their services to the Artillery Department, but had received a reply that the State factories would suffice. Members of the Council made a tour of the State and private factories, and discovered at the Petrograd arsenal a million and a half time fuses, alleged to be of an obsolete pattern. As a matter of fact, they turned out to be perfectly adaptable to the new shells, and when tested gave 90 per cent, of bursts. After a discovery like this the output of shells could be immediately increased without waiting for new plant. From the very first month of the Council's work, the supply of munitions at the front was doubled, and continued to increase progressively.

* * *

CHAPTER IX

That summer a congress of the War Industries Committee met in Moscow. Public workers and business men responded heartily to the appeal addressed to them and fell to work with a will. Similar committees, with the help of the Zemstvos and municipalities, began to be formed throughout Russia, mainly composed of Zemstvo workers and factory managers. All kinds of factories, workshops and craft schools were adapted by them for production of war material. We knew in May that according to approximate estimates a sufficient quantity of munitions would be available in three months to arrest any further advance of the enemy. The enlistment of public services in war work and the creation of the Special Council was welcomed by the nation; a sigh of relief swept over the front, and the gall of recent defeats was mitigated by the hope of a brighter future. The possibility of working for the army and taking an active part in preparing its future successes helped people to bear the bad news from the front, where our retreat still continued.

I must here go back a little. The Duma met on July 19. The atmosphere was tense, and a storm was brewing. The Cadets and Left wing intended to move a series of interpellations. The Octobrists were opposed to this, saying this was no time for argument, when all energy should be concentrated on productive work. A number of Cadets proposed to raise the question of a Government responsible to the Duma. It required a good deal of persuasion to make them desist. P. N. Miliukoff supported the Octobrists on all questions, even against the Progressive party. In the House all efforts were directed towards the formation of a solid majority. This was crowned with a success which exceeded our expectations: we managed not only to unite several parties within the Duma, but also to reach an agreement with the Centre of the Council of the Empire. While the Left wing insisted on a responsible Cabinet, and the Right declared that this subject should not be broached, the Centre agreed that mention of a responsible Cabinet should be made not in the form of a demand but as a wish, and that at present "such persons should be called to power as enjoyed the confidence of the nation." Such a Government could work excellently with the Duma, as the war, contrary to all expectations, had smoothed away all petty controversies among the separate Centre parties, and an agreement had been reached which yielded a majority, united in the so-called Progressive bloc, which gave the Government firm support.

At a secret sitting on July 20 it was decided to call to account all persons who were to blame for the inadequacies in the equipment of the army. A law was passed providing for the formation of special committees attached to the Ministers for War, Transport, Commerce and Industry, Agriculture and the Interior, and including members of the Duma and the Council of the Empire, and representatives of trade and industry. The Cadets wanted to move a motion for the organization of a special Ministry of Supplies; the Government, on the other hand, sought to make the Special Council subordinate to the Cabinet. Fortunately, both these schemes were rejected and the Special Council Bill was passed in its already existing form, i.e., it was subordinate to the Crown alone, and the Minister for War was responsible for its acts.

Grand Duke Sergei Mikhailovitch (1869-1918)
Adjutant General in the Artillery Department

He was a first cousin to Alexander III. He resigned as head of the Artillery in January 1916 amid the scandal of arms dealing by his aides including his mistress the ballerina Kshesinskaia. When the Bolsheviks took power, they rounded up the few Romanovs that had not escaped Russia and imprisoned them at a camp in Alapayevsk. As the White Army approached the camp, Sergei and others of his extended family were executed.

CHAPTER X

The Emperor as Commander-in-Chief—Increasing Influence of the Empress—Goremykin dissolves the Duma—A. D. Samarin's Dismissal—The Putiloff Works—The British and our Mercantile Marine.

OUR troops in the meantime continued their retreat, which seemed as if it would never end. We abandoned Przmysl and Lvoff, and held out against furious attacks on the line Lublin-Kholm, thus covering our troops in the Warsaw region and escaping from the grip of iron in which the Germans threatened to hold us. The fortress of Novo-Georgievsk, while holding up the enemy's advance, was doomed. It held out heroically, was taken by assault, and few of its defenders escaped alive. Our other fortresses, Kovno, Ossovets and Brest Litovsk, offered scarcely any resistance and surrendered almost without fighting. Here, too, the treason and criminal negligence of the higher command staff and the War Ministry were fully revealed. The fortresses were badly built, the brick forts good for nothing, and the commandants of the fortresses totally incompetent. General Grigorieff, whether from stupidity or purposely, surrendered the fortress of Kovno almost without fighting. And it was of this fortress that Savitch, a member of the Duma, said in the Defence Commission that "it was a nut the Germans would find hard to crack." The "nut" proved to be a pack of cards.

As early as the end of April the Germans, simultaneously with their advance in Galicia, began to press on the Baltic front and, though with some difficulty it is true, succeeded in occupying Shavly, Libau and Mitau, and endeavoured to break through towards Riga. Vilna, too, was in the enemy's hands, and repeated attacks were made on Dvinsk. In the south we had a success near Tarnopol and warded off an advance on Kieff. There was panic in Kieff, the evacuation of the place was begun, and the population, preparing to flee, retarded the sowing of the winter crops. Trenches were being dug in the province of Podolsk, and the people were only awaiting orders from the Government to retreat into the interior of the country.

Confidence in the Grand Duke began to waver. The inefficiency of the higher command, the absence of plan, the retreat, bordering on flight—all tended to prove the incompetence of the Chief of the Staff, General Yanushkevitch. The Grand Duke ought long ago to have replaced him by Alexeieff, who had been Chief of the Staff to General Ivanoff during our advance in Galicia, and was now Commander-in-Chief on the Western front. Literally everyone advocated that name. I wrote of this to the Grand Duke, urging him to remove Yanushkevitch and appoint Alexeieff in his place.

In the meantime, rumours of the Emperor's intention to dismiss the Grand Duke Nicolai Nicolaevitch and assume the supreme command himself became more persistent. This, it was said, was the desire of the Empress, who detested the Grand Duke, and wished to remove the Emperor from the direction of internal affairs in order to govern herself while he was at the Stavka. The desire to remove the Grand Duke Nicolai Nicolaevitch from the supreme command was regarded as a great mistake by the Duma and the general public. The consequences of this insane plan could easily be imagined. Already our series of misfortunes had given rise to endless rumours, in which the truth was closely intermingled with the most fantastic lies, and in which the name of the Empress recurred more and more often. Something had to be done to avert the approaching calamity. Goremykin obviously knew of the Emperor's decision, but kept silence, neither daring nor wishing to oppose the intrigues hatched in the Palace.

It should be mentioned here that after my visit to Tsarskoe Selo and the Stavka someone spread the rumour of my coming appointment to the Premiership. My relations with Goremykin became, in consequence, more strained. It was not the time, however, for personal differences, and I determined to persuade Goremykin and the President of the Council of the Empire to wait on the Emperor and urge him to abandon his decision and leave the Grand Duke Nicolai Nicolaevitch at his post. Before doing so I wished to speak to Krivoshein, and telephoned to him at his villa on Elagin. He replied rather brusquely that he was busy and unable to see me. I

CHAPTER X

insisted that time was precious, that I had to see the Prime Minister and him, Krivoshein, and would come to Elagin immediately. Krivoshein greeted me with an ill concealed sneer, which betrayed his apprehension.

"I suppose you have come to preside over us," he said.

"No," I answered, "over you I will never preside."

My proposal that the Emperor's decision should be opposed was, of course, rejected. Goremykin spoke in the same strain as Krivoshein, talked of the sacred will of the Sovereign, said he could not interfere in military questions, and so on. I called on the President of the Council of the Empire, Kulomsin, and repeated all my arguments, but he also refused and, in the course of our conversation, tried to remember the name of thee courtier who on his bended knees implored the Emperor Alexander I in 1812 not to assume the supreme command of the army but to appoint Kutuzoff. There remained but one chance—to solicit an audience and entreat the Emperor myself.

Princess Z. N. Yusupoff called on the Dowager Empress and entreated her to use her influence over her son when he came to inform her of his decision.

During the audience at Tsarskoe I spoke to the Emperor of the unanimous desire to see General Alexeieff in Yanushkevitch's post. To my horror I received the following reply:

"I have irrevocably decided to dismiss the Grand Duke Nicolai Nicolaevitch and place myself at the head of the troops."

"Sire, against whom are you raising your hand? You are the supreme arbiter, and who is to judge you in the event of failure? How can you place yourself in such a position and forsake the capital at such a time? In case of misfortune, you yourself, Sire, and the whole dynasty may be in danger."

The Emperor would not listen to any arguments, and declared firmly: "I know; I may perish, but I will save Russia."*

After the audience I sent a letter to the Emperor, once again repeating all my arguments and entreating him to revoke his decision.

On August 21 the joint Special Councils held their first sitting at the Palace, the first sitting after the Bill was passed by the Duma.

* M. V. Rodzianko often recounted this scene, and his own feelings. He returned from Tsarskoe feeling quite ill and overpowered by the Emperor's insistence. He had a heart attack in consequence.

The Emperor, who presided, delivered a very good speech. I replied on behalf of the Duma. On August 23 an Imperial order was published to the Army and Navy announcing the Emperor's decision to assume the supreme command. Many people were terrified by this act. Princess Z. N. Yusupoff came to us in tears and said to my wife: "This is dreadful. I feel it is the beginning of the end: it will bring us to revolution." Contrary to the general fears and expectations this change produced no particular impression in the Army. Perhaps it was mitigated by the fact that munitions were arriving in plenty and the army had a feeling of greater security.

The formation of the Progressive *bloc* in the Duma and the Council of the Empire, as well as the occasional Speeches criticizing the policy of the Government, displeased Goremykin, and he began to impress the Emperor with the necessity of dissolving the Duma. Relations between the Duma and the Government became particularly strained after the Duma had accepted the bill for the creation of Special Councils attached to the ministries, widening its scope by its amendments, and passed to the bill for combating German aggression. This bill, as proposed by the Government, appeared to have been drafted with the purpose of discrediting the Duma. It was presented in such a form that the Duma was bound to reject it and consequently could be declared to be pro-German. To pass the bill as drafted by the Government was likewise impossible, since it was aimed mainly against the German settlers, i.e., small landowners, whom it was undesirable to irritate in war-time. Besides, the deportation of so large a number of settlers would lead to a reduction of the area under cultivation in South Russia. Finally, no mention was made in the bill of engineers, factory directors and staff, important traders, bankers and other more influential Germans.

The Emperor left for the army, and the direction of internal affairs passed into the hands of the Empress. Ministers, particularly I. L. Goremykin, waited on her with reports, and an impression arose that she had secretly been made Regent. Soon after the Emperor's departure Goremykin went to the Stavka and secured the Emperor's consent to dissolve the Duma.

At a Cabinet meeting on August 27 Goremykin spoke of the

CHAPTER X

necessity of dissolving the Duma, on the plea that it unsettled the public and impeded the work of government. The Duma meanwhile was busy debating a number of urgent questions directly bearing on the war, such as the Refugees Bill, German Aggression Bill, and others. The Cabinet disagreed with Goremykin, who was supported only by the Minister for Justice, Khvostoff. When Goremykin announced that he had already obtained the Emperor's provisional sanction to a dissolution, the Ministers proposed, in order not to cause too much irritation in the country, that a compromise should be arrived at; they should come to an agreement with the President of the Duma by which the latter would himself break off the sittings on the pretext that it was necessary for members to take part in the elections of the Zemstvo members of the Council of the Empire. But Goremykin refused any kind of compromise and, without warning, went to the Stavka again and brought back an ukase for the dissolution of the Duma. When he announced at the next meeting of the Cabinet that he had in his possession an ukase for the dissolution of the Duma, the Ministers were indignant and rebuked him sharply for going to the Stavka on such an important matter without previously consulting them. Goremykin attempted to close the debate and end the sitting, and, failing to do this, he left the meeting and went away without taking leave of anyone. The Ministers, left without a president, decided to present their resignation in a body; Polivanoff and Scherbatoff offered to wait on the Emperor and transmit the written resignations of their colleagues, stating they all declined to serve with Goremykin.

In those days Goremykin almost daily sought inspiration at Tsarskoe from the Empress, who, with her entourage, was again wholly under Rasputin's influence. Goremykin's wife became an open follower of Rasputin and was not ashamed to avow it. On receiving the Ministers at the Stavka the Emperor took the petitions brought by Polivanoff and Scherbatoff, tore them in pieces and said: "This is childishness. I do not accept your resignations. As for Ivan Loginovitch,* I have confidence in him."

Scherbatoff and Polivanoff left the Stavka without having achieved anything, and Goremykin acquired greater power than before. On September 2 Goremykin telephoned me in the evening saying he had important business to discuss, but was too tired to come himself. That evening a good many members of the Duma

* Goremykin.

had assembled at my flat, and were discussing the persistent rumours of Goremykin's intention to dissolve the Duma. This appeared so im-possible and improbable that, on learning of our telephone con-versation, the deputies expressed the belief that the Premier had probably asked me to call for the purpose of refuting this rumour. Goremykin, however, at once staggered me by handing me the Imperial ukase.

"Here is the ukase for the prorogation of the session of the Duma," was his greeting: "you will read it to-morrow."

Feeling very angry, I retorted sharply:

"I am surprised that you should disturb me to transmit such unpleasant news; it could easily have been done by telephone."

Nothing more was said. Obviously Goremykin had purposely hurried on the prorogation of the Duma so as not to allow the members to come to an understanding, and to take advantage of the sharp and heated debates which might possibly take place to dissolve the Duma altogether. The deputies who awaited my return at my house were astounded and indignant. We decided to warn the party leaders at once and request their presence at the Duma at nine o'clock next morning instead of eleven.

I was at the Duma at eight in the morning. The Senioren-Convent was immediately called, at which full vent was given to the general indignation. Feeling ran very high, and some of the speeches were almost of a revolutionary character. Some went so far as to refuse to submit to the prorogation and demanded that we should proclaim ourselves a Constituent Assembly. It needed a great deal of eloquence and calmness to persuade the hotheads to curb their anger and not to ruin the Duma and the country by playing into Goremykin's hands. I was greatly helped by Dmitriukoff; the poor fellow actually fainted.* Fortunately, Miliukoff shared my view and promised to persuade his party to abstain from sharp utterances. I purposely retarded the opening of the plenary sitting to let the indignation cool down in party discussions. I, myself, on learning of the ukase the evening before, had passed through a similar state of anger and indignation.

When I took the chair at eleven o'clock, there was such a hubbub in the hall as had never been heard there before; it was like a huge hive that had been disturbed. The excitement of the deputies had spread to the public in the gallery, where it was apparently ex-

* Dmitriukoff shot himself shortly after the Revolution.

CHAPTER X

pected that the Duma would lose its self-control, and sensational developments were anticipated. Officers in the gallery sat pale and anxious. It seemed as if the Duma could not but respond to the challenge and the insulting prorogation of its work at a time when it was occupied with important bills relating to the war.

The effect of perfect calm on the opening of the assembly was all the more impressive; the hubbub ceased, and in the midst of the tense silence the approach of a moment of tremendous import could plainly be felt. The reading of the ukase took place amid complete silence, and when, according to custom, I proclaimed "His Imperial Majesty—Hurrah!" the deputies cheered as loudly and loyally as ever and began slowly to disperse. The public, too, dispersed in silence; everyone suddenly seemed to feel a kind of assurance and realized that this has been the right course of action, and that the Government's petty desire to provoke agitation had failed because the Duma had shown itself to be above such provocation and given proof of statesmanship and wisdom.

Public bodies throughout the country behaved in a similar manner. The Lord Mayor of Moscow issued an appeal to factory workers urging them calmly to proceed with their work, so vitally necessary for the war. Zemstvos and Assemblies of the Nobility throughout Russia passed resolutions appealing to the Emperor to listen to the voice of the nation and appoint a Cabinet endowed with firm authority and enjoying the country's confidence.

The key was set by the Assembly of Nobles of Moscow, which determined to send a delegation to the Stavka to wait on the Sovereign. Unfortunately the Emperor refused to receive them. It seemed as if all Russia was imploring the Emperor for one and the same thing, and that it was impossible not to understand and ignore the appeal of the suffering country. I sent a report to the Stavka in which I endeavoured to prove the necessity of removing Goremykin and listening to the voice of the nation, which had sacrificed so much and deserved to be heard.

Persons were found, however, who hastened to weaken the impression produced by this unanimous impulse. The president of the United Nobility, Strukoff, wrote to the Emperor a letter, in the name of what purported to be the whole nobility, alleging that the situation was not as bad as was represented by certain groups, affirming the nation's confidence in the Government and the whole nobility's readiness to lay down their lives and devote their energies to fulfilling the will of those whom the Emperor had entrusted with authority. For some time this letter remained unknown to the public, and when at last it was circulated and the Assemblies of Nobles began to discuss it and censured Strukoff's action, it was already too late. The resolution of loyal subjects petitioning for a firm Government composed of persons enjoying public confidence was represented by Strukoff as a revolutionary act, and subsequent explanations of the nobles that Strukoff had acted without authority were disregarded.

Instead of persons enjoying the confidence of the nation being summoned to form a Government, the two popular Ministers, Samarin and Scherbatoff, were compelled to resign, while the next session of the Duma was repeatedly adjourned. Samarin's resignation was due to the following incident. Barnabas, Bishop of Tobolsk, had discovered in his diocese the relics of a certain John, and without waiting for him to be canonized by the Synod, held services in his honour as a saint. On Samarin's motion the Synod inquired into the case and resolved that Bishop Barnabas should be summoned to Petrograd to explain himself. Barnabas arrived and attended the sitting of the Synod, but declined to give explanations, saying tersely: "I've nothing to tell you." He quitted the assembly forthwith and disappeared, so that for a long time nothing was known of his whereabouts. During that time Barnabas lived at the flat of Prince Andronikoff, one of Rasputin's friends.

Samarin wanted to raise a fresh point concerning the bishop's disobedience to the Synod and deprive him of his rank, but the Synod was given to understand that Barnabas was to be left alone. The latter meanwhile produced an autograph letter from the Emperor authorizing the offering of special prayers to Saint John and the holding of services in his honour—a proceeding in direct contradiction to all canonical regulations. Samarin then waited on the Emperor at Tsarskoe Selo to present a detailed report on the case. As the written report was very long, Samarin asked whether the Emperor would not prefer a verbal summary. By way of an answer the Emperor reminded him that he, Samarin, was due at a Cabinet meeting, and said he would keep the report to read at leisure. Samarin left and arrived at the meeting of the Cabinet, but before he had time to take part in it, was called aside by Goremykin, who handed him a letter from the Emperor in which he was instructed to inform Samarin of his dismissal from the post of High Procurator of

CHAPTER X

the Synod.

Samarin left for Moscow. There he was given a triumphant welcome at the Assembly of the Nobles then in session and universally acclaimed. The Minister of the Interior, Prince Scherbatoff, resigned of his own free will soon after Samarin. He frankly admitted that he was utterly sick of the everlasting intrigues which prevented any useful work.

Samarin was succeeded by Volgin, a man scarcely above the commonplace, while Khvostoff, an extremely conservative member of the Duma, was appointed in place of Scherbatoff. In an interview with the representatives of the Press he announced his desire to win public confidence, and launched a campaign against the high cost of living. He went to Moscow, organized the unloading of goods trucks with the help of the garrison, made a great fuss and got himself talked about, and at first appeared to have done something. He was exceedingly cordial to me, called frequently, and among other things alluded to his campaign against Rasputin. He urged that the latter should be fought with his own weapons, and for that object wished to introduce a monk named Mardary into the Palace. He thought the best way to render Rasputin harmless was continually to intoxicate him, for which purpose he, Khvostoff, had already advanced 5,000 roubles from his own private resources.

By this time a shortage of various commodities had begun to be felt in the towns, owing partly to the great number of refugees, but more often to the Government's inefficiency. To combat the high cost of living fixed wholesale and retail prices were introduced, but as these were below market prices, the traders, to avoid losses, either concealed the goods or sold them surreptitiously. The disorder on the railways, particularly the abhorrent system of bribery, served to raise prices still higher. The overhead charges for transport frequently exceeded the value of the goods transported. A. F. Trepoff, who succeeded Rukhloff as Minister for Ways and Communications, only increased the muddle, because, as he owned himself, he had never had anything to do with transport.

As a result Petrograd was threatened with famine. The Government then decided to suspend all passenger traffic between Moscow and Petrograd for six days in order to rush goods trains to the capital. This measure, however, had little effect, as no one had thought of organizing an increased transport of supplies from other districts to Moscow. Passenger traffic was stopped, but the goods trucks returned from Moscow half empty. It might almost have been thought that instead of really doing something, the Ministers merely wanted to make a show of their zeal.

Meanwhile the Special Council was hard at work organizing the war supplies, and important results had already been achieved. Both the Zemstvos and the war industries committees rendered valuable assistance, and despite the Government's obstruction, the supply of munitions and other necessaries increased daily. An event occurred at that time in the Special Council which clearly revealed the disastrous influence of irresponsible persons even in the matter of war supplies. One of the largest munition factories was the Putiloff works in Petrograd. The chief shareholder, Putiloff, who was also manager of the Russo-Asiatic Bank, wishing to obtain a State subsidy of 36,000,000 roubles, resorted to the following manoeuvre. The Russo-Asiatic Bank refused further credits to the Putiloff works. The board then applied to the Government asking for a subsidy and threatening to close the works if it did not get it. As the works were producing munitions and other war material, it was reasonable to expect that the subsidy would be granted, even to the amount of 36,000,000 roubles. The whole intrigue was perfectly clear to all well-informed persons.

Instead of a subsidy being granted, I proposed that the works should be commandeered. A resolution to that effect was passed almost unanimously by the Special Council, but, quite unexpectedly, an Imperial order was received to revise the case. This was done with the help of Rasputin, with whom Putiloff was on good terms. At the next Council meeting, all the members of the Government voted against the commandeering, one of them. Admiral Giers, openly saying, "I was ordered to vote against it." The votes of the members of the Duma and the Council of the Empire were divided. The best and firmest among them were unfortunately absent "for worthy reasons." The proposal that the works should be commandeered was rejected. I found myself almost alone; the power of gold was against me.

The case of the Putiloff works was not unique. The Special Council was continually in collision with the influence of irresponsible persons, who put obstacles in its way.

At the beginning of the war a special committee was formed in London to deal with all orders for war supplies abroad. This co-

CHAPTER X

mmittee included a number of business men, both British and Russian, and was at first presided over by the Grand Duke Mikhail Mikhailovitch and later by General Hermonius. Before the Special Council was created this committee's activities were controlled by no one. At the time of its formation the British Government had stipulated that all our orders for war supplies abroad should be given through that committee, thus preventing us from being masters of the situation and making us dependent on the arbitrary discretion of British business men. Orders placed in America were never punctually executed, which gave rise to continual and unexpected complications and negotiations. The ships which carried the supplies to Archangel had to be convoyed by British cruisers as a safeguard against the attacks of German submarines. The next step was that the British proposed to take over our entire mercantile marine on the pretext of convenience and unity of command. Had this been agreed to, we should have renounced our mercantile marine and placed ourselves in heavy bondage to the British. General Headquarters had agreed to such an arrangement. I raised the question at the meeting of the Special Council on January 2, 1916, proving that an agreement of the kind could not be concluded without the knowledge of the Special Council. My motion was seconded only by Gurko, the rest of the members stood aloof, probably because the motion would be contrary to the wishes of the Emperor.

After the meeting I was visited by the British Ambassador, Sir George Buchanan, and the Military Attaché, General Knox. I told them frankly that the British were taking advantage of our difficulties and forcing the Emperor's consent to a transaction obviously detrimental to Russian interests. "This is blackmail," I said; "it is unworthy of a great nation and an Ally. The Russian people will not tolerate such a humiliation, and it will have to be spoken of from the tribune of the Duma." I repeated these arguments at my next audience with the Emperor. The British ceased their insistence, and the matter sank into oblivion. At the same time, Grigorovitch, foreseeing complications with England, had entered into negotiations with Japan, These were crowned with success, and on the payment of their expenses for repairs the Japanese Government returned to us the warships *Variag*, *Peresviet* and *Poltava*, sunk during the Japanese war. After a long voyage round Africa, which was kept strictly secret, these ships reached Archangel, and we obtained our own convoys for our merchant ships.

The ukase which prorogued the Duma had mentioned November as the latest date for the re-opening of the session; Goremykin's attitude, however, lent colour to the persistent rumours that the date of its meeting was quite problematic. As a matter of fact November was nearly over, and nothing as yet heard of the re-opening. The work of the Budget Commission was in full swing. Deputies were restless and asked me to make the actual situation clear. At my audience with the Emperor I spoke again of Goremykin, of how he handicapped all work, impeded activity in the rear; I mentioned the activities of the bankers in the matter of war supplies from the factories. When I asked that the summoning of the Duma should be accelerated. The Emperor replied: "Yes, all right, I will speak of it to Ivan Loginovitch."

Not half an hour after my return from Tsarskoe Selo, I received an Imperial rescript. In this document, addressed to the President of the Duma, mention was made of the efficient work of the Budget Commission, and it was stated that on the termination of this work a report would be made by the President of the Duma and the legislative chambers would be convened. This letter placed me in an absolute quandary. The work of the Budget Commission always proceeded parallel to that of the plenary sitting of the Duma, and the re-opening of the session in no way depended on the termination of the work of the Commission. The Imperial letter had followed on my audience with the Emperor, and the impression it made was as if some compromise had been reached. As a matter of fact it was another ruse on the part of Goremykin, who wanted to lower the prestige of the President of the Duma in the eyes of the representatives of the people. The deputies were, of course, surprised, but it is doubtful whether anyone believed that the postponement of the session had taken place with my consent. At the same time rumours were circulated that the President of the Duma was about to receive some high honour. These rumours were justified, and on December 6* I learnt I had received the Order of St. Anne, first class. It should be mentioned that prior to this the Minister of War, Polivanoff, had, without my knowledge, sent my

---

* The feast of St. Nicholas—the Emperor's name day.

name in for a decoration in view of my special services for the army, but his petition was refused. The present honour was obviously conferred to emphasize my supposed compliance in the question of the summoning of the Duma. In order to leave no doubt that the honour conferred did not concern my work in the Special Council, the ukase stated that the Order was conferred on the "Warden of the Novomoskovskaia Gymnasium for Boys," i.e., not on the President of the Duma.

Aleksey Andreyevich Polivanoff (b. 1855-1920)
Minister of War (1915-1916)
Chief of Staff (1905-1912)

General Polianoff was promoted from deputy war minister to bolster the war effort. He was among the military leaders that tried in vain to dissuade the Tsar from taking over the supreme command of armed forces in September 1915.

For his concerns, and for previously being overly supportive of the Duma, he was also one of the senior staff that was removed from office by the Tsar on the recommendation of the Tsarina (March 1916).

CHAPTER XI

Strikes—The Inventor Bratoliuboff and Mme. Brasova—Letter to Goremykin—The Maid of Honour M. A. Vasilchikova.

AFFAIRS in the country were going from bad to worse. Profiteering, bribery and other abuses were flourishing on an unprecedented scale. In the towns prices were soaring up owing to the disorganization of transport. Strikes began to occur at the munition factories, followed by arrests, mainly of those workmen who were in favour of order and opposed to the stoppages.

I visited the Putiloff works with some of the members of the Duma to see how orders were being executed and attempt to parley with the men. The workmen listened most attentively to what we said, were perfectly frank with us, and urged that the strike was not in the least a political one, but was entirely due to the discrepancy between the wages and the rise in the cost of living. After I had had a talk with the board of managers, the workmen's claims were satisfied, but soon afterwards the men who had spoken with us were arrested. These arrests led to further unrest, and it was only after insistent pressure on our part that the workmen were released.

The Bratoliuboff affair came to light about December of the same year. A certain Bratoliuboff approached the Grand Duke Mikhail Alexandrovitch, alleging that he had invented an apparatus for throwing inflammable liquid from a long distance. In order to construct this apparatus special plant was needed, which, he alleged, had to be brought over from America. For this purpose the inventor claimed a subsidy of 30,000,000 roubles. Having secured the patronage of Mme. Brasova (the Grand Duke's morganatic wife), Bratoliuboff succeeded in gaining an influence over Mikhail Alexandrovitch. The latter went to the Emperor and persuaded him to sign a rescript in the name of the Grand Duke, authorizing Bratoliuboff to draw the desired sum by instalments from the State Bank. Tests of the new apparatus were arranged at the Grand Duke's wish. The results proved highly unsatisfactory; the inflammable liquid could not be projected to any distance, but the five soldiers

CHAPTER XI

who manned the apparatus received fatal injuries.

Lukomsky, the Assistant Minister for War, reported this affair to Polivanoff. Polivanoff hastened to explain to the Grand Duke that all grants for war orders had to be passed through the Special Council and the Minister for War. The Grand Duke admitted his error, apologized with the greatest sincerity and called immediately on the Emperor, after which steps were taken to prevent Bratoliuboff from cashing the draft. It turned out, however, that this bold inventor had already called at the bank, and, when doubt was expressed there as to the validity of his claim, produced a photograph of the rescripts addressed to the Grand Duke. The bank then advanced about 2,000,000 roubles.

It transpired later that this Bratoliuboff was backed by a gang of profiteers who were aiming at enriching themselves at the expense of the State. Bratoliuboff was exposed, but Lukomsky was soon dismissed from the post of Assistant Minister for War. According to reliable information his discharge was due to his part in the Bratoliuboff affair.

Prince Lvoff, president of the All-Russian Zemstvo Union, arrived in Petrograd at the beginning of December. He called on me and sat till three o'clock in the morning talking of affairs in Moscow, where public feeling was taking a distinctly revolutionary turn. The most well intentioned people spoke openly of the Government's corrupttion and did not scruple to lay all the blame on the Emperor and Empress.

At this very time General Russky was recalled from the front and removed from active participation in the war. No one believed in his alleged illness, and all were certain that he owed his disgrace to the influence of the German party, which resented his stern measures in the Baltic provinces. General Plehve was appointed in his stead.

Public indignation was growing against Goremykin, who was held responsible for the general confusion and who, whenever he was asked any question in connection with the war, invariably replied: "The war does not concern me. It is the War Minister's business."

Petitions and persuasions addressed to the Emperor with the object of securing Goremykin's removal had no effect. After my interview with Prince Lvoff, and under the impression produced by instances of appalling disorder in the interior of the country quoted at a meeting of the Special Council, I determined to write personally to Goremykin. I wrote at once, during the meeting, as follows:

"Dear Ivan Loginovitch,

"I am writing under the impression of what I have just heard at to-day's meeting of the Special Council concerning the catastrophic state of the railway transport. This question had already been raised by the members of the first Special Council and a commission formed to deal with the matter, but its work was confined to talk, references and estimates, and the catastrophe which was then merely foreshadowed has now become a reality.

"The President of the Special Council has doubtless informed you of conditions in the munition factories, where a stoppage is imminent, and also of the prospect of a famine with which the population of Petrograd is menaced, and which may lead to unrest and consequent disorders.

Both I myself and the members of the Special Council are fully persuaded that our country is heading for ruin owing to the Government's apathy and complete lack of initiative in taking the steps necessary to avert the terrible calamities which are approaching. I consider it the bounden duty of the Council of Ministers, of which you are President, immediately to give proof of that solicitude for the destinies of Russia which, as a body of statesmen, it is its duty to show. A year ago the members of the Special Council had already foreseen what is happening now, and you, Ivan Loginovitch, cannot deny that I myself have warned you more than once. The only answer, however, that I ever got from you was that this was no concern of yours and that you could not interfere in matters concerning the war.

"Such answers are now inadmissible. The fatal end of the war is approaching, but a general disintegration in all branches of our national life, coupled with a lack of essential commodities, is growing in the rear of our national armies. The victorious spirit of the people and their faith in their own powers are being crushed by the inactivity of the Government.

Your paramount duty is, without losing a moment, to manifest at last the greatest zeal to remove all obstacles from the path to victory.

"I beg definitely to state that we, the members of the Imperial Duma, possess a merely consultative voice, and cannot, therefore, be held responsible for the inevitable and imminent collapse.

"If the Council of Ministers fails to take such steps as may yet save our country from disgrace and humiliation, the entire responsibility will rest upon you. If you, Ivan Loginovitch, feel that you lack strength to bear this heavy burden, and to use all available means to help the country to emerge on to the high road to victory—have the courage to own this and make way for younger and more energetic men.

"The decisive hour has struck; events, stem and inexorable, are

CHAPTER XI

drawing near, pregnant with consequences which may prove fatal to Russia's honour and dignity. Do not tarry, I earnestly beg of you—the Fatherland is in danger."

I read this letter, before sending it, to members of the Duma, who approved of its contents, and it was despatched to the Prime Minister. One of the members, without my knowledge, made a copy of it, which was circulated in Petrograd, and people spoke of it to me everywhere. On receipt of the letter Goremykin read it to the members of the Cabinet, and resenting its "harsh tone," declared that he would inform the Emperor of its contents.

After receiving the name-day honours I solicited an audience from the Emperor, but he replied that he was leaving for the southern front and would see me in three weeks' time. The audience took place at the end of December. The work of the Budget Commission was terminated, and the deputies insisted on the Duma being convened. In spite of the approaching Christmas holidays I despatched a report on the work of the Commission and again solicited an audience. This time my request was gratified. I proffered my thanks for the honours received, urged the necessity of immediately convening the Duma, spoke of the depressing effect produced by the recent congress of the ultra-Conservatives and, wishing to avoid misrepresentations, showed the letter I had written to Goremykin.

To all this no definite reply was vouchsafed.

In addition to all the disquieting events which caused unrest to spread among the people, persistent rumours began to be circulated of Germany's offer of a separate peace and of alleged secret parleys to that effect. This appeared all the more probable seeing that early in September I received from M. A. Vasilchikova, maid of honour to the Empresses, then in Austria, a very strange letter urging me to promote the cause of peace between the belligerent countries. The letter was written in incorrect Russian and made the impression of having been translated from the German. The envelope bore neither stamp nor postmark, and had been delivered by some stranger. Similar letters—seven in all—had been sent to the Emperor, the Grand Duchess Marie Pavlovna, the Grand Duchess Elizabeth,* A. D. Samarin, Prince A. M. Golitzyn and the Minister for Foreign Affairs, Sazonoff. I immediately communicated this letter to the last-named, who replied that he had received a similar one himself, as had also the Emperor. He advised me, as he had advised the Emperor, to throw it in the waste-paper basket. I could not but ask Sazoroff how he could tolerate that Mlle. Vasilchikova should retain her Court rank.

To everyone's surprise M. A. Vasilchikova made her appearance in Petrograd in December. At Tornea she was met by a special courier, and rooms were reserved for her at the Astoria Hotel. This I learnt from Sazonoff, who added that he thought all this was done by order from Tsarskoe Selo. In Petrograd, Mlle. Vasilchikova was boycotted by all her former friends. On the other hand she paid frequent visits to Tsarskoe, where she was received, though this fact was kept secret. When, in connection with current rumours, the question of a separate peace was raised in the Budget Commission, the Minister of the Interior, Khvostoff, stated that such rumours were actually being circulated by unknown persons, that the question had never been discussed by the Government, and that had the contrary been the case he would not have remained at his post for a moment. After this I thought it necessary to read Mlle. Vasilchikova's letter to the members of the Commission and mention the fact of her arrival in Petrograd. Khvostoff, looking extremely ill at ease, was obliged to own that she had actually stayed in Petrograd, but that by then she had been deported. Khvostoff told me privately after the sitting that the day after her arrival Mlle. Vasilchikova went to Tsarskoe (to see whom he did not say), and how he had himself searched her rooms at the Astoria. He found, among other things, a letter addressed to her from the Emperor Francis Joseph and other documents testifying to her having visited the Kaiser at Potsdam, received instructions from the Chancellor, Bethmann-Hollweg, concerning her activities in Petrograd, and stayed for a month with the Duke of Hesse, from whom she brought two letters to his sisters—the Empress Alexandra Feodorovna and the Grand Duchess Elizabeth. The Grand Duchess returned hers unopened. This we learnt from her mistress of the household, Countess Olsufieff.

The Emperor, it was said, was seriously displeased by Mlle. Vasilchikova's sudden arrival, and ordered her to be banished to Solvychegodsk.† Instead of this Mlle. Vasilchikova lived unmolestted on the estate of her sister, Mme. Miloradovitch, in the province of Tchernigoff.

* Sister of the Empress Alexandra Feodorovna.
† A remote town in north-eastern Russia.

CHAPTER XII

The Metropolitan Pitirim and Sturmer—The Emperor in the Duma—Bad Meat and Food Shortage—Arrival of MM. Viviani and Thomas—The Prime Minister's Dinner—Russian Parliamentary Delegation—A Dictatorship Scheme.

On January 14, 1916, Mgr. Pitirim, the newly-appointed Metropolitan of Petrograd, notified me by telephone of his desire to call on the President of the Duma. Pitirim, after occupying episcopal sees in various provinces, later became Exarch of Georgia and finally, through Rasputin, succeeded in gaining the confidence of the Empress and was appointed Metropolitan of Petrograd in succession to Mgr. Vladimir. He was a notorious intriguer, and very circumstantial rumours were current regarding his morality. He at once began to play a part in public life; Ministers visited him, his opinions were quoted, and his name recurred continually in the Press. He found time to visit the Emperor at the Stavka and, according to the papers, was there entrusted with a message to the President of the Duma concerning the date for the reopening of the House.

The Metropolitan arrived at my flat accompanied by the priest Nemertzaloff, a member of the Duma, whom he had obviously brought to be a witness of our interview, and launched at once into politics.

"I come to express my admiration of your Excellency's letter to the Prime Minister Goremykin. I must tell you that its contents are known at the Stavka."

"That is no news to me, Vladiko; I myself submitted a copy of it to his Majesty."

Pitirim here remarked soothingly:

Ivan Loginovitch will not stay long; he is too old. His post will probably be filled by Sturmer."

"Yes, so I heard. But it is doubtful whether this will mean any change. Moreover, a German name has a noxious ring nowadays."

"He will change his name to Panin."

"Such a deception will satisfy no one. . . You remember, Vladiko, the saying about a 'baptized Jew,' and so on?"

Pitirim began talking about the Duma, and tried to convince me of his desire to come to an understanding and work shoulder to shoulder with the representatives of the people. This, I remarked, was hardly possible, as beyond the Budget Estimates of the Holy Synod there was no point of contact between the Duma and the Metropolitan.

The Metropolitan apparently felt rather ill at ease and kept glancing to Nemertzaloff. Our conversation drifted to Church reform, and I said frankly:

"Reform is absolutely necessary. If you, Vladiko, wish to earn the gratitude of the Russian people, you must spare no effort to purify the Orthodox Church from the pernicious influence of the *khlysty* and the interference of the enemies of Orthodoxy. Rasputin and men like him must be expelled, and your own name cleared from the opprobrium* of being looked upon as a nominee of Rasputin."

"Who told you that?" asked Pitirim, turning pale; and, as if cross-examining me, he inquired whether I had ever spoken of Rasputin to the Emperor.

"Yes, many a time. . . As for you, Vladiko, your very looks betray you."

I could see by his face that the Metropolitan disbelieved me. Our conversation dropped at this point, and we parted.

Pitirim's words came true; Goremykin resigned and was succeeded by Sturmer, whose appointment roused universal indignation. Those who had known him before had no respect for him, while his German name, coupled with the rumours of a separate peace, made an unfavourable impression on the population generally. His appointment was regarded by all as further proof of Rasputin's influence over the Empress and as a direct challenge to public opinion.

The opening of the Duma was fixed for February 9. Rumours were current that members belonging to the Extreme Right intended to create a disturbance which would necessitate the sitting being brought to a close. Our relations with the new Ministers were still uncertain. Contrary to the custom by which newly-appointed Premiers paid a call on the presidents of the legislative chambers, Sturmer made an attempt to send for me by telephone, but was told that the President of the Duma was waiting for him at home. Sturmer called

* Harsh criticism.

CHAPTER XII

at once and bore himself obsequiously.

The glad news of the capture of Erzerum from the Turks was received on February 4. This splendid victory was entirely due to General Yudenitch, who, contrary to orders from G.H.Q., took the fortress by assault. This military success cleared the air and facilitated a reconciliation between the members of the Duma and the Government.

The Allied ambassadors and numerous foreigners engaged in providing war supplies plied me with questions, being anxious to know what truth there was in the rumours of a final dissolution of the Duma. These rumours had alarmed them exceedingly. Something had to be done to dissipate these rumours, raise the moral of the nation and pacify public opinion. I thought it absolutely necessary that the Emperor should be persuaded to pay a visit to the Duma. The strained relations between the representatives of the people and the Government might lead to undesirable demonstrations from both Right and Left, which it would be difficult to avert, while the Emperor's presence in the Duma would disarm both factions.

But who could persuade the Tsar to take such a step? The first thing to be done was to approach Sturmer and extract from him a promise not to hinder or dissuade the Emperor. Sturmer, a true bureaucrat at heart, was horrified at the mere idea, but nevertheless promised not to interfere, particularly after I explained to him the personal advantage to himself: the public might think that the brilliant suggestion had come to the Emperor from the new Premier. I next decided to seek the aid of a certain Klopoff, an old patriot and idealist, whom the Emperor had known and been fond of for years, and who had access to his person. Klopoff also used to visit me. He consented to my request and wrote a letter to the Emperor setting forth the arguments in favour of a visit to the Duma. He soon received the following reply:

"Lord, give Thy blessing. Nicholas."

On February 9, half an hour before the opening of the Duma, Sturmer arrived with the announcement that the Emperor would come to the Duma direct from the Stavka. The Senioren-Convent was immediately assembled to hear the good news, which created joyful surprise among the members irrespective of parties. Everyone wished to take it as a good omen for the future. It was decided to treat this important event in the history of the Duma with all the solemnity due to the occasion. An intimation of the Imperial visit, together with an invitation to attend the solemn Te Deum, was sent to the ambassadors of the Allied Powers. The news spread rapidly through the town, and people repeated joyfully: "The Emperor is in the Duma . . . Thank God, now there will be a change for the better." The Duma staff were besieged for permits to attend the sitting, and the gallery was packed with spectators as never before.

It is interesting to note that the evening before the priest Nemértzaloff came to my room with a message from the Metropolitan Pitirim informing me of his desire to celebrate the Te Deum at the opening of the Duma. He was told that there existed a Duma chaplain and assistant clergy who enjoyed universal respect, and that there was no reason to alter the customary procedure.

All the members of the Duma were in attendance. The representatives of the Allied Powers, members of the Council of the Empire and senators were assembled in the Catherine Hall. The President of the Duma, with his two deputies, met the Emperor in the porch. The Emperor arrived in a car with the Grand Duke Mikhail Alexandrovitch and Count Fredericks. After an exchange of greetings the Emperor passed into the Catherine Hall amid prolonged cheers. He was met by the officiating clergy and kissed the cross. The Emperor was deadly pale and his hands were trembling with agitation. The Te Deum was intoned; the choir sang beautifully, the whole atmosphere was imbued with reverence and solemnity. The members of the Duma and even spectators in the gallery joined in singing: "Lord, save Thy people." This impressive spectacle appeared to quiet the Emperor's agitation, and the strained look on his face gave way to one of calm satisfaction. When the deacon proclaimed:

"May all who have laid down their lives on the field of battle be in everlasting remembrance," the Sovereign knelt, followed by all the people.

After the Te Deum the Emperor came up to me, his eyes full of tears.

"Mikhail Vladimirovitch, I should like to say a few words to the members of the Duma. Shall I speak here, do you thinks or , in some other place?"

"I think this is the best place, your Majesty."

"Then order the lectern to be removed, please."

After conversing for a few minutes with the Allied ambassadors, the Emperor turned to the deputies who crowded around him. His

CHAPTER XII

speech, delivered in a firm, clear voice, made a good impression, and thundering "hurrahs" were the reply to the gracious words of the Sovereign.*

The national anthem was then sung by the assembly, and after a short address of welcome by the President of the Duma, the Emperor passed through a side door into the assembly hall. The deputies, entering through a door at the back, had by this time filled the hall, and the Emperor was again greeted with long and continuous cheers. He examined everything with interest, asked how the seats were allotted to the various parties, entered his name in the "golden" visitors' book lying in the semi-circular hall, and passed on.

I took advantage of our being alone at some distance from the rest to draw the Emperor's attention to the enthusiasm displayed by the members of the Duma.

"Your Majesty," I said, "do make the most of this joyous occasion and proclaim here, at once, your will to grant a responsible Ministry. You cannot fathom the full magnitude of an act which will have the beneficent effect of pacifying the country and bringing the war to a victorious end. By doing so you will write a page of gold in the history of your reign."

After a short silence the Emperor said;

"I will think it over."

We were passing the doors leading to the Ministerial pavilion.

"What is that?" the Emperor asked.

"The Ministers' rooms, your Majesty, and the further you keep away from them the better."

The Emperor did not enter the pavilion.

After addressing a few cordial words to the members of the Duma staff, the Emperor, surrounded by a crowd of deputies, moved towards the doors. Before leaving he repeatedly thanked the deputies for their welcome, and, turning to me, said:

"This has all been very pleasant. This is a day I shall never forget."

Everyone flocked to the porch, and the Imperial car drove off amid thundering cheers from the deputies, which were taken up by the crowds who lined the street and greeted the Emperor with enthusiasm.

The Grand Duke Mikhail Alexandrovitch remained in the Imperial box till the Duma rose for the day. The same evening the

* This speech was completely distorted by the Court censorship.

Emperor drove to the Council of the Empire. There everything passed off in an atmosphere of cold officialdom, and the enthusiasm and solemnity which attended the reception at the Duma were entirely lacking. The contrast was so marked that it excited general comment.

The Government statement, read out by Sturmer after the Emperor's departure, was a most depressing document. His rendering of it was very indistinct, and the long-winded and incoherent phrases contained no indication of the Government's intentions. The Prime Minister left the tribune amid dead silence, and only a few members on the Extreme Right wing tried to applaud. From the very outset Sturmer revealed himself as an utter nonentity, and soon became the object of Purishkevitch's witticisms and raillery. It was then that he launched his famous bon-mot on the "Ministers' leap-frog," and nicknamed Sturmer a "*Kivatch** of eloquence," comparing him with Tchichikoff, the hero of Gogol's novel *Dead Souls*, who, after calling on all the dignitaries of the town, sat long in his gig pondering whom else to visit. The comparison was most appropriate, as from the time of his appointment Sturmer had been making a ceaseless round of the Ministries and delivering speeches.

The Minister for War, Polivanoff, received an ovation, and his businesslike and comprehensive speech was attentively listened to. An equally cordial reception was vouchsafed by the Duma to Sazonoff and Grigorovitch. The sitting closed with a resolution read out on behalf of the Progressive *bloc*, expressing the desire for the appointment of a Government enjoying the confidence of the nation, which would assist in organizing the country for decisive victory, re-establish order at home, and arraign all those who were to blame for our misfortunes at the front. This statement was couched in firm language, such as would compel the Government to listen to the voice of the nation.

The debates that followed were carried on in a similar strain; many speeches contained demands for Sukhomlinoff's prosecution. The most forcible were those of V. Bobrinsky, Maklakoff and Polovtzeff. The latter, after speaking of Miasoiedoff and the Minister for War and saying that the former had obtained his due, ended his speech with the following words: "But where is the criminal who deceived us all by his false assurances of our seeming preparedness for this terrible war; who by so doing has torn the laurels from the

* A waterfall in Northern Russia.

CHAPTER XII

brow of our gallant army and trampled them in the mire of treachery and spoliation; who placed himself between the avenging sword of justice and the traitor Miasoiedoff? It was he, the Minister for War, who staked his head on Miasoiedoff's innocence. Miasoiedoff was executed, but where is the head of his patron? On shoulders adorned with the Imperial insignia."*

Our Allies took due note of the importance of the Emperor's visit to the Duma, and telegrams of congratulation were received from the British House of Commons and the French Chamber of Deputies, testifying that the Imperial visit was interpreted as a token of the Tsar's union with his people and as a menace to Germany, which had been building hopes on our internal dissensions. The whole of the Imperial Family approved of the Emperor's act. The Empress alone was displeased; prompted by her evil genius, she had harshly protested against her consort's decision.

A few days before the reopening of the Duma, a rumour was spread that Rasputin had been murdered at the restaurant "Villa Rode." Everyone rejoiced, but it turned out that he had only been badly mauled. It became known later that Sturmer had ordered Rasputin to be guarded as if he were a member of the Imperial Family, and, without Polivanoff's knowledge, placed four military cars at his disposal. Khvostoff boasted that he had arranged that Rasputin should be systematically poisoned with drink; but already the feeling was in the air that Khvostoff's days were numbered, that the Empress and Sturmer were giving him the cold shoulder and wished to replace him by his Assistant Minister Bieletsky, who was on intimate terms with Rasputin and directly responsible for his safety. To avoid the humiliation of a dismissal Khvostoff, as he admitted, handed in his resignation. The Emperor refused to accept it. But after Rasputin's adventure at the "Villa Rode," and the exposure of a tangled affair concerning the mission of a certain Rzhevsky, who was sent to purchase documents from Iliodor, both Khvostoff and Bieletsky were dismissed.

I heard later from M. Bakhmetieff, an engineer back from America, of what had appeared in the American Press concerning Iliodor, who had sold to the *American Magazine* the letters of the Empress he had wrested from Rasputin.

Our ambassador had endeavoured to repurchase these documents but failed, and lost 10,000 roubles he had paid out.

* The A.D.C.'s to the Emperor wore his initials on their shoulder straps.

The Government by its actions did its best to dispel the favourable impression made by the Emperor's visit to the Duma. It continued the old policy, or rather the old disintegration. Within the Duma itself the members of the Extreme Right raised their heads. Markoff II permitted himself coarse sallies against public organizations, which he accused of spreading unrest and profiteering. Such accusations were of course flung at random, unsupported by facts or evidence, and with the sole object of sowing dissension and mistrust of these bodies. These members were dissatisfied with the congress held by the ultra-Conservatives at Nizhni-Novgorod, and started preparations for another one, for which they intended to enlist the help of the clergy and peasants. The chief promoter of this scheme was Stcheglovitoff, late Minister for Justice, and the necessary funds were liberally provided for by the Government. At the same time rumours of a forthcoming dissolution of the Duma and of fresh changes in the Government still persisted.

Taking advantage of the Emperor's arrival at Tsarskoe Selo, I asked for an audience and was received on February 24, 1916. The audience lasted an hour and a half. I spoke of everything with complete frankness, of the intrigues of the Ministers, who, aided by Rasputin, ousted one another; of the continuous absence of a firm policy, of the widespread abuse and contempt of public opinion and the nation's feelings. There would come a limit to all patience, I added. I mentioned the exploits of D. Rubinstein, Manus and other heroes of the rear, their connection with Rasputin, the orgies and debauchery of Rasputin himself. His proximity to the Emperor and the Imperial family, and the influence he exercised on important affairs of State were, I said, the despair of all honest men. Rasputin's role as a German agent was now also no longer open to doubt.

"Had your Majesty's Ministers," I said, "been men of independent views, whose sole aim was the good of the country, Rasputin's presence would not have really mattered. The evil lies in the fact that the members of the Government owe their posts to him and involve him in their mutual intrigues. I find myself once again obliged to submit to your Majesty that this cannot go on much longer. No one tries to open your eyes with regard to the part played by this disreputable *starets*. His presence at the Imperial Court undermines the nation's confidence in the Crown; it may have fatal

CHAPTER XII

consequences for the fate of the dynasty, and turn the hearts of your subjects against their Sovereign."

All these unpleasant home truths were heard by the Emperor in silence, with occasional marks of surprise. His demeanour, however, remained gracious and affable throughout. When I interrupted my report, he turned to me with the question:

"What, do you think, will be the end of the war? Shall we win?"

I replied that the army and the people could be fully trusted, but that the war was being protracted and victory delayed through the incompetence of the higher command and the bad policy pursued at home.

This report apparently made some impression: on February 27 an order was issued for Rasputin's deportation to Tobolsk.

A few days later, on the demand of the Empress, the order was countermanded.

On March 1 Imperial sanction was obtained for the bringing of Sukhomlinoff's case before the First Department of the Senate with a view to deciding the question of his criminal prosecution. On signing the warrant the Emperor remarked: "The sacrifice has to be made."

Three weeks later, the First Department issued a resolution ordering a preliminary inquiry into the case to be held, and personal detention to be applied to General Sukhomlinoff, in conformity with the act of indictment. This decision was reported by the chief criminal investigator to the Minister for Justice, who gave his consent to Sukhomlinoff's arrest. The ex-Minister for War was imprisoned in the Alexeievsky ravelin in the fortress of Peter and Paul. His wife, who had played such an important part in all his voluntary and involuntary connections with persons convicted of espionage, not only remained at liberty but was allowed interviews with her husband. She obtained. through Rasputin, an audience of the Empress, and thenceforward enjoyed her patronage.

On March 3, the Minister of the Interior, Khvostoff, who had broken his neck in combating Rasputin's clique, was dismissed from his post.

Strikes went on at the factories, causing great apprehension both at home and at the front. General Alexeieff wrote me that the arrival of supplies for the army was disorganized. Again there was a shortage of boots, and a complete stoppage in the supply of munitions also was feared. The troops on the northern front, nearest to the capital, were suffering from scurvy, due to malnutrition.

The question concerning the commandeering of the Putiloff works was at last dealt with by the Special Council. Not an audience passed with the Emperor but I reminded him of the necessity for revising the incorrect decision. As soon as the works were commandeered, the old members of the board were removed and replaced by competent and trustworthy men. The workers, who were made military conscripts, were thus deprived of the right to strike.

On March 15, the Minister for War, Polivanoff, was dismissed from his post without an Imperial rescript.* He had just returned from the Stavka, where he had been graciously received by the Emperor; the intimation that he was relieved of his office came as a complete surprise both to himself and to everyone else. The explanation was sought in the commandeering of the Putiloff factory, or in the charge brought against Polivanoff of having inspired the alleged political resolutions of the war industries' committee. Polivanoff's own explanation was far simpler: he had ordered the four military cars given to Rasputin by Sturmer to be taken away. The Empress, who had always mistrusted him, heard of this and insisted on his dismissal. Shortly before this Polivanoff had said: "I now see how to bring order into our military affairs after the Sukhomlinoff chaos and win the war."

The news of Polivanoff's downfall was received with profound consternation. The Press was lavish in its praises of the late Minister, and enumerated the beneficent effects of his work during his comparatively short term of office. In the Duma and in society people spoke everywhere of irresponsible influences, of the Ministerial leap-frog, the enemy's gradual penetration and concerted attacks on all those who were useful to Russia and dangerous to the Germans.

All eyes were turned to the representatives of the people, who at the time enjoyed the popularity and confidence of the nation. But the Duma already realized that with Rasputin's presence at the Court and the ever-increasing influence of the Empress, success at the front and order at home were becoming impossible.

Polivanoff's successor was General Shuvaeff, a good and honest man, but inadequately equipped to fill such a post at such a time. His manner of presiding over the meetings of the Special Council rendered them tedious and confused. After Polivanoff's resignation

* A sign of disgrace.

CHAPTER XII

the Grand Duke Sergei Mikhailovitch launched an intrigue against the Special Council, and tried to persuade the Emperor to abolish it. Continual disputes arose in the Council under Shuvaeff's chairmanship, and it seemed as if he was purposely provoking a clash to obtain a pretext for closing it altogether.

The chaos in the country was becoming appalling. A meat shortage was beginning to make itself felt in Petrograd; nevertheless, cartloads of rotting carcases being conveyed to soap factories could be met in the streets. These carts were seen by the population in broad daylight, and the sight aroused general indignation; at a time when no meat was to be found on the market, rotting carcases were being openly conveyed practically to the rubbish heap.

Members of the Special Council inspected the municipal cold storage warehouses, beyond the Baltic railway station. The refrigerators were in order and the meat in good condition, but mounds of rotting carcases were piled up all around. This was the meat intended for the use of the army. There was nowhere to store it. When the purveyors asked permission to build new refrigerators, they obtained neither permission nor the necessary funds. As usual, the different Ministers were unable to agree: the Commissariat placed the orders for meat and the railway companies carried it, but there was nowhere to store it, and it was not allowed to be placed on the market. All this was as stupid as many other things. Everybody seemed to conspire to bring about Russia's ruin.

The members of the Special Council reported to the meeting on all they had seen, and I wrote to Alexeieff, and then only did the meat question receive attention. Hundreds of tons had, of course, already perished. It was the same with the meat supply from Siberia: but here thousands of tons instead of hundreds were lost, owing to the inadequacy and disorganization of the transport arrangements. Those responsible for this were, of course, never discovered; each laid the blame on someone else, and all together on the general state of chaos.

Polivanoff believed the meat scandal to be due neither to chance nor to disorganization, but to deliberate action in pursuance of a German programme.

General Russky returned from Kislovodsk in the middle of April. He went to the Stavka to ask for an appointment at the front, but obtained no definite answer, and languished in Petrograd doing nothing. In the meantime operations on the northern front under Kuropatkin were taking a turn for the worse, and we sustained needlessly heavy casualties near Riga.

The question of increasing the output of hand grenades and special guns for destroying barbed wire entanglements was raised in the Special Council. Such guns were extensively used on the French front, and General Joffre, on learning that we had none, despatched an expert engineer to Russia, under whose supervision one of the munition factories was adapted for their construction. At the front everyone was delighted with these guns; I myself saw some of them in action on the northern front with excellent effect.

Nevertheless, the Grand Duke Sergei Mikhailovitch ordered their manufacture to be stopped. I heard of this from the French Military Attaché, the Marquis de la Guiche, whose statement was confirmed by General Manikovsky, the head of the Artillery Department. Once more the whole matter had to be raised in the Special Council, advantages proved which one might think would be patent to all, and the influence of irresponsible persons combated.

A short paragraph appeared in the Press concerning the appointment of a certain official as acting secretary to a special committee composed of five Ministers under the presidency of Trepoff. No one had any idea that this Committee existed, who were the five Ministers concerned, or upon what questions they conferred. I asked for an explanation from Sturmer concerning the nature and legal status of this institution, which had sprung into being without the knowledge of the Duma.

No answer was vouchsafed. A few days later, at a banquet in honour of the French Ministers, Sturmer drew me aside and said he was unable to answer my letter, because the Committee had been set up secretly by the Emperor's desire.

The details of the affair were as follows. After the creation of the Special Council of Defence composed of public workers, the authority of the Minister for War, as chairman, extended practically to all Government departments, where matters directly concerned with the war were involved. The Council made a decision, the Minister for War confirmed it, and the departments were bound to carry it out. The Cabinet remained, as it were, in the background. Such procedure, notwithstanding its excellent results, could not fail to displease certain Ministers and officials; so they persuaded the Emperor to appoint a kind of committee of five Ministers. They had

CHAPTER XII

not the courage to do it while Polivanoff was still in office, because he stood for law and order and the public good; he lost his post for that very reason.

The setting up of a Ministerial Committee, the lack of confidence in, and the secret control over the Special Council of public workers, aroused profound indignation among the members of the Council. They entrusted me with the mission of telling Sturmer that if the committee of five were not abolished, all the members of the Special Council of Defence would resign publicly, explaining the motives for their resignation—a step which would be pregnant with consequences. Sturmer hastened to declare that he, too, considered the committee of five to be illegal, and would report in that sense to the Emperor.

MM. Viviani and Thomas, representing the French Government, arrived at Petrograd at the beginning of May. The Duma gave a banquet in their honour. There was an exchange of speeches, with mutual assurances of friendship and readiness to fight together to a finish.

Next day Thomas expressed the wish to have a long talk on the organization of war supplies. He spent the evening at my house, and amazed a member of the Special Council, S. I. Timasheff, by his minute knowledge of the state of affairs in Russia. After speaking of the defects of our war supplies system and enumerating all our weak points, he concluded with the following significant witticism: "*La Russie doit être bien riche pour se permettre le luxe d'un gouvernement comme le vôtre, car le premier ministre—c'est un désastre, et le ministre de la guerre—une catastrophe...*"

On bidding farewell to the French statesmen next day, I asked one of them: "*Dites-moi, Monsieur, sincérement votre opinion, qu'est ce qui vous manque en Russie?*"

The Frenchman replied: "*Ce qui nous manque? C'est l'autocratie de votre gouvernement, car si j'ose vous dire encore, M. le président, la Russie doit être bien forte moralement pour supporter, pendant le temps sérieux que nous passons, cet état de douce anarchie qui régne dans votre pays et se jette aux yeux.*"

On May 12 Sturmer gave a big dinner to which all the Ministers, several members of the Council of the Empire and a few ultra-Conservative members of the Duma were invited. I accepted the invitation in order to take advantage of the intimate surroundings to give free vent to my feelings of anxiety and indignation. After dinner, when coffee was served in the drawing room, I addressed the company somewhat as follows:

"Just think of what is taking place . . . In these momentous days, when the spirit of the nation and the gallantry of our army stand revealed in all their beauty, when torrents of blood are being freely shed—the Government reveal themselves as incapable of leadership and, in pursuit of their own interests, never get farther than a petty control over public organizations. You, the representatives of the Government, see nothing, realize nothing, and clinging to your powers and privileges, remain the passive spectators of the great patriotic upheaval which sweeps the country irrespective of parties and nationalities. . . . When the people long for work in order to ensure final victory, and ask for a firm and wise Government, you spend your time in trying to discover an imaginary revolution. . . . You organize Monarchist congresses, persecute public organizations, provoke endless inter-departmental disputes and intrigues, which paralyze the work of administration, and deliver the country into the hands of self-seekers. . . . Bribery, extortion, plunder are growing on all sides, and nothing is being done to prevent it. Persons who deserve the gallows continue to remain in high favour, and instead of patriotism, personal patronage and vested interests are the moving springs of the Government's actions. . . ."

I reminded them of Maklakoff and the case of the army boot supplies, and of Goremykin who, during the retreat of 1915, kept repeating that the war "did not concern him."

"The whole nation," I said, "has rallied to the motto: 'Everything for the war,' but the Government pursues its course of petty officialdom. completely out of touch with the great events of the moment. . . ." I pointed out the Government's utter incompetence to foresee or deal with the stupendous problems of reconstruction with which the nation would be faced after the end of the war, and which were already engaging the attention of the more advanced Allied statesmen. "You should realize," I said, "that you are neither beloved nor trusted by the nation. . . . In your senseless search for a bogey revolution, you are murdering the living soul of the people and creating unrest and discontent which sooner or later may breed an actual revolution. . . . The time will come when you will be called upon to render an account of your deeds. . . ."

CHAPTER XII

Prince V. M. Volkonsky told me afterwards that my words had produced on the Ministers the effect of a thunderbolt.

Shortly after this Sturmer went to the Stavka, and the committee of the five Ministers was abolished. (A few months later, however, a similar committee was appointed, consisting of six Ministers.)

The Imperial ukase for the reopening of the Duma was issued on May 16. April 27 being the tenth anniversary of the summoning of the first Duma, I had to mark the event in my inaugural address. I said that despite the errors committed by the first two Dumas, the principle of national representation as a component factor of Russia's body politic had become profoundly engrained in the public consciousness. I emphasized the merit of the Emperor Nicholas II, who had granted a constitution to Russia. The Cabinet in a body was conspicuous for its absence, owing, it was said, to the expectation of violent anti-Government speeches.

The session proved dull and colourless; attendance was irregular and insufficient for voting. Members of the Extreme Right made inopportune sallies in the hope of provoking adjournments, and the whole atmosphere was so full of uncertainty as to render work practically impossible. The state of perpetual conflict came to nothing, the Government refused to hear reason, disorder was increasing, and the country rapidly going to ruin. All hopes were centred in the Duma, but unfortunately it was unable to do anything. We all suffered acutely from the general depression which pervaded the country.

A fresh success was achieved on the Caucasian front, but simultaneously the news arrived of the terrible hardships endured by the troops, whose strength there was insufficient. Appeals for reinforcements were disregarded by the Stavka.

In General Polivanoff's opinion we ought to have exercised our main pressure on the Caucasian front and advanced on Constantinople, which could have been captured with the aid of our Allies at Salonica. This plan was also spoken of in the French Press. A different view, however, prevailed at the Stavka, where jealousy of the Grand Duke Nicolai Nicolaevitch was the guiding principle. He had only to express an opinion, for an exactly contrary decision to be made by the Stavka. None of his requests were ever carried out. This ill-feeling being entirely mutual, anyone who was dismissed from the Stavka was sure to obtain a post in the Caucasus.

* * *

General Brusiloff started his successful offensive on our western front, where his armies took 480,000 prisoners. Our success was of immense importance to the Allies. For the second time we relieved the enemy's pressure on Verdun, where, for months past, both the French and Germans were exhausting their forces in the fruitless attempts of the latter to capture the fortress. Italy, too, was saved by our advance, and large Austrian contingents were transferred from the Italian front to ours.

Officers who took part in Brusiloff's offensive attributed our success to the fact that operations were started thirty-six hours before they were timed to do so by the Stavka. Rumours of espionage at the Stavka were current in the army, the enemy appearing to be always aware of our movements beforehand. These suspicions unfortunately received frequent confirmation.

Our parliamentary delegation made a tour of the Allied countries during May and June, and was everywhere welcomed with great enthusiasm and honours. Before they started, I warned Protopopoff, who was senior member of the delegation, that it might be treated with insufficient courtesy by members of our foreign Embassies. This, I regret to say, proved correct. Our Ambassador in London, Count Benckendorff, neither came himself nor sent any of his secretaries to welcome the delegates on their arrival. The delegates were particularly struck by this behaviour, because they received a most courteous welcome from the British; the King placed his special train at their disposal and many high officials met them at the terminus. When Protopopoff called at the Embassy, Benckendorff was barely civil to him, and explained the absence of members of the Embassy by his not having received any instructions from Petrograd. Nevertheless, in all their public speeches and private conversations, our Allies never omitted to emphasize their particular confidence in the Russian Duma. Protopopoff, judging by the report he presented and by Miliukoff's account of his behaviour, bore himself as head of the delegation with tact and dignity. Our delegates were particularly impressed by the ideal organization of the rear in all the Allied countries, and by the united efforts of the peoples for the carrying on of the war.

The only discordant note of the tour was Protopopoff's tactless interview with a German agent. On the return journey Protopopoff

CHAPTER XII

was delayed at Stockholm, and after the departure of the rest of the mission he, in a private capacity, had an interview with Herr Warburg, an emissary of Herr von Lucius, German Minister at Stockholm.

The incident was taken up by the Press, and I was obliged to request Protopopoff to explain his conduct before the Duma. Protopopoff did not deny having had an interview with the First Secretary of the German Legation, to whom he emphasized the impossibility of Russia's making peace before the complete victory of the Allies. When Herr Warburg attempted to exculpate Germany and lay the blame for the war on Great Britain, Protopopoff had cut him short, saying he could not permit any incrimination of the Allies in his presence.

The Duma expressed itself satisfied by this statement, and I wrote an explanatory letter on the Stockholm incident to the Press.

The fact that our offensive was confined to the south-western front under General Brusiloff, and was unsupported in all the other sectors, caused general bewilderment at the front. Meanwhile, the break-through near Baranovitchy failed, and the advance appeared to be checked.

As a counter-balance to Brusiloff's successes, affairs in the Special Council for Defence were once more entering a critical stage, and misunderstandings between the members and the Minister Shuvaeff were becoming more acute. His incompetence to fill a responsible post became increasingly obvious; he was completely under Court influence and blindly obedient to orders emanating from Tsarskoe Selo. In spite of his undoubted honesty and probity, he was bewildered by all the conflicting currents of opinion and incapable of smoothing over difficulties. When, under the influence of the Grand Duke Sergei Mikhailovitch, a campaign was started at the Stavka against General Manikovsky, the energetic head of the Artillery Department, Shuvaeff failed to support him, and Manikovsky was only saved by the intervention of members of the Duma and of the Council of the Empire.

On June 24 I went to the Stavka to report to the Emperor. Before the audience I called on General Alexeieff. Rumours were current in Petrograd that Alexeieff was drafting a scheme for the establishment of a dictatorship in the rear to deal with all matters concerning internal government and war supplies. Shortly before my visit to the Stavka, I learnt from General Manikovsky that the scheme had already been drafted and a report on it presented to the Emperor by General Alexeieff. To confirm his statement Manikovsky gave me a copy of this report. It amounted virtually to the establishment of a dictatorship for restoring order in the rear, and with the right to cancel the orders of the Ministers and of the Special Council. The effects of such a step may easily be imagined, especially when one realized that the idea of a dictatorship emanated from the Grand Duke Sergei Mikhailovitch, who obviously reserved the important and responsible post of dictator for himself.

I asked General Alexeieff whether what I had heard of the scheme was true, and produced the copy of the report. Alexeieff owned to having submitted a similar document to the Emperor, and insisted on learning the source from which I had obtained such confidential information. He added that he could not carry on the war with any chance of success when there was neither system nor coordination in the Government and when operations at the front were paralyzed by the chaos in the rear.

I agreed with Alexeieff on the justice of his complaints, but pointed out that were the necessary powers given to the Prime Minister, a dictatorship could be avoided. On the other hand, the appointment of a man like the Grand Duke Sergei Mikhailovitch would be tantamount to the ruin of the whole war supply organization. He would again be surrounded by his former associates and collaborators, and nothing but ill would come of this to the army and the whole country.

"Tell the Grand Duke Sergei Mikhailovitch from me," I said to Alexeieff, "that if he does not cease intriguing in the sphere of munitions supplies, I, as President of the Duma, will expose his activities from the tribune of the Duma. I have more than sufficient evidence concerning them in my possession."

Our talk having then drifted to conditions at the front, I told Alexeieff of the troops' desire to see Russky reinstated as commander. Alexeieff agreed with me on some points, disapproved of Evert and Kuropatkin, but said with regard to Russky that he could not appoint him anywhere.

This was my first meeting with Alexeieff; so far we had only corresponded. He produced the impression of being a clever and highly expert officer, but lacking in determination and broad

CHAPTER XII

political outlook.

The Emperor as usual accorded me a gracious reception, and heard all my unpleasant news of disorder in the rear without murmur or contradiction. In reporting on the work of the Duma I pointed to the desire of the ultra-Conservatives to create a conflict over the question of German aggression. The bill as drafted by the Government was rejected, as it did not secure the real object; to combat German aggression in the rear was certainly necessary, but to raise the whole question of land tenure during the war was a dangerous proceeding. Some sort of system was imperative; the taking of land from one group of owners for distribution among disabled soldiers, however, was a great risk which might lead to agrarian disorders.

The Emperor here interposed by saying that the distribution of land among the soldiers was his own idea.

"Nevertheless, your Majesty, permit me to disagree with you, and most humbly to beg that this bill may be revised."

Our conversation having touched on Poland, I reminded the Emperor that its future status was still unsettled, and that the Poles were becoming increasingly anxious, as they saw the Government's growing oblivion of the Grand Duke Nicolai Nicolaevitch's proclamation.

The Poles had told me, before I left for the Stavka, how the Empress had said in the course of a conversation with Count Zamoisky: "*L'idée de l'autonomie de la Pologne est insensée; on ne peut le faire sans donner les mémes droits aux provinces Baltiques.*"

I then passed on to the question of a dictatorship, and said I felt obliged to warn the Emperor against taking such a step. To my surprise the Emperor appeared to have completely forgotten Alexeieff's scheme.

"What dictatorship?" he asked.

I handed him the copy of the report. The Emperor glanced at it carelessly and said:

"Yes, I have a copy of this among my papers."

My opinion, in short, was that a dictatorship would not attain the object in view, while detracting from the authority of the Sovereign. The Emperor listened attentively and asked:

"What steps would you advise for restoring order in the rear?"

"Your Majesty, I have but one solution to recommend, which is the same as I proposed before; grant a responsible Ministry. By doing so you will merely extend the rights you have given already in granting the Constitution, but your own authority will remain immutable. Only the responsibility will no longer rest with you but with the Government, and you will continue as before to ratify the laws, dissolve the legislative bodies, and determine questions of war and peace."

The Emperor replied: "Very well, I will think it over." He added, "Whom would you recommend as Prime Minister?"

"You will be surprised, your Majesty, but the man I would recommend is Admiral Grigorovitch. In a short time he put his own department in excellent order."

"That is true, but that is a different sphere of action, and he would be out of place as Prime Minister."

"Believe me, Sire, he would be better than Sturmer."

Speaking of the disorder in the Ministries of Ways and Communications and of Commerce, the Emperor again asked:

' And who are your candidates for these posts?"

I named the engineer Voskresensky and Protopopoff, deputy-president of the Duma.

The Emperor made no objections and, as was his custom, made notes in his pocket book.

At the close of my report I mentioned two other items; the Ministerial defence of the so-called Kuznetsk enterprise, in which Trepoff—a brother of the Minister—had an interest, and the relief of disabled soldiers. The shareholders of the Kuznetsk works, who enjoyed the patronage of the Ministers Trepoff and Prince Shakhovskoy, were trying to obtain huge allotments of State lands, rich in mineral ore, in the Urals, and for their exploitation asked for a subsidy of twenty million roubles, which they promised to repay in five years without interest. The Imperial Duma refused a grant for what appeared to be a purely speculative concern.

The problem of the care of disabled soldiers had not yet been worked out. The Emperor requested that a detailed scheme should be submitted to him which could then be laid before the legislative chambers.

After the audience I was invited to dine at the Imperial table. Notwithstanding this gracious act of courtesy, I realized that my report had failed to produce the desired impression: a kind of indifference or weariness was noticeable in the Emperor's attitude towards everything that was taking place.

CHAPTER XII

In the interval between the audience and dinner I spoke of this with M. P. Kaufman,* who said to me: "I would advise you to wait on the Empress and try to make her hear reason by explaining to her the true state of affairs. Perhaps you may achieve something in that quarter."

Mikhail Vassilivitch Alexeieff

Chief of the Imperial General Staff on the northwestern front

Chief of Staff (1900-1900)

Formerly:
- Governor General of Eastern Siberia
- Governor of Russian Manchuria

General Alexeieff was the Chief Commander of land and sea forces in the Pacific, at the same time.

A veteran of the Russ-Turko War of 1877 in service of Alexander II. He was the first Russian viceroy in the Far East. In 1885 he reached the rank of Captain and entered the Academy of the General Staff on his 30th birthday. Next to the Tsar, he was probably the most powerful Russian that had served in the Russian empire. A Russian newspaper said that he was, "*the instrument of the will and purpose of the Tsar.*"

In one account, the Tsar telegraphed him "*I give you full power to maintain, if necessary, the prestige of Russia by force of arms.*" And, according to British adjutant major-general Sir john Hanbury Williams, "*To him, indeed, it was due that the Germans got no farther than they did.*"

---

* Red Cross delegate at the Stavka and member of the Council of the Empire.

CHAPTER XIII

Dismissal of Sazonoff—Sturmer as Dictator—The Guards on the Stokhod—Aircraft from Abroad.

THE Ministerial leap-frog still continued. Sazonoff, the Minister for Foreign Affairs, was summarily dismissed and Sturmer appointed in his stead while retaining the Premiership. Khvostoff, Minister for Justice, received the post of Minister of the Interior, and Makaroff that vacated by Khvostoff. No one could explain the cause of Sazonoff's disgrace. One of the Foreign Ministry officials told me it was due to Sazonoff's report on Poland, in which he insisted on the settlement of the Polish question, and the removal of the chief opponent of Poland's autonomy—Sturmer. But in my opinion the real cause lay deeper.

With regard to the Minister for Justice, Khvostoff, it was said that he had suffered on account of Sukhomlinoff, because he had refused to suspend the investigation into his case. Khvostoff had been summoned to the Empress, who for two hours had urged him to release Sukhomlinoff. At first she persisted in asserting his innocence, and finally, raising her voice, demanded that he should be released from the fortress, repeating incessantly: "*Je veux, j'exige qu'il soit libéré.*" (Ed. 'I demand that he be released.')

Khvostoff replied that he was unable to do so, and on the Empress asking him, "Pourquoi pas, si je vous l'ordonne?" said, "*Ma conscience, Madame, me défend de vous obéir et de libérer un trắitre.*" (Ed. 'My conscience, Madam, forbids me from obeying you and freeing a traitor.')

Khvostoff, after this interview, realized that his days were numbered, and his transference to the post of Minister of the Interior was but an interlude in order to save appearances. The Empress appointed Makaroff in his stead in the hope of finding him more pliant, but such, fortunately, did not prove to be the case.

On my return from the Stavka I had an interview with Sturmer concerning the dictatorship scheme. He professed complete igno-

CHAPTER XIII

rance on the subject. A week later he departed for the Stavka bearing a letter from the Empress.

It was revealed at a meeting of the Special Council that the despatch of several artillery supply columns ordered by the Council had been countermanded by Sturmer. This Council, at the time of its formation, had by Imperial ukase been placed above the Council of Ministers. The members demanded explanations from the Minister for War. The latter then produced a secret document—an Imperial ukase appointing Sturmer dictator with full powers. A delegation of members was immediately chosen to wait on Sturmer and express the Council's indignation to him. He ceased from that time to tamper with the work of the Special Council, but continued to interfere in all other branches of the administration.

The authorities arrested D. Rubinstein, the chairman of the board of a private bank, who was known to be on intimate terms with Rasputin, also Rubinstein's two brothers, Stembo, a journalist, and the lawyer Wolfson, solicitor to the Countess Kleinmichel— all of them on the charge of profiteering, gambling on the Stock Exchange with a view to lowering the value of Russian securities, and of acts of open treason, such as the sale to Germany of war supplies ordered by us abroad.

These events almost coincided with the resignation of the Minister for Agriculture, Naumoff, the last member of the Cabinet chosen from among public workers. With the assistance of the Zemstvos he had drafted a scheme for organizing the food supply throughout the country. The scheme, which had been debated in and approved by the Duma, was nevertheless rejected by the Cabinet under pressure from Sturmer.

My wife and I left Petrograd on July 12 for the southern front, stopping at Kieff on our way. That city was now the residence of the Empress Marie Feodorovna, who had retired there from all the cares and trials which beset her at Petrograd and Tsarskoe. I visited her, and she detained me for two hours, talking of the work of the Red Cross. On my remarking that instead of spending only a week in Kieff as originally intended, she had prolonged her stay for months, the Empress replied: "Yes, it is so nice here; I am going to stay as long as I like" Afterwards she said: "Vous ne pouvez pas vous imaginer quel contentement pour moi aprés cinquante ans que je devais cacher mes sentiments—c'est de pouvoir dire á tout le monde combien je déteste les allemands."*

On July 16 I went to visit General Brusiloff at Berditcheff in company with V. A. Maklakoff and M. I. Tereschenko. Everything was going on well on his front, munitions were plentiful, and the Commander-in-Chief seemed to be full of confidence concerning the state of his armies. There was but a temporary shortage in the supply of heavy shells, due to a great outlay during the advance.

General Kaledin, in command of the Eighth Army, whom I visited at Lutsk, repeatedly expressed his astonishment at General Besobrasoff's† behaviour. The latter acted independently of everyone else and never co-ordinated his operations with those of his neighbours. Kaledin also strongly disapproved of the appointment of the Grand Duke Paul‡ as a corps commander. The Grand Duke did not execute the orders even of his immediate superiors, and his presence merely tended to increase the already existing confusion.

Speaking of the Kovel operations, Kaledin remarked: "Had I the Guards at my disposal, I would have captured Kovel; it was not so strongly fortified as now, and the Austrians did not dispose of large forces at that point. The Stavka failed to carry out its original plan."

Kaledin was loud in praising the fresh contingents of young soldiers, who were well trained and all of them picked men.

From Lutsk we went to Torchin, where the Zemstvo Union hospital unit, attached to the "Iron Division," was at work. All along the road we met convoys of covered waggons carrying the wounded, and traces of the Austrians' recent occupation were to be found on all sides. At Torchin we saw huge quantities of war trophies: piles of hand grenades and shells, and rows of guns of various calibres. The heavy guns had been captured where they stood, turned about and fired after the retreating enemy. A flying unit had been despatched from the Zemstvos' dressing station for work within a mile of the line of battle. The casualties were very heavy, and doctors and nurses had been working for two days without respite. The corps commander, General Kashtalinsky, said that fresh attacks were ex-

---

* (Previous page) Ed. 'You can't imagine how happy it is for me after fifty years that I have had to hide my feelings—from being able to tell everyone how much I hate the Germans.'

† Gen. Besobrasoff was in command of the so-called Imperial Guards joint contingent, consisting of two corps.

‡ Uncle of the Emperor Nicholas II, commanding the 1st Guards Corps.

CHAPTER XIII

pected and that the Austrians were already carrying out an artillery preparation. In fact, towards evening a bombardment began which reminded one of uninterrupted thunder-bursts, with occasional terrific explosions.

A continuous stream of peasants' carts filled with wounded plodded along the road from Rozhistche. Many of the seriously wounded were lying without even a straw litter, and groaned aloud. The Red Cross delegate to the Eighth Army, H. H. Lerche, had said to us at Lutsk: "Notice the evacuation of wounded from the Guards. God knows what's happening there."

At Rozhistche great numbers of the wounded could be seen lying about everywhere: in the houses and gardens, on the ground, in sheds. Many had been wounded in the place itself during enemy air raids and by the explosion of pyroxilene fuses stacked in the open beside the hospital. G. M. Khitrovo, the head of the Red Cross, was killed like this, as he rushed to rescue the wounded from a hut which had caught fire from the explosion. The Army Medical Service, under Professor Veliaminoff, was short of the most necessary drugs and surgical appliances. General Besobrasoff's staff was over-crowded with officers. Judging by his account of conditions at the front, complete chaos reigned in his sector.

On my return journey I again met General Kaledin at Lutsk. He did not conceal his indignation at the enormous casualties sustained by the Guards coupled with negligible results. "Such a senseless sacrifice of human lives cannot be justified, and such splendid men, too!" he said.

We arrived at Rozhistche hoping to see our son, whose regiment had taken part in all the fighting, where the Guards had lost 33,000 men killed and wounded. Besobrasoff gave us leave to send for our son by telephone, his regiment having been withdrawn to the second line. We had to wait till daybreak on the second day. We sat on a bench in the road till late at night, listening in anxious expectancy to the roar and din of the battle, after the harrowing experiences of the day. The night was very dark, and my wife went to get some rest in the hut of Mme. Mestcherinova, who, true to herself, was never far behind the Preobrazhensky Regiment. Of her three sons who served there, one was already killed. Sleep was impossible. My wife soon rejoined me, and we visited three field hospitals—one bearing the name of Rodzianko, where my nephew's wife (an Englishwoman) was doing splendid work. The second was the British hospital run by Lady Muriel Paget, and the third belonged to the Kaufman Association. The staffs were everywhere working with the utmost self-denial, but it was impossible to admit all the wounded for want of room. The men all belonged to the Guards, splendid stalwart young fellows, from the latest "Polivanoff" drafts. They answered our questions cheerfully, but the "old men" complained that such heavy casualties were needless, as the men were sent to attack barbed wire entanglements without a preliminary bombardment. They treated me with complete confidence, and spoke gently and sadly of the bad staff work.

With Mme. Mestcherinova we were present at Khitrovo's funeral. He was laid in a temporary grave, and, after the ceremony, we stayed for the burial of some soldiers who had died in hospital. They were brought without coffins, stark naked, and laid in rows in a common grave. It was a harrowing sight. The priest gabbled carelessly through the burial service, and when we asked him not to hurry and ourselves began to sing, he looked at us in surprise and read the prayers properly. Before going away the priest thanked us, saying with a sigh: "We do nothing else but bury—it's pitiful to see," and made a despairing gesture.

Our son came straight to Lutsk and, after an hour's rest, began to narrate his experiences. Criminal incompetence, lack of cooperation in the higher command, and chaotic disaccord had resulted in a senseless slaughter of our crack regiments. Not only officers but the men saw clearly that, notwithstanding the heroism of the Guards, victory under the existing conditions was impossible. The Grand Duke Paul, corps commander, disobeyed the order he received to encircle a given point by a flank manoeuvre, and sent the Preobrazhensky and the Imperial Rifle Regiments to make a frontal attack on the Rai-Mesto heights. The troops found themselves in a swamp, where many men perished. While they were floundering through the bog, German aeroplanes hovered overhead and bombarded them at close quarters. My son sank up to the armpits and was with difficulty extricated by his men. The wounded could not be brought out, and all perished in the swamp. These marshes extended to the foot of the hill, which was covered with barbed wire. Our artillery fire was weak and failed to destroy the entanglements; the shells fell short of them, or dropped among our own men. General Rauch, in command of the cavalry division, instead of obeying orders from headquarters and attacking the enemy from the

CHAPTER XIII

rear, withdrew his regiments. As a matter of fact, each commander acted on his own, and many men were sacrificed in vain. Nevertheless, the gallant Guards fulfilled their task and, though bled white, succeeded in capturing the heights, which they were then ordered to abandon.

My son, usually so calm and self-possessed, was terribly excited and kept repeating to me: "You must tell the Emperor. It is a crime to sacrifice these men for nothing. . . . The higher command is absolutely rotten. Everyone in the army feels that for no reason whatever matters are going from bad to worse. The men are spleendid, guns and munitions plentiful, but the generals lack brains. The want of aeroplanes, too, is very bad. No one trusts either the Stavka or his own chiefs. All this may end by creating resentment and disruption. We are willing to die for Russia, for our Mother country, but not for the caprice of the generals, who sit in safe places during the fighting; few of them are ever seen in the firing line, and it is we who die. Both men and officers think that if things are not changed, we shall never win. The eyes of people in high quarters must be opened."

Under the impression of all we had seen and heard, I wrote a detailed letter to Brusiloff, who, adding to mine a report of his own, despatched both to the Stavka. The result of this was that General Besobrasoff, his chief staff officer, Count Ignatieff, the Grand Duke Paul and Professor Veliaminoff were removed from their posts.

At the very next meeting of the Special Council I raised the question of our air force. Shuvaeff objected to this, fearing criticism of the activities of the Grand Duke Alexander Mikhailovitch.* When the members of the Council, nevertheless, determined to discuss the matter, Shuvaeff closed the meeting without further explanations. The Grand Duke's name was connected with many cases of abuse. Aeroplanes unfit for service were purchased, the receiving committee did not even trouble to open the cases on arrival, and machines were despatched to the front which could not be flown or were very dangerous. The Grand Duke's chief assistant. Colonel Fogel, enjoyed a very doubtful reputation. All orders were placed through him and he was practically at the head of our air force. When, in June, the question came up before the Special Council,

* Cousin of the Emperor and married to his sister the Grand Duchess Xenia. This grand duke was at the head of the Air force.

information was asked for as to the exact number of aircraft actually at the front as compared with those which should be there according to estimate. The reply took long in coming, and when at last it did arrive, it turned out that most of the aeroplanes were training ones and attached to the aviation schools.

The Special Council then proposed that the shortage should be made good by the purchase of aircraft from abroad. A long time elapsed; appeals for aeroplanes came repeatedly from the front, and still nothing was heard of the order. To the Special Council's reiterated inquiry the Aviation Department replied that the orders were placed in France and the machines were due to arrive shortly. A little later a statement came to the effect that France had refused to execute the order. In the meantime I received information that the alleged order had actually never been placed, and that the Grand Duke Alexander Mikhailovitch had caused all negotiations to be cancelled. I then determined to collect all the data concerning our air force organization. Valuable assistance was rendered me by two of our prominent flying officers, one of whom was at the head of the flying school and had received three Crosses of St. George* for distinguished war service. Moreover, I received numerous letters from members of the service at the front.

A conclusive report was drawn up containing precise figures of the orders given, with the dates of their execution, enumerating all the instances of abuse, casualties among the personnel, and so forth. The whole system of our air force administration stood revealed, together with the appalling state of the service. Copies of this report were sent by me to the Emperor, the Grand Duke Alexander Mikhailovitch, and all the members of the Special Council.

The whole matter was brought up again at the following meeting of the Special Council in the absence of Shuvaeff. I acquainted the assembly with the contents of my report, recounted all my experiences at the front, and added that such authorities as Brusiloff, Kaledin and Sakharoff had begged that most serious attention should be given to the state of our air force. While the Germans hovered over our lines like birds pelting us with bombs, we were powerless to prevent them. The enemy was perfectly aware of our dispositions, while our own aerial reconnaissance was practically non-existent.

I urged on the Council the impossibility of relying further on the Aviation Department and the Grand Duke, and proposed that we

* The Russian V.C., which had four grades.

CHAPTER XIII

should take the initiative in ordering aircraft from abroad. The Council agreed to this, and in view of Shuvaeff's disinclination to negotiate the affair with the Allies, the task was entrusted to me. Shuvaeff gave me the war code cipher, and I telegraphed to General Joffre through the medium of our Military Attaché in Paris, Count Ignatieff. The reply was long in coming, and the French Military Attaché, the Marquis de La Guiche, told me that according to their secret information, Count Ignatieff had kept back my telegram and not delivered it to Joffre. I requested La Guiche to send a telegram in French cipher direct to Joffre and to the Minister of Supplies, Thomas. I also inquired of Shuvaeff by what right a Military Attaché had taken the liberty of censoring a telegram from the President of the Duma, sent with the knowledge of the Minister for War, and in war cipher. Ignatieff's reply was peculiar: he had been unwilling to agitate the Generalissimo by submitting to him the telegram of the President of the Duma. Meanwhile, a reply was soon received to La Guiche's telegram, informing us that the orders had already been placed and the aeroplanes would be delivered shortly. Joffre's reply made an excellent impression on the Special Council.

This episode, however, did not end here. I left Petrograd for a short holiday in the country. A few days later I received a telegram saying that the Budget Commission insisted on my pressing the Government for a speedy convocation of the Duma. The same telegram announced the arrival of my private secretary, V. Sadykoff. To my great surprise Sadykoff brought me, besides the report of the Budget Commission, a letter from General Alexeieff notifying me of the Emperor's desire that I should "abstain from direct interference in war matters which did not concern either the President of the Duma or a member of the Special Council."* My secretary drew my attention to the fact that the envelope containing the letter bore no seal and was not inscribed "confidential," although such seals and inscriptions were put on the most unimportant letters. Sadykoff said that on opening this envelope he decided at once to bring it me, in the country, without consulting anyone, as he knew I was due to go to the Stavka before returning to Petrograd, and, not knowing the contents of the letter, would find myself there in a very awkward position. My conscience did not enable me to accede to the Emperor's desire. It would mean that I should have to remain silent

* See Appendix No. III.

during the Council's debates on war supplies, and in general behave, according to Goremykin's maxim, as if the war "did not concern me."

At my next audience I submitted my views to the Emperor and explained that in conformity with the law establishing the Special Council, it behoved* me, as a member of it, to take an active part in all matters connected with army supplies and equipment, adding that he had obviously been misinformed with regard to my interference in the business.

The Emperor replied: "Yes, you were right, and the matter was not correctly represented to me."

The Emperor's reply gave me complete satisfaction

Dmitry Savelyevich Shuvaeff (b. 1854-1937)
Minister of War (1916-Jan 1917)
Chief Quartermaster (1909-1916)

General Shuvayeff head of the Chief Quartermaster Department and was promoted to War Minister following the dismissal of Alexei Polivanoff.

He was a victim of the Red Terror in Soviet Russia and was arrested in early December 1937, more than ten years after his retirement, and executed two weeks later.

* A duty or responsibility for someone to do something.

CHAPTER XIV

Protopopoff becomes Minister—The President of the Duma states his Terms—A Greek Prince—Refusal of an Audience—A Visit to Sturmer.

AMONG Sturmer's particularly intimate associates was a certain Manusevitch-Manuiloff, a former collaborator of Ratchkovsky's and a journalist on a small scale connected with Rasputin's clique, to whose influence Sturmer partly owed his own promotion. He was with Sturmer in the capacity of private secretary. Taking advantage of his position, he levied blackmail on the banks, which propitiated* him by bribery. Count Tatistcheff, manager of the Soedinenny (Union) Bank, together with the Minister A. A. Khvoston, determined to catch Manuiloff out. A bribe was offered him, but each of the 500-rouble notes was marked by Ivan Khvostoff, the Minister's nephew. All this took place during Sturmer's absence at the Stavka. A search was made at Manuiloff's flat, and the 500-rouble notes found almost intact; only a part of them had disappeared. Manuiloff was arrested.

When Sturmer heard that Manuiloff had been arrested, he refused to believe it. Having ascertained the truth of it, he again left for the Stavka. What he said there no one ever knew, but he returned to Petrograd with Khvostoff's dismissal in his pocket. He summoned Khvostoff to the telephone and announced: "You brought me the unpleasant news of Manusevitch-Manuiloff's arrest; now I have news for you: you are no longer Minister of the Interior."

Khvostoff (senior) was succeeded as Minister of the Interior by Protopopoff, Deputy-President of the Imperial Duma.

Since Protopopoff's return from abroad and the interview with the German emissary at Stockholm, his name had begun frequently to appear in the Press. A paragraph was inserted in one of the papers announcing Protopopoff's intention of editing, with the assis-

* To regain the favour of.

tance of several banks, a newspaper called *Volia Rossii*. Litvinoff-Falinsky, Tereschenko, and many others warned me that Protopopoff was surrounded by shady characters, that his name was coupled with that of Rasputin, and that the latter's clique was supporting his candidature for the post of Minister of the Interior. Protopopoff's appointment might appear to be popular, because he had had a certain amount of success as head of the parliamentary delegation and was even a member of the Progressive *bloc*.

The actual appointment created general bewilderment, but in his very first interview with representatives of the Press, Protopopoff showed his hand by declaring that he entered the Cabinet as a member of Sturmer's Government and pursued no separate programme. Protopopoff had lately been avoiding me and did not show himself at the Duma. At last I got him on the telephone and insisted on his coming to lunch with me. I put the question to him point blank: "

Tell me frankly, Alexander Dmitrievitch, are the rumours of your appointment correct? You place me in a very awkward position—I must know what post my deputy is about to accept."

"Yes, I was offered the post of Minister of the Interior," replied Protopopoff, "and accepted it."

"Who offered it you?"

"Sturmer, at the desire of his Majesty the Emperor."

"What? . . . And you consent to become a member of Sturmer's Cabinet?"

"Why, you recommended me yourself."

"Yes, I recommended you as Minister for Commerce in Grigorovitch's Cabinet, but not as Sturmer's Minister of the Interior."

"I feel," Protopopoff said, "that you are angry with me."

"I am, very angry indeed. You have acted treacherously towards the Duma. You are going to serve in a Government which the Duma considers incompetent and detrimental to Russia's interests; and this you do after having signed the resolution of the Progressive *bloc*. Moreover, you openly confess that you have no other programme but that of the Prime Minister, Sturmer. You will be called upon to explain yourself before the Duma—let me tell you that."

"I hope," said Protopopoff, "that I shall succeed in bringing about some changes in the present state of affairs. Believe me, the Emperor is willing to do all that is good, but is being prevented."

"So be it; but how will you be able to do anything against Sturmer

CHAPTER XIV

and Rasputin? You will merely compromise both yourself and the Duma. You haven't sufficient strength for the fight, and will never dare speak outright to the Emperor."

After Protopopoff's appointment a rumour spread that the President of the Duma was to be offered the dual post of Premier and Minister for Foreign Affairs. The story was soon confirmed. I received an unexpected visit from Protopopoff, who announced:

"Do you know, Mikhail Vladimirovitch, at the Stavka they want to appoint you Minister for Foreign Affairs."

"How can I be Minister for Foreign Affairs?" I asked with a smile.

"You will have assistants who know the technique of the business."

"Am I also expected to combine this office with the Premiership?"

"Yes, that too, of course." ,

It was time to put a stop to this farce.

"Look here," I said, "you are executing a commission; you have been sent to learn my views on the subject. In that case, tell the Emperor, here are my terms: I alone shall have power to choose the Ministers. I must be appointed for a term of not less than three years. The Empress must renounce all interference in affairs of State and remain at Livadia* till the end of the war. None of the Grand Dukes shall be permitted to take any active part in affairs or allowed at the front. The Emperor must be reconciled with all the Ministers whom he has unjustly offended. Polivanoff must be appointed the Emperor's assistant at the Stavka, and Lukomsky Minister for War. Weekly conferences on all matters connected with the war must be held at the Stavka, at which I shall be present, with the right of a casting vote on all questions not of a purely strategical character."

Protopopoff looked staggered at my words, and, unable to imagine how he would ever have the courage to transmit them, I came to his assistance.

"If the Emperor sends for me, I will tell him all this myself."

"Oh yes, I know you'll tell him," Protopopoff kept repeating, scratching his head.

I asked him to put my terms in writing, and he put them down in his note-book.

"Please add, that I will accept this post on condition that all these terms are made public in the Duma. . ."

Dining with me a few days later, Protopopoff spoke in very high terms of the Empress.

* The Imperial estate in the Crimea.

"She is an uncommonly strong-minded, authoritative and clever woman. You really ought to go and see her, Mikhail Vladimirovitch."

Instead of an answer, I felt his pulse and asked:

"Where did you dine yesterday?" (Shortly before this his special Ministerial secretary, Greve, who had served under Stolypin, had informed me that the day before Protopopoff had dined at Tsarskoe Selo, presumably with Mme. Vyrubova, and spent the evening at Sturmer's.)

Protopopoff looked abashed.

"Now then, tell me, where did you dine last night?" I went on with my interrogation.

"Who told you?"

" That is my own business; my secret service is better than yours. . . . Well, my dear fellow, where did you dine?"

"You probably know already," replied Protopopoff.

"And you spent the evening with Sturmer."

"You know that, too?"

"I know everything, as you see. Tell me, why do you do such things? Why do you compromise yourself? Such things cannot be kept secret. You propose that I should go and see the Empress. I would not go and see her for worlds. You want people to say that I, too, am seeking her patronage, and perhaps also that of Vyrubova and Rasputin. I cannot follow that path."

The Empress's visits to the Stavka became increasingly frequent, and when at Tsarskoe, she received the Ministers, who presented their reports to her.

Under the influence of the Metropolitan Pitirim and Rasputin, a certain Raeff, the principal of a Higher College for Women, was appointed Procurator of the Holy Synod. A delegation of the Synod, in which this Raeff took part, presented the Empress with an ikon and a "blessed *gramota*" (address) signed by the Metropolitan Pitirim and other ecclesiastical dignitaries who were members of the Synod, extolling the Empress's work of mercy among the wounded and invoking the blessing of God on her labours.

This address was published in the Press, but failed to produce the desired impression. The Empress never had been popular, and when Rasputin's influence over her, and her own interference in affairs of State, became more widely known, public resentment was aroused. The Empress was spoken of as "that German woman," and was looked upon as the moving spirit of the Emperor's unsuccessful

CHAPTER XIV

and ill-fated policy.

Prince Nicholas of Greece, the husband of the Grand Duchess Helena Vladimirovna,* arrived at Petrograd via Vienna and Berlin on what was purported to be a secret mission. His visit lasted several months. He went to the Stavka, and Alexeieff complained that on coming one day to make his customary report to the Emperor, he found the Prince and the Grand Duchess Marie Pavlovna† in the study. The Emperor proposed that Alexeieff should report in their presence, but the latter refused to do so, and requested that the interview should be strictly private. Alexeieff considered the Prince's presence at the Stavka out of place, and was of opinion that he ought to be interned and not allowed to return, and more especially, prevented from again passing through Berlin and Vienna. On the demand of the military authorities Prince Nicholas eventually travelled not via Tornea to Sweden, but direct to England via Archangel. He arrived in Greece in the very thick of the disturbances. We saw a paragraph later in the papers stating that "at the Court of King Constantine the mission of Prince Nicholas was considered to have been most successfully accomplished."

On assuming office Protopopoff had declared that the organization of the food supply would be his main task. At a Cabinet meeting he proposed that matters relating to the food supply should be transferred from the Ministry of Agriculture to that of the Interior. This proposal was opposed by the Press and the Zemstvo delegates working in the supplies organizations, as they justly feared increased pressure on the part of governors, police officials and so forth in the event of the organizations passing into the hands of the Ministry of the Interior. The majority declined to work under the control of that body.

These apprehensions were soon justified. The following incident took place in the province of Ekaterinoslav. The governor sent a telephone message to the chairman of the Zemstvo Board, Herberg (who was also plenipotentiary of the Ministry of Agriculture for food supplies) requesting him to authorize the purchase by the agents of the Ministry of the Interior of a consignment of one and a half million poods of barley for the Kalashnikoff corn exchange in Petro-

* First cousin to the Emperor.
† The Prince's mother-in-law.

grad. Fearing that the activities of inexperienced outside agents would inevitably lead to an increase in prices and abuse, Herberg offered to buy and despatch the barley himself; but the governor stood his ground and added that he was merely transmitting an order of the Minister of the Interior, which, if disobeyed, would lead to reprisals. To this Herberg replied that, as chairman of the Zemstvo Board, he was not entitled to receive notifications from the governor on matters of food supply and that, as plenipotentiary, he was subordinate to the Ministry of Agriculture. Herberg's reply was transmitted to Protopopoff, and the latter determined to deport Herberg to Siberia on the pretext of his having a German name. This was averted by a mere chance. A certain Magdenko, justice of the peace of the Novo-Moskovsk district (in the province of Ekaterinoslav) and an old fellow-officer of Protopopoff's, paid a call on the Minister. Protopopoff spoke to him of Herberg and of his intention to deport him. Magdenko implored Protopopoff to desist, saying it would provoke an outburst of indignation throughout the province, where Herberg, who had recently celebrated the twenty-fifth anniversary of his Zemstvo service, was exceedingly popular. It was only after insistent entreaties and persuasions that Protopopoff consented to cancel his decision, and, in Magdenko's presence, tore up the signed order of deportation.

Protopopoff's behaviour was in general becoming very peculiar, and at times he made the impression of not being quite normal. He arrived at a meeting of the Duma Budget Commission wearing the uniform of Chief of the Gendarmerie. He was received with marked coldness by the Duma, and his food supply scheme rejected. It was also condemned by the Unions of Towns and Zemstvos. Protopopoff pressed for an interview with his former fellow-members in the Duma and asked my assistance in the matter. He evidently hoped that an interview would be arranged solely with members belonging to the Zemstvo-Octobrist group, but I purposely invited the leaders of all parties included in the Progressive *bloc*. Protopopoff's behaviour that evening was most extraordinary: he rolled his eyes, repeating in a kind of unnatural ecstacy, "I feel that I shall save Russia, I feel that I alone can save her." Shingareff, a doctor by profession, was of opinion that Protopopoff was simply suffering from creeping paralysis. Protopopoff remained with me till three o'clock in the morning, as if unable to leave, until finally I almost forced him to go home to bed.

CHAPTER XIV

In spite of Protopopoff's endeavours to assure everyone that he was the man who could save Russia, the deputies did not trust him, his scheme was condemned by the Budget Commission, and when in its final stage it was laid before the Council of Ministers, it was also rejected by the latter, and the food supply organization was left under control of the Ministry of Agriculture.

On October 27 the Anglo-Russian Flag Association held a formal meeting. This society had been founded a year before by M. M. Kovalevsky, who was also its first chairman. After his death I was elected in his place. The meeting was held in the Town Hall. Major Thornhill's speech produced an excellent effect. He drew a graphic and vivid sketch of the Russian soldier and spoke with much humour of Germany's efforts to provoke a quarrel between Great Britain and Russia. Great Britain, he said, was out to conquer not territory, but the noble heart of the Russian people; it was for him as an Englishman to say, he added, that such a conquest would also be to our advantage.

Shingareff, who narrated the impressions of his tour with the parliamentary delegation, laid stress on the wonderful solidarity and mutual confidence which existed in England between the Government and the people. This statement was greeted with applause, which grew louder when he added that there was no room there for powers of darkness and irresponsible influences. When one of the speakers mentioned the name of the late Minister Sazonoff, also a member of the society, the assembly cheered again and called on him to give him an ovation, but he was not present in the hall.

I received the Emperor's reply to my request for an audience. The following note was written in his own hand on my petition: "I direct the Prime Minister to inform the President of the Duma that he may be received after the reopening of the session to present a report dealing with matters relating to the session only." There was no signature. The document was enclosed in an envelope addressed to me and sealed with the "small seal." Obviously the Emperor had by mistake placed a document intended for Sturmer in an envelope addressed to Rodzianko.

Next day Sturmer rang me up on the telephone. He had been at the Stavka the day before and there learnt that the Emperor had sent his reply to the wrong man by mistake.

"Mikhail Vladimirovitch, have you received a document from his Majesty in which he desires me to inform you that he is unable to receive you?"

"Yes, I received it."

"What do you intend to do?"

"That is my business."

"But what am I to do? I must transmit his Majesty's command to you."

"That is your own affair. I cannot take it upon myself to advise you in anything."

"Could we not consider that I have given you the message by telephone?"

"I do not think his Majesty's command ought to be transmitted by telephone."

"Then what am I to do?"

"I really don't know."

"Could you send me that document?"

"A copy, yes, but I will keep the original, as I have received it from the Emperor in an envelope addressed in my name and under seal."

"What do you intend to do with regard to this refusal?"

"I am not bound to give you an account of my actions."

Next day Sturmer, after all, sent me an official intimation of the Emperor's message. It was a repetition of the incident which had occurred a few years before during Kokovtzeff's Premiership.

That same day or the next, two members of the Duma met Verevkin, the Assistant Minister for Justice, who asked them: "Whom does the Duma propose to elect as President?" The deputies replied that the re-election of the present President was practically certain. Verevkin looked surprised. "What," said he, "after the Emperor's refusal to receive him?" The deputies, though unaware of this, replied that it would not prevent a re-election. They straightway came to see me and repeated the conversation.

I determined, in order not to strain further the already tense atmosphere of the Duma, to conceal from the members both General Alexeieff's letter concerning the aeroplanes and the Emperor's reply to my request for an audience. But when the Government itself began to circulate rumours to that effect, I sent for the leaders of the parties forming the Progressive *bloc* and acquainted them with all the facts.

CHAPTER XIV

The Duma was due to assemble on November 1. The members of the Progressive *bloc* held continual conferences, at which a resolution, in strong terms, was drafted, stating the need of forming a Government supported by a majority in the Imperial Duma. The Progressives insisted on demanding a responsible Ministry, but, thanks to Miliukoff, the final resolution was couched in more moderate language. The motive for this was that were the demands of the *bloc* rejected, the latter would either be compelled to work with the same Government, or have recourse to revolutionary methods. Two days before the opening of the Duma I received a visit from the Minister for Education, Count Ignatieff. It appeared that the Government was already in possession of a copy of the resolution of the bloc. The Ministers were exceedingly perturbed by the fact of its containing the word "treason."* The Cabinet, so Count Ignatieff informed me, had held a special meeting on account of it and decided to request the President of the Duma to erase that word, as otherwise the Duma would have to be dissolved. I could not give Count Ignatieff any definite promise.

A similar request was made to me by Sturmer, on the eve of the opening of the Duma. On the plea of illness he asked me to call on him. At first I decided not to go, and wrote Sturmer a letter. I thought better of it afterwards and resolved to have a personal explanation. I handed to him a resolution passed by the chairmen of the provincial Zemstvo Boards, in which they reiterated all that had many times been pointed out to the Government: its incapacity to make the most of the nation's patriotic enthusiasm, its perpetual conflict with the representatives of the people all through the war, its incompetence under present conditions to bring the war to a victorious end, and the fact that the principal danger with which the country was menaced lay not outside but within.

"Such is the opinion of Russia's most conservative men," I told Sturmer, "the opinion of persons of ripe experience, that of the whole of Russia's Zemstvos. This resolution is similar to that of the Progressive *bloc*, and thus enables you to know the mind of all Russia. Co-operation with public workers is for you impossible, and without such cooperation the war cannot be won. Everyone feels that the Government is driving the country to ruin. One must speak nothing but the truth now, for we are living through terrible times."

* It transpired after the Revolution that the Government was informed of all that went on in the Duma by the deputy P. N. Krupensky.

Having read the resolution, Sturmer asked:
"What am I to do?"
"Resign."
"How do you mean—resign?"
"Just take a pen, write, and sign."
Sturmer was extremely annoyed.
"So that is the advice you give me!"

Alexander Dmitrievich Protopopoff (b. 1866-1918)
Minister of Interior (Sep 1916 to Feb 1917)
Vice-president of Duma (1914-1916)

A Duma official and later Government minister that had the rare support of the Tsarina because of his acceptance of Rasputin. His leaning towards peace talks with Germany, by association linked the Tsarina to this treachery, and the Duma severely criticised him for it. He became mentally unsound and was asked to step down by Prime Minister Alexander Trepov, but refused. He helped dissolve the Duma and it was not until the Provisional Government was in place that he was finally removed as Interior Minister. He was arrested and incarcerated at the famous Taganka Prison in Moscow for political prisoners. Almost a year since his arrest, he was certified sane and executed in October 1918.

CHAPTER XV

The "Junge Zarin": Miliukoff's Speech and its Consequences— Sturmer and Protopopoff demand the Dissolution of the Duma—Markoff II makes a Scene—After Rasputin's Murder— Protopopoff as Spiritualist.

A FEW days before the opening of the Duma the German Governor-General of Warsaw issued a proclamation announcing the decision of the German and Austrian Emperors to create out of the Polish provinces annexed from Russia an independent State under an hereditary constitutional monarch. This was but another of Wilhelm's cunning moves. Poles living in neutral countries passed resolutions protesting against such a violation of international law and the settlement of the destiny of whole provinces before the end of the war and the conclusion of a general peace. They treated this act as a clever manoeuvre for the conscription of a Polish army. The Russian Poles thought likewise. A statement was read out at the very first sitting of the Duma protesting, in the name of the Polish "Kolo,"* against the German act, and expressing their hope for the ultimate victory of the Allies, the unification of all Polish territory and the restoration of a free Poland.

Unfortunately, after Sazonoff's resignation, our own Government displayed absolute indifference with regard to the Polish question. More than this, it seemed purposely to be creating a feeling that Russia was not bound by the promise contained in the Grand Duke Nicolai Nicolaevitch's manifesto, nor did it find the right word to say at this juncture. No statement was made in the Duma in reply to that read by Garusevitch on behalf of the "Kolo," while in the Council of the Empire. Protopopoff, as if suddenly remembering that he had something to say, asked leave to speak at the moment when members were already dispersing at the end of the sitting. They were asked to return to the hall, and Protopopoff, ascending the tribune, made a brief statement to the effect that with regard to the Polish question

* The Polish group in the Duma.

the Government still adhered to the principles enunciated in the manifesto of the Grand Duke Nicolai Nicolaevitch and in a subsequent declaration made in the Duma by Goremykin. Such a statement, of course, failed to satisfy anyone, nor could it counteract the effect of the Kaiser's proclamation.

The Cabinet, including Sturmer, were present at the opening of the Duma. After listening to the presidential address Sturmer rose and, amid shouts from the Left wing of "Down with the traitor Sturmer," quitted the assembly, followed by the rest of the Ministers. They were all alleged to be hastening to the opening of the Council of the Empire, which was fixed for 2 p.m. instead of 8 p.m. as was the custom. Kulomsin, President of the Council of the Empire, was ill, and his deputy, Golubeff, had fixed this early hour at Sturmer's request, because Sturmer and Protopopoff, having no statements to make, were unwilling to listen to disagreeable home truths in the Duma.

I had caught a chill the day before, felt very unwell, and having with difficulty got through my inaugural address, gave up the chair to my deputy, Varun-Secret. This fact, trivial in itself, was pregnant with unpleasant consequences. Miliukoff, in the course of his speech, read out a passage from a German newspaper. Varun-Secret, who apparently had not heard what Miliukoff was reading, and overlooked the fact that the use of foreign languages on the tribune of the Duma was prohibited by the order of procedure, did not call Miliukoff to order. Yet the passage quoted by Miliukoff contained a broad hint at the active part taken by the Empress Alexandra Feodorovna in Sturmer's appointment to the Premiership, while Sturmer himself was openly called a traitor. The passage read was as follows: "*Das ist der. Sieg der Hofpartei, die sick um die junge Zarin gruppiert.*" ("This is a victory of the Court party, grouped around the young Tsaritsa.")

That same night, at 2 a.m., I received the following letter from Sturmer:

> "Dear Mikhail Vladimirovitch,
> "Information has reached me that at to-day's sitting of the Imperial Duma, Miliukoff, a member of the Duma, took the liberty of quoting a paragraph from a newspaper edited in one of the countries with which we are at war, in which paragraph mention was made of the august name of her Imperial Majesty the Empress Alexandra Feodorovna in an inadmissible juxtaposition with the names of

certain other persons; and that no steps were taken by the presiding member for putting a stop to such proceedings.

"Attaching, as I do, exceptional importance to this event, hitherto unknown in the annals of the Imperial Duma, I entertain no doubt but that you will take decisive measures, and would be greatly obliged if you could let me know your decision on the matter."

Simultaneously Sturmer wrote me another letter asking for a copy of the stenographic report of the speech as actually delivered, uncensored by the President, and adding that "this speech may be the subject of a judicial investigation."

The head of the Duma secretariat, Glinka, told me that the ministers held a conference that night At Sturmer's house. The Premier urged the dissolution of the Duma, but eventually they decided to send me the above letters, while the Minister for Justice, Makaroff, did not consider that Miliukoff's speech contained anything criminal and refused to bring him to justice.

After Sturmer's letters I also received one from Count Fredericks, Minister of the Imperial Court. He reminded me that I held the rank of Chamberlain, and asked to be informed of the steps I intended to take in connection with the mention of the Empress's name. To Sturmer I replied that the President of the Duma was not bound to render account of his actions to the Prime Minister, and forwarded him a verbatim copy of Miliukoff's speech in full. I wrote a similar official reply to Fredericks, but as he was a man whom I esteemed, I added a private letter in which I told him that in the stenographic reports intended for the Press the Empress's name was not mentioned.

At the next sitting of the Duma, Varun-Secret made a statement in which he explained his conduct of the day before by his ignorance of the German language and by the fact that in the stenographic report of Miliukoff's speech submitted to him the German quotation was omitted. Nevertheless, Varun-Secret admitted himself to be guilty of inattention to the words of the speaker and resigned his office of Deputy- President of the Duma.

That same day, I believe, I received a letter from the Chief Committee of the All-Russian Union of Towns. It reiterated still more forcibly all that had been said in the resolution of the chairmen of the provincial Zemstvo Boards. The letter ended with an entreaty that I should tell the Duma that in the opinion of the Committee the decisive hour had struck, and that it was urgently necessary to insist on obtaining a Government which would lead the nation to victory in union with the people.

On November 3 I was re-elected President by 232 votes against 58. The Right Wing voted against me, the Left abstained, as usual. On November 5 an event occurred which created a profound impression not only in the Duma, but throughout the country. In the course of Markoff's speech, in which he endeavoured diligently, but unsuccessfully, to parry Maklakoff's attacks on Sturmer, Shuvaeff and Grigorovitch, Ministers for War and Marine respectively, entered the assembly hall. They notified the President of their desire to make a statement. After Markoff II had finished speaking, Shuvaeff mounted the tribune and said, showing great emotion, that he, as an old soldier, trusted in the gallantry of the Russian army, and that owing to the unanimous support of the nation and the representatives of the people, the army was now properly equipped and supplied with all necessaries. He quoted figures showing the increase in munitions since the formation of the Special Council for Defence. His speech ended in an appeal for the Duma's continued support and confidence. Grigorovitch's brief statement was equally effective. The meaning attributed to their joint demonstration was as follows: If the other Ministers choose to steer clear of the Duma, we, the representatives of the services, desire to make common cause with the nation."

When the Ministers descended from their box into the hall, they were at once surrounded by deputies, who shook hands with them. Shuvaeff found himself among the Cadets and, gripping Miliukoff's hand, repeatedly said: "I thank you." Involuntarily one asked oneself, whether Shuvaeff and Grigorovitch had acted on their own intitiative or had made sure of a permission from the Stavka. It is significant that even such an Ordinary event as a Minister's cordial visit to the Duma produced an impression on the country; telegrams of sympathy and joy addressed to the Duma and the Ministers themselves began to pour in from all sides. The Government, led by Sturmer, remained absolutely indifferent: Shuvaeff and Grigorovitch, it appeared, had not consulted the Stavka, and visited the Duma at their own risk.

After this Sturmer and Protopopoff pressed the Empress for the dissolution of the Duma.

* * *

CHAPTER XV

On my re-election I solicited an audience of the Emperor. At the same time I forwarded to him a copy of the resolution of the Zemstvos and Towns as well as the full text of Miliukoff's speech, including the German quotation. The reply was long in coming.

Trepoff, the Minister for Ways and Communications, desired to make a statement on the Murmansk railway. The construction of this important strategic railway had just been completed, and Trepoff prided himself on its having begun to function during his tenure of office. He hoped to gain the approval of the Duma, and perhaps share the popularity of Grigorovitch and Shuvaeff. He was quite out of place as Minister for Communications, and not always unbiassed in the matter of the direction of new railway lines, in which private companies were interested.

Trepoff asked Shingareff, chairman of the Duma Commission for Defence, to fix a date for his statement and was invited by the latter to come next day. As soon as the members of the Commission learnt that Trepoff's report had been placed on the agenda, the majority declined to hear him, and announced their intention of making a disturbance in the event of his arrival. In the meantime Trepoff had already arrived and was waiting in the Ministerial pavilion. Shingareff was vainly trying to persuade the members to give the Minister a hearing. At last, in despair, he asked me by telephone to come to the Duma. I had great trouble in proving to the deputies that once the chairman of a commission had invited a Minister to make a statement, members were not entitled to turn him out. Trepoff was kept waiting for two hours. When finally admitted before the Commission, he hurried through his statement, asked whether there would be any questions and, as no one replied, left the Duma.

On November 9 Sturmer and Grigorovitch left for the Stavka. Fresh changes were expected. Eventually Sturmer was dismissed and Trepoff appointed Premier. It was said that Sturmer received notice of his dismissal at Orsha before reaching the Stavka. As soon as the Empress heard of this she immediately started for Headquarters, accompanied by Protopopoff.

Trepoff called on me the day after his appointment and assured me of his desire to work in collabo-ration with the Duma, adding that he felt capable of overcoming the influence of Rasputin. I told him that the first thing for him to do was to dismiss Protopopoff, Shakhovskoy and A. Bobrinsky (Minister of Agriculture), as otherwise he would never be trusted.

The Duma recess was drawing to a close, but beyond Sturmer's dismissal no further changes had taken place. The reopening of the Duma was again deferred. It was generally believed that Trepoff would profit by the interval to remove several other Ministers and prepare a statement on the policy of the Government. Rumours were current that he had accepted the Premiership on condition of Protopopoff's resignation, but this unfortunately proved incorrect; the only minister to be dismissed was A. Bobrinsky, who, as Minister for Agriculture, was succeeded by Rittich.

At last, on November 15, I was received in audience by his Majesty, to whom I presented a detailed report on the same subject as before. I remained with the Emperor for an hour and three-quarters.

The Duma reassembled on the 19th. Trepoff read out the Government statement, which contained no programme and took refuge in commonplaces. He made public our agreement with the Allies on the subject of our annexation of the Dardanelles after the war. Rittich was obliged to own that he had had no time to acquaint himself with the food supply organization during his short term of office, and was therefore unable to submit any scheme to the Duma. The deputies criticized both Trepoff and Rittich severely, and set themselves to work out a comprehensive system for improving the country's food supply. I was very sorry that for political reasons the Left wing had at once launched an open campaign against Rittich. I always looked on him as an eminently capable and hard-working man, having had occasion to collaborate with him when I was chairman of the Agrarian Commission. I had then learnt to appreciate him as a perfectly honest and experienced worker. His appointment unfortunately came too late, and he was in bad company.

A disturbance occurred in the Duma during the sitting of November 22. It had obviously been planned beforehand, because the serjeants-at-arms heard members of the Right asking each other in the gallery: "Has the row come off yet?"

Markoff II, having obtained leave to speak, intentionally used language calling for reprimand from the chair. I stopped him several times and finally ruled him out of order. On quitting the tribune, Markoff approached the presidential chair and, waving his papers and shaking his fist in my face, uttered distinctly; "You scoundrel, scoundrel, scoundrel . . ."

At first I did not even realize what had happened. Then, having

CHAPTER XV

notified the Duma of the insult directed at its President, I gave up the chair to my senior deputy.

Count Bobrinsky, after making a statement on the incident, moved that the severest punishment allowed for by the procedure, i.e., suspension for fifteen sittings, be applied to Markoff. The motion was carried unanimously. Markoff asked for leave to make a statement and announced: "I re-affirm what I said before. I wished to insult your President, and in his person to insult you all, gentlemen. Insulting allusions to exalted personages were made in this place, which none of you resented, through the medium of your President, who is partial and not a gentleman. . . . I insult you all!"

On the way from the hall to my room I caught sight of Markoff's retreating figure. My first impulse was to overtake him, but luckily I was prevented from doing so by my confessor, the Duma chaplain. I regained my self-possession and together we entered my room. It was already crowded with deputies. Dmitriukoff, a highly-strung, nervous man, embraced me with tears in his eyes. Bobrinsky tried to soothe me, and Markoff I came up to me saying that though he was Markoff II's uncle he begged not to be "associated with his nephew." My son George, an officer in the Preobrazhensky Regiment, who was in the gallery with several brother officers, rushed downstairs to the telephone to ask his colonel's permission to challenge Markoff to a duel. As soon as I heard of it, I forbade him to do so. I sent for Panchulidzeff and D. Dashkoff, two of my own old brother officers in the Chevaliers Gardes, and asked them to act as my seconds.

That same evening the Duma met for the election of the presidential body. I was re-elected by the majority against 26 votes. The Zemstvo-Octobrist group decided that the utterances of Markoff II were unworthy of notice and that he should not be shaken hands with. This resolution was endorsed by all the parties included in the Progressive *bloc*. The deputies Savitch and Kapnist arrived at my house with a copy of this resolution, which they handed me in the presence of my seconds, Panchulidzeff and Dashkoff. My seconds considered that under the circumstances Markoff II could not be regarded as a man enjoying the right to fight a duel.

After this unfortunate episode, in which Markoff II figured merely as somebody's mouthpiece, I began to receive numerous letters and telegrams from acquaintances and strangers, from assemblies of the Zemstvos and the Nobility assemblies, provincial and district Zemstvo Boards, municipalities and so forth. The Council of Professors of Petrograd University honoured me by electing me a member of the University *honoris causa*. The Ekaterinoslav Municipal Council sent me the following telegram: "Congratulations on brilliant victory over base sally of henchman of Ministerial lobby."

There could be no doubt but that Markoff's bout had been premeditated; clearly the desire existed to degrade the President of the Duma and trample him in the mud. It turned out otherwise.

A few days later the French Ambassador presented me, in the name of the President of the French Republic, with the Grand Cordon of the Legion of Honour.

At one of the next sittings a wonderfully powerful and inspiring speech was delivered by Purishkevitch. Disassociating himself from the Extreme Right, he spoke of the influence of the powers of darkness, and appealed to the Ministers present in the Duma. "You must," he said, "go at once to the Stavka, throw yourselves at the Emperor's feet, and implore him to credit the full horror of Rasputin's influence, the dire consequences of the present state of affairs, and to change his policy."

As all the stenographic reports of proceedings at the Duma were strictly censored, the members' speeches appeared in the Press with large blank spaces and reached the public in a completely distorted form. Evil-intentioned persons even began to fabricate certain speeches by inserting passages of their own, and sold separate copies for a few roubles.

A sharp change of front became manifest in the Council of the Empire. There, too, the members at last realized the impossibility of supporting such a Government. Eugene Trubetzkoy appealed to the members of the Synod to remember the cross which they wore on their breast, and taking up their cross, to go to the Tsar and implore him to deliver the Church and the Government from unclean influences. Like the Duma, the Council of the Empire passed a resolution declaring that it was the duty of the Government to listen to the voice of the nation and entrust power to men who enjoyed the confidence of the country. (How many times had all this been said already! . . .) A similar resolution was carried by the congress of the United Nobility.

All Russia thought alike and desired the same thing, yet the Government's policy remained unchanged. On the contrary, the acute

CHAPTER XV

divergency between Government and people appeared to be intentionally emphasized. The Pan - Zemstvo Congress in Moscow was prohibited at the last moment, in spite of Protopopoff's assurances to the Press of his favourable attitude towards the Zemstvos and public workers in general. The delegates to the congress held meetings in private houses and handed over their rights to the committee presided over by Prince Lvoff.* In the papers blank columns appeared in place of the reports communicated by telephone from Moscow.

A notice appeared in the Press that Princess S. N. Vasilchikova, wife of a member of the Council of the Empire, was about to leave Petrograd for her estate in the province of Novgorod. The Princess's departure, as everyone understood, was not voluntary. Soon it became known that Princess Vasilchikova had written a letter to the Empress about Rasputin. Kaufman-Turkestansky, High Steward to the Imperial household, suffered in a similar fashion. He was Red Cross delegate at the Stavka. He had the courage to speak to the Emperor and entreat him to dismiss Protopopoff and appoint a man trusted by the nation. The Emperor agreed. The Empress arrived at the Stavka. Kaufman was due to leave for a time. He was bidden a most cordial farewell, but on reaching Petrograd he received from the Emperor an intimation that he was released from his duties as Red Cross representative at the Stavka.

A whole group of members of the Left had been suspended for from eight to fifteen sittings a few days before the Markoff episode. They had created a disturbance during the reading of the Government statement and had prevented Trepoff from speaking. After Markoff's suspension, the question was raised that the punishments meted out had been equal, while the offences were by no means equal. I intended to move in the Duma that the term of suspension of the deputies of the Left should the reduced. At this juncture a delegation arrived from the Petrograd factory workers, announcing that they had come to "demand" a reprieve for the suspended deputies. I had a long talk with them about the state of the country, and, with regard to their claim, told them frankly what my intention had been, but that in view of the "demand" put forward by the workers I did not consider it possible to act under pressure from outside.

* Prime Minister of the first Provisional Government in 1917.

Quite unexpectedly and illegally Dobrovolsky, the Minister for Justice, dismissed the case of Manusevitch-Manuiloff, which had already been heard by Court and jury. This was a proceeding unheard of in Russian jurisprudence. It was done by Imperial command.

On December 16 the Duma rose for the Christmas recess.

An event occurred on the night of December 17 which may justly be considered, as marking the beginning of the second Revolution—the murder of Rasputin. No doubt the perpetrators of this murder acted from patriotic motives. They saw that all legal methods of fighting the dangerous favourite led to nothing, and thought it their sacred duty to deliver the Imperial Family and Russia from the hypnotic power in which they were held enthralled. The result, however, was exactly contrary to the anticipation. The people saw that the fight for Russia's interests was only possible by means of terroristic acts, as legal methods failed to attain the desired aim. The knowledge that a Grand Duke, a member of the highest aristocracy, and members of the Duma had taken part in Rasputin's murder seemed to emphasize this fact.

At the same time, Rasputin's power and influence appeared to be confirmed by the extraordinary severity of the punishment meted out by the Emperor to members of the Imperial Family. A number of Grand Dukes were banished from the capital to the army and other places. The papers were prohibited by the censor from writing of the *starets* Rasputin and of *startsy* in general. Editors, however, while paying heavy fines, published all the minutest details of the case. As if in defiance of public opinion, the policy of the Government became still more reactionary, and confidence was bestowed only on Rasputin's followers. The clamour roused by this terroristic act only served to make it generally popular, and the conviction steadily grew that since persons closely connected with the Imperial Family and members of the aristocracy had taken part in it—matters had indeed reached a climax.

Ever since the winter of 1913-14 society had talked of little else but of the influence exercised by the "powers of darkness." It was stated openly and definitely that the appointment of Ministers and other officials depended on these "powers of darkness," whose medium was Rasputin. The Court entourage either could or would not realize the fatal consequences such a state of affairs might have for the dynasty. Indignation was practically universal—but so were

CHAPTER XV

silence and submission. Such was the state of mind of Russian society when the world war broke out. The universal outburst of patriotic enthusiasm which swept the country relegated all internal troubles and apprehensions temporarily to the background. It seemed as if at the prospect of a cruel war, which claimed such heavy sacrifices from everyone, all differences had disappeared and the whole community, in singleness of purpose had rallied round the motto of "War to a victorious end."

The Rasputinites, however, did not rest. They soon resumed their intrigues, which aimed at placing the Government in opposition to public opinion. In order to shake the Government's confidence in the nation, the legend of the growth of revolutionary tendencies was carefully and adroitly circulated. There were at the time absolutely no grounds for such fears, but the Russian public was immediately made suspect by the Government, and this policy of no confidence was continued right up to the outbreak of the Revolution. As most of the Ministers were Rasputin's nominees, I am justified in asserting that this policy of alienating the Government from the nation originated with his circle. Patriotic enthusiasm soon gave way to keen apprehension, and the fatal word "treason," first whispered secretly, soon sounded loudly and ominously throughout the country. Defeatists raised their heads, and the criminal, treacherous propaganda of their ideas soon became widespread, affecting all the weak and vacillating members of the community.

I here close the narrative of Rasputin's career and of the part played by him in the history of the Russian Empire. I can vouch for the truth of all the facts I have alleged. These facts adjust themselves into a definite and intricate pattern, showing the enormous influence this man exercised on the trend of public affairs through the medium of the Empress Alexandra Feodorovna. The case leaves no room for doubt. What always struck me, who closely observed these phenomena, was the strict correlation in all the acts of the Rasputinites. It seemed as if they were pursuing some well thought out and definite plan.

I am far from asserting that Rasputin himself was the inspirer and leader of the nefarious activities of his clique. Though clever and astute by nature, he was after all only an illiterate and uneducated peasant, with a limited outlook on life and absolutely devoid of any political ideas—world politics were simply beyond his power of comprehension. He was, therefore, incapable of guiding the political opinions of the Imperial couple. Had he alone been an intimate of the Court, the whole affair would have been limited to donations, presents, perhaps to instances of patronage extended to a certain number of suppliants—nothing more. On the other hand, the wicked idea of "treason" on the part of the Empress Alexandra Feodorovna must be rejected once and for all. This charge was absolutely repudiated by the commission under Muravieff which was appointed by the Provisional Government for the purpose of elucidating this matter in the light of documentary evidence.

That the Empress Alexandra Feodorovna may have thought a separate peace with Germany would serve Russia's interests better than a prolongation of the war on the side of the Allies, is certainly possible, but this was never actually established. Still less has anyone the right to speak of "treason" to the Allied cause on the part of the Emperor Nicholas II. He sealed his loyalty to his pledge by dying a martyr's death.

But at the same time it was perfectly clear that the whole internal policy of the Imperial Government from the outbreak of the war had inevitably and methodically led the country to revolution, to confusion in the minds of the citizens and to the complete political and economic collapse of the State.

One has but to recall the "Ministerial leapfrog." Five Ministers of the Interior had succeeded one another between the autumn of 1915 and that of 1916; Prince Scherbatoff was followed by A. N. Khvostoff, who was succeeded in turn by Makaroff, the elder Khvostoff, and lastly Protopopoff. Their average term of office was about two and a half months. How was any serious home policy possible under such circumstances? Three Ministers for War were changed during the same period—Polivanoff, Shuvaeff and Beliaeff, and four Ministers for Agriculture—Krivoshein, Naumoff, Count A. Bobrinsky and Rittich. The regular work of all State departments connected with the war was inevitably interrupted by these continual changes. No good could come of it: chaos, contradictory orders, general confusion, absence of guiding will power, lack of determination and firmness of purpose were not conducive to victory.

The people looked on, felt something was wrong, the conscience of the nation was stirred, and simple-minded folk drew the logically sound conclusion: a war is on, yet no one seems to care for our brothers, the soldiers in the ranks, who are being slain in their thousands, while there is chaos everywhere, due to the incompetence

CHAPTER XV

and carelessness of the Ministers and generals appointed by the Tsar.

All that happened during the war was not merely the result of bureaucratic negligence, caprice and unlimited power, or of incapacity to cope with the stupendous difficulties raised by the war. It was the outcome of a well thought out and systematic campaign for creating disruption in the rear of our army. And for those who were working consciously towards that end, Rasputin proved a most convenient tool.

For this reason I affirm that those who were in a position, and whose duty it was, to combat this evil phenomenon have sinned heavily against their Mother country, for not only did they not oppose Rasputin, but they used him as a means to attain their own selfish interests at the expense of Russia.

It is interesting to note that agents of the Okhrana who stood on duty near Rasputin's house and whom he had dismissed before the arrival of Yusupoff's car on the fatal night, returned to their post next morning knowing nothing of the murder. Rumours of Rasputin's murder had spread long before it had actually taken place, and after the event the police rushed in all directions. Even my sons were suspected, and under the pretence of a burglary a search was made in my flat. The front door latch was forced, the contents of drawers and cupboards overhauled; none of the clothes were taken, but all the papers and letters scattered about.

It was hoped that the murder would have a salutary effect, the warning taken to heart at Tsarskoe Selo, and the Government brought to its senses, or at least frightened. Actually the reverse was the case. As if to spite the public, all Rasputin's adherents were promoted. Protopopoff's appointment as Minister of the Interior received Imperial confirmation, as if to emphasize the Emperor's approval of his policy; Trepoff resigned; Count Ignatieff, Makaroff and the Assistant Minister of the Interior, Prince Volkonsky, did likewise. Trepoff was succeeded by the old Prince N. D. Golitzyn. Ignatieff's and Volkonsky's resignations were temporarily not accepted, but a few days later they read in the papers of their dismissal. The Duma learnt of the peculiar role played at the Ministry of the Interior by General Kurloff, who held no official post and was looked upon as the organizer of Stolypin's assassination. In the absence of Protopopoff, who scarcely attended to his duties and was perpetually at Tsarskoe, Kurloff signed documents "p.p. Minister of the Interior." In the meantime, as no decree concerning his appointment had been published by the Senate, Government institutions declined to acknowledge such documents. Kurloff's appointment, it appeared, had been kept secret even from the Senate. The Government had actually come to this. Exposure by the Duma had no effect, and Kurloff remained at his post.

On January 1, 1917, corresponding changes were made in the Council of the Empire. Kulomsin was relieved of the presidency and replaced by Stcheglovitoff, and a number of ultra-reactionary men nominated members of the Council. Nevertheless, the Government failed to alter the spirit of the Upper Chamber. The recent supporters of the Government, "right or wrong," now declared themselves against Protopppoff. When the rumour arose that Sturmer would be included in the list of newly-nominated members of the Council, the Conservatives announced that they would not admit him into their group. Trepoff was elected chairman of the Right group, as if to emphasize the members' approval of his stand against Protopopoff and the motives which led to his resignation from the Cabinet.

The whole policy of the Government during this period consisted of a series of inefficient reprisals coupled with inaction. After the Duma rose for the Christmas holidays rumours became current that it would not be summoned on January 9, which was the date fixed for its reopening. The Imperial warrant on the appointment of Prince Golitzyn contained a phrase recommending "friendly relations with the legislative chambers and the necessity of collaborating with them in their work." This, however, in no wise prevented Protopopoff from obtaining, without Golitzyn's knowledge, a postponement of the Duma session till January 14. Protopopoff not only continued to be an important personage at Tsarskoe, but apparently posed as Rasputin's successor. It was said that he held spiritualist *séances* and even evoked Rasputin's spirit.

CHAPTER XVI

Disruption in the Rear—Krymoff urges a Coup d'État—Luncheon with the Grand Duchess Marie Pavlovna—Visit of the Grand Duke Mikhail Alexandrovitch—Audience of January 7.

THE supply organization was going from bad to worse. The towns were short of food, the peasants could not buy boots; yet all felt that there was plenty of everything in Russia, and that the shortage was due to the chaos prevailing throughout the country. While Moscow and Petrograd had no meat, the papers wrote of large consignments of frozen meat which had accumulated at the railway stations in Siberia. All these stocks of over half a million poods were bound to be spoilt as soon as the thaw set in. All efforts on the part of Zemstvo organizations or private persons were wrecked by the criminal indifference or incompetence of the authorities. Each Minister or senior official laid the blame on someone else, and those actually guilty could never be discovered.

For the improvement of the food supply in the large centres the Government could think of nothing more effective than a temporary suspension of passenger traffic. This, too, proved a scandalous failure. After one of these stoppages the locomotives were found to be out of order: the water had not been let out, frost had set in and the pipes burst; instead of improving, the transport became still worse. The Zemstvos and trade organizations attempted to convene special food supply conferences, but these were prohibited by the Government. The local supply officials, who vainly sought to obtain instructions in the various Ministries, used to come in despair to consult the President of the Duma, who, in the absence of the Duma itself, embodied the principle of national representation. Many of the Government's measures provided food for peculiar and melancholy reflections: it seemed as if the authorities were consciously working on behalf of Germany and against Russia. Closer investigation of the sources from which such measures emanated led inevitably to

Protopopoff and through him to the Empress.

At the beginning of January (1917) General Krymoff arrived from the front and asked to be given an opportunity of unofficially acquainting the members of the Duma with the disastrous conditions at the front and the spirit of the army. A large number of members of the Duma, the Council of the Empire and the Special Council assembled at my flat. The gallant General's tale was listened to with profound emotion. His was a painful and grim confession. There could be no hope of victory, said Krymoff, until the Government had changed its course, or given way to another which the army could trust. The progress of the war was heavily handicapped and all temporary successes brought to nought by conditions in the rear. Krymoff wound up his statement more or less as follows:

"The spirit of the army is such that the news of a *coup d'état* would be welcomed with joy. A revolution is imminent, and we at the front feel it to be so. If you decide on such an extreme step, we will support you. Clearly there is no other way. You, as well as numbers of others, have tried everything, but the Emperor attaches more weight to his wife's nefarious influence than to all honest words of warning. There is no time to lose."

Krymoff ceased speaking, and for a few seconds an ominous and painful silence filled the room. It was first broken by Shingareff.

"The General is right. A coup *coup d'état* is urgent. But who will have the courage to undertake it?"

Shidlovsky said fiercely:

"No need to pity or spare him, when he is driving Russia to ruin."

Many members of the Duma agreed with Shingareff and Shidlovsky; heated arguments arose on every side. Someone quoted Brusiloff's words: "If I had to choose between the Emperor and Russia, I follow Russia."

The most implacable of all proved to be Tereschenko. His words greatly agitated me, and I rebuked him.

"You do not take into account," I said, "what will follow on the Emperor's abdication. . . . I shall never countenance a revolution. . . . I have taken the oath of allegiance. . . . I desire you not to speak this way in my house. . . . If the army can insist on an abdication, let it do so through the medium of its leaders; as for me, I will continue to act, not by violence, but by persuasion, to the very last."

The conference lasted far into the night. One felt the gathering of the storm, and the future loomed dark and menacing: some fatal

CHAPTER XVI

destiny seemed to be drawing the country into a fathomless abyss.

About the same time I had a peculiar interview with the Grand Duchess Marie Pavlovna.

One night, about 1 a.m., the Grand Duchess summoned me on the telephone.

"Mikhail Vladimirovitch, could you come and see me at once?"

"Your Highness, I really don't know whether it would be convenient at such a late hour. . . . To tell you the truth, I was just going to bed."

"I must see you on an urgent matter. I will send my car to fetch you. Do come, please."

I felt puzzled by such insistence, and asked if I might give my answer in a quarter of an hour. The President of the Duma calling on a Grand Duchess at one o'clock in the morning—it would savour too much of a conspiracy.

Exactly a quarter of an hour later the telephone bell rang again and Marie Pavlovna's voice was heard asking:

"Well, are you coming?"

"No, your Highness, I cannot come to you now."

"Then come to lunch to-morrow."

"At your service, thank you. I will come tomorrow."

On my arrival next day I found the Grand Duchess and her sons, as if assembled for a family council. They were all most cordial to me, and not a word was said about the "urgent matter." At last we passed into the Grand Duchess's boudoir, the conversation still revolving round trivial topics. Cyril Vladimirovitch, turning to his mother, said:

"Why don't you speak?"

The Grand Duchess then began to talk of the general state of affairs, of the Government's incompetence, of Protopopoff and of the Empress. On mentioning the latter's name she became more and more excited, dwelt on her nefarious influence and interference in everything, and said she was driving the country to destruction; that she was the cause of the danger which threatened the Emperor and the rest of the Imperial Family; that such conditions could no longer be tolerated; that things must be changed, something done, removed, destroyed. . . .

Wishing to understand more precisely what she was driving at, I asked:

"What do you mean by 'removed'?"

"Well, I don't know. . . . Some attempt must be made . . . . The Duma must do something. . . . She must be annihilated. . . ."

"Who?"

"The Empress."

"Your Highness," said I, "allow me to treat this conversation as if it had never taken place, because if you address me as the President of the Duma, my oath of allegiance compels me to wait at once on his Imperial Majesty and report to him that the Grand Duchess Marie Pavlovna has declared to me that the Empress must be annihilated."

The idea of the Emperor's compulsory abdication had been persistently circulated in Petrograd since the end of 1916. Persons belonging to the highest society frequently urged upon me that it was the duty of the Duma and of its President to make themselves responsible to the country and save the army. After Rasputin's death such talk became still more insistent. Many people were sincerely convinced that I was preparing a *coup d'état* with the support of officers of the Guard and the British Ambassador, Sir George Buchanan. I was profoundly indignant at this, and whenever people hinted or spoke openly to me of a *coup d'état*, I invariably repeated the same denial:

"I will not be a party to any venture, both on principle and because it is impossible to involve the Duma in an inevitable collision. The legislative chambers cannot be concerned in palace revolutions, and I have neither the will nor the power to raise the people against their Tsar."

Resentment, indignation and complaints became universal, and found vent at political meetings, at drawing-room parties, in casual talks in the theatres, shops or even trams, but no one went beyond talk. Meanwhile, had all been united, had the clergy, the men of science and of business, and representatives of the upper classes together presented a petition or even a demand to the Emperor to listen to the voice of the nation, perhaps something might have been attained. Instead of this, some cringed and fawned, others safeguarded their own interests or clung to their posts, some kept silent, confining themselves to grumbling, gossip, and underhand threats of a revolution.

Strange as it may appear, certain members of the Imperial Family also sought the aid of the President of the Duma, demanding that he should go, prove, and persuade.

CHAPTER XVI

The Emperor's immediate circle also realized the magnitude of the approaching danger, but they too, even the Emperor's own brother, were both irresolute and powerless.

One afternoon the Grand Duke Mikhail Alexandrovitch called unexpectedly at my flat.

"I should like to speak to you of what is going on, to ask your advice as to what is to be done. We realize the situation perfectly," said the Grand Duke.

"Yes, your Highness, the situation is so grave that there is not a moment to lose, and Russia must be saved at once."

"Do you think there will be a revolution?"

"The people realize that while the war is on, a revolution would be fatal to the army, but the danger lies elsewhere. The Government and the Empress Alexandra Feodorovna are driving the country to a separate peace and disgrace; they are delivering us into Germany's hands. This the nation will not tolerate. Should such rumours be confirmed, a most terrible revolution will break out, and will sweep away the Throne, the dynasty, all of you and us too. There is yet time to save Russia. Even now your brother's reign may attain unsurpassed grandeur and glory, but if this is to happen, the entire policy of the Government must undergo a radical change. Ministers must be appointed whom the nation trusts, not men whose very presence in the Government is an insult to public feeling. I am sorry to have to tell you that this can only be done on condition that the Empress is removed. She exercises a deplorable influence on all appointments, even those in the army. She and the Emperor are surrounded by shady, incompetent evil persons. Alexandra Feodorovna is fiercely and universally hated, and all circles are clamouring for her removal. While she remains in power, we shall continue on the road to ruin."

"Do you know," said Mikhail Alexandrovitch, "Buchanan told my brother exactly the same thing. The whole family realizes Alexandra Feodorovna's evil influence; she and my brother are surrounded by traitors. All the decent people have gone. . . . But, things being so, what is to be done."

"Your Highness, you, as the Emperor's only brother, must tell him the whole truth, point out the pernicious results of the Empress's interference, seeing that the country looks on her as a pro-German, who is not concerned for Russia's interests."

"Do you think a responsible Ministry necessary?"

"The general demand is only for a strong Government, and no

mention is made anywhere of a responsible Ministry. The country's desire is to see at the head of the Cabinet a man enjoying the confidence of the nation. Such a man would form a Ministry responsible to the Tsar."

"Only you, Mikhail Vladimirovitch, could be that man; everybody trusts you."

"If I were indispensable, I should be willing to devote all my energies to my country's service, but again on one condition the removal of the Empress from all interference in affairs of State. She must go, for owing to the Emperor's unfortunate lack of will power it is quite useless to fight her. The Emperor's refusal to receive me is due to the influence of the Empress and Protopopoff. There are also grounds for belief that the Duma will be dissolved and fresh elections held. I am informed that owing to disruption in the rear, disaffection is spreading to the troops. The army is losing its self-control. . . . If all the sacrifices and suffering endured, and the blood shed, prove in vain—there will be a terrible reckoning."

"Mikhail Vladimirovitch, you must see the Emperor and once again tell him the whole truth."

"I entreat you to persuade your august brother to receive me before the opening of the Duma. For God's sake, your Highness, use your influence to get the Duma summoned and Alexandra Feodorovna and her set put out of the way."

Our talk lasted for over an hour. The Grand Duke agreed to all I said and promised to help.

The Grand Duke Mikhail Alexandrovitch was not the only one to realize the menacing state of affairs; it was clearly understood by other members of the Imperial Family. The Grand Duke Nicolai Mikhailovitch had said to me long before, "Goodness knows what they are doing with their insane policy. They want to drive the whole Russian public to desperation."

I determined once more to solicit an audience and on January 5 wrote to the Emperor:

"I take the liberty of asking permission to wait on your Imperial Majesty. In the awful hour our Mother country is passing through, I deem it my duty as a loyal subject and President of the Imperial Duma to lay before you in full the knowledge of the calamity which is threatening the Russian State. I implore you, Sire, to command my presence and hear me out."

The reply came next day, and on January 7 I was received by the

CHAPTER XVI

Emperor.

Shortly before this the customary New Year's Day reception was held at the Palace. I knew I should meet Protopopoff and resolved not to shake hands with him. On entering I asked the Masters of the Ceremonies, Baron Korff and Tolstoy, to warn Protopopoff not to approach me. Either they did not tell him, or Protopopoff took no heed of the warning, but I noticed that he was following me with his eyes as if intending to approach me. To avoid a meeting I moved to another part of the hall and stood with my back towards Protopopoff's group. Notwithstanding this, Protopopoff showed a bold front and, approaching me with a cordial greeting, held out his hand. I replied:

"Nowhere and never."

Protopopoff seemed nonplussed, and, at a loss what to do, took me in a friendly manner by the elbow, saying:

"My dear fellow, surely we can come to an understanding."

I felt disgusted with him.

"Leave me alone; you are repellent to me," I said.

This incident, though not in full detail, appeared in the Press. Protopopoff, it was added, intended to challenge me to a duel. However, nothing happened.

My first act, on being received by the Emperor, was to apologize for my behaviour in the Palace to a guest of the Emperor's. To this the Emperor replied:

"Yes, it was not right—at the Palace...."

I remarked that Protopopoff had not greatly felt the insult, as he had sent no challenge.

"What, hasn't he challenged you?" asked the Emperor, looking surprised.

"No, your Majesty.... As Protopopoff is unable to defend his honour, next time I will simply thrash him."

The Emperor laughed.

I then passed on to my report.

"Your Majesty was able to gather from my second report that I consider the state of the country to have become more critical and menacing than ever. The spirit of the people is such that the gravest upheavals may be expected. Parties exist no longer, and all Russia is unanimous in claiming a change of Government and the appointment of a responsible Premier invested with the confidence of the nation. It is necessary to organize, on the basis of mutual confidence between the Government, the legislative chambers and public bodies, the work for the attainment of victory over the enemy and order at home. To our shame, chaos reigns everywhere. There is no Government and no system, neither is there, up to the present, any coordination between the front and the rear. At every turn one is confronted with abuse and confusion. The nation realizes that you have banished from the Government all those in whom the Duma and the people trusted, and replaced them by unworthy and incompetent men. The constant changes of Ministers at first created confusion among the officials, which finally gave place to complete indifference. Think, your Majesty, of Polivanoff, Sazonoff, Count Ignatieff, Scherbatoff, Naumoff—all of them honest and loyal servants of yourself and of Russia, who were dismissed for no cause or any fault whatever. . . . Think of such venerable statesmen as Golubeff and Kulomsin. They were removed for the sole reason that they refused to silence honest men in the Council of the Empire. As if purposely, everything is being done to the detriment of Russia and the advantage of her enemies. No wonder monstrous rumours are afloat of treason and espionage in the rear of the army. Sire, there is not a single honest or reliable man left in your entourage; all the best have either been eliminated or resigned, and only those who have bad reputations have remained. It is an open secret that the Empress issues orders without your knowledge, that Ministers report to her on matters of State, and that by her wish those whom she views with disfavour lose their posts and are replaced by incompetent and inexperienced persons. Indignation against and hatred of the Empress are growing throughout the country. She is looked upon as Germany's champion. Even the common people are speaking of it. . . ."

"Give me facts," said the Emperor, "there are no facts to confirm your statements."

"There are no facts, but the whole trend of policy directed by her Majesty gives ground for such ideas. To save your family your Majesty ought to find some way of preventing the Empress from exercising any influence on politics. The heart of the Russian people is tortured by the foreboding of awful calamities, the people are turning away from their Tsar because they see that after all their suffering and bloodshed fresh trials are in store for them."

Touching upon events at the front, I reminded the Emperor that as long ago as 1915 I had entreated him not to assume the supreme

CHAPTER XVI

command; that now the entire responsibility for our reverses in Rumania was attributed to him.

"Your Majesty," I continued, "do not compel the people to choose between you and the good of the country. So far, the ideas of Tsar and Motherland were indissoluble, but lately they have begun to be separated."

The Emperor pressed his head between his hands, then said:

"Is it possible that for twenty-two years I tried to act for the best, and that for twenty-two years it was all a mistake?"

It was a hard moment. With a great effort at self-control, I replied:

"Yes, your Majesty, for twenty-two years you followed a wrong course."

In spite of these frank words, which it could not be pleasant to hear, the Emperor bade me a kind farewell and manifested neither anger nor even displeasure.

My memory here involuntarily recalls another audience, in which the true nature of the Emperor Nicholas II stood revealed more clearly than at any other time. Those who considered him to be a false and callous man are mistaken. He was merely weak and easily led by another's stronger will.

I remember how tired the Emperor looked after hearing one of my reports.

"Have I wearied your Majesty?"

"Yes, I didn't have my sleep out last night. I went out woodcock shooting this morning. How lovely it was in the woods!"

The Emperor went up to the window. It was early spring. He stood silently looking out. I, too, stood respectfully at a distance. Then the Emperor turned to me:

"How is it, Mikhail Vladimirovitch? I was in the woods to-day.... It is so quiet there.... One forgets all these intrigues and paltry human restlessness.... My soul felt so peaceful.... One is nearer to Nature there, nearer to God...."

A man who felt like this could not be callous and deceitful.

Shortly before my audience on January 3, I summoned Samarin from Moscow. He had just been elected President of the United Nobility. It should be noted that rumours of my impending arrest and banishment were persistently current at the time. They were confirmed to me by a member of the Government. I felt bound to impart this information to those of my associates who in my absence would take upon themselves the defence of Russia's dignity and honour and protect the representatives of the people from undeserved insult.

Samarin arrived, accompanied by two members of the Council of the Nobility—Karpoff and Prince Kurakin. He also had asked for an audience. He was determined, to lay before the Emperor the resolution of the United Nobility and explain its full significance. He spoke with intense emotion of how he felt it to be his duty to tell the Emperor the plain truth. On the eve of his visit to Tsarskoe he sat with me till late at night; he never, to the last moment, abandoned his faith in the ultimate triumph of truth and justice, and his belief that, at last, we should be granted a hearing.

Samarin's visit to me was followed by those of Prince Lvoff, Tchelnokoff and Konovaloff. They all approved of my actions and upheld my view that it was time to speak the whole truth, however unpalatable it might be.

After my report and that of Samarin's rumours again arose that Trepoff would be invited to form a Cabinet of "confidence" chosen from among the members of the legislative chambers. These rumours were taken up by the Press, but they soon died down. Protopopoff remained at his post, continued his frequent visits to Tsarskoe Selo, and everything went on as before. There was even some talk of the Duma being dissolved till the end of the war, after which fresh elections would take place. What seemed to be preparations for an election campaign were set on foot. As neither the clergy nor the nobility could be relied upon, Protopopoff conceived the idea of rallying the peasants to the Government. A bill was drafted providing for the distribution of land to peasants—Knights of the Order of St. George—in holdings amounting to 30 dessiatines (about 80 acres) to be compulsorily expropriated from private landowners.

The nobility of ancient Novgorod held its provincial assembly. The spirit which animated the members found expression in a resolution vividly reflecting their feelings of anguish and fear for the future of Russia. It was hoped that a direct appeal addressed to the Emperor by members of the ruling class would produce the desired effect. The marshal of the nobility of Novgorod, Budkevitch, was unanimously elected to lay the resolution personally before the Sovereign. Unfortunately, the Emperor did not find time to receive

CHAPTER XVI

Budkevitch, and the resolution was handed in through Protopopoff. The result of this was that the Governor of Novgorod, Islavin, was summoned to Petrograd to give explanations, and was dismissed from his post.

Alexander Feodorovich Trepoff (b. 1862-1928)
Prime Minister (Nov 1916 to Dec 1916)
Minister of Transport (Oct 1915 to Dec 1916)

Trepoff is mainly known for holding the fort in between the presidencies of Sturmer and Golitsyn but he achieved much more than that, for example being one of the authors of the Manifesto of 17 October 1917. He also spent 23 years within the Ministry of the Interior (1869-1892).

His two brothers held senior positions and his brother-in-law was General Alexander Mossolov, the Court Chencellor. Despite this, Trepoff was another minister despised by the Tsarina, not least for his attempts to drive Rasputin away.

CHAPTER XVII

Entente Delegates in Petrograd—Police and Machine Guns—The Last Audience—Labour Arrests—The Emperor agrees to a Responsible Ministry—His Sudden Departure—Adrift.

AN Allied Mission arrived in Petrograd towards the end of January for the purpose of co-ordinating operations during the approaching spring campaign.

Joint conferences were held with the Allied delegates, at which the absolute ignorance of Beliaeff, the Minister for War, was fully revealed. He and also some of our other Ministers found themselves in an extremely awkward situation with reference to our Allies; they had failed on many points to reach a preliminary understanding among themselves, and were not up-to-date even concerning their own departments. This was particularly noticeable with regard to orders placed abroad. After listening for a long time in silence to our Ministers' arguments. Lord Milner finally asked: "What is the amount of the orders you intend to place?" He was told. "And how much tonnage do you require for the transport of the material?" On receiving the answer, he remarked: "Then let me tell you that you are asking for one-fifth of the tonnage required."

The Allied delegates expressed their regret that Russia's remoteness, and her independence of the united Allied command in the West, prevented their obtaining sufficient information concerning us. The Minister Pokrovsky then proposed that a special commissioner should be appointed who would represent Russia in the West and rank above our ambassadors. Sazonoff, the newly-appointed Russian Ambassador in London, who was present at the conference, resented this, and an argument ensued between him and Pokrovsky. The foreign delegates saw clearly that we had no unity, no system, and no understanding of the seriousness of the situation. This made them most indignant. Lord Milner, a cool and collected man, could scarcely control his feelings. He kept throwing himself back in his chair and groaned audibly. Every time the chair

CHAPTER XVII

cracked, and he was offered another.

The French delegates also seemed very nervous, and obviously dissatisfied with us. As far back as January, 1916, when the members of the French mission, Doumergue and Castelnau, had visited Tsarskoe Selo, they had seen there, to their amazement, the heavy guns sent from France to the Russian front.

I was informed that the Petrograd police were being trained in machine gun firing. Large quantities of machine guns, instead of being despatched to the front, were distributed to the police divisions. At the same time a very peculiar order was issued, on the strength of which the troops of the Petrograd military district were excluded from the command of the northern front field army, and made directly subordinate to the Government under the commander of the military district. Some secret purpose, it was said, underlay this strange proceeding. According to persistent rumour; the Empress desired a separate peace at all costs, and Protopopoff, who was her ally, conceived the idea of provoking food riots in Petrograd and Moscow in order to suppress them and thus obtain a lawful excuse for starting peace negotiations.

So persistent were these rumours that they created grave consternation not only among members of the Duma, but also among the representatives of the Allies. Members of the Special Council for Defence resolved to raise the question of the French artillery and machine guns at the earliest meeting of the Council. They asked Beliaeff, the Minister for War, by what right he had handed over, without sanction from the Special Council, such an enormous quantity of war material to the Minister of the Interior. Beliaeff promised to give a reply in the course of the meeting, but did not, and on the question being put to him a second time, tried to close the debate. My protest against the War Minister's action was seconded by Stishinsky, Gurko and Karpoff, members of the Council of the Empire, who urged that the Minister had no right to evade answering questions put to him by the Council.

Having failed to obtain the desired information, the members decided to resort to extreme measures and request the Emperor to preside over the next meeting. The resolution on that point was carried unanimously, especially as the Emperor had promised that he would preside over particularly important meetings. Beliaeff, however, held his ground and declined to submit the Council's resolution to the Emperor on the plea that it was inopportune to harass his Majesty with questions which were not of primary importance. The members then drew up a written petition, which I despatched with my customary report.

No answer was given. . . .

On February 10 I was received in audience by the Emperor. I started on my journey with a heavy heart. Beliaeff's evasiveness and delay in replying to important questions put by the Special Council, the Emperor's unwillingness to preside—all this boded no good.

The unusual coldness with which I was received showed me that I could not even, as usual, frankly set forth my arguments in the course of conversation. I therefore proceeded to read my written report. The Emperor's attitude was not merely indifferent, but positively harsh. During the reading of the passage which dealt with the shortage of food supplies in the army and the towns, the arming of the police with machine guns, and the general political situation, the Emperor seemed absent-minded and finally interrupted me:

"Couldn't you get through with it quicker?" he said sharply: "the Grand Duke Mikhail Alexandrovitch is expecting me to tea."

When I mentioned the terrible conditions in which our prisoners of war were kept and the report on the subject made by the Red Cross nurses who had visited Germany and Austria, the Emperor said:

"This does not concern me at all. There is a special committee for this presided over by the Empress Alexandra Feodorovna."

Concerning the machine guns for the police, the Emperor remarked apathetically:

"Strange, I've heard nothing about it."

But when I mentioned Protopopoff, he said irritably:

"Protopopoff was your deputy-president in the Duma. Why do you dislike him now?"

I explained that since he became Minister, Protopopoff had positively gone mad.

In the course of our talk about Protopopoff and home policy in general, I alluded to Maklakoff.

"I very much regret Maklakoff," said the Emperor, "he at least was certainly not out of his mind."

"He had none to get out of, your Majesty," I could not refrain from saying.

CHAPTER XVII

On my speaking of the menacing state of the country and the prospect of a revolution, the Emperor again interposed:

"My information is directly contrary to yours. As to the spirit prevailing in the Duma—if the Duma permits itself such harsh utterances as last time, it will be dissolved."

I was obliged to conclude my report.

"I consider it my duty. Sire, to express to you my profound foreboding and my conviction that this will be my last report to you."

"Why?" the Emperor asked.

"Because the Duma will be dissolved, and the course the Government is taking bodes no good. There is still time; it is still possible to change everything and grant a responsible Ministry, That, apparently, is not to be. You, your Majesty, disagree with me, and everything will remain as it is. The consequence of this, in my opinion, will be revolution and a state of anarchy which no one will be able to control."

The Emperor said nothing and curtly bade me farewell.

The opening of the Duma was fixed for February 14. A few days earlier I learnt that a delegation of Petrograd workmen meant to attend the first meeting in order to put forward some demands. At the same time I heard that an unknown individual posing as Miliukoff was making a round of the factories and inciting the workmen to riot. Miliukoff wrote a letter to the Press denouncing the impostor and warning the workers against provocation. This letter was suppressed by the war censor, and it was only after repeated requests on my part that the commander of the Petrograd military district, General Khabaloff, realized the expediency of allowing Miliukoff's statement to be published. He also issued an appeal to the workers on his own account, urging them to keep calm and threatening reprisals in case of riot.

Immediately before the opening of the Duma, members of the Labour group in the war industries committee were arrested. They were men of moderate views, and the Government's motives for arresting them seemed incomprehensible. Neither were all arrested; two members remained at liberty. They addressed an appeal to the workers, entreating them to keep calm whatever happened. This appeal, like Miliukoff's letter, was not allowed to appear in the Press.

The opening of the Duma passed off quietly. There were no signs of any Labour delegation, but large police forces had been mustered in the neighbouring courtyards. In order not to add more fuel to the already smouldering fire, I limited my inaugural speech to a mention of the army and its loyal fulfilment of its duty. Instead of dealing with the general political situation, the debates were diverted to the food supply, the Minister for Agriculture, Rittich, having intimated his desire to make a statement. He made a long speech, was supported by the Centre and severely criticized by the Cadets. It was clear from his speech that in the short space of time he had been in office he had been able to do very little, and that the food supply organization was in a state of chaos. Owing to the disorganization of transport the towns were threatened with famine, while large quantities of meat, butter and corn had accumulated in Siberia. The apportionment system for the provision of supplies from the different provinces was defective. The corn-growing districts supplied too little, while excessive charges were laid upon those which themselves lacked grain. The peasants, terrified by various apportionments, registrations and rumours of requisitions, had begun to conceal their supplies of grain or hastened to sell them off to middlemen.

In the Duma spirits were at a low ebb. Even Purishkevitch's speech lacked verve. The Duma felt itself powerless, weary of the useless struggle, almost reduced, indeed, to the role of passive spectator. Yet, despite everything, the Duma clung to its old position and did not proceed to an open rupture with the Government. Its sole weapon was the spoken word—and this was emphasized by Miliukoff when he said that the Duma " would act with words, and with words only."

The Duma was in session for nearly a week. I learnt casually that the Emperor had summoned several of the Ministers, including Golitzyn, and expressed his desire to discuss the question of a responsible Ministry. The conference ended in the Emperor's decision to go to the Duma next day and proclaim his will to grant a responsible Ministry. Prince Golitzyn was overjoyed and came home in high spirits. That same evening he was again summoned to the Palace, where the Emperor announced to him his intention to leave for the Stavka.

"How is that, your Majesty?" asked Golitzyn, amazed. "What about a responsible Ministry? You intended to go to the Duma tomorrow."

"I have changed my mind. . . . I am leaving for the Stavka to-

CHAPTER XVII

night...."

Golitzyn explained this sudden departure by the Emperor's desire to avoid further reports, conferences and deliberations.

The Emperor left.

The Duma continued with the debate on food supplies. Outwardly everything appeared quite quiet. Suddenly something seemed to snap, and the State machine jumped off the rails....

Something happened—that something which those at Court, though often warned, did not believe in, and which now, implacable and menacing, suddenly arose before us all....

Nikolai Dmitriyevich
Golitsyn (b. 1850–1925)

Prime Minister
(Jan 1917 to Mar 1917)

Governor of Tver Oblast
(1897–1903)

Governor of Kaluga Oblast
(1893–1897)

Governor of Arkhangelsk
Oblast (1887–1893)

Golitsyn reluctantly accepted the position at the bequest of the Tsar and Tsarina but avoided appearances in the Duma and Government as much as possible, and as the Duma and Soviet were competing for control at that time, he didn't last for long as Prime Minister. He lasted just two months, because the February Revolution occurred and a Provisional Government subsequently installed Georgy Lvov for its Chairman.

Over the next few years he was imprisoned in St Petersburg and arrested two more times after that, until in Moscow in 1925, he was imprisoned and executed a few months later for involvement with a counter-revolutionist group.

APPENDIX I

M. V. RODZIANKO'S SPEECH AT THE CELEBRATION OF THE TERCENTENARY ANNIVERSARY OF THE HOUSE OF ROMANOFF, 1913.

Three centuries ago, when it seemed as if the Russian State had come to an end, your august ancestor, Mikhail Feodorovitch Romanoff, was called to the throne by the will of Divine Providence, the blessing of God and the unanimous voice of the people.

Inspired by their unity with their crowned leader, and beneath the shelter of the Holy Orthodox Church, the Russian people defended their native land from the daring attacks of her foes. Great in those days was the service of the Tsar—great, too, is the solemn day we are now celebrating.

Three centuries of the glorious reign of the House of Romanoff testify, that beneath the sceptre of the august successors of the first Tsar of the now reigning House, Holy Russia valiantly withstood all the trials with which she was afflicted, grew, gathered strength, expanded, and attained her present state of greatness.

The heart of the Russian Tsars, so filled with love, always palpitated with joy at all the joys and successes of the Fatherland, and was filled with profound sorrow in the year of troubles and misfortune. The good of the Russian Sovereign was the good of the people, his grief was the people's grief, and the Russian people now, as three hundred years ago, reverently venerate and unreservedly love their Tsar. O great Sovereign, manifold are your labours and your care for the good of the people, and unwearied your solicitude for them. Believing, as of yore, that the strength of the Motherland lies in close unity of Tsar and people, believing in their statesmanship and wisdom, you have summoned the men chosen by the nation to participate in legislative construction. And the members of the Imperial Duma, the chosen of the people, inspired by the confidence of the Monarch, are infinitely rejoiced personally to lay at the feet of your Imperial Majesty their most loyal congratulations on the occasion of this supremely momentous festival of the Russian State.

Accept therefore, Sire, this holy ikon of Christ the Saviour as a blessing from the people, as a visible token of those heartfelt prayers which are offered to-day in all the remotest parts of Russia for the health and happiness of your Majesty and all the Reigning Family.

May the blessing of the All-Highest be upon you, may He guard His Anointed beneath His heavenly pall, for the happiness and joy of all the Russian nation.

APPENDIX II

M. V. RODZIANKO'S SPEECH AT THE OPENING OF THE IMPERIAL DUMA ON JULY 26 (O.S.) 1914.

His Majesty the Emperor has been most graciously pleased, in this hour of trial which has befallen the Fatherland, to summon the Imperial Duma in the name of the Russian Tsar's unity with his loyal people. The Imperial Duma has given its reply to its Sovereign at to-day's reception. We all know well that Russia did not want war, that the Russian people are alien to aspirations for conquest, but destiny itself has drawn us into war. The die is cast, and we are now fully confronted with the problem of safeguarding the integrity and unity of our State. It is good to see, in the midst of a tempestuous vortex of events unparalleled in the history of the world, the calm and dignified assurance which has possessed all without exception, and which has emphasized before the whole world the majestic strength of the Russian spirit. We are able to say, calmly and without challenge: "Hands off! Dare not touch our Holy Russia." Our people are gentle and peaceful, but terrible and powerful when forced to defend themselves. "See,"—so may we say—"you thought that we were torn by dissensions and antagonisms, and yet all the nationalities inhabiting Russia are united in one family when their common Fatherland is threatened with danger."

And the Russian paladin will not bow his head in discouragement whatever trials befall him. His powerful shoulders will bear any burden, however heavy; and once again will our Motherland, one and undivided, be glorified with peace and plenty in all the lustre of her indomitable greatness. Gentlemen, members of the Imperial Duma! At this hour, all our thoughts and wishes are directed to our frontiers, where our gallant army and glorious navy are fearlessly advancing to battle. Our thoughts are there, where our children and brothers, with the bravery inherent to them, are defending the greatness of the Fatherland. God the Almighty be with them, defend and strengthen them, while our own heartfelt wishes of success and glory will always be with these our heroes. We who stay at home must work without respite to provide for the families left without their breadwinners; and those in the army know that in deed, and not merely in word, we shall look to it that they shall want for nothing.

APPENDIX III

LETTER FORM GENERAL ALEXEIEFF TO
M. V. RODZIANKO.

DEAR MIKHAIL VLADIMIROVITCH*, You have addressed, through the intermediary of our attaché in France, a telegram to General Joffre and M. Albert Thomas concerning the supply of aeroplanes for the Russian army, and have determined, according to your own lights, both the type and quantity of the machines, without any relation to the general programme worked out by common agreement between ourselves and the French and British Governments. Copies of the correspondence conducted by you, though after the despatch of your telegram, were forwarded by you to the Grand Duke Alexander Mikhailovitch. On this correspondence being submitted to his Majesty the Emperor, his Majesty commanded me to notify you of his wish that you should abstain from direct interference in war matters which do not concern either the President of the Imperial Duma or a member of the Special Council. A business possessing several masters, each deeming himself to be independent of the others, equally competent and invested with full powers, is liable to come to ruin in a very short time. I beg to assure you of my absolute respect and loyalty.

MIKHAIL ALEXEIEFF.

---

* In Russian official correspondence the customary address was: "Milostivy Gosudar" ("Gracious Sir"), followed by the name and patronymic.

APPENDIX IV

M. V. RODZIANKO'S SPEECH AT THE INDUSTRIALISTS' CONGRESS, 1915.

GENTLEMEN: On my way to attend this meeting, I encountered more than one unit of young recruits now being trained and preparing to fill the places of the fallen. I have travelled 2,000 versts, visited Galicia, been in close contact with the army, and can find no suitable words to express my profound emotion and my infinite reverence for these brave soldiers, for the indomitable spirit which I have everywhere witnessed, and with which the young men now in training are animated, knowing it to be their duty fearlessly to march into the field of battle. It is, therefore, the first and most important duty of citizens of the Russian State to give the army a complete and perfect assurance that perfect calm reigns in the rear; that the interior of our peaceful homeland, as yet untroubled by the effects of the war, is ready to devote all its strength to the task of assisting them, and working for their needs and their glory. We must, too, convey to them the certainty that here, in the rear, there is no room for parties or dissensions, but only one desire—for victory over the enemy.

I am happy, gentlemen, to testify that this is now the watchword firmly established among the members of the Imperial Duma. The representatives of the people realized this by instinct, and you can bear witness that the absence of parties, and complete unanimity, are a continuous feature of all our sittings. I may say that this unity, this absence of all party principles, are equally manifest in the small meetings we now frequently hold in connection with the business of the Imperial Duma. I am perfectly well aware that the industrial world, industrial circles, are a class and a sphere of immense importance to the State. You represent the masters and rulers of that vast sphere of the economic life of the State which in its future high grade of progress will enable us not only to defeat the enemy in the field, but will give us power to prove what Russia is capable of achieving. Henceforth all Russian citizens must have but one watch-word: Everything for the army, everything for victory over the enemy. Everything must be done in order to overthrow by our united efforts those who dare challenge Russia's greatness. I take the liberty of expressing a wish that henceforth there may be no party divisions, aspirations or ambitions, but one unanimous thought, directed towards productive work for assisting our army completely to enfranchise Russia from all assaults of alien influence. Allow me to greet you in these words and express the certainty that so it will be in deed.

INDEX

Abalaksky monastery, 394
Adrianople, fall of, 447, 450
Agapit, Archbishop, 444, 456–458
Akimoff, 472
Alexander I, Emperor, 392, 501
Alexander III, Emperor, unveiling of memorial to, 436
Alexander Mikhailovitch, Grand Duke, 483, 543-544
Alexandra Feodorovna. Empress ; tendency towards mysticism, 391–2 ; falls under Rasputin's influence, 397 ; unbounded influence over Emperor, 415 ; insists on dissolution of Duma, 416 ; letter to Rasputin, 417 ; alleged intimacy with Rasputin, 427 ; despair at Rasputin's dismissal and anger with Rodzianko and Gutchkoff, 430 ; opposes reception of members of Duma by Emperor, 436 ; nominal president of Supreme Council, 475 ; Grand Duke Nicolai Nicolaevitch complains of her influence, 478 ; desire for Grand Duke's dismissal, 500 ; protests against Emperor's visit to Duma, 523 ; condemns Polish autonomy scheme, 535 ; demands liberation of Sukhomlinoff, 538 ; attacked by Miliukoff in Duma, 558–9 ; vindicated against "treason" charge, 568 ; necessity of removal, 575–6, 577–8, rumoured desire for separate peace, 583
Alexeieff, General, 500, 501, 525, 527, 533–4, 551, 554
Alexeyenko, 454, 460
All-Russian Zemstvo Union, 513
Altshuller, 482
American Magazine, 523
Andronikoff, Prince, 506
Anglo-Russian Flag Association, 553
Anthony, Metropolitan, 399, 403, 410
Anthony, Bishop of Tobolsk, 421, 431–2
Antioch, Patriarch of, 445
Archangel, 495–6, 509
Army Medical Department, 474–7
Artillery Department, 419, 485–7, 495–6
Aviation Department, 544–5

Badmaieff, 416
Bakhmetieff, 523
Balashoff, 434, 441
Balkan war, 447–451
Baranovitchy, 533
Bark, 473
Barnabas, Bishop, 403–4, 427, 506
Beatty, Admiral, 466
Beliaeff, 456, 582, 583
Benckendorff, Count, 532
Beresina, battle of, 476
Berezkin, 431–2
Besobrasoff, General, 540, 541
Bethmann-Hollweg, 516
Bieletsky, 523
Bobcheff, 448
Bobrinsky, Count A., 561, 563, 568
Bobrinsky, V., 494, 522
Borodino, anniversary celebrations, 438
Brasova, Madame, 512
Bratoliuboff, 512–3
Brest Litovsk, 477, 499
British squadron at Reval, 466–7
Brusiloff, General, 482, 532, 533, 539, 544
Buchanan, Sir George, 509, 574–5
Budkevitch, 580
Bulgaria, Russian sympathy with, 447–8

Cadet Party, 439, 441, 451, 490, 497–8, 586
Castelnau, 583
Caucasian front, 531
Constantine, King, 551
Constantinople, 449, 453, 531
Cyril Vladimirovitch, Grand Duke, 573

Damansky, 399, 426–428, 430
Daneff, 448
Daniloff, General, 476, 487
Dashkoff, D., 563
Dediulin, General V. N., 398, 426
Derevenko, 422, 425
Dmitrieff, General Radko, 447–449, 482, 485
Dmitrieff (priest), 444

INDEX

Dmitriukoff, 487, 504, 563
Dnieper rapids, visit to, 456
Dobrovolsky, 565
Doumergue, 583
Drachevsky, 451
Dragomiroff, Vladimir, 485
Dreadnoughts, purchase of, 463–465
Dudykevitch, 483
Dumbadze, General, 409
Dunajetz, river, 482
Dvinsk, 499

Ekaterinoslav, Bishop of, 444, 456
Elizabeth, Grand Duchess, 403, 515–516
Erzerum, 453, 519
Essen, Admiral, 468
Eulogius, Bishop, 437, 483
Evdokimoff, 474–5
Evert, General, 534

Fedoroff, 465, 467
Feofan, Bishop, 393-4, 399, 401, 421
Fersen, Baron, 445
Filaret Nikititch, 445
Finland, Bishop of, 404 ; question of, 437 ; port of Hangö, 468
Floristchevo hermitage, 421
Fogel, Colonel, 543
Francis Joseph, Emperor, 516
Fredericks, Count, 436, 440, 520, 559

Galicia, campaign in, 482–5, 499–500
German Aggression Bill, 502, 535
Germans in Duma, 481
Germany, announcement of state of war with, 471
Giers, Admiral, 508
Glinka, J. V., 434, 483, 559
Godneff, 460
Golitzyn, Prince A. M., 473
Golitzyn, Prince N. D., 569-70, 586
Golos Moskvy, 412
Golovina, Madame, 434
Golubeff, no. 578
Goremykin, I. L., 397, 473, 475, 478, 480–1, 495, 500 ; urges dissolution of Duma, 502–4 ; 505, 501 ; M. V. Rodzianko complains to Emperor of, 510 ; M, V. Rodzianko's strong letter to, 513–5 ; 517–8 ; resignation, 518 ; 546
Grazhdanin, 454, 458
Greece, Prince Nicholas of, *see* Nicholas
Grevé, 550
Grigorieff, General, 499
Grigorovitch, Admiral, 464, 522, 536, 560–1
Guards, heavy losses of, 541
Guiche, Marquis de la, 528, 545
Gurko, 509, 583
Gutchkoff, A. I., 413, 416, 421, 426, 430, 455, 458, 460, 482

Hangö, port of, 467–8
Helena Vladimirovna, Grand Duchess, 551
Herberg, 551–2
Hermogen, Bishop, 395, 399, 401–6, 410, 412–14, 416, 417. 420, 434
Hermonius, General, 509
Hesse, Duke of, 435, 516

Ignatieff, Count (Minister), 555, 569, 578
Ignatieff, Count (staff officer), 543
Ignatieff, Count (Military Attaché), 545
Iliodor, 401, 404, 406, 410, 412, 416, 421, 523
Industrialists' Congress, 490
Islavin, 516
Ivanoff, General, 482, 485, 500
Izvolsky, P. P., 407

Japan, Russian warships returned by, 509
Joffre, General, 528, 545

Kaiser (William II), 467, 516, 558
Kaledin, General, 540, 544
Kamensky, 426
Kapnist, 563
Kargopol, bishopric of, 403
Karpoff, V. L, 426, 434, 580, 583
Kashtalinsky, General, 540
Kaufman-Turkestansky, 537, 565

INDEX

Kazan Cathedral, 445–7
Kerensky, 490
Khabaloff, General, 585
Kharitonoff, 458
Khitrovo, G. F., 541–2
Khlysty, sect of, 395, 406, 412, 421–3, 429, 431
Kholm, 499 ; province of, 437
Khomiakoff, 460
Khvostoff, A. A. (senior), 503, 538, 547
Khvostoff, A. N. (junior), 442, 507, 516, 523, 525
Khvostoff, Ivan, 547
Kieff, 455, 499
Kleinmichel, Countess, 539
Klopoff, 519
Knox, General, 509
Kokovtzeff, V. N., 409, 416, 418, 433, 436, 443, 448, 454–5, 458, 461, 554
Koliubakin, 481
"Kolo," Polish, 557
Kolokol, 462
Konovaloff, 580
Korff, Baron, 438, 441, 445, 577
Korniloff, General, 484
Kovalevsky, 447, 553
Kovel, operations near, 540
Kovno, 499
Kovzan, 438
Kremenchug, 456
Krivoshein, 478, 501, 568
Krupensky, P. N., 555
Krymoff, General, 572
Kshesinskaia, 486
Kulomsin, 501, 570
Kurakin, Prince, 580
Kurloff, General, 569–70
Kuropatkin, General, 528, 534
Kutuzoff, 501
Kuznetsk enterprise, 536

Lemberg, *see* Lvoff
Lerche, H. H., 541
Letchitsky, General, 482
Litvinoff-Falinsky, 486, 487–8, 496, 548
Livadia, 409, 455, 549
Lodz, battle of, 476

Lublin, 499
Lucius, Herr von, 533
Lukianoff, 407, 409
Lukomsky, 513, 549
Lutsk, 540-1
Lvoff, Prince G. E., 490, 513, 565, 580
Lvoff, V. N., 414
Lvoff (Lemberg), 483–4, 499

Magdenko, 552
Makaroff, 414, 538, 569
Maklakoff, B., 490–1, 522, 560
Maklakoff, N. A., 443–4, 450, 453, 461 ; growing influence at Court, 465 ; obstruction of war work, 479–81 ; 483, 486 ; patronage of Germans, 487 ; 490–2 ; M. V. Rodzianko urges Emperor to dismiss him, 492 ; 493 ; dismissal, 494 ; 530, 584–5
Maklakoff, V. A., 540
Mandryka, 406
Manikovsky, General, 495, 528, 533
Manus, 524
Manusevitch-Manuiloff, 547, 566
Mardary, 507
Marie, Grand Duchess, 416
Marie Feodorovna, Dowager Empress, conversation with M. V. Rodzianko about Rasputin, 416-8 ; efforts to improve Red Cross organization, 474–5 ; 501 ; talk with M. V. Rodzianko at Kieff, 539
Marie Pavlovna, Grand Duchess, 515, 551, 573–4
Markoff, 454, 524, 560, 562–5
Masonic Congress at Brussels, 412
Medvied, Yaroslav, 394
Mestcherinova, Madame, 541–2
Mestchersky, Prince, 452
Miasoiedoff, Colonel, 481–2, 488, 522–3
Mikhail Alexandrovitch, Grand Duke, 512, 520, 521, 575–6, 584
Mikhail Feodorovitch Romanoff, 445
Mikhail Mikhailovitch, Grand Duke, 509
Military Medical Academy, 452–3
Miliukoff, P. N., 441, 473, 490, 497, 555, 558–60, 585
Milner, Lord, 582
Miloradovitch, Madame, 516

INDEX

Mitia, 401, 402
Murmansk railway, 561

Nauheim, 437, 469
Naumoff, 539, 568, 578
Nemertzaloff, 517–8
Nicholas II, Emperor, appoints Rasputin lamp-keeper, 395; falls under Rasputin's influence, 398; attitude towards Bishop Hermogen, 405–6, 420; ignores Mgr. Anthony's representtations concerning Rasputin, 410–11; complete domination by Empress, 416; listens to M. V. Rodzianko's denunciation of Rasputin, 420–4; orders M. V. Rodzianko to examine Rasputin documents, 426; refuses to receive M. V. Rodzianko, 432; receives members of Duma, 436; receives M. V. Rodzianko, 439–40; receives members of Duma, 441–2; listens to M. V. Rodzianko's complaints against Ministers, 443, 453–4; discusses purchase of Dreadnoughts with M. V. Rodzianko, 463; hesitation over mobilization orders, 469–70; words to crowd before Winter Palace, 471; speech to Chambers, 472; visit to Galicia, 483–4; agrees to formation of Special Council of Defence, 488–9; emotion on hearing M, V. Rodzianko's report on Sukhomlinoff, etc., 492–3; decision to assume supreme command, 501; refuses to dismiss Goremykin and prorogues Duma, 502–3; visit to Duma, 520–1; rebuke to M. V. Rodzianko, and subsequent explanation, 454–5; refuses to receive M. V. Rodzianko, 553–4; receives M. V. Rodzianko, 577–9, 584; leaves Petrograd, 494
Nicholas of Greece, Prince, 551
Nicolai Mikhailovitch, Grand Duke, 576
Nicolai Nicolaevitch, Grand Duke, 473, 474–5; complains of Empress's influence, 478; visit to Galicia with Emperor, 483–4; on munitions shortage, 485–7; dismissal, 500; at loggerheads with Stavka, 531; 535, 557
Nikititch, Filaret, 445
Nizhni-Novgorod, 524

Novgorod, Governor of, 570
Novo-Georgievsk, 499
Novoseloff pamphlet, 412–5, 422–3

Octobrist party, 448, 455, 459–60, 497
Ogonek, 423
Oldenburg, Prince Alexander Petrovitch of, 475–7
Olga, Grand Duchess (d. of Nicholas II), 416
Olga Alexandrovna, Grand Duchess, 416
Olsufieff, Countess, 516
Orloff, Madame, 427
Oseroff, General, 416
Ossovets, 499
Ostroukhoff, Professor, 445
Ourusoff, Prince, 456, 457

Paget, Lady Muriel, 542
Pan-Zemstvo Congress, 565
Panchulidzeff, 563–4
Papus, 392, 393
Parish Schools' Credits Bill, 437–8
Paul, Grand Duke, 540–3
Petroff, 494
Philippe, 392
Pitirim, Metropolitan, 398, 517–8, 550
Plehve, General, 513
Podolsk, province of, 500
Pokrovskoe, 393, 409, 467
Pokrovsky, 582
Poland, status of, 358, 538, 557
Polish language in schools, 461
Polivanoff, General, 494–5, 503, 510, 513, 522, 526-7, 531, 549, 568, 578
Polovtzeff, 522
Progressive *bloc* in Duma, 497, 502, 552, 554–5, 563
Protopopofl, A. D., 487, 491; heads parliamenttary delegation to Allied countries, 532–3; becomes Minister of Interior, 547–9; sounds M. V. Rodzianko regarding acceptance of Premiership, 549; eccentric conduct, 552–3; presses Emperor for dissolution of Duma, 560; 561, 565, 569; poses as Rasputinas successor, 570; 572, 573, 576 rebuffed by M. V. Rodzianko, 577; 580–1, 584

INDEX

Przmysl, 482, 483–4
Purishkevitch, V. M., 405, 522, 564, 586
Putiloff, 488, 508 ; works, 512

Raeff, 550
Rai-Mesto, 542
Rasputin, Gregory, introduction to Imperial Court, 393 ; origin and career, 393–6 ; establishes influence over Empress, 397–8 ; supporters and opponents, 399 ; rapidly acquires followers, 400 ; violent scene with Bishop Hermogen, 401–2 ; unsuccessfully proposed by Sabler as candidate for priesthood, 402 ; interview with Stolypin and departure from St. Petersburg, 407–8 ; reinstated at Court, 409 ; affair of Imperial children's nurse, 410 ; his confederates, 411 ; attacked in Novoseloff pamphlet, 412–5 ; denounced by M. V. Rodzianko to Empress Marie Feodorovna, 417, and to Emperor, 420–4 ; further proofs against, 431 ; exiled to Tobolsk, 434–5 ; rumours of return, 443 ; expelled from Kazan Cathedral by M. V. Rodzianko, 446 ; praised by organ of Synod, 462 ; stabbed at Pokrovskoe, 467 ; again banished and again returns, 495; 503, 507, 508, 517, 518 ; assaulted at " Villa Rode," 523 ; deportation ordered and countermanded, 525 ; 539, 547–8, 550 ; murder, 566–7 ; review of activities, 567 ; police action after murder, 569
Ratchkovsky, 392, 547
Rauch, General, 542
Red Cross organization, 474–8, 484
Retch, 451, 473
Reval, British squadron at, 466
Rittich, 562, 586
Rodionoff, 402, 416, 434
Rodzianko, George, 563
Rodzianko, M. V., elected member of Council of the Empire, 391 ; collects evidence against Rasputin, 396, 397 ; appeals for leniency for Bishop Hermogen, 405 ; dispute with Minister of Interior over Novoseloff pamphlet, 414 ; denounces Rasputin to Empress Marie Feodorovna, 417–8, and to Emperor, 419–20 ; presented to Tsarevitch, 424–5 ; interviews with Damansky and Archpriest Vasilieff, 426–429 ; attacked by Empress, 430 ; examines Rasputin documents at Emperor's orders, 431–2 ; further audience of Emperor refused, 433 ; re-elected President of Duma, 439 ; audience of Emperor, 439–40 ; expels Rasputin from Kazan Cathedral, 446–7 ; speech at dinner to Bulgarian guests, ; complains to Emperor of Ministers' conduct, 453–4, 461–2 ; conversation with Archbishop Agapit, 456–8 ; re-elected President of Duma, 458 ; approaches Emperor about purchase of Dreadnoughts, 463–5 ; delivers address of welcome on board British flagship, 472–3 ; learns of Emperor's hesitation over mobilization orders, 469–70 ; speech at Winter Palace, 472–473 ; efforts to improve Red Cross organization, 474–7; conversation with Grand Duke Nicolai Nicolaevitch, 477–8 ; efforts to improve supply of footwear for army, 478–9; visit to Galicia, 483–4 ; conversation with Grand Duke Nicolai Nicolaevitch on munitions shortage, 485–7 ; scheme for creation of Special Council, 488-90; begs Emperor to dismiss Sukhomlinoff, Maklakoff, etc., 493–4 ; rumour of coming appointment to Premiership, 500 ; receives Order of St. Anne, 510 ; strong letter to Goremykin, 514–5 ; asks Emperor to grant responsible Ministry, 521 ; again denounces Rasputin to Emperor, 524–5 ; denounces Government at Stunner's dinner, 530 ; conversations with Emperor and Alexeieff at Stavka, 533 ; visit to front, 540–2 ; secures dismissal of Besobrasoff, etc., 543 ; states to Protopopoff terms on which he will accept Premiership, 549 ; advises Sturmer to resign, 555 ; re-elected President of Duma, 560–1 ; insulted by Markoff in Duma, 563 ; conversation with Grand Duchess Marie Pavlovna, 573–4 ; rebuffs Protopopoff, 577 ; frank report to Emperor, 577–9 ; last audience of Emperor, 584–5

INDEX

Rodzianko, Nicholas, 484
Romanoff, Mikhail Feodorovitch, *see* Mikhail
Romanoff tercentenary celebrations, 444-7
Rozhistche, 541
Rubinstein, D., 524, 539
Rukhloff, 496, 507
Rumania, reverses in, 579
Russkoe Slovo, 455
Russky, General, 482, 513, 527, 534
Russo-Asiatic Bank, 508
Rzhevsky, 523

Sabler, V. K., 398, 399, 402-4, 428, 437, 443, 488, 492, 494-5
Sadykoff, V., 545
Sakharoff, General, 544
Samarin, A. D., 495, 506, 515, 579
San, river, 484-5
Saratoff, Bishop of, *see* Hermogen
Savitch, 460, 487, 499, 563
Savitsky, 453
Sazonoff (friend of Rasputin), 422, 427
Sazonoff (Minister for Foreign Affairs), blamed for Russia's attitude in Balkan war, 447, 450; explanations to members of Duma, 451; overcomes Emperor's hesitation regarding mobilization orders, 470; 473, 481, 515, 522; dismissal, 538; 553, 578, 582
Scherbatoff, Prince N. B., 494-5, 503, 506-7, 568, 578
Selivanoff, General, 482
Serajevo, assassination at, 469
Sergei Mikhailovitch, Grand Duke, 419, 486, 492, 495, 527, 528, 533-4
Sergius, Bishop of Finland, 404
Shakhovskoy, Prince, 487, 561
Shakhovysky, 496
Shaliapin, 441
Shidlovsky, Nicholas, 460
Shidlovsky, Sergei, 460
Shingareff, 552-3, 561
Shubinsky, 426
Shuvaeff, 480, 526-7, 533, 543-5, 560, 561, 568
Socialists in Duma, 439, 441, 464
Soldau, battle of, 481-2

Solvychegodsk, 516
South-Western Provinces Zemstvos Act, 408
Special Council of Defence, 488-90, 494-5, 498, 508-9, 511, 513, 526-7, 528-9, 533, 543-4
Stcheglovitoff, 488, 492, 495, 534, 570
Stchepkin, 444
Stembo, 539
Stetsenko, 465
Stishinsky, 583
Stolypin, P. A., among Rasputin's opponents, 399; interview with Rasputin, 407-8; resignation offered and withdrawn, 408; assassination, 409; 411, 423 unveiling of memorial to, 455-6; 550, 569
Strukoff, 505
Sturmer, B. V., one of Rasputin's circle, 517; succeeds Goremykin as Premier, 518; 519, 522-3; dispute with Special Council over " committee of five, " 528, 529; takes over Ministry for Foreign Affairs, 538; 539, 547-8, 550, 553-4; advised by M. V. Rodzianko to resign, 555-6; 558-60; presses Empress for dissolution of Duma, 561; dismissal, 561-2; excluded from Conservative group in Council of Empire, 570
Sukhomlinoff, General, illegal proceedings of, 452-3; complains of Emperor's hesitation over mobilization orders, 469-71; 475, 478; calming assurances regarding war material, 481; alleged connection with Miasoiedoff, and growing indignation against, 482; dismissal urged by M. V. Rodzianko, 486, 488, 492; dismissed, and later found guilty of peculation and State treason, 494; 496, 522; imprisoned, 525; release demanded by Empress, 538
Sumarokoff, Count, 416

Tagantzeff, Senator, 493
Taneieff, A. S., 399, 425, 427
Tatiana, Grand Duchess, 416
Tatistcheff, Count, 547
Tchelnokoff, 580
Tchemoduroff, 525
Tchernigoff, province of, 453, 516

INDEX

Tereschenko, M. L, 540, 548
Thomas, M., 529, 545
Thornhill, Major, 553
Timasheff, S. I., 529
Tobolsk, 393, 431; Bishop of, 421; Governor of, 431
Tolstoy, Count, 445, 577
Torchin, 540
Trepoff, 507, 528, 536, 561–2, 569–70, 580
Trubetzkoy, Eugene, 564
Trubetzkoy, Prince G. N., 473
Tsar, see Nicholas II
Tsarevitch, 395, 397, 409, 410–2, 422, 424–5, 439–40, 465
Tsaritsa, see Alexandra Feodorovna
Tsaritsin, 406, 443
Tumanoff, Prince, 434

Union of the Russian People, 441
Utine, 488

Varun-Secret, 494, 558–9
Vasilchikova, M. A., 515–6
Vasilchikova, Princess S.N., 565
Vasilieff, Archpriest, 399, 428–9, 430
Vechernie Vremya, 430, 462
Veliaminoff, Professor, 541, 543
Verevkin, 554
Viborg manifesto, 441
"Villa Rode," 523
Vilna, 500
Viviani, M., 529
Vladimir, Mgr., 517
Voeikoff, General, 399
Volgin, 507

Volia Rossii, 548
Volkonsky, Prince V. M., 416, 418, 429, 454, 530. 569
Vorontzoff-Dashkoff, Count, 419
Voskresensky, 536
Vyruboff, 475
Vyrubova, Madame, 399, 408–9, 430, 434, 467, 550
Vyshnegradsky, 488

War Industries Committee, 497
Warberg, Herr, 533
Warsaw, M. V. Rodzianko's visit to, 475–7
Witte, Countess, 427
Wolfson, 539
Wolkoff, General, 476

Xenia Alexandrovna, Grand Duchess, 483

Yalta, 409
Yanushkevitch, General, 487, 500, 501
Yudenitch, General, 519
Yusupoff, Prince, 416, 418, 465, 569
Yusupoff, Princess, 418, 430, 501–2

Zamoisky, Count, 535
Zemstvos, in South-Western Provinces, 408; in Western Russia, 437; co-operation in war work, 478–80, 497, 539–40, 571
"Zemstvo-Octobrists," 460, 552, 563
Zhirovetsky monastery, 404
Zvegintzoff, 460, 466

END OF BOOK 2

VOLUME & SERIES INFORMATION

This volume:

	Words	Pages	Images
Introduction:	9,560		
Book I:	141,532	337	6
Book II:	77,935	206	13
Total word count:	229,027		

Comparisons:	Ulysses	265, 222
	Pride and Prejudice	122,685

Volume III editions
All versions with Black & White images

Ebook   ISBN: 978-1-80517-626-8
Paperback ISBN: 978-1-80517-623-7 (cream paper, matt cover)
Hardback ISBN: 978-1-80517-624-4 (groundwood paper, dust jacket)
Hardback ISBN: 978-1-80517-625-1 (cream paper, gloss cover)

Series editions

Nicholas II – Tsar to Saint
The Memories of a Russian Yesteryear Volume 1
The Memories of a Russian Yesteryear Volume 2
The Memories of a Russian Yesteryear Volume 3

VOLUME & SERIES INFORMATION

NICHOLAS II – TSAR TO SAINT
THE RULER THAL LOST A DYNASTY

ebook
ISBN: 978-1-80352-908-0

Paperback
B&W on Groundwood paper
ISBN: 978-1-80352-799-4

Paperback
B&W on Cream paper
ISBN: 979-8-85465-243-8

Hardback
B&W on Groundwood paper
with dust jacket
ISBN: 978-1-80352-911-0

Hardback
B&W on Cream paper
ISBN: 979-8-85221-513-0

Pages: 546 / Illustrations: 203

From the back Cover:

Why was Russia's Imperial Family murdered? What part did they play in the revolution that gave rise to the Bolsheviks and transformed Russian Orthodoxy and State in to the Soviet Union? Tony Abbott takes us back to the pivotal moment in 1894 when Nicholas Alexandrovich Romanov became Tsar and there existed a real opportunity for Russia to modernise and become an industrial power and world leader. This is an incredible story of two rulers very much in love, who unwittingly created the circumstances that collapsed their dynasty.

Through first hand commentaries and with over 200 images, the events around the twenty-three year reign of Nicholas II are presented with clear and acute observations. What emerges is a fascinating insight of the man who made history by helping to bring about the revolution of an empire and the demise of his dynasty.